I0125993

Yours Very Truly

Frederick C. Pierce.

Yours Truly

Ford A. Pierce.

HERITAGE BOOKS

AN IMPRINT OF HERITAGE BOOKS, INC.

Books, CDs, and more—Worldwide

For our listing of thousands of titles see our website
at
www.HeritageBooks.com

A Facsimile Reprint
Published 2016 by
HERITAGE BOOKS, INC.
Publishing Division
5810 Ruatan Street
Berwyn Heights, Md. 20740

Copyright © 1882 Frederic Beech Pierce
47 Broad Street, Boston, Mass., U.S.A.

Originally published

Worcester:
Press of Chas. Hamilton
311 Main Street
1882

— Publisher's Notice —
In reprints such as this, it is often not possible to remove blemishes from
the original. We feel the contents of this book warrant its reissue despite
these blemishes and hope you will agree and read it with pleasure.

International Standard Book Numbers
Paperbound: 978-0-7884-1720-7
Clothbound: 978-0-7884-6318-1

Pierce Genealogy

BEING THE
RECORD OF THE POSTERITY OF
THOMAS PIERCE,
AN EARLY INHABITANT OF
CHARLESTOWN,
AND AFTERWARDS CHARLESTOWN VILLAGE (WOBURN),
IN NEW ENGLAND,
WITH
WILLS, INVENTORIES, BIOGRAPHICAL SKETCHES, ETC.

Frederic Beech Pierce

Assisted and Edited by

Frederick Clifton Peirce, Esq.

Author of the *Peirce Genealogy, History of Grafton, History of
Barre*, Compiler of the *Gibson and Harwood Genealogies*, Resident
Member of the New England Historic-Genealogical Society,
and Corresponding Member of the Wisconsin and
Kansas State Historical Societies.

HERITAGE BOOKS
2016

TO

THE PIERCE FAMILY,

THIS WORK IS

MOST RESPECTFULLY DEDICATED

BY THEIR FRIEND,

THE AUTHOR.

Concerning this nepular history, then;

is it a human invention or is it a

divine record. Is it "a tale told by

an idiot signifying nothing," or is it a

plan of infinite imagination signifying

immortality?

      Prof. BENJAMIN PEIRCE,
          of Harvard University.

AUTHOR'S PREFACE.

Two years ago I obtained of Frederick C. Pierce, Esq., of Barre, Mass., all the papers which he had compiled in relation to the family of Thomas Pierce of Charlestown, who was admitted to the church there 21 (12) 1634–5, and who was probably born in England in 1596. He had collected a mass of matter to which has been added as much more, at great expense, time and trouble. In the task of compiling the new matter and properly arranging the whole for the printer, Mr. F. C. Pierce has rendered valuable assistance. He has also corrected the proof sheets and attended to other minute details of the work, for which he has my sincere thanks.

I take this opportunity to tender my thanks and acknowledgments to all those who have so kindly furnished me with information and statistics. My thanks are especially due to Miss Mary F. Pierce of Cambridge, and John Ward Dean, the efficient and courteous librarian of the New England Historic-Genealogical Society.

The matter of spelling the name of Pierce or Peirce, has been the subject of considerable writing and discussion, as will be seen in the article by Prof. James Mills Pierce below. It is entirely a matter of fancy or preference. There are in existence autographs of the original Thomas, as being spelled in three different ways— Pierce, Peirce and Pieirce. By following down the autographs of the family, which the author at much pains and cost has collected, it will be seen that different members of the same family have spelled it, and do spell it, in different ways. Some of the descendants of Samuel[3], Benjamin[3], sons of Sergt. Thomas, of Woburn, one of the descendants of Benjamin, being the Miss Mary F. above alluded to, have always spelled it Peirce. The descendants of Isaac, of Boston, who married Grace Tucker, have invariably spelled it Peirce. The matter of not belonging to the same family on account of not spelling the name the same way, as has been brought forward by some of my correspondents, has no force whatever.

The author has always spelled his name Pierce, and hoping that he has not given any great offence to the members of the family spelling it the other way, has decided to publish his work under the name—PIERCE.

Very respectfully,

FREDERIC B. PIERCE.

47 Broad Street, Boston.

The *spelling* of the name of Pierce is generally supposed to have no significance in determining relationships. Certainly a great variety in this regard
will be found in printed and written documents, from the settlement of New
England until now. But my observation leads me to believe that a high
degree of uniformity exists in the spelling, *as used by persons bearing the
name*, in any one family connection. Thus the descendants of Robert of
Woburn, and I believe nearly the whole body of the descendants of John
of Watertown, from the beginning to the present day, almost everywhere use
the spelling *Peirce;* though John himself appears to sign his will *Pers* or *Perss*
in an antiquated hand resembling German *Schrift*. The spelling Pearse in
the will of his wife Elizabeth is not written by the testator, who signs only
by *mark*. On the other hand, the descendants of Samuel of Charlestown and
of Sergt. Thomas of Woburn most commonly employ the spelling *Pierce*,
which is also, I *think*, that of the signature of the will of Thomas, senior, of
Charlestown, which may, however, be *Peirce* or *Peerce*. In the old *pronunciation* of the name, according to the tradition prevalent in several branches
of the family of John of Watertown, the vowel-sound was the same that we
now hear in the words *pear, heir* and *their;* and this pronunciation is remembered by living persons as having been sometimes used by old-fashioned
people. This was probably quite independent of the spelling. The same
sound was, according to A. J. Ellis, used in the verb *to pierce*, in the 17th
century, and by some in the 18th century. On the other hand, the verb may
be occasionally heard with the pronunciation *perce* (or *purse)*, which is now
the prevalent pronunciation of all forms of the surname in the neighborhood
of Boston.

Let me add that the great number of families of this name among the early
settlers of New England makes it exceedingly difficult to trace the different
lines. Savage is guilty of many omissions under this name, and has committed
some decided mistakes. The perplexity in which all printed authorities
leave the subject make the matter very difficult for the author.

JAMES MILLS PEIRCE.

Cambridge, Mass.

THE ENGLISH FAMILY.

In the History of the "Peirce Family, of Watertown," written by my friend Mr. Frederick C. Peirce, of Barre, Mass., he alludes to John Pers, the ancestor of that branch in this country, as being "John Pers, of Norwich, Norfolk County, England, weaver."

As yet the ancestry in England of the Peirce family has not been followed out in an authentic manner; but in the "History of Norwich, Norfolk County, England," under the head of St. Peter's Church, in that town, we find the following in relation to the family living there then :—"Sparks Chantry, in this church was granted, July 23rd, in the 4th of Edward VI., with all its lands and rents, &c., in the tenure of Robermore, to Nicholas le Strange. And in the 23rd of Elizabeth, Peter Perse, cousin and heir of Humphrey Cony, late of this town, held part of these lands, being son of Thomas Perse, son of Margaret Perse, sister of John Cony, father of Humphrey."

It will be seen by this that there was a family by the name there at that time, and that also there was a Thomas in the family. It is reasonable to suppose therefore that our Thomas was of this family, and that he was brother of the John alluded to, and also of Robert, of Dorchester, as the same coat of arms is found in that family.

IRISH BRANCH OF PIERCES.

There was one branch of the Pierce family which went into Ireland from England during the reign of Queen Elizabeth. This branch went from Northumberland County, England. Several of the members were soldiers with Oliver Cromwell, and went with him to Ireland in 1649, and settled at Glencanny on Hillywater, two miles from

Enniskillen, and the farm upon which they located is still in the pos-
session of the family—owned and occupied by William Pierce, Esq.
Seven members of this family were in the battle of the Boyne, in
1690. Four or five were members of the celebrated Enniskillen
Dragoons. In the old family bible at Enniskillen, translated by Beza
and published by Barker, London, 1599, is the following record:—
"Sarah, b. Nov. 16, 1694; Elizabeth, b. April 22, 1698; Edward, b.
July 23, 1701; Henry, b. April 9, 1704; John, b. Aug. 17, 1707;
William, b. Nov. 14, 1709; Mary, b. May 14, 1712; Cromwell, b.
—— 18, 1715; Peter, b. —— 16, 1718." The early family records
and also the early parish records at Glencanny I am informed were
destroyed. The family were members of the Church of England.
Edward, b. 1701, m. in Dublin, Frances Brassingtin, dau. of Marmaduke. In 1737, with his wife and three children he sailed for America
—two of the children died on the passage over—and he landed in
Philadelphia. He purchased a farm in Delaware County, Pa., and
finally settled in Paoli, Chester County, Pa., where he died. His
descendants now reside in Pa.

JOHN PIERCE OF LONDON.

The first patent granted by the Council of Plymouth, of land in
New England, was to John Pierce of London, and his associates,
dated June 1, 1621. This was a roaming patent granting 100 acres
for each settler already transplanted and such as should be transported;
the land to be selected by them under certain restrictions. Pierce
located at Broad Bay, and afterwards found one Brown at N. Harbor,
with an Indian deed of the territory, and they joined their titles and
continued the settlement already begun at N. Harbor and Pemaquid,
which became prosperous and populous as the extensive remains at
these points strongly indicate.

Thomas Weston was associated with Pierce in this enterprise, and
both were doubtless men of influence in those days. John Pierce's
son Richard Pierce was a resident at Pemaquid, or rather Muscongus,
and married Elizabeth Brown. Richard Pierce's children were Richard,
William, Joseph, Elizabeth who m. Richard Fulworth, George, Margaret who m. Nathaniel Ward, and Francis.

B

PIERCE PROCLIVITIES.

A prominent and distinguishing trait of character in the Pierce
Family is casually exposed to view by the Historian Babson, in his description of the tumultuous proceedings occasioned by the violent party
spirit that prevailed in the country after the embargo of President
Jefferson in 1806. "At a town meeting held in Gloucester, the two
political parties struggled for the mastery through the day and amid
darkness until half-past ten at night, and the floor of the church
wherein the meeting was held he describes as presenting a scene of
wild confusion and discord worthy of Pandemonium itself. The
leaders of each party entertained their friends with unbounded hospitality, and each had its own place of refreshment for general resort."
But he adds:—"The Democrats not unreasonably expected success as
they had the influence of the Pierce family." Young ducks do not
take to the water more naturally than the Pierce family throughout
the country to democratic principles. Indomitable perseverance is
also a trait that marks their character in every department of life, and
has generally crowned their efforts with ultimate success, though
attained after repeated and sometimes very mortifying failures.

                                            GEN. E. W. PEIRCE.

A GENEALOGICAL DICTIONARY

Of the First Settlers in New England, by the Name of Pierce (however spelled), showing three generations of those who came before May, 1692, on the basis of Farmer's and Savage's Registers.

ABRAHAM, Plymouth, 1623, had share in the division of cattle 1627 ; one of the original purchasers of ancient Bridgewater in 1645, by wf. Rebecca had *Abraham,* b. Jan., 1638 ; *Isaac,* b. 1661 [?] ; *Rebecca ; Mary; Alice,* bap. Barnstable, July, 21, 1650, d. Duxbury, 1673. Haz. I., 326 ; Baylies II., 254. Peirce Genealogy by Gen. Peirce. Davis, Morton's N. E. Mem., 382. 2 Coll. Mass. Hist. Soc., VII., 138.

ABRAHAM, Jr., s. of the preceding, of Duxbury, ad. freeman 1670, by wife Hannah had *Abraham ; John ; Samuel.* He d. Jan., 1718.

ANTHONY, Watertown, eldest s. of John of Watertown, b. in England, ad. freeman Sept. 3, 1634, he *had two wives, Sarah and Ann,* the first d. 1633, and the second Jan. 20, 1682-3. He d. May 9, 1678. Ch. *John,* "eldest son ; " *Mary,* b. Oct. 20, 1633 ; *Mary,* b. 1636, m. Ralph Read of Woburn ; *Jacob,* b. Sept. 15, 1637 ; *Daniel,* b. Jan. 1, 1639-40, d. Watertown, 1723 ; *Martha,* b. April 24, 1641 ; *Joseph; Benjamin,* b. 1649 ; *Judith,* b. July 18, 1650, m. John Sawin, 16 Feb., 1667. *Peirce Genealogy, F. C. Peirce, pp.* 21-2.

AZERIKAM, or AZRAKIM, Warwick, came from Weymouth, s. of *Ephraim,* b. Jan. 4, 1672. Ch. *Samuel* and *Tabitha,* and perhaps others.

BENJAMIN, Scituate, s. of Capt. Michael, m. 1678, Martha, dau. of James Adams, had *Martha, Jerusha, Benjamin, Ebenezer, Persis, Caleb, Thomas, Adams, Jeremiah,* and *Elisha,* all b. between 1679 and 1699.—*Deane's Scituate.*

BENJAMIN, Watertown, s. of Anthony, b. 1649, m. Jan. 15, 1677-8, Hannah, dau. of Joshua Brooks of Concord. Ch. *Hannah,* b. Dec. 25, 1679 ; *Benjamin,* b. April 29, 1682, d. Nov., 1683 ; *Grace,* b. Jan. 4, 1685 ; *Sarah,* b. Jan. 1, 1687-8 ; *Samuel,* b. Aug. 22, 1689 ; *Lydia,* b. Oct. 3, 1692 ; *Hannah,* b. Jan. 2, 1699-1700, freeman, 1690. —*Brooks' Medford. Peirce Genealogy, F. C. Peirce, p.* 28.

BENJAMIN, Sr. of Woburn, s. of Thomas, Jr. (or John) of the same, by wf. Mary (dau. of Benjamin Reed), had *Benjamin*, b. Aug. 28, 1689, d. 27 Nov., 1713 ; *Mary*, b. Jan. 29, 1691-2 ; *Esther*, b. Oct. 25, 1696 ; *Rebecca*, b. Oct. 10, 1698 ; *Deborah*, b. Dec. 5, 1700 ; *Thomas*, b. Nov. 23, 1702 ; *Zurishaddai*, b. June 22, 1705. He d. 1739, leaving widow Mary.

DANIEL, Watertown and Newbury, blacksmith, came in the *Elizabeth*, from Ipswich, Suffolk County (called of London by Coffin in History of Newbury, p. 314), in 1634, aged 23 ; freeman May 2, 1638, by wife Sarah had *Daniel*, b. May 15, 1642 ; *Joshua*, b. May 15, 1643 ; *Martha*, b. Feb. 14, 1648. He sw. fidel. 1652, and m. 2nd, Dec. 26, 1654, Ann (Goodale), wid. of Thomas Milward, and d. leav. good est. Nov. 27, 1677. His wid. d. Nov. 27, 1690, and wife's dau. (not *his dau.* as Savage says) Rebecca Milward m. a Thorpe.—*Gen. Reg.*, Vol. XXIX, No. 115.

DANIEL, Groton, afterwards of Watertown, s. of Anthony, by wf. Elizabeth had *Elizabeth* (m. Mixer), b. May 16, 1665 ; *Daniel*, b. Nov. 28, 1666 ; *John*, b. Aug. 18, 1668 ; *Ephraim*, b. Oct. 15, 1673 ; *Josiah*, b. May 2, 1675 ; *Joseph ; Abigail*, b. Jan. 3, 1681 ; *Hannah* (m. Smith), bap. and *Benjamin*, bap. Jan. 16, 1686-7 ; *Mary*, who m. a Scripter (see Daniel's will).—*Bond's Watertown. Butler's Groton.*

DANIEL, Newbury, s. of Daniel, same, by wife Elizabeth, had *Daniel*, b. Dec. 20, 1663 ; *Anne*, b. May 22, 1666 ; *Benjamin*, b. Feb. 20, 1668-9 ; *Joshua*, b. Oct. 16, 1671 ; *Thomas*, b. May, 1674 ; *Martha*, b. Feb. 26, 1676-7 ; *Sarah*, b. Oct. 3, 1679 ; *George*, b. March 5, 1682-3 ; *Mary*, b. April 14, 1685 ; *John*, b. Oct. 16, 1687 ; *Katherine*, b. Sept. 18, 1690 ; was a Captain, Rep. 1682-3, of the Council of Safety on the Rev. 1689, Col. of one of the Essex Regts., Rep. under the new Charter in the import. yr. 1692, and d. April 22, 1704, accord. to his gr. Stone, and not as Farmer, Savage and Hutchinson say, viz. (Jan. 22, and April 4), *Gen. Reg.* Vol. XXIV., No. 115. His wid. d. Dec. 9, 1709, and his s. Daniel, and his wf. Joanna and dau. Joanna all d. 1690. Savage is in error about his dau. Joanna, he had none—and also the date of his wf.'s death (1690), for he d. 1704, and men. in will his "loving wf. Elizabeth."

EDWARD, Watertown, and Wethersfield, Conn., 1639, died in Simsbury, Conn., s. p., Conn. Pub. Rec. May, 1743.—*Bond's Watertown.*

EPHRAIM, Weymouth, prob. s. of Capt. Michael of Scituate, by wf. Hannah, dau. of John Holbrook, had *Azrikam*, b. Jan. 4, 1672 ; prob. Ephraim ; and perhaps others.

GEORGE, Boston, a smith, m. Mary, dau. of Richard Woodhouse, had *Mary*, b. June 20, 1660, and he d. Dec. 7, 1661.

GEORGE, Portsmouth, R. I., m. April 7, 1687. Alice, dau. of Richard Hart, had *Susanna*, b. Aug. 21, 1688 ; and per. others.

GILES, Greenwich, R. I., 1687.

ISAAC, Boston, tailor, s. of Samuel of Woburn, b. March 22, 1687, m. Grace, dau. of Lewis Tucker of Casco, May 5, 1708. She was b. 1680.

JAMES, Boston, killed in youth by lightning, at Plymouth, 1660.

JAMES, Woburn, s. of Thomas, Jr., b. 1659, m. Elizabeth Kendall, and had *Elizabeth*, b. Oct. 11, 1688 ; *James*, b. Feb. 28, 1690 ; *Rebecca* and *Mary*.

JEREMIAH, East Greenwich, R. I., b. in Eng. prob. Feb. 7, 1679, m. Abigail Long, and had eight ch.

JOHN, the patentee under the Pres. and Counc. for N. E., June 1, 1621, though connected with the Pilgrims of Plymouth, never came, in my opinion, to this shore, yet Willis seems contrary, I., 13. After most respectful consideration of the document referred to in his note I am constrained to express a confidence, that the London clothworker never succeeded in accomplishing, though he undertook, a voyage to Plymouth, the ship being put back in distress. My judgement seems to have confirmation by what is read in Bradford, 140, his son *Richard* came over and settled in Pemaquid, or rather Muscongus.

JOHN, Dorchester, mariner, came from Stepney, Middsx. Co., Eng., by wf. Parnell had *Joseph*, b. Sept. 30, 1631 ; *Abigail*, b. July 17, 1633 ; *John*, b. March 3, 1634, d. March 30, 1634 ; *Nehemiah*, b. July 12, 1637, d. Sept., 1639. His wf. Parnell d. Sept., 1639.

JOHN, Dorchester, adm. freeman 1631, selectman 1633-6-41, prop. of lands, 1656, Rep. Mar., 1639, rev. to Boston, 1642; his first wife Mary d. July 12, 1647, and he m. then, Aug. 10, 1654, Rebecca Wheeler, wid. of Thomas Wheeler. Ch. *Nehemiah ; Samuel ; Mehitable ; Mary ; Marcy ;* and *Exercise.* He was a cooper and d. Sept. 17, 1651. See *Hist. Dorchester*, p. 71. Savage has these two last Johns confounded.

JOHN, Watertown, freeman, March, 1638, a man of good estate, pro-jected settlement at Sudbury and Lancaster, d. May 9, 1661 ; and his will of March 4, 1658, was pro. the Oct. 1, following. In it he pro-vides for wf. Elizabeth, eldest s. Anthony, and other ch. which he does not name ; but his wid. in her will of March 15, 1666-7, pro. April 2, supplies the deficiency, naming ch. Anthony, John, Robert, Esther Morse, wf. of Joseph, Mary Coldam prob. res. in Lynn, besides gr. chil. Mary Ball, and ano. Ball, Esther Morse, and the chil. of Anthony and Robert; he also had ch. Judith, who m. Francis Wy-man ; and Elizabeth, who m. John Ball, Jr. ; the two latter d. bef. their father.   See Peirce Gen. by F. C. Peirce, Esq.

JOHN, Boston, Woburn, Wethersfield, Conn., s. of John, Water-town, by wf. Elizabeth had John and Elizabeth, tws. b. June 16, 1643, d. young; John, b. Nov. 23, 1644 ; Joseph, b. Sept. 12, 1646 ; Thomas, b. May 3, 1649.

JOHN, Gloucester, husbandman, freeman, 1651, he m. Nov. 4, 1643, Elizabeth ——, who d. July 3, 1673, he then m. Sept. 12, 1673, Jane Stanwood who d. Aug. 18, 1706, his ch. were Mary, b. Sept., 1650, and John, b. July 14, 1653.   He d. Dec. 15, 1695.

JOHN, Boston, s. of Anthony, cannot be the one adm. as an inhabt. Feb. 28, 1643, as Savage states ; m. April 15, 1656, Ruth, dau. of Nathaniel and Alice Bishop, b. April 14, 1639, and had Hannah, b. June 30, 1660, d. July 28, 1662 ; Ruth, b. Nov. 22, 1662 ; Hannah, b. Nov. 1, 1665 ; Sarah, b. June 1, 1668, d. young ; Ell [?], b. April 15, 1670 ; Rebecca, b. April 12, 1672, d. infant ; Nathaniel, b. April 10, 1678 ; Rebecca, b. Feb. 15, 1679 ; Sarah, b. Sept. 9, 1682.   His will is dated Oct. 21, 1682.—Suff. Prob. VI., p. 389.

JOHN, Hartford, Conn., 1640, a youth who prob. rev. soon.

JOHN, Charlestown, 1652, s. of Thomas, Sen., of same, but I do not think (as Savage suggests) that he is the one who had a wife Elinor and rev. to Kittery, for John and Elinor were inhabitants of the Colony as early as 1639 ; but it seems to me prob. that he died soon after his father (1666) and that he is the "unkle John" named in the will of Samuel, Charlestown.

JOHN, Boston, mason or bricklayer, by wf. Isabell, had Samuel, b. Jan. 14, 1659, d. same day ; Mary, b. March 13, 1661, m. William Wilson ; Sarah, b. Aug. 10, 1665 ; Jacob, and d. June 20, 1664 ; Joseph.

JOHN, Woburn, yeoman, ensign, s. of Thomas, Jr., b. 1643, m. July 5, 1663, Deborah Convers, dau. of James, had *Deborah*, b. Oct. 30, 1666 ; *John*, b. Jan. 26, 1671, m. Mary Parker ; *Thomas*, b. Dec. 23, 1673 ; *James*, b. Aug. 6, 1674, d. Sept. 13, 1685 ; *Daniel*, b. Oct. 7, 1676, m. Dinah Holt ; *James*, b. Oct. 8, 1686 ; *Ebenezer*, b. 1687 ; *Joseph*, b. Aug. 24, 1688, m. Mary ——— ; *Ruth*, b. 1690.

JOHN, Salem, lieut., 1675, See Felt., II., 497.

JOHN, Springfield, m. 1677, Lydia, dau. of Miles Morgan, had *Nathaniel*, b. 1679; *John*, b. 1683 ; *Jonathan ;* rev. to Enfield, there had *Lydia*, b. 1693, and he d. Sept., 1696, leaving the wf. and these ch.

JOHN, York, 1680, took o. of alleg. next yr., had sevl. yrs. bef. m. Phebe Nash, wid. of Isaac.

JOHN, Gloucester, s. of John, same, m. Mary, dau. of Robert Ratchell of Boston, had *Rachel, John, Stephen,* and *Silas ;* he rev. from G. in 1682.—*Babson.*

JOHN, Woodbury, s. of John, Jr., of Wethersfield, b. 1644, m. Ann Huthwitt, the defrauded orphan, had *John*, b. Sept. 10, 1683, m. Comfort Jenner ; *Elizabeth*, b. Aug. 10, 1685, he d. Nov. 19, 1731.— *Cothren.*

JOHN, Scituate, s. of Capt. Michael, same, m. 1683, Patience, dau. of Anthony Dodson, had *Michael, John, Jonathan, Ruth, Jael, David,* and *Clothier*, b. bet. 1684 and '98.—*Deane.*

JONATHAN, Woburn, s. of Robert, of same, b. 1663, m. Nov. 19, 1689, Hannah Wilson, had *Hannah*, b. March 8, 1691, d. Sept. 13, 1693 ; *Jonathan*, b. May 11, 1693, d. July 7, 1694 ; he d. June 17, 1694.

JOSEPH, Woburn, s. of Thomas, Jr., m. June 24, 1681, Mary Richardson. He d. s. p. 1716 ; soldier in 1675.

JOSEPH, Watertown, s. of Anthony, had wf. Martha, and m. 2nd, 1698, Elizabeth (Kendall) Winship, freeman 1690, April 18. Ch. *Joseph*, b. 1669 ; *Francis*, b. 1671 ; *John*, b. 1673 ; *Mary*, b. 1674 ; *Benjamin*, b. 1677 ; *Jacob*, b. 1678 ; *Martha*, b. 1681 ; *Stephen*, b. 1683 ; *Israel*, b. 1685 ; *Elizabeth*, b. 1687.

JOSHUA, Newbury, s. of Daniel, Sen., m. May 7, 1668, Dorothy, dau. of Maj. Robert Pike, had *Sarah*, b. March 18, 1668-9, m. Dr. Humphrey Bradstreet ; *Joshua*, b. Jan. 14, 1670, m. Elizabeth Hall.— *Gen. Reg.*, July, 1875, p. 278.

MARMADUKE (Percy), Salem, 1639, charged with killing his apprentice. Winthrop I., 318-19. He came, 1637, from Sandwich in Kent,
with wf. Mary and servt.—*Boyd's Sandwich,* p. 752 ; *Felt,* I., 169 ;
Ib., II., 458.

Capt. MICHAEL, Hingham, Scituate. Ch. *Persis, Benjamin, John,
Ephraim, Elizabeth, Deborah, Ann, Abia, Ruth ;* he m. a second
wf. Ruth, was a capt. of great bravery, in command of 50 Eng. and
20 friendly Indians from Cape Cod, in Philip's war, and was with
most of them killed March 26, 1676, at Pawtucket fight in Rehoboth—
Deane's Scituate, pp. 122, 325.

NATHANIEL, Woburn, s. of Robert of the same, was sol. in K.
Philip's War and was in the memorable battle at the falls of the Conn.
River, May 19, 1676 ; m. Dec. 27, 1677, Hannah Convers, had
Nathaniel, b. Feb. 2, 1678-9 ; his wf. d. Mar., 1678. He m. 2nd,
Elizabeth (Pierce) Foster,* wid. of Hopestill of Charlestown and dau.
of Thomas Pierce, Jr., and had *Mary, Hannah, Ichabod, Robert.*

NEHEMIAH, Boston, cooper, 1661 ; art. Co. 1671 ; m. 1684, Ann, wid.
of Samuel Mosely, eldest dau. of Isaac Addington and d. 1691.
Admr. was giv. Apr. 28 of this yr. to his wid.

NEHEMIAH, Boston, by wf. Phebe had *Phebe,* b. Aug. 31, 1663 ;
Mary, b. Aug 21, 1673.

RICHARD, Portsmouth, R. I., had prob. other ch. besides Susanna,
who m. Dec. 4, 1673, George Brownell.

RICHARD, Pemaquid, s. of John, m. Elizabeth Brown. He was a
carpenter ; he is, I think, the man to whom in Jan., 1642, an Indian
Sagamore made large gr. of lands and islands, as may be seen in Genal.
Reg. XIII., 365 ; took o. of fidel. 1574. Ch. *Richard, William,
Joseph, Elizabeth* who m. Richard Falmoth, *George, Margaret* who
m. Nathaniel Ward, and *Francis.*

RICHARD, Boston, printer, m. Aug. 27, 1680, Sarah, dau. of Rev.
Seaborn Cotton. *Thomas' Hist.* I., 282. For Benjamin Harris, book-
seller, he pub. Sept. 25, 1690, the *first* No. of a newspaper, of wh. the
sec. never appeared. *See Felt,* II., 14.

RICHARD, Tiverton, R. I., m. Susannah Wright and had 12 ch.
His will prov. 1677. He is the ancestor of nearly all the R. I.
Pearces.

---

*She had been prev. m. to Thomas Whittemore, of Woburn.

ROBERT, Dorchester, m. Ann, dau. of John Greenway, and had *Deborah*, b. Feb., 1640, d. few wks. ; was freeman May 18, 1642, and d. Jan. 6, 1665, leav. only s. Thomas, and Mary who m. Apr. 15, 1650, Thomas Hearing (not Haven), town records of Dedham see. His wid. d. Dec. 31, 1695, "the oldest person prob. that ever liv. in Dor." says the History, p. 261, aged "about 104 years." Of his will good abst. is in Gen. Reg. XIII., 154. Some of the bread brot. over from Eng. by him is still in the poss. of his des. in Dor.

ROBERT, Ipswich, m. Abigail, dau. of Mark Symonds of the same.

ROBERT, Watertown, s. of John, same, freeman 1650 ; rev. to Woburn ; m. Mary Knight. Ch. *Judith, Mary, Nathaniel, Elizabeth, Jonathan, Joseph, John,* and *Benjamin.*

ROBERT, Charlestown, s. of Thomas, Sen., same, m. Feb. 18, 1657, Sarah Eyre.

SAMUEL, Malden, s. of Thomas, Sen., of Chast., by wf. Mary, had *Mary,* b. June 20, 1656 ; *Thomas,* b. Jan. 7, 1658, m. Elizabeth Hall ; *John,* b. Aug. 10, 1659, d. ; *Joseph,* b. Aug., 1660, d. bef. 1678 ; *Jonathan,* b. 1661, m. Mary Lobdell ; *John,* b. 1664, m. Elizabeth Mudge ; *Elizabeth,* b. Oct. 16, 1666 ; *Persis,* b. Jan. 30, 1668 ; *Abigail,* b. Apr. 16, 1670, d. bef. 1708 ; *Hannah,* b. Dec. 28, 1671 ; *Benjamin,* b. Aug. 15, 1675, d. bef. 1678 ; *Samuel,* m. Mary Orton.

SAMUEL, Boston, cooper, 1672.

SAMUEL, Woburn, s. of Thomas, Jr., same, freeman 1684 ; m. Dec. 9, 1680, Lydia Bacon, and had *Samuel,* b. Nov. 25, 1681, m. Abigail Johnson ; *Lydia,* b. May 25, 1683 ; *Joseph,* b. Mar. 28, 1685, d. young ; *Isaac,* b. Mar. 22, 1687, m. Grace Tucker ; *Abigail,* b. Feb. 27, 1689; *Sarah,* b. June 22, 1691; *Ruth,* b. Feb. 14, 1693; *Tabitha,* b. Aug. 28, 1697, d. Sept. 30, 1697 ; *Tabitha,* b. Mar. 10, 1700.

STEPHEN, Chelmsford, s. of Thomas, Jr., Charlestown, by wf. Tabitha Parker, had *Jacob, Benjamin, Sarah, Tabitha, Stephen.*

STEPHEN, Chelmsford, s. of Stephen, same, by wife Esther Fletcher, had *Robert, Oliver, Esther, William, Stephen, Tabitha, Remembrance, Sarah, Mary,* and *Benjamin,* the gr.-father of Pres. Franklin Pierce of the U. S.—*Gen. Reg.* VII., 10.

THOMAS, Charlestown, from England, adm. to Church 1634, freeman 1635, by wf. Elizabeth had *John, Samuel, Thomas* b. 1618, *Robert, Mary, Elizabeth, Persis,* and *Abigail.* He d. Oct. 7, 1666.

c

THOMAS, Charlestown Village *alias* Woburn ; m. May 6, 1635, Elizabeth Cole, often styled " Sergt. Thomas," selectman, Woburn, 1660 ; had ch. *Ensign John*, b. Mar. 7, 1643 ; *Thomas*, b. June 21, 1645 ; *Elizabeth*, b. Dec. 25, 1646 ; *Joseph*, b. Sept. 22, 1648, d. Feb. 27, 1649 ; *Joseph*, b. Aug. 13, 1649 ; *Stephen*, b. July 16, 1651 ; *Samuel*, b. Feb. 20, 1654, d. Oct. 27, 1655 ; *Samuel*, b. Apr. 7, 1656 ; *William*, b. Mar. 7, 1658 ; *James*, b. May 7, 1659 ; *Abigail*, b. Nov. 20, 1660 ; *Benjamin*, m. Mary Reed.

THOMAS, Setauket, L. I., 1661, had that year a commission as a magistrate of Conn.

THOMAS, Dorchester, only s. of Robert of Dorchester, m. Mary, dau. of George Proctor, and had nine ch., of wh. were *Thomas*, bap. Oct. 26, 1662 ; *Mary*, b. Apr., 1665 ; *John*, b. Oct. 26, 1668 ; besides *Samuel*, killed Dec. 16, 1698, by the fall of a tree. His wf. d. Mar. 22, 1704, æ 62, and he d. Oct. 26, 1706, æ 71. He was the ancestor of the late well-beloved Rev. John Pierce, D.D., of Brookline, Harvard Coll. 1793.

THOMAS, Gloucester, had wf. Ann, who d. Jan. 26, 1668, perhaps dau. Elizabeth d. July 3, 1673.

WILLIAM, Boston, a distinguished shipmaster, made more voyages than any other person in the same years to and from Boston, was killed by the Spaniards at Providence in the Bahamas, July 13, 1641. *Winthrop* II., 33. Prince says in *Annals* II., 69, he was the ancestor of Rev. James, a distinguished theologian of Exeter, Eng., who d. 1730.

WILLIAM, Boston, came in the *Griffin* and arrived Sept. 4, 1633, with Cotton, Hooker, Gov. Haynes, and other churchmen ; was made freeman May 14, following ; often a selectman ; d. 1661. He had early m. Sarah, dau. of William Colbron, had dau. Sarah, nam. Sarah Colpit in the will of her gr.-f. But I fear that name is wrong, at least such name is not known in Boston. See the note in *Winthrop* I., 109.

WILLIAM, Barnstable, 1643.

WILLIAM, Boston, 1653, a mariner, d. 1669, leaving small property to his wid. By wf. Esther had, *William*, *Nathaniel*, *Moses*, *Mary* b. Dec. 10, 1656, d. young ; *Martha* and *Mary*, tws., b. May 16, 1659, both d. young ; *Ebenezer*, b. Mar. 16, 1661 ; *Esther*.

WILLIAM, Falmouth, 1680, on the second destruction of the town, 1690, rev. to Milton. *Willis* I., 163.

WILLIAM, Suffield, m. 1688, Esther Spencer, had *Thomas*, b. 1688. WILLIAM, Woburn, s. of Thomas, Jr., m. Apr. 8, 1690, Abigail Sommers *nee* Warren; was a soldier in 1675, and d. 1720, leaving ch. *Sommers*, b. Feb. 16, 1697, m. Martha Holt of Andover, and Eve, b. Oct. 30, 1694, d. Aug. 1, 1695.

Fifteen of this name, in its various forms, had, in 1834, been gr. at Harvard, five at Yale, and ten at other New England Colleges.

COLLEGE GRADUATES BY THE NAME OF PEIRCE, ETC.

HARVARD UNIVERSITY.

NAME.	GRAD.	NAME.	GRAD.
NATHANIEL PEIRCE,	1775	WILLIAM AMBRAS PEIRCE,	1860
BENJAMIN PEIRCE,	1801	BENJAMIN MILLS PEIRCE,	1865
HENRY PEIRCE,	1808	EDWARD FOSTER PEIRCE,	1866
CYRUS PEIRCE,	1810	WARREN PEIRCE,	1869
WARREN PEIRCE,	1811	RICHARD PEIRCE,	1724
PROCTOR PEIRCE,	1814	DANIEL PEIRCE,	1728
AUGUSTUS PEIRCE,	1820	JOSIAH PEIRCE,	1735
DANIEL H. PEIRCE,	1820	CHARLES PEIRCE,	1744
BENJAMIN PEIRCE,	1829	JOHN PEIRCE,	1793
CHARLES HENRY PEIRCE,	1833	JOHN TAPPAN PEIRCE,	1831
THOMAS NELSON PEIRCE,	1836	JACOB PEIRCE,	1849
JAMES ROBINSON PEIRCE,	1838	EDWARD LILLIE PEIRCE,	1852
GEORGE WASHINGTON PEIRCE,	1846	LOUIS PEIRCE,	1853
JOSHUA RINDGE PEIRCE,	1851	ALBION PEIRCE,	1860
JAMES MILLS PEIRCE,	1853	GEORGE WINSLOW PEIRCE,	1864
CHARLES SAUNDERS PEIRCE,	1859	HUMPHREY PEIRCE,	1866
BENJAMIN FRANKLIN PEIRCE,	1860	GARDNER CARPENTER PEIRCE,	1866

YALE COLLEGE.

NAME	GRAD	NAME	GRAD
JOHN PEIRCE,	1777	THOMAS WILSON PEIRCE,	1868
SETH PEIRCE,	1806	DWIGHT EDWARD PEIRCE,	1875
GEORGE EDMUND PEIRCE,	1816	AMOS PEIRCE,	1783
MOSES PEIRCE,	1816	CYRUS PEIRCE,	1802
JOHN GILKEY PEIRCE,	1825	JOHN BARNARD PEIRCE,	1861
LEONARD PEIRCE,	1826	LUTHER HILLS PEIRCE,	1858
GEORGE TABER PEIRCE,	1843	FRANKLIN WILLIAMS PEIRCE,	1876
GRANVILLE TOUCEY PEIRCE,	1855	REUBEN HENRY PEIRCE,	In College

DARTMOUTH COLLEGE.

GEORGE PEIRCE,	1780	MARIS BRYANT PEIRCE (Indian),	1840
BENJAMIN FRANKLIN PEIRCE,	1795	EPAMINONDAS JAMES PEIRCE,	1845
PROCTOR PEIRCE,	1796	JOHN SABIN PEIRCE,	1851
WARREN PEIRCE,	1799	EDWIN PEIRCE,	1852
DAVID PEIRCE,	1811	CLAUDIUS BUCHANAN PEIRCE,	1854
CHARLES PEIRCE,	1825	GEORGE PEIRCE,	1860
SAMUEL PEIRCE,	1835	GARDNER CARPENTER PEIRCE,	1863

WILLIAMS COLLEGE.

CHARLES PEIRCE,	1857	EDWARD ARTHUR PEIRCE,	1858

AMHERST COLLEGE.

NEHEMIAH P. PEIRCE of Enfield, Conn.
ASA C. PEIRCE of Hinsdale.
GEORGE ALEXANDER OTIS PEIRCE of Watertown.
HENRY R. PEIRCE of Northampton.
WILLIAM MARTIN PEIRCE of Hadley.

EDWARD WILLARD PEIRCE of North Abington.
GARDNER CARPENTER PEIRCE of North Abington.
HENRY THOMPSON PEIRCE of Lancaster.
OTIS PEIRCE of Stoughton.

PHILLIPS EXETER ACADEMY.

MARK WENTWORTH PEIRCE,	1798	JAMES PEIRCE,	1845
OLIVER P. PEIRCE,	1820	HERBERT H. D. PEIRCE,	1864
CHARLES H. PEIRCE,	1828	WILLIAM PEIRCE,	1868
SILAS S. PEIRCE,	1842	JOSHUA RINDGE PEIRCE,	——
GEORGE H. PEIRCE,	1843	ROBERT CUTTS PEIRCE,	1856
JOSHUA WINSLOW PEIRCE,	——	JOSEPH WENTWORTH PEIRCE,	——

The following is a list of places in the United States named Peirce :—

Peirce, DeKalb Co., Illinois.
Peirce, Will Co., Illinois.
Peirce, Callaway Co., Missouri.
Peirce, Washington Co., Indiana.
Peirce, Page Co., Iowa.
Peirce, Morrison Co., Minnesota.
Peirce, Stone Co., Missouri.
Peirce, Texas Co., Missouri.
Peirce, Peirce Co., Nebraska.
Peirce, Clermont Co., Ohio.
Peirce, Stark Co., Ohio.
Peirce, Armstrong Co., Pa.
Peirce, Kewanee Co., Wisconsin.

Peirce City, Shoshone Co., Idaho.
Peirce City, Lawrence Co., Missouri.
Peirce, Goochland Co., Virginia.
Peirce's Bridge, Grafton Co., N. H.
Peirce Station, Obion Co., Texas.
Peirceton, Anderson District, S. C.
Peirceville, DeKalb Co., Illinois.
Peirceville, Ripley Co., Indiana.
Peirceville, Van Buren Co., Iowa.
Peirceville, Wyoming Co., Pa.
Peirceville, Kansas.
Peirce's P. O., New York.

ILLUSTRATIONS.

Pages 1-14 do not exist in the
original

FAMILY HISTORY.

PIERCE COAT OF ARMS.

Three Ravens rising sable.
Fesse-hummette.
Motto—*Dixit et Fecit:* (He said and he did).
Crest—Dove with olive branch in beak.

PIERCE PEDIGREE.

ORIGIN OF THE NAME OF PIERCE IN ENGLAND.

PETER claims our attention next. When we consider how important has been the position claimed for him it is remarkable that in an age when, so far as England was concerned, this respect was more fully exacted than any other, his name should be so rarely found, rarely when we reflect what an influence the ecclesiastics of the day themselves must have had in the choice of the baptismal name, and what an interest they had in making it popular. It is to them, doubtless, we must refer the fact of its having made any mark at all, for "Peter" was odious to English ears. It reminded them of a tax which was the one of all least liked, as they saw none of its fruits. It is to country records we must look for the "Peters" of the time. The freer towns would none of it. Among the rude peasantry ecclesiastic control was wellnigh absolute; in the boroughs it was proportionately less. I have already quoted an instance of 133 London names where Peter is discovered but once to thirty-five Johns. In the Norwich Guild already mentioned, the proportion, or rather disproportion, is the same. To 128 Johns, forty-seven Williams, forty-one Thomases, thirty-three Roberts, and twenty-one Richards, there are but four Peters. On the other hand, in Wiltshire, out of 588 names we find sixteen Peters to ninety-two Johns. This wide difference of ratio I find to be fully borne out in all other groups of early names. Thanks then to the ecclesiastics it did exist, and its relics at any rate are numerous enough. It is hence we get the shorter Parr, Piers, Pierce, Pears, Pearse, and Peers. It is hence with the patronymic added we get Parsons, Pearsons, Pierson, and the fuller Peterson. It is hence once more with the pet desinences attached we get our Perrins and Perrens, our Perrets, Perretts, Parrots, and Parrets, our Peterkins, Perkins, Parkins and Parkinsons, besides our Perks and Perkes innumerable.—[*English surnames, their sources and significations, by Charles Wareing Bardsley, A. M.*, 1875], pp. 88-9.

1. THOMAS PIERCE, the emigrant ancestor of this branch of the Pierce family, came from England to this country in 1633-4, with his wife Elizabeth Pierce, and settled in Charlestown, Mass. He was b. in England in 1583-4; d. Oct. 7, 1666. His wife Elizabeth was b. in England in 1595-6.

3

The wife of Thomas was admitted to the church at Charlestown Jan. 10, and he Feb. 21, 1634–5. He was freeman May 6, 1635. Sept. 27, 1642, he was one of the twenty-one commissioners appointed by the Great and General Court, " to see that Saltpetre heapes were made by all the farmers of the colony."

INVENTORY: House, etc., £60; 12 acres, £48; 8 acres commons, £32; 6 acres, £20; 10 acres marsh, £30; 5 commons, £30; total, £413.

Children, b. in Charlestown :—

2. i.   JOHN, probably the one admitted to the Church of Charlestown Aug. 22, 1652. He is not the one (as Savage suggests) who had a wife Elinor and removed to Kittery, for John and Elinor were inhabitants of the colony as early as 1639. He was a " Mariner," and probably returned to England and died there, as nothing can be found of his children in this country. He signed a deed in " Charltowne " the 27th of the 6th MO., 1655, as " John Pierce, Mariner, Doe for my selfe, my wiffe," &c. ; in this property conveyed was " a quarter of a cows common, which I bought of my sister, widdow Persis Bridges."
There was a Capt. " John Pierce," who made several voyages between the colonies and England, who is supposed to be this one.
It seems to me very probable that John died in England soon after his father, and that he is the " Unkle John " named in Samuel's will.

ESTATE.—John Pierce of London, mariner, buys of Grace Smith, house and garden, late of I. Cole—s., street; w., common; E., John Waff; N., James Brown: 1648. To R. Mousal, house : also ¼ common " bo't of widow Bridges, my sister " and hay-lot : 1655. John Pierce of Wapping, Middlesex, mariner, of W. Bates, power to sell, 1669.

3. ii.   SAMUEL; m, Mary ———.
4. iii. THOMAS, Jr., b. 1608 [?]; m. May 6, 1635, Elizabeth Cole.
5. iv.   ROBERT; m. Feb. 18, 1657, Sarah Eyre.
6. v.   MARY; m. Peter Jeffs and had child Elizabeth.
7. vi.   ELIZABETH; m. Randall Nichols.
8. vii. PERSIS; m. William Bridge and had a child Mary. She m. 2nd, John Harrison. She was admitted to the church of Charlestown, Nov. 30, 1643.
9. viii. ABIGAIL, b. June 17, 1639.

ESTATE.—Grant, 4 acres planting ground, 1635–6.

POSSESSIONS, 1638, 10 lots : (1) 5 acres in West end—bd. w., Richard Sprague; E., Edward Burton, common; N., highway; s., church land; with dwelling-house. (2) 1 acre South Meade—E., creek; w., church land; N., E. Burton; s., Nowell. (3) 1 acre South Meade—s., Camb. fence; E., John Woolrich; N. w., M. Bastow. (4) 4 acres Linefield—s. w., Camb. line; s. E., Will Baker; N. w., common, swamp; N. E., Brooks. (5) 4 cow commons. (6) 5 acres woods Mystic field. (7) 3 acres Mystic marshes—w., North River; E., woods; N., widow Nash; s., Chubuck, J. Brimsmead. (8) 1 acre Mystic Long Meadow. (9) 15 acres woods Mystic field—N. E., Mrs. Coytemore; s. w., E. Richardson, J. Hodges; N. w., R. Palgrave; s. E., J. Hubbard.

(10) 62 acres Waterfield—N. W., Joshua Tedd, Rice Morrice, J. Hodges, George Felt; S. W., E. Frothingham; S. W., James Hubbard; N. E., R. Palgrave.

THOMAS PIERCE'S WILL.

Cambridge in New England, Novemb. 7th, 1665.

I, Thomas Pierce of Charlestown, aged about 82 years, being throw the goodness of ye Lord of souud judgment & memory, and in some measure of bodily health, do ordaine & hereby declare my last Will and testament, in manner and form following; viz: my soul, which I believe is imortall, I do desire humbley and believeingly to resign it unto the father of spirits, who gave it to mee, and to remit both body and soul into the everlasting mercyes of God, the father, Sonne, and Holy Ghost. My body I desire it may be decently interred, at the discretion of my loving wife whom I do ordaine and make sole Executrix of this my Will. And for my outward Estate wherewith the Lord hath gratiously blessed mee, I do dispose thereof as follows, viz: to Harvard College twenty shillings to be payed within one year after my decease. To Mary Bridge, and Elizabeth Jeffs, two of my grand-children now dwelling with mee I do give ten pounds apiece, to be paid by my Executrix as soon as she can with convenience, but not to be compellable thereto for and during to years after my decease. The residue of my estate, my just debts and funerall expenses being first payed, I do give and bequeath unto my loving wife Elizabeth, to have and to hold the same during her life, and at her pleasure to be helpfull to any of my children as shee shall see meet in her discretion, by giveing or lending to them any part thereof: And before her deceased I do give her power to make her will, and by the same to bequeath any part thereof by gift or legacy as shee shall see meet, and after her decease such part thereof as shall be by her unexpended, and not disposed of by her before her decease, I do will and bequeath ye same in manner following—viz: To all my grand-children I do give ten groates apeece, and the remainder to be equally divided among my children. My will is that the younger shall have eaquell with the eldest, I have *formerly* done for them according to my ability: Finally I do nominate my loving friends, Mr. Ri: Russell & Mr. Thomas Danforth*, and my sonne Jno. Pierce overseers of this my will; by whose advice and consent of them or the more part of them I do give my Executrix full power to settle all my lands on such of my sonnes, as shall approve themselves in the feare of God, and duty to their aged mother, and on such conditions as they shall meet /also I do nominate Lift. Randall Nicholls [this name is in place

---

*A note at time of proof shows that this will was executed at Thomas Danforth's house in Cambridge. Thomas Danforth was Treasurer of Harvard College, 1650-68. The inventory of Thomas Pierce's property taken Oct. 23, 1666, £413 5 s., was filed Mar. 22, 1666-7 by his widow Elizabeth Pierce aged about 71, appd. by Richard Lowden, Richard Jackson, Thomas Welch (?).

of one erased, I think—Lowden] to be added to my overseers above named,/ provided always it is my declared will y^t my Executrix shall not a=lienabe or dispose of any of my Lands so as to deprive all my sonnes of the same, but I do give her power by the advice of my overseers as above is expressed to dispose of the whole to any one of my sonnes according to her discretion, but not to divide the same into parcels. In witness whereof I do hereunto sett my hand and seale the day and year first above written.

3. SAMUEL^2 PIERCE (*Thomas*^{1}); m. Mary ——, b. 1631, d. July 17, 1705, of small-pox. He d. Sept., 1678. He was of Malden, but removed to Charlestown between 1666 and 1669. He joined the Charlestown church Dec. 5, 1669 (Savage) and Jan. 16, 1670, brought to baptism, Samuel, Thomas, Joseph, Jonathan, John, Mary, Elizabeth, and Persis. His wife Mary joined the church, Mar. 27, 1670. Their son, Samuel, is, I think, the one to whom the widow, Mary, gave the land in Charlestown, as he moved from Malden.

Children :—

10. i. MARY, b. June 20, 1656; m. John Lynde and d. Dec. 22, 1690, leaving issue.
11. ii. SAMUEL, Jr.; m. Mary Orton, b. 27 (6), 1648.
12. iii. THOMAS, b. Jan. 7, 1658; m. Elizabeth Hall, b. 18 (7), 1658; and she m. 2nd, John Oldham, b. 1652, d. Oct. 14, 1719. He d. Aug. 4, 1693, of fever.
13. iv. JOHN, b. Aug. 10, 1659; d. "very soon" (Savage).
14. v. JOSEPH, b. Aug., 1660; d. bef. 1678.
15. vi. JONATHAN, b. 1661; m. Dec. 4, 1683, Mary Lobdell.
16. vii. JOHN, b. 1664; m. Feb. 4, 1691, Elizabeth Mudge.
17. viii. ELIZABETH, b. Oct. 16, 1666; m. Jan. 3, 16—, John Cuttice. They had one child, Elizabeth. After the death of Cuttice the widow m. Isaac Cleveland of Charlestown.
18. ix. PERSIS, b. Jan. 30, 1668; m. Mar. 26, 1690, John Sheppard; m. 2nd, William Rand of Charlestown, who was wounded at Quebec, and d. Feb. 9, 1746. She d. June 25, 1748.
19. x. ABIGAIL, b. Apr. 16, 1670; d. before May 31, 1708. Abigail Pierce of Charlestown, spinster, will dated Apr. 23, 1707, proved May 31, 1708, leaves all her "goods and estate" to "my three sisters, viz: Elizabeth Cleveland, Persis Rand and Hannah Counce." Total Inventory of Estate £77—19—09.
20. xi. HANNAH, b. Dec. 28, 1671; m. Jan. 29, 1695, Samuel Counce, b. July, 1671. She d. 1714.
21. xii. BENJAMIN, bap. Aug. 15, 1675; d. bef. 1678.

ESTATE.—Samuel Pierce of Malden buys of T. Brigden, 2¾ acres, 1666. To A. Hill, 2 acres, 1670-1, rec. 1698-9. Of James Goodin, house, etc., 1677.

WILL, Sept. 8, pro. 17 (10), 1678, devised to son *Thomas*, house and two acres—N. W., on highway; and all meadow from Sprague's marsh to Bullard's bridge. 4 acres plowland before door—two lots, two acres each. Hay-lot at Camb. line. Meadow adj. Bullard bridge—E., common; w., creek. To *Thomas*, four cow-commons, he to pay to *Joseph* and the four daus. To *Jonathan*, great lot—w., Camb. line; s., widow Gold; N. W. and N. E., Chas. common. Marsh bet. widow Lynde and Bullard bridge—w., T. Welch; E., creek. Two commons. To *John*, house and malt-house at Neck, and land

except house-plot for Joseph, 30 by 40, between dwelling-house and creek—
N. E., Sprague's marsh; N. W., C. Goodwin. One acre bo't of James Goodin,
formerly of E. Drinker. Two cow commons.

WIDOW MARY grant eight commons, 1681. Eleven acres in three parcels,
two by her house, other between James Russell and the watering-place and
Thomas Danforth, 1681. Consents to Jonathan Pierce sale, 1700.

EXTRACT FROM SAMUEL PIERCE'S WILL.

Samuel Pierce of Charlestown (draught of will Sept. 3, 1678, signed
but not sealed, and witnessed by Christopher Goodwin and Benjamin
Sweetser; will, almost a transcript of the other, Sept. 5, 1678, signed
and sealed and witnessed by Benjamin Sweetser and Alc. Roper,
proved Dec. 17, 1678) names his wife (Exec.), his sons Thomas, Jonathan and John, his "dafters" Elizabeth, Percis, Hannah, Abigaiell (all
these daughters under age), his d. Mary (not named in the draught,
and last in the will), his s. Joseph (for whom he only provides that
Thomas shall have £5 and John shall pay him £10), his son's "Unkle
John", as having given John Jr. £10 (only in draught), and Edward
Wilson and Samuel Frothingham overseers. Inventory of Estate of
Samuel "deceased" taken Sept. 27, 1678, contains among other items
the following:—

A Bible and other books . . . . £1—00—00
Dwelling hous & barn & orchard & 26 axkars of upland, 7
axkars of marsh . . . . .331—00—00
By his arms . . . . 2—00—00

Total . . . . £659—10—00

Apprized by John Cutter, Lawrence Dowse, Nov. 20, 1699.

A petition of "John Lynde of Malden who married with Mary, one of the
daughters of Samuel Pierce, late of Charlestown deceased, of William Rand
of Charlestown who m. with Persis, another of the dau. etc., of Samuel
Counts, who m. with Hannah, another of the daus.,——and of Abigail, a
fourth daughter—shewith that whereas the said Samuel Pierce dyed intestate
and at his death left a very valuable estate both Real and Personall, of which
Administration hath not yet been committed to any person according to Law,
nor any Legal settlement made of the same, Wee therefore —— pray that
administration —— may be committed to the widow of the deceased who
yet survives or to some other of next of kin, that so ye Petrs. who have been
many years kept out of their right, may have their portions." Hereupon the
Judge of Probate ordered Mary Pearse and Jonathan and John Pearse of
Charlestown, "the surviving sonus," to appear before him on Nov. 28, 1699,
when he appointed a farther hearing for Dec. 4, of which I find no record.
But John Pierce was probably appointed admr. Mar. 9, 1705, John Pierce of
Charlestown admr. de bonis non, cum fest. annexo of Samuel Pierce late of C.
deceased, gives bonds in £300, with Jno. Cutter and James Lowden, both of
C., to render account of admr. on or before Mar. 9, 1706, and the same day he
exhibited inventory of Est. not administered £25—10—00. Mar. 14, 1706,
Abigaill Pierce rendered her account for nursing her mother in her sickness
from 1698 to her death, Jan. 17, 1705-6, £10—12—0. May 12, 1707, John
Pierce admr. de bonis non, renders account of which he speaks of Mary as
relict of the deceased.

4. THOMAS[2] PIERCE, Jr. (*Thomas[1]*), b. 1608; m. May 6, 1635, Elizabeth Cole, d. Mar. 5, 1688. He d. Nov. 6, 1683. They res. in Charlestown Village, now Woburn. He was often styled Sergt. Thomas.

Sergt. Thomas Pierce was admitted into the church at Charlestown, Feb. 21, 1634; was in Woburn as early as 1643; was taxed there, 1645; was selectman of Woburn, 1660, and repeatedly afterwards of the committee for dividing the common lands in Woburn; he was one of "the right proprietors," chosen Mar. 28, 1667; and also of the General Courts' Committee appointed for the same purpose in 1668.

[signature: Thomas Pierce]

Children :—

21½. oi.   ABIGAIL, b. Aug. 17, 1639.
22. i.   JOHN, b. Mar. 7, 1643; m. July 5, 1663, Deborah Convers.
23. ii.   THOMAS, b. June 21, 1645; m. Eliza ———; m. 2nd, Mar. 24, 1680, Rachel Bacon.
24. iii.   ELIZABETH, b. Dec. 25, 1646; m. Nov. 9, 1666, Thomas Whittemore*, d. Mar. 10, 1670, leaving Joseph, b. Aug. 14, 1667; m. 2nd, Hopestill Foster; m. 3rd, Mar. 23, 1680, Nathaniel Peirce. See *Peirce Genealogy*, by Frederick C. Peirce, Esq.
25. iv.   JOSEPH, b. Sept. 22, 1648; d. Feb. 27, 1649.
26. v.   JOSEPH, b. Aug. 13, 1649; m. June 24, 1681, Mary Richardson, b. Jan. 15, 1657, d. 1720. He d. 1716, leaving no issue. He was a soldier in 1675. They had an adopted dau., Hannah, who m. a Nichols and a Lynde.

[signature: Joseph Peirce]

Joseph Pierce, senior, of Woburn, husbandman (will dated May 27, 1715, entered for probate Nov. 28, 1716), names his wife Mary (exec.); his wife's father, Theophilus Richardson, late of Woburn, deceased; the three eldest ch. of his adopted dau. Hannah Lynde, formerly Hannah Nickols; his "cozen" Nathan Richardson, "that now liveth with me"; his bro. Benjamin Pierce; his bro. Samuel Pierce; his "cozen" Ichabod Pierce; his "cozen" Sumors Pierce, s. to his bro. William and his "cozen" Deborah Richardson, "who now liveth with me." Witnesses, Samuel Baker, Sen., Timothy Snow, John Russell, Jun.

Mary Pierce, widow of Joseph, late of Woburn (will dated Jan. 20, 1716–17, pro. June 16, 1721), names cousin Nathan Richardson, "that now liveth with me " (Exec.); cous. Deborah Richardson, "that now liveth with me"; cous. Thos., s. to her bro. Benjamin Pierce. June 8, 1721, Articles of agreement between John Richardson of Woburn and his s. Nathan, on the one part, and the heirs of Joseph Pierce, late of Woburn, on the other. The former giving bonds to James Pierce, Benjamin Pierce, Joseph Whittemore and Timothy Snow, all of Woburn. The administration of the will of Mary Pierce, Joseph's widow,

---

* Thomas Whittemore was taxed in the Rate of the Country, assessed in Woburn Aug. 26, 1666, and is reckoned among those who were entitled to a share of the common lands of the town in 1668, but not being taxed in the Rate for the Meeting-house in 1672, he appears to have previously removed to some other place; or, more probably as Mr. Savage thought, to have died in Mar., 1670, for the "5th of Apr. that year his wife had administered."

was committed during the minority of the Exec. to James Pierce, John Pierce and Timothy Snow.

Savage calls this Joseph, "prob. s. of Thomas." The opinion seems to me correct, for the following reasons: John of Woburn is not known to have had any son Benjamin, Samuel or William : Thomas of Woburn had sons Samuel and William. The parentage of Benjamin of Woburn, who had a son Thomas, is doubtful. He is not a son of Robert, and may have been son of either Thomas or John—probably the former. Again, the only Ichabod Pierce we know was the son of Nathaniel, a son of Robert and his second wife Elizabeth Foster, who was, says Savage, "perhaps the widow of Hopestill Foster." If this conjecture is correct, she was, before her first marriage to Thomas Whittemore, Elizabeth Pierce, "prob. d. of Thomas Pierce," and this relationship would explain Joseph's calling Ichabod "cozen" (i. e., as commonly used at that day, Nephew). On the whole, therefore, it appears that the hypothesis of Joseph's being the son of Thomas is that which best explains the various facts of the case. At the same time, we must regard Benjamin who m. Mary Reed, William who m. Abigail Somers, and Elizabeth the second wife of Nathaniel Peirce, as children of Sergt. Thomas Pierce.

27. vi.   STEPHEN, b. July 16, 1651; m. Nov. 18, 1676, Tabitha Parker.
28. vii. SAMUEL, b. Feb. 20, 1654; d. Oct. 27, 1655.
29. viii. SAMUEL, b. Apr. 7, 1656; m. Dec. 9, 1680, Lydia Bacon.
30. ix.   WILLIAM, b. Mar. 7, 1658; m. Apr. 8, 1690, Abigail Sommers nee Warrin.
31. x.   JAMES, b. May 7, 1659; m. Elizabeth Kendall.
32. xi.   ABIGAIL, b. Nov. 20, 1660; m. Feb. 18, 1684, George Reed, Jr., b. Sept. 14, 1660, d. Jan. 20, 1756. She d. Sept. 7, 1719, and he m. 2nd, May 24, 1721, Mrs. Sybil Rice. Ch. Abigail, b. Feb. 6, 1686; Ebenezer, b. Mar. 6, 1690; George, Jr., b. Aug. 2, 1697, d. Oct. 6, 1697; Eliza, b. June 4, 1700, m. Christopher Paige.
33. xii. BENJAMIN; m. Mary Read. (Not named by Savage).

INVENTORY of the Estate of Sergt. Thomas Pierce, late of Woburn, who deceased upon the 6th of Nov., anno dom. 1683. Amount £440. Appraisers : Matthew Johnson and James Convers.

ESTATE.—Thomas Pierce of Woburn sells Thomas Richardson, forty acres formerly of John Cole—s. E., Mount Discovery; N., Mr. Graves; W., T. R.; E., Samuel Richardson, Aberjona river; ack. 11 (8) 1650. Of T. Burgess, 20 acres, 1662. With R. Lowden, of J. Smith Exr., four and one half acres, 1674. Same to J. Dexter, 1677, rec. 1684. Of R. Lowden, two acres, 1680. Of B. Davis, three acres, 1682.

11.   SAMUEL[3] PIERCE (Samuel[2], Thomas[1]) ; m. Mary Orton, b. June 26, 1648. Res. in Charlestown. His estate was inventoried March 30, 1691, at £169. Children :—

34. i.   MARY, b. Dec. 1, 1683.
35. ii.   JOHN, b. Feb. 17, 1686.
36. iii. NEHEMIAH, b. Nov. 11, 1688.
37. iv.   BARIAH, b. Feb. 7, 1689.

15.   JONATHAN[3] PIERCE (Samuel[2], Thomas[1]), b. 1661 ; m. Dec. 4, 1683, Mary Lobdell, b. 1663, d. Dec. 18, 1744, buried at Copp's Hill. They res. in Charlestown, where he d. July 4, 1722 ; on the 16th of July of this year, adm'n of his estate was given to his widow Mary. The persons interested in the estate were, May 23, 1723-4, the widow Mary ; Joseph, the third son, "the eldest now alive"; Benjamin and

Isaac, of full age; John and Stephen, minors (Isaac Smith guardian);
Mary, who m. Isaac Smith; Martha, who m. John Steele of Boston;
Elizabeth, who m. Abraham Smith; Humphrey Scarlet, who m. the
widow of Samuel; the eldest s. of Jonathan who left one dau.; the
three [?] ch. of a dead son, Jonathan, whose widow had died. Thos.
Webb was admr.

Jonathan peirc

Children:—

38. i.　MARY, b. Sept. 4, 1686; m. Nov. 22, 1709, Isaac Smith of
　　　　　　Reading. She d. 1740.
39. ii.　SAMUEL, b. Feb. 19, 1687; m. Feb. 5, 1711, Mehitable Harrise.
40. iii.　JONATHAN, b. Oct. 18, 1689; d. Oct. 18, 1689. "Dead born."
41. iv.　JONATHAN, b. Jan. 24, 1690; m. Mary Webb.
42. v.　THOMAS, b.. Mar. 29, 1693; d. young.
43. vi.　JOSEPH, b. Jan. 25, 1694; m. May 17, 1715, Mary Mellens.
44. vii.　MARTHA, b. Jan. 5, 1696; m. John Steele of Boston.
45. viii.　BENJAMIN, b. Sept. 30, 1698; m. Mary ———.
46. ix.　SARAH; bap. at Cambridge, July 28, 1699.
47. x.　ELIZABETH, b. June 29, 1700; m. Nov. 5, 1720, Abraham Smith.
48. xi.　ISAAC, b. June 27, 1702; m. Agnes Kent.
49. xii.　JOHN, b. Dec. 23, 1703; m. Elizabeth ——— and Mary Hoppings.
50. xiii.　JACOB, b. Aug. 24, 1705; d. Aug. 24, 1705.
51. xiv.　STEPHEN, b. Jan. 24, 1706; m. May 20, 1728, Elizabeth Rand.

ESTATE.—Grant, 10½ acres—N. W., range; N. E., John Pierce; S. E., Capt.
Wheeler; S. W., Thomas Pierce; 1685. Buys of B. Bunker 6 acres, 1699—1700,
rec. 1708. To Samuel Whittemore, 16½ acres—W., range; E., Mr. Wheeler;
N., S. W.; S., John Pierce; with Mary Pierce, Sr.; 1700, rec. 1703. To S.
Counce, house, 1704, of John Pierce, three acres, 1707. To Joseph Kent,
same, 1707. With John P. to W. Richardson, wood-lot, 12 acres No. 56
between Burt and Wilder, 1707. To A. Ireland, 6 acres of Bunker, 1708. To
Spencer Phipps [27] lots, 1709, 1710. To son, Samuel, house and 30 acres,
etc., 1713. Of Mehitable, widow of Saml. P., the same, 1714-15. To C.
Chambers, mort. same lots, 1715-16.

ADMIN.—To widow, July 16, 1722.

INVENTORY.—House and 10 acres, being 4 acres meadow, 3 acres orchard,
3 acres plowland—N., road; S., field; E., common; W., D. Russell. 19½ acres
pasture—N., fieldway; W., Asbury; S., Banister; S. E., Col. Phipps' way.
Two acres marsh. Two acres upland—N., fieldway; W., Pierce; S., E. Lynde;
E., creek. 1½ acres and 6 acres, being 7½ acres woods, 1st Div., 2nd, range,
Mystic side.

DIVISION: To widow, S. W. part of house, 1½ acres orchard and meadow,
2 acres of upland, 2¼ acres woods, 6 acres of the 19½.
WIDOW deeds to children all right to husband's estate, 1728.

HEIRS sell to Joseph Pierce, N. E. end of house, and cellar under N. W. end,
⅔ barn at W. end, and 8¾ acres—N., road; E., watering-place to Bullard's
bridge; S., fieldway; W., Asbury. 13½ acres—W., Asbury; Russell and widow's
thirds; S., Col. Lynde, Col. Phillips and Asbury; S. W., Banister. ¼ of 5
acres woods gr. Drinker's house, No. 45, 3¼ acres, lot, No. 56, gr. Thomas
Pierce, 1724-5. Heirs (by Joseph and John Pierce attorneys) to N. Tufts,
1½ acres orchard—N., road; W., D. Russell; E., N. T.; S., brook. 6 acres—N.,
fieldway; W., Asbury; S., Tufts; E., way to S. Phipps. ¼ of barn, the S. E.
part. 2¼ acres, N. end of six-acre lot, 1728-9.

16. John³ Pierce (*Samuel²*, *Thomas¹*), b. 1664; m. Feb. 4, 1691, Elizabeth Mudge, b. Mar. 12, 1674, bap. in 1691. She was adm. to the church Aug. 21, 1715. He d. in Charlestown, Sept. 28, 1716. John Pierce of Charlestown, yeoman (will dated Sept. 27, 1716, proved Nov. 8, 1716), names his w. Elizabeth (Exec.), his three sons, John, George and James (none of age), and his six daughters, Elizabeth, Hannah, Mary, Abigail, Sarah and Mercy (all Pierce). William Rand is a witness and gives bonds for the Executrix. [The widow's estate was administered in 1748]. In 1752, the following were the heirs of this estate:—John Pierce of Stow, housewright: James Pierce, Charlestown, yeoman; the heirs of Elizabeth Lee, dec'd, represented by Joseph Lee of Boston, sailmaker; Hannah Fillebrown, w. of Isaac Fillebrown of Charlestown, yeoman; Sarah Prentice, w. of Ebenezer Prentice of Cambridge, housewright; the heirs of Abigail Osborn, dec'd, who m. Thos. Osborn and had s. Thomas and dau. Elizabeth; the heirs of Mary Reed, dec'd; Mercy Prentice, the w. of Jonas Prentice of Cambridge, husbandman. Among those interested in the estate were John Truman, mariner; Thomas Hudson, carter; and Samuel Haley, goldsmith, all of Boston.

John pierce

Children:—

52. i. ELIZABETH; bap. Mar. 12, 1693-4; m. Dec. 5, 1717, Joseph Lee of Boston. She d. prior to 1725, for he then m. his second wife.
53. ii. HANNAH, b. Aug. 4, 1694; m. Dec. 25, 1718, Isaac Fillebrown of Charlestown. She d. Dec. 27, 1773.
54. iii. MARY, b. June 11, 1696; m. Timothy Reed, Jr., and d. Apr. 7, 1745, æ 49.
55. iv. JOHN, b. Aug. 8, 1698; m. Susanna Marrett.
56. v. GEORGE, b. Nov. 21, 1700; d. Oct. 1, 1716.
57. vi. JAMES, b. Aug. 12, 1703; m. Mary Prentice and Alice Fessenden.
58. vii. SARAH, b. Oct. 3, 1706; d. July 25, 1709.
59. viii. SARAH, b. Oct. 29, 1711; m. Aug. 21, 1735, Ebenezer Prentice.
60. ix. ABIGAIL; bap. Feb. 27, 1708; m. Oct. 24, 1734, Thomas Osborn, and had Thomas and Elizabeth. She d. prior to 1752.
61. x. MERCY, b. June 22, 1714; m. Apr. 22, 1736, Jonas Prentice of Cambridge.

ESTATE.—Grant 7 acres—N w., range; N. E., P. Tufts; s. w., Timothy Wheeler; s. E., Jonathan P.; 1685. Sells Isaac Fowle, ¾ acre near Training-field, 1696-7, rec. 1734. To Jonathan Fosdick, house, 1699. To Samuel Whittemore 8 acres—N. w., rangeway; s. w., Jonathan P.; s. E., Mr. Wheeler; N. E., Peter Tufts; 1699, rec. 1703. Of S. Counce, qt. cl. his wife's share estate that Samuel Pierce left son Thomas, 1699, rec. 1726. Of C. Crosswell, 8 acres, 1701, rec. 1726. Of John Cutler, 1 acre, 1704. Of John Lynde's heirs, W. Rand, S. Counce, Isaac Cleveland by agent, and Abigail Pierce; rights in Samuel and Thomas P.'s estates, 1706. Of S. Counce, 1 acre, 1707. To Jonathan Pierce, 3 acres, 1707; with Jonathan P. to W. Richardson, woods, 1707. Exchanges with Joseph Whittemore: gives 1¼ acres—s. w., road; N. w., N. Salisbury, P. Fowle, W. Brown; N. and N. E., Mystic river;

s. e., town; receives 3¾ acres late of Joseph Frost and gr. ch. of Thomas White—n. e., highway; s. e., town, James Russell; s. w., J. R.; n. w., J. Whittemore; n., highway : 1709. To William Smith, 7 acres 2nd Div., common—n. w., range; n. e., W. S,; e. s., James Tufts; s. w., Samuel Whittemore; 1709, rec. 1718.

Will—Sept. 27 (pro. Nov. 7), 1716, devised to wife, the house and lot bo't of Whittemore, during life; to John, George and James, house and land and to pay their six sisters' moneys.

Elizabeth (widow's) Admin. to son John, March 9, 1748. The dower set. to John, he to pay bros. and sisters, 1752.

22. Ensign John[3] Pierce (*Thomas[2], Thomas[1]*), b. May 7, 1643; m. July 5, 1663, Deborah Convers, b. July 25, 1647. He was a resident of Woburn and was a yeoman. His will was dated Apr. 26, 1716, lodged Friday, Apr. 8, 1720, names his Dear and loving wife Deborah, his s. John, Daniel, Ebenezer, James, his dau. Ruth and the ch. of his dau. Deborah Wilson, dec'd, his s. Josiah Exec. Witnesses, Kundul Goodwin, Nathaniel Nickols and Ebenezer Flagg.

John Pierce

Children, b. in Woburn :—

62. i. Deborah, b. Oct. 30, 1666; m. a Wilson.
63. ii. John, b. Jan. 26, 1671; m. 1697, Mary Parker.
64. iii. Thomas, b. Dec. 23, 1673; d. bef. 1716.
65. iv. James, b. Aug. 6, 1674; d. Sept. 13, 1685.
66. v. Daniel, b. Oct. 7, 1676; m. July 3, 1705, Dinah Holt.
67. vi. James, b. Oct. 8, 1686. He was taxed in Woburn in 1707-8-11-13, and then his name disappears from the lists.
68. vii. Ebenezer, b. 1687; m. Mary ——.
69. viii. Joseph, b. Aug. 24, 1688. He paid his last tax in Woburn in 1711.
70. ix. Ruth, b. 1690.
71. x. Josiah, b. June 10, 1691; m. Hannah Thompson.

23. Thomas[3] Pierce, Jr. (*Thomas[2], Thomas[1]*), b. June 21, 1645; m. Eliza ——; m. 2nd, Mar. 24, 1680, Rachel Bacon, b. June 4, 1652. He d. Dec. 8, 1717. They res. in Woburn. The following is an abstract of his will, dated Nov. 26, 1717 :—

Thomas Pierce, husbandman, &c. *Imps.* After my & my wife Rachel's decease I give my whole estate to my three children, viz :
To my son Timothy Pierce of Plainfield
To my daughter Rachel
" " " Abigil, All my housing and lands in Woburn, both real and personal estate. They to pay the several legacies.
To my daughter Abigill 14£ in 6 months to make her equal to Rachel.
Item. With reference to my son Thomas' children, although I gave to my son Thomas in the time of his life his full part and portion out of my esteat, notwithstanding, out of my good will and tender affection which I do bear towards them his children, I do give & be-

queath unto Thomas the eldest son of my son Thomas as aforesaid deceased, 40 shillings, and to Ebenezer 40 shillings, and to Amos 5 shillings and to Mary 5 shillings, and to Rachel 5 shillings to be paid in one year after my decease : And to Mary, she that was the relicke widow of my son, I give 5 shillings in token of my love to her in one year.

I make Timothy Pierce, & my son in law David Roberts Executors.

Thomas perce

Witnesses.
{ JOSEPH KNIGHT.
{ JACOB FOWLE.
{ JOHN RUSSELL.

Children, b. in Woburn :—

72. i.   THOMAS, b. Feb. 12, 1670; m. Feb. 27, 1692, Mary Wyman.
73. ii. TIMOTHY, b. Jan. 25, 1673; m. May 27, 1696, Lydia Spaulding;
         m. 2nd, Oct. 12, 1709, Hannah Bradhurst.
74. iii. ELIZABETH, b. Jan. 5, 1676; d. Feb. 15, 1699.
75. iv. RACHEL, b. July 24, 1681; m. Jesse Osmer.
76. v.   ABIGAIL, b. Apr. 14, 1685; m. David Roberts.
77. vi. ISAAC, b. Dec. 23, 1686; d. Dec. 28, 1686.
78. vii. EBENEZER, b. Dec. 10, 1687; d. May 25, 1688.
79. viii. PHEBE, b. Feb. 13, 1689; d. July 12, 1707.

27. STEPHEN[3] PIERCE (*Thomas*[2], *Thomas*[1]), b. July 16, 1651 ; m. Nov. 18, 1676, Tabitha Parker, d. Jan. 31, 1742. He d. June 10, 1733. They res. in Chelmsford. His will, dated June 7, 1732, proved July 23, 1733, names his wife Tabitha, his s. Jacob, his s. Jacob's eldest s. Stephen, Robert Pierce, and Thomas Pierce, his s. Benjamin's s. Stephen Fletcher, his dau. Tabitha's eldest, his s. Stephen, his s. Benjamin, his dau. Sary (Sarah), his dau. Tabitha, his eldest s. Jacob (to whom he gives no land, because he went away when he was young and learned a trade and so was not profitable to the estate). He made his w. and his s.-in-law William Fletcher, his Execs.

Tabitha Pierce, widow of Stephen of Chelmsford (will Nov. 18, 1735, lodged Dec. 20, 1744, on citation of Judge of Prob.), names her gr. dau. Sarah Wheeler, her dau. Fletcher, her dau. Wheeler, her s. Stephen and s.-in-law William Fletcher (Execs.), her gr. s. Oliver Pierce. Witnesses : Eleazer Tyng, Benjamin Parker, Tabitha Fletcher.

Stephen Peirce

Children, b. in Chelmsford :—

80. i.   STEPHEN, b. 1679; m. Jan. 5, 1707, Esther Fletcher.
81. ii. BENJAMIN, b. June 4, 1682; m. ——— ———.
82. iii. SARY (Sarah), b. Mar. 25, 1686; m. a Wheeler.
83. iv. TABITHA, b. Feb. 24, 1689; m. William Fletcher.   Ch. Stephen.
84. v.   JACOB; m. ——— ———.

29. SAMUEL[3] PIERCE (*Thomas*[2], *Thomas*[1]), b. Apr. 7, 1656; m. Dec. 9, 1680, Lydia Bacon, b. Mar. 6, 1656, d. Dec. 5, 1717. They res. in Woburn, where he d. July 5, 1721.

July 28, 1721, Samuel Pierce of Woburn, admr. of est. of his late father, Samuel, giving bonds with Benj. Pierce, wit. Ebenezer Johnson, and Isaac Pierce, agreements of the children of the dec'd (July 17, 1721), signed by Peter Waite (as guardian to his two ch.), Ruth Pierce, Hannah Pierce, Tabitha Pierce, Samuel Pierce, Isaac Pierce, Timothy Snow, Abraham Hill. Witnessed by Joseph Wright, Ebenezer Peck, and Josiah Converse. (Joseph Whittemore and Cabel Blodget, to Peter Waite signing). Inv. £167—17—00.

Samuel Peirce senr

Children, b. in Woburn :—

85. i. SAMUEL, Jr., b. Nov. 25, 1681; m. June 14, 1705, Abigail Johnson.
86. ii. LYDIA, b. May 25, 1683; m. Timothy Snow.
87. iii. JOSEPH, b. Mar. 28, 1685; d. young; not mentioned in father's will.
88. iv. ISAAC, b. Mar. 22, 1687; m. May 5, 1708, Grace Tucker.
89. v. ABIGAIL, b. Feb. 27, 1689; m. May 22, 1718, Peter Waite, b. Jan. 20, 1689, d. Dec. 8, 1721, in Medford, leaving by his 2nd wife, Peter, Jr., b. Apr. 21, 1720, d. June 15, 1794, leaving a large family, and Jonathan, b. Mar. 24, 1721.
90. vi. SARAH, b. June 22, 1691; m. Peter Waite. She d. Aug. 16, 1717, leaving Sarah, b. Jan. 15, 1713, and Mercy, b. Apr. 28, 1716.
91. vii. RUTH, b. Feb. 14, 1693; m. Abraham Hill.
92. viii. TABITHA, b. Aug. 28, 1697; d. Sept. 30, 1697.
93. ix. TABITHA, b. Mar. 10, 1700.

30. WILLIAM[3] PIERCE (*Thomas*[2], *Thomas*[1]), b. Mar. 7, 1658; m. Apr. 8, 1690, Abigail Summers *nee* Warrin, d. June 4, 1726. He res. in Woburn and was a soldier in 1675. He d. Aug. 22, 1720. Nov. 14, 1720, articles of agreement between Abigail Pierce, wid. of the late William of Woburn, dec'd, and her son, Summear (Sommers), s. of the same. Wit. John Pierce and John Russell. Children :—

94. i. EVA, b. Oct. 13, 1694; d. Aug. 1, 1695.
95. ii. SOMMERS, b. Feb. 16, 1697; m. Mar. 3, 1726, Martha Holt of Andover.

31. JAMES[3] PIERCE (*Thomas*[2], *Thomas*[1]), b. May 7, 1659; m.* Elizabeth Kendall, b. Jan. 15, 1653, d. Oct. 16, 1715. He res. in Woburn and d. Jan. 20, 1742.

James Peirce

Children :—

96. i. ELIZABETH, b. Oct. 11, 1688.

---

* By this marriage a *lusus naturæ* of an extra finger or toe, and sometimes both, was produced, and this has ever since appeared in this branch of the family.

97. ii. JAMES, b. Feb. 28, 1690; m. Hannah ———, and Phebe ———.
98. iii. REBECKAH, b. Sept. 16, 1692; m. Feb. 12, 1714, Nathaniel
      Winship.
99. iv. MARY, b. ———; m. Lea F. Kendall.

33. Sergt. BENJAMIN[3] PIERCE (*Thomas*[2], *Thomas*[1]); m. 10 (8),
1688, Mary Reed, b. Oct. 15, 1670, d. June 17, 1746. He d. Sept. 25,
1739, in Woburn.
    Mary Pierce of Woburn, Mar. 10, 1739, admit. admrx. of Est. of her
late husb., Benjamin Pierce, late of Woburn, dec'd, int.: giving bonds
in £1500, with Samuel Richardson and Thomas Belknap, husbandmen,
all of Woburn. Inventory of estate taken 20th, and presented 24th
Mar., 1739–40, amounting to about £325 (land £195), apprized by
David Wyman, Thomas Belknap and James Proctor. Mary (no date)
declares the estate insolvent. Thomas, Sept. 30, 1740, "one of the
heirs, complains of improper administration, after hearing on Oct. 6,
the Judge was of the opinion that the inventory ought to be amended"
so as to include property not taken account of.

Benjamin Peirce

Children, b. in Woburn:—

100. i. BENJAMIN, b. Aug. 28, 1689; m. Martha ———.
101. ii. MARY, b. Jan. 29, 1692.
102. iii. ESTHER, b. Oct. 25, 1696; m. Mar. 31, 1718, Edward Walker, b.
      1694, d. Dec. 6, 1787. She d. Sept. 23, 1761, leaving nine
      children.
103. iv. REBECCA, b. Oct. 10, 1698.
104. v. DEBORAH, b. Dec. 5, 1700; m. Sept. 25, 1722, Samuel Dunton.
105. vi. THOMAS, b. Nov. 23, 1702; m. Hannah Locke and Lydia Gibbs.
106. vii. ZURISHADDI, b. June 22, 1705; m. July 24, 1728, Abigail Johnson.

39. SAMUEL[4] PIERCE (*Jonathan*[3], *Samuel*[2], *Thomas*[1]), b. Feb. 19,
1687; m. Feb. 5, 1711, Mehitable Harrise, b. Feb. 8, 1690. He d.
Apr. 24, 1714. Mehitable Pierce of Charlestown, May 19, 1714,
admit. admx. of Est. of her late husband Samuel, late of Charlestown,
intest., giving bonds in £200 with Edward Thomas and Edward
Stevens, both of Boston. Wit. Thos. Foxcraft and Rebeckah Rost.
Inv. £380—04—11, taken May 25, 1714, by Edward Thomas and
Joseph Kent. A bond given by dec'd June 8, 1713, describes him as
of Boston, shipwright. They res. in Charlestown, and she m. 2nd, in
1718, Humphrey Scarlet.

Samuel Peirce

Child:—

107. i. REBECCA, b. Mar. 30, 1713. (Per Probate).

ESTATE.—Deed from father, house, etc., 1713. To W. Brattle, treasurer
of Harvard College, mort. lots, 1713–14, dis. by widow 1714–15.

ADMIN. to widow, May 19, 1714.

41. JONATHAN[4] PIERCE, Jr. (*Jonathan[3], Samuel[2], Thomas[1]*), b. Mar. 29, 1693; m. Nov. 27, 1712, Mary Webb, d. prior to 1722-3. They res. in Boston and he d. bef. 1722.

Children :—

108. i.   SARAH, b. Sept. 28, 1714.
109. ii..   MARY, b. Dec. 13, 1716.
110. iii. SUSANNA, b. May 9, 1719; d. 1721.
111. iv.   JONATHAN, b. July 17, 1721.

ESTATE.—Admin. to Thomas Webb, Nov. 20, 1721.

2nd, Admin. to widow Elizabeth Webb, May 22, 1729. (Suffolk Prob.)

43. JOSEPH[4] PIERCE (*Jonathan[3], Samuel[2], Thomas[1]*), b. Jan. 25, 1694; m. Mary Mellens, May 17, 1716. He d. 1750-2. He was a fisherman and joiner. They lived in Boston.

Children :—

112. i.   ELIZABETH, b. ———; m. ——— Robbins.
113. ii.   JOSEPH, b. Sept. 21, 1721; m. Mary Pierce.
114. iii. MARTHA, b. Oct. 6, 1723; m. ——— Davidson.
115. iv.   SUSANNA, b. June 1, 1726; m. ——— Beach.
116. v.   JONATHAN, b. Oct. 6, 1728; d. June 15, 1730.
117. vi.   RUTH, b. Dec. 30, 1730; m. ——— Williams.
118. vii. JONATHAN, b. Nov. 27, 1735.
119. viii. MARY, b. June 23, 1741.
120. ix.   JOSIAH, b. Oct. 19, 1742.

ESTATE.—Mort. to W. Rand and Nathaniel Tufts, ⅔ of father Jonathan's estate, 30 acres, made up of house and 10 acres—N., road; s., way over Bullard's bridge; N. w. and w., J. Asbury, D. Russell. 16 acres—N., highway between house-lot; E., way to Spencer Phipps', Camb. line; w. and N. w., J. A. 4 acres marsh—E., creek; s., J. Lynde; N. w., way to S. P.; N., way over bridge. ½ wood-lot, 1st Div., 2½ acres—s. and w., Jonathan P., dec.; w., Asbury; E., Lynde; 1723-4. Mort. to C. Chambers, lots, 1724. Of Pierce heirs, 1724-5. Of father's heirs, 1724-5. To N. Tufts, same, 1724-5. With bro. John, of mother, all right in father's estate, 1728. With bro. John, and in behalf of bro. Benjamin, to Daniel Russell, 2 acres marsh, 2 upland—N., fieldway; w., way to Col. Phipps'; s., Nathaniel Tufts, J. Lynde, 1728.

45. BENJAMIN[4] PIERCE (*Jonathan[3], Samuel[2], Thomas[1]*), b. Sept. 30, 1698; m. Mary ———. He was a housewright. They lived in Stratford, Conn. Children :—

121. i.   MARY, b. Apr. 4, 1727.

ESTATE—joins deed with father's heirs to bro. Joseph, 1724-5.

48. ISAAC[4] PIERCE (*Jonathan[3], Samuel[2], Thomas[1]*), b. June 27, 1702; m. June 21, 1722, Agnes Kent. He d. prior to 1746, for in

that year she was published to Robert Stone. They res. on Deer Island, Boston Harbor. He was a fisherman and ropemaker.

Isaac Pierce

Children :—

122. i. ISAAC, b. Apr. 3, 1723; m. Miriam James.
123. ii. AGNES, b. May 17, 1724; m. —— Lobdell.
124. iii. JOANNA, b. Apr. 6, 1727.
125. iv. JOHN, b. June 23, 1729; d. young.
126. v. THOMAZIA, b. Jan. 8, 1731.
127. vi. MARY, b. Jan. 7, 1733.
128. vii. ELIZABETH, b. Apr. 8, 1736.
129. viii. JOHN, b. May 19, 1738.
130. ix. JOSHUA, b. Aug. 28, 1740.

ESTATE.—Sells bros. John and Joseph, rights, 1728.

49. JOHN[4] PIERCE (*Jonathan*[3], *Samuel*[2], *Thomas*[1]), b. Dec. 23, 1703; m. Elizabeth ——, who owned the covenant Mar. 20, 1725–6; m. 2nd, Jan. 15, 1735, Mary Hoppings, bap. June 16, 1717. Res. Boston. He was a potter.

John Pierce

Children :—

131. i. ELIZABETH, b. Feb. 19 (bap. Mar. 20), 1725.
132. ii. MARY, b. Nov. 19, 1727.

ESTATE.—With bro. Joseph buys of heirs, 1728–9.

51. STEPHEN[4] PIERCE (*Jonathan*[3], *Samuel*[2], *Thomas*[1]), b. Jan. 24, 1706; m. Elizabeth Rand, May 20, 1724, b. Sept. 22, 1706. She d. Aug. 15, 1779. He d. Sept. 23, 1785. He was a leather-dresser. Stephen and his wife were both buried in Old Reading. He received war aid at Reading æ 71 with his daughter æ 45 in 1775. He was admitted to the Charlestown church Feb. 15, 1729–30. Res. Charlestown and Reading. Children :—

133. i. STEPHEN, b. Apr. 5, 1729; m. Harriet Gullison.
134. ii. ELIZABETH, b. Dec. 3, 1731; d. unm. in 1800.
135. iii. MARY, b. Mar. 26, 1734; m. Samuel Damon.
136. iv. JONATHAN, b. 1735; bap. Feb. 3, 1735; d. soon.
137. v. JONATHAN, b. 1737; bap. Oct. 23, 1738.
138. vi. SAMUEL; bap. Apr. 20, 1740; m. Harriet Larkin and Jemima ——.
139. vii. MARTHA, b. 1742; m. John Harrison.

ESTATE.—Taxed 1727–1773 (ex. 1738): and in 1766, for son Samuel. Buys of John Griffin, house, 1732–3. To E. Sumner, 1744, rec. 1759. Buys of Thomas Fluker, house, 1768. Of J. Hancock, qt. cl. same, 1768. To T. F., mort. 1768, dis. 1771. To Abigail Stevens, mort. 1769, dis. 1773. Claimed for loss of 1775.

ADMIN.—To Samuel, June 3, 1800.

INVENTORY.—1 acre lot, begin. at N. W. corner of R. Miller, run. N. W., bd.
W., Main street, 157; N. W., Oliver Holden, 312; N. E., O. H., 120; S., R. M.,
300.

HEIRS.—Samuel, Elizabeth and Mary Damon sell to J. Harrison, 1798.

55. JOHN[4] PIERCE (*John[3], Samuel[2], Thomas[1]*), b. Aug. 8, 1698;
m. Sept. 27, 1722, Susanna Marrett, b. 1698. He d. April, 1753.
Res. Stow. No children. She m. 2nd, Jonathan Loring of Marlboro,
and d. there in 1798. She was the sister of Mrs. Judah Morris of
Harvard University.

ESTATE.—John Pierce added to tax list, Oct. 2, 1721; taxed 1727. Deed
with bro. James of S. Counce estate, late of Samuel Pierce, 1738-9.

WILL.—April 26, 1753, pro. Mar. 31, 1755, devised to wife use during life of
real estate, except that from father occ. by bro. James; to James ⅓ estate
from father then to his ch.; to John, son of James, one farm land and buildings; to Thomas Osborn, nephew, the other half; the niece Elizabeth Osborn,
legacy; Dr. Samuel Brigham, Jr., bondsman for widow, the Ex'x. Children of
bro. James shared his house and 9 acres—s., Camb. road; E., James P.; N.,
range; w., Menotomy road.

57. JAMES[4] PIERCE (*John[3], Samuel[2], Thomas[1]*), b. Aug. 12, 1703;
m. Mary Prentice, Feb. 10, 1731, b. Oct. 8, 1705; m. 2nd, Mrs. Alice
Fessenden (pub.) Feb. 9, 1760. Res. Charlestown. Children :—

140. i.   MARY, b. Dec. 5, 1731; m. Oct. 19, 1753, Nathaniel Tufts, and
           2nd, Abraham Frost.
141. ii.   ABIGAIL, b. 1732; m. June 6, 1764, Isaiah Tufts, b. 1740, d. May
           1, 1773.
142. iii. ELIZABETH, b. Feb. 10, 1734; m. Nov. 15, 1764, Wm. Tufts, b.
           1720, d. Nov. 2, 1773.
143. iv.   JOHN, b. Dec. 14, 1735.
144. v.   SUSANNA, b. Oct. 12, 1737; m. Samuel Choate.
145. vi.   JAMES*, b. Dec. 27, 1739; m. Mary Frost, and d. Sept. 23, 1815,
146. vii. GEORGE, b. Oct. 30, 1743. He was a soldier in B. Locke's Co. in
           Rev. War, in 1778.
147. viii. HANNAH, b. Nov. 10, 1745; m. Mar. 9, 1772, Caleb Rand, b. 1751,
           d. Oct. 9, 1807. She d. May 13, 1802.
148. ix.   SAMUEL, b. Oct. 23, 1748. He was a soldier in B. Locke's Co.,
           and prob. d. bet. 1778-82, as his estate (which he rec'd from
           his father) was admin. to Samuel Tufts, Nov. 7, 1782.

ESTATE.—Taxed 1727-1766 (ex. 1738, 1739, 1762); abated Dec. 2, 1742.
buys of Joseph Lynde, at Wildredge hill, 1728-9. Of Theophilus Ivory, 1½
acres, 1732. Of W. Rand, 3-6 of 2 acres—w., Camb. road; N. W., range; on
all other sides by J. P.: 1734-5, rec. 1738. With bro. John of S. Counce,
1738-9.

WILL, Jan. 19 (pro. May 7), 1771, devised to wife Alice use of real estate in
Chas. and Medford; to dau. Hannah and "other children"; legacy to widow
Abigail Bodge.

INVENTORY.—(1) 20 acres Wildredge's hill, £180. (2) ½ of house and 17
acres—s. E., Camb. road; w., Menotomy road; N., range; N. E., J. P.: £181.
(3) Lands in Medford.

———

* ESTATE.—Sells John Stone, 8½ acres—w., range; N., Abigail Shed heirs;
E., Nehemiah Rand, S. Shed; s., James and John P., 1783. To S. Shed, 3
acres—s., road; N., John Stone; E., S. S.; w., Mary Frost, S. Choate, 1789.

ADMIN. to Samuel Tufts, April 6, 1781.

INVENTORY.—6 acres 20 rods mowing—s., Camb. road; E., S. Shed; N., J. P.; W., S. Choate, Mary Frost. 8 acres 45 rods—W., range; N., heirs of E. Shed; E., Nehemiah Rand, S. Shed; S., S. Choate, etc.

DIVISION.—To Elizabeth, 3¾ acres 6 rods of 1st lot. To James, 8 acres 45 r. To Mary, 1 acre 5 r. 1st lot. To Susanna, 1 acre 49 r. 1st lot. These heirs sold Jonathan Hastings, 7 acres 26 poles, 1772. They rec'd of estate of Uncle John P., viz.: Mary Frost, house and 60 rods of land. Susanna Choate, 1 acre 27 rods. George P., 1 acre 14 rods. Abigail Tufts, 1 acre 22 rods. Hannah Rand, 1 acre 30 rods. James P., 1 acre 44 rods. Samuel P., 1 acre 61 rods. Elizabeth Tufts, 1 acre 62 rods.

ROYAL MORSE and wife, heirs of Hannah Rand, complained in 1815 that S. Tufts had made no account. It soon appeared at Court.

63. JOHN[4] PIERCE (*John*[3], *Thomas*[2], *Thomas*[1]), b. Jan. 26, 1671; m. Mary Parker in 1697. He d. 1735. Res. Woburn.

[signature: John Peirce]

Children :—

149. i. THOMAS, b. Aug. 11, 1698; d. Dec. 18, 1698.
150. ii. MARY, b. Jan. 6, 1702; m. Solomon Wyman.
151. iii. ABIJAH, b. Aug. 6, 1716; d. Aug. 14, 1716.

In the Name of God Amen, I John peirce of Woobourn in the County of Middle[x] within His Maj[st] province of y[e] Massachussets Bay in New England Husbandman, being aged : but of perfect mind and memory thanks be given to God therefor, calling to mind the mortality of my Body and knowing that it is appointed for all men once to Dye Do make and ordain this my Last will and Testament. that is to say principly and first of all I give and Recomend my soul into y[e] Hands of God that gave it hooping through y[e] merits Death and passion of my saviour Jesus Christ to have full and free pardon of all my sins., and to Inherit Everlasting Life, and my Body I commit to y[e] Earth to be Burried in Christian Decent Burial at y[e] Discretion of my Executor[x] hereafter Named Nothing Doubting but at y[e] Generall Resurrection I shall Recive the same Again by y[e] mighty power of God ; and as Touching such worldly Goods and Estate wherewith it hath pleased God to Bless me with all in this Life I give Demise and Disspose, of of y[e] same in y[e] following manner and form : that is to say

First. I will that all my Just Debts that I Do owe to any parson or persons whatsoever, be well and Truly paid in Conveniant time by Executor[x] hereafter Named.   .   .   .   .   .   .

Item. To Mary my Dear and well Beloved Wife Whom I Likewise make and ordain my only and sole Executor[x] of this my Last Will and Testament I give and Bequeath the use and Improvement of all my Housing and Lands (not Dissposed of) During y[e] Term that she shall Remain my Widow : And also y[e] use and Improvement of all my moveable Estate which I shall not Disspose of in this my Last will and Testament And also she paying out of y[e] same the Legacies that I shall order her to Do herein : And if my said Wife shall See Cause to

5

Mariy Againe then she shall have a fether Bead and y[e] furniture belonging to y[e] same, and also fifty pounds more att her Choice out of my moveable Estate : but if she shall Dye my Widow then she shall have y[e] Liberty of Dissposing of my moveable Estate amongst my Grand Children Children of my Daughter Mary Wyman : that is to say y[e] Remainder that I do not Dispose of in this my Last will and Testament.   .   .   .   .   .

Item. To my well beloved and Dutyfull Daughter Mary Wyman I give and Bequeathe y[e] sum of Teen pounds or to y[e] vallue thereoff to be paid to her out of my moveable Estate by my afore Named Executor[x].

Item. To my Grand Daughter Mary Wyman I give and Bequeath a feather Bead with y[e] furniture, that is one of my fether Beads that I Now have.   .   .   .   .   .   *Item.*

Item. To my Cousen John Peirce son of my Brother Daniell peirce I give and Bequeath my Gunn or fire Lock.

Item. To my Grand son John Wyman Eldest Son of my Daughter Mary I give and Bequeath all and Singuler my Housings and Lands wheresoever and whatsoever to him his heirs and assigns for ever he paying out to y[e] Rest of my Daughter Marys Children to each and every of them Teen pounds apeace : upon mariage or when they shall Arive to y[e] Age of Twenty and one years but it is to be understood that my afore said Grand son is not to come into possession of Any of my Housing or Lands untill my afore said Wife shall mary or at her Decease : and if my afore s[d] Grand son shall Dye before that he shall Arive to y[e] Age of Twenty and one years that then all my Housing and Lands shall be Equally Devided Amongst y[e] surviving children of my afore s[d] Daughter Mary Wyman.   .   .   .   .

And further my Will is that my Son in Law Sollomon Wyman shall have and I give unto him all my wearing apparile—And I do hereby utterly Disallow Revoke and Dissanull all and every other and former Testaments Wills and Legacies Bequests and Executors by me in any way, before this Time Named Willed and Bequeathed Rectifying and Confirming this (and y[e] foregoing page) and no other to be my Last Will and Testament. In Witness where off I y[e] said John peirce have hereunto sett my hand and seal this Teenth Day of Aprile Annoye Domini one thousand seven hundred thirty and five and in y[e] Eight year of his Maj[st] Reign &c.   .   .   .   .

Signed sealed pronounced and Declared ⎤
  by y[e] said John Peirce as his Last |
  Will and and Testament in presence |
  of us the Subscribers viz:— . . ⎬ JOHN PEIRCE (Seal)
   -   SAMUEL NEVERS |
      EBENEZER JOHNSON |
      JOHN RUSSELL ⎦

66. DANIEL[4] PIERCE (*John*[3], *Thomas*[2], *Thomas*[1]), b. Oct. 7, 1676 ; m. Dinah Holt, July 3, 1705, b. May 23, 1681. Res. Woburn, Wilmington and Harvard. Children :—

152. i. ABIGAIL, b. May 18, 1706 ; m. Ephraim Buck, Jr.

153. ii.　THOMAS, b. Oct. 30, 1707; m. Hannah Thompson.
154. iii.　SARAH, b. May 30, 1709; m. Daniel Albert.
155. iv.　JOSEPH, b. May 5, 1711; m. Abigail Green.
156. v.　DANIEL, b. June 23, 1714; m. Sarah Buck.
157. vi.　JOHN, b. May 23, 1716; m. Hannah Stone and Hannah Houghton.
158. vii.　DINAH, b. Nov. 2, 1719.
159. viii.　KEZIAH, b. May 9, 1723.

68.　EBENEZER[4] PIERCE (*John*[3], *Thomas*[2], *Thomas*[1]), b. 1687; m. Mary ———. He d. May, 1766. They res. in Woburn and Wilmington.

Children :—

160. i.　MARY, b. Feb. 21, 1708; m. July 8, 1730, Samuel Wyman.
161. ii.　DEBORAH, b. Nov. 4, 1709; m. Mar. 11, 1729, Increase Wyman.
162. iii.　EBENEZER, b. Sept. 11, 1711; m. Feb. 25, 1742, Mary Stowe.
163. iv.　JONATHAN, b. July 28, 1713; d. 1739.
164.　　ELIZABETH,　　　　　　　　　　　　　　m. ——— Johnson.
v.　　　　　　　　　　　　　　twins, b. Sept. 8, 1715,
165.　　RUTH,　　　　　　　　　　　　　　m. Feb. 24, 1737, Ephraim Kendall.
166. vi.　JOSHUA, b. May 2, 1718; m. Lois ———.
167. vii.　REBECCA, b. Apr. 7, 1720; m. Oct. 31, 1740, Jacob Barrett.
168. viii.　NATHAN, b. Sept. 12, 1723.

In the name of god Amen 8th Day of September : A. D. 1757 I Ebenezer peirce of wilmington in y⁶ County of Middlesix Gentleman being weake of Bodey but of perfict mind & mimory thanks be givin to god therefor : and calling to mind the mortality of my Bodey, and Knowing that it is appointed to men once to Die. Do make and ordain this my Last will & testement : That is to Say first of all I Recomend my Soul into y⁶ hands of God who gave it : and my Bodey I Recommend to be buryed in a Christian maner at y⁶ Discretion of my wife & my Executer hereafter named : nothing Doubting but at y⁶ Generall Reserrection I shall Recive y⁶ Same again by y⁶ mighty power of god : And touching Such Worldly Estate where with it haith pleased god to Bless me in this Life : I give Demise & Dispose of y⁶ Same in y⁶ following manner & form :

First I will & ordain that all my Just Debts & funerall Charges be paid by my Executer here after named out of my moveable Estate :

Imprimis I give and bequeath to my true and Loveing Wife Mary peirce the use and Improvement of all my Real and personal Estate : inCluding quick Stock Husbandry vtensals : money : notes of hand : book Debts & Bonds : where Ever any of y⁶ Same is or may be found : During her naturall Life : and if my Said Loveing wife shall find it of necessity to Sell away aney of y⁶ Said Real or personal Estate for her Comforttable Subsistance : I will & ordaine y⁶ Same to her & her assigns for Ever and at her Decease what of my Estate Remains I will and ordain it Shall be disposed of in y⁶ following mannor

Item. I will and bequeath to my Dutifull Son Nathan peirce five Shillings to be paid to him by my Executor in one year after my Decese and y[e] Reason why I give my Dutifull Son Nathan nomore in this my Last will is: because I have already given him his portion of my Estate.

Item. I will and Bequeath all the Remainder of my Estate at my wife Decese to be Divided to & among my Dutifull Childeren whose names is hereafter written : in Such mannor & form as y[e] Law has provided in Case of Intestats. (Viz) one Duble Share to my Eldist Son Ebenezer peirce : one Single Share to y[e] Childeren of my Son Joshua peirs Decest : one Single Share to my Daughter Mary Wyman : one Single Share to y[e] Childeren of my Daughter Debro wyman Decest : one Single Share to my Daughter Elisabeth Johnson : and one Single Share to my Daughter Rebeckah Barritt : and I will & ordain that the Share that might have gon to my Daughter Ruth Kindal Shall be Delivered to y[e] Children of y[e] Said Ruth Kindal as they arive to full age : by my Executer : and in Lue of my Said Daughters her porsion of my Said Estate I will & Bequeath to her my Daughter Ruth Kindal five Shillings to be paid to her in one year after her mothers Decese by my Executor.

Finally. I do hereby nominate & appoint that my Son Ebenezer peirce shall be the only & Sole Executer of this my Last will and testement vtterly Revokeing and making void all other wills and Executers by me in anie wise made or named heretofore Declaring this and this only to be my Last will and Testament in witness whereof I the said Ebenezer peirce Have hereunto Set my hand and affixed my Seal the Day and yeare above written.

Signed Sealed pronounced
  & Declared By the Said
  Ebenezer peirce to be his
  Last will & testement
  in the presence of us   EBENEZER PEIRCE (Seal).
  y[e] Subscribers—
REUBEN BUTTERS
SAMUEL FRENCH
WILLIAM BUTTERS Junier.

71. JOSIAH[4] PIERCE (*John[3], Thomas[2], Thomas[1]*), b. June 10, 1691 ; m. Hannah Thompson, b. June 28, 1691. They res. in Woburn. He was styled "Lieut."

Children :—

169. i.   JOSIAH, b. Mar. 30, 1720 ; m. Aug. 15, 1752, Ruth Dorr ; m. 2nd, Jan. 15, 1756, Mrs. Ruth (Simonds) Thompson.
170. ii.   JOHN, b. Aug. 13, 1724 ; m. ——— ———.
171. iii. HANNAH, b. Dec. 6, 1728 ; d. Oct. 23, 1755.

72. THOMAS[4] PIERCE (*Thomas[3], Thomas[2], Thomas[1]*), b. Feb. 12, 1670 ; m. Mary Wyman, Feb. 27, 1692, b. June 25, 1674. He d. between 1704 and 1708. Res. Woburn, and removed to Plainfield, Conn., where he was Deacon of the 1st Church in 1742.

Children :—

172. i. THOMAS, b. Oct. 10, 1696; m. Mary Parkhurst.
173. ii. EBENEZER, b. Sept. 10, 1698; m. Lydia ———.
174. iii. ELIZABETH, b. July 23, 1700; d. July 5, 1704.
175. iv. AMOS, b. Aug. 3, 1702; m. Mary Spaulding and Widow Pyer.
176. v. JOHN, b. Feb. 10, 1704; m. ——— ———.

73. TIMOTHY⁴ PIERCE (*Thomas³, Thomas², Thomas¹*), b. Jan. 25, 1673; m. May 27, 1696, Lydia Spaulding, d. Mar. 23, 1705; m. 2nd, Oct. 12, 1709, Hannah Bradhurst, b. Dec. 14, 1682, d. Apr. 2, 1747. They res. in Plainfield, Conn., and he d. May 25, 1748. The following is a copy of his will, dated Apr. 12, 1748 :—

After all my just Debts and funeral charges are all paid, I give and dispose of the same in the following manner. I give to the widow Mary Pierce, my daughter-in-law, the sum of forty shillings in Bills of credit at tenor, and I give to each of the children of my son Timothy Pierce, deceased, the sum of twenty shillings apeace in Bills of credit at tenor, with what I have given to my son Timothy in his life-time, as the full of their portion of my estate. I give to my son Nathanel Pierce the sum of fifteen pounds in Bills of credit at tenor with what I have already given him, which makes the full of his portion out of my estate. I give to my daughter Phebe Smith my Negro girl Dinah and the sum of one hundred pounds of my in doore movable estate at inventory price at the rate of all tenor bills with what I have given her, which makes the full of her portion of my estate. I give to the two children of my Grandaughter Lydia Cortland, deceased. To each of them ten pounds in Bills of credit at tenor, to be paid by my executor, to each of them. The son at twenty-one years of age and the daughter at eighteen years of age or at marriage day, and if at eighteen one of the sᵈ two children dyes before the time to receive, then the surviving one to have the other ten pounds, and if both sᵈ children should die before the sᵈ time to receive, The sᵈ legacies then I give it to my son Ezekiel and to his heirs. I give and bequeath all the remainder of my estate Both Real and personal of what kind soever to my son Ezekiel Pierce and his heirs forever, and I do make and appoint my sᵈ son Ezekiel the sole Executor of this my last will and testament Ratefying and confirming this and no other to be my last will and testament. Signed, sealed, published, pronunced and declared by the sᵈ Timothy Pierce as his last will and testament the day and year first written.

Tims peirce

Children :—

177. i. TIMOTHY, Jr., b. Oct. 7, 1698; m. June 12, 1723, Mary Wheeler.
178. ii. NATHANIEL, b. June 3, 1701; m. Feb. 20, 1723, Elizabeth Stevens and Mrs. Simonds.
179. iii. JEDEDIAH, b. Feb. 23, 1703; d. Feb. 21, 1746.
180. iv. LYDIA, b. Mar. 10, 1705; m. Dr. Joseph Perkins.
181. v. BENJAMIN, b. June 7, 1710; m. Hannah Smith; m. 2nd, July 15, 1737, Naomy Richards; m. 3rd, Aug. 31, 1758, Sarah Mills; m. 4th, Jan. 28, 1762, Sarah Holt.

182. vi.   EZEKIEL, b. Jan. 8, 1712; m. Feb. 11, 1736, Lois Stevens.
183. vii. PHEBE, b. Feb. 19, 1714; m. John Smith.
184. viii. HANNAH, b. May 8, 1717; d. Sept. 3, 1727.
185. ix.   ABEL, b. June 17, 1720; d. Sept, 4, 1736.
185½ x.   JABEZ, b. ———, m. Susannah Sheppard.

Timothy Pierce was one of Plainfield's most prominent men. Judge of Probate, Col. of Militia, and member of the Governor's Council.

80.   STEPHEN[4] PIERCE (*Stephen[3]*, *Thomas[2]*, *Thomas[1]*), b. 1679; m. Esther Fletcher, Jan. 5, 1707, b. 1681. He d. Sept. 9, 1749. Res. Chelmsford, Mass.

Stephen· Peirce

Children :—

186. i.   ROBERT, b. Jan. 19, 1708; m. Mary ———.
187. ii.   OLIVER, b. May 15, 1709; m. Ann Hunt and Hannah Adams.
188. iii. ESTHER, b. April 25, 1711; m. Nathan Richardson.
189. iv.   WILLIAM, b. May 7, 1713; m. Sarah ———.
190. v.   STEPHEN, b. April 10, 1715; m. Betsey Bowers.
191. vi.   TABITHA, b. Feb. 28, 1716; m. ——— French.
192. vii. REMEMBRANCE, b. Feb. 11, 1719; m. ——— Parker.
193. viii. SARAH, b. Jan. 10, 1720; d. Jan. 19, 1745.
194. ix.   MARY, b. Dec. 14, 1722; unm. in 1750.
195. x.   BENJAMIN, b. Nov. 25, 1726; m. Elizabeth Merrill.

81.   BENJAMIN[4] PIERCE (*Stephen[3]*, *Thomas[2]*, *Thomas[1]*), b. June 4, 1682; m. ——— ———. He d. Sept. 9, 1749. Res. Chelmsford. Children :—

196. i.   ROBERT; d. Sept. 6, 1783.
197. ii. THOMAS.

84.   JACOB[4] PIERCE (*Stephen[3]*, *Thomas[2]*, *Thomas[1]*); m. ——— ———. Res. Chelmsford. Child :—

198. i.   STEPHEN, b. 1698; m. Rachel Harrod.

85.   SAMUEL[4] PIERCE (*Samuel[3]*, *Thomas[2]*, *Thomas[1]*), b. Nov. 25, 1681; m. Abigail Johnson, June 14, 1705. She d. March 16, 1787. He d. Jan. 26, 1774. Res. Woburn and Wilmington, Mass., and Mansfield, Conn.

Samuel parce—

Children :—

199. i.   SAMUEL, b. June 3, 1706; m. Abigail ———.
200. ii.   JOSIAH, b. July 13, 1708; m. Miriam Cook.
201. iii. ABIGAIL, b. Feb. 28, 1711; m. Zeph. Wyman.
202. iv.   ESTHER, b. Feb. 7, 1715; m. Shubel Dimick.
203. v.   SETH, b. Nov. 30, 1716; m. Elizabeth Nye.
204. vi.   ENOCH, b. March 22, 1719; m. Mary Mason.

88.   ISAAC[4] PIERCE (*Samuel[3]*, *Thomas[2]*, *Thomas[1]*), b. Mar. 22,

1687; m. Grace Tucker, dau. of Lewis Tucker,'of Casco, Me., May 5, 1708. Res. Boston.

Isaac Peirce

Children :—

205. i. ISAAC, b. Apr. 12, 1709; d. June 25, 1709.
206. ii. SARAH, b. May 22, 1710.
207. iii. LYDIA, b. Sept. 1, 1712.
208. iv. MARY, b. Dec. 7, 1713.
209. v. ELIZABETH, b. May 17, 1715.
210. vi. SAMUEL, b. Apr. 11, 1719; d. 1803; buried at Copp's Hill, Boston.
211. vii. ISAAC, b. Oct. 12, 1722; m. Mary Hardy.

95. SOMMERS⁴ PIERCE (*William³*, *Thomas²*, *Thomas¹*), b. Feb. 16, 1697; m. Martha Holt, Mar. 3, 1726. They res. in Andover, Mass., and moved to Pomfret, Conn. Taxed in Woburn to Nov. 28, 1726.

Summer Pearce

Child :—

212. i. WILLIAM, b. Mar. 16, 1727; m. Hannah ——.

97. JAMES⁴ PIERCE (*James³*, *Thomas²*, *Thomas¹*), b. Feb. 28, 1690; m. Hannah ——; m. 2nd, Phebe ——. She d. 1776. He d. Dec. 21, 1773. Res. Woburn.

James peirce

Phebe peirce

Children :—

213. i.   REBECCA, b. Oct. 8, 1711; d. young probably,—not mentioned in her father's will.
214. ii. PHEBE, b. Sept. 28, 1713; m. Feb. 1, 1746, Jona. Locke, b. 1717, d. June 10, 1799. She d. Mar. 2, 1793. Ch. : Jonathan, Jr., b. Sept. 12, 1746, d. infant; Phebe, b. Mar. 1, 1748, m. Aaron Tay; Jonathan, Jr., b. Nov. 29, 1749, m. Mary Frost; James, b. Apr. 7, 1752, m. Sally Sommers; Josiah, b. Feb. 3, 1753, m. Elizabeth Richardson.
215. iii. JAMES; m. Mar. 17, 1753, Phebe Tottingham.
216. iv. JOSHUA, b. Apr. 1, 1722; m. Feb. 18, 1749, Susan Reed; m. 2nd, Oct. 27, 1753, Esther Richardson.
217. v.   JACOB, b. Sept. 15, 1724; m. Aug. 18, 1752, Abigail Kendall.
218. vi. KEZIAH, b. Oct. 10, 1726; m. July 2, 1747, Richard Cutter, b. Mar. 9, 1725. She d. Dec. 19, 1788. Ch. : Thomas, b. May 29, 1748, m. Betsey Sands; Ruhumah, b. Mar. 6, 1750, m. Daniel Smith; Keziah, b. Nov. 10, 1751, m. a Wyatt; Hannah, b. Jan. 16, 1754, m. a Hobbs; Richard, b. Mar. 26, 1756, m. Miriam Brown; Seth, b. Apr. 14, 1758, m. Abiah Tallant; Susannah, b. Oct. 14, 1760, m. Wm. Fletcher; Rhoda, b. Dec. 4, 1762, m. Benjamin

Teel; Lucy, b. June 19, 1765, m. James Roby and Nathan Fisk; John, b. Apr. 14, 1767, m. Miriam Butler. They res. in Woburn, Mass., and Hudson, N. H.

219. vii.   MARY, b. June 24, 1730; m. July 7, 1750, Nathan Richardson, Jr., b. Apr. 21, 1725, d. Sept. 21, 1817. She d. Jan. 11, 1773. Ch. : Abel, b. Jan. 12, 1750, m. Ann Tufts; Nathan, b. 1753, m. Lydia Whittemore; Mary, b. Jan. 24, 1755, d. Oct. 10, 1759; Mary, b. Apr. 16, 1761, d. Dec. 8, 1762. They res. in Woburn.

220. viii. ESTHER, b. Mar. 14, 1733; m. May 10, 1751, Ammi Cutter, b. Oct. 27, 1733, d. Apr. 19, 1795. She d. Jan. 8, 1772, in Woburn. Ch. : Esther, b. Nov. 10, 1751, d. Dec. 18, 1751; John, b. Oct. 25, 1753, m. Lucy Adams; Ammi, b. Oct. 3, 1775, m. Esther Winship; Lydia, b. Oct. 26, 1757, m. Jonathan Teel; James, b. Dec. 14, 1759, m. Anna H. Russell, Mehitable Cutter, Lydia Adams and Mrs. Rebecca Parker; Benjamin, b. Nov. 7, 1761, m. Ann Wyeth; Jonas, b. Oct. 13, 1763, m. Lydia Frost; Esther R., b. Sept. 26, 1765, m. Ebenezer Hall; Ephraim, b. Oct. 31, 1767, m. Deborah Locke; Frances, b. Dec. 30, 1769, m. Walter Russell.

221. ix.   EUNICE, b. Feb. 19, 1735; m. Mar. 30, 1756, Oliver Richardson, b. Aug. 15, 1706, d. Apr. 7, 1795. She d. Apr. 5, 1774. No issue.

222. x.   SUSANNA, b. May 22, 1736; d. May 23, 1736.

223. xi.   SUSANNA; m. John Tay.

In the Name of God Amen this Fifteanth Day of March one thousand Seven Hundred and Sixty Nine and in the Ninth year of his majestis Rain I James Peirce of woburn In the County of middlesex and Province of the masichusets bay In Newingland Youman Being of Parfict mind and memory Thanks Beto God their For yet calling to mind the mortality of my Body that it is appointed For all men once to Die Do mak and ordain this my last will and Testement whereby Principally and First of all I Give and Recomend my sole Into the Hands of God that Gave it and my Body I Recomend to the Durst to be Buryed by a Decant Christon Buryal at the Dscresion of my Executer hear after to be Named Nothing Doubting butt I shall Reseav the same again at the General Reseretion by the mighty Power of God. and as Touching my worly Estat it Hath Pleased God to Bless me with In this life I dispose of In the Following manner—

Imprs.   I do Give and Bequeathe unto Phebee my Dearly Beloved wife the uce and Improvement of the one half of my Real Estate wheare as I have sold the one half to my sone Jacob Peirce here to fore I Do Give the Improvement of the other half to my d wife so long as she Remain my wido and also the Improvement of all my houshold stuf or In Dore movable that I Do Not Hear after Dispose of

I Give and Bequeath unto my Two sons each of them one Shilling lawfull money Namely James and Joshua to be Paid by my Executer Imeadetly after my Deseas having Given each of them their Full Portion bear to fore   .   .   .   .

Itam   I Give and Bequeath unto my Son Jacob whome I ordain Sole Executer of this my last will and Testement to him and his Heirs and assigns for Ever all my Real Estat In woburn or Elswhare my Right in the metting house in the First Parish my Comb and Tackling all my Carpentors Tolls Flex comb Stilyards Half Bushel half Peck and a large meal chest and all such of my Parsonell Estat that I have Not

other wise Disposed of by this will He paying all my gust Debts and
Funeral charges of me and my wife and the several Legacies ordered
in this my last will . . . .

Itam I Give and Bequeathe unt my six Daughters namly Phebee
Kesiah Mary Easther Eunice and susanah all my houshold stuf after
the deseas of me and my wife that is Not otherwise Disposed of in this
will to be eaquelly Dovided amongst them. also my will is and I do
order my Executter above Naned to Pay unto my six Daughters above
Named Imedatly after the Deceàs of me and my wife Towards their
Funerah Habit six Pounds thirteau shillings and Four Pence lawfull
mony to be Equell Devided amongst then . . .

Itam. I Give and Bequeath unto my Daughter Phebee six shillings lawfull mony wich I order my Ex^tr above Named to Pay with in
Two years after the Deseas of me and my wife . . .

Itam. I Give and Bequeathe unto my Daughter Kesiah Twelve
Shillings lawfull mony which I order my Executer above Named to
Pay in Two years after the Decest of me and my wife . .

Itam. I Give and Bequeth unto my Daughter Mary Forty shillings lawfull mony which I order my Executter to Pay in Two years
after the Decece of me and my wife.

Item. I Give and Bequeath unto my Dauhter Easther six pounds
Seventean Shillings lawfull mony which I order my Executter to Pay
in Two years after the Deseas of me and my wife.

Itam. I Give and Bequeth unto my Daughter unice Forty Pounds
lawfull mony to her her Heirs and asigns which I order my Ex^tr above
Named to Pay in one year after the Deseas of me and my wife also I
Give this my Daughter one Fether Bead and the Furnetuer their to
Belonging the same that she Now loges upon also Two small Putter
Platters and three Putter Plats and I order my Executter above Named
to Provid and Bring in to her Imeadetly after the Decase of me and my
wife Four Bushels of Endion Corn and Two Bushels of Rje and one
hundred and 20 and Twenty Pounds of Good Pork. . .

And wheiras I Did Give to my Daughter Susanah In a late will
which I Now Disnowl the sum of Five Pounds Fourteen shillings and
Two Pence lawfull mony she Having Reseaved of my Executter above
Named that full sum with her Full Part of the Six Pounds Thirtean
Shillings and Four Pence which I Gave to my six Daughters for there
Funeral Habit. as by the Recip of her Husband John Tay Baring
Dat February the 11, 1769 may be mad more fully to appear so that I
Give nothing to her In this my last will saving her Equall Part with
the Rest of her sisters In my houshold stuff. . . .

Further My will is and I Do order my Executter above Named to
lett my wife have the uce and Improvement of Two Good Cows and
Find a hors and cary my s^d wife to meeting and Elsewhare as she shall
have occasion and also lett her have full liberty of setting In my Puee
In the meetting house so long as she shall Remain my wido. . .

Also my will is that my Executter above Named shall have the
liberty to ocepy and Improve that Part of my Rail Estat which I have
Given the Improvment of to my s^d wife Paying a Reasunable Rent to

6

her yearly and Every year. and if they Do Not agree how much the
Rent shall be it shall be left to three Inditerant men to say how much
the Rent shall be and the s^d Execntte shall have the Refusel of Im-
proving he Paing the rent they sett it at and if he Refuse to Give the
same she shall have full libourty to lett the same to sum other Parson.

And I Do Hearby utterly Disallow and Nulefye all and Every other
Former Wills and Testements legacies Bequeats In any manner by me
Named willed and Bequethed Rattifying and Confirming this and and
only this to be my last will and Testement In Confirmation where of I
have Hearunto sett my hand and afixed my seal the Day and year First
mentioned.

Signed sealed Published and
    Pronunced by the above said
    James Peirce to be his last
    will and Testement In   his
    presence of us   JAMES ⋈ PEIRCE (Seal)
    SAMUEL WYMAN   mark.
    NATHAN RICHARDSON
    JOSIAH PARKER.

100. Benjamin[4] Pierce (*Benjamin[3]*, *Thomas[2]*, *Thomas[1]*), b. Aug.
28, 1689; m. Martha ———. He d. Nov. 27, 1713. Res. Woburn.

Children :—

224. i.   Benjamin, b. Apr. 26, 1712; m. Oct. 26, 1732. Phebe Thompson,
        b. 1704, d. Aug. 11, 1787; m. 2nd, Dec. 9, 1787, Jerusha Rich-
        ardson, d. 1799. He d. June 11, 1788.
225. ii.   Martha, b. Apr. 5, 1714. (Posthumous.)

105. Thomas[4] Pierce (*Benjamin[3]*, *Thomas[2]*, *Thomas[1]*), b. Nov.
23, 1702 ; m. Nov. 5, 1722, Hannah Locke, b. July 11, 1701, d. bef.
Jan. 24, 1743, for at that time he m. 2nd, Lydia Gibbs. He d. Mar.
10, 1768. He first went to Leicester, then to Hopkinton. His wife
was admitted to the church in that town in 1730, by letter from the
church at Leicester. In 1747, he resided in Framingham. Thomas
Pierce of Framingham, yeoman, advanced in age (will, Feb. 22, 1768,
pro. Apr. 5, 1768), names his w. Ledy (Exec.), his children, viz: Jonathan, John, Elizabeth, Mary, Martha, Mehitable, his s. Thomas, his s.
Benjamin, the heirs of his s. Timothy dec'd, his s. James, his d.
Hannah Ballard, his dau. Hephzibah Dolby (Dolbier). Agreement of
children and heirs signed by Mary Pierce, Thomas, Martha, Jonathan,
John, Elizabeth (all Pierce), Hannah Ballard, William Ballard, Hitte
Pierce. John (over 14) was put under guardianship Apr. 5, 1768.

A very singular error was five times repeated on the Middlesex Probate records in 1747, where guardians were appointed to the children
of the first wife, her father having deceased, leaving the children
property. In the records of the appointment of guardian, it is recited
that they were "the children of Thomas Pierce, late of Framingham,

deceased," when in fact he did not die till twenty-one years after. It was the wife who had "deceased."

Thos Pearce

Children :—

225A. i. HANNAH, b. Feb. 1, 1723; m. Aug. 25, 1741. William Ballard,* d. in Framingham, Dec. 10, 1802. Ch.: Beulah, m. Sam'l Ballard; Anna, m. Ephraim Pratt; Esther, m. Jona. Flagg. Jr.; Ebenezer, d. unm.; Sarah, m. A. M. Chandler.

225¼. ii. BENJAMIN, b. 1725; m. May 7, 1752, Mary Lamson.

225⅓. iii. THOMAS, b. 1727; m. Apr. 26, 1750, Mary Haven.

225B. iv. EBENEZER, b. Dec. 22, 1728; d. bef. 1748; not mentioned in father's will.

225C. v. HEPZIBAH, b. Apr. 18, 1731; m. in King's Chapel, Boston, Feb. 18, 1760, Benjamin Dolbier. They res. in Newton, Weston and Templeton. Ch.: James, b. Nov. 5, 1760; Timothy, b. Mar. 23, 1762; Samuel, b. Jan. 13, 1764; Nathan, b. Dec. 23, 1765; Lydia, b. Oct. 19, 1767; Umphre, b. Jan. 1, 1769.

225½. vi. TIMOTHY, b. Mar. 31, 1734; m. Mar. 27, 1755, Abigail Knap.

225D. vii. JAMES, b. Oct. 22, 1737.

225E. viii. PHEBE, b. July 22, 1739; d. Mar. 1, 1755.

225F. ix. ELIZABETH, b. Nov. 30, 1744; m. Apr. 25. 1771, Silas Haven.

225¾. x. JONATHAN, b. Dec. 4, 1745; m. Lydia ———; res. Framingham. Ch. Jonathan, b. July 28, 1788.

225G. xi. MARY, b. Aug. 7, 1748; m. July 1, 1772, Amos Stimpson.

225H. xii. MARTHA, b. June 25, 1749.

225⅞. xiii. JOHN, b. Oct. 20, 1751; m. Mar. 3, 1773, Mary Brown.

225J. xiv. MEHITABLE, b. July 21, 1758.

106. ZURISHADDAI[4] PIERCE (*Benjamin[3], Thomas[2], Thomas[1]*), b. June 22, 1705; m. July 24, 1728, Abigail Johnson. They d. bef. 1762, in Woburn.

Josiah Johnson, Esq., of Woburn, was, Mar. 29, 1762, appd. guardian to Benjamin (15 years old in May, 1761), and Hannah Pierce, ch. of Zurishaddai, late of Woburn, died, giving bonds with Benjamin Reed, Esq., of Lexington.

Zurishaddai Pirce

Children :—

226. i. ABIGAIL, b. June 22, 1729.

227. ii. MARTHA, b. Jan. 13, 1731; d. young.

228. iii. MARY, b. Jan. 10, 1733.

229. iv. JONATHAN, b. May 22, 1737.

---

* Was b. at Lynn, the son of William, gr. son of Nathaniel, and gr. gr. son of William, all of Lynn. William, Sen., is supposed to have come from England in the *James*, 1634, then aged 32; was made a freeman May 2, 1638; was a member of the Quarterly Court at Salem, the same year. His ch. were John, Nathaniel and Elizabeth. He d. before March 1, 1641, making a nuncupative will, by which he gave half of his estate to his wf. and half to his child. The name was sometimes spelled Ballord. (For a further account of the Ballards see Lewis' History of Lynn, and Barry's Hist. of Framingham). William, Jr., who m. Hannah Pierce, was a miller; his house was destroyed by fire in 1797, and he d. Dec., 1802, at an advanced age.

230. v.   MARTHA, b. Sept. 1, 1742; m. Aug. 8, 1769, Samuel Woolsy.
231. vi. BENJAMIN, b. Apr. 27, 1746.
232. vii. HANNAH.

113.   JOSEPH[5] PIERCE, Jr. (*Joseph*[4], *Jonathan*[3], *Samuel*[2], *Thomas*,[1]),
b. Sept. 21, 1721; m. Mar. 20, 1744, Mary Pierce; d. Nov. 5, 1807.
They res. in Chelmsford.   He d. June 14, 1796.

Joseph Peirce

Children :—

233. i.   SILAS, b. July 22, 1744; m. Mar. 26, 1771, Lucy Spaulding; m. 2d,
          Apr. 12, 1774, Elizabeth Barron; m. 3rd, Dec. 7, 1786, Lydia
          Richardson; m. 4th, Dec. 28, 1797, Sarah Goodhue; m. 5th,
          Sept. 1, 1800, Bridget Putman; m. 6th, November 20, 1806,
          Hannah Littlehale.
234. ii. WILLARD, b. Dec. 1, 1746; m. Mar. 23, 1780, Olive Kemp.
235. iii. LEVI, b. Feb. 20, 1747; m. Jan. 3, 1776, Remembrance Fletcher.
236. iv. THANKFUL, b. June 9, 1751; m. Samson Walker; d. 1828, in
          Andover, Vt.   Ch. : Thankful, m. Eli Burnhap; Sarah, m. James
          Heald; Mary, m. John Felton; Hannah, m. —— Gibson;
          Rachel, m. Daniel Lamson; Amy, m. John Hall; Jesse, m. Lois
          Holt; Pierce, d. unm.; Nathaniel, d. unm.
237. v.   MARY, b. May 16, 1755; d. Oct. 28, 1826.
238. vi. SARAH, b. Dec. 30, 1759; m. Jan. 24, 1780, Amos Byam, and
          2d, —— Parkhurst.
239. vii. RACHEL, b. May 15, 1762; m. May 6, 1784, Nathaniel Harwood, and
          2nd, —— Bowers.
240. viii. JOANNA, b. Mar. 24, 1764; m. June 16, 1785, James Marshall.
          They res. in Chelmsford, and had James.

In the Name of God amen the Twenty second day of April in the
year of our Lord one thousand Seven hundred and Ninety Six I, Joseph
Peirce of the Town of Chelmsford in the county of middlesex and
Commonwealth of massachusetts yeoman being Infirm in Body but in
Perfect mind and memory and thanks be given to God for so Grait a
Blessing but Bairing in mind the certenty of Death and the uncertenty
of the Time there of but knowing it is appointed unto all men once to
die I do make and ordain this as my Last Will and Testament that is
to Say Principly and above all I Give and Recommend my Sole into
the hands of God that Gave it and my Body I Recommend to the
Earth to be Buryed in a Decant and christian manner at the Discretion
of my executer nothing Doubting but at the General Resurection I
shall Receive the Same again by the mighty Power of God . . .
and touching Such Worldly Estate where with it hath Pleased God to
Bless me in this Life I Give and Dispose of it in the following manner
and form viz .   .   .   . it is my Will and order that all my Just
Debts and Funeral Charges Should be payed and Satisfied by my
Executor hear in after Named to be Payed out of my Estate
   Item I give and bequeath unto my well beloved wife mary the
Improvement of all my Estate Borth Rieal and Personal that I shall die
Seazed and Possessed of after my Just Debts and Funeral Charges are
Payed During her Natural Life.   .   .   .   .
   Item I Give unto my Two Sons Willard and Levi the Sum of

Thirty three Dollars to Each of them or their Heirs to be Payed by my Executor hear after named within one year after the Death of my Said wife . . . .

Item I Give unto my Daughters hearafter named viz to Thankfull Mary Sarah Rachel and Joanna or their Heirs the Sum of thirty three Dollar to Each of them to be payed by my Executor hear after Named within one year after the death of my Said wife.

Item it is further my will that my Daughter Mary before mentioned have the Improvment of my middle Room and the Sellr unter the Same So Long as She Shall Remain unmarried after the death of my Said wife.

Itam it is my Will further that at the Death of my Said wife that all my Household furniture Should be Equilly Devided among my Children

Itam it is my Will that my Executor Should pay the Funeral Charges of my Said wife.

Turn over

Itam furthermore at the Deces of my Said wife I do give unto my Son Silas or his heirs the whol of the Estate Borth Reail and personal that shall then be left by my Said wife that I Died Seazed and possessed of.

and I do Like wise Constitute and ordayn my Said Son Silas my Sole Executor of this my Last Will and Testement and I do Confirm this and no other to be my Last Will and Testement in witness wher of I do hear unto Set my hand and Seal this twety Second day of April in the year of our Lord one thousand seven hundred and Ninety Six

Signed Sealed and Delivered
in presence of us
Henry Coburn   JOSEPH PEIRCE (Seal)
Samuel Procter.
Benj[a] Spaulding

A Copy, Attest, J. H. TYLER, Register.

122. ISAAC[5] PIERCE (*Isaac[4], Jonathan[3], Samuel[2], Thomas[1]*), b. Apr. 3, 1723 ; m. Miriam James, Aug. 8, 1746.* She d. ———. He d. Jan. 7, 1792. Res. Boston.

Children :—

241.   i.   ISAAC, b. June 23, 1747; d. at sea.
241½. ii. ERASMUS, b. Sept. 22, 1748; m. Mrs. Susan (Hewes) Hinckley.
242.   iii. MIRIAM, bap. April 7, 1751; m. Robert Hewes.
242½. iv. AGNES, b. June 22, 1753; m. ——— Lobdell.

*Miriam James, the wife of Isaac Pierce, was a daughter of Demetrius James, a Scotchman, who set up a fishery at Nantasket. The Indians murdered all the family but the wife and Miriam (aged 8 years), who jumped into a boat and fled to Boston. Erasmus James, brother of Demetrius, came with him to this country and set up a distillery at Boston.

243. v.   BETSEY, b. Oct. 12, 1754; m. Benjamin Thompson.
243½. vi. JOSEPH, b. Feb. 29, 1756; m. Sally Pease.
244. vii. SARAH, bap. Sept. 4, 1757; d. young.
244½. viii. DELIVERANCE, b. Oct. 11, 1758; d. young.
245. ix. SARAH,   } bap. March 8, 1761. { d. young.
245½. x.   DELIVERANCE, }
246. xi. JOANNA, bap. July 25, 1762.
246½. xii. JOHN, bap. Aug. 14, 1763; m. Mrs. Sarah Lobdell.
247. xiii. JAMES, b. Sept. 7, 1764; m. Polly Peacock.
247½. xiv. ANNIE, b. ——; m. Joseph Daniel Clark.
248. xv. SARAH, bap. Sept. 20, 1767.

130. JOSHUA[5] PIERCE (*Isaac[4], Jonathan[3], Samuel[2], Thomas[1]*).
b. Aug. 28, 1740 ; m. Sarah Saunders, July 7, 1763. Res. Boston.
Children :—

248½. i.   SARAH, bap. April 29, 1764.
249. ii. SUSANNA, bap. Jan. 10, 1768.
250. iii. JOSHUA, bap. July 2, 1769.

133. STEPHEN[5] PIERCE (*Stephen[4], Jonathan[3], Samuel[2], Thomas[1]*),
b. Apr. 5, 1729; m. Jan. 3, 1753, Harriet Gullison. He and his dau.
were aided in Reading, 1780. She d. Jan. 3, 1800. He d. prior to
1800. Children :—

251. i.   HANNAH, bap. Mar. 21, 1756; m. —— Shepherd.
252. ii. STEPHEN, b. Apr. 18, 1757; prob. d. bef. 1780.

138. SAMUEL[5] PIERCE (*Stephen,[4] Jonathan[3], Samuel[2], Thomas[1]*),
bap. Apr. 20, 1740 ; m. July 24, 1770, Hannah Larkin, b. Apr. 3, 1738,
d. May 17, 1784, and was buried on Copp's Hill; m. 2nd, Jemima
——. He res. in Boston, and had his store on Fleet street. He d.
1803.

Jamuel Pierce

Children :—
253. i.   SAMUEL, b. Aug. 17, 1785; m. Abigail Winslow.
254. ii. BETSEY; m. —— Wilder.

ESTATE—claimed, at Reading, for loss of 1775, sells with heirs to James
Harrison, 1799.

ADMIN. to B. Hurd, May 5, 1803, left land on Main street, next to Harrison,
bounds 15, 19, 3, 52, 12, 71 ft. Settled on widow.

ADMR. sell G. Alexander, ½ house, 1804.

HEIRS, Samuel Pierce, painter, of Boston, and Betsey Pierce, of Reading,
sell to N. R. Holden, lot on Main street, 1819.

153. Capt. THOMAS[5] PIERCE (*Daniel[4], John[3], Thomas[2], Thomas[1]*),
b. Oct. 30, 1707 ; m. Hannah Thompson, July 27, 1732. She d. Aug.
14, 1767. He d. May 19, 1790. Res. in Wilmington. Children :—
255. i.   JACOB, b. Nov. 18, 1738.
256. ii. ESTHER, b. Aug. 27, 1741; m. Joseph Harnden.

155. JOSEPH[5] PIERCE (*Daniel[4], John[3], Thomas[2], Thomas[1]*), b.
May 5, 1711 ; m. Abigail Green, Nov. 10, 1742, b. Apr. 2, 1713. Res.
Woburn. Children :—

257. i. JONATHAN, } twins, b. Nov. 17, 1743; { m. Lettice Warren.
258. ii. DEBORAH, }
259. iii. JOSEPH, b. Apr. 20, 1746.
260. iv. BARZILLAI, b. Nov. 17, 1750; m. Isabel Howe.

156. DANIEL[5] PIERCE (*Daniel[4], John[3], Thomas[2], Thomas[1]*), b. June 23, 1714 ; m. Sarah Buck, Dec. 23, 1741, b. Apr. 3, 1717. She d. May 13, 1758. He d. Apr., 1795. Res. in Harvard and Lunenburg. Children :—

261. i. DAVID, b. Oct. 3, 1742; m. Mrs. Sarah Mainer [?].
262. ii. ABIGAIL, b. Nov. 5, 1744; d. Sept. 6, 1746.
263. iii. REUBEN, b. March 7, 1747; m. Mary Wood.
264. iv. SAMUEL, b. May 21, 1749; m. Abigail Carter and Elizabeth Whiting.
265. v. JACOB, b. Aug. 3, 1751; m. Rebecca Whitcomb.
266. vi. SARAH, b. Aug. 3, 1754; d. Mar. 3, 1771.
267. vii. ABIGAIL, b. Apr. 1, 1756.
268. viii. KEZIAH, b. May 13, 1758; m. July 20, 1781, Jno. Holt of Jaffrey, N. H.

157. JOHN[5] PIERCE (*Daniel[4], John[3], Thomas[2], Thomas[1]*), b. May 23, 1716 ; m. Hannah Stone, Nov. 22, 1744. He m. 2nd, 1747, Hannah Houghton, b. 1729. She died Apr. 17, 1811. He d. 1779. They united with the Harvard church in 1745. He left home during the Rev. war, and it was supposed he was killed in New York in 1779. Res. Harvard and Bolton. Children :—

269. i. HANNAH, b. Aug. 18, 1745; d. Oct. 21, 1745.
270. ii. MENIEH, b. Oct. 19, 1748; m. Elisha Houghton.
271. iii. HANNAH, b. May 6, 1750; d. Oct. 14, 1750.
272. iv. HANNAH, b. Oct. 25, 1751; m. Lemuel Burnham.
273. v. THOMAS, b. Oct. 2, 1754; d. June 14, 1757.
274. vi. LUTHER, b. May 16, 1764; d. 1832; unm.
275. vii. JOHN, b. May 22, 1759; m. Dinah Sawyer.
276. viii. CALVIN, b. Mar. 1, 1766; m. Betsey Brown and Mrs. Lucy Bridge.

162. EBENEZER[5] PIERCE, Jr. (*Ebenezer[4], John[3], Thomas[2], Thomas[1]*), b. Sept. 11, 1711 ; m. Feb. 25, 1742, Mary Stowe, b. Mar. 22, 1719 ; d. Aug. 7, 1801. He d. Mar. 2, 1805. They res. in Sutton and Millbury.

Eben' Peirce

Children :—

277. i. MARY, b. Feb. 4, 1743; m. Feb. 21, 1788, Capt. Abijah Burbank and had no issue.
278. ii. EBENEZER, b. June 9, 1745; m. Eunice Loomis.
279. iii. SARAH, b. July 18, 1747; d. Dec. 9, 1769.
280. iv. RUTH, b. Feb. 27, 1748; d. Sept. 30, 1750.
281. v. RUTH, b. Nov. 25, 1750; d. Oct. 21, 1782.
282. vi. DEBORAH, b. Oct. 28, 1752; m. July 5, 1786, Samuel Small. Ch.: Hannah, m. David Phillips; Sarah; Aaron, m. Sally Stone; Luther.
283. vii. JOHN, b. Apr. 20, 1754; m. Oct. 5, 1775, Lucy Snow.
284. viii. LYDIA, b. Feb. 19, 1756; m. Mar. 23, 1774, Jedediah Barton. Ch.: Rufus, m. Nancy Goddard; Silence, m. Jenison Barton; Lucretia, m. H. B. Harback; Aaron, m. a Park; Pliney, m. a Clemence; Livey, m. a Clemence.

285. ix. JONATHAN, b. Sept. 17, 1757; m. Apr. 15, 1781, Lydia Bowman.
286. x. DAVID, b. Aug. 16, 1760; m. Dec. 9, 1783, Sarah Bridges.
287. xi. AARON, b. Apr. 16, 1762; m. Sept. 8, 1790, Hannah Greenwood.

166. JOSHUA[5] PIERCE (*Ebenezer[4], John[3], Thomas[2], Thomas[1]*), b. May 2, 1718; m. Lois ———. He d. Oct., 1745. Res. Lancaster.*

Joshua peare

Children:—

288. i. JOSHUA, b. May 17, 1741; m. Lydia Goodrich.
289. ii. JONATHAN, b. Jan. 20, 1744; m. Elizabeth Cooper and Mrs. Lydia Francis.

169. JOSIAH[5] PIERCE, Jr. (*Josiah[4], John[3], Thomas[2], Thomas[1]*), b. Mar. 30, 1720; m. Aug. 15, 1752, Mary Dorr, b. 1717, d. Nov. 11, 1753; m. 2nd, Jan. 15, 1756, Mrs. Ruth (Simonds) Thompson. She was the mother of Benjamin Thompson, the Count de Rumford of Bavaria, Germany. She d. 1811. They res. in Woburn. He d. Aug. 18, 1799, in Baldwin, Me.

Josiah Peirce

Children:—

290. i. MARY, b. Oct. 26, 1753; d. Dec. 28, 1753.
291. ii. JOSIAH, b. Aug. 27, 1756; m. Mar., 1787, Phebe Thompson.
292. iii. HANNAH, b. Sept. 12, 1758; d. Dec. 24, 1762.
293. iv. RUTH, b. Dec. 31, 1761; m. Clement Neal of Portsmouth, N. H., and d. 1826.
294. v. JOHN, b. May 26, 1764; m. Rebecca Wilson.
295. vi. HANNAH, b. Jan. 15, 1768; m. June 12, 1791, Bernard Douglass, and d. 1803.

170. JOHN[5] PIERCE (*Josiah[4], John[3], Thomas[2], Thomas[1]*), b. Aug. 13, 1724; m. ——— ———. Res. St. Johnsbury, Vt. Children:—

296. i. DANIEL; b. 1742; m. Mercy Gates.
297. ii. JOSEPH, b. 1749; m. Margaret Gates.
298. iii. THOMAS, b. 1756; m. Abigail ———.

172. THOMAS[5] PIERCE (*Thomas[4], Thomas[3], Thomas[2], Thomas[1]*) b. Oct. 10, 1696; m. Mary Parkhurst,† b. Nov. 30, 1703. She d. Nov. 30, 1789. He d. Jan. 18, 1762. Res. Plainfield, Conn.

The following is a copy of his will: "As touching my worldly goods wherewith it hath pleased God to bless me in this life I give and bequeath of the same in the following manner. I give and Bequeath

*Joshua Pierce was a captain of artillery in the French and Indian war, and was killed in action in October, 1745, by being struck by a cannon ball in the stomach. He had on his person, when killed, a sword which he had previously taken from the body of a French officer, bearing the date of 1414. This same sword was worn by his two sons in the Revolutionary war, at different times, one under General Washington and the other under General Lafayette. It is still in possession of the family.

† Mary Parkhurst was the first white child born in Plainfield.

to Mary my beloved wife the use of my Dwelling house except that part hereafter mentioned, and the use & improvement of one half of my house place with half the use & improvement of all my land in the General field except what is now on the High plain During her Natural Life & also both my Negro man & woman and that my Negro man be free after my s^d wife's decease only he shall be under the care of my son John and shall be maintained by my s^d son when he is Incapable of Providing for himself. Likewise I give to my s^d wife all my household goods except what is hereafter disposed of and one third of all my farming impliments During her Natural life and one yoke of Oxen four cows forty sheep and all my swine meaning that my household goods except what is hereafter mentioned be at her own disposal, and also the above mentioned creatures and likewise my shorel mare and her year old colt and also a 2 years old colt that come of my "Cutler" mare so called.

I give and bequeath unto my son John Pierce all my home Place above mentioned except what is on the high plain above and with-all Priviledges their unto Belonging to be to him his heirs & assigns forever. Except the use & improvements above bequeathed to my s^d wife of one half therein of as above and also four acres Hereafter Disposed of Likewise. I give and Bequeath unto my s^d son the land I had from Mr. Wm. Dean which land lyes North of Moosup River and contains about sixty five acres to be at his disposal in order to pay my just Debts and the legacies hereafter mentioned also I give unto my s^d son my Clock after my wife's deceased and the other two thirds of my farming impliments and the hole of them after my s^d wife's decease and the remaining part of my stock and creature Except what is here in other wise disposed of.

I give and bequeath unto my daughter Lois the wife of Andrew Backus one half of my Winthrop & Gerald farm lying North of s^d Moosup River for quanity & quality to be to her & to the heirs of her body forever with all priviledges to same, belonging likewise.

I give to s^d Andrew Backus all my land lying on the high plain above Being North from the house that William Lovejoy now lives in to be to him & his heirs forever to be Disposed of by him for his best advantage and also one heifer coming three years old.

I give unto my daughter Eunice the other half of my s^d Winthrop & Gerald farm tobe to her & to the heirs of her body forever with all the priviledges to the same Belonging but if she shall die without such heir or heirs then my s^d daughter Lois and her heirs shall have the same Likewise. I give to my s^d daughter Eunice all my land in Kent in the County Litchfield containing three Hundred and fifteen acres to be disposed of to the best advantage for her by my Executor hereafter Named and if she shall die without an heir as above s^d or before she shall have occation for s^d Land then my son John above named shall have the same. Likewise I give her my riding horse and a new side sadle Three cows with calf and twenty sheep and two feather beds and furniture the one which stands in the west chamber, and the other my Executor hereafter named shall provide for her and fifty five pounds in lawful

7

money in four months after she shall be Eighteen Years of age to be paid to her by my s^d Executor & Six large New Silver Spoons which are now in the house and also the west Chamber of my Dwelling House with the Priviledges thereinto belonging so long as she shall remain unmarried only it is to be understood that the widow Ruth Gerald is to have her fire wood off my s^d Winthrop & Gerald farm during her life.

I give to my sister Rachel the wife of Jesse Osmer four punds lawful money in six months after my decease. I give to my cousin Samuel Pierce four acres of Plow land to be measured of to him by my Executor to be to him & his Heirs forever. I give to Stephen the son of my cousin John Pierce three pounds in lawful money to be paid by my Executors. I give to my Beloved friend Elizabeth Spalding five pounds lawful money to be paid by my Executor.

I give to each of my cousin Asa Kingsbury's children one Ewe and lamb out of those sheep that is now in s^d Asa custody.

I give to the Congregationals Comonly known by the name of the " Seperate Church " in s^d Plainfield the sum of thirty pounds in lawful money to be paid in three years after my decease by my. s^d Executor.

And I do hereby appoint and ordain my son John Pierce my sole Executor.

Themy Peivee

Children :—

299. i.   JOHN, b. Feb. 10, 1724; m. Zeuriah Spalding.
300. ii.   PHINEAS. b. Sept. 28, 1725; d. May 9, 1751.
301. iii.   STEPHEN, b. Oct. 31, 1727; d. May 12, 1751.
302. iv.   SUSANNA, b. May 19, 1730; d. May 9, 1751.
303. v.   LOIS, b. Aug. 19, 1732; m. Andrew Backus.
304. vi.   TIMOTHY, b. May 22, 1734; supposed d., as not spoken of in will above.
305. vii.   MARY, b. Dec. 7, 1735; d. Nov. 10, 1748.
306. viii. ESTHER, b. Oct. 17, 1740; d. Nov. 16, 1746.
307. ix.   EUNICE, b. Jan. 30, 1744; m. Isaac Knight.

173.   EBENEZER[5] PIERCE (*Thomas[4], Thomas[3], Thomas[2], Thomas[1]*), b. Sept. 10, 1698; m. Lydia ———. He d. 1739. Res. Plainfield, Conn. Children :—

308. i.   LEMUEL, b. Nov. 16, 1730; m. Dorcas Spalding.
309. ii.   LYDIA, b. July 27, 1732; d. Aug. 17, 1737.
310. iii.   ANNESEPH, b. Apr. 17, 1734.
311. iv.   TEMPERANCE, b. July 23, 1736.
312. v.   WILLIAM, b. 1738.
313. vi.   ELIZABETH.

Thomas Pierce was appointed guardian of Lemuel and William in 1738.

175.   AMOS[5] PIERCE (*Thomas[4], Thomas[3], Thomas[2], Thomas[1]*), b. Aug. 3, 1702; m. Mary Spaulding, d. Feb. 24, 1768; m. 2nd, Widow Pyer. He d. 1791. They res. in Killingly and Canaan, Conn. Children :—

314. i.   KEZIAH, b. Feb. 4, 1727; m. John Franklin.

315. ii. THOMAS, b. July 2, 1729; m. Nov. 19, 1755, Olive Green.
316. iii. ICHABOD, b. Mar. 12, 1731.
317. iv. MARY, b. July 24, 1733; m. Samuel Howe.
318. v. LUCY, b. Sept. 12, 1735; m. Samuel Forbes. She d. Oct. 8, 1813, leaving one ch. Abigail, m. John Adams.
319. vi. RUTH, b. July 25, 1737; m. —— Turner, and d. June 13, 1760.
320. vii. SILAS, b. Oct. 9, 1739. He died Sept. 3, 1760, and left a son Joseph.
321. viii. AMOS, b. Sept. 6, 1742; m. Lois Fellows.
322. ix. ELIZABETH, b. Sept. 6, 1744; m. Nathaniel Lawrence.
323. x. ESTHER, b. Jan. 16, 1747; m. Rev. Mr. Campbell.
324. xi. EDWARD, b. Jan. 24, 1749; d. Apr. 24, 1749.
325. xii. PHINEAS, b. Jan. 24, 1751; m. Oct. 10, 1771, Ruth Gaines; m. 2nd, Jan. 13, 1803, Ruth Beebe.

176. JOHN[5] PIERCE (*Thomas[4]*, *Thomas[3]*, *Thomas[2]*, *Thomas[1]*), b. Feb. 10, 1704; m. —— ——. Res. Plainfield, Conn., and Wyoming, Pa.

In a deed given by John Pierce he recites as source of title : which lands I received from my Hon[d] father, Thomas Pierce, of Plainfield, Conn.

Child :—

325½. i. JOHN, b. Feb. 18, 1750; m. Tamar Tift.

177. TIMOTHY[5] PIERCE, Jr. (*Timothy[4]*, *Thomas[3]*, *Thomas[2]*, *Thomas[1]*), b. Oct. 7, 1698; m. June 12, 1723, Mary Wheeler. They res. in Plainfield, Conn. He d. bef. 1761.

Timothy Pierce

Children :—

326. i. LYDIA, b. Nov. 1, 1724; m. Oct., 1742, Rev. Thos. Stevens.
327. ii. MARY, b. Nov. 15, 1728; m. Oct, 1, 1747, Reuben Spaulding, b. Feb. 24, 1727, d. Jan. 10, 1765. She d. 1826. Ch.: Mary, b. June 19, 1748, m. Ebenezer Parkhurst; Azel, m. Mary Cole; Reuben, b. Dec. 15, 1758, m. Jerusha Carpenter; Pedew, d. young; Phineas, d. young.
328. iii. HANNAH, b. Sept. 8, 1730.
329. iv. PHEBE, b. May 27, 1732; m. Dec. 6, 1779, John Parkhurst.
330. v. TIMOTHY, Jr., b. May 22, 1734; m. Aug. 8, 1754, Eunice Fish; m. 2nd, Hannah Gilkey.
331. vi. AZEL.
332. vii. JOSIAH, b. 1745; m. Lydia Sheppard.
333. viii. SARAH; m. Dec. 26, 1758, Squire Sheppard.

178. NATHANIEL[5] PIERCE (*Timothy[4]*, *Thomas[3]*, *Thomas[2]*, *Thomas[1]*), b. June 3, 1701; m. Feb. 20, 1723, Elizabeth Stevens, b. 1707, d. July 13, 1748; m. 2nd, Mrs. Simonds. He d. 1775. They res. in Plainfield and Pomfret, Conn.

Nathaniel Pierce

Children :—

334. i.   RUTH, b. Nov. 27, 1725; m. ——— Coit.
335. ii. NATHANIEL, b. Mar. 19, 1728; m. Priscilla Sheppard.
336. iii. EZEKIEL, b. Dec. 18, 1730; m. Esther Blodgett.
337. iv. PHEBE, b. Feb. 5, 1732; d. Apr. 13, 1751.
338. v.   ELIZABETH, b. Nov. 30, 1736; d. July 13, 1748.
339. vi. JEDEDIAH, b. Feb. 22, 1740; m. Apr. 11, 1764, Susanna Eaton.
340. vii. WILLARD, b. Mar. 6, 1743; m. Jerusha Pellett.

181. Capt. BENJAMIN[5] PIERCE (*Timothy*[4], *Thomas*[3], *Thomas*[2], *Thomas*[1]), b. June 7, 1710; m. Hannah Smith, d. Sept. 25, 1736; m. 2nd, July 15, 1737, Naomy Richards, d. July 20, 1757; m. 3rd, Aug. 31, 1758, Sarah Mills; m. 4th, Jan. 28, 1762, Sarah Holt. He was captain in the Revolutionary war, and d. Feb. 7, 1782. He res. in Brooklyn, Conn.

Benjamin Pierce [signature]

Children :—

341. i.   NEHEMIAH, b. May 27, 1730; m. May 3, 1759, Lydia Sheppard.
342. ii. HANNAH, b. Feb. 5, 1733; m. 1764, Isaac Burton; d. Dec., 1841.
          Ch.: Nehemiah P., b. June 30, 1796; Jos. H., b. Sept. 27, 1791;
          Isaac, b. Mar. 21, 1768; Benjamin, b. Aug. 3, 1789; Hannah,
          b. Apr. 10, 1798; David, b. Mar. 31, 1801; Sarah, b. June 5,
          1804; Louisa, b. June 8, 1808. They res. in Lisbon, Vt.
343. iii. OLIVER, b. June 27, 1736; d. unm. in Coventry, June 27, 1837, aged
          101 years.
344. iv. OLIVE, b. Mar. 29, 1738; m. ——— Abbott.
345. v.   RUFUS, b. Sept. 27, 1740; d. Dec. 23, 1741.
346. vi. RACHEL, b. Feb. 19, 1742; m. Dec. 28, 1760, John Gilbert, b. 1746;
          d. Sept. 30, 1785. She d. 1827. They res. in Brooklyn and
          Pomfret, Conn. Ch.: John W., b. Oct. 11, 1770, m. Mrs. Augusta
          Ames; Dorcas and Delight, b. Oct. 23, 1772, m. Charles Dabney
          and John Dresser; Hannah, b. Oct. 27, 1774, m. Christopher
          Hyde; Perigrine, b. Jan. 4, 1777, m. Charity Bruce; Esther, b.
          Apr. 2, 1779, m. Zadoc Eaton; Wyllys, b. Apr. 2, 1782, m. Sally
          Kingsbury; Septimus and Sarepta, b. Oct. 2, 1783, m. Sally
          Barker and Lodana Pearl, and Calvin Tucker; Jasper, b. Nov.
          14, 1785, m. Elizabeth H. Rose.
347. vii. LYTE, b. July 23, 1745; d. Sept 21, 1804.
348. viii.DELANO, b. Nov. 19, 1748; m. Nov. 1, 1770, Abigail Hammond.
349. ix. TIMEUS, b. June 3, 1751; m. May 4, 1779, Elizabeth Grosvenor.
350. x.   RUFUS, b. Sept. 7, 1753; m. Sarah Whitney.
351. xi. DIADEMA, b. Apr. 14, 1756; m. Timothy Prince.

182. Major EZEKIEL[5] PIERCE (*Timothy*[4], *Thomas*[3], *Thomas*[2], *Thomas*[1]), b. Jan. 8, 1712; m. Feb. 11, 1736, Lois Stevens, b. 1718, d. June 25, 1762. Major Pierce was Town Clerk of Plainfield, Conn., from 1749 to 1754, and of Wyoming, or Westmoreland, Penn., at the first town-meeting of that town. He res. in Plainfield, Conn., and Wyoming, Penn.

Major Ezekiel Pierce, as Town Clerk of Westmoreland, Pa., makes the following Entries :

April 25, 1772, Major Ezekiel Pierce appointed one of a committee to admit settlers in 6 mile Townships.

Oct. 2, 1772. Major Ezekiel Pierce appointed one of a committee to provide a habitation for Rev. Jacob Johnson for the winter. Abel Pierce chosen Constable for Kingston township for 1772. March 30, 1773. Major Ezekiel Pierce one of a committee to receive bonds given for settling rights. June 21, 1773. Major Ezekiel Pierce apppointed one of a committee to assist in regulating the settlement of the Towns and to redress grievances.

Ezekiel Peirce Clerk

Children :—

352. i. ABEL, b. Dec. 15, 1736; m. Ruth Sheppard.
353. ii. ALICE, b. Nov. 17, 1738; d. unm.
354. iii. DANIEL, b. Jan. 30, 1740; taken prisoner at Wyoming.
355. iv. LYDIA, b. Feb. 17, 1743.
356. v. JOHN, b. Mar. 10, 1745; killed July 3, 1778.
357. vi. TIMOTHY, b. June 23, 1747; m. Hannah Gore.
358. vii. HANNAH, b. Jan. 25, 1749; d. unm.
359. viii. PHINEAS, b. Jan. 17, 1751.
360. ix. LOIS, b. May 6, 1753.
361. x. PHEBE, b. Sept. 15, 1755.

The History of Wyoming has the following : Major Ezekiel Pierce, the father of the Pierce family, was the ready writer of early days and for a succession of years clerk of the town, the records being in his handwriting. He had five sons all grown to manhood when he moved from Plainfield, Conn. to Wyoming in 1771—and must therefore been advanced towards the decline of life. Their names were Abel, Daniel, John, Timothy and Phineas. When in June, 1778, the two independent companies were consolidated into one under Capt. Spaulding, Timothy and Phineas were commissioned 1st and 2nd lieutenants. Timothy was one of the three who rode all night before the battle, arrived after the troops had marched out, followed and fell. John also was slain in the engagement.

185½. JABEZ[5] PIERCE (*Timothy[4]*, *Thomas[3]*, *Thomas[2]*, *Thomas[1]*), b. ——; m. Susannah Sheppard, Jan. 27, 1748; b. ——. Res. Plainfield, Conn. Children :—

361¼. i. LYDIA, b. July 23, 1749.
361½. ii. STEPHEN, b. Nov. 19, 1751.

186. ROBERT[5] PIERCE (*Stephen[4]*, *Stephen[3]*, *Thomas[2]*, *Thomas[1]*), b. Jan. 19, 1708; m. Mary ——, d. June 5, 1761. They res. in Chelmsford.

Robert Peirce

Children :—

362. i. EPHRAIM, b. Jan. 1, 1733; m. Oct. 2, 1760, Bridget Parker.
363. ii. WILLIAM, b. Oct. 29, 1735; m. Mar. 19, 1761, Elizabeth Pierce.
364. iii. MARY, b. Aug. 5, 1742; m. Jan. 29, 1765, Joseph Dunn.

187. OLIVER[5] PIERCE (*Stephen[4], Stephen[3], Thomas[2], Thomas[1]*), b. May 15, 1709; m. Mar. 21, 1733, Ann Hunt; m. 2nd, July 14, 1714, Hannah Adams. They res. in Chelmsford.

Oliver perce

Children :—

364¼. i. ELIZABETH, b. Dec. 30, 1734; m. Oliver Bowers.
364½. ii. ANN, b. Sept. 13, 1736.
365. iii. OLIVER, b. May 20, 1742; m. Dec. 21, 1769, Deborah Stevens.
366. iv. HANNAH, b. Feb. 5, 1744; m. Feb. 27, 1772, John Dunn.
367. v. SYBELL, b. Oct. 5, 1746; m. June 8, 1775, Silas Spalding, b. Oct. 30, 1746, d. Mar. 7, 1846. She d. Nov. 6, 1834. They res. in Chelmsford, Mass., and Hollis, N. H. Ch.: Sybil, b. Feb. 14, 1776, m. Thad. Wheeler; Sally, b. Mar. 8, 1777, m. Josiah Blood; Silas, b. May 30, 1779, m. Dorcas Chandler; Simeon, b. Feb. 7, 1782, m. Hannah Dow; Rebecca, b. Apr. 10, 1785, m. Charles Eastman and Josiah Blood; Esther, b. Jan. 30, 1787, m. Jona. T. Wheeler.
368. vi. ESTHER, b. Aug. 23, 1748; m. May 10, 1770, Ephraim Parkhurst.
369. vii. JONAS, b. Jan. 22, 1750; m. Betsey Dunn.
370. viii. JONATHAN, b. Apr. 7, 1752; m. Hannah Perham; m. 2nd, Nov. 27, 1788, Esther Spalding; m. 3rd, Jan. 18, 1810, Lydia Conant; m. 4th, July 26, 1821, Molley Batchelor.
371. ix. STEPHEN, b. Aug. 15, 1754; m. Hannah Marshall.
372. x. RUTH, b. Sept., 1756; m. May 6, 1783, Andrew Spalding, b. Feb. 10, 1761. Ch.: Nabby, b. Dec. 2, 1783, m. Thos. Hutchins; Anna, b. July 10, 1785, m. Samuel Perham; Polly, b. Apr. 10, 1792, m. Dr. Asa Byam; Ruth, b. May 26, 1794, m. King Parkhurst; David, b. Jan. 15, 1796, d. Feb. 24, 1798; Phebe, m. Benjamin P. Hutchins; Hannah, m. Oliver Hutchins.
373. xi. OLIVE, b. July 13, 1759; m. Dec. 1, 1791, Abijah Spalding, b. Nov. 12, 1759; no issue.

189. WILLIAM[5] PIERCE (*Stephen[4], Stephen[3], Thomas[2], Thomas[1]*), b. May 7, 1713; m. Sarah ——. He d. May 16, 1754. They res. in Groton.

Wm Pewce

Children :—

374. i. SARAH, b. Nov. 3, 1740; m. Samuel Shattuck.
375. ii. WILLIAM, b. May 27, 1742. He ran away from home when a small boy, and nothing further was ever known of his whereabouts.
376. iii. JOHN, b. Jan. 26, 1743; m. Tobathy Porter.
377. iv. LUCY, b. Apr. 20, 1745; m. —— King.
378. v. ELIZABETH, b. May 7, 1747; m. Joseph Hartwell.
379. vi. LYDIA, b. Nov. 8, 1748; m. Peter Waite.
380. vii. SILAS, b. July 27, 1750; m. Hannah Woods, b. Sept. 4, 1764. He d. Nov. 22, 1809. He res. in Peterboro', N. H.

Captain Silas Pierce was born in Shirley in 1750, and died in Peterboro', N. H., Nov. 22, 1809. He married Hannah Woods, daughter of General Woods of Pepperell. He purchased in

1790 the farm of Asa Pierce of Peterboro', N. H., with the exception of the widow's third, and a part of the Hogg or Sheppard farm. He was an officer in the army of the Revolution during the war. The late Gov. Benj. Pierce of N. H. was his cousin, and said to have been his waiter in the army for a time. Captain Pierce was wounded in the left arm, in consideration of which a pension was granted him. His arm was rendered stiff by the wound. He was a short, thick-set man with a Roman nose and commanding personal presence. After the war he moved to Peterboro', and went into trade at Hunt's Corner, soon failed by some bad management of a partner, and was left burdened with debts. He and his wife now laid aside all show of gentility, to which they had before made some claim; moved into a log-house on the hill east of the house of the Hayes family; went to work,—he as a layer of stone-wall for fence, she as a weaver. They soon moved into better quarters, but still humble, near the house which he afterwards built, in which Moses Fairbanks now lives. They both worked very hard for many years, paid off all their old debts, and purchased of real estate and acquired the means, with the aid of a small property left to Mrs. P. by the will of her father, to pass the latter years of their lives in comparative ease and comfort. But he did not live long to enjoy his improved condition. They were both much respected. The widow Pierce married James Brazer, Esq., of Groton, Mass., a wealthy merchant of that place. They had no issue.

380¼. viii. OLIVER, b. Mar. 4, 1752; d. Mar. 4, 1752.
380½. ix. ANNA, b. Mar. 3, 1756; d. Aug. 18, 1775.

190. STEPHEN[5] PIERCE, Jr. (*Stephen[4], Stephen[3], Thomas[2], Thomas[1]*), b. Apr. 10, 1715; m. Feb. 6, 1745, Betsey Bowers. They res. in Chelmsford. Children:—

381. i. SARAH, b. Dec. 20, 1745; m. John Stevens.
382. ii. LUCY, b. Oct. 14, 1748; m. Stephen Saunders.
383. iii. BETSEY, b. Nov. 17, 1751; m. Ephraim Adams.
384. iv. ROBERT, b. Apr. 13, 1754; m. Mary Trull. He was in the Revolutionary war after the battle of Bunker Hill.
385. v. ANN, b. Oct. 19, 1756.
386. vi. STEPHEN, b. Feb. 5, 1759; m. Dec. 25, 1787, Phebe Trull.

195. BENJAMIN[5] PIERCE (*Stephen[4], Stephen[3], Thomas[2], Thomas[1]*), b. Nov. 25, 1726; m. Elizabeth Merrill of Methuen, b. Feb. 22, 1728; she m. 2nd, a Bowers. He d. June 16, 1764. They res. in Chelmsford.

Benja Peirce

Children :—

387. i. REBECCA, b. Feb. 24, 1746; m. Solomon Corey.
388. ii. JESSE, } twins, b. Dec. 25, 1748; { d. young.
389. PHEBE, } { m. Edward Foster.
390. iii. LYDIA, b. Sept. 11, 1750.
391. iv. LEAFEY, b. May 1, 1752; m. —— Dodge.
392. v. SUSANNA, b. Nov. 11, 1754; d. Dec. 11, 1775.
393. vi. BENJAMIN, b. Dec. 25, 1757; m. May 24, 1787, Elizabeth Andrews; m. 2nd, Feb. 1, 1790, Ann Kendrick.
394. vii. ESTHER, b. June 12, 1761; m. Timothy Kendall.
395. viii. MERRILL, b. Jan. 29, 1764; m. Dorcas Barker.

A Inventory of the Estate of M^r. Benjamin Pierce Late of Chelmsford, in the County of middlesex Yeoman. Deceast taken by us the
Subscribers July ye 19th A. D: 1764 as the Same was Shown to us.
and by us apprized, we being appointed and Sworn for that purpose
which is as followeth—

      Imprimas

Wearing apparel : a thin old Coat and Jacket 9/8 Leather Breetches 15/	£1—4—8
Item a Great Coat 18/ old Coats 2/8 old Shirt 3/	1—3—8
Item Stockens & Shoes 3/9 woolen mittens 1/6 old hat 1/6	0—4—9
Item a Gun 12/ Books 2/8	0–14—8
Item Best Bed and furniture 37/4 other bed and furniture 32/8	3–10—0
Item and old Bed and furniture 21/ Pueter Vessels 13/6	1–14—6
Item a Small Iron pot and Skillet 6/ frying pan 2/4	0—8—4
Item Earthen and Tin Vessels 1/i1 Glass Bottles 1/7	0—3—6
Item old knives and forks 1/4 a Raisor 1/	0—2—4
Item old Table 2/ a chest with Drawers 12/ a Box 2/8	0–16—8
Item old Chairs 2/ Bread trough 1/2 a Seeive 1/ a Riddle 1/6	0—5—8
Item A Loome and furniture 37/ Spinning wheele 3/8	2—0—8
Item wooden Dishes 1/10 pails /8 wooden Bottle /8	0—3—2
Item old Tongs 1/10 Iron tramel 4/ meal sack 1/10	0—7—8
Item a Sope Tub and Sope 4/ Cyder Casks 11/	0–15—0
Item Dry Casks and wooden Lumber 7/ a pair of Sheers /6	0—7—6

Husbandry Tools.

One half of an old Cart wheels and Irons	0–16—0
Item old plough & Irons 6/ Small chain 4/ old axes 4/	0–14—0
Item Shovels 2/4 Iron forks 1/ old hoes 1/4	0—4—8
Item Scyths and tackling 7/4 old Sickels 2/ a Sled 4/	0–13—4
Item one third part of a grind stone 2/ Rakes 1/3	0—3—3
Item Iron fetters 2/4 hames 1/6 old Iron 7/6	0–11—4
Item Sheeps wool	0—9—4

Quick Stock.

A Colt £3—12—0 A heifer £2—2—8	5–14—8
Item one Sheep and three Lambs 21/ three Swine 48/	3—9—0
Item A Note of hand from William Frentch of	8—0—0
Item A Note of hand from John Richardson of	0—6—0
	35—4—4

Brought over   35—4—4

All the Lands and Buildings that belonged to the Said Deceased we
   apprized at one Hundred and Seventeen pounds and Ninteen
   Shillings   117—19—0

All the aforesaid Sums are in Lawfull money   £153—3—4
which is humbly submitted by us

                 EPHR^M SPAULDING   ⎫
                 JOSEPH PEIRCE Junr. ⎬ Commi*tee*
                 WM. PEIRCE   ⎭

The S^d Estate appears
to be in Debted aboute
Seven Hundred pounds old ten^r.

the apprizers Charg
Eph^m Spaulding for apprizeing & writing   6/
Joseph Peirce   3/
Wm. Peirce   3/

Middlesex ss July 31 1764 Mrs Elizabeth Pierce the admin^x exhibited the foregoing Inventory on Oath.

                                S. Danforth J. prob.
    A Copy. Attest. J. H. Tyler, Register.

Middlesex ss. Chelmsford December 18th 1770
I hereby certify that Benjamin Peirce, a minor upwards of fourteen years of Age, Son of Benjamin Peirce late of Chelmsford afore sd. Husbandman, deceased, & of Elizabeth Peirce his then wife, now Elizabeth Bowers, came before me and nominated, elected and made choice of William Peirce of Chelmsford aforesaid, Gentleman to be Guardian of his Person & Estate untill he shall attain his Age of Twenty one years.

                              Oliver Fletcher, Just Pac^s.

To the honourable Samuel Danforth Esqr Judge of the Probate of Wills &c for the County of Middlesex.
                    A Copy, Attest, J. H. Tyler, Register.

198. STEPHEN[5] PIERCE (*Jacob*[4], *Stephen*[3], *Thomas*[2], *Thomas*[1]), b. 1698; m. Rachel Harrod, 1722. He d. July 6, 1761. Res. in Groton, Mass.

Children :—

396. i.   RACHEL, b. Oct. 21, 1723.
397. ii.   STEPHEN, b. Nov. 6, 1725; d. Mar. 6, 1733.
398. iii. JONATHAN, b. April 11, 1727; m. Ruth Gilson.
399. iv. ELIZABETH, b. May 26, 1729; d. March 10, 1802.
400. v.   SUSANNA, b. May 30, 1731.
401. vi. MARY, b. June 24, 1732.
402. vii. SARAH, b. Aug. 18, 1733; d. June 1, 1737.
403. viii. ISAAC, b. Feb. 24, 1734; d. May 24, 1737.
404. ix. STEPHEN, b. Oct. 16, 1736.
405. x.   THANKFUL, b. June 5, 1744.

199. SAMUEL[5] PIERCE (*Samuel*[4], *Samuel*[3], *Thomas*[2], *Thomas*[1]), b.

8

June 3, 1706; m. Abigail ———. She d. 1796. Res. Woburn, Mass., Mansfield, Conn., Holden and Charlemont, Mass. He bought land in Mansfield, Conn., 1734. Children :—

406. i. ABIGAIL, b. Sept. 22, 1733; m. Samuel Garfield. Ch.: Samuel, b. March 5, 1757; Joseph, b. Sept. 19, 1758; Daniel, b. Sept. 29, 1760; Josiah, b. Oct. 12. 1762; Abigail, b. Aug. 28, 1764; Enoch, b. Sept. 28, 1766; Elisha, b. April 25, 1769; John, b. July 26, 1771; Elizabeth, b. Sept. 15, 1773; Silas, b. Jan. 19, 1776. He d. Jan. 12, 1792. She d. Jan. 23, 1816.
407. ii. ELIZABETH, b. May 10, 1742; m. ——— Leonard.
408. iii. SAMUEL, b. July 31, 1743; m. Anna ——— and Mrs. Willard.
409. iv. RUTH, b. Nov. 6, 1745; m. Moses Rice.
410. v. GERSHOM, b. Apr. 14, 1747; d. at Albany in Rev. Army, 1777.
411. vi. JUDITH, b. Apr. 16, 1749; m. David Lynds.
412. vii. JOSIAH, b. March 7, 1751; m. Miriam Pierce [421].
413. viii. SETH, b. March 30, 1753; d. 1781, unm.
414. ix. RELIEF, b. Apr. 2, 1755; m. Dr. Daniel Nelson.
415. x. ESTHER; m. ——— Birch.

200. JOSIAH[5] PIERCE (*Samuel[4], Samuel[3], Thomas[2], Thomas[1]*), b. July 13, 1708; m. Miriam Cook, Nov. 17, 1743, b. 1716. She d. June 27, 1795. He d. Feb. 10, 1788. Res. Hadley, Mass.

Josiah Peirce

Children :—

416. i. JOSIAH, b. Oct. 11, 1745; m. Lucy Fairfield.
417. ii. HANNAH, b. Nov. 19, 1747; d. Jan. 31, 1841.
418. iii. SAMUEL, b. Nov. 11, 1749; m. Anna Cook.
419. iv. WILLIAM, b. June 21, 1752; d. unm. Jan. 11, 1832.
420. v. DAVID, b. Sept. 27, 1754. Turned out after the battle of Lexington, went with Arnold to Canada and d. there Dec. 28, 1775.
421. vi. MIRIAM, b. March 1, 1757; m. Josiah Pierce [412].

203. SETH[5] PIERCE (*Samuel[4], Samuel[3], Thomas[2], Thomas[1]*), b. Nov. 30, 1716; m. Nov. 10, 1743, Elizabeth Nye of Tolland, b. 1680, d. May 14, 1749. He d. Dec. 5, 1794. They res. in Mansfield, Conn. Children :—

422. i. SETH, b. Sept. 12, 1744; m. Apr. 17, 1767, Bethiah Fields; m. 2nd, 1813, Patty Rindge.
423. ii. ELIZABETH, b. June 2, 1748; m. Bennett Fields.
424. iii. ENOCH.
425. iv. DAU.; m. a Nye of Montpelier, Vt.

204. ENOCH[5] PIERCE (*Samuel[4], Samuel[3], Thomas[2], Thomas[1]*), b. Mar. 22, 1719; m. Mar. 10, 1743, Mary Mason, b. Feb., 1719, d. Oct. 24, 1783. They res. in Mansfield, Conn. He d. Mar. 2, 1806. Children :—

426. i. MARY, b. Apr. 17, 1745; m. T. Eldridge.
427. ii. SUSANNA, b. May 3, 1747; d. May 23, 1804.
428. iii. ENOCH, Jr., b. Aug. 23, 1749; m. Dec. 14, 1783, Experience Storrs; m. 2nd, Oct. 31, 1792, Molly Snow.
429. iv. HANNAH, b. Nov., 1751; d. Feb. 10, 1817.
430. v. SAMUEL, b. June 24, 1755; m. Joanna Babcock.
431. vi. JOHN, b. Mar. 22, 1754; d. Jan. 17, 1816.

211. ISAAC[5] PIERCE, Jr. (*Isaac*[4], *Samuel*[3], *Thomas*[2], *Thomas*[1]), b. Oct. 12, 1722; m. Jan. 5, 1745, Mary Hardy, dau. of Joseph and Sarah (Pickering) Hardy, of Salem, Mass. He d. in Boston, Dec. 20, 1811. Boston gave to the army of the Revolution no family more patriotic, devoted and self-sacrificing than that of Isaac Pierce, Jr. and his four sons.

Isaac Pierce

Children :—

432. i.   JOSEPH, b. Dec. 25, 1745; m. Apr., 1771, Ann Dawes.
433. ii.   ISAAC, b. Jan. 17, 1748; d. Oct. 10, 1750.
434. iii. JOHN, b. Sept. 28, 1750.
         Captain John Pierce died at Fort McHenry, Walnut Hills, near Vicksburg, Miss., July 22, 1798, of a climatic disease contracted while in garrison at Fort Adams on the left bank of the Mississippi River, at which place he had been for some time stationed. Com. Lieut. in Kern's Artillery in 1776. 2nd Lieut. in Callender's Company, Crane's Artillery, Sept. 12, 1777. Captain's Lieut. Sept. 12, 1778, serving in Rhode Island. He saw much active service, beginning with the siege of Boston and ending only with the close of the war in 1783. Reentering the service of his country under confederation he was commissioned Lieut. in 1787; Lieut. Artillery in 1789; and Captain Oct., 1791.
         John Pierce signed the roll and became a member of the Cincinnati in 1783, at the cantonment of the Massachusetts line on the banks of the Hudson River.
434½. iv. ISAAC, b. Dec. 25, 1753.
         Major Isaac Pierce died Feb. 27, 1781; he was aide-de-camp to Major Gen. Gates with the rank of Major.

[*Force's American Archives, Fourth Series*, Vol. 6, p. 761.]

Parole Gates.

Countersign " Mifflin."

HD'Q'S., NEW YORK, *June* 7, 1776.
   The honorable, the continental Congress, have been pleased to appoint Horatio Gates, Esq., Major General, and Thomas Mifflin, Esq., Brigadier General in the army of the United Colonies. They are to be obeyed as such.
          *   *   *   *
   Walter Stewart and Isaac Pierce, Esquires, are appointed Aides-de-camps to Major-General Gates. All orders, written or verbal, delivered by either of them, are to be considered as coming from the Major-General, and obeyed as such.

[*Fifth Series, Vol.* 1, *p.* 181—1776.]

ISAAC PIERCE to COLONEL BUELL.

HEADQUA'TERS, TYCONDEROGA, *July* 30, 1776.
   SIR:—
      You are immediately upon receipt of this, to set out for this place, in order to join your regiment.
          By the General's command.
                    ISAAC PIERCE, Aid-de-camp.

[*Fifth Series, Vol.* 1, *p.* 828—1776.]

TYCONDEROGA, *Aug.* 7, 1776.

GENERAL GATES TO GENERAL WASHINGTON.

SIR :—

Major Pierce being extremely ill of a fever, leaves me and my Secretary more writing to do than we can possibly accomplish.

With my most respectful compliments to your Excellency,

I am, Sir, your most obedient, humble servant,

HORATIO GATES.

To His Excellency GENERAL WASHINGTON.

435. v. HARDY, b. July 20, 1756; d. Nov. 5, 1776.

Lieut. Hardy Pierce was Lieut. in Knox's Artillery, and was a friend of Lafayette. He was killed at Fort Lee, New Jersey.

LIEUT. HARDY PIERCE.

(By Josiah Throop.)

To Mr. ISAAC and Mrs. MARY PIERCE.

When you recount the qualities that shone
Conspicuous in an amiable son,
Especially his fortitude and zeal,
Above his years, to save the common weal
And then reflect by what a sudden stroke
The prospect of your future joys was broke,
Your grief stands justified as reason's bar
And virtue must approve each generous tear.
Yet heaven afford some comfort, some defence,
Against this seeming frown of Providence;
In the bright list of heroes see his name,
Enrolled by the kind hand of deathless fame.
For when New England estimates the cost
Of civil discord by the sons she's lost;
When Freedom is established in the land,
And Peace and Confidence walk hand in hand,
Then those who in the glorious cause were slain,
In every grateful heart shall rise again.
Their names shall live and flourish on the stage,
Till time itself shall perish with old age.
If this reviving thought yield no relief,
Throw back the gloomy curtain of your grief,
And by the penetrating eye of Faith,
Scatter the melancholy shades of Death;
Pass by a day or two that hangs between,
And views Time's grave, important, final scene.
See this young Warrior, in his Heaven-built car,
Crowned with the Triumphs of a righteous war
In which he fell, while by Almighty wrath,
Each sceptered Tyrant dies a second death,
Behold the dazzling glories of the train
Of heroes, who in Freedom's cause were slain;
Each an immortal crown of victory wears,
Blazoned with sunbeams, interspersed with stars,
In which some mystic mark is fixed, to tell
The Heaven-defended cause in which they fell;
While in the midst we see young PIERCE appear,
Let this calm every sigh, dry every tear.

436. vi. SARAH, b. Nov. 24, 1758; d. Jan. 25, 1777.
437. vii. MARY, b. Apr. 7, 1761; probably d. young.

438. viii. GRAFTON, b. Sept. 12, 1763; probably d. young.

212. Lieut. WILLIAM[5] PIERCE (*Sommers*[4], *William*[3], *Thomas*[2], *Thomas*[1]), b. Mar. 16, 1727; m. Hannah ———. He was a Lieutenant in the Provincial militia, when the country was under British rule, for a number of years. He d. July 22, 1818. Res. Wilton, N. H., and Andover, Vt. Children:—

439. i. WILLIAM; m. Sarah Holt.
440. ii. BENJAMIN, b. May 18, 1762; m. Dorcas Lovejoy.
441. iii. TIMOTHY, b. Feb. 4, 1765; m. Phebe Carlton.
442. iv. ASA; d. Sept. 15, 1776, in Rev. army.

215. JAMES[5] PIERCE (*James*[4], *James*[3], *Thomas*[2], *Thomas*[1]); m. Mar. 17, 1753, Phebe Tottingham, b. June 30, 1728. She d. Nov. 18, 1797. He d. 1777. Res. in Woburn. Children:—

443. i. JAMES; d. in Rev. army in 1783.
444. ii. SAMUEL; d. in Rev. army in 1783.
445. iii. PHEBE; m. Jan. 1, 1782, Henry Farrase, a Prussian soldier.
447. iv. NATHAN, b. 1759; m. Sarah Leathe.
448. v. ABEL, b. 1767; m. Ruth Parker.

In the Name of God Amen this fourth day of April 1777 I James Peirce of Wobourn in the County of Middlesex and State of the Massachusetts Bay in New England yeoman being Sick and weak of Body but of Sound mind and Memory Thanks be given to God therefor calling to Mind the Mortallity of My Body knowing that it is appointed unto all Men Once to die do make and publish this my last Will and Testament in the which principally and first of all I Give and Bequeath my Soul into the hand of God who gave it hoping for Eternal Redemption though the alone mirit of Jesus Christ and my Body I Recommend to the Earth to be buried in a decent Christian Burial at the Charge and Discretion of my Executrix hereafter named nothing doutbing but I shall receive the same again by the mighty Power of God at the general Resserection and as to Such worldly Estate with which it hath pleas[d] God to bless me in this Life I Give & Dispose of the same in the following manner namely
I Give unto my dearly beloved Wife Phebee the sole use and Improvement of all my real Estate in Wobourn afores[d] for and during her natural Life and all my personal Estate where Ever I Give to her to her own disposal and I order this my Wife Phebee to pay all my Just Debts and funeral Charges and to provide for and bring up my three youngest Children namely Nathan Abel & Phebee until they arive to lawfull age to act for them selves provided they shall see fit to abide with her solong
and as to my real Estate after the decease of my said Wife Phebee I Give the same to be Divided among all my Children namely James Samuel Nathan Abel and Phebee according to form of Law
and I appoint and ordain my said Wife Phebee sole Exec[x] to this my lest Will and Testament and I hereby Revoak and Nullify all former Wills and Testaments and Exec[x] by me heretofore made and named holding for Stable this Will and Testament and this Exec[x] here in by

me named and these only I confirmation whereof I have hereunto Set
my hand and affix^d my Seal the day and date above written.
Sign^d Seal^d publish^d pronounc^d
and declared by the said James
Peirce to be his last Will and Testament

in presence of

JONATHAN LOCK
OBADIAH KENDALL
SAMUEL WYMAN Jun.
JOSIAH JOHNSON

A Copy, Attest, J. H. Tyler, Register.

216. JOSHUA[5] PIERCE (*James[4]*, *James[3]*, *Thomas[2]*, *Thomas[1]*), b.
Apr. 1, 1722; m. Feb. 18, 1749, Susan Reed; m. 2nd, Oct. 27, 1753,
Esther Richardson, b. Aug. 6, 1727, d. June 1, 1819. He d. in Woburn,
Feb. 13, 1771.

Children :—

449. i.   ESTHER, b. Apr. 16, 1754; m. Richard Marshall, b. Feb. 14, 1751,
d. Jan. 4, 1834. She died Feb. 27, 1842. Ch. b. in Bradford,
N. H.: Richard, Jr., b. Sept. 15, 1773, m. Hannah Lawrence,
Mrs. Mary Jameson and Mrs. White; Esther, b. Feb. 16, 1776,
m. Josiah Melvin; Ruth, d. 1805; Polly, m. Willard Lane;
Susan, b. Mar, 10, 1785, m. Isaac Kendall and Mark Gould;
Sarah, b. 1789, m. Asa Sargent; Nathan R., b. June 10, 1792, m.
Abigail Hawks; Cummings, b. June 1, 1796, m. Polly Bagley,
Betsey Bagley and Lucy Farnum.
450. ii. JOSHUA, b. Sept. 16, 1756; m. Dec. 25, 1781, Sarah Lund.
451. iii. SUSANNA, b. July 4, 1758; m. Mar. 10, 1780, Reuben Spalding, b.
Sept. 6, 1761, d. Mar. 20, 1798. She d. Feb. 24, 1809 in Hudson,
N. H. Ch.: Reuben, Jr., b. Mar. 2, 1781, m. Hannah Barrett;
Susannah, b. May 20, 1783, m. Jeremiah Smith; Sarah C., b.
Jan. 31, 1785, m. Reuben Coburn and James Wilson; Joshua P.,
b. Apr. 15, 1787, d. Jan. 10, 1826; Esther R., b. Feb. 21, 1789,
m. Robert Patterson; Suel, b. Apr. 6, 1791, d. Aug. 10, 1851;
Willard, b. Mar. 18, 1793, d. Jan. 16, 1868; Dustin, b. July 27,
1795, m. Rachel Rupert; Alfred, b. Aug. 10, 1797, d. Dec. 10,
1811.
452. iv. PHEBE, b. May, 3, 1761; m. a Searles and a Pearsons.
453. v.   NATHAN, b. Sept. 11, 1766; m. Phebe Cummings.
454. vi. JAMES, b. Sept. 8, 1768; m. Mary Stacy.
455. vii. DANIEL, b. Aug. 8, 1763; m. Hannah Marsh.

217. JACOB[5] PIERCE (*James[4]*, *James[3]*, *Thomas[2]*, *Thomas[1]*), b.
Sept, 15, 1724; m. Aug. 18, 1752, Abigail Kendall, b. Feb. 27, 1730,
d. May 28, 1816. He d. in Woburn, Nov. 14, 1774.

Children :—

456. i.   ABIGAIL, b. Apr. 16, 1753; m. Abijah Kendall.   She d. Jan. 3, 1838.
457. ii. JACOB, b. Dec. 28, 1755; m. Oct. 13, 1783, Martha Johnson.
458. iii. EPHRAIM, b. Mar. 8, 1758; m. Nov. 30, 1782, Mrs. Abigail Porter.
459. iv. ELIZABETH, b. Jan. 9, 1762; d. June 18, 1804.
460. v.   SAMUEL, b. Aug. 7, 1764; d. unm. May 20, 1824.
461. vi. HEMAN, b. Feb. 16, 1768; m. July 4, 1793, Mary Bowen.
462. vii. SUSANNA, b. Sept. 18, 1769; d. Apr. 15, 1811, unm.

An Inventory of the Real Estate of Mr Jacob Pierce late of Woburn
Deceas^d Intestate   £   s.   d.
Dwelling House Sixty Pounds   60:   0:   0
Barn forty Pounds   40:   0:   0
One Hundred & two acres of Land caled the Homstid
on which the afore mentioned Buildings stand Bounded
as follows viz at the South Westerly Corner on the
Road leading from Samuel Wyman Esq to m^r Daniel
Reed, Southerly by land of the Widow Hannah Johnson
and a few Rods on land latly Thomas Reeds, Easterly ⎫
a small part on Nathan Richardson but chiefly on land ⎬ 680 : 0 : 0
latly the afore Said Thomas Reed, Northerly on Mr. ⎭
Tylor's land in part and part on Esq Wyman's land
Westerly on Said Esq. Wyman's Land in part and part
on the Land of James Pierce to the Road first mentioned
Estemated at Six pounds thirteen Shillings & four pence
per Acre all Six hundred & Eighty Pounds.
Ten Acres of Pasture Land known by the name of ten
acres lying near Josiah Parkers Bounded Westerly on
Nathan Kendall Southerly on Esq. Johnsons land and
else where on land of Josiah Parker and Thomas Wright
Estemated at Six Pounds thirteen Shillings and four ⎫
pence per acre all Sixty Six Pounds thirteen Shillings ⎬ 66 : 13 : 4
& four pence   ⎭
Two acres called the Horn pond meadow bounded Southerly on Said Horn Pond and land of ye afore s^d Thomas
Reeds Northerly on Capt Belknaps meadow and meadow ⎫
of Mr Zebediah Wyman Deces^d Estemated at Six pounds ⎬ 13 : 6 : 8
thirteen Shillings & four pence per acre all thirteen ⎭
pounds Six shillings & Eight pence
Pew in Woburn meeting House thirteen Pounds Six
Shillings & Eight pence   13 : 6 : 8
                                                                ――――――――――――――
                Sum total of the Inventory   £873 : 6 : 8

Having finished the Inventory We Proceed to Set to Abigail Widow
of Jacob Pierce late of Woburn Deceas^d her Thirds (or Dower)
which are as follows viz.
                                                                £   s.   d.
The East end of the Dwelling House with half the ⎫
Cellar under said House & an equal Priviledge in all the ⎬ 30 : 0 : 0
Stair ways & fore door in said House Prised at thirty ⎭
Pounds

	£	s.	d.

The East end of the Barn to the midle of the floor way
and yard before the Same from the middle of s^d floor
way to Stake near the west post of the bars leading into
said yard at thirteen Pounds Six Shillings & eight pence
} 13 : 6 : 8

One third of the Pew at four pounds Eight Shillings and
eleven pence The New Pasture being about twelve
} 4 : 8 : 11

acres & an half together with about fourteen acres and
an half more being the southerly & easterly part of the
Homestid Bounded as follows viz. begining with the
fence at the West end of the House running Westerly
with said fence to the New Pasture then run north westerly till it comes to ye Peach orchard (leaving said Peach
orchard to the two thirds) thence forward to Esq.
Wyman's east corner then Westerly by said Wyman's
land to James Pierce's land then Southerly by said
Pierce's land to the Road bounded Southerly by s^d Road
and by land of ye Widow Hannah Johnson to land latly
} 195 : 6 : 8

Thomas Reeds Easterly by Nathan Richardson till it
comes to the lane leading to the House then crost s^d lane

	£	s.	d.

by and with s^d land of Thomas Reed about thirty one
rods to a heap of Stones then turning and running near
West Seventeen rods to a heap of Stones; thene a few
Degrees more Southerly to another heap of Stones about
the same distance thence running Southerly by a Walnut
marked to a heap of Stones by the east post of the bars
then running to the West Post of s^d bars from thence
to the East side of the Close a few rods east of the Barn
& from said Close to the corner near the House and so
on by the back of the House to the first Bound excepting the West half of the Garden which is bounded by
Stakes and Stones in lieu of which the wd is to have a
small yard top of ye Hill back of ye House, Prised at
Seven Pounds & almose five Shilling per acre being one
Hundred & ninety five Pounds Six Shillings & eight
pence   turn over.   195 : 6 : 8

Six acres of Wood land Bounded as follows Viz. Northerly twenty Rods on Esq. Wyman West thirty five Rods
on said Esq. Wymans then runing Easterly about thirty

	£	s.	d.

Seven Rods to a heap of Stones and Stake from thenc
about thirty five Rods Northerly to the first bound being
a stake and stones at eight Pounds per acre all forty
eight Pounds   48 : 0 : 0
Brought over £243 : 2 : 3   243 : 2 : 3

Sum total of the Widows Thirds   £291 : 2 : 3

Having Set to the Widow her Thirds (or Dower) in the
foregoing Manner We now proceed with the Residue of
s^d Estate as follows viz

We Set to Jacob the Eldest Son of Jacob Pierce late

	£	s.	d.
of s^d. Woburn deceas^d the remaining two thirds as fol-			
lows			
The West half of the House and half the Cellar at £30 :	30 :	0 :	0
The West two thirds of the Barn at £26 : 13 : 4	26 :	13 :	4

To Sixty nine acres the Residue of the Homestid ⎫
Bounded South and West by the Widows Third as ⎪
described in Seting of her Dower & in other parts as ⎪
bounded in the foregoing inventory Prised at Six ⎬ 436 : 13 : 4
pounds Six Shillings & near Seven pence per acre all ⎪
four hundred & thirty Six pounds thirteen Shillings and ⎪
four pence ⎭

Ten acre Pasture at Six pounds thirteen Shillings & four pence per acre all Sixty Six pounds thirteen Shillings & four pence bounded as in the foregoing inventory	66 :	13 :	4
Two acres called Horn Pond meadow at Six pounds thirteen Shillings & four pence per acre all thirteen Pounds Six Shillings & eight pence bounded as in the foregoing inventory—	13 :	06 :	8
Two thirds of the Pew eight pounds seventeen Shillings & nine pence—	8 :	17 :	9
Sum total of the two thirds	£582 :	4 :	5

The conveniences of flowing turning or conveying the water the well and watering places the severall usual ways and Passages for all needful uses be improved by the owners of the thirds and two thirds as each shall have occasion leaving gates and bars as they are found.

abgial peirce		Woburn December 24th 1777.
Jacob Peirce		Having finished the work your
her		Honor appointed us we Sub-
Abigail X Pierce	Countersigners	scribe our Selves your Honor
mark		Humble Servant
Joshua Walker		Sam^{ll} Belknap ⎫
as Garden for		Saml Thompson ⎬ Appr
fiue of his		Daniel Reed ⎭ sers.
children		

A Copy, Attest, J. H. Tyler, Register.

Woburn August 28 1787
Rec^d of James Wyman Guardien To Susa Pierce Forty two Shillings, one fifth of a Note given by Capt Walker a former Guardien

Rec^d : by me   abigail peirce—Mother to s^d
                                        Susa

Middlesex ss. Cambridge, 7 Oct. 1790. I order this discharge to be recorded.

                          Oliver Prescott, J. prob.

Woburn October 4th 1790
Rec^d of James Wyman Guardien to my Daughter Susea pierce Now Arived at the age of Twenty one years,   *   *   *   *   & has
9

binn under my Care for four years past the sum of two pounds Seven Shillings & 5ᵈ one fifth of a State Note, in full of all Demands against Said Guardien on her part—State Note 2-7-5   Recᵈ: per me

abigail peirce

Middlesex ss Cambridge in Probate Court 7 Oct. 1790   I order this discharge to be recorded
JACOB PEIRCE   OLIVER PRESCOTT, J. prob.

Woburn March 20ᵗʰ 1778
Then Recived of Mʳˢ Abigail Pirce Administratrix of the the Estate of Mʳ Jacob Pirce Late of said woburn Desest as Garden for the Children hearafter named Viz
For Ephraim the Sum of Eleven pounds ten Shillings and one peny half peny. for Elizabeth the Like Sum of £11—10—1-2 for Samuel the Like Sum of £11—10—1-2, for Heman the Like Sum of £11—10—1-2. for Susey the Like Sum of £11—10—1-2 Lawfull money assined to Each of them by the honorable Judge for the County of middlesex in his Decree on the Personal Estate of the afore Said Deseased. and Likewise I have Recived in addition to the above Said Sums the Sum of fourteen Shillings and nine pence for Each of the Children above Said which makes in the whole the sum of Sixty one pound four Shillings and four pence half peney in full for their Several Shears in the parsonal Estate of their honoured Father Desest as above Said I say
Rceivᵈ by me   JOSHUA WALKER
                                                      as Guardian
Test
Jacob Peirce
Samˡˡ Belknap

Middlesex 4 Dec. 1783 I accept of this discharge & order it to be recorded.
                                         OLIVER PRESCOTT J. prob.

Woburn March yᵉ 20ᵗʰ 1778
Then Recived of my Honoured mother Mʳˢ Abagail Pirce Administratrix on the Estate of of my honoured Father Mʳ Jacob Pirce of said woburn Late Deseast the Sum of twenty three pounds and three pence Lawfull money that was assined me by the honoured Judge for the County of middlesex in his Decree on the parsenal Estate of the afore said Deseased and Likewise I have Recivᵈ. one pound nine Shillings and Six pence in addition to the above Said Sum which I acknoledge to be in Full for my Double Share of Said Parsonal Estate Recivᵈ. by me.   JACOB PEIRCE

Test
    Joshua Walker
    Samˡˡ Belknap.

Middlesex 4 Dec. 1783. I accept of this discharge & order it to be recorded
                                         OLIVER PRESCOTT J. prob.

Woburn March 20th 1778

Then Recived of my Hounard mother Mrs Abigail Pirce Adminis-
tratix on the Estate of my hounared Father Mr Jacob Pirce Late of
Woburn Desest the Sum of Eleven pounds ten Shillings and one peny
half peny Lawfull money that was assined me by the honorable Judge
for the County of middlesex in his Decree on the parsonal Estate of
the afore said Deceased and Likewise I have Recived fourteen Shillings
and nine pence In addition to the above Said Sume which I acknoledge
to be in full for my Share of said parsonal Estate

Recived by me

Test
  Joshua Walker
  Sam^{ll} Belknap

her
ABIGAIL X PIRCE
mark

Middlesex 4 Decr. 1783   I accept of this discharge and order it to be
recorded
OLIVER PRESCOTT. J. prob.

Balance of the account of Joshua Walker guardian to Ephraim,
Elizabeth, Samuel, Susa & Heman all children of Jacob Pierce late of
Woburn in the County of Middlesex yeoman, deceased, allowed on 5
Decr 1783, & to be distributed among the Children is £34—2—4¾
One fifth part for each child is £6—16—5¾
Attest JAMES WINTHROP Reg^r

Middlesex 5 Decr. 1783. Having examined this account & seen the
vouchers, and sworn the Guardian, I allow there-of. And having considered the advancements to several of the said children, & the allow-
ances made to some of them by consent of the said Guardian & the
other heirs as by an account on file; I order the said Guardian to pay
them or their legal Representatives respectively as follows: viz. Ephraim £5.4.7¼, Elizabeth £3.16.5¼; Samuel £9.10.7¾ Susa £5.18: 11¾,
& Heman £9.8.2¾, which sums will be in full of their respective shares.
OLIVER PRESCOTT J. Prob.

     Copy examined, Attest

JAMES WINTHROP Reg^r.

Woburn January 12th 1786
Received of James Wyman Guardian to Samuel Pierce Nine pound,
teen Shilling, & Seven pence three farthing; also thirty Six Shillings
the fifth of a State note; and two pounds three Shillings one fifth of a
Note given by Capt Walker a former guardien; as alowed by the
Judge Decr 5th 1783 In full of the above
Guardien SAMUEL PEIRCE

Woburn Decem 8th 1787
Rec^d of James Wyman Guardien to Susa pierce five pound, Eighteen

Shilling Eleven pence three farthing also a further Sum of Twenty Eight Shilling & 6^d—as Intrest it being for Taking care of my Daughter Susa and money pd to Docters

Rec^d by me   abigail peirce

Medford March 31st 1790

Rec'd of James Wyman Guardian to Heman Pearse Nine pounds Eight Shillings two pence three farthings as allow'd by the Judge Decr 5th 1783   Also Fifty Spanish Mill'd Dollars Rec'd p^r me

HEMAN PIERCE

Middlesex ss. Cambridge in Probate Court 7 Oct 1790   I order the above written discharge to be recorded.

OLIVER PRESCOTT J. prob.

A Copy, Attest, J. H. TYLER, Register.

225¼. BENJAMIN[5] PIERCE (*Thomas*[4], *Benjamin*[3], *Thomas*[2], *Thomas*[1]), b. 1725; m. May 7, 1752, Mary Lamson, b. May 11, 1731. She was the daughter of John Lamson by his second wife, Abigail. They came from Reading in 1714, his wife Elizabeth bringing a certificate from that church June 6, 1714. It is probable he was the son of Joseph Lamson of Charlestown, whose will, dated July 16, proved Sept. 21, 1722, mentions his wife Dorathy, and his sons Joseph, John, William, Nathaniel and Caleb; the two last executors.

Benjamin Pierce was a large land owner in Weston. For 17 years he held several town offices, and in 1781 he lent the town 135 pounds. He served in Capt. Samuel Lamson's company on the 19th of April, 1775, and was in the battles of Ticonderoga, White Plains and Crown Point. Tradition says he had a sister who married a Dolbier. Sept. 1, 1759, he informs the Selectmen that he has taken into his family Hepsebah Pierce of Woburn, last from Hopkinton. Hepsebah Pierce, dau. of Thomas and Hannah (Locke) Pierce, was married to Benjamin Dolbier at King's Chapel in Boston, Feb. 18, 1760. Aug. 28, 1760, he informs the Selectmen that he has taken into his house Abigail Ballard. His sister Hannah m. William Ballard, Jr. In 1774 he was chosen on the committee of correspondence.—[See Bond, page 1067]. In 1777 was on a committee of five to see that every one abide by a report, which he had helped draw up to the General Court, to regulate the price of certain articles. In 1781 he received 33 pounds 1 shilling 8 pence for his services in Rhode Island. Children :—

463. i.   HANNAH, b. Mar. 1, 1753; m. —— Jewell. No issue.
464. ii. MARY, b. Dec. 17, 1754; m. Oct. 31, 1776, Andrew Benjamin. Ch. : Levi, Stephen, and Sally.
465. iii. BENJAMIN, b. Oct. 21, 1756; m. Nov. 28, 1782, Eunice Jones.
466. iv. JOHN, b. Sept. 18, 1758; m. Mary Webb.
467. v.   AMOS, b. Aug. 5, 1760; m. Mar. 3, 1789, Hepsibah Smith.
468. vi. CALEB, b. Feb. 27, 1763; said to have rem. to Mt. Holley, Vt.
469. vii. ASA, b. Sept. 21, 1765.
470. viii. STEPHEN, b. Oct. 2, 1768; m. —— ——.
471. ix. LUCY, b. Aug. 29, 1773; m. —— Weeks and settled in Winchendon.
472. x.   SARAH, b. Aug. 6, 1774; m. —— Robbins and went west.

225⅛. THOMAS⁵ PIERCE (*Thomas⁴, Benjamin³, Thomas², Thomas¹*), b. 1727; m. Apr. 26, 1750, Mary Haven. They res. in Hopkinton and Framingham. Children:—

473. i. HANNAH, b. Mar. 22, 1755; m. ―――― Fletcher.
474. ii. JOSEPH, b. July 12, 1757; m. Hannah Green.
475. iii. ANNE, b. July 20, 1759.
476. iv. ELIAB, b. Sept. 5, 1761; m. Lydia Wood.
477. v. THOMAS, b. Dec. 5, 1763; m. Sally Derry.
478. vi. LYDIA, b. Mar. 6, 1766; m. John Woods.
479. vii. MARY, b. Sept. 4, 1768; m. ―――― Marshall.
480. viii. MOSES H., b. Mar. 15, 1771; m. Dec. 6, 1792, Anna Rice.

225½. TIMOTHY⁵ PIERCE (*Thomas⁴, Benjamin³, Thomas², Thomas¹*), b. Mar. 31, 1734; m. Mar. 27, 1755, Abigail Knap. He d. in Southborough bef. 1768. (See his father's will). Children:—

481. i. PHEBE, b. Jan. 10, 1756.
482. ii. TIMOTHY, b. Apr. 18, 1757.

225⅞. JOHN⁵ PIERCE (*Thomas⁴, Benjamin³, Thomas², Thomas¹*), b. Oct. 20, 1751; m. Mar. 3, 1773, Mary Brown. They res. in Weston.

John Pierce, born in Weston in 1751, was a soldier in the Revolutionary War and personally acquainted with Gen. Washington, and a Lieutenant in his army. His daughter although but three years old at the time of Washington's death well remembered her father wearing crape on his arm. After Independence had been declared Mr. Pierce returned to his business in Weston, that of Inn-keeper; his Hotel was burned containing $5000 in Continental money which he and his brothers had received for their services while in the army.

233. SILAS⁶ PIERCE (*Joseph⁵, Joseph⁴, Jonathan³, Samuel², Thomas¹*), b. July 22, 1744; m. Mar. 26, 1771, Lucy Spalding, d. July 31, 1773; m. 2nd, Apr. 12, 1774, Elizabeth Barron, d. Mar. 23, 1786; m. 3rd, Dec. 7, 1786, Lydia Richardson, d. Dec. 4, 1796; m. 4th, Dec. 28, 1797, Sarah Goodhue, d. May 31, 1799; m. 5th, Sept. 1, 1800, Bridget Putman, d. May 12, 1805; m. 6th, Nov. 20th, 1806, Hannah Littlehale, d. May 21, 1837. He d. Apr. 14, 1828. They res. in Woburn and Chelmsford. Children:—

483. i. MARY, b. July 24, 1772; d. Mar. 4, 1773.
484. ii. JOSEPH, b. Mar. 5, 1775; m. May 28, 1805, Nancy Hollis.
485. iii. OLIVE, b. Oct. 23, 1776; m. David Parker. They had a son Joshua, who resided in Londonderry, Vt.
486. iv. RHODA, b. Sept. 14, 1779; m. Feb. 9, 1802, Zachariah Spalding, b. Sept. 14, 1774; d. May 16, 1838. She d. in Ludlow, Vt., May 16, 1838. Ch.: Ephraim, b. Dec. 10, 1802, m. Julia Brooks; Rhoda, b. Jan. 7, 1805, d. Sept. 10, 1856; Benj. P., b. Nov. 26, 1807, m. Anna W. Whitcomb and Marian Read; Silas B., b. Sept. 26, 1810, m. Grena B. Gilbert; Anson, b. July 3, 1813, m. Lucy A. Brown; Mary, b. Mar. 2, 1816, m. Parkhurst B. Dunn; Emily, b. Dec. 10, 1820, m. Ambrose L. Adams; Olive C., b. Dec. 15, 1823, m. Dr. J. N. Moore.
487. v. SARAH, b. May 28, 1799; d. May 31, 1799.

234. WILLARD⁶ PIERCE (*Joseph⁵, Joseph⁴, Jonathan³, Samuel²,*

Thomas[1]), b. Dec. 1, 1746 ; m. Mar. 23, 1780, Olive Kemp. He d. Sept. 21, 1825. They res. in Merrimack, N. H. He was in the Revolutiouary war seven years. She was b. Mar. 12, 1744, d. Nov. 12, 1810. No. children.

235. LEVI[6] PIERCE (*Joseph*[5], *Joseph*[4], *Jonathan*[3], *Samuel*[2], *Thomas*[1]), b. Feb. 20, 1747 ; m. Jan. 3, 1776, Remembrance Fletcher, b. Dec. 23, 1752, d. Dec. 30, 1833. They res. in Temple, N. H., where he d. Oct. 18, 1799.

Children :—

488. i. LEVI, Jr., b. July 22, 1778; m. Sept. 18, 1804, Rhoda Cutler.
489. ii. REMEMBRANCE, b. Apr. 23, 1781; m. Isarance Long.
490. iii. RACHEL, b. Jan. 2, 1786; m. Peter Wakefield.
491. iv. MARY, b. July 29, 1789; m. William Reynolds.
492. v. JOSEPH, } twins, b. May 2, 1790; { m. Elizabeth Dunklee.
493. vi. SALLY, } { d. Dec. 1, 1818.

241½. ERASMUS[6] PIERCE (*Isaac*[5], *Isaac*[4], *Jonathan*[3], *Samuel*[2], *Thomas*[1]), b. Sept. 22, 1748 ; m. Sept. 13, 1778, Mrs. Susan (Hewes) Hinkley. Was an officer in the Revolutionary war. She d. 1795. He d. 1804. Res. Boston. He was a distiller like his father, carrying on the business for some time, when he became a tallow chandler. At the time of the war he turned all his property into Continental money and gave it to his intended wife to take care of and keep if he did not return. After the war was over and Continental money worth nothing he raked open the fireplace and placed all he could find against the back log and watched it burn. His eldest daughter remembered the circumstance and used to talk about it. Children :—

494. i. PATTY, b. July 14, 1779; m. Samuel C. Hills and Jonathan Simonds.
495. ii. ERASMUS J., b. Oct. 29, 1780; m. Elizabeth Messenger.
496. iii. INFANT, b. June 14, 1782; d. June 14, 1782.
497. iv. JOHN, b. May 1, 1783; d. Oct., 1792.
498. v. NANCY, b. June 26, 1785; m. Caleb Hartshorne; d. leaving no issue.
499. vi. BETSEY, b. June 27, 1787; d. Oct., 1788.
500. vii. PETER, b. Feb. 29, 1789; m. Gwenthalla Morris and Elizabeth Luuberg.
501. viii. DANIEL, b. May 28, 1791; m. Mary Ann Taylor.

243½. JOSEPH[6] PIERCE (*Isaac*[5], *Isaac*[4], *Jonathan*[3], *Samuel*[2], *Thomas*[1]), b. Feb. 29, 1756 ; m. Sally Pease, b. June, 1761. She d. June 24, 1826. Res. Boston. Children :—

502. i. JOSEPH, b. July 30, 1783; m. Sally Hatch.
503. ii. SALLY; d. in infancy.

504. iii. ISAAC, b. Apr. 7, 1788; m. Alice Barstow and Nancy Brack.
505. iv. JAMES, b. Dec. 28, 1790; m. Abigail Waite and Nancy Waite.
506. v. SARAH; m. George Jackson.
507. vi. LUCRETIA.
508. vii. CHARLES; d. 5 years old.
509. viii. WILLIAM; d. in infancy.

246½. JOHN[6] PIERCE (*Isaac[5]*, *Isaac[4]*, *Jonathan[3]*, *Samuel[2]*, *Thomas[1]*), baptized Aug. 14, 1763; m. Dec. 29, 1791, Mrs. Sarah Lobdell. She was said to have been for many years the handsomest lady in Boston. No children.

247. JAMES[6] PIERCE (*Isaac[5]*, *Isaac[4]*, *Jonathan[3]*, *Samuel[2]*, *Thomas[1]*), b. Sept. 7, 1764; m. Dec. 11, 1791, Polly Peacock. Res. Boston. Children:—

510. i. ELINOR; d. age 17.
511. ii. MARY, b. 1798; d. 1798.
512. iii. JAMES I. C. C.
513. iv. MARY; m. Timothy B. Miller.

253. SAMUEL[6] PIERCE (*Samuel[5]*, *Stephen[4]*, *Jonathan[3]*, *Samuel[2]*, *Thomas[1]*), b. Aug. 17, 1785; m. Dec. 17, 1809, Abigail Winslow, b. Nov. 21, 1792. She d. Sept. 1, 1834. He d. Aug. 12, 1853. Res. Boston. Children:—

514. i. ELIZA ANN, b. Dec., 1810; m. John Hanaden.
515. ii. JOHN W., b. Oct. 4, 1812; m. Lydia Ann Osborn.
516. iii. SAMUEL, b. Aug. 11, 1814; m. Rebecca P. Dorell, Caroline Tufts and Mary Payson.
517. iv. ABIGAIL, b. Sept. 19, 1816; m. Nahum H. Wilbur.
518. v. STEPHEN, b. Sept. 2, 1818.
519. vi. EDWARD K., b. Sept. 21, 1820; m. Margaret E. Bass.

257. JONATHAN[6] PIERCE (*Joseph[5]*, *Daniel[4]*, *John[3]*, *Thomas[2]*, *Thomas[1]*), b. Nov. 17, 1743; m. Lettice Warren, 1778. Children:—

520. i. BARZILLAI, b. Dec., 1779; m. Jane Turner and Sarah Hix.
521. ii. JONATHAN, b. 1782; m. Olive Ford.
522. iii. HANNAH, b. 1784; m. Benj. Simmonds.
523. iv. MARY, b. 1786; m. Alex. Mitchell.
524. v. JOSEPH, b. 1789; d. at Plattsburgh, war of 1812.

260. BARZILLAI[6] PIERCE (*Joseph[5]*, *Daniel[4]*, *John[3]*, *Thomas[2]*, *Thomas[1]*), b. Nov. 17, 1750; m. Isabel Howe, Apr. 13, 1775. He was taxed in Hollis in 1775 and 1781. Res. in Hollis, N. H., and ——— ———. Child:—

525. i. BARZILLAI; m. Lucy ———.

261. DAVID[6] PIERCE (*Daniel[5]*, *Daniel[4]*, *John[3]*, *Thomas[2]*, *Thomas[1]*), b. Oct. 3, 1742; m. Apr. 10, 1742, Mrs. Sarah Mainer. She d. 1771. He d. Apr. 6, 1821. Res. in Chesterfield, H. N., and Norridgewock, Me. Children:—

526. i. SIMON, b. Mar. 1, 1764; m. Hepzibah Wood.
527. ii. CALVIN, b. Feb. 10, 1766; m. Deborah Blackwell.
528. iii. LUTHER, b. May 12, 1768; m. Susanna Gray.
529. iv. DAVID, b. Sept. 20, 1771; m. Olive Russell.
530. v. CHARLES, b. Mar. 10, 1775; m. Abigail Ayer.
531. vi. PETER, b. Aug. 12, 1777; m. Elizabeth Blackwell.
532. vii. ALICE; m. Eleazer Whipple.

263. REUBEN[6] PIERCE (*Daniel[5]*, *Daniel[4]*, *John[3]*, *Thomas[2]*, *Thomas[1]*), b. Mar. 7, 1747; m. Jan. 1, 1771, Mary Wood. Reuben Pierce accidentally killed himself at Lunenburg or Leominster in the woods while loading logs by stepping forward and lifting to shove one back after it was loaded. He d. Dec. 30, 1821. Res. Leominster, Mass. A. A. Pierce of St. Albans, Vt., his grandson, has in his possession a powder-horn that was worn by Reuben Pierce at the battle of Lexington, April 19, 1775, when he was wounded. Children:—

533. i.   MARY, b. Sept. 20, 1771; m. Simeon Tyler.
534. ii.   SARAH, b. Aug. 28, 1773; d. Feb. 7, 1778.
535. iii.   ABIGAIL, b. Oct. 2, 1774; d. Feb. 9, 1778.
536. iv.   REUBEN, b. Feb. 5, 1778; d. Feb. 16, 1778.
537. v.   REUBEN, b. Sept. 10, 1779. Was a sea captain.
538. vi.   SARAH, b. Sept. 4, 1781; d. unm.
539. vii.   ZEBEDIAH, b. Dec. 23, 1784; m. Phebe Tyler.
540. viii.   ABIJAH, b. Oct. 7, 1788; m. Sally Maynard and Elvira (Maynard) Jewett.

264. SAMUEL[6] PIERCE (*Daniel[5]*, *Daniel[4]*, *John[3]*, *Thomas[2]*, *Thomas[1]*), b. May 21, 1749; m. Jan. 10, 1774, Abigail Carter, b. 1751, d. Feb. 28, 1777; m. 2d, Elizabeth Whiting, b. June 27, 1751, d. Oct. 23, 1823. He d. Dec. 27, 1824, in Jaffrey, N. H.
Tradition says : Abigail, the wife of Samuel, rode from Jaffrey to Leominster on horseback to visit her friends, and carried her second and youngest son, Samuel, who was then only four months old. She was there taken sick and died ; her husband was sick at Jaffrey at the time of her death, and was unable to attend her funeral, and never saw her again. Children :—

541. i.   ASAPH, b. July 9, 1774; m. Feb. 10, 1797, Hannah Stickney.
542. ii.   SAMUEL, Jr., b. May 9, 1776; m. Feb. 21, 1806, Hetty Brooks.
543. iii.   BETSEY, b. Mar. 29, 1779; m. Jacob Pierce, Jr. [551.]
544. iv.   CALEB, b. Jan. 30, 1781; m. Feb. 20, 1805, Lucy Gale.
545. v.   ANNIE, b. Apr. 12, 1783; m. Dec. 18, 1806, Benjamin Frost, b. Dec. 1, 1778, d. Mar. 9, 1825. She d. in Jaffrey, N. H., Oct. 28, 1834. Ch. : Cyrus, b. May 12, 1807, m. Cynthia May and Betsey McCoy; Annie, b. Dec. 20, 1808, m. Edward M. Lawrence; Eliza, b. Oct. 17, 1811, d. Apr. 14, 1835; Benjamin, Jr., b. June 25, 1813, m. Lydia M. White; Joseph P., b. June 19, 1815, m. Sarah E. Cutter and Sarah A. Osgood; Albert, b. Mar. 20, 1817, m. Mary Boutelle; Silas P., b. Feb. 9, 1820, m. Betsey E. Mason; Caleb W., b. Feb. 9, 1822, m. Mrs. Rhoda D. Burgin.
546. vi.   ABIGAIL, b. Oct. 4, 1785; m. Feb. 17, 1812, Jude Carter, b. July 8, 1781. They res. in Jaffrey, N. H., and in Penn. Ch. : Liberty, b. Dec. 22, 1812; Sylvester, b. Sept. 4, 1815; Abigail, b. July 25, 1817.
547. vii.   SARAH, b. Sept 3, 1787; m. Mar. 12, 1812, Joel Fisk, b. 1787, d. Jan. 19, 1823; m. 2nd, Sept. 10, 1825, James Bridges. They res. in Jaffrey, N. H. She d. Feb. 20, 1836, leaving no issue.
548. viii.   LUCY, b. Nov. 28, 1789; d. Nov. 28, 1789.
549. ix.   JOSEPH, b. Mar. 23, 1792; m. Dec. 18, 1821, Esther (Jaquith) Pierce.
550. x.   SILAS, b. Jan. 4, 1795; m. May 7, 1818, Esther Jaquith. He d. July 29, 1819. His widow m. his brother.

265. JACOB[6] PIERCE (*Daniel[5]*, *Daniel[4]*, *John[3]*, *Thomas[2]*, *Thomas[1]*), b. Aug. 3, 1751; m. Feb. 19, 1777, Rebecca Whitcomb.

They res. in Leominster and Jaffrey, N. H. He d. Aug. 11, 1827. Jacob Pierce went to Jaffrey, N. H., in the spring of 1777; he had purchased his land prior to this time, and had erected thereon a log cabin. He was brought up in Leominster by a man named Carter. He was orderly sergeant in the War of the Revolution, and was at the battle of Bunker Hill. He borrowed his brother Samuel's gun because it was lighter and a better one than his, and he said he fired it seventeen times in that battle, and it became so hot that he could hardly hold it in his hands; he said he took good sight at men before he fired, but never knew or never wanted to know whether he killed any one or not. He was in Charlestown when the foundation for Bunker Hill monument was laid.

Children :—

551. i. JACOB, Jr., b. Apr. 28, 1778; m. Nov. 27, 1800, Mary Sawtell; m. 2nd, Nov. 17, 1813, Electa Evans; m. 3rd, Jan. 18, 1818, Betsey Pierce [543]; m. 4th, Mar. 23, 1823, Sally Garfield.
552. ii. BENJAMIN, b. Feb. 2, 1782; m. Aug. 1, 1813, Sally Erskine.
553. iii. REUBEN, b. Sept. 4, 1787; m. Mar. 9, 1814, Lydia Holden; m. 2nd, May 21, 1823, Florilla Sweetland.
554. iv. MOSES, b. June 22, 1793; m. Betsey Jewett.
555. v. JOSIAH, b. Mar. 15, 1795; d. Apr. 11, 1795.
556. vi. REBECCA, b. Dec. 2, 1799; d. Dec. 13, 1823.
557. vii. KEZIAH, b. Sept. 29, 1783; m. Feb. 6, 1806, Alvin Jewell. She d. Nov. 12, 1824.
558. viii. DEBORAH, b. Oct. 4, 1785; m. Oct. 19, 1826, Alvin Jewell.
559. ix. MARIAN, b. July 6, 1789; m. Nov. 29, 1812, Benjamin Hale, b. Sept. 19, 1790, d. Feb. 12, 1832. She d. in Jaffrey, N. H., Apr. 26, 1863. Ch. : Triphosa, b. Oct. 8, 1813; Almira; Benj. O., m. Maria Spalding and Lydia Spalding; Jacob M. and Moses.
560. x. DANIEL, b. Apr. 2, 1791; d. Apr. 22, 1808.
561. xi. NANCY, b. July 10, 1796; m. Apr. 24, 1823, Sewell Hosmer. They had a son, Granville, res. in Fitchburg.
562. xii. JOSIAH, b. June 19, 1798; m. Feb. 9, 1824, Pauline Erskine.
563. xiii. TRIPHOSA, b. Apr. 15, 1800; d. May 19, 1802.

275. JOHN[6] PIERCE (*John[5], Daniel[4], John[3], Thomas[2], Thomas[1]*), b. May 22, 1759; m. May 16, 1799, Dinah Sawyer, b. 1772. She d. June 12, 1825. He d. Sept. 12, 1828. Res. Harvard, Mass. Children :—

564. i. ELIZA, b. Apr. 17, 1801; d. June 16, 1818.
565. ii. JOHN, b. Oct. 13, 1803; m. Sarah Parker and Louisa Percy.
566. iii. STILLMAN, b. Apr. 23, 1809; m. Sarah French.

276. CALVIN[6] PIERCE (*John[5], Daniel[4], John[3], Thomas[2], Thomas[1]*), b. Mar. 1, 1766; m. Jan. 12, 1786, Betsey Brown, b. 1771. She d. 1817. He m. 2nd, Mar. 31, 1818, Mrs. Lucy Bridge. She d. 1827. He d. 1832. Res. Bolton, Mass. Children :—

567. i. JOHN, b. Mar. 23, 1786; m. Sally Brigham.
568. ii. RUFUS; d. 1817.

569. iii. DANIEL; d. 1827.
570. iv. BETSEY; m. Thorndike Chase.
571. v. MARY; m. John Chase.
572. vi. SOPHRONIA, b. May 13, 1806; m. Luther W. Houghton.
573. vii. CALVIN. 574. viii. SOPHIA. 575. ix. LOUISA. 575½. x. LUCY.

278. EBENEZER[6] PIERCE (*Ebenezer*[5], *Ebenezer*[4], *John*[3], *Thomas*[2], *Thomas*[1]), b. June 9, 1745; m. Eunice Loomis, b. Oct. 10, 1750. She d. Feb. 26, 1826. He d. Aug. 1, 1802. Res. Peru, Mass.

Children :—

576. i. SARAH, b. Oct. 28, 1772; m. Levi Allen.
577. ii. JOHN, b. Aug. 21, 1774; m. Sarah Frissell.
578. iii. EUNICE, b. Oct. 8, 1775; m. William Stevens.
579. iv. MARY, } twins, b. Jan. 13, 1777; { m. Isaac Stevens.
580. v. MARTHA, } { m. Joshua Minor.
581. vi. ASA, b. Mar. 25, 1779; m. Caroline Worthington.
582. vii. LYDIA, b. Jan. 23, 1781; d. Oct. 23, 1800.
583. viii. RUTH, b. Jan. 20, 1783; m. Col. Reid.
584. ix. JERUSHA, b. Oct. 6, 1786; m. Col. Reid.
585. x. EBENEZER, b. Mar. 28, 1788; m. Electa Phillips.
586. xi. ENOCH, b. Apr. 17, 1791; m. Mary Moseley.

283. JOHN[6] PIERCE (*Ebenezer*[5], *Ebenezer*[4], *John*[3], *Thomas*[2], *Thomas*[1]), b. Apr. 20, 1754; m. Oct. 5, 1775, Lucy Snow, b. 1756, d. May 11, 1823. He d. Sept. 20, 1832. They res. in Millbury.

Children :—

587. i. JOHN, b. July 14, 1776; d. Oct. 20, 1796.
588. ii. BETSEY, b. Oct. 29, 1777; m. Dec. 1, 1802, Elias Lovell. Ch. : Elias, m. Eliphal Newton; John, m. Ellen ———; Styra, m. Benj. Sumner; Alden; Adeline, m. John Davidson.
589. iii. LUCY, b. Mar. 25, 1779; m. Aug. 19, 1801, Andrew Waters. Ch. : Lucy, m. a Pardee; Louisa, m. a Goodale.
590. iv. LUTHER, b. Oct. 14, 1781; m. Mar. 23, 1803, Clarissa Reed; m. 2nd, Aurilla Terry.
591. v. CALVIN, b. Dec. 12, 1784; m. Sept. 28, 1808, Sophronia Colton.
592. vi. CLARISSA, b. Nov. 6, 1787; m. Oct. 6, 1808, Luther Stiles, d. June 13, 1857. She d. in Elgin, Ill., Mar. 5, 1865. Ch. : Lydia S., b. Sept. 9, 1811, d. Nov. 5, 1831; Eliza J., b. Feb. 24, 1814, m. Ralph Grow; Mary S., b. Mar. 6, 1816, d. Feb. 22, 1830; Luther C., b. Mar. 7, 1819; Martha W., b. Apr. 25, 1821, d. Oct. 21, 1833; Cornelius C., b. Jan. 12, 1824; Harriet W., b. June 8, 1826; Sarah L., b. June 6, 1828, d. Dec. 22, 1833; Mary P., b. Sept. 15, 1830.
593. vii. HERVEY, b. Oct 24, 1790; d. Sept. 20, 1796.
594. viii. POLLY, b. Mar. 7, 1792; m. June 23, 1811, Jared Brainard. Alive at last accounts and had never worn spectacles.
595. ix. HERVEY, b. Mar. 26, 1797; m. July, 15, 1819, Linia Stone.
596. x. JOHN W., b. May 20, 1801; d. Aug. 1, 1803.

285. JONATHAN[6] PIERCE (*Ebenezer[5]*, *Ebenezer[4]*, *John[3]*, *Thomas[2]*, *Thomas[1]*), b. Sept. 17, 1757 ; m. Apr. 15, 1781, Lydia Bowman, b. Jan. 8, 1763, d. June 28, 1841. He d. Aug. 20, 1808. They res. in Southboro'.

Jenathan Peirce

Children :—

597. i. LYDIA, b. Feb. 4, 1782; m. Asa Holt.
598. ii. NANCY, b. June 30, 1783; m. —— Ford.
599. iii. NATHAN, b. Jan. 6, 1785.
600. iv. JONATHAN, b. Apr. 21, 1788.
601. v. LAVINA, b. Feb. 9, 1790; m. July 11, 1813, William Robbins, b. Apr. 24, 1791. She d. Sept. 2, 1868. Ch. : Lavina, b. Aug. 25, 1814, d. Aug. 11, 1844; William, b. Apr. 14, 1816, d. June 21, 1819; Charles, b. Nov. 28, 1817. He is a physician and resides in Worcester.
602. vi. AARON, b. Feb. 15, 1793.
603. vii. LINA, b. July 16, 1794.
604. viii. LOLA, b. Nov. 20, 1799 ; d. Oct. 13, 1837.

286. Dea. DAVID[6] PIERCE (*Ebenezer[5]*, *Ebenezer[4]*, *John[3]*, *Thomas[2]*, *Thomas[1]*), b. Aug. 16, 1760 ; m. 1783, Sarah Bridges, b. Apr. 1, 1760. She d. Aug. 31, 1820. He d. Sept. 12, 1816. Res. Barnard and Woodstock, Vt.

David Peirce

Children :—

605. i. NATHAN, b. Nov. 24, 1784; m. Sally Richmond.
606. ii. DAVID, b. Mar. 26, 1786; m. Ruth Downer and Mary S. Gardner.
607. iii. AARON, b. Nov. 23, 1787; m. Sarah Hough.
608. iv. SALLY, b. Oct. 22, 1789 ; d. Jan. 23, 1812.
609. v. ANNA, b. July 3, 1791; m. Charles Carpenter.
610. vi. BETSEY, b. July 13, 1793 ; m. Abner Harlow.
611. vii. DANA, b. Sept. 7, 1795 ; m. Deadama Paul.
612. viii. EDMUND, b. Aug. 19, 1797; m. Louisa Stane.
613. ix. POLLY, b. Sept. 6, 1799 ; m. Sanford Sessions and Warren Harlow.
614. x. LUCY, b. Feb. 2, 1802; d. Oct. 30, 1802.
615. xi. FANNY, b. Sept. 22, 1803 ; m. —— Barstow.

287. AARON[6] PIERCE (*Ebenezer[5]*, *Ebenezer[4]*, *John[3]*, *Thomas[2]*, *Thomas[1]*), b. Apr. 16, 1762 ; m. Sept. 8, 1790, Hannah Greenwood, b. Dec. 27, 1764 ; d. Dec. 9, 1837. He d. Sept. 7, 1833. They res. in Millbury, Mass.

Aaron Pierce was a man much esteemed and trusted by his townsmen, holding offices of trust, and representing the town in the General Court one or more sessions. His grandson, Mr. Geo. L. Chase of Hartford, Conn., has in his possession a Commission issued by Governor Samuel Adams, which sets forth that " confiding in the ability, discretion and integrity of Aaron Pierce, by and with the consent of the Council, do appoint him Justice of the Peace for the County of Worcester," which office he held for many years.

Aaron Peirce

Children :—

616. i. SALLY, b. June 10, 1791; m. Dec. 9, 1819, Paul C. Chase, b. 1790. Ch.: Leonard P., b. 1820, m. Mary Goddard; Lydia P., b. 1822, m. H. Derby P. Bigelow; Geo. L., b. 1828, m. Calista Taft; David B., b. 1829, m. Melissa Simmons; Hannah G., b. 1831, m. Perley Whipple; David M., b. 1832.

617. ii. LYDIA, b. Sept. 9, 1792; m. Oct. 25, 1813, David Gordon. Ch.: Leander, m. Sarah Wheeler; Emeline, m. Fred. Sargent; Lydia, m. Alphonza Busnell; Fred., m. Louisa ——— ; Hannah, m. Frank Crosby; Frank, m. Martha Crosby.

618. iii. LEONARD, b. Dec. 8, 1793; d. Sept. 20, 1796.

619. iv. HANNAH, b. July 9, 1796; d. infant, July 12, 1796.

620. v. LEONARD, b. Jan. 11, 1798; m. Nov. 15, 1831, Mary Putnam.

621. vi. AARON, b. Aug. 8, 1802; m. Sophronia Scott.

622. vii. MARY S., b. Dec. 4, 1806; m. Nov. 10, 1831, Calvin Temple. Ch.: Joseph, b. Oct. 12, 1839, m. Lucia Kingman; twins, b. July 15, 1834, d. July 15, 1834; Caroline, b. Jan. 29, 1836, d. Sept. 29, 1836; Mary, b. Apr. 15, 1837, d. Nov. 12, 1842; Sarah, b. Oct. 23, 1842, d. Jan. 20, 1852. They res. in Reading.

288. Lieut. JOSHUA[6] PIERCE (*Joshua*[5], *Ebenezer*[4], *John*[3], *Thomas*[2], *Thomas*[1]), b. May 17, 1741; m. Nov. 27, 1766, Lydia Goodrich, b. Aug. 1, 1740. She d. Jan. 25, 1826. He d. Nov. 5, 1812. Res. Leominster, Mass.

Joshua Pierce was a Lieutenant under General Washington during the Revolutionary war, and wore a sword which was taken from a French officer in the French and Indian war, which bears date 1414. After the war he settled in Lancaster, Mass., as a farmer. Children :—

623. i. THOMAS S., b. Sept. 13, 1767; m. Dolly Boutelle.

624. ii. JOSHUA, b. April 19, 1769; d. unm.

625. iii. KATHERINE, b. May 6, 1771; m. Sylvester Ropes.

626. iv. JONATHAN, b. April 26, 1773. Res. New York State.

627. v. ASA, b. Aug. 5, 1775; m. Deborah Joslin and Martha J. Richardson.

628. vi. PHINEAS, b. Nov. 29, 1778; d. unm. June 20, 1836.

629. vii. DAVID, b. July 17, 1781; m. ——— ———.

630. viii. ELIAS, b. Nov. 5, 1784; d. unm. Sept. 25, 1834.

289. Capt. JONATHAN[6] PIERCE (*Joshua*[5], *Ebenezer*[4], *John*[3], *Thomas*[2], *Thomas*[1]), b. Jan. 20, 1744; m. Dec. 28, 1766, Elizabeth Cooper, b. Jan., 1738. She d. May 21, 1806. He m. 2nd, April 27, 1809, Mrs. Lydia Francis, b. Jan., 1742. She d. July 31, 1834. He d. Sept. 2, 1825. Res. Lancaster and Boston.

Jonathan Pierce settled in Newport, R. I., and was Captain of the Royal Artillery of Warren, R. I., before the breaking out of the Revolutionary war, but then with others of his command joined the American forces. As a consequence his property was confiscated and a price set on his head. He entered the Revolutionary Army as Captain under General Lafayette, and was at the battles of Yorktown and

Brandywine, in which he wore the sword taken by his father in the French and Indian war. After the war he was in the employ of the Government, and at the time of his death held the post of armorer at Charlestown Navy Yard. Children:—

631. i. CURTIS, b. March 3, 1769; d. Jan., 1775.
632. ii. JONATHAN, b. Jan. 3, 1772; d. Oct. 19, 1772.
633. iii. JONATHAN, b. Oct. 18, 1809; m. Elizabeth B. Leavitt.
634. iv. JOSHUA H., b. July 24, 1812; d. unm., 1869.

291. JOSIAH[6] PIERCE, Jr. (*Josiah[5]*, *Josiah[4]*, *John[3]*, *Thomas[2]*, *Thomas[1]*, b. Aug. 27, 1756; m. March, 1787, Phebe Thompson*, b. Dec. 31, 1762, d. Feb. 27, 1839. He d. in Baldwin, Me., Jan. 23, 1830, where he had settled in 1785.† Children:—

635. i. HANNAH, b. Apr. 27, 1788; d. Sept. 23, 1873.
636. ii. PHEBE, b. Sept. 29, 1789; d. Nov. 11, 1800.
637. iii. JOSIAH, Jr., b. Aug. 15, 1792; m. Eveline Lewis.
638. iv. RUTH, b. Mar. 24, 1794; m. Ira Crocker. They res. in Portland, Me. and had one son, who left two ch. She d. Mar. 16, 1875.
639. v. NANCY, b. Jan. 7, 1796; m. 1822, Rev. Charles Freeman of Limerick, Me., and had two ch., Phebe E., b. Mar. 26, 1823, m. —— Sanborn; Charles M., b. Mar. 21, 1825. She d. Sept. 2, 1825.
640. vi. HARRIET, b. Mar. 2, 1798; d. June 14, 1829.
641. vii. SARAH R., b. Jan. 2, 1800; m. Dr. William B. Gooch. She d. Dec., 1851, leaving one dau., Mrs. Elizabeth Clark of Elizabeth, N. J.
642. viii. PHEBE T.. b. Mar. 17, 1801; d. July 22, 1803.
643. ix. DANIEL T., b. Mar. 15, 1803; m. Frances E. B. Lewis.
644. x. GEORGE W., b. Dec. 2, 1805; m. Ann Wadsworth Longfellow, sister of Henry W., the Poet. He d. Nov. 15, 1835, without issue.

---

* She was dau. of Daniel Thompson of Woburn, who was killed at the battle of Lexington.

† Josiah Pierce (son of Josiah Pierce and Ruth Thompson, widow of Benj. Thompson, and mother of Count Rumford), born at Woburn, Mass., Aug. 27, 1756, died at Baldwin, Me., Jan. 23, 1830, was a man remarkable for his ability, energy, success in life, and superior physical and moral character. His father, Josiah Pierce, possessed 50 acres of tillage land in Woburn, opposite Col. Baldwin's place (inherited from his ancestor who settled there, as to 40 acres as a settler, and by acquisition of 10 acres more from some other settler), and also a lot of 30 acres (called "Wood-acre"), acquired by purchase. Josiah Pierce (born 1756), accompanied his half-brother Benj. Thompson (Count Rumford) in his escape from America, but took some part in the American Revolution, crossed Charlestown Neck during the engagement at Bunker Hill, with supplies for the troops, and was a member of a Company of Minute-men, and afterwards was an officer of the State in Shays' Rebellion. About 1780, he was engaged in the business of Col. Loammi Baldwin, and a partnership was formed between them under the name of "Baldwin & Pierce," through which they purchased the rights of several grantees to lands in Maine, chiefly in Flintstown (afterwards Baldwin), Maine; the partnership was dissolved in 1802. Meanwhile Josiah Pierce came to Baldwin about 1785, and then stopped at a settler's (Lowell's), where forty carcasses of deer killed on the hills near by, were in the house. Bears were frequently seen there then. Now a railway passes through those grounds, and it is rarely that one sees a partridge or squirrel. He set up a potash factory, a corn-mill, and timber-sawing mill, and built a house, square, old-fashioned, of the Massachusetts

294. JOHN[6] PIERCE (*Josiah*[5], *Josiah*[4], *John*[3], *Thomas*[2], *Thomas*[1]),
b. May 26, 1764 ; m. Rebecca Wilson, Aug. 17, 1788. He d. Sept.
21, 1838. Res. Woburn, Mass. and Hiram, Me. Children :—

645. i.   JOHN, b. Feb. 2, 1789 ; m. Ruth Powers.
646. ii.   JOSIAH, b. Nov. 8, 1790 ; m. Mary Hancock.
647. iii. REBECCA, b. July 29, 1792 ; m. Mar., 1825, Mark Rounds, and d.
            May 30, 1877.
648. iv.   BENJAMIN T., b. Aug. 18, 1794 ; m. Nancy Young.
649. v.   WILLIAM, b. April 1, 1796 ; m. Betsey Larrabee.
650. vi.   TIMOTHY C., b. Mar. 14, 1798 ; d. Aug. 1, 1798.
651. vii. TIMOTHY C., b. Jan. 6, 1800 ; m. Olive Pingree.
652. viii. DANIEL, b. Feb. 7, 1802 ; m. Abigail Hancock.
653. ix.   LEVI, b. April 27, 1804 ; unm ; res. Hiram, Me.
654. x.   RUTH, b. Feb. 5, 1807 ; m. July 4, 1828, John Johnson.

296. DANIEL[6] PIERCE (*John*[5], *Josiah*[4], *John*[3], *Thomas*[2], *Thomas*[1]),
b. 1742 ; m. Mercy Gates, b. 1748. She d. Mar. 26, 1827. He d.
July 16, 1821. Res. Westmoreland, N. H. and St. Johnsbury Centre,
Vt Children :—

667. i.   DANIEL, b. Jan. 27, 1768 ; m. Abigail Gilson.
668. ii.   ARETAS, b. Jan. 2, 1770 ; m. Rebecca Blood.
669. iii. MERCY, b. Aug. 6, 1771 ; m. Phineas Day.
670. iv.   SALLY, b. June 10, 1773 ; m. Thomas Peck.
671. v.   BETSEY, b. Feb. 17, 1775 ; d. unm.
672. vi.   NATHANIEL, b. Aug. 8, 1777 ; m. Betsey McManus.
673. vii. LEVI, b. May 24, 1779 ; m. Polly Fowler.
674. viii. ABEL, b. Aug. 12, 1781 ; m. Mercy Allen.

---

pattern (which is still standing), came back to Massachusetts and was married in March, 1787, to Phebe Thompson (dau. of Daniel Thompson who was
killed at the battle of Lexington), carried her to Baldwin on a pillion, and
lived there till his death. When he closed his partnership with Col. Baldwin
in 1802, he took the lands in Maine, and his partner the debts to them on
account—and he held afterwards during most of his life a large extent of tim-
bered land (10,000 acres or more), and employed it usefully. He bought up
his father's and mother's property in Woburn, and they came to live near him
in 1791, and died in Baldwin. His business increased and gradually became
chiefly that of manufacturing or supplying lumber or deals. At one time he
owned thirty saw-mills. In politics he was a Federalist of the old school, and
was by some called a Tory, from his old-fashioned ways. He was a Justice
of the Peace, and had much to do in that capacity. He was almost always on
horseback, the roads being bad at first, and from custom afterwards. To the
close of his life he wore the old fashioned queue, tied with black ribbon, and
was careful of his dress, usually wearing a suit of gray cloth. His house was
open to all guests, and his hospitality was famous through all the country
round. He sometimes employed as many as a hundred men, on his farm of
400 acres, and on other work in the neighborhood. Although without a
classical education, he was very fond of books, and read and knew almost all
the best literature of his time, preferring metaphysics, and having as favorite
authors Dugald Stewart, Brown, Burke, Locke, Pope, and Adam Smith.
His conversation was remarkably pleasant and entertaining. It is said that
when he went to Portland on business and stopped at an hotel, twenty or
thirty of the old citizens would gather there to hear him talk. He gave all
his children a good liberal education. Two of his three sons graduated at
Bowdoin College. He was physically very superior, very strong, never ill,
six feet in height, erect, broad-backed, and firm. He left a large family, well-
trained, and well-placed—a memory still honored—a considerable property,
and an example of the solid old Massachusetts Federalist.

675. ix. REUBEN, b. May 25, 1783; m. Abigail Cobb.
676. x. JOEL, b. July 16, 1785; d. young.
677. xi. LOIS, b. 1786; m. Nahum Stiles.

297. JOSEPH[6] PIERCE (*John[5], Josiah[4], John[3], Thomas[2], Thomas[1]*),
b. 1749; m. Margaret Gates. He d. Jan. 20, 1803. Res. Bolton,
Mass., Westmoreland, N. H., and St. Johnsbury, Vt. Children:—

655. i. JOSEPH, b. May 15, 1773; m. Susanna Lawrence.
656. ii. EPHRAIM, b. June 8, 1775; d. unm. 1815.
657. iii. TIMOTHY, b. Aug. 20, 1776; rem. to New York State.
658. iv. JOTHAM, b. ——— 12, 1778; m. Mary R. Cobb.
659. v. ASA, b. Feb. 25, 1781; rem. to Belvidere, Ill.
660. vi. MARTIN, b. June 5, 1783; m. Abigail Sanderson.
661. vii. LEONARD, b. July 28, 1785, m. Nancy Norris.
662. viii. WILDER, b. Jan. 3, 1788; m. Nancy Parsons.
663. ix. ALFRED, b. Aug. 9, 1790; m.———.
664. x. SHUBAL, b. Apr. 10, 1793; m. Mary A. Barnard.
665. xi. ALMIRA, b. May 18, 1796; m. Horace Huntoon.
666. xii. THOMAS, b. Feb. 11, 1799; m. Olive Martin.

298. THOMAS[6] PIERCE (*John[5], Josiah[4], John[3], Thomas[2], Thomas[1]*), b. 1756; m. Abigail ———, b. April, 1753. She d. Dec. 12, 1836. He d. Dec. 14, 1832. Res. St. Johnsbury, Vt.

Thomas Peirce

Children:—

678. i. THOMAS, b. 1780; m. Betsey Sanderson and Mrs. (Roberts) Flint.
679. ii. ORPHA; m. Israel Peirce. See *Peirce Genealogy* by Frederick C. Pierce, Esq.
680. iii. ABIGAIL.
681. iv. SALLY; m. Jacob Sanderson.
682. v. DIANTHE; m. Philip Goss.

299. JOHN[6] PIERCE (*Thomas[5], Thomas[4], Thomas[3], Thomas[2], Thomas[1]*), b. Feb. 10, 1724; m. Dec. 24, 1750, Zeruiah Spalding, b. Dec. 24, 1726. She d. Nov. 20, 1808. He d. Sept. 24, 1780. Res. Plainfield, Conn.

John Peirce

Children:—

683. i. SUSANNA, b. Nov. 3, 1751; d. Sept. 22, 1776.
684. ii. JOHN, b. Aug. 19, 1753; d. Nov. 24, 1834.
685. iii. ESTHER, b. April 1, 1755; d. Oct. 24, 1790.
686. iv. MARY, b. April 5, 1757; m. John Cleveland.
687. v. PHINEAS, b. Jan. 15, 1759; d. unm. Oct 14, 1801. He was High Sheriff of Windham Co., Conn., at his death.
688. vi. PRISCILLA, b. April 24, 1761; m. Daniel Gordon.
689. vii. THOMAS, b. April 8, 1763; m. Baradill Fox.
690. viii. STEPHEN, b. June 2, 1765; d. Nov. 24, 1822.
691. ix. SPALDING, b. Feb. 29, 1768; m. Nabby Bacon.
692. x. SYLVESTER, b. Sept. 17, 1770; m. Eunice ———.

308. LEMUEL[6] PIERCE (*Ebenezer*[5], *Thomas*[4], *Thomas*[3], *Thomas*[2], *Thomas*[1]), b. Nov. 16, 1730; m. Feb. 10, 1756, Dorcas Spalding, b. Aug. 9, 1735. He d. 1821. Lemuel was in the Revolutionary War. Res. Plainfield and Sterling, Conn. Children:—

693. i. PARNEL, b. Apr. 17, 1758; d. Sept. 27, 1761.
694. ii. OLIVE, b. Apr. 9, 1760.
695. iii. PHINEAS; m. Rowena Harris.

315. THOMAS[6] PIERCE (*Amos*[5], *Thomas*[4], *Thomas*[3], *Thomas*[2], *Thomas*[1]), b. July 2, 1729; m. Nov. 19, 1755, Olive Green, d. Nov. 6, 1822. He d. Mar. 30, 1811. Children:—

696. i. SAMUEL, b. Sept. 22, 1756; m. Hannah White.
697. ii. TRYPHENE, b. June 22, 1758; m. a Peats and had Lewis and Betsey.
698. iii. RUTH, b. Oct. 8, 1759; m. Abner Miller and had William, Heber, Betsey, Olive and Polly.
699. iv. SARAH, b. Nov. 20, 1761.
700. v. JOHN, b. Apr. 20, 1764; m. Nov. 28, 1798, Sally Daboll; m. 2nd, June 10, 1822, Mary Smith.
701. vi. ESTHER, b. Oct. 17, 1766; m. a Caldwell and had James, Samuel, Milo, Margaret, Beulah, Lavinia, Fidelia, and Oby. She d. Apr. 16, 1812.
702. vii. OLIVE, b. July 30, 1770; m. ——— Bull and d. Apr. 16, 1812, leaving Lucy, Mittie, Henrietta, Olive, Cynthia, Norman, Buell, and William.
703. viii. SILAS, b. Feb. 24, 1772; m. Lois Kelsey.
704. ix. BEULAH, b. Aug. 7, 1774; d. July 12, 1790.
705. x. CYNTHIA, b. Dec. 22, 1775.

321. AMOS[6] PIERCE, Jr. (*Amos*[5], *Thomas*[4], *Thomas*[3], *Thomas*[2], *Thomas*[1]), b. Sept. 6, 1742; m. Lois Fellows, d. Feb. 28, 1820. He d. Feb. 13, 1807, in Canaan, Conn. Children:—

706. i. MARY, b. Apr. 14, 1773; d. Feb. 12, 1793.
707. ii. ICHABOD, } twins, b. Nov. 12, 1775; { m. a Whitney.
708.   EDWARD, } { d. Feb. 24, 1802.
709. iii. ANNA, b. Oct., 1778; m. a Freeman and a Hill. She d. Apr. 12, 1828. Had Daniel, Orrin, Edward, Silas and Lois.
710. iv. STEPHEN, b. June 15, 1780; d. infant.
711. v. SAMUEL, b. Mar. 27, 1783; m. Sally Gorham.
712. vi. BETSEY, b. Apr. 8, 1785; m. Samuel Williams; d. Aug. 23, 1836.
713. vii. WILLIAM, b. Feb. 25, 1787; m. Jan. 19, 1813, Polly Loveland.
714. viii. LAURA, b. Aug. 3, 1789; m. Silas Williams; d. Mar. 30, 1826.
715. ix. CANDACE, b. Oct. 14, 1792; m. Isaac Gifford. Ch.: Ferdando; res. Olena, Ohio.

325. PHINEAS[6] PIERCE (*Amos*[5], *Thomas*[4], *Thomas*[3], *Thomas*[2], *Thomas*[1]), b. Jan. 24, 1751; m. Oct. 10, 1771, Ruth Gaines, b. 1751, d. Nov. 9, 1802; m. 2nd, Jan. 13, 1803, Ruth Beebe. He d. Dec. 1, 1808. Children:—

716. i. KEZIAH, b. July 1, 1773; m. ——— Austin.
717. ii. CANDACE, b. Oct. 14, 1775; d. Sept. 13, 1777.
718. iii. HULDAH, b. Aug. 8, 1777; d. Oct. 7, 1777.
719. iv. RHODA, b. Aug. 4, 1779; m. John Rawson. She d. Sept. 20, 1862. Ch.: John P., b. Aug. 4, 1801, d. 1863; Julia; Hiram; Horace; Stephen; Mary, b. Oct. 2, 1812, m. C. P. Van Ness.
720. v. PHINEAS, b. Aug. 16, 1781; m. Annie Kellogg.

721. vi.　ELIZABETH, b. May 1, 1783; d. May 5, 1783.
722. vii.　AMOS, b. July 31, 1784; m. Mary Sanford and ———— ————.
723. viii.　ABIRAM, b. May 20, 1786; m. Jan. 8, 1809, Sarah Satterlee.
724. ix.　WILLIAM, b. Apr. 20, 1788; d. May 9, 1788.
725. x.　LUCY, b. May 20, 1789; m. Ashel Smith.
726. xi.　STEPHEN, b. June 18, 1791; m. Edith Low.
727. xii.　HORACE, b. Nov. 16, 1803; m. Mary Perkins.
728. xiii.　RUTH, b. Oct. 12, 1805; m. Luke Perkins.
729. xiv.　HARRY, b. Feb. 20, 1808; m. Alma Phelps.

325½. JOHN[6] PIERCE (*John[5], Thomas[4], Thomas[3], Thomas[2], Thomas[1]*), b. Feb. 18, 1750; m. Tamar Tift. He d. Oct. 11, 1804. Res. Wyoming, Penn.

John Pierce

Children:—

730. i.　PELATIAH; m. Polly ————.
731. ii.　ELIZABETH: m. Elihu Parrish.
732 iii.　LUCRETIA; m. John Bowman.
733. iv.　THANKFUL; m. Nathaniel Hartsouf.
734. v.　JOHN, b. Feb. 27, 1792; m. Susanna Shupp.
735. vi.　TAMAR.

[Petition in John Pierce Est.]
Whereas John Pierce, Blacksmith, late of Kingston Tp. dec[d], died siezed of land in Kingston Tp. and Plymouth Tp., Luzerne Co., leaving a widow Tamar Pierce and issue—
Pelatiah, Elizabeth intermarried with Elihu Parrish, Lucretia intermarried with John Bowman, and Thankful intermarried with Nathaniel Hartsouf, and John and Tamar, minors.
John Pierce and Tamar Pierce, minor children of John Pierce late of Kingston Township, dec[d], pray for appointment of guardians.
John chooses Stephen Hollister.
Tamar chooses Elihu Parrish.

330. TIMOTHY[6] PIERCE, Jr.(*Timothy[5], Timothy[4], Thomas[3], Thomas[2], Thomas[1]*), b. May 22, 1734; m. Aug. 8, 1754, Eunice Fish. He m. 2nd, Feb. 28, 1765, Hannah Gilkey, b. 1731. She d. Dec. 19, 1819. He d. Feb. 2, 1813. Res. Plainfield, Conn.

Timothy Pierce

Children :—

736. i.　TIMOTHY, b. Sept. 13, 1756; d. at sea, 1775.
737. ii.　PALMER, b. Oct. 8, 1761; m. Eunice Kimball and **Lydia Burton**.
738. iii.　HANNAH, b. Aug. 26, 1768; d. Feb. 21, 1846.
739. iv.　JOHN L., b. Aug. 15, 1770; m. Apame Thomas.
740. v.　EUNICE, b. Oct. 8, 1772; d. Sept. 5, 1863.

11

332. JOSIAH[6] PIERCE (*Timothy*[5], *Timothy*[4], *Thomas*[3], *Thomas*[2], *Thomas*[1]), b. 1745; m. Lydia Sheppard. He d. Aug. 1, 1805.

Children :—

741. i.   JOB, b. Mar. 22, 1770; m. Jerusha Mery and Mary E. Pitkin.
742. ii.   AZEL, b. June 26, 1773; m. Eliza Brewster.
743. iii. POLLY, b. Apr. 1, 1775; m. John Morgan.
744. iv.   JOSIAH, b. July 21, 1777; d. Jan., 1813.
745. v.   SHEPPARD, b. Apr. 29, 1780; m. Sarah Colbaugh.
746. vi.   LYDIA, b. July 23, 1782: m. —— Pratt and Theophilus Meyer.
747. vii. CHESTER, b. Nov. 25, 1785; d. 1799.
748. viii. DOLLY, b. Mar., 1788; d. June 18, 1842.
749. ix.   AUGUSTUS, b. Sept., 1790; d. May, 1825.

335. NATHANIEL[6] PIERCE, Jr. (*Nathaniel*[5], *Timothy*[4], *Thomas*[3], *Thomas*[2], *Thomas*[1]), b. Mar. 19, 1728; m. Sept. 24, 1754, Priscilla Sheppard, b. 1734, d. Nov. 10, 1827. He d. July 13, 1808. They res. in Pomfret, Conn., and Royalton, Vt.

Nathl Pirce

Children :—

750. i.   ELIZABETH, b. May 4, 1756.
751. ii.   MARTHA, b. Mar. 1, 1758.
752. iii. PHEBE, b. Jan. 13, 1760.
753. iv.   WILLARD, b. Jan. 28, 1762; m. July 22, 1784, Susanna Waldo.
754. v.   LUCY, b. Dec. 28, 1764; m. Mar. 11, 1784, Phineas Parkhurst. Ch. : Lucy A., m. Jason Allen; Harriet, m. Rev. Geo. G. Ingersoll; Susan, m. John Wright; Nancy, m. Asa Francis; Sarah; Phineas. Jr., m. Persis Kendall; Horace, d. 17 years old.
755. vi.   BESTER; m. May 21, 1795, Lois Stevens; m. 2nd, 1798, Sally Burroughs; m. 3rd, 1818, Miss McChenney.
756. vii. PRISCILLA; m. Dec. 29, 1785, Standish Day.
757. viii. ISAAC, b. 1774; m. Dec. 22, 1797, Polly Smith.
758. ix.   CALEB; m. Betsey Fogg.

336. EZEKIEL[6] PIERCE (*Nathaniel*[5], *Timothy*[4], *Thomas*[3], *Thomas*[2], *Thomas*[1]), b. Dec. 18, 1730; m. July 8, 1749, Esther Blodgett. He d. Sept. 11, 1751. Res. Plainfield, Conn. Children :—

759. i.   SARAH, b. Feb. 6, 1750; m. —— Leonard.
760. ii.   EZEKIEL, b. Feb. 17, 1752.

339. JEDEDIAH[6] PIERCE (*Nathaniel*[5], *Timothy*[4], *Thomas*[3], *Thomas*[2], *Thomas*[1]), b. Feb. 22, 1740; m. Apr. 11, 1764, Susanna Eaton, b. Aug. 24, 1744. She d. June 23, 1831. He d. Dec. 31, 1826. He was in the Revolutionary war. Res. Plainfield, Conn.
Children :—

761. i.   JOSEPH, b. Aug. 19, 1765; m. Roxanna Perrin.
762. ii.   ESTHER, b. Nov. 22, 1766; m. Benj. Tuckerman.
763. iii. RUTH, b. Aug. 23, 1768; m. Mar. 1, 1798, Ebenezer Cole. She d. in Morristown, Vt., May 15, 1852.
764. iv.   WILLIAM, b. Sept. 5, 1770; m. Hannah Baker.
765. v.   LOIS, b. Feb. 14, 1772; m. Dec. 1, 1796, Joseph Safford. She d. in Royalton, Vt., Sept. 14, 1798.
766. vi.   ELISHA, b. Nov. 27, 1774; m. Polly Baker.
767. vii. LUCY, b. Dec. 9, 1776; d. May 15, 1859.

768. viii. JEDEDIAH, b. Feb. 4, 1779; d. Sept. 3, 1798.
769. ix. EATON, b. Apr. 22, 1781; d. Aug. 9, 1798.
770. x. SUSANNA, b. Mar. 29, 1783; d. June 23, 1855.
771. xi. EBENEZER, b. Feb. 20, 1784; m. Mary Fales.
772. xii. MARY, b. Feb. 16, 1787.

340. WILLARD[6] PIERCE (Nathaniel[5], Timothy[4], Thomas[3],
Thomas[2], Thomas[1]), b. Mar. 6, 1743; m. Jerusha Pellett. She d.
Feb. 19, 1815. He d. Apr. 11, 1826. Res. Plainfield, Conn.
Children:—

773. i. EDITH, b. 1764; m. —— Herrick.
774. ii. JAMES, b. Mar. 13, 1766; m Elizabeth Fuller.
775. iii. JERUSHA, b. 1768; m. Nathan Parker.
776. iv. HEZEKIAH, b. 1770; m. —— White.
777. v. ANNIS, b. 1772; m. —— Frink.

341. NEHEMIAH[6] PIERCE (Benjamin[5], Timothy[4], Thomas[3],
Thomas[2], Thomas[1]), b. May 27, 1730; m. May 3, 1759, Lydia Sheppard, b. Oct., 1731, d. Oct. 22, 1809. He d. Oct. 12, 1783. They res.
in Plainfield and Coventry, Conn. Children:—

778. i. DANIEL, b. July 24, 1760; d. Apr. 22, 1769.
779. ii. BENJAMIN, b. Sept. 4, 1762; m. Dec. 24, 1786, Lydia Gurley.
780. iii. HANNAH, b. May. 10, 1766; m. 1784, Isaac Barton, d. 1841. They
had eight children.
781. iv. FREDERICK, b. July 22, 1768; m. 1802, Rebekah Blood.
782. v. NEHEMIAH, b. May 10, 1771; m. Apr. 14, 1794, Clarissa Williams;
m. 2nd, Jan. 8, 1844, Nancy Ladd.
783. vi. LYDIA, } twins, b. Dec. 4, 1774; { m. Aaron Loomis. She d. in 1847, and left seven children.
784. vii. LUCY, } { d. young.
785. viii. LUCY, b. May 30, 1776.

348. Capt. DELANO[6] PIERCE (Benjamin[5], Timothy[4], Thomas[3],
Thomas[2], Thomas[1]), b. Nov. 19, 1748; m. Nov. 1, 1770, Abigail
Hammond, b. Aug. 22, 1753, d. Jan. 1, 1812. He d. Oct. 28, 1835.
The res. in Coventry, Conn. He was Captain in the Revolutionary
war.

Children:—

786. i. BETSEY, b. May 15, 1771; m. Nov. 20, 1791, Benjamin Gilbert, b.
Aug. 17, 1767, d. Jan. 12, 1835. She d. Oct. 10, 1863. Ch.:
Henry, b. Aug. 25, 1792, d. Mar. 28, 1804; Betsey, b. June 5, 1794,
m. Jona. Davis; John P., b. Nov. 15, 1797, m. Sarah L. Daw-
son; Joseph, b. May 20, 1800, m. Harriet Williams and Sophia
H. Merchant; Horace, b. July 30, 1802, m. Sarah Hall; George
H., b. Feb. 15, 1806, m. Phebe Farnum and Elizabeth Hooker;
Emily F., b. Nov. 22, 1812, m. Thos. R. Baxter.
787. ii. ABIGAIL, b. July 9, 1773; d. Mar. 9, 1795.
788. iii. OLIVE, b. Feb. 25, 1776; m. Daniel Litchfield.
789. iv. ERASTUS, b. Jan. 22, 1780; m. Feb. 9, 1800, Hannah Cady.
790. v. ELIAS, b. Jan. 29, 1781; m. Feb. 10, 1813, Lydia Thompson.

791. vi. BENJAMIN, b. Sept. 1, 1783; d. unm. July, 9, 1839.

Benj= Pierce

792. vii. DELANO, Jr., b. July 19, 1786; m. Nov. 22, 1813, Anna Nichols.
793. viii. LOIS, b. Oct. 6, 1790; m. Nov. 13, 1809, Jonathan Parkhurst. b. Nov. 29, 1784, d. Nov. 27, 1851. She d. Dec. 3, 1857. Ch.: Abigail, b. Feb. 21, 1812, m. Alfred Palmer; Chas. S., b. Nov. 7, 1813, m. Hannah Graves; Harriet, b. Aug. 9, 1816, m. Cleveland Warren and Geo. W. Ellison; Caroline, b. Oct. 18, 1818, m. Alfred Palmer; Lucretia, b. Dec. 8, 1820, m. Edmond L. Warren; Pierce, b. Oct. 31, 1823, d. Dec. 5, 1841; Miner H., b. Nov. 18, 1827, m. Martha Steer.

349. TIMEUS[6] PIERCE (*Benjamin[5]*, *Timothy[4]*, *Thomas[3]*, *Thomas[2]*, *Thomas[1]*), b. June 3, 1751; m. May 4, 1779, Elizabeth Grosvenor. He d. Sept. 27, 1802. They res. in Brooklyn and Coventry, Conn.

Timeus Peirce

Children:—
794. i. SOPHIA, b. Feb. 13, 1780.
795. ii. PAYSON G., b. Sept. 10, 1781; m. Mary Shepard.
796. iii. RIZPAH, b. July 19, 1783; m. Samuel L. Whipple.
797. iv. RUFUS, b. June 20, 1785; d. Feb. 24, 1786.
798. v. RUFUS, b. Dec. 24, 1786; m. ――― ――― and moved to Akron, Ohio.
799. vi. OLIVER, b. Feb. 12, 1789; m. ――― ――― and lived in Providence, R. I. and moved West.
800. vii. BETSEY, b. Apr. 2, 1792; d. Apr. 2, 1792.

350. RUFUS[6] PIERCE (*Benjamin[5]*, *Timothy[4]*, *Thomas[3]*, *Thomas[2]*, *Thomas[1]*), b. Sept. 7, 1753; m. May 16, 1776, Sarah Whitney. He d. Aug. 10, 1784. Res. Brooklyn, Conn. Children:—
801. i. SEPTIMUS, b. Mar. 13, 1777; m. ――― ――― and moved to Middletown, Vt.
802. ii. DEBORAH, b. June 2, 1779; m. Thomas Goodale.
803. iii. NAOMI, b. June 3, 1781; m. Titus Goodale.
804. iv. SARAH, b. July 10, 1783; m. ――― Herrick.

352. ABEL[6] PIERCE (*Ezekiel[5]*, *Timothy[4]*, *Thomas[3]*, *Thomas[2]*, *Thomas[1]*), b. Dec. 15, 1736; m. Ruth Sheppard, b. 1733. She d. 1820. He d. May 23, 1814. Res. Wyoming, Penn. His only son Chester was the first man killed in the "Pennamite and Yankee War" (1784). His oldest daughter married, as his second wife, Capt. Daniel Hoyt, grandfather of the Governor of Pennsylvania, but left no children, and lived to be over 90 years old. The other married Lord Butler, eldest son of Col. Zebulon Butler who commanded the American forces the day of the Wyoming Massacre. Mrs. Butler had five sons, viz: Pierce, John, Chester, Zebulon, Lord, and three daughters, viz: Sylvinia who m. Judge Garrick Mallory, Ruth Ann who m. Judge Conyngham, who lived until July, 1879, and Phebe who m. Dr. Alex. Donaldson. Many of the descendants of the above are well

known. Mrs. Butler died Oct. 28, 1834. In the possession of the family are an old teapot, and an old apron which was worked for Mrs. Ruth (Sheppard) Pierce, by her sister "Aunt Dolly Cobb," as she was called.

Ab. L. P. ived

Children :—

805. i.   SYLVANIA, b. Apr. 5, 1758; m. Capt. Daniel Hoyt.
806. ii. CHESTER, b. 1762; killed July 20, 1784.
807. iii. POLLY, b. Oct., 1763; m. May 30, 1786, Gen. Lord Butler.

357. Lieut. TIMOTHY[6] PIERCE (*Ezekiel*[5], *Timothy*[4], *Thomas*[3], *Thomas*[2], *Thomas*[1]), b. June 23, 1747; m. Hannah Gore, b. May 28, 1752. He d. July 3, 1778. Lieut. Timothy Pierce was killed at the massacre at Wyoming, Penn., after riding all night; he was one of the first "Key Keepers." Res. Wyoming, Penn. Of the twenty-five or thirty officers and privates who left the company in New Jersey, with or without leave, and hastened to Wyoming to participate in the battle of July 3, 1778, Lieut. Timothy Pierce was one, and he went into the battle after riding all night, "merely snatching a bite to eat as he left the house to join the forces." Children :—

808. i.   CLARISSA; m. Alward White.
809. ii. POLLY.

362. EPHRAIM[6] PIERCE (*Robert*[5], *Stephen*[4], *Stephen*[3], *Thomas*[2], *Thomas*[1]), b. Jan. 1, 1733; m. Oct. 2, 1760, Bridget Parker. He d. Mar. 6, 1798. He was in the Revolutionary War. Res. Chelmsford, Mass. Children :—

810. i.   EPHRAIM, b. Sept. 1, 1761.
811. ii. REBECCA, b. Oct. 31, 1763.
812. iii. ROBERT, b. Sept. 24, 1767.
813. iv. PARKER, b. Aug. 19, 1770.

363. WILLIAM[6] PIERCE (*Robert*[5], *Stephen*[4], *Stephen*[3], *Thomas*[2], *Thomas*[1]), b. Oct. 29, 1735; m. Mar. 19, 1761, Elizabeth Pierce. He d. 1782. Res. Chelmsford. Children :—

814. i.   MARY, b. Nov. 10, 1761; m. Oliver Perham.
815. ii. DOLLY, b. Oct. 31, 1763.
816. iii. ELIZABETH, b. Sept. 21, 1765.
817. iv. WILLIAM, b. Oct. 7, 1767.
818. v.   ANN, b. Jan. 30, 1770.
819. vi. BRADLEY, b. May 4, 1772; d. Aug. 30, 1775.
820. vii. SYBIL, b. Sept. 13, 1775.

365. OLIVER[6] PIERCE (*Oliver*[5], *Stephen*[4], *Stephen*[3], *Thomas*[2], *Thomas*[1]), b. May 20, 1742; m. Dec. 21, 1769, Deborah Stevens. She d. Oct. 27, 1837. He d. Jan. 21, 1821. Res. Chelmsford.

Oliver Pierce 2d

Children :—

821. i.   RUTH, b. July 2, 1773; m. —— Parkhurst.

822. ii. HANNAH, b. July 3, 1774; d. Feb. 25, 1851.
823. iii. REBECCA, b. Jan. 1, 1780; d. Nov. 18, 1789.
824. iv. OLIVER, b. July 2, 1783; d. unm. Aug. 19, 1863.
825. v.   ABIGAIL, b. Feb. 7, 1792.

369. Capt. JONAS[6] PIERCE (*Oliver*[5], *Stephen*[4], *Stephen*[3], *Thomas*[2], *Thomas*[1]), b. Jan. 22, 1750; m. Betsey Dunn. She d. 1819. He d. Sept. 18, 1833. Capt. in Revolutionary Army, eight months' men, and enlisted after the Battle of Lexington, April 19, 1775. Res. E. Chelmsford.

Children :—

826. i.   JONAS, b. Jan. 20, 1780; m. ———— ————.
827. ii. BETSEY, b. May 7, 1782; m. Daniel Tuck.
828. iii. SARAH, b. Sept. 8, 1784; m. Timothy Reed.
829. iv. POLLY, b. Feb. 17, 1787; m. Levi Farr.
830. v.   OLIVER, b. Nov. 7, 1789; d. 1817.

370. JONATHAN[6] PIERCE (*Oliver*[5], *Stephen*[4], *Stephen*[3], *Thomas*[2], *Thomas*[1]), b. Apr. 7, 1752; m. Dec. 13, 1781, Hannah Perham, b. 1763, d. 1787; m. 2nd, Nov. 27, 1788, Esther Spalding, b. Dec. 17, 1753, d. Jan., 1806; m. 3rd, Jan. 18, 1810, Lydia Conant, b. 1754, d. 1815; m. 4th, July 26, 1821, Molley Batchelor, b. 1751, d. Sept. 17, 1822. He d. Oct., 1822. They res. in Chelmsford and Townsend. He was in the Revolutionary Army for eleven days after the battle of Bunker Hill.

Children :—

831. i.   RICHARD W., b. Oct. 15, 1782; m. Nov. 4, 1804, Sarah Farrar; m. 2nd, Apr. 28, 1835, Susan Keep.
832. ii. LUCY W., b. Apr., 1784; m. Oct. 14, 1802, Abel Spalding, b. Sept. 6, 1777, d. Nov. 16, 1860, in Jaffrey, N. H., where she d. July 18, 1856. Ch.: Abel, Jr., b. Sept. 14, 1803, m. Mary A. Templeton and Mary A. Stoughton; Richard, b. Oct. 10, 1804, m. Nancy French and Elvira Stratton; Alvah, b. Sept. 9, 1807, m. Ambra Tower; Lucy, b. July 14, 1809, m. Luke French; Meriel, b. Feb. 3, 1812, m. Benj. O. Hale; Erastus, b May 31, 1815, m. Mahala Baker and Mary E. Bush; Eri, b. Nov. 4, 1816, d. Mar. 30, 1817; Lydia, b. May 22, 1818, m. Benj. O. Hale; Eri J., b. Oct. 17, 1821, m. Betsey F. Holt, Lucy A. Jones and Maria R. Ellis; Hannah E., b. Feb. 1, 1823, m. Saml. Stoughton; Benj. F., b. Dec. 31, 1825, d. May 23, 1836. Res. Jaffrey, N. H.
833. iii. HANNAH, b. Mar. 6, 1786; m. John Clement, b. Mar. 11, 1782, d. Sept. 15, 1867. She d. Mar. 6, 1847. Ch.: Hannah, b. Nov. 9, 1805, d. Sept. 22, 1829; Nancy, b. Feb. 18, 1807, d. May 11, 1809; John P., b. Oct. 14, 1808; Nancy, b. Sept. 29, 1810, d. June 10, 1838; Jonathan P., b. July 7, 1812, d. June 3, 1863; Lucy W., b. July 6, 1815; Rachel P., b. June 16, 1820, d. Aug. 7, 1844; Moses, b. June 13, 1824.

371. STEPHEN[6] PIERCE (*Oliver*[5], *Stephen*[4], *Stephen*[3], *Thomas*[2], *Thomas*[1]), b. Aug. 15, 1754; m. July 30, 1777, Hannah Marshall, b. 1755, d. Sept. 27, 1855. He d. Apr. 16, 1826. Res. Chelmsford, Mass.

Know all men by these presents
That I Stephen Pierce of Chelmsford in the County of Middlesex and Commonwealth of Massachusetts yeoman being indisposed in body but of a sound and disposing mind and memory thanks be to God there for do make ordain publish and declare this to be my last will and testament in manner and form following that is to say.

And first of all I commend my soul to God who gave it being my body I commit to the grave to be intered in decent Christian burial according to the custom of my country, and with regard to such worldly estate wherewith God in his good providence has been pleased to bless me in this life, I do dispose of that as follows to wit.

1st I order and direct that all of my just debts and funeral charges be paid out of my estate in convenient time after my decease by my Executer hereafter named

2nd I order and direct that my Executer shall maintain and support my wife provide everything necessary for her in sickness and in health during her life

3d I give and bequeath unto all my children one dollar each.
I give and bequeath unto Jonathan my youngest son all of the rest residue and remainder of my estate of every kind.

Carried over

Brought over
And lastly I do hereby nominate constitute and appoint my son Jonathan Pierce sole executor of this my last will and testament hereby revoking all former wills by me made

In testimony whereof I have hereunto set my hand and seal this twenty seventh day of August in the year of our Lord one thousand eight hundred and twenty five—

Signed sealed and pronounced
by the said Stephen Pierce to
be his last will and testament
in presence of us
Jno. C. Dalton
Sprake Livingston
Elijah Hall.

STEPHEN PEIRCE (Seal)
A Copy, Attest, J. H. TYLER, Register.

Children :—

834. i. HANNAH, b. Dec. 7, 1778; m. Samuel Butterfield.
835. ii. JOHN, b. June 20, 1783; d. unm., 1824.

836. iii. STEPHEN, b. Apr. 5, 1786; m. Apr. 12, 1814, Abigail Bateman
and Mary Cory.
837. iv. PATTY, b. Jan. 21, 1788; m. Abel Marshall.
838. v. JESSE, b. Feb. 2, 1790; m. Hannah Harrington.
839. vi. MOSES, b. Jan. 22, 1792; m. Mary Barron.
840. vii. MARSHALL, b. Nov. 14, 1793; m. Mary Stearns.
841. viii. JONATHAN, b. Oct. 16, 1796; m. May 7, 1827, Mrs. Hannah H.
Pierce, his brother's widow.
842. ix. LYDIA; m. Charles Cutler.

376.   Capt. JOHN[6] PIERCE (*William*[5], *Stephen*[4], *Stephen*[3], *Thomas*[2],
Thomas[1]), b. Jan. 26, 1743; m. Tobathy Porter, b. 1757, d. Apr. 23,
1831. He d. July 7, .1812. Res. Chesterfield, N. H.   He was a
cooper in the French and Indian war and was made Captain of the
company raised around Chesterfield, N. H., at the breaking out of the
Revolutionary war—and tradition states that he and his two Lieutenants
started ahead of the company and as they neared the British forces at
Bennington, Vt., found themselves between a company of Hessians
who were bathing in a stream and the main body of the British.
Carefully crawling upon the bathers, who had their arms stacked, they
separated and representing themselves as three companies he called
upon them to surrender, which they did, and he marched them as
prisoners into the American lines.

Children :—

843. i. WILLIAM, b. Oct. 8, 1776; m. Ruth Hubbard.
844. ii. TWINS, b. Sept. 14, 1779; d. Sept. 15, 1779.
845. iii. JOHN, b. June 1, 1780; m. 1799, Judith Thompson.
846. iv. SILAS, b. June 23, 1781; d. Mar. 25, 1783.
847. v. EZEKIEL P., b. Apr. 20, 1785; m. Mar. 1, 1808, Susanna Porter.
848. vi. EBENEZER, b. June 22, 1788; m. Alpha Randall.
849. vii. ESTHER, b. Sept. 29, 1791; m. Samuel Thompson, b. Dec. 4, 1781.
She d. Mar. 13, 1874, leaving Silas, b. Mar. 6, 1815, m. Elizabeth C. Tefft; Lucy M., b. Nov. 20, 1819, d. Feb. 27, 1853;
Diantha, b. Jan. 25, 1812, m. Geo. Chamberlin; Larkin, b. Mar.
12, 1817, d. Nov. 3, 1854; Elmira, b. Sept. 29, 1814, m. Samuel
Chamberlin; Emily J., b. May 17, 1826.
850. viii. LUCY, b. Feb. 27, 1799, m. Hubbard Wheeler, and had Eliza;
Davis; Melinda, m. Eph. Hunt; Parker.

The following is the inscription on John Pierce's monument:—

" In memory of

Mr. John Pierce, who died July 7th, 1812, aged 69[ys].

Though greedy worms devour my skin,
And gnaw my wasting flesh,
When God shall build my bones again,
He'll build them all afresh."

The home farm including the Island	$2000	00
One out lot	0200	00
One horse 35 two oxen 65	0100	00
One cow 16 00 two cows 13 each	42	00
Two 2 year olds heifers 13 each	26	00
One heifer 11 00 part of a steer 10 00	21	00
One year old heifer 6 50, one half of an year old heifer 3 25	9	50
Two calves 7 00 one half of two hogs and nine pigs 14 20	21	20
12 sheep & seven lambs	24	00
Two 4 year old oxen	56	00
Hay 66 00 Wheat 14 00 Rye 11 00	91	00
Flax & flax seed 6 00 old Rye & corn 3 25	9	25
Slaigh & harness 17 00 cart yrons 15 00	32	00
Grain Barn 83 50 Horse hams & collars 2 50	86	00
* _____ _____ _____		
Three axes 1 67 Beetlerings 0 33	2	00
Three chains 6 75 two shovels & 2 forks 1 00	7	75
One grindstone 2 50 on hansaw 1 67	4	17
One set of coopers tools containing five shaves 2 jointers one foreplain one ax one adds one plow and a number of other articles it being all that belongs to set tools	9	00
One cross cut saw 1 67 two staples & rings 0 83	2	50
Two hoes 58 one saddle & bridle 8 50	9	08
One woman's saddle 8 three old saddles & saddle bags 1 00	9	00
One hetchel 1 00 old Iron 1 00	2	00
One pair steelyards 1 00	1	00
One foot wheel 2 00 one wooling wheel 2 50	4	50
Two bushel of beans 1 33	1	33
Three bags 1 25 one set of measures 0 40	1	65
Soules 1 06 Lambskin 25	1	31
One chees tub 1 00 two pickle tubs 1 00	2	00
7 wheetstones 50 half barrell of vinegar 1 00	1	50
11 Barlls cider 11 00 one Brake 0 75	11	75
36 old Barrels & one hogshead	12	00
4 wash tubs & old cask &c	4	00
4 pails one churn 4 cans & other wooding ware	2	00
One meal chest & one chees press	1	75
Hollow ware with a pair of flats	4	00
Andiron & crans tramels 4 44 fire shovels & tongs 1 67	6	11
tosting iron & chopping knife	0	67
One pare hand bellowes 0 50 one clock 10 00	10	50
Bed & window curtings 1 25 crockery ware 2 86	4	11
Glass bottles & glass ware 2 50 Books 4 00	6	50
8 pounds of wooling yarn 2 00 two & ½ of cotton 50	2	50
11 pounds of tow yarn 1 75 one & ¾ of Factory yarn 1 31	3	06
* _____ _____ _____		
Articles for Bed quilt unfinished	1	00

---

* So obliterated, could not decipher these lines.

12

One towel 0 25 one cloths brush & walet 0 34	0 59
Three cyths & tackling 2 00	2 00
First Bed with Beding bedsted and cord	15 00
2d & 3d Bed beding bedsted and cord 9 50 each	19 00
4th Bed bedsted & cord with anticate & Beding	7 00
One case of Draws 6 00 one clothes Basket and cloths hors } 0 75 twelve chairs 4 00	10 75
One stand table 0 83 twenty 8 pounds of wool 16 00	16 83
191 pounds of cheese 9 00 two old blankets 0 75	9 75
Knives & forks 1 25 tin ware 1 35	2 60
Puter 4 95 Brass kettle & old Brass 6 00	10 95
4 trayes 3 milk pans & all other brown artharn	2 00
2 wooding Bollds & salt morter	0 83
One tabeste 0 85 one table 5 00 one Dto 1 00	6 83
One candle stand 0 50 clothsreel 0 25	0 75
One Loom and all the utensils belonging thereto	11 50
One chest with one Draw 2 00 one chest 0 50	2 50
One chest 1 00 one chest 1 25	2 25
One Desk 12 00 one Looking glass 1 50	13 50
7 towels 0 50 four tables cloths 1 00	1 50
2 table clothes 4 00 five towels 2 50	6 50
7 pair of pillow cases 2 00 8 wooling sheets 15 00	17 00
14 sheets	7 75
Waring apparel one pair of panterloons	2 00
One coat 4 00 one great coat 1 00	5 00
One out side coat 4 50 one hat 2 50	7 00
One coat 1 50 five Jackets 4 33	5 83
2 pair of panteloons two pare Breeches	2 75
Stockings & mittings 1 25 five shirts 2 75	4 00
One hankerchief 0 33 one pair knee buckels and two Riens } 0 75 one pair of Boots 0 50	1 58

Cash on hand.   Notes and interest.

One against Levi Mead, gr.	117 04
2 against Eben Peirce	95 56
1 against Simon Willard	3 44
One pew in the meeting house in Chesterfield	30 00
	$3233 92

(A copy *verbatim et literatim*).

386.   STEPHEN[6] PIERCE (*Stephen*[5], *Stephen*[4], *Stephen*[3], *Thomas*[2], *Thomas*[1]), b. Feb. 5, 1759 ; m. Dec. 25, 1787, Phebe Trull.   He enlisted in the Revolutionary Army after the Battle of Lexington.   Res. Chelmsford.   Children :—

851. i.   BENJAMIN, b. Dec. 7, 1790.
852. ii.   PAMELIA, b. Aug. 9, 1792.
853. iii.   THOMAS.   854. iv.   EBENEZER.   855. v.   JOEL.

392. Gov. Benjamin[6] Pierce, Jr. (*Benjamin[5]*, *Stephen[4]*, *Stephen[3]*, *Thomas[2]*, *Thomas[1]*), b. Dec. 25, 1757 ; m. May 24, 1787, Elizabeth Andrews, b. 1768, d. Aug. 13, 1788 ; m. 2nd, Feb. 1, 1790, Ann Kendrick, b. 1768, d. Dec. 10, 1838. He d. Apr. 1, 1839. Res. Hillsboro, N. H.

Benjamin Pierce [signature]

The first account we read of in the History of New Hampshire is that in 1813 some contention took place between two parties, called Republicans and Federalists, in which Benjamin Pierce, Sheriff of Hillsborough, was removed from office. To this place he was again appointed. At this time debtors were imprisoned and Gen. Benjamin Pierce interested himself in behalf of three aged prisoners who had been in jail four years. Their names were Moses Brewer, Isaac Lawrence and George Laney. Speaking of General Pierce, Barstow, the historian, says :—"He fought for liberty and enjoyed it. In his character were united the generosity of the soldier with the liberal sentiments of enlightened philanthropy." This liberation took place on the 20th of November. Sixty-one years before this time, Gen. Pierce was born at Chelmsford, Mass., and was the son of a farmer. On the memorable 19th of April, 1775, while he was plowing in the field, a horseman rode up to the door, and having delivered a brief message, hastened onward to alarm the country. Leaving the plow, young Pierce immediately set out on foot for Lexington ; he found on his arrival that the British troops had fallen back upon Boston, and he proceeded to Cambridge. It was here that young Pierce, then but eighteen years of age, enlisted as a private in the army of the revolution, and attached himself to the regiment of Col. Brooks. He was in the midst of the battle of Bunker Hill and from that time to the close of the revolution he followed the fortunes of his regiment, fought whenever it was called into action, and was invariably distinguished and commended by his superior officers for gallantry and good conduct. He rose from the ranks to the command of a company, which he held at the disbanding of the army in 1784. He returned to his native village and found that his nine years' pay in Continental money had so much depreciated that it would not suffice for the purchase of a farm. He was therefore obliged to go into the wilderness where lands were cheap and begin the cultivation of wild land. In the autumn of 1786, President Sullivan having resolved to form the militia of the county of Hillsborough into a brigade, sought out the veteran soldier, then far into the woods, and commissioned him as a Brigade-Major. He immediately took the necessary steps for the perfect organization and discipline of the several regiments. He had already served more than eight years in the regular army and he continued to serve Massachusetts and New Hampshire for twenty-one years in the militia, leaving it finally in the capacity of a Brigadier-General. The regiment which furnished a Miller, a McNiel, was for many years commanded by him, and many other valuable officers who have distinguished 'themselves in the public service have been proud to say that they received their first lessons in military discipline from the veteran General Pierce in the Militia of Hillsborough. From 1789 to 1802 he was a Representative to the General Court, and in 1803 was elected to the Council, where he continued six years, five of which were passed in the council of Gov. Langdon. It was not until 1827 that he was elected Governor of the State of New Hampshire and was re-elected in 1829, having been omitted one year on account of his opposition to John Quincy Adams. At the commencement of the last war with Great Britain his spirit entered into the contest, but the infirmities of age admonished him that he could hasten to the battle field no more. Two of his sons with his consent and advice entered the public service. He was noted for his integrity of character. At his death the public felt the loss of a man who had faithfully served his fellow men and his country.

A VISIT TO THE PIERCE MANSION.

The traveler, as he passes through Hillsborough, N. H., will notice on the old turnpike leading from Francestown through the upper village, and not far from what was once the terminus of the Contoocook Valley railroad, a stately, old-fashioned farmhouse. It is a square, commodious, two-story structure, with an L, also two stories, and a barn attached, and all painted white. Externally the building presents an appearance no different from many other old houses scattered up and down our country towns, but when once your footsteps have taken you up the walk to the entrance door, our word for it, you will not regret that you have strayed to its portals. Built during the last decade of the eighteenth century, it was for forty years the residence of Governor Benjamin Pierce, and the place where his yet more illustrious son was born on a late November day, seventy-four years ago. So the old house has a history, and a rare one, too, which fairly challenges our inquiry.

It was in 1785 that Col. Benjamin Pierce, a patriot of the revolution, who fought all through the battles of that bloody struggle, came to Hillsborough and erected a log cabin near the spot where the mansion now stands. He purchased a hundred-and-fifty-acre lot, and commenced clearing it, married and remarried, his first wife dying within a year after their union. It was up-hill work at first, but industry and perseverance brought success, and the pioneers prospered. The log cabin was pulled down to make way for a better house. Acres were added to the original purchase and Benjamin Pierce became a man of means, the squire of the village, and a rising politician. Nine children played around his door, the seventh of whom became the fourteenth president of the United States.

The Pierce mansion stands in the midst of grounds which in former years, were laid out with elegant taste, and embellished with fruit-trees, and shrubbery. Some handsome, stately trees embowered the venerable roof. Around the front side of the building extends a piazza; that at the end, facing the highway, is covered by a balcony, which forms a glorious retreat in the warm summer days. Here, in the ancient time the governor's guests were accustomed to retire for the purpose of tea or punch drinking. A visitor arriving in a carriage either alighted at the front entrance, or passed by the broad drive under the shade of thrifty maples to the swarded courtyard. Emerging from the east entrance door the old proprietor mounted his horse to ride to Exeter court-house where, as a member of the New Hampshire assembly, he long served his fellow-citizens of Hillsborough. At a later day he rode in a coach which carried him in state to the capitol at Concord, the people all flocking along the way to get a glance at " the governor."

Along the east side of the mansion extends an inclosed garden of half an acre or more, with walks, a summer-house, and in the centre an artificial pond, now choked with *débris* and weeds, but in the old governor's time well stocked with trout. These grounds must always have been a favorite resort of the family and their guests. On one of the trees an acute eye can still decipher a wound in the bark said to have been the linked names of Hawthorne and Franklin Pierce, cut there by the former in their college days. In the summer-house, covered by climbing grapevines, have sat grave judges and courtly scholars, and doubtless its walls might whisper of many a love-tryst.

Entering the house by the south door we step into a large hall, which formerly extended through the middle of the mansion, but has since been shortened. The walls of this room are lined with family portraits, those of the governor and his lady, President Pierce, Gen. John McNeil and wife, and their daughter, Col. and Mrs. C. E. Potter. We notice the broad stairway and the elaborately-carved balusters, and are transported to the time when a powdered, dignified gentleman used to go up and down the stairs, and when a merry group of children played upon this very floor, among whom was a boy with hazel eyes and brown, curly locks, who, less than fifty years afterwards, was to sit among the great rulers of the earth, in the place which Washington had occupied before him, and which Jefferson, Adams, Van Buren and Jackson adorned. What a lesson for the young is exhibited by the life, stranger than any romance, of the simple country youth, who, from an humble station, rose by honest and persevering toil to be the peer of kings!

On the left of the hallway is the great parlor, with its large chandeliers, its heavy cornice, its massive hearthstone, with antique brass andirons, and its walls covered with the original paper put on more than eighty years ago. This paper is very thick and extends from ceiling to floor, embossed in gorgeous colors, with landscapes, tournaments, marine views and civil festivals. The room teems with historic associations. Here were married all of the governor's children, and brilliant ceremonies attended some of these events. Beautiful and antique relics are distributed about, war trophies of the Pierces and McNeils, Mexican curiosities, curious old mirrors and chairs, and a host of articles too numerous to specialize, which are now the property of Mrs. Potter.

There are eight rooms on the ground floor of the square part. In the northeast corner, now used as a sleeping-room, is the apartment where Franklin Pierce was born. His cradle is still preserved here, and in this room is also the old governor's sideboard, which oldtime hospitality required should be always garnished with wines or a huge bowl of punch. That was in the ante-Washingtonian days, when men could drink their pint of Antigua without fearing any enemy but the gout, and when the aroma of good old Xeres was not distateful to the ladies.

The second floor is provided with six chambers, all opening on a spacious and airy hall. None of these rooms demand special description. Descending to the cellar, we have pointed out to us the various compartments of the old governor's domestic repository. Everything is on a grand scale. In the wine-cellar there were annually stored twenty casks of wine and fifty barrels of cider—the good old New England beverage. The potato-bin will accommodate three hundred bushels of tubers. The founder of this mansion was a great man in his day, and with but one exception, was probably the most popular gov ernor ever elected in New Hampshire. Even to-day, after a lapse of forty years, his very name touches the heart almost to a burst of enthusiasm. His personal appearance, as it has been preserved by the portraits on the walls of the mansion, is indicative of the man. There is something of the look of a Jackson in that face. The jaws have the same lion-like solidity, the lips are firm and the nose identical with that same feature which we observe on the medals of the Roman imperators, but the eyes have a merry gleam, and the rubicund visage, and the thick-set, portly figure tell more plainly than words can of the good-natured, good-living, hospitable squire, whose name could rally more voters to the polls than that of any other man in the State, after John T. Gilman.

One would hardly think, gazing at the house, that it had been the scene of so much romance and glory. Yet in some of these old rooms, the embryo statesman and president must have slept and ate and studied through all his boyhood days. Out of some of those windows looked the eyes that were to gaze on the splendors of the White House and the varied scenes of foreign lands. In this very yard sang the voice which was to stir listening senates with its tones. Around this place centre all of the associations connected with his youthful years. Here was the theatre of his early sports, here his school-days began, here he had his first visions of future eminence, or of the possibility of it. Through this very door he passed with his college honors upon him ; the friend of Stowe, of Hawthorne, of Longfellow, and others equally known to fame. Great men, statesmen, writers, divines and soldiers have been domiciled under this roof. Nearly all of the leading men of New Hampshire for fifty years visited at Squire Pierce's house. Isaac Hill, Charles H. Atherton, Ebenezer Webster, Judge Woodbury and John T. Gilman were more than guests of the governor. And, afterwards, Hawthorne, Dr. Appleton, the McNeils, and others came to see the young lawyer, their friend. John McNeil, in particular, was long a visitor there, coming every Sunday night, to pay his addresses to a certain staid, beautiful maid, who afterwards became his wife. There were several fair daughters in the house of Pierce, but Elizabeth, the eldest, was the queen of the family. At all the sewing-bees and tea assemblies of the countryside Elizabeth Pierce was the belle among the village maidens. Many of the leading young men of the place had a desire for her fair hand and the heart that went with it. But John McNiel, the son of an old comrade-in-arms of her father, tall, handsome and manly, was the favored suitor. Who would not like to know the particulars of that courtship? When Alphonso and Juliana, after flirting with and kissing half-a-dozen other girls and men, engage themselves nowadays, between the pauses in the waltz, and hie away the next morning to announce the fact to all their friends, the story does not seem sweet at all. But it was different in the early days of our century. Young lovers saw each other only in the presence of others ; letters were studied and formal, and the engagement was kept secret according to custom. Human hearts, however, are the same in all ages, and love was as strong and fiery then as now, though hidden under modest reserve. Many a time, undoubtedly, John and Elizabeth walked arm-in-arm along this path, talking the same old story that lovers always have. One almost envies them the delicious thrill of the sacred secret when their hands touched in the stately quadrille, or their eyes told the sweet, unspoken story. They were married on Christmas day, 1811. John McNeil became a general and a famous New Hampshire worthy, and his Elizabeth made a most true wife and loving mother. Both died before their famous relative went into the White House.

On the opposite side of the road stands a long, low building, in good repair. This was formerly the old horse-shed, in one corner of which a room was finished as a law office, where the future president first "set up in business." It was in the year 1827 that young Pierce began his practice of law in this place. Few who saw the young attorney then imagined they were looking on the future chief magistrate of the nation. Not much above the middle size, nervous and hesitating in speech, he did not even look as though he would succeed as a lawyer. Indeed, his first effort as an advocate was a marked failure. But there were elements of greatness in the young man, and he could not be discouraged. Said he to a friend who condoled with him, "I will try nine hundred and ninety-nine cases, if clients will continue to trust me, and if I fail just as I have to-day, will try the thousandth. I shall live to argue cases in this court-house in a manner that will neither mortify myself nor my friends." He made his assertion good, and even as a lawyer Franklin Pierce had few superiors. George Barstow, Esq., was the last practitioner of law who used the office. The innovation of railroads left the old village out in the cold and carried its business to other places, and the law-office of an American president is now devoted to the humble use of a carriage-house.

The old house still remains in the family, practically speaking. Governor Pierce died in 1839, and some years prior to that event

Franklin had removed to Concord. The homestead became the property of Mrs. McNeil, with whom it remained until her death, in 1852. Her daughter, Fanny Maria McNeil, inherited it and lived in the old mansion many years with her talented husband, the Hon. Chandler E. Potter. For the last few years the property has been owned by General Samuel Andrews, a nephew of Governor Pierce's first wife.

FROM THE HISTORY OF PRESIDENT PIERCE.

Benjamin Pierce was a native of Chelmsford, Mass. He never received a liberal education; in fact, he was almost entirely a self-educated man, gaining his knowledge more from men than from books. At the early age of seventeen he bade farewell to his plow, and enlisted as a common soldier in the great war of the American Revolution. On the 19th of April, 1775, the revolutionary committee sent couriers out in every direction; one of them drove up before the farm-house of the uncle of Benjamin, and told his brief tale of the news of the battle of Lexington. The simple account of the courier was all that was needed to fire the brave heart of the young farmer, and he shouldered his musket, and with the blessings of his parents, started on foot for the seat of war. He soon arrived in Boston, where he enlisted as a private in the regiment commanded by Colonel Brooks. He was in the great battle of Bunker Hill, the 17th of June following, and there distinguished himself by his bravery. In one of the many important actions in which he was subsequently engaged, during the hottest of the battle, when the leaden rain was fiercest, Benjamin Pierce saw the flag of his regiment wave to and fro, and as if the bearer were unable longer to uphold it. Although the act was accompanied with the greatest danger, he rushed forward, and grasping it, held it proudly in its proper place, while the old bearer dropped dead at his feet. And until the action was finished and the victory complete, he continued to uphold it. The brave action was noticed, and the next morning the young farmer was rewarded with an ensigncy. His superior bravery, and his military talents, attracted attention, and when the Revolutionary War was brought to a termination, he quitted the army with the rank of captain. Such was the wretched pecuniary condition of the treasury, that the soldiers were paid off for their services in a depreciated currency, and Captain Peirce found that he possessed only about $200. He was necessitated, therefore, to retire to the wilderness, where land was cheap, and purchase himself a farm. In the fall of the year 1786, General Sullivan, who was then a resident of New Hampshire, determined upon forming the militia of Hillsborough county into a brigade, and appointed Benjamin Pierce a brigade-major. His services were of great value to the militia of New Hampshire, and he finally rose to a brigadier-general. In 1789, he was elected from Hillsborough to sit in the House of Representatives at Concord, and continued to represent that town in the House for twelve consecutive years. In 1803, he was elected a member of the Governor's Council, in which office he continued until 1809, when he was appointed Sheriff of Hillsborough county. This office he occupied for four years. For many years following he was either Sheriff of the county or he was a member of the Governor's Council. In 1827, Benjamin Pierce was elected Governor of the State of New Hampshire; in 1828, in times of great political agitation, he was for once defeated in his election, but was triumphantly re-elected again in 1829.

Without the advantages of early education, without opulent and powerful friends, Benjamin Pierce grew to be the most influential man in New Hampshire. His influence in the county of Hillsborough was overwhelming, and indeed through the State. He was, in fact, a man of great native talent. Shrewd, good-natured, and possessed of common-sense, he soon took his position as a leader of men. In personal appearance he was striking, He was rather short, and thick-set, had a rigid, honest-looking face, resembling, to a degree, the best portraits of Gen. Jackson. He was a universal favorite—fearless, frank-hearted, entirely devoid of all aristocratical pride—he was calculated to please the great body of the people.

In the jail at Amherst, N. H., there were three aged prisoners, viz.: Moses Brewer, Isaac Lawrence, and George Lancy; one of them had remained there for four years, in the closest confinement, all for the non-payment of a trifling debt. When Benjamin Pierce was elected Sheriff of the county, one of his first acts was to appoint a day for the releasement of these prisoners. The people thought the occasion worthy of a public meeting, and when the day arrived, Nov. 20, 1818, a large number attended.

FROM THE HISTORY OF THE CINCINNATI SOCIETY.

Benjamin Pierce was born in Chelmsford, Mass., Dec. 25, 1757. Losing his father when he was but six years of age, he labored on the farm of his Uncle Robert until April 25, 1775, when he enlisted in Ford's company of Bridge's Regiment and was in the battle of Bunker Hill. He was orderly-sergeant of Jackson's (8th) Regiment, and was promoted ensign for gallantry at Bemis Heights, Oct. 7, 1777; he was subsequently commissioned lieutenant, July 7, 1782. He was a prisoner in New York, and was grossly insulted by a British officer, whom he ran through the body in a duel. After the evacuation of New York, in 1786, he commenced clearing land for a farm in the valley of the Contoocook River in N. H. He was representative to the General Court in 1789 and 1802. Successively Major, Colonel and in 1805 Brigadier-General of Militia. Member of the Council 1803 to 1809 and 1814 to 1818. Sheriff of Hillsborough 1809 to 1814 and 1818 to 1823. Governor of N. H. 1827 and 1829, and Vice-President of the Mass. Society of the Cincinnati, from 1836 to his death at Hillsborough, N. H., April 1, 1839.

13

Children :—

856. i. ELIZABETH A., b. Aug. 9, 1788; m. Gen. John McNeil. She d.
Mar. 27, 1855. Children : John W. S., b. 1817, d. Sept. 10,
1837.* Elizabeth A., m. Capt. G. W. Benham; Frances, m.
Col. Chandler E. Potter, of Manchester; Benjamin P., d. June
12, 1853.

The death of Mrs. McNeil, widow of the late Gen. John
McNeil and daughter of the late Gov. Pierce, of New Hampshire, was announced some weeks since. Mrs. McNeil inherited
the same strength of mind, nobleness of soul, and generosity of
heart of her father, in whose bosom patriotism, liberality and
charity ever burned. A portion of her life was spent in the
wilds of the west, whither she followed him in whom she had
" garnered up her heart." She was bland in her manners, and
possessed a richly endowed mind; and the christian generosity
which was extended to all without distinction, made her the
friend of the needy who always found relief at her hands. She
was proud of her country, and was ready to make great sacrifices
for its protection and advancement when public services called
her husband beyond the pale of civilization, in the flush and enthusiasm of her youth, and with the devotedness and self-sacrificing spirit of the best and truest of her sex, she shared his
dangers and sufferings with a high sense of woman's duties.
Fit consort for such a man she has followed many loved ones

---

*Lieutenant McNeil was the son of General John McNeil, of Boston, Massa-
chusetts, and grandson, on his mother's side, of the late General Benjamin
Pierce, of Hillsborough, New Hampshire. He was born on the Island of
Mackinaw, Michigan Territory, February 17, 1817. He remained several years
with his parents at Chicago, Illinois, while his father was commandant of the
United States troops of that station. In 1824, he returned with his parents to
New England; was at West Point; spent some time in the office of
Hon. Franklin Pierce, at Hillsborough, New Hampshire, and entered the
United States Army in the spring of 1838, as Lieutenant of a company in the
2d Regiment of Dragoons. He recruited through the summer, and in the
following winter was ordered to Florida. He continued in the service, and
was out in several skirmishes till the fall of 1837, when he fell in a fight with
the Seminole Indians on the morning of September 10.

The circumstances of that encounter were these : General Hernandes on
the 7th set out an expedition from Head-Quarters, at Picolata, in the vicinity
of St. Augustine, against a body of Indians that had taken a position about
sixty miles to the southwest. In the absence of their superior officers, the
command of the battalion, under the direction of General Hernandes, was
given to Lieutenants McNeil and Peyton. On the evening of the 9th the battalion approached the Indians, who occupied a position deemed almost
impregnable by reason of a swamp and thicket that surrounded them.
The battalion halted till dawn of day (Sabbath morning), when the
attack was made in two columns, headed respectively by Lieutenants
McNeil and Peyton. The savages had time to give but one fire before they
were surrounded and taken. While McNeil was advancing at the head of his
column, he saw their chief, Uchee Billy, level his rifle at him; and at the
moment he drew his pistol, the rifle of the chief was discharged, the bullet
passing through his pistol hand and taking effect in the abdomen. McNeil remained on the field through the action; and when the Indians were secured,
he was carried on a litter to the camp, about ten miles distant. The next day
the battalion set out for St. Augustine, but McNeil died on the way, Monday
night at 10 o'clock. His remains were carried to St. Augustine, and buried
with the honors of war; after which the officers of the army met and passed
resolutions expressive of their sense of his character as a soldier and as a

to the mansions of rest, and slowly waited till her spirit took
its flight to that brighter world on high. " Then shall the dust
return to the earth as it was: and the spirit shall return unto
God who gave it." Eccles. XII : 7. During her severe illness,
her youngest daughter, like the ministering angel of mercy,
watched over her, "smoothed her dying pillow," and with
words of heavenly cheer and comfort, " soothed the pain and
anguish of her disease." Soon, ah! too soon, and that which
was born of the flesh gave way, and the earthly tabernacle sank

---

man. Though only about twenty years of age when he fell, he was as brave
an officer as ever commanded troops. Had he lived, and circumstances con-
curred, there is every reason for believing that he would have worthily emu-
lated the bravery and generalship of his distinguished father.

"To the memory of

Lieutenant JOHN W. S. MCNEIL, *of the United States Army, who fell in an*

engagement with the Seminole Indians, near St. Augustine, Florida,

September 10, 1837.

In that wild land drenched by our bravest blood,
Poured out in torrents like the Autumn rain,
Of all the young and gallant multitude
Whose bones have whitened many a fatal plain,
Repose no nobler relics of the slain
Than thine, McNeil, the generous, mild, and brave!
Why should we mourn his early fate in vain?
For he has gone into a glorious grave,
Wet by the grateful tears of those he died to save.

And when the turf was laid upon his breast,
His country's cannon thundered o'er his head
A requiem fitting for the Soldier's rest—
There sleeps he on his gory-mantled bed
Among a nation's unforgotten dead;
Fain would I rest where he is sleeping now!
The patriot's life-blood for his country shed
Blooms up afresh in the perennial glow
Of Laurels twined by Fame around his glittering brow.

The generous flame that burned within his soul
Was lit by nature at a kindred fire:
Sprung from a race that never brooked control,
Rightly to glorious deeds he might aspire,
The highborn offspring of a noble sire!
And she who, with a mother's untold grief,
Yearns o'er his early tomb with vain desire,
Was daughter of New Hampshire's bravest chief,
Late gathered to his rest like the o'erripened sheaf.

And as the Spartan matrons searched of yore
The bodies of their sons in battle slain,
And when they found the mortal wounds *before*
Knew they fell bravely, and in gladsome train
Exulting bore them from the bloody plain
With proud though bitter joy,—so now may they
Lament *his* loss with no complaining strain;
Though pierced, he sank not through the well-fought day,
Till Victory's joyous shout wafted his soul away!

MAY 3, 1842."

in death while that which is spiritual still exists, binding soul to soul. Never was a mother worn down with the fatigues of an eventful life and the workings of disease, more blest than was Mrs. McNeil in the untiring attentions of the child of love. All that purest affection could prompt submissive hands procured, but finite love, though stronger than death, could not save. Child of sorrow, thou art surrounded by many dear friends, and thou art supported with the consciousness of having administered to the wants of a sick and dying mother. God has blessed you in that mother, dearly beloved by all her children.

Another Relic.

The good sword of a brave man was recently deposited among the mementoes of the revolution in the museum at Independence Hall. It was borne by Benjamin Pierce (father of President Franklin Pierce), who rallied at Lexington to defend his country, and thence continued in the army, fought at Bunker Hill, at Long Island and at the siege of Yorktown. He remained in the service until the final disbanding of the army, at West Point, in 1784. He retired in command of his company and continued in the line of well-earned promotion; was twice elected Governor of New Hampshire. His granddaughter, Mrs. C. E. Potter, of Hillsborough. N. H., is the depositor.

857. ii. BENJAMIN K., b. Aug. 29, 1790; m. ―――― La Flambou; m. 2nd., Amanda ―――― ; m. 3rd., ―――― Reed.
858. iii. NANCY M., b. Nov. 2, 1792; m. Feb. 16, 1815, Gen. Solomon McNeil. She d. Aug. 27, 1837, leaving Anna, b. July 17, 1817, m. Tappan Wentworth, of Lowell; Solomon, b. 1819; John, b. Nov. 6, 1822, m. C. M. Morse, and res. in Winchester, Mass.
859. iv. JOHN S., b. Nov. 5, 1796; m. Marietta O. Putthoff.
860. v. HARRIET B., b. 1800; m. June 25, 1822, Hugh Jameson. She d. Nov. 24, 1837.
861. vi. CHARLES G., b. 1803; d. June 25, 1828, in Utica, N. Y.
862. vii. FRANKLIN, b. Nov. 23, 1804; m. Nov. 10, 1834, Jane M. Appleton.
863. viii. CHARLOTTE; d. infancy.
864. ix. HENRY D., b. Sept. 19, 1812; m. Susan Tuttle.

394. MERRILL[6] PIERCE (*Benjamin[5], Stephen[4], Stephen[3], Thomas[2], Thomas[1]*), b. Jan. 29, 1764 ; m. Dorcas Barker, b. 1771, d. July 23, 1840. He d. Dec. 17, 1816, in Hillsboro, N. H. Children:―

865. i. POLLY, b. Sept. 30, 1794; m. Dec. 25, 1823, Moses Chapman, b. Mar. 16, 1796, d. Mar. 3, 1859. She d. July 11, 1867, in Peterboro, N. H. Ch.: Albert P., b. Mar. 29, 1826, m. Mary Blanchard; Jackson, b. Oct. 18, 1824, m. Ann Black; Walter D., b. Dec. 13, 1836, d. May 20, 1858; Jerome B., b. Jan. 25, 1832, d. Oct. 25, 1863; Martin Van B., b. Oct. 3, 1834, d. Sept. 29, 1865; Julia A., b. Jan. 22, 1828, m. George Handy; Adaline P., b. Aug. 11, 1830, d. Sept. 14, 1848; Harriet M., b. Apr. 11, 1839, d. June 17, 1864.
866. ii. MARY A. A., b. Sept. 4, 1803; m. Nov. 22, 1826, William B. Kimball, b. May 24, 1801. She d. Feb. 5, 1849, in Peterboro, leaving Mary A., M. D., b. Aug. 31, 1827; Elizabeth, b. Sept. 17, 1830.

867. iii. ADALINE; m. Nov. 23, 1831, Benjamin B. Cushing, b. Sept. 29, 1808. She d. Nov. 10, 1870, in Marlboro, N. H. Ch.: Elizabeth P., b. Aug. 24, 1832, d. Apr. 17, 1835; Adaline P., b. Mar. 7, 1834, d. May 2, 1842; Ann B., b. Oct. 26, 1837, m. J. J. Durham; Benj. P., b. Sept. 22, 1849, m. Louisa Lawrence. Mrs. (Pierce) Cushing was a woman of remarkable traits of character, endearing herself to both young and old. The Physician who attended her having become so much attached to her wept like a child when she died. She was only in Marlboro, N. H., for one year, and the Congregational minister remarked that she was no ordinary woman.
868. iv. LOUISA A., b. Aug. 31, 1809; m. Dec. 25, 1851, Thomas McCoy, d. Mar. 10, 1870. She d. without issue in Sharon, N. H., Nov. 22, 1873.
869. v. NANCY, b. 1812; m. Col. E. P. Emerson of Nashua, N. H. Ch.: William B., b. June 20, 1835, m. Abby M. Presby; Edward M., b. July 25, 1843, d. 1865; Jessie D. P., b. June 13, 1845, m. Geo. H. Taylor, A. M.
870. vi. MERRILL; m. Mary Dickinson.
871. vii. JESSE; d. unm.
872. viii. ELIZABETH M., b. Dec. 10, 1816; m. 1836, Cornelius G. Fenner, b. Aug. 6, 1800. Ch.: Elizabeth, b. Aug. 14, 1837, m. Rev. F. M. Baker; Arthur P., b. Sept. 2, 1839, d. 1840; Arthur P., b. Sept. 10, 1841, d. 1843; Arthur P., b. Feb. 6, 1844, unm., and res. in Boston, P. O. Box 1495.

398. JONATHAN[6] PIERCE (*Stephen[5], Jacob[4], Stephen[3], Thomas[2], Thomas[1]*), b. April 11, 1727; m. Nov. 10, 1750, Ruth Gilson, b. Mar. 21, 1728. He d 1785-6. Res. Groton. Children :—

873. i. JONATHAN, b. Dec. 3, 1751; m. Abigail Prescott.
874. ii. BENJAMIN, b. June 5, 1754; m. Rebecca Wright.
875. iii. RUTH, b. June 10, 1757; d. young.
876. iv. MOLLY, b. March 25, 1759; d. Jan. 12, 1766.
877. v. STEPHEN, b. Aug. 13, 1761; d. Jan. 14, 1766.
878. vi. JOSEPH, b. May 15, 1764; d. Jan. 20, 1766.
879. vii. RUTH, b. April 17, 1767; m. —— Fletcher.
880. viii. SOLOMON, b. Sept. 2, 1771.

408. SAMUEL[6] PIERCE (*Samuel[5], Samuel[4], Samuel[3], Thomas[2], Thomas[1]*), b. July 31, 1743; m. Anna —— ; m. 2nd, Mrs. Willard. Res. Herkimer, N. Y. Children :—

881. i. SAMUEL, b. June 11, 1779; m. —— Butler.
882. ii. GERSHOM, b. Jan. 16, 1781.
883. iii. HANNAH K., b. April 2, 1783.
884. iv. ABIGAIL F., b. June 7, 1789.
885. v. JAMES, b. Aug. 19, 1792.

412. JOSIAH[6] PIERCE (*Samuel[5], Samuel[4], Samuel[3], Thomas[2], Thomas[1]*), b. March 17, 1751; m. March 13, 1783, Miriam Pierce [421], b. March 1, 1757. She d. May 5, 1845. He d. May 10, 1845. Res. Charlemont, Mass. Children :—

886. i. SETH, b. March 19, 1784; d. April 6, 1784.
887. ii. SETH, b. June 16, 1785; m. Cynthia Hawkes.
888. iii. JOSIAH, b. June 18, 1787; m. Jemima Thornton.
889. iv. DAVID, b. Oct. 14, 1789; m. Providence ——.

890. v.   MIRIAM, b. May 16, 1792; d. unm. Sept., 1879.
891. vi.   RICHARD, b. June 9, 1794; m. Sally Rudd.
892. vii. JUDITH, b. Dec. 6, 1796.

416. JOSIAH[6] PIERCE (*Josiah*[5], *Samuel*[4], *Samuel*[3], *Thomas*[2], *Thomas*[1]), b. Oct. 11, 1745; m. 1771, Lucy Fairfield, b. Feb. 26, 1745. She d. April 6, 1845. He d. March 22, 1834. Res. Hadley, Mass. Children :—

893. i.   LUCY, b. July 1, 1773; d. Sept. 26, 1775.
894. ii.   DOLLY, b. Oct. 29, 1774; m. Rufus Shumway.
895. iii. ANNE, b. May 7, 1776; m. Andrew Dunnakin.
896. iv.   LUCY, b. April 26, 1778; m. Elijah White.
897. v.   DAVID, b. March 31, 1780; m. Miriam Cook.
898. vi.   ELIHU, b. Jan. 27, 1782; m. Nancy Dunnakin.
899. vii. JOB, b. July 8, 1785; m. Thankful Fairfield.

418. SAMUEL[6] PIERCE (*Josiah*[5], *Samuel*[4], *Samuel*[3], *Thomas*[2], *Thomas*[1]), b. Nov. 11, 1749; m. April 3, 1794, Anna Cook, b. 1758. She d. March 1, 1825. He d. Jan. 12, 1796. Res. Charlemont, Mass. No Children.

Sam¹ Pierce

422. SETH[6] PIERCE, Jr. (*Seth*[5], *Samuel*[4], *Samuel*[3], *Thomas*[2], *Thomas*[1]), b. Sept. 12, 1744; m. Apr. 17, 1767, Bethiah Fields, b. 1745, d. Sept. 18, 1807; m. 2nd, 1813, Patty Rindge, d. 1829. He d. in Homer, N. Y., in 1835. Children :—

900. i.   SARAH, b. Nov. 20, 1767; m. Royal Storrs.
901. ii.   LUCINDA, b. Sept. 14, 1769; m. Nov. 27, 1788, Thomas Welch, b. Feb. 17, 1757, d. Mar. 20, 1832. She d. in Enfield, Conn., Jan. 25, 1854. Ch.: Martha, b. Feb. 24, 1790, d. Feb. 2, 1854; Harriet, b. Feb. 20, 1792, d. June 15, 1811; Jerusha, b. Jan. 14, 1794, m. Jesse Cordy; Marcus, b. Nov. 27, 1795, d. Apr. 7, 1872; Lucas, b. Dec. 19, 1797, m. Alma Pierce; Clarissa A., b. Mar. 25, 1800, d. Oct. 4, 1802; Damia, b. July 19, 1702, m. Dennis R. Olmstead; Clarissa A., b. May 14, 1803, m. Lewis Chapin; Caroline M., b. Apr. 8, 1807, m. Calvin King; Bennett S., b. July 25, 1809, m. Elizabeth Kilborn; Harriet, b. Sept. 18, 1811, m. Geo. C. Wilson.
902. iii. BENNETT, b. Sept. 12, 1771; d. Mar. 17, 1773.
903. iv.   GORDON, b. Aug. 31, 1773; m. 1796, Thirsa Smalley.
904. v.   BENNETT, b. July 14, 1775.
905. vi.   SAMUEL, b. May 23, 1777; d. Aug. 26, 1778.
906. vii. SAMUEL, b. May 20, 1779; m. Persis Barrows.
907. viii. ELIJAH, b. Apr. 27, 1781; m. Feb. 8, 1801, Patty Moulton.
908. ix.   SETH, b. Feb. 17, 1784.
909. x.   DANIEL, b. Mar. 16, 1786.
910. xi.   ELIZABETH, b. Sept. 12, 1788; m. Chester Collins.
911. xii. BELA, b. Apr. 13, 1792.

428. ENOCH[6] PIERCE, Jr. (*Enoch*[5], *Samuel*[4], *Samuel*[3], *Thomas*[2], *Thomas*[1]), b. Aug. 23, 1749; m. Dec. 14, 1783, Experience Storrs, b. 1751. She d. Aug. 31, 1789; m. 2nd, Oct. 31, 1792, Molly Snow.

She d. Dec. 5, 1811. He d. Nov. 6, 1828. Res. Mansfield, Conn., and North Pitcher, N. Y. Children :—

912. i. ESECK, b. 1784; d. Jan. 4, 1786.
913. ii. ALGERNON, b. Jan. 17, 1786; m. Phebe Evans.
914. iii. SOPHRONIA, b. July 5, 1788; m. Given Atwood.
915. iv. EXPERIENCE, b. Aug. 16, 1793; m. A. A. Starks.
916. v. ENOCH, b. July 17, 1795; m. Laura Dean.
917. vi. EARL, b. April 3, 1798; m. Olive Stearns.

430. SAMUEL⁶ PIERCE (Enoch⁵, Samuel⁴, Samuel³, Thomas², Thomas¹), b. June 24, 1755; m. May 28, 1778, Joanna Babcock. Res. Mansfield, Conn., and Derwinter, Chenango Co., N. Y. Children :—

918. i. ANNA, b. April 24, 1779; m. Enoch Eldridge.
919. ii. MARY, b. Oct. 7, 1781; m. Samuel Finch.
920. iii. SARAH, b. Nov. 16, 1787; m. Samuel Eldridge.
921. iv. OLIVE, b. Sept. 7, 1791; d. unm.
922. v. JOANNA, b. April 24, 1793; m. Charles Hyde.
923. vi. AUELIA, b. April 14, 1796; m. Moses Smith.
924. vii. EUNICE, b. July 28, 1800.

432. Capt. JOSEPH⁶ PIERCE (Isaac⁵, Isaac⁴, Samuel³, Thomas², Thomas¹), b. Dec. 25, 1745; m. Apr. 6, 1771, Ann Dawes, b. May 19, 1753, d. Mar. 4, 1812. He d. Jan. 1, 1828. She was dau. of Col. Thos. Motley and sister of the late Hon. J. Lathrop Motley, the historian, and minister to England.

Joseph Pierce died in Boston Jan. 1, 1828; was graduated at the Boston Latin School, 1756. Joseph was a prominent merchant of the times and a man of great integrity, and possessed considerable influence with his fellow-citizens. Feeble health and a young and increasing family prevented his taking an active part in the struggle for liberty, which, however, received the aid both of his purse and his influence. From his store on the north side of State street he witnessed the "massacre" of Nov. 5, 1770. In connection with the sufferings of the inhabitants of Boston during the siege he often spoke of the fact that rats were eaten, occasionally, to appease hunger. He was the founder of the Provincial Grenadier corps and its commander on the occasion of its first parade, June 8, 1772, Henry Knox, afterwards Major-General and Secretary of War, being second in command. The splendid uniform, military appearance, drill, and the efficiency of its corps, are of traditional renown. It elicited the commendation of the British officers then in Boston, and received the special notice of Gov. Gage on his public entry into Boston in May, 1774. He was the friend and correspondent of Gov. Knox, with whom he afterwards associated himself in the proprietorship of large tracts of land in Maine. Knox's letters were unfortunately lost in 1811 by the burning of a store in which they were deposited. Capt. Pierce, from his personal acquaintance with the leaders of the Revolution and the principal officers of the army, and having himself participated in the early events of the contest, was, in his old age, full of reminiscences and anecdotes relating to them, and was consequently a most interesting and instructive companion. Res. in Boston. Children :—

925. i.   HANNAH, b. 1771; d. 1775.
926. ii. J. HARDY, b. March 8, 1773; m. Frances Temple Cordis and Abby Robinson.
927. iii. ANN, b. Aug. 11, 1774; m. John Lathrop, Jr.
928. iv. THOMAS, b. Oct. 4, 1775; d. Oct., 1776.
929. v.   HANNAH, b. Oct. 5, 1777; d. Sept., 1778.
930. vi. LUCY, b. Feb. 17, 1779; d. March 9, 1779.
931. vii. HARDY, b. July 17, 1780; d. Oct. 15, 1780.
932. viii. ISAAC, b. Dec. 13, 1781; d. March 16, 1793.
933. ix. HANNAH D., b. Jan. 3, 1783; m. Thomas P. Kettell.
934. x.   LUCY, b. Oct. 28, 1785; d. Oct. 28, 1785.
935. xi. ELIZABETH S., b. Oct. 25, 1787; m. Fitch Pool Putnam.
936. xii. MARIA, b. Oct., 1789; d. Aug. 11, 1874.
937. xiii. FRANCIS, b. Aug. 31, 1792; d. Sept. 2, 1792.

439. WILLIAM[6] PIERCE (*William[5], Sommers[4], William[3], Thomas[2], Thomas[1]*); m. Mar. 30, 1780, Sarah Holt. Res. Wilton, N. H., and Weston, Vt. Children :—

938. i.   ROXANNA; m. Wm. Campbell.
939. ii. ASA, b. Dec. 6, 1788; m. Hannah Higgins.
940. iii. SALLY; m. John Kimball.
941. iv. PHEBE; d. unm.
942. v.   WILLIAM, b. Sept. 20, 1785; m. Mary Moncrief.
943. vi. BETSEY; m. —— Lockwood.
944. vii. HANNAH; m. Charles Lockwood.
945. viii. LYDIA; m. Aaron Blanchard.
946. ix. POLLY; d. unm.
947. x.   CALVIN; d. unm.

440. BENJAMIN[6] PIERCE (*William[5], Sommers[4], William[3], Thomas[2], Thomas[1]*), b. May 18, 1762; m. Oct. 27, 1785, Dorcas Lovejoy, b. April 16, 1762. She d. Aug. 15, 1817. He m. 2nd, Feb. 8, 1820, Mrs. Nabby F. Dodge. She d. Aug. 28, 1865. He d. May 9, 1847. Benjamin Pierce was born in Wilton, N. H., and enlisted in the Revolutionary Army when but 18 years old and served during the war. He enlisted first for 3 mo. and then for 3 years. The war ended just before his time expired. He was stationed at West Point when Arnold sold out to the British. Soon after he was detailed as one of Gen. Washington's life guard and remained in that position till the close of the war. He assisted in moving Gen. Washington and family to Mt. Vernon, after the Declaration of Independence was signed and sealed. Res. Andover and Londonderry, Vt.

Children :—

948. i.   DORCAS, b. Jan. 22, 1786; m. Jan. 15, 1809, Thomas Hall. He d. July 13, 1835, and she d. Sept. 7, 1853. Res. South Londonderry.

Ch. : Harriet K., b. Jan. 18, 1812, m. Joseph Carlton; James
P., b. Feb. 23, 1815, m. Susan Dodge; Henry B., b. Oct 18,
1817, m. Melita Mason; Sally A., b. April 7, 1822, m. John Fel-
ton; John K., b. Feb. 23, 1825, m. Nancy Wilbur.

949. ii. POLLY, b. April 29, 1787; m. July 26, 1810, Daniel Dodge.
Daniel Dodge removed to Londonderry, Vt., from Andover,
Vt., in 1817. They purchased one of the first rights of Dr.
Samuel Thomson, to practice his system of medicine, and Polly
(Pierce) Dodge was often called to N. H. to visit the sick,
going the entire distance on horseback. She was familiarly
known as the " old Steam Doctor Woman" for miles around
her home; her success was excellent. She d. Dec. 20, 1851.
Ch. : Polly, b. Aug. 12, 1811, m. Sumner Wait; Dorcas, b. Mar.
12, 1812, m. Solon Richardson.

950. iii. JAMES, b. Aug. 17, 1789; m. Dec. 5, 1811, Mary Walker, and d. s.
p., April 12, 1813.

951. iv. ABIEL, b. Mar. 21, 1791; m. Nancy Holt; m. 2nd, Hannah K. Manning.

952. v. ASA, b. Mar. 17, 1793; m. Betsey Dodge.

953. vi. ALVAH, b. Oct. 6, 1796; m. Dolly Baker.

954. vii. NANCY, b. Dec. 2, 1798; m. Sept. 30, 1830, Isaac Jewett, d. 1852;
m. 2nd, David Putnam. She d. Aug. 4, 1862.

955. viii. ALANSON, b. Aug. 27, 1801; m. Hannah Bulton.

956. ix. ABEL, b. April 1, 1804; m. Harriet Dodge.

957. x. ABIGAIL, b. Nov. 25, 1820, m; April 7, 1842, George C. Mason, b.
Sept. 18, 1811. Res. Farmer, Ohio. Ch. : Sabrina E., b. Aug.
1, 1845, d. April 28, 1856; Welcome G., b. July 1, 1847, m. Emma P. Hauser; Frank P., b. Dec. 21, 1851, unm.; Harland J.,
b. June 13, 1854, unm.

958. xi. JAMES, b. Dec. 22, 1822; d. Oct. 21, 1842.

959. xii. LUCY, b. June 17, 1825; m. Sept. 11, 1851, Daniel P. Chittenden.
Ch. : Abbie J., b. June 1, 1852, d. June 2, 1863; Deelbert D., b.
Sept. 23, 1859, d. June 8, 1863; Willie E., b. April 11, 1857;
Flora A., b. Aug. 2, 1861. Res. N. Springfield, Vt.

960. xiii. BENJAMIN F., b. Feb. 7, 1828; m. May 8, 1851, Julia Ewing, b.
Mar. 16, 1830. Res. s. p., Bethlehem, Penn.

441. TIMOTHY[6] PIERCE (*William[5]*, *Sommers[4]*, *William[3]*, *Thomas[2]*,
Thomas[1]), b. Feb. 4, 1765 ; m. May 5, 1785, Phebe Carlton. Res.
Wilton, N. H. Children :—

960¼. i. TIMOTHY, b. Aug. 15, 1785; d. Sept. 21, 1787.
960½. ii. HANNAH, b. Oct. 27, 1789.

447. NATHAN[6] PIERCE (*James[5]*, *James[4]*, *James[3]*, *Thomas[2]*,
Thomas[1]), b. 1759; m. July 24, 1781, Sarah Leathe, b. Nov. 8, 1755.
She d. Aug. 20, 1850. He d. Nov. 14, 1841. Res. Woburn.
Children :—

961. i. SARAH, b. Jan. 29, 1783; m. Ephraim Brown.
962. ii. SUSANNA, b. Feb. 26, 1785; d. 1815.
963. iii. NATHANIEL, b. Mar. 27, 1787; m. —— Woods.
964. iv. NATHAN, b. July 8, 1789; d. Dec. 23, 1806.
965. v. JAMES, b. June 7, 1790; m. Polly Wood.
966. vi. SAMUEL, b. 1800; m. —— Merriam; m. 2nd, Priscilla E. Moore.
967. vii. PHEBE, b. May 28, 1798; m. John Scadding.
968. viii. JOSIAH, b. 1804; m. Ellen Davis ; m. 2nd, Polly Baker.

448. ABEL[6] PIERCE (*James[5]*, *James[4]*, *James[3]*, *Thomas[2]*,*Thomas[1]*),

14

b. 1767; m. Mar. 14, 1792, Ruth Parker. He d. in Woburn, May 22, 1838.

Children :—

969. i. HARRIET, b. March 23, 1793; m. April 19, 1812, Samuel Wyman.
970. ii. ABEL, Jr., b. Aug. 14, 1795; d. Mar. 17, 1796.
971. iii. ABEL, Jr., b. Jan. 25, 1797; m. April 4, 1822, Almira Russell; m. 2nd, Jan. 17, 1840, Mary C. Dickson; m. 3rd, Jan. 17, 1849, Eliza Dickson.
972. iv. CHARLES, b. Feb. 23, 1800.

Charles Peirce

973. v. FRANKLIN, b. Mar. 21, 1802; d. Feb. 20, 1837.
974. vi. MARY A., b. Dec. 22, 1804; m. May 26, 1824, Bradley Simonds, b. Dec. 19, 1799. They res. in Lexington and Ashby. Ch. : Frank, Nathan, Calvin, Bradley, Mary, Hattie, Sarah, Sophronia.
975. vii. WILLIAM, b. April 30, 1807; m. June 19, 1828, Lydia Sleeper; m. 2nd, May 12, 1856, Jane Clark.
976. viii. GEORGE W., b. July 14, 1819; m. Sept. 26, 1840, Eliza B. Hutchinson; m. 2nd, Hannah C. Merrill.
977. ix. SEWELL W., b. Dec. 11, 1813; m. Feb. 7, 1839, Margaret R. Adams.
978. x. ELIZA, b. 1816; m. Mar. 30, 1830, Samuel Cook, and had a Samuel, Jr.

450. JOSHUA[6] PIERCE, Jr. (*Joshua[5], James[4], James[3], Thomas[2], Thomas[1]*), b. Sept. 16, 1756 ; m. Dec. 25, 1781, Sarah Lund, b. July 6, 1763 ; d. Oct. 20, 1851. He d. in Hudson, N. H., Sept. 24, 1857.

Joshua Pierce

Children :—

979. i. JOSHUA, b. Feb. 27, 1783; d. Feb. 10, 1784.
980. ii. JOHN, b. April 22, 1785; d. Oct. 11, 1825.
981. iii. JOSHUA, b. July 9, 1787; m. Mar. 10, 1810, Dolly Hutchins.
982. iv. JAMES, b. Mar. 31, 1792; m. April 11, 1821, Belinda Cross.
983. v. JOSEPH B., b. Oct. 4, 1794; d. unm. Jan. 7, 1841.
984. vi. ABRAHAM, } b. Nov. 6, 1798; { d. Aug. 18, 1804.
985.   ISAAC, } { d. Nov. 24, 1798.
986. vii. COSMORE, b. Aug. 28, 1802; d. Jan. 31, 1804.

453. NATHAN[6] PIERCE (*Joshua[5], James[4], James[3], Thomas[2], Thomas[1]*), b. Sept. 11, 1766; m. Phebe Cummings, b. July 8, 1768 ; d. June 14, 1860. He d. Jan. 29, 1853, in Bradford, N. H.

Children :—

987. i. NATHAN, Jr., b. Jan. 15, 1789; m. Abigail Graves.
988. ii. SUSAN, b. May 5, 1792; d. Sept. 13, 1797.
989. iii. MARY, b. July 12, 1794; d. Aug. ——, 1863.
990. iv. CUMMINGS, b. 1796; d. Dec. 1, 1801.
991. v. SUSAN, b. Feb. 7, 1799; m. Enos Collins.
992. vi. DANIEL, b. July 17, 1801; m. Lucy Wheelock.
993. vii. CUMMINGS, b. May 22, 1803; m. Caroline Dowlin.
994. viii. STEPHEN C., b. Nov. 4, 1807; m. Martha Collins.

454. James[6] Pierce (*Joshua*[5], *James*[4], *James*[3], *Thomas*[2], *Thomas*[1]), b. Sept. 8, 1768 ; m. Jan., 1795, Mary Stacy, b. Dec. 20, 1774 ; d. Sept. 15, 1847. He d. Feb. 4, 1849, in W. Swanzey, N. H. Children :—

995. i. ALVAH; b. July 30, 1795; m. Leafee Miller.
996. ii. AVERY, b. April 6, 1797; d. Oct. 16, 1798.
997. iii. POLLY, b. July 20, 1799; m. Solomon Fields, and d. Oct. 28, 1837.
998. iv. DANIEL, b. Oct. 24, 1801; m. Ursula Caldwell.
999. v. ENOCH C., b. Nov. 8, 1803; d. Nov. 22, 1815.
1000. vi. SARAH C., b. Mar. 2, 1806; m. Feb. 10, 1837, Charles Greene, b. Feb. 5, 1803. She d. in W. Swanzey, Sept. 10, 1876. Ch. : Charles, b. Oct. 22, 1838; Rexford, b. Sept. 14, 1840; Mary, b. Aug. 17, 1842; George, b. Jan. 30, 1844; James, b. Jan. 24, 1846.
1001. vii. NANCY, b. July 5, 1808; d. June 28, 1853.
1002. viii. JAMES, Jr., b. Sept. 24, 1810; m. Jan. 1, 1839, Chloe Holbrook.
1003. ix. WILLIAM, b. Jan. 6, 1813; m. Mar. 13, 1844, Martha M. Whitcomb.

455. Daniel[6] Pierce (*Joshua*[5], *James*[4], *James*[3], *Thomas*[2], *Thomas*[1]), b. Aug. 8, 1763 ; m. Hannah Marsh, b. 1765. She d. Jan. 13, 1842. He d. previous to 1830. She m. 2nd, Dea. Jabez True. Res. Hudson, N. H.

Daniel Pierce

Children :—

1004. i. SAMUEL, b. Mar. 25, 1784; m. Abigail Davis.
1005. ii. SARAH, b. Mar. 12, 1786; m. Eben Dustin.
1006. iii. DANIEL, b. May 31, 1789; m. Clarissa Hardy.
1007. iv. ROBERT F., b. Oct. 5, 1790; m. Sarah Harvey.
1008. v. ISAAC, b. July 13, 1793; m. Mary Floyd.
1009. vi. JOSHUA; m. Apr. 3, 1817, Sarah Barnard.
1010. vii. WILLIAM M., b. June 15, 1806; m. Lois C. Kenniston.
1011. viii. ABIGAIL; m. Morrill Clement.

457. Jacob[6] Pierce, Jr. (*Jacob*[5], *James*[4], *James*[3], *Thomas*[2], *Thomas*[1]), b. Dec. 28, 1755 ; m. Oct. 13, 1783, Martha Johnson, b. Dec. 20, 1763 ; d. Oct. 2, 1849. He d. Oct. 2, 1825. They res. in Woburn.

Jacob Pierce

Children :—

1012. i. MARTHA, b. Dec. 20, 1784; m. Feb. 17, 1807, Joseph Gardner, b. Aug. 8, 1780, d. April 13, 1858. She d. Sept. 9, 1869. They had Joseph, b. Feb. 13, 1809, m. Nancy Hodgton; George, b. Sept. 21, 1814, m. Mary C. Gardner; Mary, b. Oct. 1, 1820, m. Ebenezer L. Pierce; Martha, b. July 2, 1816, m. Allen Lincoln.
1013. ii. MARY, b. Nov. 7, 1786; m. May 29, 1810, Rev. Timothy F. Rogers, of Bernardston. She d. July 5, 1846. Ch. : Mary, m. John Morey; Timothy and William.

1014. iii. JACOB, Jr., b. June 20, 1789; m. Sept. 26, 1816, Melicent Law-
             rence.
1015. iv. RUFUS, b. Oct. 9, 1791; d. unm. April 12, 1845.

458. EPHRAIM[6] PIERCE (*Jacob*[5], *James*[4], *James*[3], *Thomas*[2],
Thomas[1]), b. Mar. 8, 1758 ; m. Nov. 30, 1782, Mrs. Abigail Porter, b.
June 18, 1756; d. Jan. 9, 1840. He d. May 17, 1810. They res. in
Stoneham.

Children :—

1016. i.   EPHRAIM, b. Oct. 2, 1783; m. May 3, 1806, Sarah Leathe.
1017. ii. ABIGAIL, b. Jan. 5, 1786; m. Dec. 3, 1807, John Alden.
1018. iii. SAMUEL, b. July 6, 1788; d. April 24, 1813.
1019. iv. BETSEY, b. Aug. 2, 1790; m. April 18, 1811, James Steele and had
            a son John.
1020. v.   TIMOTHY, b. Oct. 2, 1792.

1021. vi. POLLY, b. April 1, 1795; m. Feb. 20, 1820, Onesimus Hadley, and
            d. May 28, 1831, in Stoneham.
1022. vii. WILLIAM, b. Mar. 8, 1798; d. July 3, 1832.

460. SAMUEL[6] PIERCE (*Jacob*[5], *James*[4], *James*[3], *Thomas*[2], *Thomas*[1]), b. in Woburn, Aug. 7, 1764 ; was the fifth child and third son of
Jacob and Abigail (Kendall) Pierce. He always lived in Woburn,
and for some time taught school there, and a good many stories and
anecdotes are told of him by persons now living who were his scholars.
A pocket-book with a great many of his school bills, and memoranda of
articles bought for the school, private papers, &c., in it, just as he left
it when he died, is in the possession of Fred. B. Pierce, 47 Broad
street, Boston. It was found among the effects left by his brother,
Jacob Pierce of Woburn, and given to the present owner by Mr.
Ebenezer L. Pierce of Woburn.

461. HEMAN[6] PIERCE (*Jacob*[5], *James*[4], *James*[3], *Thomas*[2] *Thom
as*[1]), b. Feb. 16, 1768; m. July 4, 1793, Mary Bowen, b. 1771, d. Oct.
14, 1828. He d. in Reading, Vt., Mar. 17, 1818.

Children :—

1023. i. JOSEPH, b. 1796; d. June 24, 1830, unm.

1024. ii. HENRY, b. Nov. 25, 1798; m. Mary Newton.
1025. iii. JAMES, b. Mar. 7, 1803; m. Oct. 15, 1828, Mary Slayton.
1026. iv. SAMUEL B., b. Aug. 14, 1806; m. Dec. 17, 1829, Hannah R. Homer.
1027. v. CHRISTRANY, b. Aug. 10, 1814; d. Apr. 4, 1816.

465. BENJAMIN[6] PIERCE, Jr. (*Benjamin[5], Thomas[4], Benjamin[3], Thomas[2], Thomas[1]*), b. Oct. 21, 1756; m. Nov. 28, 1782, Eunice Jones, dau. of Abraham and Mercy (Gale) Jones, at Wayland (formerly East Sudbury), b. July 1, 1755. He was a farmer; was a soldier in the Revolution, was in the battles of White Plains, Ticonderoga, Crown Point and other places. He died Jan. 13, 1819.

Children :—
1028. i. EUNICE, b. Nov. 19, 1786; m. 1818, William Spring. He d. Apr. 12, 1823. Ch.: Eunice, b. 1819, m. Stephen Seaverens; Geo., b. Feb. 1, 1821, m. Mary A. Starr; Mary R., b. Mar. 21, 1823.
1029. ii. BENJAMIN, Jr., b. June 15, 1788; d. 1792.
1030. iii. LOIS, b. Oct. 18, 1789; d. Oct. 10, 1856.
1031. iv. LUTHER, b. Aug. 21, 1791; m. Jan. 6, 1818, Betsey Brackett.
1032. v. BENJAMIN, b. Jan. 3, 1794; m. Mar. 10, 1818, Almira Harrington.
1033. vi. MARTHA, b. Aug. 20, 1795; m. Oct. 9, 1817, Samuel Hews. She d. Jan. 26, 1874. Ch.: George, b. July 10, 1827; Henry A., b. Jan. 20, 1828; Samuel G., b. Aug. 12, 1830, d. 1833.
1034. vii. MARY, b. Sept. 26, 1797; d. Dec. 15, 1867.

466. JOHN[6] PIERCE (*Benjamin[5], Thomas[4], Benjamin[3], Thomas[2], Thomas[1]*), b. Sept. 18, 1758; m. Mary Webb, b. Feb. 28, 1766, d. Dec. 21, 1816. They res. in Weston, Mass. and East Embden, Me. He d. Apr. 19, 1837.

Children :—
1035. i. JOHN, Jr., b. Jan. 16, 1789; m. 1815, Ann Cragin; m. 2nd, Oct. 22, 1822, Sarah Spalding.
1036. ii. DAVID W., b. Feb. 7, 1791; m. May 12, 1819, Ruth Andrews.
1037. iii. BENJAMIN, b. Mar. 6, 1795; m. Dec. 18, 1817, Hannah Cragin; m. 2nd, May 30, 1841, Lois H. Bartlett.
1038. iv. MARY T., b. Mar. 5, 1797; m. Henry Moore, b. June 3, 1799, d. June 13, 1863. No issue.
1039. v. SARAH W., b. July 14, 1801; m. ——— Cleveland, and d. May 2, 1835, in Embden, leaving Thaddeus S., b. Aug. 31, 1818; res. Calais, Ohio.

467. AMOS[6] PIERCE (*Benjamin[5], Thomas[4], Benjamin[3], Thomas[2], Thomas[1]*), b. Aug. 5, 1760; m. Mar. 3, 1789, Hepsibah Smith, b. Aug. 31, 1761. They res. in Ashburnham. She d. Oct. 3, 1873. He d. Dec. 30, 1872.

Children :—

1040.   i.   HEPSIBAH, b. June 8, 1791; d. Oct. 3, 1793.
1041.   ii. AMOS, Jr., b. Aug. 1, 1794; d. July 18, 1849.

Amos Pierce

1042.   iii. LUCY, b. Apr. 8, 1798; d. Oct. 24, 1814.
1043.   iv.   JAMES, b. Aug. 20, 1801; m. Martha W. Warren.

470. STEPHEN[6] PIERCE (*Benjamin[5]*, *Thomas[4]*, *Benjamin[3]*, *Thomas[2]*, *Thomas[1]*), b. Oct. 2, 1768; m. —— ——. Res. Dublin and Chesterfield, N. H. Children:—

1043.   i.   MARY M., b. —— ——; m. Jan. 21, 1821, Solomon Blodgett.
             Ch. : Mary W., b. Jan. 11, 1822; Walter M., b. Dec. 11, 1823.
1044.   ii. LUCRETIA; m. 1827, Cyrus Powers.

474. JOSEPH[6] PIERCE (*Thomas[5]*, *Thomas[4]*, *Benjamin[3]*, *Thomas[2]*, *Thomas[1]*), b. July 12, 1757; m. Hannah Green, b. Dec. 28, 1764. She d. Dec. 18, 1840. He d. June 4, 1809. She m. 2nd, Stephen Dyre. Res. Hubbardston, Mass., and Chester, Vt. Children :—

1045.   i.   LEVI, b. June 27, 1785; m. Betsey Eaton and Eunice Green.
1046.   ii.   CLARISSA, b. Oct. 7, 1789; d. Nov. 20, 1868.
1047.   iii. ABEL G., b. Feb. 10, 1792; m. Susan H. Rice.
1048.   iv.   LYDIA, b. May 17, 1795; d. Sept. 9, 1796.
1049.   v.   LYDIA, b. June 10, 1797; d. Sept. 30, 1816.
1050.   vi.   MYRA, b. Jan 3, 1800; d. April 4, 1878.

476. ELIAB[6] PIERCE (*Thomas[5]*, *Thomas[4]*, *Benjamin[3]*, *Thomas[2]*, *Thomas[1]*), b. Sept. 5, 1761; m. Lydia Wood, b. April 5, 1759. She d. Oct. 12, 1833. He d. Nov. 30, 1851. Res. Putney, Vt. and Fairfield, N. Y.

He was born of poor but respectable parents, in the town of Hopkinton, Middlesex Co., Mass. He lived for about a year with his maternal uncle, Noah Havens, in the south part of Dedham, Mass., when he was about ten years old. His parents at that time moved to Hubbardston, Worcester Co., about 40 miles. Thinking they were going so far that all intercourse of communication would be cut off they took Eliab with them. When nearly eighteen Eliab enlisted in the Militia Co. then doing duty in R. I., where he served under sordid officers and was cheated out of his rations and most of his pay. The next summer he re-enlisted and went to West Point and vicinity, where he served under Benedict Arnold.

Eliab Pierce.

Children :—

1051.   i.   IRA, b. March 28, 1794; m. Mary J. Brown.
1052.   ii. ACHSA, b. Feb. 2, 1800; d. Dec. 2, 1855, unm.

477. THOMAS[6] PIERCE (*Thomas[5], Thomas[4], Benjamin[3], Thomas[2], Thomas[1]*), b. Dec. 5, 1763 ; m. Feb. 12, 1792, Sally Derry, b. Dec. 23, 1766, d. April 2, 1840. He d. Oct. 13, 1850. Res. Putney, Vt., Fairfield and Ashford, N. Y.

Thomas Peirce

Children :—

1053. i. LISSETA, b. Nov. 19, 1792; d. Feb. 24, 1879.
1054. ii. HENRIETTA, b. Nov. 16, 1794; m. Bradford Joslin.
1055. iii. CHAUNCEY, b. Sept. 17, 1796; m. Lydia Wells.
1056. iv. SARAH, b. Oct. 20, 1798, d. Sept. 19, 1860.
1057. v. THOMAS, b. Dec. 8, 1800; m. Catherine Weber and Mary Etta Scobey.
1058. vi. BETSEY, b. Feb. 11, 1803; m. Sylvester Perry.
1059. vii. GIFFORD, b. Feb. 2, 1805; m. four times.
1060. viii. MARY, b. Nov. 21, 1808; m. Jacob Myers.

480. MOSES H.[6] PIERCE (*Thomas[5], Thomas[4], Benjamin[3], Thomas[2], Thomas[1]*), b. Mar. 15, 1771 ; m. Dec. 6, 1792, Anna Rice. He d. July 30, 1846. Res. Hubbardston. Children :—

1061. i. PATTY, b. March 5, 1793 ; m. June 9, 1811, Silas Davis.
1062. ii. JOHN, b. Feb. 15, 1795 ; d. Oct. 7, 1798.
1063. iii. HAVEN, b. Nov. 12, 1797 ; m. Hannah Rice.
1064. iv. LEVI, b. Jan. 7, 1799 ; m. Mary M. Clark.
1065. v. ASA, b. Sept. 13, 1800 ; m. Harriet Wheeler.
1066. vi. MARGARET, b. Oct. 7, 1802 ; d. Sept. 4, 1823.
1067. vii. J. HERVEY, b. Nov. 23, 1804 ; m. Eunice Davis.
1068. viii. MARY M., b. 1807 ; d. unm. Aug. 28, 1865.
1069. ix. DEXTER, unm.
1070. x. MELISSA ; m. —— Bryant.

484. JOSEPH[7] PIERCE (*Silas[6], Joseph[5], Joseph[4], Jonathan[3], Samuel[2], Thomas[1]*), b. Mar. 5, 1775 ; m. May 28, 1805, Nancy Hollis, b. Aug. 23, 1785, d. Nov. 11, 1861. He d. Mar. 28, 1835, and she then, Mar. 12, 1841, m. Abijah Carter. He (Jos.) res. in Chelmsford, Lowell and Fitchburg. Children :—

1071. i. HARRIET, b. Aug. 16, 1806 ; m. June 2, 1829, Ross C. Stevens, b. Mar. 26, 1806, d. Jan. 19, 1876, in Marlboro. Ch. : Mary E. P., b. Nov. 19, 1842, m. Rufus L. Cooper.
1072. ii. JOSEPH, b. Feb. 1, 1817 ; m. May 1, 1838, Sarah S. Sawyer. They res. in Fitchburg and have had no issue.
1073. iii. JAMES, b. June 19, 1819 ; m. June 4, 1844, Ellen L. Weatherbee ; m. 2nd, Aug. 13, 1864, Elvira Sibley.

488. LEVI[7] PIERCE, Jr. (*Levi[6], Joseph[5], Joseph[4], Jonathan[3], Samuel[2], Thomas[1]*), b. July 22, 1778 ; m. Sept. 18, 1804, Rhoda Cutter, d. Sept., 1850. He d. Aug. 28, 1838. Children, b. in Temple, N. H.:—

1074. i. RHODA, b. Aug. 16, 1806 ; m. Dec. 6, 1825, Howard S. Blood. Ch. : George H., Levi H., Emily P. She d. June, 1838, in Temple, N. H.
1075. ii. HANNAH, b. July 25, 1808 ; d. July, 1867.
1076. iii. EMILY, b. Mar. 18, 1811 ; m. May 27, 1834, Joseph Spear. Ch. : Joseph A. and Edward H. She d. Mar. 30, 1837, in N. Ipswich, N. H.

1077. iv. LOUISA, b. Feb. 4, 1814.
1078. v. LEVI A., b. Sept. 2, 1818; m. Nov. 27, 1847, Rachel A. Lovejoy.

492. JOSEPH[7] PIERCE (*Levi[6], Joseph[5], Joseph[4], Jonathan[3], Samuel[2], Thomas[1]*), b. May 2, 1790; m. Dec. 27, 1810, Elizabeth Dunklee, b. May 10, 1789, d. Aug. 9, 1855. He was adopted one month before he was named by his uncle Willard Pierce of Merrimac, N. H. He d. June 24, 1825. He was a sea Captain and sailed from Boston. Jonas Chickering, afterwards the famous piano-forte builder, was at one time a mate of his. Children:—

1079. i. ELIZABETH D., b. Sept. 23, 1811; m. Apr. 15, 1830, Ralph Burns.
1080. ii. MARY B., b. Feb. 1, 1813; m. John S. Marshall, and d. Aug. 17, 1853.
1081. iii. SUSANNAH T., b. Jan. 13, 1815; m. Mar. 14, 1838, Freeman C. Sewell.
1082. iv. ELECTA, b. Mar. 13, 1817; d. Jan. 17, 1849, unm.
1083. v. JOSEPH B., b. Mar. 10, 1819; m. Mary B. Cummings. Res. White River Junction, Vt.
1084. vi. SOPHIA, b. Dec. 8, 1821; m. Jan. 24, 1850, Charles Wilson, d. Aug. 23, 1859.
1085. vii. PHEBE W., b. Mar. 14, 1825; d. Apr. 15, 1831.

495. ERASMUS J.[7] PIERCE (*Erasmus[6], Isaac[5], Isaac[4], Jonathan[3], Samuel[2], Thomas[1]*), b. Oct. 29, 1780; m. April 3, 1809, Elizabeth Messenger, b. July 29, 1783, d. Oct. 5, 1836. He d. Aug. 26, 1852. Res. Philadelphia, Pa. Children:—

1086. i. ERASMUS J., b. May 21, 1810; d. May 21, 1810.
1087. ii. MARY E. M., b. Oct. 19, 1815; m. Wm. A. Drown.
1088. iii. CATHERINE A. C., b. Sept. 1, 1822; m. Henry D. Landis.
1089. iv. EPAMINONDAS J., b. Oct. 24, 1823; m. Susan Savery.

500. PETER[7] PIERCE (*Erasmus[6], Isaac[5], Isaac[4], Jonathan[3], Samuel[2], Thomas[1]*), b. Feb. 29, 1789; m. Dec. 25, 1821, Gwenthalla Morris, b. Sept. 9, 1802, d. April 24, 1824; m. 2d, July 19, 1825, Elizabeth Lunberg, b. March 9, 1809, d. March 3, 1867. He d. Aug. 29, 1872. Res. Benoyn, Pa. Children:—

1090. i. ERASMUS J., b. Oct. 7, 1822; d. June 11, 1823.
1091. ii. ELIZABETH M., b. April 20, 1824.
1092. iii. CAROLINE M., b. Nov. 16, 1826; m. John M. Bradford.
1093. iv. ROBERT M., b. Aug. 19, 1828; m. Elizabeth G. Hodgson.
1094. v. PETER, b. Nov. 23, 1830; d. Jan. 20, 1832.
1095. vi. MARY E., b. Nov. 7, 1832; d. Oct. 3, 1844.
1096. vii. ADELAIDE B., b. Jan. 27, 1835.
1097. viii. ARABELLA L., b. Feb. 5, 1838.
1098. ix. WILLIAM A. D., b. July 9, 1840.
1099. x. CLARISSA, b. Aug. 9, 1842; d. July 12, 1845.

501. DANIEL[7] PIERCE (*Erasmus[6], Isaac[5], Isaac[4], Jonathan[3], Samuel[2], Thomas[1]*), b. May 28, 1791; m. Aug. 19, 1819, Mary Ann Taylor. He d. 1873. She m. 2nd, Seth Hyatt. Res. Washington, D. C.

Daniel Pierce

Children :—

2000. i. SUSAN S., b. Dec. 28, 1820; m. E. Rufus Ward.
2001. ii. MARY A., b. Oct. 11, 1829; m. John Willis.
2002. iii. HANNAH; d. infancy.
2003. iv. EMELINE, b. July 4, 1834; m. Wm. G. Bishop.
2004. v. HARVEY L., b. Aug. 24, 1839; m. —— Perrington.

502. JOSEPH[7] PIERCE (*Joseph[6], Isaac[5], Isaac[4], Jonathan[3], Samuel[2], Thomas[1]*), b. July 30, 1783 ; m. Aug. 14, 1808, Sally Hatch, b. Jan. 3, 1787, d. Sept. 22, 1841. He d. Feb. 27, 1863. Res. Cincinnati, Ohio.

Captain Joseph Pierce was born in Boston, on the 30th of July, 1783, and was consequently nearly eighty years of age at his demise. At an early age he chose a sailor's life and went to sea. He pursued this adventurous career for many years, during which he circumnavigated the globe, visiting nearly all the important places of the world. As early as 1802, while employed on board the armed ship *Juno* of Bristol, R. I., he entered the Oregon river and Puget's Sound on the Pacific coast—points then almost unknown to commerce. During the war of 1812, he was engaged in the naval service of our country; in what capacity we are not informed, but if we mistake not he was taken prisoner and suffered confinement, for a time, in one of the noted dungeons of England. In 1818 he emigrated to the West and engaged in the navigation of the western waters, and for many years was known as one of the most successful commanders on the rivers. Identifying himself with this pursuit he ever afterward retained a deep interest in all the improvements which have characterized our river trade. No man in the community was better posted in all matters pertaining to steam power, the machinery, equipments, architecture and finish of our river craft. It is nearly or quite a quarter of a century since his first appointment, by the Insurance Companies of Cincinnati, as Inspector of Steamboats; which position he continued to occupy till his death, without intermission. His previous life and occupation pre-eminently qualified him for the duties of this department—and the length of time he filled the place bespeaks the confidence reposed in him by the institutions he served.

Politically, Capt. Pierce was a Whig of the Henry Clay school, and stood firm and unshaken in his faith through all the vicissitudes of the party and its leader. The principles he then embraced he retained to the last; yielding only to the imperious demands of fate which, for the time being, swept them in part from the political platforms of the day. He could never sympathize in any degree with the radicalism of any party. Above all personal or party considerations, his country and its government, whether administered by political friends or foes, occupied the first place in his affections; and unsparing and terrible were his denunciations of him who dared, in his presence, to suggest even the possibility of a dismemberment of the great family of States. No heart ever beat in truer loyalty than his. His patriotism was untarnished by a single corrupt thought. When the present rebellion was inaugurated, the highest regret he entertained was that age and phys-

15

ical disabilities prevented him from taking up arms for the defense of his country. To his dying hour his purest earthly aspiration was expressed in the wish that this Government, consecrated by the sacred blood of our fathers, might survive the shock of civil war under which it now trembled, and stand forth before the world an exemplification of the principles on which it is founded, furnishing in all time to come proofs of a higher civilization than has been elsewhere attained—a monument of the wisdom which laid its foundations in blood.

Socially, Captain P. was in the highest sense genial; his eventful life and its stirring incidents, rendered him capable of affording pure entertainment to the social circle. When the Spring Grove Cemetery was orgrnized (nearly twenty years ago), he became one of the original lot owners—selecting the spot where he desired his remains might repose after life's journey was accomplished. His interest in its preparation was for a time intense. At great expense he provided a vault and erected a monument, which was among the most creditable structures, in its early days, of this now almost unequalled "city of the dead." The remains of his wife, deceased many years before, he removed from Boston and placed them in the only niche in the vault, besides the one prepared for himself. He procured a coffin for his own body, made strictly after his own instructions, and accurately adapted to the place it was intended finally to occupy. A silver plate to be adjusted to the same was also procured, and suitable inscriptions of his name, date of birth, with a blank for the date of his death, and appropriate masonic emblems (of which fraternity he was a member), all engraved on the same so that the least possible additional service, preparatory to his burial, would be required. This plate for safe keeping, he placed in a frame and hung it in his room. On the back of the frame he had attached in manuscript in his own handwriting, the form of an epitaph, which he designed for his monument after his decease. This recounted briefly the date of his birth—the principal events of his life—and leaving a blank space for the date of his death, it closed with a declaration of his religious faith in the certainty of "*future happiness and in the existence of a just God.*"

Children :—

2005. i.   JOSEPH, b. May 23, 1809; m. Mary Thrives.
2006. ii. SALLY ANN, b. March 20, 1811; d. April 1, 1816.
2007. iii. WILLIAM H., b. Feb. 23, 1813; m. Eveline Jackson, Elizabeth Garrison and Mrs. Elizabeth Jacques.
2008. iv. JAMES W., b. March 25, 1814; m. Eliza Woods.
2009. v.   SALLY ANN, b. Sept. 23, 1820; m. Oct. 3, 1837, Lewis Worthington, b. Feb. 24, 1808. She d. April 1, 1876, leaving one son, Lewis Sedam Worthington, b. Mar. 21, 1839. He graduated from Yale College in the class of 1860, M. D. of Miami University, Cincinnati, Ohio, March, 1871, M. D. of the Paris, France,

School of Medicine, Aug., 1875. He resides in Paris at 36 Rue des Ecuries d'Artois.

2010. vi. CHARLES J., b. April 12, 1823; d. Nov. 3, 1834.
2011. vii. FRANKLIN, b. Aug. 28, 1825; d. April 27, 1826.
2012. viii. BENJAMIN F., b. June 2, 1827; m. Frances A. Rockinfeld.
  ix. SALLY, b. July 15, 1818; d. July 15, 1818.
  x. JOSIAH, b. Feb. 5, 1817; d. Feb. 15, 1817.

504. ISAAC[7] PIERCE (*Joseph*[6], *Isaac*[5], *Isaac*[4], *Jonathan*[3], *Samuel*[2], *Thomas*[1]), b. April 7, 1788; m. June 25, 1809, Alice B. Barstow, b. Sept. 24, 1790, d. 1818. He m. 2nd, Dec. 24, 1818, Nancy Brack, b. Dec. 8, 1800. He d. Aug. 8, 1830. Res. Charlestown, Mass.
Children :—

2013. i. ISAAC, b. Aug. 26, 1810; d. 1847, unm.
2014. ii. ALICE B., b. Jan. 3, 1813; m. John Campbell and d. June 3, 1847.
2015. iii. CHARLES, b. Oct. 1, 1815; m. Hannah Eaton.
2016. iv. GEORGE B., b. Jan. 3, 1818; d. Apr. 27, 1818.
2017. v. JOSEPH, b. Nov. 21, 1819; m. Elizabeth Huff.
2018. vi. GEORGE J., b. Sept. 30, 1821; m. Emeline C. Canterbury.
2019. vii. SARAH E., b. Feb. 8, 1824; m. Silas Morse.
2020. viii. NANCY, b. April 26, 1826; m. Daniel Rhoades and d. Mar. 17, 1869.
2021. ix. EDWARD F., b. Feb. 22, 1828; m. Harriet E. Deguio.
2022. x. BENJAMIN A., b. Dec. 8, 1830; d. Nov. 13, 1850.

505. JAMES[7] PIERCE (*Joseph*[6], *Isaac*[5], *Isaac*[4], *Jonathan*[3], *Samuel*[2], *Thomas*[1]), b. Dec. 28, 1790; m. Aug. 7, 1813, Abigail Waite, b. Dec. 30, 1790, d. Jan. 16, 1822; m. 2nd, Dec. 1, 1822, Nancy Waite, b. June 17, 1793, d. July 8, 1873. He d. March 24, 1863. Res. Boston.

Children :—

2023. i. NANCY W., b. March 19, 1814; d. March 20, 1814.
2024. ii. NANCY W., b. Feb. 25, 1815; d. Sept. 12, 1816.
2025. iii. SARAH A. J., b. June 22, 1817; m. Daniel Tourtellott.
2026. iv. HARRIET N., b. Oct. 7, 1818.
2027. v. JAMES W., b. July 8, 1820; m. Sarah E. D. B. Wilson.
2028. vi. ABIGAIL, b. Jan. 15, 1822; d. Jan. 16, 1822.
2029. vii. ABIGAIL W., b. Nov. 3, 1823; m. Wm. H. Lyon and Francis H. Barrett.
2030. viii. THOMAS P., b. Nov. 30, 1825; m. Anna Clapp.
2031. ix. NANCY W., b. Aug. 20, 1827; m. Samuel Walker.
2032. x. WILLIAM J., b. April 19, 1829; m. Sarah L. Bunten.
2033. xi. ISAAC, b. Dec. 27, 1830; m. Jennie Hayes.
2034. xii. JOSEPH, b. Oct. 1, 1832; d. Sept. 27, 1833.
2035. xiii. MARY B., b. Jan. 9, 1834; m. George W. Booth.
2036. xiv. JOSEPH, b. Aug. 26, 1835; m. Emily A. Norwood.

515. JOHN W.[7] PIERCE (*Samuel*[6], *Samuel*[5], *Stephen*[4], *Jonathan*[3], *Samuel*[2], *Thomas*[1]), b. Oct. 4, 1812; m. June 5, 1836, Lydia Ann Osborn, b. Nov. 8, 1815. Res. Boston, No. 5 Milford street.

Children :—

2037. i.   GEORGE W., b. March 24, 1841; unm; res. with parents. He is a lawyer at 12 Equitable Building, Boston, having graduated from Harvard University in the class of 1864.

George W. (Winslow) Pierce

2038. ii. ANNIE L., b. July 13, 1845; m. Nov. 14, 1871, Joseph Southwick, b. Aug. 6, 1841. Res. s. p. No. 126 W. Concord street, Boston.
2039. iii. LIZZIE M., b. April 16, 1849; unm.
2040. iv. HEZEKIAH C., b. Dec. 26, 1854; d. Mar. 10, 1861.

516. SAMUEL[7] PIERCE (*Samuel[6], Samuel[5], Stephen[4], Jonathan[3], Samuel[2], Thomas[1]*), b. Aug. 11, 1814; m. July 15, 1833, Rebecca P. Dorell, d. April 29, 1862; m. 2nd, Jan. 1, 1863, Caroline Tufts, d. Dec. 6, 1871; m. 3rd, May 15, 1872, Mary Payson. Res. Westboro, Mass. Children :—

2041. i.   S. WINSLOW, b. July 19, 1835; m. Fannie Whitney.
2042. ii.   REBECCA, b. April 7, 1837; m. L. Remington.
2043. iii. SARAH, b. Jan. 8, 1841; d. Aug. 24, 1841.
2044. iv.   MARY E., b. Jan. 15, 1844; m. John Beaman.
2045. v.   SARAH, b. Sept. 7, 1851; m. Charles Howe.
2046. vi.   HARRIET R., b. March 13, 1865.
2047. vii. ARTHUR, b. Jan. 30, 1867.

519. EDWARD K.[7] PIERCE (*Samuel[6], Samuel[5], Stephen[4], Jonathan[3], Samuel[2], Thomas[1]*), b. Sept. 21, 1820; m. Aug. 17, 1845, Margaret E. Bass, b. May 6, 1826, d. Jan. 15, 1862. He d. Aug. 23, 1870. Res. Boston, Millbury and Worcester. Children :—

2048. i.   E. HENRY, b. July 2, 1847; m. Luella Lake.
2049. ii.   J. ELIZABETH, b. March 25, 1849.
2050. iii. CHARLES A., b. Feb. 11, 1852; d. Nov. 19, 1853.

520. BARZILLAI[7] PIERCE (*Jonathan[6], Joseph[5], Daniel[4], John[3], Thomas[2], Thomas[1]*), b. Dec., 1779; m. Jan. 10, 1802, Jane Turner, b. 1779, d. Mar. 4, 1833; m. 2nd, Dec. 29, 1833, Sarah Hix, b. 1787, d. July 12, 1860. He d. Oct. 24, 1861. Res. So. Thomaston, Me. Children :—

2051. i.   WILLIAM, b. Jan. 13, 1803; m. Jane Spratt.
2052. ii.   ISRAEL S., b. Jan. 1, 1805; m. Mary Snow.
2053. iii. JOHN, b. Feb. 1, 1807; d. unm. Sept. 30, 1846.
2054. iv.   JANE, b. Dec. 28, 1809; m. Eliphalet Martin.
2055. v.   JOSEPH S., b. Feb. 5, 1811; m. Margaret Snow.
2056. vi.   ARCHIBALD, b. Jan. 24, 1813; d. May 7, 1835.
2057. vii. GEORGE W., b. May 13, 1816; m. Nancy F. Martin and Harriet N. McLane.
2058. viii. NANCY C., b. Nov. 14, 1819; d. Mar. 28, 1843.
2059. ix.   CHARLES G., b. June 12, 1823.

524. JOSEPH[7] PIERCE (*Jonathan[6], Joseph[5], Daniel[4], John[3],*

Thomas², *Thomas¹*), b. 1789; m. ——— ———; d. 1814. She m. 2nd, Samuel Putnam. Child :—

2060. i. JOSEPH, b. 1812; d. at sea, 1842.

525. BARZILLAI⁷ PIERCE (*Barzillai⁶*, *Joseph⁵*, *Daniel⁴*, *John³*, *Thomas²*, *Thomas¹*); m. Lucy ———. Res. Lunenburg, Mass. Child :—

2061. i. STEPHEN, b. July 21, 1809; d. Oct. 13, 1809.

526. SIMON⁷ PIERCE (*David⁶*, *Daniel⁵*, *Daniel⁴*, *John³*, *Thomas²*, *Thomas¹*), b. March 1, 1764; m. Nov. 10, 1787, Hepzibah Wood, b. July 3, 1771, d. Aug. 23, 1842. He d. April 9, 1814. Res. Chester ville, Me.

Children :—

2062. i. LUCY, b. Oct. 16, 1788; d. Jan. 28, 1789.
2063. ii. CYRUS, b. Aug. 18, 1793; m. Julia Sewall.
2064. iii. LUCINDA, b. Sept. 20, 1797; m. Luther Pierce [2083].
2065. iv. LAVINIA, b. Mar. 28, 1800; m. Wm. O. Bradbury.
2066. v. CEPHAS, b. Sept. 30, 1802; d. June 8, 1803.
2067. vi. RUFUS, b. Aug. 30, 1804; d. July 31, 1805.
2068. vii. PHEBE, b. June 6, 1806; m. Sumner Russell.
2069. viii. ABNER, b. Jan. 17, 1809; m. Abigail Walton.
2070. ix. JULIA A., b. May 30, 1812; m. Angi Sanborn.

527. CALVIN⁷ PIERCE (*David⁶*, *Daniel⁵*, *Daniel⁴*, *John³*, *Thomas²*, *Thomas¹*), b. Feb. 10, 1766; m. April 4, 1790, Deborah Blackwell, b. Jan. 23, 1772, d. Jan. 29, 1849. He d. Oct. 7, 1814. Res. Bingham, Me.

Children :—

2071. i. MOSES C., b. May 4, 1791; m. Temperance Savage.
2072. ii. NATHANIEL, b. March 25, 1793; m. Andrew Baker.
2073. iii. SARAH, b. Feb. 16, 1795; m. Simon Piper.
2074. iv. JAMES S., b. Feb. 3, 1797; m. Mercy B. Hale.
2075. v. JOSHUA B., b. Feb. 19, 1799; m. Hannah Bean.
2076. vi. ELIZABETH, b. Feb. 28, 1801; m. Mark Langley.

2077. vii. SUSANNAH, b. May 5, 1803; d. Jan. 17, 1804.
2078. viii. SUSAN, b. Sept. 26, 1804; m. Edmund Spalding.
2079. ix.   EZEKIEL, b. Jan. 17, 1807; m. Content B. Pierce [2116].
2080. x.   CHARLOTTE, b. Feb. 28, 1809; m. Edward L. Eldridge.
2081. xi.   LOVINIA, b. May 2, 1811; m. Heman McIntire.

528. LUTHER[7] PIERCE (*David*[6], *Daniel*[5], *Daniel*[4], *John*[3], *Thomas*[2], *Thomas*[1]), b. May 12, 1768; m. 1793, Susanna Gray, b. April 22, 1766, d. April 8, 1835; m. 2nd, Oct., 1835, Mrs. Martha Kimball, d. Nov. 18, 1853. He d. Jan. 14, 1846. Res. Solon, Me.

Luther Pierce

Children :—

2082. i.   JOHN, b. May 2, 1795; m. Rachel L. Nudd.
2083. ii.   LUTHER, b. Feb. 8, 1797; m. Lucinda Pierce [2064], and Mary S. Burns.
2084. iii. JESSE, b. Jan. 17, 1799; m. Catherine Reed.
2085. iv.   SALLY, b. Jan. 17, 1802; m. Luther Chaney.

529. DAVID[7] PIERCE (*David*[6], *Daniel*[5], *Daniel*[4], *John*[3], *Thomas*[2], *Thomas*[1]), b. Sept. 20, 1771 ; m. 1794, Olive Russell, b. Nov. 15, 1779, d. Sept. 22, 1819. He d. June 20, 1844. Res. Norridgewock, Me.

David Peirce

Children :—

2086. i.   ISAAC R., b. Oct. 15, 1795; m. Eliza Chute.
2087. ii.   SAMUEL D., b. Jan. 18, 1797: m. Lucy Barstow.
2088. iii. OLIVE R., b. Jan. 26, 1801; d. May 13, 1817.
2089. iv.   RUFUS W., b. Dec. 31, 1805; m. Sally Hosmer and Martha Nutting.
2090. v.   MARY, b. Oct. 8, 1808; d. Oct., 1819.
2091. vi.   MARTHA, b. Jan. 7, 1810; m. Dec. 22, 1830, James Young. They had nine children, four of which number are now living. He d. Dec. 22, 1869.
2092. vii. CALEB S., b. Jan. 13, 1812; m. Eliza Young.
2093. viii. SIMON D., b. June 10, 1813; m. Sarah A. Parsons.
2094. ix.   BETSEY, b. June 16, 1816; d. 1818.
2095. x.   CALVIN, b. July 13, 1818; m. Julia A. Swan.

530. CHARLES[7] PIERCE (*David*[6], *Daniel*[5], *Daniel*[4], *John*[3], *Thomas*[2], *Thomas*[1]), b. March 10, 1775 ; m. Abigail Ayer, b. July 7, 1779, d. Aug. 5, 1864. He d. April 11, 1851. Res. Bingham, Me.

Charles Peirce

Children :—

2096. i. ALICE, b. Jan. 15, 1798; m. Roby Marston.
2097. ii. MAHALA, b. Feb. 13, 1799; m. Abraham Smith.
2098. iii. CHRISTIAN, b. Nov. 21, 1800; m. Daniel Strickland.
2099. iv. SALLY, b. March 7, 1802; m. Samuel Atwood.
2100. v. HARRY, b. July 23, 1803; m. Fidelia Quint.
2101. vi. PETER, b. Nov. 20, 1804; m. Lydia Watters.
2102. vii. WILLIAM, b. April 22, 1806; m. Anula Quint.
2103. viii. HEPZIBAH, b. Nov. 27, 1807; m. James Kincade.
2104. ix. LUCY, b. Jan. 1, 1810; m. Abraham Smith.
2105. x. HARRIET, b. Aug. 19, 1811; m. Cyrus Robinson.
2106. xi. ABIGAIL, b. May 26, 1813; m. Abner Albee.
2107. xii. POLLY, b. June 8, 1815; m. William Norton.
2108. xiii. CHARLES T.; m. Polly Strickland.
2109. xiv. BETSEY; m. Obed Allen.
2110. xv. ELIAS M.; m. Mary E. Allen.

531. PETER[7] PIERCE (*David[6], Daniel[5] Daniel[4], John[3], Thomas[2], Thomas[1]*), b. Aug. 12, 1777; m. Aug. 6, 1799, Elizabeth Blackwell, b. April 2, 1785, d. Dec. 6, 1838. He d. Dec. 18, 1858. Res. Moscow, Me.

Children :—

2111. i. ALVIN B., b. Aug. 13, 1800; m. Sally Baker.
2112. ii. DEBORAH, b. Jan. 17, 1802; m. William Robinson.
2113. iii. CHARLES, b. Nov. 25, 1804; m. Hannah R. Jones.
2114. iv. DORCAS, b. May 1, 1806; m. Ucebus Whitcomb.
2115. v. HEMAN, b. Dec. 15, 1808; m. Achsah Holman.
2116. vi. CONTENT B., b. Aug. 12, 1810; m. Ezekiel Pierce [2079].
2117. vii. SIMON, b. Feb. 10, 1813; m. Betsey Graves.
2118. viii. ADRA, b. Aug. 6, 1816; m. William Fentaman and Roger Smith Howes.

539. ZEBEDIAH[7] PIERCE (*Reuben[6], Daniel[5], Daniel[4], John[3], Thomas[2], Thomas[1]*), b. Dec. 23, 1784; m. Sept. 17, 1807, Phebe Tyler, b. Sept. 6, 1785, d. Jan. 28, 1829. He d. March 12, 1828. Res. Jaffrey, N. H.

Children :—

2119. i. REUBEN, b. Dec. 9, 1809; m. Cornelia Jewell.
2120. ii. REBECCA, b. March 31, 1811; m. Dec. 15, 1835, Elijah Smith, b. Jan. 9, 1812. Ch.: Rebecca, b. Aug. 31, 1840.
2121. iii. ALMIRA, b. June 3, 1823; m. Dec. 7, 1843, Benj. B. Davison, b. 1818, d. Nov. 16, 1861.

540. ABIJAH[7] PIERCE (*Reuben[6], Daniel[5], Daniel[4], John[3], Thomas[2], Thomas[1]*), b. Oct. 7, 1788; m. Sept. 20, 1817, Sally Maynard, b.

Oct. 4, 1798, d. Oct. 6, 1840 ; m. 2nd, June, 1842, Mrs. Elvira (Maynard) Jewett, b. July 23, 1806. He d. Oct. 23, 1870. Res. Jaffrey, N. H.

Abijah Pierce

Children :—

2123. i. ABIJAH A., b. March 9, 1818; m. Caroline Marole.
2124. ii. LEWIS L., b. March 28, 1820; m. Christina M. Billings.
2125. iii. REUBEN P., b. Feb. 19, 1823, d. Aug. 2, 1827.
2126. iv. SARAH, b. June 3, 1826, d. Dec. 7, 1829.
2127. v. MARY C., b. Sept., 1828; m. Aug. 29, 1846, George F. Follansbee, b. July 26, 1825, d. Sept. 27, 1858. Ch.: Ella M., b. July 3, 1847, m. Addison Peirce, Jr. (see Peirce Genealogy); Annie S., b. Jan. 29, 1850, m. John H. Steele; Geo. W., b. Nov. 19, 1853; Fred. A., b. July 20, 1855; Ida M., b. Nov. 10, 1857. They res. in Peterboro', N. H., Pierpont, O., and E. Jaffrey, N. H.
2128. vi. REUBEN P., b. June 4, 1831; m. Charlotte ——, and Susan Davis.

541. ASAPH[7] PIERCE (*Samuel[6], Daniel[5], Daniel[4], John[3], Thomas[2], Thomas[1]*), b. July 9, 1774; m. Feb. 10, 1797, Hannah Stickney, b. Dec. 24, 1773, d. Dec. 29, 1836. Asaph Pierce was a tall, energetic and powerful man, full of ready wit and a great lover of horses and cattle. It was his custom for many years to drive an ox team from Montpelier, Vt., to Boston and back twice a year, besides carrying on his farm, carrying down such produce as would sell well in Boston and returning with merchandise for the merchants in Montpelier. He d. Feb. 9, 1840. Res. Barre, Berlin and Moretown, Vt.

GRAVESTONE INSCRIPTION:
" Here lies beneath this grassy sod,
An aged friend and father dear,
On earth he strove to walk with God,
In Heaven, we trust, he's joined the choir."

Children :—

2129. i. PHEBE, b. Jan. 4, 1798; d. Dec. 8, 1813.
2130. ii. SAMUEL, b. Dec. 23, 1799; m. Matilda Bailey.
2131. iii. KIMBALL, b. Jan. 12, 1802; d. May 19, 1804.
2132. iv. LATTACE, b. Oct. 26, 1804; m. Girdon Gurley.
2133. v. ROXANNA, b. Jan. 20, 1806; m. David Dodge.
2134. vi. HANNAH, b. Dec. 13, 1809; m. Uriah Howe.
2135. vii. REBECCA, b. Nov. 13, 1812; m. Ira Cameron, and d. June 20, 1872.

542. SAMUEL[7] PIERCE, Jr. (*Samuel[6], Daniel[5], Daniel[4], John[3], Thomas[2], Thomas[1]*), b. May 9, 1776; m. Feb. 21, 1806, Hetty Brooks, b. Dec. 26, 1777, d. April 7, 1866. He d. in Jaffrey, N. H., April 8, 1858.

Saml Pierce

Children :—

2136. i. LUKE C., b. Jan. 11, 1807; m. May 5, 1836, Margaret Smith; m. 2nd, Dec. 16, 1851, Hester E. Lammons.

2137. i. LUTHER B., b. Jan. 11, 1807; m. Sept. 29, 1831, Mary A. Wilson.
2138. ii. SAMUEL W., b. Aug. 31, 1808; m. Apr. 27, 1837, Mary Dutton; m. 2nd, Sept. 28, 1847, Martha Plummer.
2139. iii. EURIDYCE, b. Oct. 11, 1810; d. Sept. 2, 1863.
2140. iv. CHARLES W., b. May 27, 1812; m. May 27, 1835, Abigail G. Going.
2141. v. ROSINA, b. Dec. 19, 1813; m. Edwin F. Wheeler, d. Aug. 6, 1863, in E. Jaffrey, N. H. Ch.: John F., b. Sept. 21, 1844; James A., b. Mar. 12, 1849, m. Maddelon P. Emery; Mary J., b. Sept. 27, 1853, m. Frank P. Wellman.
2142. vi. ASAPH, b. Nov. 17, 1815; d. Sept. 10, 1818.
2143. vii. HETTY, b. May 28, 1818; d. July 16, 1819.
2144. viii. NANCY, b. Jan. 2, 1820; m. Mar. 23, 1843, James H. Holt, b. Aug. 16, 1818. Res. in Milton, N. H. Ch.: Samuel P., b. Sept. 9, 1844; James A., b. May 22, 1847, m. Mary E. Dodge; Nathaniel K., b. Nov. 24, 1855; Charles D., b. Nov. 29, 1857; Emma R., b. Sept. 21, 1863.
2145. ix. ASAPH, b. Feb. 25, 1823; m. Feb. 7, 1846, Fanny D. Jewell. They res. in Hudson, Mich., and have no children.

544. CALEB[7] PIERCE (*Samuel[6], Daniel[5], Daniel[4], John[3], Thomas[2], Thomas[1]*), b. Jan. 30, 1781; m. Feb. 20, 1805, Lucy Gale, b. Dec. 19, 1785, d. May 10, 1873. He d. Aug. 30, 1850. They res. in Alstead, N. H., Lyme, N. Y., and Flint, Mich. Children :—

2146. i. FANNY, b. June 29, 1806.
2147. ii. LUCY, b. Apr. 23, 1808.
2148. iii. CALEB W., b. Feb. 28, 1810; m. Nov. 2, 1835, Mary M. Miles.
2149. iv. MARY W., b. Mar. 21, 1815; m. D. W. Montague.
2150. v. SILAS R., b. June 27, 1817; m. Apr. 24, 1844, Mary A. Wolverton; m. 2nd, Jan. 3, 1851, Caroline Crocker.
2151. vi. HARRIET, b. May 21, 1819; m. Aug. 26, 1873, Marion Williams, b. Sept. 31, 1809. They res. in Flint, Mich., and have had no issue.
2152. vii. CHARLES G., b. Dec. 19, 1822; d. 1824.

549. JOSEPH[7] PIERCE (*Samuel[6], Daniel[5], Daniel[4], John[3], Thomas[2], Thomas[1]*), b. Mar. 23, 1792; m. Dec. 18, 1821, Esther (Jaquith) Pierce, d. Mar. 29, 1866. He d. Apr. 20, 1860. They res. in Auburn, Mass. Children :—

2153. i. FREDERICK S., b. Sept. 10, 1822; m. Dec. 10, 1848, Martha Tolman; m. 2nd, Jan. 29, 1853, Mary A. Grant.
2154. ii. SARAH E., b. Mar. 12, 1824; m. Aug. 26, 1850, George Eddy. She d. Dec. 10, 1858. Ch.: Frank J., b. Jan. 25, 1854, d. Aug. 13, 1864. Res. Byron, Ill.
2155. iii. SAMUEL J., b. Dec. 1, 1825; d. Sept. 9, 1827.
2156. iv. SAMUEL S., b. July 14, 1828; m. April 9, 1851, Stella L. Clark.
2157. v. DIANTHA M., b. June 18, 1830; unm.
2158. vi. ESTHER L., b. July 29, 1832; m. Nov. 27, 1851, Hollis R. Clark, b. April 20, 1832. Ch.: Herbert W., b. Oct. 18, 1852, m. Ella A. Brown; Ida L., b. Nov. 20, 1854; Ella E., b. Sept. 29, 1860, d. July 13, 1862; Nettie L., b. Sept. 11, 1862; Minneola E., b. Sept. 22, 1865; Howard P., b. Dec. 22, 1867. Res. No. 105 Canal street, Providence, R. I.
2160. vii. SILAS, b. Nov. 27, 1835; d. Oct. 22, 1840.
2161. viii. EMILY, b. Sept. 19, 1837; d. Oct. 15, 1837.

551. JACOB[7] PIERCE, Jr. (*Jacob[6], Daniel[5], Daniel[4], John[3], Thomas[2], Thomas[1]*), b. Apr. 28, 1778; m. Nov. 27, 1800, Mary Sawtell, b. Aug. 27, 1778; d. Oct. 7, 1812; m. 2nd, Nov. 17, 1813,

16

Electa Evans, b. Feb. 20, 1815, d. Apr. 1, 1817 ; m. 3rd, Jan. 18, 1818, Betsey Pierce, b. Mar. 29, 1779 [543], d. Mar. 10, 1823 ; m. 4th, Mar. 23, 1823, Sally Garfield, b. 1782, d. Sept. 4, 1872. He d. May 18, 1828. They res. in Westminster, Mass. Children :—

2162. i. POLLY, b. Oct. 20, 1801 ; m. John Colburn, and d. Dec. 25, 1822, leaving two children.
2163. ii. TRIPHOSA, b. Aug. 7, 1803 ; m. Moses Templeton, and d. Nov. 12, 1852.
2164. iii. JACOB S., b. Mar. 22, 1805 ; d. Jan. 27, 1820.
2165. iv. ORVILLE W., b. Dec. 6, 1806 ; m. Amanda Templeton and Mrs. Lydia Flanders.
2166. v. DANIEL, b. Aug. 24, 1808 ; m. Oct. 18, 1836, Almira Black.
2167. vi. TRYPHENE, b. June 27, 1812 ; m. Sept. 25, 1834, Willard Booth, b. Aug. 3, 1811. Ch.: Alvin O., b. Aug. 15, 1836, d. Jan. 2, 1871 ; Orville W., b. June 3, 1838, m. Martha M. Corlet ; Mary A., b. July 4, 1841, m. A. Henshaw ; Lucy J., b. May 28, 1843, m. Chas. Pillsby ; Sarah E., b. Nov. 29, 1845, m. Albint Litchfield ; Hatty E. W., b. Nov. 9, 1847, m. Aaron B. Bixby ; Lydia M., b. June 13, 1851, m. John Spalding.
2168. vii. ELECTA, b. Feb. 20, 1815 ; d. Apr. 30, 1853.
2169. viii. JOSEPH, b. Apr. 30, 1816 ; d. June 12, 1817.
2170. ix. JACOB L., b. May 6, 1822 ; d. Oct. 11, 1823.
2171. x. SARAH R., b. Dec. 24, 1823 ; m. ——— ——— ; m. 2nd, Oct. 16, 1849, Leonard R. Peirce.
2172. xi. SAMUEL G., b. Jan. 13, 1825 ; m. Nov. 29, 1853, Almira E. Kimball.

552. BENJAMIN[7] PIERCE (*Jacob[6]*, *Daniel[5]*, *Daniel[4]*, *John[3]*, *Thomas[2]*, *Thomas[1]*), b. Feb. 2, 1782 ; m. Aug. 1, 1813, Sally Erskine, b. 1782, d. Dec. 27, 1851. He d. May 16, 1864. They res. in Pulaski, N. Y. Children :—

2173. i. BENJAMIN, Jr., b. Dec, 8, 1814 ; m. Feb. 13, 1838, Louisa A. R. Scott.
2174. ii. HILLMAN, b. June 9, 1815 ; m. Nov. 26, 1869, Sarah A. Wood.
2175. iii. MARSHAL, b. Nov. 30, 1819 ; m. May 15, 1849, Sarah A. Stowe.

553. REUBEN[7] PIERCE (*Jacob[6]*, *Daniel[5]*, *Daniel[4]*, *John[3]*, *Thomas[2]*, *Thomas[1]*), b. Sept. 4, 1787 ; m. Mar. 9, 1814, Lydia Holden, b. Nov. 19, 1785, d. Jan. 15, 1823 ; m. 2nd, May 21, 1823, Florilla Sweetland, b. Aug. 25, 1805. He res. in North Bloomfield, N. Y., and d. June 26, 1857.

Reuben Pierce engaged in the war of 1812 and was taken prisoner at Black Rock, near Buffalo, New York, and taken to jail at Montreal, Canada. He was finally liberated when peace was declared. He was a fine man and respected by all who surrounded him.

Children :—

2176. i. IMOGENE, b. Mar. 11, 1815 ; m. Apr. 5, 1835, David Shaddock, b. Sept. 5, 1809. Ch.: Albert, b. Sept. 12, 1836, m. Huldah Barnhart ; George G., b. July 19, 1838, m. Phebe Raynols ; Henry H.,

b. May 11, 1841; Reuben R., b. Nov. 29, 1843, m. Fanny Palmer; Benj. F., b. Mar. 26, 1845; Seranno B., b. Dec. 4, 1848, m. Alice Moses; Sarah J., b. Dec. 19, 1850, m. Nelson Cloon; Bruce H., b. Apr. 11, 1853; Mary L., b. Sept. 1, 1861. Res. W. Bloomfield, N. Y.

2177. i. BENJAMIN W., b. May 31, 1825; m. Oct. 21, 1847, Salina Wiggins.
2178. ii. AMOS E., b. Apr. 12, 1827; m. Jan. 7, 1851, Emily Foote, b. Jan. 10, 1828. They res. at No. 1521 N. Eleventh street, St. Louis, Mo., and have no children.
2179. iii. MARCIA L., b. Aug. 9, 1829; m. June 13, 1855, A. Jay Carmichael, b. July 22, 1823. Ch.: Asahel A., b. June 12, 1856, d. Apr. 17, 1857; John J., b. Aug. 21, 1858; Amos O., b. May 23, 1861; William B., b. Apr. 15, 1864. Res. N. Weston, N. Y.
2180. iv. SIVILLA L., b. Aug. 11, 1831; m. Apr. 14, 1857, Henry H. Clark, b. June 10, 1834, d. Jan. 29, 1865. She d. July 12, 1862, and he m. Mar. 24, 1863, Mary A. Pierce, his sister-in-law. He had no children.
2182. v. DANIEL K., b. Aug. 2, 1833; d. July 2, 1836.
2183. vi. ROSANNA O., b. Oct. 17, 1835; m. Jan. 13, 1861, William W. St. John, b. May 9, 1828. Ch.: Frank N., b. Nov. 2, 1865; Fred. Y., b. Jan. 10, 1871. Res. Bunceton, Mo.
2184. vii. MARY A., b. Mar. 2, 1838; m. Henry H. Clark [see iv.]; m. 2nd, Apr. 12, 1866, Columbus White, b. June 12, 1826. Ch.: Rosa M., b. Feb. 15, 1867; Frank A., b. Oct. 7, 1870; Grace E., b. Oct. 12, 1871; Dean S., b. Oct 7, 1873, d. Mar. 15, 1877; Dickie, b. Apr. 28, 1875, d. Apr. 10, 1876.
2185. viii. FRANKLIN K., b. Nov. 11, 1841; m. Mar. 16, 1871, Mrs. Sarah Raines.
2186. ix. FLORA L., b. Apr. 27, 1844; m. Jan. 28, 1861, Eli H. Babcock, b. Oct. 15, 1838. Ch.: John R., b. June 15, 1862; Amos A., b. Oct. 8, 1866; Marion F., b. Aug. 4, 1869; Daisy A., b. Nov. 30, 1871. Res. Canandaigua, N. Y.
2187. x. KATE R., b. Aug 8, 1846; unm.; N. Bloomfield, N. Y.
2188. xi. CHARLES R., b. May 17, 1849; m. Apr. 24, 1869, Mary A. Woodward.

554. MOSES[7] PIERCE (*Jacob[6]*, *Daniel[5]*, *Daniel[4]*, *John[3]*, *Thomas[2]*, *Thomas[1]*), b. June 22, 1793; m. Betsey Jewett. Res. Oshkosh, Wis. Children :—

2189. i. LUCY; m. Albert Wilson. Res. Baraboo, Sauk Co., Wis.
2190. ii. ELVIRA, b. Jan. 26, 1829.

562. JOSIAH[7] PIERCE (*Jacob[6]*, *Daniel[5]*, *Daniel[4]*, *John[3]*, *Thomas[2]*, *Thomas[1]*), b. June 19, 1798; m. Feb. 9, 1824, Pauline Erskine, b. Dec. 25, 1801. They res. in Mexico, N. Y.

Children :—

2191. i. ORILLA R., b. Jan. 29, 1825.
2192. ii. S. MARIA, b. Apr. 13, 1826; m. Oct. 5, 1847, Stephen F. Emery, b. June 25, 1823. They res. in Mexico, N. Y., and have no children.
2193. iii. AUGUSTA J., b. Nov. 29, 1828; m. Dec. 25, 1850, Louisa A. Evarts.

565. JOHN[7] PIERCE (*John*[6], *John*[5], *Daniel*[4], *John*[3], *Thomas*[2], *Thomas*[1]), b. Oct. 13, 1803 ; m. Dec. 8, 1828, Sarah Parker, b. Jan. 4, 1803, d. Jan. 1, 1845 ; m. 2nd, Nov. 3, 1845, Louisa Percy, b. June 12, 1810. Res. Boston.

Children :—

2194. i.   SARAH E., b. Nov. 18, 1829 ; m. H. A. Stone.
2195. ii.   JOHN, b. Dec. 18, 1831 ; d. Dec. 24, 1836.
2196. iii. GEORGE, b. Aug. 27, 1833 ; d. Oct. 10, 1835.
2197. iv.   FRANCES M., b. Nov. 4, 1834 ; m. —— Thompson.
2198. v.   HARRIET, b. Aug. 4, 1836 ; d. Aug. 29, 1836.
2199. vi.   LOUISA T., b. July 26, 1837 ; m. A. Fawcett.
2200. vii. JOHN, b. Nov. 18, 1839.
2201. viii. ELLEN, b. Aug. 4, 1842 ; m. H. E. Adams.
2202. ix.   EMILY, b. Nov. 16, 1843 ; m. Chales Tarr and J. B. Clark.

566. STILLMAN[7] PIERCE (*John*[6], *John*[5], *Daniel*[4], *John*[3], *Thomas*[2], *Thomas*[1]), b. April 23, 1809 ; m. Sarah French. He d. 1872. Res. Cambridge. Children :—

2203. i.   WILLIAM ; m. —— ——.
2204. ii. ANNIE ; m. E. Holt.

567. JOHN[7] PIERCE (*Calvin*[6], *John*[5], *Daniel*[4], *John*[3], *Thomas*[2], *Thomas*[1]), b. March 23, 1786 ; m. July 1, 1814, Sally Brigham, b. Feb. 2, 1791, d. Feb. 28, 1873. He d. April 28, 1853. Res. Bolton. Children :—

2205. i.   SUSAN M., b. Nov. 30, 1815 ; m. Levi Johnson.
2206. ii.   HARRIET E., b. Nov. 19, 1817 ; d. June 2, 1821.
2207. iii. JOHN E., b. Aug. 22, 1819 ; m. three times.
2208. iv.   ALBERT, b. May 17, 1821 ; m. Abigail Moody.
2209. v.   ADDISON B., b. May 16, 1826.

577. JOHN[7] PIERCE (*Ebenezer*[6], *Ebenezer*[5], *Ebenezer*[4], *John*[3], *Thomas*[2], *Thomas*[1]), b. Aug. 21, 1774 ; m. April, 1796, Sarah Frissell, b. May 6, 1778, d. May 15, 1858. He d. in Peru, Mass., Sept. 14, 1820.

Children :—

2210. i.   JOHN, b. June 12, 1797 ; m. Laura Barrett.
2211. ii.   SALLY, b. May 4, 1799 ; d. May 17, 1857.
2212. iii. LYDIA, b. Feb. 2, 1801 ; m. Royal Cushing. Ch. : Mary, m. Geo. Berkus ; Sarah, b. 1844, d. Nov. 6, 1862.
2213. iv.   ERASTUS, b. Aug. 17, 1802 ; d. Nov. 19, 1803.
2214. v.   ERASTUS, b. Jan. 8, 1805 ; m. Apr. 3, 1833, Sophia Morgan.
2215. vi.   MARSHALL, b. Mar. 1, 1807 ; m. Mary Francis.

2216. vii. ASHLEY, b. Jan. 6, 1810; m. Mary McGee.
2217. viii. JUDITH, b. Oct. 29, 1814; d. Apr. 30, 1872.
2218. ix. EUNICE, b. Jan. 9, 1812; d. May 7, 1812.
2219. x. LEWIS, } twins, b. July 14, 1817; { m. Mary Aiken.
2220. xi. LUCIUS, } twins, b. July 14, 1817; { m. Matilda Spencer.
2221. xii. EUNICE, b. Apr. 18, 1819; m. Milton Nash, by whom she had no children; d. Apr. 13, 1852.

581. ASA[7] PIERCE (*Ebenezer*[6], *Ebenezer*[5], *Ebenezer*[4], *John*[3], *Thomas*[2], *Thomas*[1]), b. Mar. 25, 1779; m. Feb. 25, 1807, Caroline Worthington, b. 1779, d. July 23, 1862. He d. Sept. 1, 1819, in Peru. Children:—

2222. i. MARTHA C., b. Jan. 30, 1809; m. Mar. 12, 1834, Fred. Curtis. Ch.: Worthington, b. Dec. 12, 1835; Sarah, b. Mar. 2, 1837; Clinton, b. Dec. 17, 1838; Arthur, b. Apr. 11, 1841; Frank, b. May 2, 1850.
2223. ii. WARREN, b. Nov. 25, 1811; m. Clemence Morgan and Abigail Wright.
2224. iii. JULIET, b. Mar. 2, 1813; d. May 13, 1817.
2225. iv. HARRIET, b. Feb. 22, 1815; m. Levi Phillips. No issue.
2226. v. ELBRIDGE G., b. Aug. 26, 1816; m. Electa Rockwell.
2227. vi. ASA C., } twins, b. July 17, 1819; { m. Oct. 24, 1855, Mary Wilson.
2228. vii. CAROLINE, } twins, b. July 17, 1819; { d. Nov. 10, 1819.
2229. viii. FRANK, b. May 15, 1817; d. Feb. 11, 1819.

585. EBENEZER[7] PIERCE, Jr. (*Ebenezer*[6], *Ebenezer*[5], *Ebenezer*[4], *John*[3], *Thomas*[2], *Thomas*[1]), b. Mar. 28, 1788; m. May 22, 1816, Electa Phillips, b. Apr. 16, 1794, d. May 15, 1872. He d. July 15, 1865, in Peru, Mass.

Ebenezer Peirce

Children:—

2230. i. FIDELIA, b. June 16, 1817; m. May 5, 1840, Lyman Granger, b. Sept. 19, 1817. Ch.: Chole A., b. Aug. 27, 1842, m. Davis Bartlett; Helen E., b. Mar. 27, 1844, d. June 1, 1868; Idella E., b. June 16, 1846, d. Mar. 3, 1868.
2231. ii. AARON, b. June 6, 1819; m. Martha Thompson.
2232. iii. CHOLE, b. July 29, 1822; d. Feb. 12, 1838.
2233. iv. EUNICE, b. Apr. 15, 1827; m. Samuel Watkins.
2234. v. MARTIN, b. Mar. 21, 1833; m. Mar. 4, 1853, Malvina M. Thompson.

586. ENOCH[7] PIERCE (*Ebenezer*[6], *Ebenezer*[5], *Ebenezer*[4], *John*[3], *Thomas*[2], *Thomas*[1]), b. Apr. 17, 1791; m. May 28, 1821, Mary Moseley; d. Oct. 31, 1856, in Pittsfield. Children:—

2235. i. ARTHUR G., b. Feb. 19, 1822; m. Mar. 17, 1853, Dolly Thompson.
2236. ii. DAVID S., b. Aug. 22, 1825; m. Aug. 9, 1853, Charlotte Todd.
2237. iii. DWIGHT G., b. Sept. 17, 1831; d. Nov. 28, 1837.
2238. iv. MARY, b. Aug. 28, 1834; d. Sept. 5, 1861.

590. LUTHER[7] PIERCE (*John*[6], *Ebenezer*[5], *Ebenezer*[4], *John*[3], *Thomas*[2], *Thomas*[1]), b. Oct. 14, 1781; m. March 23, 1803, Clarissa

Reed, b. Mar. 12, 1780, d. July 9, 1824 ; m. 2nd, May 31, 1825, Aurilla Terry, b. May 6, 1786, d. Sept. 12, 1866. He d. Nov. 14, 1861. Res. Grafton, Mass., and Thompsonville, Conn.

Children :—

2239. i.   LUTHER, b. June 23, 1804; m. Mary A. Ashley.
2240. ii.   CLARISSA R., b. Dec. 17, 1805; m. 1844, Wm. Wood. Res. Warren.
2241. iii. LUCY C., b. Aug. 19, 1807; d. Aug. 18, 1835.
2242. iv. JOHN H., b. May 18, 1809; m. March 6, 1831.
2243. v.   CHARLOTTE R., b. July 7, 1811; m. Stephen Sibley. Res. Auburn.
2244. vi. MARTHA R., b. May 18, 1813; m. Rev. S. P. Robbins, and d. 1841.
2245. vii. PAULINE, b. June 15, 1812; m. Isaac B. Lee. Res. Longmeadow.
2246. viii. NEHEMIAH P., b. Aug. 28, 1817; m. Frances A. Ely.
2247. ix. FRANCIS R., b. Oct. 22, 1821; m. Cynthia E. Hitchcock and Marietta E. Tuttle.
2248. x.   EBENEZER, b. March 24, 1826; m. Charlotte Kimball.

591. CALVIN[7] PIERCE (*John*[6], *Ebenezer*[5], *Ebenezer*[4], *John*[3], *Thomas*[2], *Thomas*[1]), b. Dec. 12, 1784 ; m. Sept. 28, 1808, Sophronia Colton, b. Oct. 14, 1786, d. Feb. 19, 1866. He d. June 23, 1812. Res. Millbury, Mass.

Children :—

2249. i. SOPHRONIA, b. Sept. 18, 1809; d. April 27, 1826.
2250. ii. CALVIN W., b. May 5, 1811; m. Catherine Lathrop.

595. HERVEY[7] PIERCE (*John*[6], *Ebenezer*[5], *Ebenezer*[4], *John*[3], *Thomas*[2], *Thomas*[1]), b. March 26, 1797 ; m. July 15, 1819, Linia Stone, b. Aug., 1796, d. April 23, 1870. He d. April 16, 1851. Res. Millbury, Mass.

Children :—

2251. i. ANDREAS W., b. April 29, 1820; m. Mary Putnam.
2252. ii. SARAH S., b. March 23, 1824; m. Robert Jones.

605. Dea. NATHAN[7] PIERCE (*David*[6], *Ebenezer*[5], *Ebenezer*[4], *John*[3], *Thomas*[2], *Thomas*[1]), b. Nov. 24, 1784 ; m. Oct. 8, 1806, Sally Richmond, b. Oct. 23, 1781, d. Sept. 16, 1854. He d. Oct. 23, 1849. Res.

Barnard, Brandon, Vt., and Whitehall, N. Y. Dea. Pierce was a native of Southborough, Mass. At the age of 17 he united with the Congregational Church at Barnard, Vt. About 40 years before he died, he removed to Brandon, Vt., where he was soon after elected a deacon. For more than twenty-five years, he was an elder in the Presbyterian Church in Whitehall. His singular consistency of christian character commanded the respect of all. The following testimonial of his worth was placed on the records of the church of which he was the oldest member : " In recording the death of Dea. Nathan Pierce, the senior member of this body, this session would express their sincere regards for the integrity and christian principle which marked his character, as also the high estimation in which they held his discreet counsels and earnest prayers. While they mourn their own loss in his removal as well as that of his family, the church and the community of which he was a member, they record their humble gratitude for the clear evidence he left that for him to die was gain. When asked in his last hours if he had any wish to express, he answered, 'only that the name of the Lord be glorified.'"

Children :—

2253. i. NELSON, b. Aug. 24, 1807; d. May 30, 1809.
2254. ii. EMILY, b. April 21, 1809; d. June 27, 1812.
2255. iii. PERSIS, b. Feb. 27, 1812; m. J. J. Howard.
2256. iv. EDMOND D., b. April 24, 1813; d. July 9, 1814.
2257. v. WELLINGTON B., b. July 6, 1815; d. Aug. 26, 1816.
2258. vi. SARAH A., b. Aug. 24, 1820; m. John D. Hunt.

606. Judge DAVID[7] PIERCE (*David*[6], *Ebenezer*[5], *Ebenezer*[4], *John*[3], *Thomas*[2], *Thomas*[1]), b. March 26, 1786; m. Oct. 5, 1819, Ruth Downer, b. Jan. 8, 1797, d. June 23, 1833; m. 2nd, Dec. 17, 1834, Mary S. Gardner, b. Jan. 11, 1804, d. May 24, 1871. He d. Aug. 17, 1872. Res. Woodstock, Vt. David Pierce was born in Southboro', Mass. He graduated at Dartmouth College in 1811. He taught the Royalton, Vt., Academy from 1811 to 1812. Read law with Hon. Charles Marsh (D. C. 1786), at Woodstock, Vt. Began practice there in 1816. After some years, he left the profession and was devoted to scientific pursuits. Had a part in the construction of the " Horizontal and Perpendicular machine." Was chosen by the Vermont Legislature Auditor of State Accounts in 1823 and was re-elected annually for twenty-three years. Was Judge of the Windsor County Court from 1846 to 1856. Judge Pierce published much on financial concerns and against the doctrine of secession by South Carolina in 1833.

Children :—

2259. i. JOHN D., b. Aug. 1, 1820; d. Aug. 29, 1820.
2260. ii. JASON B., b. Dec. 13, 1821; m. Harriet Lemmix.
2261. iii. MAEIA D., b. June 21, 1824; m. H. B. White.

607. Dr. AARON[7] PIERCE (*David*[6], *Ebenezer*[5], *Ebenezer*[4], *John*[3], *Thomas*[2], *Thomas*[1]), b. Nov. 23, 1787 ; m. Dec. 28, 1819, Sarah Hough, b. March 21, 1797, d. Oct. 3, 1842 ; m. 2nd, July 9, 1844. Mary Billings, b. Feb. 8, 1799, d. Feb. 13, 1879. He d. June 1, 1860, Res. Barton, Vt.

SKETCH OF DR. AARON PIERCE.

BY MRS. J. K. COLBY.

Dr. Aaron Pierce was the son of Deacon David and Sally Pierce, of Barnard, Vt. He was born Nov. 23, 1787. He died June 1, 1860, aged 72 years. "His father's family embraced eleven children. It was a household penetrated with much of the Puritan spirit." If there was sometimes an apparent want of gentleness in it, there was always evidence of strong christian love and principle. The support of such a large family from a farm of little natural fertility, required hard work and strict economy. The life which was the result of these conditions, gave to the family a large share of that robustness which has distinguished the New England character.

Aaron, the third son in this family, labored on the farm until he was 22 years of age. He then fitted for college intending to enter at Middlebury, Vt., and after completing his undergraduate course to study for the ministry. Alarming symptoms of lung disease, however, compelled a change in his cherished plan for life, and led him to begin the study of medicine. After studying for a time with a physician of experience in his native town he attended lectures at the Dartmouth Medical School, at Hanover, N. H., but, like many, at that time, did not include surgery in his course, and began the practice of his profession at Cornish, N. H.

In this place, Dec. 29, 1819, he was united in marriage to Sarah Hough, daughter of Thomas Hough and Sarah Kimball, of Lebanon, N. H., a woman of most lovely christian character. She was born at Lebanon, N. H., March 21, 1797, and died at Barton, Vt., Oct. 3, 1842. [For genealogy of Houghs, see history of New London, Conn., by E. M. Caulkins]. To them were given ten children.

On the 9th of July, 1844, Dr. Pierce was united in marriage to Mary Billing, who was born at Lebanon, N. H., Feb. 8, 1799, and died at Barton, Vt., Feb. 13, 1879.

Although he remained in Cornish only a few years—a more lucrative practice being offered to him in Weathersfield, Vt., he was long remembered there with respect and affection. After practising eleven years in Weathersfield, he removed to Irasburgh, Vt. From this place he removed in 1842 to Barton, Vt., where, for a time, he united to some extent the practice of both towns—Irasburgh and Barton.

His personal appearance commanded respect. He was a little more than six feet in height and well proportioned. He was always dignified in his bearing. His convictions were strong, and, if he thought occasion required it, they were apt to be expressed with far more regard for the truth than for the opinion of others. He was sometimes abrupt to a degree approaching harshness. An anecdote illustrating this characteristic is related of him soon after he went to Irasburgh. A woman in a neighboring town who had an idiotic child, hearing that a physician of skill and experience had come to reside near her, summoned Dr. Pierce. He looked at the child, examined it for a few minutes, but remained silent. The mother then asked, "Can you do anything for my child?" "Nothing, Madam, your child is a fool!" was the reply.

To his family, though sometimes stern in discipline, he was affectionate and confiding.

"In his profession, he was skilful and successful. His counsel was often sought and highly valued. A physician who knew him well, says of him, that his information was extensive, that he ranked among the first physicians in the region where he resided and was second to none. His information was well digested into serviceable knowledge," which he was quick to apply as occasion offered. He was a diligent student of medical books, and was a regular subscriber to the most approved medical journals. The extreme accuracy of his information never permitted him to pass unnoticed a mistake even in pronunciation or quotation, and if made by one of his family, it never failed to receive correction even during his last sickness. He was enthusiastically fond of his profession, still he never lost his love for that of his first choice. More than thirty sermons were found among his papers after his death. These were written during his residence in Irasburgh, and most, if not all, were read by him on the Sabbath, at intervals, when the church was without a pastor. Neither did he lose his love for the employment of his boyhood—farming. In every place where he resided after leaving Cornish, he owned some land, and enjoyed much the care of its cultivation. Though diligent in his profession, he left only a small property. This was not due to any want of accuracy in book-keeping, neither to failure in collecting his bills, nor in the practice of strict economy ; but to the *small* fees which the time and region where he practised allowed, and the still smaller returns in *cash*.

In politics, Dr. Pierce was a decided Whig. Earnestly opposing Jackson's Bank and Indian policy, and predicting, at an early period, civil war as the result of the slavery conflict, he found himself in hearty sympathy with the anti-slavery party. Still he never took an active, public part in relation to any of these questions. He had no political ambition to gratify. He held no office in state or church. His profession was his life work.

In religion, Dr. Pierce was an earnest christian. A member of the Congregational Church, he labored to advance its interests wherever he lived, and to the utmost of his ability he aided the spread of the gospel. Whenever it was possible, he was present at the services of the sanctuary, leading for many years the choir of singers with his own rich tenor voice. In the social meeting, he was a helper. "His christian experience was mature, founded on a sound basis of Biblical knowledge." He loved the Bible, and his "Scott" bears the marks of diligent use.

17

He also loved the Calvinistic doctrines, but he did not teach them at second hand. He could state and defend them ably from the Bible. His reading was largely of a religious character, well chosen, digested and made his own. His thoughts on moral and religious subjects and on other topics which interested him, were well defined and clearly expressed, both in writing and conversation. "His mind was of a high order."

Toward the close of his life he suffered several years from abnormal action of the heart, and, at times, from inflammation of the kidneys. A cold, increasing the trouble of the heart, occasioned his death.

A true child of the Puritans, he gave to his generation the service of a good citizen, a trusted physician and a spiritually minded man.

Aaron Pein

Children :—

2262. i.   SARAH A., b. Nov. 8, 1820; d. July 10, 1822.
2263. ii.   SARAH A., b. May 6, 1822; m. James K. Colby. Ch. : Lucy J. ; James F. ; Edward A., Principal of St. Johnsbury Academy.
2264. iii. EMELINE K., b. July 23, 1824; m. A. K. Gray and M. Pearson.
2265. iv.   EDWARD M., b. March 29, 1826; d. May 8, 1826.
2266. v.   EDWARD P., b. Aug. 13, 1827; d. June 26, 1839.
2267. vi.   HENRY M., b. July 14, 1829; d. July 18, 1830.
2268. vii. ELLEN M., b. March 15, 1832; missionary at Aintab, Turkey.
2269. viii. HENRY H., b. April 6, 1836; m. Sarah Kirkland.
2270. ix.   EDWARD G., b. Sept. 8, 1839; d. June 13, 1860.

611. Dea. DANA[7] PIERCE (*David[6], Ebenezer[5], Ebenezer[4], John[3], Thomas[2], Thomas[1]*), b. Sept. 7, 1795; m. June 10, 1819, Diademia Paul, b. Dec. 5, 1798, d. Oct. 4, 1873. He d. March 23, 1870. Res. Woodstock, Vt.

Died at his residence in Woodstock, Vt., Monday evening, the 23rd instant, Dea. Dana Pierce, at the age of seventy-four.

Dana Pierce was born in Lancaster, Mass., the 7th of September, 1795. In the winter of 1796-97, his parents removed to Barnard, Vt., and there settled. Dana Pierce was brought up in that town and spent there nearly thirty-nine years of his life. On the 10th of June, 1819, he married Diademia Paul. He united with the Congregational Church in Barnard, in the autumn of 1822, and was elected a deacon in that church in June, 1825. In April, 1835, he removed to Woodstock and settled on the farm now owned by Henry C. Johnson. On the 2nd of July, 1841, he was chosen a deacon in the Congregational Church in this place, which office he actively filled to the very close of his life. Deacon Pierce was a model of an industrious farmer, faithful always to his vocation, believing in its dignity, and drawing his inspiration as well as the means of subsistence from the soil he cultivated. To whatever work was to be done he applied himself vigorously, and never spared his strength in the hours of toil. Believing that every good thing is the gift of Divine Providence he realized as truth that children are an heritage of the Lord, and that happy is the man who has filled his quiver with them ; having himself in the course of a long life met the smiles of numerous offspring of his own, most of whom are still living to revere his memory. Though Deacon Pierce shared in the frailties that are the common lot of humanity, you could not but feel that there was an odor of sanctity about him to give the world assurance of the honesty of his professions. Here was no vain show of religion, but the substance, proven in the sincere piety that adorned his whole life. A little stern, perhaps, he stood in the eye of the beholder a rugged oak, breasting the storms of life, but with branches ever raised Heavenward as if reaching after the serene atmosphere above. Firm in his faith, yet without enthusiasm, he was possessed with a deep settled conviction that it was his duty and his special privilege to live for the glory of God. His humanity, however, was such as to persuade him that at best he imperfectly fulfilled his calling. We honor him for his integrity. We thank him for his example, and we especially thank him for proving anew that a New England deacon is not necessarily the embodiment of cant and hypocrisy, and we deem the church happy which has been permitted to count such a man among its members.— [*Woodstock Paper.*

Children :—

2271.	i.	NELSON M., b. May 18, 1820; m. Cynthia A. Brown.
2272.	ii.	DELIA M., b. Feb. 11, 1822; m. Dec. 28, 1841, Ira Atwood, and d. Jan. 24, 1871.
2273.	iii.	WILLIAM D., b. June 9, 1824; m. Sophronia E. Sperry.
2274.	iv.	EDWIN, b. June 25, 1826; m. three times.
2275.	v.	RODNEY C., b. May 24, 1828; m. Mary R. Severance.
2276.	vi.	SARAH A., }twins, b. Apr. 14, 1830; { m. July 11, 1865, George Fisher.
2277.	vii.	JANE I., } { d. March 10, 1832.
2278.	viii.	SAMUEL N., b. May 6, 1832; m. Margaret N. Peirce. [See Peirce Gen., page 202.]
2279.	ix.	LUCIAN F.; }twins, b. Apr. 7, 1834; { m. Susan Heizer.
2280.	x.	LUCIUS, } { d. Oct. 6, 1834.
2281.	xi.	PAYSON A., b. Feb. 26, 1836; m. Frances M. Swain.
2282.	xii.	HARRIET E., b. April 28, 1838; d. April 2, 1839.
2283.	xiii.	CHARLES, b. Jan. 22, 1840; d. Sept. 7, 1862.
2284.	xiv.	WORTHINGTON W., b. June 1, 1843; m. M. J. Bennett.
2285.	xv.	DAVID G., b. Jan. 6, 1845; d. Jan. 30, 1847.

612. EDMUND[7] PIERCE (*David[6], Ebenezer[5], Ebenezer[4], John[3], Thomas[2], Thomas[1]*), b. Aug. 19, 1797 ; m. Oct. 17, 1822, Louisa Stane, d. Jan, 22, 1876. He d. June 10, 1877. Res. Barnard, Vt., and Manhattan, Kansas.

Children :—

2286.	i.	CATHERINE F., b. Jan. 18, 1825; m. R. J. Harper.

2287. ii. HENRY B., b. April 14, 1827; m. Laura A. Hoyt.
2288. iii. CLAUDIUS B., b. April 10, 1829; m. Mary E. Fairchild.
2289. iv. EDWARD E., b. Jan. 17, 1831, d. July 24, 1854.
2290. v.   ELLEN E., b. April 22, 1833; m. Geo. L. Coleman.
2291. vi. LYMAN B., b. Jan. 14, 1835; m. ———— ————.

620. Dr. LEONARD[7] PIERCE (*Aaron*[6], *Ebenezer*[5], *Ebenezer*[4], *John*[3], *Thomas*[2], *Thomas*[1]), b. Jan. 11, 1798; m. Nov. 15, 1831, Mary Le-Baron, daughter of Capt. Israel Putnam, of Sutton, d. Nov. 7, 1843.
Dr. Leonard Pierce studied medicine, practised successfully for a time in Sutton; then removed to Canton, Ill.; where he died Aug. 30, 1843.

Children :—

2292. i. MARY F., b. May 19, 1834; unm.; res. Sutton.
2293. ii. ELLEN D., b. Aug. 22, 1836; m. Nov. 16, 1864, Marius Hovey.
          Ch.: John William, b. Aug. 24, 1865; Marius, Jr., b. June 15, 1875. He res. in Sutton and is one of its most prominent men; has been Representative.

621. AARON[7] PIERCE, Jr. (*Aaron*[6], *Ebenezer*[5], *Ebenezer*[4], *John*[3], *Thomas*[2], *Thomas*[1]), b. Aug. 8, 1802; m. Feb. 14, 1839, Sophronia Scott, b. June 21, 1814. He d. Sept. 27, 1878. Res. Millbury, Mass.

Children :—

2294. i.   HANNAH, b. Aug. 3, 1845; d. Jan., 1854.
2295. ii. FLORELLA, b. July 15, 1849; m. William Robinson.
2296. iii. JOSEPH; m. Lucia Kingman.

623. THOMAS S.[7] PIERCE (*Joshua*[6], *Joshua*[5], *Ebenezer*[4], *John*[3], *Thomas*[2], *Thomas*[1]), b. Sept. 13, 1767; m. Aug. 2, 1791, Dolly Boutelle. Res. Leominster, Mass. Children :—

2297. i.   DOLLY, b. Dec. 26, 1792; d. Sept. 28, 1809.
2298. ii.   LYDIA, b. Aug. 7, 1794; d. Sept. 20, 1857.
2299. iii. AUGUSTUS, b. Dec. 29, 1795; m. Eliza Whitney.
2300. iv.   ————, b. Sept. 1, 1797; d. Sept. 1, 1797.
2301. v.   JONAS, b. Sept. 1, 1798; d. Sept. 1, 1799.
2302. vi.   THOMAS, b. Aug. 10, 1800; d. May 28, 1821.
2303. vii. HOUGHTON, b. April 20, 1802; m. Mira Snow.
2304. viii. HENRY, b. July 2, 1804.
2305. ix.   DORINDA, b. Feb. 23, 1806; d. May 28, 1828.
2306. x.   ORRISSE, b. Jan. 17, 1808; m. Smith Colburn.
2307. xi.   DOROTHY, b. Dec. 25, 1810; m. John Brigham.
2308. xii. ALMIRA, b. Feb. 23, 1813; m. Horace Cook.

627. ASA[7] PIERCE (*Joshua*[6], *Joshua*[5], *Ebenezer*[4], *John*[3], *Thomas*[2], *Thomas*[1]), b. Aug. 5, 1775; m. Dec. 2, 1800, Deborah Joslin, b. Aug.

21, 1779, d. Dec. 8, 1818; m. 2nd, Nov. 18, 1821, Martha (Joslin) Richardson, b. Jan. 28, 1790, d. Dec. 15, 1866. He d. Nov. 13, 1842. Res. Leominster, Mass.   Children :—

2309. i.   SYLVESTER, b. Jan. 24, 1802; m. Abigail Taylor.
2310. ii.   ASA, b. Feb. 14, 1803; res. Leominster.
2311. iii. JOSEPH, b. Dec. 10, 1804; m. Roxanna Bailey and Susan A. W. Goodrich.
2312. iv.   DEBORAH, b. April 7, 1808; d. April 2, 1824.
2313. v.   CATHERINE, b. June 3, 1811; m. Israel T. Nichols.
2314. vi.   FRANKLIN, b. Sept. 10, 1814; res. Holliston.
2315. vii. MARY F., b. Apr. 18, 1817; m. Thomas Harris.
2316. viii. MIRA,   } twins, b. Mar. 29, 1823; { d. April 28, 1828.
2317. ix.   MARTHA,   }   { m. Leander Archibald.
2318. x.   WILLIAM D., b. Jan. 31, 1825; m. Maria Whitney.
2319. xi.   JAMES,   } twins, b. Oct. 14, 1826; { d. Dec. 7, 1831.
2320. xii. JANE A.,   }   { m. Samuel Putnam.
2321. xiii. RUFUS E., b. Jan. 13, 1830; d. July 2, 1864.
2322. xiv. MIRA E., b. Oct. 2, 1833; res. Leominster.

629. DAVID[7] PIERCE (*Joshua[6]*, *Joshua[5]*, *Ebenezer[4]*, *John[3]*, *Thomas[2]*, *Thomas[1]*,) b. July 17, 1781; m. ——— ———. Children :—

2323. i.   VARNUM.
2324. ii.   JAMES.
2325. iii. OLIVER.

633. JONATHAN[7] PIERCE (*Jonathan[6]*, *Joshua[5]*, *Ebenezer[4]*, *John[3]*, *Thomas[2]*, *Thomas[1]*), b. Oct. 18, 1809; m. Oct. 29, 1835, Elizabeth B. Leavitt, b. Dec. 25, 1817, d. Aug. 6, 1867. Res. Chelsea, Mass.

Children :—

2326. i.   JONATHAN, b. Aug. 26, 1836; m. Hannah Warren.
2327. ii.   ABBY F., b. Sept. 27, 1838; m. Gen. Augustus P. Martin.
2328. iii. WILLIAM H., b. April 28, 1841; m. Sarah A. Moore.
2329. iv.   JOSHUA F., b. Jan. 7, 1848; d. July 28, 1848.
2330. v.   ELIZABETH L., b. Oct. 22, 1849; m. James A. Hammond.

637. Judge JOSIAH[7] PIERCE (*Josiah[6]*, *Josiah[5]*, *Josiah[4]*, *John[3]*, *Thomas[2]*, *Thomas[1]*), b. Aug. 15, 1792; m. Sept. 13, 1825, Eveline Lewis, b. Nov. 13, 1795, d. Oct. 5, 1870. He d. June 25, 1866. Res. Gorham, Me.

Hon. Josiah Pierce, late of Gorham, Maine, eldest son of Josiah and Phœbe (Thompson) Pierce, was born in Baldwin, Maine, August 15, 1792, and died in Gorham, June 25, 1866. After preparatory studies, chiefly at Bridgeton Academy, he was matriculated at Bowdoin College in the class which graduated in 1818, when he received his degree of A. B., with the honor of one of the first parts at Commencement, and an election to the Phi Beta Kappa Society. He studied law in the office of Hon. Stephen Longfellow, of Portland, Maine; was admitted to the Bar of Cumberland County, in 1821; in which year he also received the degree of A. M. from Bowdoin College, and opened his office for the practice of his profession in Gorham, where he continued to reside till his death. On the 20th of September, 1825, he married Eveline, daughter of Major Archelaus Lewis (an officer of the Revolution), and his second wife Elizabeth (Brown). Mrs. Eveline Pierce was born Nov. 13, 1795, and died Oct. 5, 1870. They had four sons and three daughters, of whom three sons and two daughters were living in 1881.

Mr. Pierce became early in life a member of the Baptist (Calvinist) church, and remained a faithful, devout, charitable, practical Christian, a diligent student and teacher of the Bible. He was a prominent member of the Democratic party, and as such represented his town in the State Legislature, in 1832 and 1833, and his county in the Senate from 1833 to 1836, being President of the Senate in 1835 and 1836. After this date he returned to a more close practice of his profession, which was at that period very considerable, and he was much esteemed as an upright, careful and able lawyer. Several young men read law in his office, most of whom attained distinction in their profession afterwards, especially the Hon. S. S. Prentiss of Mississippi.

Mr. Pierce was appointed Judge of Probate for Cumberland county in 1846, and held that office until 1857. Bringing to the place not only abundant professional ability, but an urbanity and a quick and tender sympathy for all who were in trouble "of body or estate," which were marked traits of his character; he was a faithful and efficient, an honored and beloved judge.

Mr. Pierce was a working member of the Masonic fraternity, and was Master of Harmony Lodge in Gorham, for some time, much beloved by his brethren and active in their charities. He was a useful citizen of his town, always much interested in its prosperity, and particularly well-informed as to its history. He delivered the address at the celebration of its one hundredth anniversary, in 1832, and in 1862 published a History of the Town. He was a member of the Board of Trustees of Gorham Academy and attended faithfully to its interests. He was a Trustee of Waterville College; and also an Overseer, and during the latter part of his life a Trustee, of Bowdoin College, performing his duties in this respect with great fidelity, and rarely missing attendance at the meetings of these boards. His attachment to his Alma Mater (Bowdoin) was exceedingly strong, and his three sons were educated there. He was also an active member of the Maine Historical Society, and of the New England Historic-Genealogical Society; contributed many articles to newspapers, chiefly on historical and biographical topics, and was a great reader and student through life; fond of poetry and classical literature, with a retentive memory and highly cultivated mind, a strong sense of humor, great aptitude for narrating anecdotes, and both in conversation and in public speaking was interesting, instructive and often eloquent. In person he was of medium stature, with dark curling hair and bright eyes, active in body as in mind; in manner gentle and courteous, charitable in judgment and considerate in conduct, never willingly making an enemy or alienating a friend, and living truly more for others than for himself.

Josiah Pierce

Children :—

2331. i.   JOSIAH, b. June 14, 1827; m. Martha D. Lander and Isabel
           Millett.
2332. ii. ARCHELAUS L., b. Aug. 23, 1828; d. Dec. 11, 1829.
2333. iii. EVELINE L., b. June 3, 1830; m. Judge John A. Waterman.
2334. iv. LEWIS, b. April 15, 1832; m. Emily H. Willis and Mary B. Hill.
2335. v.   NANCY, b. April 7, 1834; m. Dr. Edward H. Whittier.
2336. vi. GEORGE W., b. July 1, 1836; unm.; res. West Baldwin, Me.
           Fitted for college at Gorham Academy and "Phillips," Andover (the latter two years), and entered "Bowdoin" in 1853—graduated at Bowdoin College in 1857. He read law with his father in Gorham about one year; 1858-'59-'60 and part of '61 was in New York city in a mercantile house. From '61 to '69 in Arizona, connected with mining enterprises. From '69 to '75 Civil Engineer on various railroads. From 1875 to the present, living on the Baldwin Homestead.

Geo. W. Pierce

2337. vii. ELIZA L., b. Aug. 4, 1838; d. Apr. 13, 1879.
           The following tribute to the memory of a noble woman was written by Gov. Alexander H. Rice of Massachusetts, for the *Boston Journal :—*
           *The Woman's Prison.—How the Chaplain Lived and Died.—A Fervent Tribute to the Memory of a Maine Woman.—*Those who were at the Woman's Reformatory Prison in Sherborn on Tuesday last were witnesses of a spectacle of deep and impressive pathos. It was just enough rare in personality and circumstance to lie outside the course of common experience, and yet so tender and profound as to strike the hidden chords that sound the sacred and solemn harmonies of the uplifted soul. The Chaplain had died. She who less than a year ago came to the place a stranger, and whose remains on this day lay in the marble beauty of death, surrounded by bleeding hearts and streaming eyes. Miss Eliza L. Pierce was a native of Maine, daughter of the late Josiah Pierce, Esq., of Gorham, well connected, finely educated and endowed with intellectual gifts and graceful accomplishments which would make her welcome in any society she entered. Her nature was as guileless as a child's, and was coupled with great sweetness of disposition, courage and discretion. Upon these was built a blameless and holy life, the centre and inspiration of which was a devout personal consecration and unlimited love of God and of human beings for the Saviour's sake. Unostentatious and

almost shy in the discharge of her duties, she allowed nothing
to stand between herself and their performance. She had a
somewhat lengthy experience in saintly work in a parish church
in England, and after returning to her own country, seemed to
burn with a new desire to throw all that was valuable in her
life into the beneficent means and influences of American
society.

The Chaplaincy of the Reformatory Prison for Women had
become vacant and was waiting a suitable incumbent. Few
places are more difficult to fill. The inmates of the prison
represent nearly every form of vice and every variety of disposition and character. Nowhere would dissemblance or cant be
more immediately detected in a spiritual teacher. Nowhere
would mere formalism or insincerity sooner work spiritual
disaster. Nowhere would a heartless or mercenary service be
more instantly discovered; and, it may also be said, that
nowhere would the excellence of a simple and loving soul
which gave its efforts and its sympathy to the reckless and
unthankful, as well as to the sorrowful penitent, be more
quickly discerned or more certain of victory. Miss Pierce was
not an applicant for the place. In her first interview with the
governor, held at his request, the characteristics of the position
were fully set forth to her—its opportunities for noble work,
as well as its hardships, responsibilities, discouragements and
dangers all exposed. She listened with earnest attention, her
face becoming radiant with expectation and enthusiasm as the
recital proceeded. At its close she replied that she had consecrated her life to God and to His service in the world; that she
cared little for conspicuous position, less for salary or com-
pensation, feared neither hardship nor danger, but desired only
to spend her life absolutely for God and humanity; that she
could not, must not, take any place of ease or of doubtful use-
fulness, but desired a place of opportunity sufficient to absorb
all that she had to give.

In answer to an inquiry how soon she could enter upon her
duties if appointed, she said "Immediately;" and in four days
thereafter she was installed in the chaplaincy which proved to
be her field of final labor. Those who were witnesses of her
daily life speak of it as saintly and sincere; and the very
atmosphere of the prison seemed fragrant with the holy
influence of her presence. Every morning and every evening
the prison family assembled in the chapel for prayer and praise
under her leadership and direction. If any came reluctantly at
first, most of them came joyfully afterward; and through the
livelong day she went from workroom to dormitory, hall and
cell, inquiring into the individual weakness, sinfulness or
sorrow of each erring inmate, exhorting and persuading with
Christian faith and fortitude and with a sister's tenderness.
In this way she knew the secret history of every one of her
charge. She never betrayed their confidence and never ceased
to labor with and for them in the line of their individual
necessity.

One day in the week only did she give herself any rest, and
then it was not the repose of idleness that she sought, but
refreshment in the deeper contemplations of spiritual truth,
and in the ordinances of the church of her affection and choice.
On Sundays she held a fuller service in the chapel than on
week days, comprising prayers, Scripture lessons, psalms and
hymns, and Bible reading with simple explanation. She never
attempted preaching nor the administration of ordinances; but

she cultivated the spirit and practice of devotion, and through her example made attractive the religion which she taught with earnest simplicity. She became a universal favorite. The strong, though wayward, admired the beauty and sincerity of her character; the weak leaned upon her for guidance, and the hopeless and despairing clung to her as to a ministering angel. Even the little children in the nursery, unconscious prisoners brought into custody with their erring mothers, stretched out their tiny arms and raised their wistful eyes as she came among them, as if the innocency of their natures recognized the guilelessness of hers.

What wonder then, that this prison household sobbed and cried when the Chaplain lay dead before them? What wonder that they bowed themselves in unutterable grief, and covered with kisses the cold form, out of which had gone forever the life that had softened and sweetened a world, which, to so many of them, had been hard and unsympathizing and friendless? Let those who have known the darkness which comes over the soul when a great hope has failed, realize what to these poor, mourning women it is to look for the last time upon the brightest joy that had ever shone into their desolate lives.

The Chaplain endured her illness with fortitude and even with cheerfulness. Every care was given her which skill and loving solicitude could furnish, but she went beyond recovery; and after a brief sickness, passed away on Easter morning under such peace of mind and glory of outward circumference, as to give to her death, amid all its solemnity, the aspect of poetic beauty. She woke early in the morning and asked that the blind of a window might be opened, so that she could look out into the daylight. The rising sun was just throwing its full effulgence over the face of Nature, illuminating the earth and filling the great dome of the sky with warmth and brilliancy; and seemingly the Son of Righteousness in like manner illumined her soul with ineffable radiance. "He cometh forth as a bridegroom out of his chamber," she feebly said; and these words were her last connected utterance. A few moments later the lady superintendent of the prison entered the sick chamber with the Easter salutation: "Christ is risen;" the dying Chaplain turned toward her with an assenting smile, and that was for herself "the last of earth."

On Tuesday her funeral was attended in the chapel of the prison—the inmates and officers, the immediate relations of the chaplain, the prison commissioners, and a few friends, including the present and the last Governors of the State, constituted the assembly. The beautiful and impressive ritual of the Episcopal church was used, and the hymn,

> "There is a land of pure delight,
> Where saints immortal reign,"

was sung by the prisoners, with a tenderness and pathos seldom equaled. The Rev. Mr. Hall of the Church of the Advent, Boston, then delivered an extemporaneous address, which was notable for the absence of personal eulogy of the deceased and for its earnest presentation of the significance of death, the certainty of the resurrection, the incentives to purity and holiness of life presented in the example of Christ and the promised immortality of blessedness in Him. The preacher seemed to feel that no words spoken could equal in eloquent persuasion the example of the life which had gone from the silent form

18

before him. The crisis of the final separation showed that human nature never goes so far from rectitude as to lose hold of its instinctive virtues. As the prisoners passed from the chapel there was scarcely an eye not wet with tears. There was an evident struggle for composure among them all, and an almost equal failure as their eyes fell for the last time upon the noble and placid features of their steadfast friend. Many doubtless felt that she had given her life for them, and were almost inconsolable.

The funeral cortege passed from the prison grounds while the bell, which so often summoned to praise and prayer, tolled its mournful farewell, and the prison family, in their permitted freedom, crowded to the windows and watched the receding hearse until there was nothing left visible to them but a flood of tears. There are moments in each of our lives when we seem to be more than ourselves. The greatest of these is when we stand in the presence of the holy dead and rise to the sublime contemplations of immortality. Some who were present at the prison on Tuesday felt all of this as they stood by the lifeless form of the dead Chaplain and followed her spirit away through the victories of Easter morning.

643. DANIEL T.[7] PIERCE (*Josiah*[6], *Josiah*[5], *Josiah*[4], *John*[3], *Thomas*[2], *Thomas*[1]), b. March 15, 1803; m. April 26, 1826, Frances E. B. Lewis, b. April 3, 1809, d. Dec. 3, 1874. He d. March 15, 1856. Res. Pontiac, Mich. Children :—

2338. i.   FRANCES E. L., b. June 27, 1828; d. June 27, 1828.
2339. ii.   HARRIET, b. Nov. 19, 1829; m. Frederick Clement.
2340. iii. SUSAN A., b. Aug. 15, 1831; d. Aug. 12, 1845.
2341. iv.   FRANCES E. L., b. April 20, 1833; m. Edward K. Butler.
2342. v.   DANIEL T., b. May 15, 1835; m. Annie Pitcher.
2343. vi.   GEORGANNA, b. June 23, 1836.
2344. vii. RICHARD S., b. Aug. 29, 1839; d. Sept. 2, 1839.
2345. viii. CLARA F., b. Oct. 12, 1840; m. Frederick S. Stewart.
2346. ix.   ARTHUR D., b. March 4, 1846; d. Jan. 7, 1865.

644. GEORGE W.[7] PIERCE (*Josiah*[6], *Josiah*[5], *Josiah*[4], *John*[3], *Thomas*[2], *Thomas*[1]), b. Dec. 2, 1805; m. Nov. 26, 1832, Annie Longfellow, b. March 3, 1810; d. Nov. 15, 1835. Res. Portland, Me. No children.

George Washington Pierce was born in Baldwin, Maine. His father, born in Woburn, was half-brother of Benjamin Thompson (*Count Rumford*). Mrs. Phebe Pierce was the daughter of Daniel Thompson, who, at the fight of Lexington, was shot through the heart by a retreating British soldier.

From his earliest childhood he was remarkable for an ardent temperament, a desire for noble distinction, for lively fancy and quick intelligence, for prepossessing manners and social tact, for becoming the especial favorite of his old friends, and for easily gaining new ones. He was prepared for college, partly in the academies of Fryeburgh and Saco, and partly at home, under the tuition of Mr. Joseph Howard, now Judge of the Supreme Court of Maine. His chum through the college course at Bowdoin was the Rev. Daniel Shepley. As a member of the Pencinian Society he diligently improved its opportunities for debate and practice in writing, and among the Bowdoin students of that day, since so

distinguished at the bar, in the pulpit and in general literature as
writers and speakers, he was soon acknowledged eminent for ability in
discussion and for vigor and elegance in composition. He observed
strictly the maxim of *Apelles, Nulla dies sine lineâ*—in permitting no
day to pass without studiously writing at least a page on some subject of
present interest. Although he ranked well in the recitation room he became greater in the libraries, and was doubtless a more earnest student
of the English classics than of the college text-books. Being among
the youngest of his class, and very social, active and mirthful, he was a
loved and constant companion in the joyous and open-hearted intercourse of college gaiety and sports, but wisely avoided college dis-
grace, and was graduated honorably. His commencement exercise
was a discussion with George B. Cheever, and the two disputants were
thought to be well mated. After leaving college he never ceased to
manifest a worthy and reciprocated attachment and respect for the
officers and fellow-graduates of his *alma mater*. He chose the law. One
year of the required period was passed at Gorham, in the office of his
brother Josiah—part of another year in Portland with Mr. Longfellow—
and more than a year at the Law School in Northampton, Mass. At
Northampton, his classmate was Frank Pierce (afterwards President of
the United States). The learned and clear-minded judge Howe was
his instructor and encouraged him with many marked expressions of
interest and praise. A refined society of which the learned historian
George Bancroft, residing at Round Hill, was a leader and example,
admitted him to the communion of its courtesies and enjoyments. He
passed the Spring and Summer of 1828 at his brother's house in Gorham
—an invalid, but an active one. It was a time of warm political conflict. The presidential canvass was pending. Mr. Pierce advocated
the election of Gen. Jackson, and no one wrote more circulars or
spoke at more caucuses, or communicated more articles to the newspapers, than he did. In looking for a place to settle, the great West
seemed most strongly to invite him, and he determined to go and see
for himself. Taking Washington on his way, he remained there several
weeks. His letters to his friends at this time are filled with most
animated and graphic descriptions of the men he met and heard—of
Clay and Calhoun, and McDuffie, and Adams, and John Randolph
—of his conversations with them, of their personal appearance and
manners—of the Congress generally, the Capitol, the city and Mt.
Vernon, which he visited with deep emotion. His western tour
extended to St. Louis. In April he returned from the slow, difficult and sometimes dangerous journey, quite willing to be governed
by the friends, who advised and besought him to stay where he was.
In July, 1829, he opened an office in Portland, Me. After thus
committing himself to his profession, distinction in it became the
chief object of his care. He read law diligently, and never ceased
to do so while he lived. He admired physical accomplishments, and
acquired some skill in fencing, boxing and other manly exercises;
—became tolerably versed in the French language, and was a prominent
actor in the literary society of the town. He had already become

known to the Democratic party in the vicinity as a ready and able writer, and the services of his pen were soon desired and freely given for political articles in the *Portland Argus*, the chief journal of that party in the State of Maine. Newspapers of that day, and indeed during both terms of Gen. Jackson's administration, were savage in their attacks on men and measures connected with the hotly disputed questions between the two great parties. It was a time of revolutionary excitement throughout the world—of intense discord in the United States regarding the Bank, the tariff, internal improvements, and the right of secession—to which was added extraordinary local agitation in Maine upon the negotiations respecting the North-eastern boundary, and from the new current of speculation in the State lands,—Mr. Pierce was an increasing contributor to the *Argus* in these controversies; and once so enlisted, he could not withdraw from it. The applause of his party, his warm personal feelings, his facility in writing, the necessity of defending positions. he had taken, secured him and made him well known as a political disputant. Many young men of great ability, who have since attained high national distinction, were then in Maine, as rivals or opponents, and the leading Whig journal of the State was then edited by the Hon. James Brooks, now of the *New York Express*, with his well-known ability, in the keenest opposition to the *Argus*. Thus led into political strife Mr. Pierce continued actively engaged in all public movements of the Democrats in his county. During the years 1831 and 1832, at their caucus meetings, conventions, and festivities, he was constantly in requisition for speeches, resolutions, etc. On the 4th of July, 1832, at the great Democratic celebration, he delivered the oration. But amid all this, he endeavored to give his best thoughts and work to his profession. In September, after a warm contest, he was elected to the Legislature as Representative. In November he married Annie Longfellow, daughter of his former instructor, and sister of his classmate, Henry Wadsworth Longfellow, the poet, and at once began housekeeping. During the session of the Legislature he was constant in attendance and active and useful. One speech, in particular, on the South Carolina Resolutions was thought to be very able. In March, 1833, he was appointed County Attorney for Cumberland, and entered at once upon the duties of the office. At the following city municipal election he was chosen a Common Councilman. Such was his popularity, that the Democrats insisted on again sending him to the Legislature. He resigned, not without reluctance, the County Attorneyship, and was elected by a large majority. After another busy and useful winter at the seat of government, he returned to Portland, quite resolved to give himself, thenceforward, strictly to his profession, and to the beneficial influences of his happy and refined home. His legal practice increased and extended to all the courts, but he most esteemed and sought the liberal and technical system of civil law in the Admiralty Court. Evidences of his industry and ability may be seen in the law reports of the time. Sometimes he appears to have relieved the severe labors of his profession by literary writing for the *Magazine*. Late in the Summer of 1835, the *Argus* was enlivened by a series of letters from his pen, descriptive of the Northern journey, in which he was accompanied by his wife and her parents. At that time, Canada and the White Mountains were not quite so familiar as they are now. On the 14th of October, he was appointed the Reporter of the Decisions of the Supreme Court of Maine, an important and then lucrative office. His reputation as a lawyer—as an influential and public spirited-citizen—had become well and widely established. Conscious of natural abilities and accomplishments, certain of devoted political and personal friends, of a dignified and pleasant professional position, and of means to secure him from want, and secure in the possession of soothing and ennobling domestic life,—he was now suddenly cut off by death. Making an impression so striking and sad of bereavement to his friends, and of loss to the whole society of which he was a part, that it has never yet changed its hue. He was attacked with typhus fever and after a painful illness of four weeks, died on the 15th day of November.—[*From the forthcoming history of Bowdoin College.*

Prof. Henry W. Longfellow, writing in reference to Mr. Pierce, says :—

" I have never ceased to feel that in his death something was taken from my own life, which could never be restored. Though particular incidents have faded from my memory, the general impression of his person and character remains ineffaced and unimpared ; perhaps even more perfect and complete from the lapse of time, as distance enables us to estimate more truly the exact proportions of an object. I have before me always his tall and erect figure, in the vigor of early manhood, his frank and handsome countenance, in which sweetness and energy were mingled, and which in its outlines, though less stern and cold, much resembled the portraits of his grand-uncle, the Count of Rumford. I have constantly in my memory, also, his beautiful and manly character ; frank, generous, impetuous, gentle ; by turns joyous and sad—mirthful and serious ; elevated by the consciousness of power, depressed by the misgivings of self-distrust ; but always kind, always courteous, and, above all, noble in thought, word and deed ! Such was the friend of my youth, of whom I have said elsewhere—

' He, the young and brave, who cherished
Ardent longings for the strife,
By the road-side fell and perished,
Weary with the march of life.' "

645. JOHN[7] PIERCE (*John[6]*, *Josiah[5]*, *Josiah[4]*, *John[3]*, *Thomas[2]*, *Thomas[1]*), b. Feb. 2, 1789 ; m. Jan. 10, 1815, Ruth Powers, b. June 17, 1792. He d. Dec. 28, 1871. Res. Hiram, Me. Children :—

2347. i. NATHAN, b. June 24, 1817; d. April 12, 1840.
2348. ii. JOHN, b. Dec. 13, 1818; d. March 13, 1820.
2349. iii. MARY W., b. Sept. 22, 1822; m. Lemuel Cotton.
2350. iv. SARAH, b. Dec. 13, 1823; m. Rev. A. P. Sanborn.
2351. v. RUTH, b. April 30, 1825; m. Samuel Lewis.
2352. vi. JOHN, b. July 30, 1827; m. Harriet M. Craig.

2353. vii. HOSEA, b. Jan. 30, 1830; m. Mary Parker.
2354. viii. CLARISSA, b. April 17, 1834; m. Charles H. Tripp.

646. JOSIAH[7] PIERCE (*John[6], Josiah[5], Josiah[4], John[3], Thomas[2], Thomas[1]*), b. Nov. 8, 1790; m. Jan. 15, 1834, Mary Hancock, b. July 4, 1793, d. May 17, 1879. He d. April 16, 1863. Res. Hiram, Me. No children.

648. BENJAMIN T.[7] PIERCE (*John[6], Josiah[5], Josiah[4], John[3], Thomas[2], Thomas[1]*), b. Aug. 18, 1794; m. Nov. 17, 1829, Nancy Young, b. April 2, 1799, d. Dec. 30, 1847. He d. May 17, 1860. Res. Patten, Me. Children:—

2355. i.   BENJAMIN, b. Oct. 30, 1830; d. Feb. 23, 1831.
2356. ii. GARDNER, b. Dec. 12, 1832; d. Sept. 1, 1862.
2357. iii. ALMIRA J., b. March 25, 1834; m. Ira Morrill and J. B. Dally.

649. WILLIAM[7] PIERCE (*John[6], Josiah[5], Josiah[4], John[3], Thomas[2], Thomas[1]*), b. April 1, 1796; m. June 10, 1818, Betsey Larrabee, b. April 6, 1798, d. May 10, 1861. He d. Oct. 8, 1876. Res. Hiram, Me. Children:—

2358. i.   SUSAN, b. Oct. 10, 1819; m. Francis Meade.
2359. ii.   REBECCA W., b. Feb. 1, 1821; m. George Bumpus.
2360. iii. ELIZABETH A., b. Feb. 5, 1825; m. James Abbott and ——
        Nevins.
2361. iv.   WILLIAM B., b. July 17, 1826; m. Augusta Berry.
2362. v.   PHEBE T., b. June 9, 1829; m. Jason Clark.
2363. vi.   CHARLES W., b. July 21, 1831; m. Ann E. Scammon.
2364. vii. GEORGE W., b. March 20, 1834; unm. Res. Colorado.
2365. viii. ARTHUR, b. April 15, 1835; m. Lizzie Gile.
2366. ix.   HENRY A., b. June 10, 1842; d. Aug. 16, 1863.

650. TIMOTHY C.[7] PIERCE (*John[6], Josiah[5], Josiah[4], John[3], Thomas[2], Thomas[1]*), b. Jan. 6, 1800; m. June 10, 1824, Olive Pingree, b. Aug. 12, 1797, d. Dec. 10, 1865. He d. Jan. 26, 1856. Res. Brighton, Mass. Children:—

2367. i.   OLIVE, b. Aug. 12, 1826; m. John F. Mentzer.
2368. ii. PHEBE, b. July 8, 1829; m. Madison Clark.

652. DANIEL[7] PIERCE (*John[6], Josiah[5], Josiah[4], John[3], Thomas[2], Thomas[1]*), b. Feb. 7, 1802; m. April 6, 1823, Abigail Hancock, b. May 16, 1806. Res. Hiram, Me. Children:—

2369. i.   HARRIET W., b. Aug. 3, 1824; m. Lorin Robertson.
2370. ii.   HANNAH H., b. March 18, 1827; m. Benj. N. Craig.
2371. iii. ABIGAIL J., b. Dec. 23, 1831; m. Geo. F. Clement.
2372. iv.   DANIEL W., b. June 26, 1834; m. Lois G. Lane.
2373. v.   JOHN H., b. Dec. 31, 1837; m. Fidelia Temple and Sarah Spikins.
2374. vi.   ALDEN M., b. May 3, 1840; d. Aug. 13, 1868.
2375. vii. JULIA A., b. Feb. 3, 1843; m. Charles Roberts and Josiah
        Thurston.

655. JOSEPH[7] PIERCE (*Joseph[6], John[5], Josiah[4], John[3], Thomas[2], Thomas[1]*), b. May 15, 1773; m. 1794, Susanna Lawrence, b. June 21, 1775, d. 1852. He d. 1840. Res. St. Johnsbury, Vt. Children:—

2376. i.   HUBBARD L., b. March 1, 1795; m. Amy Spalding and Matilda
        H. Brockway.

2377. ii. LEWIS, b. Dec. 21, 1796; m. Abigail Stowell.
2378. iii. ALFREDA, b. Feb. 21, 1799; d. Oct. 25, 1816.
2379. iv. ELIZA, b. June 19, 1801; m. Wm. L. Kelley.
2380. v. CALISTA, b. May 19, 1804; m. Abel Wiley.
2381. iv. CAROLINE, b. Oct. 7, 1807; m. ———— Ramsdell.
2382. vii. HENRY M., b. April 15, 1809; d. April 17, 1813.
2383. viii. WILLARD M., b. Aug. 12, 1813; m. Lucinda C. Witherell.
2384. ix. RICHARD, b. Jan. 20, 1818; d. Sept. 15, 1818.

658. JOTHAM[7] PIERCE (*Joseph[6], John[5], Josiah[4], John[3], Thomas[2], Thomas[1]*), b. Nov. 12, 1778; m. March 1, 1804, Mary R. Cobb, b. April 5, 1782, d. June 30, 1832. He d. Aug., 1823. Res. Coventry, Vt. and Montreal, C. E. Children:—

2385. i. INFANT; d. young.
2386. ii. MARY C., b. March 25, 1807; m. Isaiah B. Johnson.
2387. iii. INFANT; d. young.
2388. iv. BRADFORD, b. 1809; d. 1815.
2389. v. LUCIUS, b. 1812; d. 1815.
2390. vi. INFANT; d. young.
2391. vii. OLIVIA; d. young.
2392. viii. INFANT; d. young.
2393. ix. CHARLES K., b. June 11, 1818; m. Sarah Barker and Mary A. Barker.
2394. x. HARRIET A., b. July 24, 1820; m. Avery H. Goss and D. H. Walworth.
2395. xi. JOTHAM, b. Jan., 1824; d. June, 1832.

659. ASA[7] PIERCE (*Joseph[6], John[5], Josiah[4], John[3], Thomas[2], Thomas[1]*), b. Feb. 25, 1781; m. ———— ————. He d. Sept., 1846. Res. Belvidere, Ill. His widow res. there in 1856. Children:—

2396. i. WILLARD.
2397. ii. DIANTHA; m. Chapin Martin; res. W. Bloomfield, N. Y.
2398. iii. ————.
2399. iv. ————.

660. MARTIN[7] PIERCE (*Joseph[6], John[5], Josiah[4], John[3], Thomas[2], Thomas[1]*), b. June 5, 1783; m. 1803, Abigail Sanderson, b. June 13, 1785, d. Feb. 25, 1843. He m. 2nd, Oct. 23, 1843, Nancy A. Cleveland, b. Aug. 2, 1796. He d. April 10, 1804. Res. Stanbridge, P. Q. Children:—

2400. i. FREDERICK, b. May 1, 1804; m. Mary Briggs.
2401. ii. VARNUM, b. Nov. 26, 1805; m. Evaline Goss.
2402. iii. EMELINE, b. April 25, 1807; m. Ray Steere.
2403. iv. CALVIN, b. Oct. 30, 1808; d, 1832.
2404. v. CURTIS, b. March 16, 1811; m. Mary Dunham and Sarah Dunham.
2405. vi. HENRY, b. Nov. 16, 1812; m. Lucinda Stockwell.
2406. vii. ALMIRA, b. Sept. 7, 1814; m. Nathaniel Hart.
2407. viii. HIRAM, b. June 7, 1818; m. Anna Beattie.
2408. ix. MILO, b. March 23, 1820; m. Amanda Baker.
2409. x. MILONA, b. Feb. 23, 1822; m. Henry Scott.
2410. xi. ALVIRA, b. May 13, 1824; d. June 13, 1825.
2411. xii. JOTHAM, b. July 29, 1826; m. March 29, 1829.

661. LEONARD[7] PIERCE (*Joseph[6], John[5], Josiah[4], John[3], Thomas[2], Thomas[1]*), b. July 28, 1785; m. March 23, 1815, Nancy Norris, b.

May 22, 1786, d. March 15, 1864. He d. May 14, 1852. Res. Brownington, Vt.

Children :—

2412. i. HARRIET M., b. Dec. 18, 1815; m. Joseph Wheelock.
2413. ii. SHUBAEL, b. Feb. 1, 1818; d. Sept. 16, 1846.
2414. iii. MARGARET, b. Aug. 23, 1820; d. July 7, 1847.
2415. iv. SALLY A., b. Oct. 10, 1822; m. Dec. 25, 1846.
2416. v. LUCINA P., b. Oct. 8, 1824; m. Daniel O. Parlin.
2417. vi. WILDER L., b. Jan. 5, 1827; d. Feb. 6, 1846.
2418. vii. ANDREW M., b. Aug. 8, 1829; m. Rodaska Paddleford.

662. WILDER[7] PIERCE, Esq. (*Joseph[6], John[5], Josiah[4], John[3], Thomas[2], Thomas[1]*), b. Jan. 3, 1788; m. June 9, 1817, Nancy Parsons, b. April 29, 1799, d. Jan. 10, 1853. He d. Sept. 30, 1866. "Wilder Pierce was born in Westmoreland, N. H., commenced mercantile business at Stanstead Plains, Canada, in 1816. In 1817, he married Nancy Parsons, daughter of Israel Parsons, of Hatfield, Mass. He retired from trade in 1837, and employed the remaining years of his life in the cultivation of his farm. He was early appointed magistrate, and was for many years actively employed in public affairs." Res. Stanstead, P. Q.

Children :—

2419. i. CHARLES W., b. April 23, 1818; m. Mary F. Horton.
2420. ii. SARAH P., b. March 14, 1820; m. Henry Keyes.
2421. iii. JOHN A., b. Sept. 12, 1823; d. July 20, 1861.
2422. iv. GEORGE, b. May 31, 1825; m. Mary M. Clapp.
2423. v. HENRY G., b. June 9, 1827; m. Mary C. Benton.
2424. vi. JULIA A., b. April 5, 1829; m. Geo. L. Goodwin.
2425. vii. CARLOS, b. May 20, 1831; m. Mary A. Mills.
2426. viii. EMMA F., b. Sept. 17, 1833; m. Henry Keyes.
2427. ix. MARTHA, b. March 1, 1836; m. Isaac Butters.
2428. x. MARY, b. April 2, 1838; m. Walter B. Cobb.
2429. xi. EMILY, b. Oct. 29, 1821; d. Feb. 26, 1832.

663. ALFRED[7] PIERCE (*Joseph[6], John[5], Josiah[4], John[3], Thomas[2], Thomas[1]*), b. Aug. 9, 1790 ; m. —— ——. H. d. April 11, 1822.

Children :—

2430. i. ——.   2431. ii. ——.   2432. iii. ——.

664. SHUBAEL[7] PIERCE (*Joseph[6], John[5], Josiah[4], John[3], Thomas[2],*

Thomas¹), b. April 10, 1793 ; m. April 7, 1825, Mary A. Barnard, b. Oct. 13, 1799. He d. Jan. 13, 1864. Res. Richmond, P. Q.

Children :—

2433. i. WILLIAM H., b. Aug. 20, 1828; d. Sept. 14, 1834.
2434. ii. CHARLES F., b. July 30, 1830; d. June 17, 1856.
2435. iii. ANN, b. Nov. 5, 1832.
2436. iv. GEORGE H., b. July 4, 1835.

666. THOMAS⁷ PIERCE (*Joseph⁶, John⁵, Josiah⁴, John³, Thomas²*, *Thomas¹*), b. Feb. 11, 1799 ; m. Jan. 4, 1826, Olive Martin, b. Nov. 24, 1806, d. March 20, 1879. He d. Jan. 22, 1880. Res. Martinsville, P. Q.

Children :—

2437. i. JAMES M., b. Nov. 1, 1826 ; m. Emily Barrar.
2438. ii. EMILY, b. March 14, 1832 ; d. Feb. 5, 1834.
2439. iii. WILLIAM A., b. Aug. 31, 1834 ; m. Maria Merrill.
2440. iv. MARY, b. July 14, 1837 ; m. Alo Kenney.
2441. v. SARAH F., b. July 13, 1840 ; m. Benj. N. Haines.
2442. vi. ALBERT C., b. Oct. 29, 1842 ; m. Minnie A. Ayer.
2443. vii. HENRY T., b. Aug. 17, 1846 ; m. Annie P. L. Manning.
2444. viii. GEORGEANNA, b. March 14, 1849 ; d. June 5, 1853.

667. DANIEL⁷ PIERCE (*Daniel⁶, John⁵, Josiah⁴, John³, Thomas²*, *Thomas¹*), b. Jan. 27, 1768 ; m. Abigail Gilson, b. June 11, 1766, d. Sept. 23, 1847. He d. Nov. 3, 1839. Res. St. Johnsbury, Vt.

Child :—

2445. i. WARREN, b. 1789 ; m. Sally McManus.

668. ARETAS⁷ PIERCE (*Daniel⁶, John⁵, Josiah⁴, John³, Thomas²*, *Thomas¹*), b. Jan. 2, 1770 ; m. Sept. 5, 1794, Rebecca Blood, b. March 8, 1775, d. Dec. 2, 1850. He d. Aug. 30, 1840. Res. Monroe, N. Y.
Children :—

2446. i. ARETAS, b. March 27, 1799 ; m. Matilda Stedman.
2447. ii. JENETTA ; m. ——— Chapman.
19

2448. iii. AMANDA; m. Hunt Farnsworth.
2449. iv. CASPER, b. May 28, 1817; m. March 18, 1841, Louisa Warren, b. April 11, 1813. Res. Holley, N. Y. No children.

672. NATHANIEL[7] PIERCE (*Daniel*[6], *John*[5], *Josiah*[4], *John*[3], *Thomas*[2], *Thomas*[1]), b. Aug. 8, 1777; m. Betsey McManus, b. Feb. 22, 1786, d. 1863. She was a daughter of Patrick and Grace McManus. He was one of the Irish soldiers that surrendered under Gen. Burgoyne. Res. Michigan. Children:—

2450.	i.	——.	2452.	iii.	——.	2454.	v.	——.
2451.	ii.	——.	2453.	iv.	——.			

673. LEVI[7] PIERCE (*Daniel*[6], *John*[5], *Josiah*[4], *John*[3], *Thomas*[2], *Thomas*[1]), b. May 24, 1779; m. 1802, Polly Fowler, b. 1779, d. Aug., 1865. He d. Oct., 1839. Res. St. Johnsbury, Vt. Children:—

2455. i. MARY, b. Sept. 19, 1804; m. Ezra Brigham.
2456. ii. MERCY, b. May 3, 1806; m. Lathrop Cole.
2457. iii. LYDIA, b. Nov., 1813; m. Loren Stone.
2458. iv. CAROLINE; d. 1840.
2459. v. LUCY, b. 1822; d. Oct., 1838.
2460. vi. MYRANDA, b. 1824; d. Jan., 1832.

674. ABEL[7] PIERCE (*Daniel*[6], *John*[5], *Josiah*[4], *John*[3], *Thomas*[2], *Thomas*[1]), b. Aug. 12, 1781; m. Dec. 29, 1805, Mercy Allin, b. May 21, 1783, d. Jan. 30, 1850. He d. Jan. 10, 1862. Res. St. Johnsbury Centre, Vt.

Abel Pierce

Children:—

2461. i. LOUISA H., b. Oct. 29, 1808; m. Orlando W. Hutchinson and Joseph Clark.
2462. ii. SALLY, b. Oct. 3, 1810.
2463. iii. JOSIAH H., b. April 26, 1814; d. Nov. 8, 1816.
2464. iv. JOSENTHIA, b. Aug. 8, 1816; m. Darius Bradley.
2465. v. ABEL A., b. April 28, 1825; m. Rosetta Ayer and Sarah McGrath.

675. REUBEN[7] PIERCE (*Daniel*[6], *John*[5], *Josiah*[4], *John*[3], *Thomas*[2], *Thomas*[1]), b. May 25, 1783; m. Dec. 4, 1807, Abigail Cobb, b. Jan. 5, 1788. She d. Sept. 26, 1868. He d. July 25, 1855. Res. St. Johnsbury, Vt.

Reuben Pierce

Children:—

2466. i. JOHN S., b. Jan. 8, 1809; m. Sarah Gould.
2467. ii. NANCY S., b. Jan. 30, 1810; m. Leonard Wright.
2468. iii. HORATIO A., b. March 7, 1812; m. Claissa Stearns.
2469. iv. FREELOVE B., b. July 4, 1822; m. John Prescott.
2470. v. PRENTISS L., b. May 5, 1829; m. Martha J. Powers.
2471. vi. CANDACE, b. July 13, 1813; m. Josiah Cobb.

678. THOMAS[7] PIERCE (*Thomas*[6], *John*[5], *Josiah*[4], *John*[3], *Thomas*[2], *Thomas*[1]), b. 1780; m. Betsey Sanderson, b. 1789, d. Oct. 21, 1842. He m. 2nd, Mrs. Melon (Roberts) Flint. She d. Oct. 12, 1850. He d. Nov. 23, 1857. Res. St. Johnsbury, Vt.

Children :—

2472. i.   HIRAM, b. June 3, 1803; m. Lois Stiles and Diantha Fuller.
2473. ii. PHEBE, b. Aug. 19, 1805; m. Willard Minot.
2474. iii. RICHARD, b. June 21, 1807; d. June 14, 1808.
2475. iv. MILO, b. June 6, 1808; m. Eliza Bennett.
2476. v.   PATTY, b. June 24, 1811; m. Lemuel Wright.
2477. vi. JABEZ, b. April 13, 1813; d. June 3, 1816.
2478. vii. LUCY, b. Feb. 24, 1815; d. Sept. 14, 1855.
2479. viii. ABIGAIL, b. May 22, 1817; m. Thomas Brigham.

689. THOMAS[7] PIERCE (*John*[6], *Thomas*[5], *Thomas*[4], *Thomas*[3], *Thomas*[2], *Thomas*[1]), b. April 8, 1763; m. Sept. 26, 1790, Baradill Fox, b. May 21, 1768, d. May 11, 1839. He d. Feb. 23, 1843.
Children :—

2480. i.   HARDY, b. Oct. 6, 1791; d. unm. Nov. 25, 1871.
2481. ii. SUSAN, b. April 13, 1793; m. Ammi Doubleday.
2482. iii. JABEZ, b. May 9, 1794; m. Ann Mary King.
2483. iv. MARIA B., b. April 15, 1799; m. Robert M. Bailey.
2484. v.   JULIA A., b. Dec. 19, 1803; m. Horatio N. Gilbert.
2485. vi. ABBY J., b. Jan. 21, 1806; m. Jared M. Root.

691. SPALDING[7] PIERCE (*John*[6], *Thomas*[5], *Thomas*[4], *Thomas*[3], *Thomas*[2], *Thomas*[1]), b. Feb. 29, 1768; m. April 18, 1799, Nabby Bacon, b. Sept. 24, 1782, d. May 14, 1872. He d. Feb. 14, 1827. Res. Paris, N. Y.

Children :—

2486. i.   ESTHER, b. Dec. 21, 1802; m. Ransom Curtis.
2487. ii. LEWIS B., b. July 18, 1805; d. Feb. 18, 1808.
2488. iii. WILLIAM L., b. Feb. 16, 1810; m. Susan Barringer.
2489. iv. PHINEAS S., b. June 7, 1812; d. July 21, 1814.
2490. v.   SYLVESTER P., b. Sept. 19, 1814; m. Cornelia Marsh.
2491. vi. SOPHIA, b. Jan. 6, 1817; d. May, 24, 1877.
2492. vii. JOHN S., b. May 8, 1819; m. Fidelia Griffith.
2493. viii. ABBY, b. Oct. 31, 1822; d. Sept. 3, 1824.

692. SYLVESTER[7] PIERCE (*John*[6], *Thomas*[5], *Thomas*[4], *Thomas*[3], *Thomas*[2], *Thomas*[1]), b. Sept. 17, 1770; m. Eunice ———, b. 1778, d. March 4, 1812. He d. Jan. 30, 1814. Res. Plainfield, Conn.
Children :—

2494. i.   MARY A.; m. ——— Fox.   2496. iii. SUSAN Z.
2495. ii. EMILY.   2497. iv. EUNICE S.

695. PHINEAS[7] PIERCE (*Lemuel*[6], *Ebenezer*[5], *Thomas*[4], *Thomas*[3], *Thomas*[2], *Thomas*[1]), b. 1768; m. 1792, Rowena Harris, b. 1778, d. April 10, 1850. He d. 1855. Res. Mansfield, Sterling and Rockville, Conn. Children:—

2498. i.   OLIVE, b. 1794; m. Sterry Angell.
2499. ii.   MARTHA; d. unm. 1856.
2500. iii. CHARLES, b. 1798; m. Emily Edson and Maria White.
2501. iv.   MARTIN, b. Sept., 1803; m. Julia Hall.
2502. v.   MARIA, b. 1805; m. Owen Green.
2503. vi.   ASA, b. 1807; d. 1810.
2504. vii. DARIUS, b. 1809; m. ——— ———.
2505. viii. ROWENA, b. 1811; d. unm. 1851.
2506. ix.   HANNAH, b. 1813.
2507. x.   BETSEY, b. 1817; m. Julius Rich.
2508. xi.   EMELINE, b. 1819; m. Austin Caswell.

696. SAMUEL[7] PIERCE (*Thomas*[6], *Amos*[5], *Thomas*[4], *Thomas*[3], *Thomas*[2], *Thomas*[1]), b. Sept. 22, 1756; m. Oct. 25, 1781, Hannah White, b. Jan. 8, 1761, d. May 24, 1846. He d. March 11, 1832. He was a soldier in the war of 1812. Res. Canaan, Conn., and Salisbury, Vt.

Children :—

2509. i.   ELIZABETH, b. Aug. 12, 1782; m. Jesse Story.
2510. ii.   THEODOTHIA, b. May 14, 1784; d. Dec. 21, 1843.
2511. iii. SUBMIT, b. April 6, 1786; m. John Weaver.
2512. iv.   ALVARES, b. Dec. 3, 1791; m. Polly Booth and Sarah M. Ryan.
2513. v.   SAMUEL, b. May 31, 1794; d. Feb. 3, 1809.
2514. vi.   RODNEY, b. April 1, 1796; m. Eliza Severance.
2515. vii. HANNAH, b. Dec. 18, 1798; m. Alvah English.
2516. viii. S. WILLIAM, b. Dec. 26, 1801; m. Eliza Bigelow.
2517. ix.   ALONZO, b. May 19, 1804; d. Aug. 19, 1826.

700. JOHN[7] PIERCE (*Thomas*[6], *Amos*[5], *Thomas*[4], *Thomas*[3], *Thomas*[2], *Thomas*[1]), b. April 20, 1764; m. Nov. 28, 1798, Sally Daboll, b. July 12, 1778, d. Sept. 24, 1817. He m. 2nd, June 10, 1822, Mary Smith, b. 1777, d. April 25, 1832. He d. April 17, 1832. Res. Canaan, Conn.

Children :—

2518. i.   HARRIET, b. June 20, 1801; m. Jan. 21, 1822, Buel Green. Res. Garrettsville, Ohio.
2519. ii.   RODNEY, b. July 12, 1807; m. three times.
2520. iii. ANDREW, b. July, 21, 1814; m. Mary A. Cleveland.
2521. iv.   JOHN D., b. May 5, 1817; m. Mary West.

703. SILAS[7] PIERCE (*Thomas*[6], *Amos*[5], *Thomas*[4], *Thomas*[3], *Thomas*[2], *Thomas*[1]), b. Feb. 24, 1772; m. 1829, Lois Weed Kelsey, b. 1780, d. May 14, 1851. He d. March 5, 1858. Res. Torrington, Conn., and Alford, Mass. No. children.

Silas Peirce [signature]

711. SAMUEL[7] PIERCE (*Amos*[6], *Amos*[5], *Thomas*[4], *Thomas*[3], *Thomas*[2], *Thomas*[1]), b. March 27, 1783; m. Aug. 23, 1807, Sally Gorham, b. July 29, 1783, d. Aug. 5, 1856. He d. May 3, 1860. Res. Elbridge, N. Y. Children:—

2522. i. AMOS, b. Dec. 5, 1808; d. April 4, 1844.
2523. ii. HENRY M., b. Aug. 11, 1810; m. Cornelia C. Campbell.
2524. iii. BETSEY, b. July 8, 1812; m. John Chase.
2525. iv. SALLY, b. 1814; d. April 18, 1842.
2526. v. MARIA, b. Aug. 18, 1816; d. July 24, 1819.
2527. vi. WILLIAM, b. Dec. 19, 1818; m. Aurelia Bowker.
2528. vii. MINERVA, b. April 8, 1822; m. James Redman.

713. WILLIAM[7] PIERCE (*Amos*[6], *Amos*[5], *Thomas*[4], *Thomas*[3], *Thomas*[2], *Thomas*[1]), b. Feb. 25, 1787; m. Jan. 19, 1813, Polly Loveland, b. Oct. 2, 1792, d. Nov. 23, 1855. He d. Oct. 19, 1864, in Canaan, Conn. Children:—

2529. i. AMOS, b. Nov. 12, 1814; m. May 13, 1841, Marianna Butler; m. 2nd, Oct. 5, 1864, Mrs. Saloma E. Lewis.
2530. ii. WILLIAM G., b. Nov. 27, 1816; m. May 1, 1843, Jane E. Adams.
2531. iii. MARY, b. Dec. 24, 1818; m. Jan. 2, 1840, John R. Elton, M. D. They res. in Vineland, N. J. Ch.: Laura P., b. Oct. 14, 1842; Mary E., b. Oct. 8, 1845, d. March, 1855.
2532. iv. LAURA, b. April 29, 1821; d. Dec. 16, 1855.
2533. v. DANIEL L., b. Jan. 1, 1824; m. June 5, 1850, Ann E. Rood.

720. PHINEAS[7] PIERCE (*Phineas*[6], *Amos*[5], *Thomas*[4], *Thomas*[3], *Thomas*[2], *Thomas*[1]), b. Aug. 16, 1781; m. 1810, Annie Kellogg, b. 1787, d. April, 1813. He d. Sept., 1815. Children:—

2534. i. FANNY, b. Jan., 1811; m. Dr. —— Cummings.
2535. ii. SAMUEL R., b. Jan. 23, 1813; m. Sylvia J. Comstock.

722. AMOS[7] PIERCE (*Phineas*[6], *Amos*[5], *Thomas*[4], *Thomas*[3], *Thomas*[2], *Thomas*[1]), b. July 31, 1784; m. 1811, Mary Sanford, b. 1790, d. Sept. 30, 1845. He m. 2nd, —— ——. He d. July 20, 1872. Res. Poultney, Vt. and Roseville, Ills.

Amos Pierce [signature]

Children:—

2536. i. CLEMENT, b. Sept. 24, 1813; m. Nancy Farr.
2537. ii. WILLIAM H., b. Jan. 23, 1816; m. Angeline Waldron and Harriet Woods.

2538. iii. MARIETTA, b. 1818; m. Henry Kelsey.
2539. iv. STEPHEN, b. Sept. 24, 1820; m. Elizabeth Hanan and Lottie
            Johnson.
2540. v.   PHEBE J., b. March 7, 1823; m. Charles W. H. Chapin.
2541. vi. ELIZA, b. March 10, 1825; d. Dec. 19, 1845.

723. ABIRAM[7] PIERCE (*Phineas*[6], *Amos*[5], *Thomas*[4], *Thomas*[3],
Thomas[2], *Thomas*[1]), b. May 20, 1786; m. Jan. 8, 1809, Sarah
Satterlee, b. March 21, 1787, d. May 7, 1848. He d. Oct. 17, 1860.

Children :—

2542. i.   CHRISTOPHER E., b. Sept. 24, 1809; m. May 7, 1838, Emeline
            Pierce.
2543. ii. WILLIAM S., b. July 9, 1811; m. Jan. 12, 1847, Sarah Hermon.
2544. iii. STEPHEN, b. Aug. 29, 1813; m. Aug. 23, 1838, Mary Ransom.
2544½. iv. MARY, b. April 5, 1816; m. Sept. 12, 1838, John Spaulding, b.
            July 29, 1814, d. Nov. 20, 1846. Ch.: Sarah E., b. July 21, 1839,
            d. Sept. 7, 1852; John A., b. May 3, 1841, m. Sarah I. Car-
            nochan; Jane P., b. April 1, 1845, m. Leroy F. Halloway;
            Francis E., b. May 24, 1847, m. Robert F. Redington.
2545. v.   JANE L., b. July 19, 1818; m. Jan. 28, 1841, John L. Johnson, b.
            Oct. 14, 1814. Ch.: Julius, b. Aug. 1, 1842, m. Henrietta Mor-
            ley; Mary, b. Aug. 24, 1844, m. Geo. W. Ray; Abiram, b. Jan.
            14, 1853, d. March 26, 1853.
2546. vi. AMOS, b. Oct. 12, 1820; m. June 1, 1843, Laura Pomeroy.
2547. vii. EMMA, b. June 9, 1824; m. April 1, 1845, Horace Pomeroy, b.
            Jan. 19, 1819. Ch.: Alice, b. Aug. 25, 1850, m. L. M. Smith;
            Jennie, b. Nov. 21, 1858; Louise, b. Aug. 14, 1861.

726. STEPHEN[7] PIERCE (*Phineas*[6], *Amos*[5], *Thomas*[4], *Thomas*[3],
Thomas[2], *Thomas*[1]), b. June 18, 1791; m. Aug. 11, 1822, Edith Low,
b. Sept. 10, 1805, d. Sept. 7, 1869. He d. Sept. 6, 1847. Res. Exeter,
Ill. Children :—

2548. i.   MARIAN, b. Sept. 10, 1823; d. May 31, 1827.
2549. ii. AMOS, b. Jan. 1, 1825; d. Jan. 1, 1825.
2550. iii. ABIRAM, b. April 30, 1826; m. Maria Draper.
2551. iv. STEPHEN, b. Nov. 8, 1828; m. Elizabeth Miller.
2552. v.   JULIA, b. June 25, 1832; m. J. M. Mills.
2553. vi. MARY, b. April 13, 1837; m. Owen Nicholson.

727. HORACE[7] PIERCE (*Phineas*[6], *Amos*[5], *Thomas*[4], *Thomas*[3],
Thomas[2], *Thomas*[1]), b. Nov. 16, 1803; m. Nov. 5, 1826, Mary Perkins, b. Nov. 28, 1805. He d. Dec. 12, 1864. Res. E. Smithfield, Pa.

Children :—

2554. i.   WALTER, b. Oct. 3, 1834; m. Lorancy Carpenter.
2555. ii. HARRY, b. Dec. 22, 1842; m. Harriet Campbell.

729. HARRY[7] PIERCE (*Phineas*[6], *Amos*[5], *Thomas*[4], *Thomas*[3], *Thomas*[2], *Thomas*[1]), b. Feb. 20, 1808; m. May 11, 1834, Alma Phelps, b. Juue 29, 1814, d. March 16, 1861. Res. E. Smithfield, Pa. Children :—

2556. i. SARAH J., b. Oct. 23, 1835; m. D. C. Holcomb.
2557. ii. CLARENCE H., b. July 29, 1838; m. Mariou Morley.
2558. iii. FANNIE, b. Nov. 10, 1841; m. W. A. Shoemaker.
2559. iv. HELEN, b. Jan. 6, 1843; m. V. C. Phelps.
2560. v. LORON, b. Oct. 10, 1846; d, May 26, 1863.
2561. vi. CLARA, b. Oct. 24, 1850.
2562. vii. CHARLES, b. Nov. 7, 1855; m. Nellie K. Wood.

730. PELATIAH[7] PIERCE (*John*[6], *John*[5], *Thomas*[4], *Thomas*[3], *Thomas*[2], *Thomas*[1]); m. Polly ———. Res. Wilkesbarre, Pa. Child :—

2563. i. JOHN, b. March 13, 1810; d. April 7, 1814.

734. JOHN[7] PIERCE (*John*[6], *John*[5], *Thomas*[4], *Thomas*[3], *Thomas*[2], *Thomas*[1]), b. Feb. 27, 1792; m. Susanna Shupp, b. Dec. 23, 1792, d. Nov. 29, 1861. He d. Sept. 28, 1836. He served in the war of 1812. Res. Wilkesbarre, Pa. Children :—

2564. i. CHARLES, b. Feb. 3, 1813.
2565. ii. PHILIP, b. Sept. 6, 1816; d. March 4, 1848.
2566. iii. EVERETT, b. Nov. 17, 1818.
2567. iv. JOHN, b. June 10, 1820.
2568. v. CATHERINE, b. April 25, 1822; m. Andrew Lamb.
2569. vi. JAMES B., b. July 16, 1828.
2570. vii. MARY, b. March 5, 1830.
2571. viii. SAMUEL, b. May 1, 1834.
2572. ix. ANDREW R., b. March 17, 1837.

737. PALMER[7] PIERCE (*Timothy*[6], *Timothy*[5], *Timothy*[4], *Thomas*[3], *Thomas*[2], *Thomas*[1]), b. Oct. 8, 1761; m. Nov. 20, 1783, Eunice Kimball. She d. May, 1791. He m. 2nd, Sept., 1792, Lydia Burton. He d. Nov. 3, 1840. Res. Norwich, Vt. Children :—

2573. i. EARL, b. Aug. 5, 1785; m. Orry Woodward.
2574. ii. PALMER, b. July 27, 1787; m. Anna A. Brewster.
2575. iii. TIMOTHY, b. June 17, 1789; d. June 22, 1820.
2576. iv. JOHN L., b. May, 1791; d. young.
2577. v. JOHN, b. Oct. 29, 1793; m. Clarissa Pratt.
2578. vi. EUNICE, b. Oct. 14, 1795; d. March, 1852.
2579. vii. LEONARD, b. Aug. 12, 1797; d. June 2, 1801.
2580. viii. CHESTER, b. Nov. 18, 1799; d. Jan. 19, 1801.
2581. ix. CHESTER, b. 1801; d. Nov. 18, 1801.
2582. x. MINERVA, b. Nov. 3, 1803.
2583. xi. JOSEPH B., b. Oct. 12, 1805.
2584. xii. MARY, b. Oct. 1, 1812.

739. JOHN L.[7] PIERCE (*Timothy*[6], *Timothy*[5], *Timothy*[4], *Thomas*[3], *Thomas*[2], *Thomas*[1]), b. Aug. 15, 1770; m. June 25, 1798, Apame Thomas, b. May, 1778, d. March 3, 1849. He d. May 13, 1813. Res. Plainfield, Conn. Children :—

2585. i. CAROLINE A., b. Feb. 19, 1800.
2586. ii. JOHN G., b. Nov. 14, 1802; m. Sarah A. Babcock.
2587. iii. ———, b. Nov., 1801; d. Dec., 1801.

741. JOB[7] PIERCE (*Josiah*[6], *Timothy*[5], *Timothy*[4], *Thomas*[3], *Thomas*[2], *Thomas*[1]), b. March 22, 1770; m. Jerusha Mery, b. April,

1780, d. May 6, 1802. He m. 2nd, Mercy Stevens. He d. 1827. Res.
Caledonia, N. Y. Children :—

2588. i.   SHEPPARD; m. Mary E. Pitkin.
2589. ii.   DOLLY.
2590. iii. JOSEPH S., b. April 22, 1802; m. Celina Strong and Elizabeth
             Branch.
2591. iv.   RICHARD.   2594. vii. WILLIAM.
2592. v.   EDWARD.   2595. viii. JOB C.
2593. vi.   JAMES.   2596. ix.   CAROLINE; m. —— Moss.

742. AZEL[7] PIERCE (*Josiah*[6], *Timothy*[5], *Timothy*[4], *Thomas*[3],
Thomas[2], *Thomas*[1]), b. June 26, 1773; m. Sept. 28, 1800, Eliza
Brewster. She d. Nov., 1834. He m. 2nd, May, 1836, Marietta Fitch.
He d. April 17, 1856. Res. Lebanon, Conn.

Children :—

2597. i.   ELIZA, b. Aug., 1801; d. July, 1805.
2598. ii.   ALFRED B., b. Jan., 1803; m. Harriet Worthington.
2599. iii. MARIA F., b. April, 1805; d. April, 1855.
2600. iv.   ELIZA A., b. July, 1807; m. Jas. F. Dolbeare.
2601. v.   EMILY, b. March, 1809; m. E. M. Worthington and Rev. Chas.
             Galpin.
2602. vi.   LYDIA, b. Jan., 1811; m. Nicholas Holland.

745. SHEPPARD[7] PIERCE (*Josiah*[6], *Timothy*[5], *Timothy*[4], *Thomas*[3],
Thomas[2], *Thomas*[1]), b. April 29, 1780. He went with his parents to
Pennsylvania when a small boy, and settled where Waverly now stands.
The writer of this article has often heard him say that his father kept the
first public inn that was kept or opened in that vicinity or section of
country. After spending several years there, he went with them to
Western New York, then known as the far-famed "Genessee Valley,"
where he spent several years, and buried his father at Caledonia, N. Y.
He then returned, and purchased, in 1806 or 1807, the property upon
which he has since lived and died, when the country here was almost
an unbroken wilderness; there being but few settlers then in Wysox,
and but one solitary log-hut where Towanda now stands. He lived
for sixty years in this vicinity, honored and respected, then he passed
away as the fruit, when full ripe, is severed from the branch by the
autumn frosts. He always entertained an almost reverential love for what
he termed the beautiful Valley of Wysox. He had traveled much in
his life, and observed much, and said it was the most lovely spot he
had ever beheld. He m. Dec. 20, 1810, Sarah Colbaugh, b. Dec. 25,
1790, d. Sept., 1850. He d. March 7, 1866. Res. Wysox, Pa.

Children :--

2603. i. EVELINE B., b. Nov. 29, 1811; m. April 24, 1830, Alonzo A. Bishop, b. March 1, 1808. Ch.: Alfred S., b. Aug. 26, 1831; Frances M., b. Jan. 23, 1833; Edward R., b. Sept. 18, 1835; S. Elizabeth, b. May 14, 1837; Mary A., b. Dec. 5, 1838, d. May 4, 1862; Jos. W., b. April 28, 1840; Shepard E., b. Aug. 21, 1846.

2604. ii. SOPHIA L., b. May 18, 1813; m. Aug. 23, 1837, Joseph Conklin, b. June 1, 1808, d. Sept. 1, 1875. Ch.: William H., b. Oct. 12, 1838; George, b. March 17, 1842.

2605. iii. CHESTER, b. March 22, 1815; m. Sept. 27, 1843, Harriet S. Lilley; m. 2nd, Oct. 29, 1855, Charlotte I. Brown.

2606. iv. DOLLY M., b. Jan. 10, 1817; m. Nov. 7, 1839, Daniel Drummond, b. June 5, 1805. Ch.: Clara M., b. March 16, 1841, d. July 24, 1871; James S., b. June 12, 1843, d. March 9, 1850; Franklin, b. May 28, 1845; Sarah, b. Oct. 17, 1846; Robert E., b. March, 1848; Mary P., b. Dec. 24, 1850; James A., b. Jan. 8, 1852; Addie M., b. Oct. 10, 1855; Eva B., b. Aug. 15, 1858; Sophia E., b. June 24, 1860.

2607. v. ELIZA E., b. July 21, 1818; m. Feb. 8, 1858, Joseph Johnson, b. Oct. 13, 1806. Ch.: Sarah A., b. March 4, 1859.

2608. vi. AMANDA, b. June 9, 1820; m. Aug. 31, 1843, J. M. Wattles, b. 1816, d. Dec. 13, 1866. Ch.: Henry L., b. June 8, 1844; John P., b. June 21, 1847; Fred'k, b. March 4, 1850; Sarah P., b. Sept. 6, 1856; Ruth, b. Nov. 7, 1857.

2609. vii. WILLIAM A., b. May 9, 1822; m. April 10, 1844, Anna M. Nagle; m. 2nd, May 25, 1863, Anna A. Newell.

2610. viii. HIRAM A., b. Sept. 20, 1824; d. Sept. 19, 1825.

2611. ix. SARAH J., b. June 18, 1826.

2612. x. SHEPPARD S., b. Mar. 2, 1828; m. June 16, 1852, Sarah A. Lilley.

2613. xi. MARY A., b. Dec. 20, 1829.

2614. xii. CHARLOTTE A., b. Sept. 11, 1831.

2615. xiii. HANNAH M., b. Oct. 2, 1834; m. Aug. 25, 1856, William H. Morgan, b. Dec. 10, 1833, d. Sept. 13, 1876. Ch.: Ida, b. March 22, 1858; Susan. b. Sept. 14, 1859; Anna, b. Oct. 11, 1861; William, b. Oct. 10, 1864; Frances, b. Sept. 3, 1867; John, b. April 9, 1872; Sarah, b. Sept. 3, 1875.

753. WILLARD[7] PIERCE (*Nathaniel[6]*, *Nathaniel[5]*, *Timothy[4]*, *Thomas[3]*, *Thomas[2]*, *Thomas[1]*), b. Jan. 28, 1762; m. July 22, 1784, Susanna Waldo, b. 1763, d. May 13, 1835. He d. in So. Royalton, Vt., Nov. 25, 1830. He was in the Revolutionary war at the age of sixteen.

Children :—

2616. i. BETSEY, b. 1785; d. young.

2617. ii. PHINEAS, b. July 13, 1787; m. Sept. 30, 1813, Charlotte S. Parkhurst.

2618. iii. ALBIGENCE, b. May 23, 1789; m. June 12, 1813, Lucy Bryant; m. 2nd, Nov. 15, 1848, Mrs. Louise Bryant; m. 3rd, Jan. 11, 1855, Mrs. Ruth Hochstrasser.

2619. iv. JOHN D., b. July 14, 1791; m. Nancy Fogg.

2620. v. LUCY, b. Dec. 25, 1793; m. Jonathan Herrick. She d. in West Loudon, N. H., Aug. 10, 1842, without issue.

20

2621. vi. BETSEY, b. July 4, 1796; m. Sept. 14, 1824, Carpenter Greenough, d. 1825; m. 2nd, May 31, 1829, Joseph L. Dewey, b. Aug. 10, 1789, d. June 30, 1873, in Hanover, N. H. Ch.; Sarah, b. 1831, d. 1861; Joseph W., b. Jan. 14, 1833. He is unm., is a celebrated Physician and has an office on Tremont-St., opp. the Museum.

2622. vii. PRISCILLA, b. April 19, 1799; m. Aug. 25, 1825, Hon. Thomas Whipple. Ch.: Priscilla, m. Dr. Frank Bonney; Celia G., b. 1833, m. John Wallace; Delia, m. Gen. Jos. C. Abbott; Phebe T., m. Benj. F. Ayer; Edgar, d. young. Res. Saratoga Springs, N. Y.

2623. viii. DANIEL W., b. Jan. 20, 1803; m. 1828, Olive Hutchinson.

755. BESTER[7] PIERCE (*Nathaniel[6], Nathaniel[5], Timothy[4], Thomas[3], Thomas[2], Thomas[1]*); m. May 21, 1795, Lois Stevens; m. 2nd, 1798, Sally Burroughs; m. 3rd, 1818, Miss McChenney. Res. Potsdam, N. Y.

Bester Pierce

Children :—

2624. i. LOIS; m. John Judd.
2625. ii. CALEB, b. Aug. 6, 1799; m. 1827, Sarah E. Farnsworth.
2626. iii. COLLINS, b. 1801; m. Mrs. Sabrina Tiffany.
2627. iv. MINERVA, b. 1804; m. 1823, Silas H. Clark, d. 1855. Ch.: Laura, d. 1851; Silas P., b. 1827, d. 1856.
2628. v. LAURA, b. 1806; m. Jesse Cogswell.
2629. vi. JOHN, b. Sept. 30, 1820; m. 1847, Marcia Hoyt.
2630. vii. ROBERT, b. June 18, 1821; m. Mary Rugg.

757. ISAAC[7] PIERCE (*Nathaniel[6], Nathaniel[5], Timothy[4], Thomas[3], Thomas[2], Thomas[1]*), b. 1774; m. Dec. 22, 1797, Polly Smith, a sister of the world-renowned Joseph Smith, the first Mormon prophet, b. 1775, d. May 24, 1844. He d. Nov. 9, 1847, in Royalton, Vt.

Children :—

2631. i. EUNICE, b. April 29, 1799; d. June 9, 1803.
2632. ii. LAURA, b. Nov. 12, 1801; d. 1803.
2633. iii. MIRANDA A., b. June 17, 1803; m. Sept. 18, 1827, Sidney S. Hemenway, b. Nov. 25, 1803. Ch.: Horace P., b. Nov. 17, 1829, m. Sarah E. Gross; Miranda P., b. Aug. 23, 1831, d. April 19, 1877. She d. Sept. 16, 1831.
2634. iv. HORACE, b. June 8, 1805; m. Feb. 17, 1836, Maria Cooley.
2635. v. JOHN S., b. March 6, 1807; m. Feb. 10, 1836, Julia Huntington.
2636. vi. SUSAN, b. June 20, 1809; m. Feb. 14, 1833, Sidney S. Hemenway [see iii], d. April 4, 1877. Ch.: Sarah A., b. Dec. 28, 1833, m. Harley Ellis; Ellen M., b. Aug. 31, 1835, m. Charles E. Morrison; Clara T., b. March 5, 1841, unm.; res. Hoboken, N. J.
2637. vii. MARY W., b. April 25, 1811; m. Sept. 27, 1847, James H. Cook, b. May 20, 1806. Ch.: Horace P., b. July 9, 1848, m. Abbie M. Colby; Oscar C., b. Oct. 1, 1850, d. Feb. 17, 1861. They res. in Barton, N. H.
2638. viii. LAURA, b. Feb. 8, 1814; m. Jan. 16, 1844, Edward W. Huntington. Ch.: Alice G., b. Sept. 20, 1847, d. April 13, 1857; Carrie M., b. July 8, 1850, m. Marshall H. Weeks. Res. Lebanon, N. H.
2639. ix. ELIZA A., b. Sept. 2, 1818; d. May 16, 1855.

758. Dr. CALEB[7] PIERCE (*Nathaniel[6], Nathaniel[5], Timothy[4], Thomas[3], Thomas[2], Thomas[1]*); m. Betsey Fogg. He d. 1813. Res. Canaan, N. H. He was a celebrated doctor, and for many years town clerk of Canaan, N. H., and his autograph was obtained from the town records.

Children :—

2640. i. NATHANIEL C.   2641. ii. BETSEY.

761. JOSEPH[7] PIERCE (*Jedediah[6], Nathaniel[5], Timothy[4], Thomas[3], Thomas[2], Thomas[1]*), b. Aug. 19, 1765 ; m. Feb. 28, 1792, Roxanna Perrin, b. Jan. 3, 1766, d. Mar. 23, 1834. He d. Aug. 9, 1835. Res. So. Royalton, Vt., and Potsdam, N. Y.

Children :—

2642. i. BETSEY, b. July 5, 1793 ; m. William Brown.
2643. ii. OLIVE, b. Dec. 23, 1794 ; m. John Patterson.
2644. iii. SETH, b. Oct. 19, 1796 ; m. three wives.
2645. iv. LOIS, b. Jan. 1, 1798 ; m. James Hebbard.
2646. v. EATON, b. June 13, 1800 ; d. Dec. 6, 1836.
2647. vi. PARNELA, b. May 26, 1802 ; m. William Patterson.
2648. vii. JOSEPH, b. June 15, 1804 ; d. July 31, 1824.
2649. viii. JOHN, b. Apr. 10, 1806 ; m. Margaret Watson.
2650. ix. SUSAN, b. Feb. 22, 1808 ; m. E. A. Hough. Died.—At the residence of her daughter, Mrs. Lydia C. Ayers, Rochester, N. Y., July 11, 1880, Mrs. Susan Pierce Hough, in the 73d year of her age. Her funeral took place from their home, July 13th; the burial from the residence of her niece, Mrs. Geo. W. Underwood, in Potsdam, Wednesday, July 14th. Mrs. Hough was born in Royalton, Vt., on the 22d day of February, 1808. Her maiden name was Susan Pierce. She removed with her parents from Vermont to Potsdam, St. Lawrence Co., N. Y., in the year 1826, being 18 years of age. Three years after—April 29, 1829—she was married to Mr. Erastus A. Hough, and became the mother of seven children, two sons and five daughters, of whom four are now living. From the time of her removal from Vermont, in 1826, until the year 1873, she remained a resident of Potsdam, where her husband and three of her daughters are buried. Then she removed to Rochester, N. Y., to live with her daughter, Mrs. Lydia C. Ayers. The next year she was stricken with paralysis, and for the last three years of her life was closely confined to the house. Yet her long confinement— during much of which she was called to endure great suffering —was borne with patience and cheerfulness, and with a Christian faith which never seemed to falter. Her elder son— Eugene K. Hough—is now residing with his wife, in Trinidad, in the West Indies. Her younger son—Sylvester E.—with his wife and child, reside in New York city. Her two surviving daughters—Mrs. Lydia C. Ayers and Miss Mary B. Hough—are

in Rochester, and have devoted themselves to the care of their mother during the last years of her life. Everything has been done, by all her children and children-in-law, that the tenderest love could suggest and the most thoughtful generosity provide, to make the suffering mother comfortable and happy. Blessed in her children, firm in her faith, sure of her Saviour's love, a member of St. Peter's Presbyterian Church, of Rochester, at the time of her death, and for more than fifty years a member of the Church of Christ; leaving behind her many mementoes of her industry and skill, wrought by her during her last years; and the rich legacy of a mother's prayers for her children, she passed up, through death, into the everlasting life, on the morning of July 11th. This date is, to the daughter, Lydia, a memorable one—and the coincidence is, indeed, remarkable— that just twenty years before the day of her mother's death, her father died—both on her birthday.

764. WILLIAM[7] PIERCE (*Jedediah*[6], *Nathaniel*[5], *Timothy*[4], *Thomas*[3], *Thomas*[2], *Thomas*[1]), b. Sept. 5, 1770; m. Dec. 27, 1796, Hannah Baker, b. Mar. 7, 1777, d. Oct. 3, 1863. He d. July 18, 1854. Res. Royalton, Vt.

William Pierce

Children :—

2651. i.   ESTHER E., b. Jan. 23, 1798.
2652. ii. DESIRE W., b. July 6, 1799; d. Oct. 4, 1876.
2653. iii. WILLIAM, b. April 15, 1801; m. Orpha B. Pierce [2668] and Hannah Brockway.
2654. iv. BESTER, b. Jan. 20, 1803; m. Sarah A. Shepard.
2655. v.   IRA, b. Jan. 20, 1805; m. Emily Shepard and Harriet J. Ashley.
2656. vi. JOHN, b. Feb. 26, 1807; d. March 8, 1807.
2657. vii. LEVI W., b. June 14, 1808; m. Maria Berndock and Celia Munson.
2658. viii. GEORGE, b. Apr. 26, 1810; d. July 31, 1845. George Pierce was a deaf mute, caused by having the spotted fever when eighteen months old. He was sent when fourteen years of age to Hartford, Conn., to the Deaf and Dumb Asylum, where he remained three years under the tuition of Prof. Galaudett. He returned to Royalton, Vt., capable to transact business for himself. He died July 31, 1845.
2659. ix. HANNAH, b. April 26, 1812; m. Arnold Welch, d. Sept. 10, 1847. Ch.: Henry C., b. July 8, 1839, m. Sarah C. Lewis of Falmouth; George P., b. Oct. 12, 1841, m. Maria H. Oliphant of Woburn.
2660. x.   CHARLES, b. April 20, 1814; m. Mary A. Griffith.
2661. xi. HENRY B., b. Oct. 6, 1816; m. Abigail M. Parish.
2662. xii. HARRIET B., b. Oct. 6, 1816; m. May 19, 1842, Harry F. Haven, d. Jan. 4, 1857.
2663. xiii. CHESTER, b. Jan. 2, 1819; m. Caroline R. Briggs.

766. ELISHA[7] PIERCE (*Jedediah*[6], *Nathaniel*[5], *Timothy*[4], *Thomas*[3], *Thomas*[2], *Thomas*[1]), b. Nov. 27, 1774; m. Jan. 2, 1800, Polly Baker, b. Sept. 8, 1775, d. March 27, 1835. He d. Aug. 20, 1835, in Royalton, Vt. Children :—

2664. i.   EDWIN, b. Oct. 27, 1800; m. Jan. 25, 1827, Susan H. Kimball.

2665. ii. STEPHEN B., b. March 3, 1802; d. Sept. 15, 1823.
2666. iii. MARY M., b. Dec. 26, 1803; d. Feb. 28, 1826.
2667. iv. SUSANNAH, b. Oct. 31, 1806; m. May 28, 1829, Wright Gifford, b.
July 19, 1805. Ch.: Levi W., b. Aug. 17, 1831, d. Feb. 22, 1832;
Elisha A., b. Dec. 16, 1832, m. Mary E. Camp; Edwin P., b.
Jan. 28, 1834, m. Lucetta J. Rowe; Mary M., b. Oct. 22, 1836,
d. Feb. 26, 1839; Susan E., b. March 7, 1849, m. Howard B.
Wright.
2668. v. ORPHA B., b. March 1, 1809; m. William Pierce, Jr. [2653].
2669. vi. ARCHIBALD T., b. Jan. 6, 1811; m. Feb. 9, 1837, Harriet N.
Baker; m. 2nd, June 2, 1862, Sarah D. White.
2670. vii. SARAH E., b. Jan. 6, 1817; m. Jan. 2, 1858, Lyman Rogers, b.
July 19, 1814, d. July 6, 1876. They had no issue. He was
found dead in a field where he had been at work, by his wife;
he died of heart disease. Res. Bethel, Vt.

771. EBENEZER[7] PIERCE (*Jedediah*[6], *Nathaniel*[5], *Timothy*[4],
Thomas[3], *Thomas*[2], *Thomas*[1]), b. Feb. 20, 1784; m. Dec. 5, 1801, Mary
Fales, d. March 23, 1839. He d. Sept. 18, 1853. Res. Royalton, Vt.

Ebenezer Peirce

Children :—

2671. i. EBENEZER F., b. Oct. 16, 1805; m. Betsey J. Luce.
2672. ii. HOSEA, b. April 26, 1808; m. Charity Russell.
2673. iii. HIRAM, b. April 12, 1816; m. Martha A. Mason.
2674. iv. MARY M., b. Feb. 5, 1821; m. Storrs Tracey.

774. JAMES[7] PIERCE (*Willard*[6], *Nathaniel*[5], *Timothy*[4], *Thomas*[3],
Thomas[2], *Thomas*[1]), b. March 13, 1766; m. Oct. 12, 1817, Elizabeth
Fuller, b. Mar. 27, 1800. He d. Feb. 1, 1851. Res. Plainfield, Conn.

James Pierce

Children :—

2675. i. ISAAC, b. April 23, 1819.
2676. ii. MARIA, b. 1821; m. Francois Lewis.
2677. iii. ANDREW A., b. July 14, 1823.
2678. iv. ANN E., b. Aug. 26, 1825.

779. BENJAMIN[7] PIERCE (*Nehemiah*[6], *Benjamin*[5], *Timothy*[4],
Thomas[3], *Thomas*[2], *Thomas*[1]), b. Sept. 4, 1762; m. Dec. 24, 1786,
Lydia Gurley, b. Jan. 6, 1767, d. Aug. 13, 1827. He d. Oct. 10, 1838,
in Brooklyn, Conn.

Benjn Pierce

Children :—

2679. i. DAVID, b. Nov. 5, 1787; m. May 15, 1832, Elizabeth Allen.

2680. il. MARCIA, b. Aug. 1, 1789; d. June 27, 1871.
2681. iii. HENRY, b. April 14, 1791; m. Sept. 2, 1817, Lucia Cleveland; m. 2nd, May, 1853, Mrs. Rev. A. E. Stowe.
2682. iv. LUCY, b. Jan. 12, 1793, d. Jan. 2, 1794.
2683. v. LUCY, b. Jan. 23, 1798, d. Oct. 18, 1865.
2684. vi. GEORGE F., } b. Apr. 14, 1802; { m. Oct. 10, 1844, Mary A. Ashley.
2685. CHAS. P., m. Feb. 29, 1832, Elizabeth Fowler.
2686. vii. JOHN H., b. Aug. 27, 1800.
2687. viii. JACOB G., b. Dec. 8, 1806; m. Sept. 20, 1836, Fanny W. Bliss; m. 2nd, May 6, 1845, Emily S. Hall.

781. FREDERICK[7] PIERCE (Nehemiah[6], Benjamin[5], Timothy[4], Thomas[3], Thomas[2], Thomas[1]), b. July 22, 1768; m. 1802, Rebekah Blood, b. 1779, d. Jan. 27, 1858. He d. Mar. 29, 1845, in Brooklyn, Conn. Res. Bridgewater, N. Y. Children :—

2688. i. FREDERICK, b. March 2, 1803; d. Apr. 11, 1835.
2689. ii. EUNICE, b. Aug. 22, 1805; m. May 6, 1851, Henry W. Osborn, d. April 3, 1860, without issue.
2690. iii. Mary A., b. Dec. 3, 1807; m. Nov. 10, 1847, Royal H. Johnson. Ch. : Fannie M., b. Feb. 6, 1849.
2691. iv. MARIA, b. Sept. 11, 1809.
2692. v. LYDIA, b. Jan. 27, 1812; m. April 1, 1840, Nathaniel W. Phillips. Ch. : Mary E , b. Sept. 12, 1851.
2693. vi. OLIVE, b. Dec. 12, 1814; m. Sept., 1838, Jonas W. Brooks. Ch. : Isadore R., b. Apr. 12, 1848, d. Apr. 6, 1854; Fred'k P., b. Sept. 22, 1854.
2694. vii. NEHEMIAH W., b. Oct. 25, 1818; m. Jan. 8, 1861, Emily Pullman.

782. NEHEMIAH[7] PIERCE, Jr. (Nehemiah[6], Benjamin[5], Timothy[4], Thomas[3], Thomas[2], Thomas[1]), b. May 10, 1771; m. April 14, 1794, Clarissa Williams, b. Feb. 15, 1772, d. July 27, 1842; m. 2nd, Jan. 8, 1844, Nancy Ladd. He d. May 6, 1850, in Monmouth, Me. He was the son of Nehemiah Pierce, an honest farmer, and was the youngest of six children, only one of whom survived him. He moved to Bath, Me., in 1807, and from thence to Monmouth, Kennebunk Co., in 1808. He married first Clarissa Williams, daughter of Dr. Jesse Williams, of Mansfield, Conn., April, 1794, who died January 27, 1842, aged 69 years, 11 months and 12 days, and by whom he had nine children. In January, 1844, he married for his second wife Nancy Ladd, of Winthrop, Me. Mr. Pierce was one of the most industrious, energetic and practical farmers in the State. He was the first who introduced the art of dairying in the State, and his farm will long live in the remembrance of the citizens of the town and State for his great perseverance and original tact in carrying forward the manufacture of the best cheese and the largest amount known at that time. He was a pious and devoted Christian and ever ready to do good whenever opportunity offered. He was a strong helper in the cause of education, as one of the trustees of the academy in Monmouth. He was secretary of the board for many years and also a great lover of the public schools. For many years he was President of the Monmouth Mutual Fire Insurance Company, the largest of any in the State. His soundness of judgment and integrity of character often found him appointed to offices of trust from the county and the executive of the State, as commissioner of

SEVENTH GENERATION.

public roads and many other important duties where decision and discretion were required.

Nehemiah Pierce

Children :—

2695. i. OLIVER W., b. Apr. 2, 1795; m. June 20, 1826, Rebecca Carlton; m. 2nd, Nov. 10, 1855, Mrs. Delia Morris.
2696. ii. BELA, b. Jan. 2, 1797; m. Mar. 27, 1822, Elizabeth Wilcox.
2697. iii. JESSE, b. Dec. 4, 1798; m. Oct. 22, 1822, Catherine Johnson.
2698. iv. CLARISSA, b. Aug. 8, 1801; m. Apr. 30, 1829, Guy Carlton. She d. March 10, 1842.
2699. v. MILTON, b. Sept. 22, 1803; d. June 10, 1827.
2700. vi. JOHN, b. Nov. 25, 1805; m. Chloe McLellan.
2701. vii. DANIEL, b. Apr. 5, 1808; m. Apr. 18, 1833, Caroline Shorey.
2702. viii. NEHEMIAH, b. June 10, 1810; d. Feb. 17, 1821.
2703. ix. MARY W., b. June 12, 1814; m. June 11, 1839, William Grows, b. Apr. 23, 1815. Ch.: John W., b. May 22, 1843, m. Isabell G. True; Joseph M., b. Dec. 22, 1844, m. Catherine A. Eldridge; Clara W., b. Aug. 19, 1847, m. Silas S. Trofant; Mary E., b. July 15, 1853, d. Apr. 6, 1857. Res. Berwick, Me.

789. ERASTUS[7] PIERCE (*Delano[6], Benjamin[5], Timothy[4], Thomas[3], Thomas[2], Thomas[1]*), b. Jan. 22, 1780; m. Feb. 9, 1800, Hannah Cady, b. 1776, d. Dec. 19, 1820; m. 2nd, June 19, 1821, Hannah Bingham, b. July 24, 1784, d. Feb. 9, 1847. He d. March 1, 1828. Res. Brooklyn, Conn. Children :—

2704. i. J. HAMMOND, b. Aug. 27, 1800; m. ——— ———.
2705. ii. DIADEMMA, b. Dec. 9, 1801; m. Wm. Scarborough.
2706. iii. EMILY, b. April 24, 1804; d. May 4, 1813.
2707. iv. ABIGAIL M., b. March 17, 1806; m. George Townsend.
2708. v. ASA S., b. June 3, 1808; d. Jan. 27, 1812.
2709. vi. LUCY M.; m. Billings Hakes.
2710. vii. ELIAS; m. Cordelia Palmer.
2711. viii. HANNAH, b. Sept. 2, 1826; m. A. A. Snow.

790. ELIAS[7] PIERCE (*Delano[6], Benjamin[5], Timothy[4], Thomas[3], Thomas[2], Thomas[1]*), b. Jan. 29, 1781; m. Feb. 10, 1813, Lydia Thompson, b. April 17, 1790, d. July 27, 1876. Res. Topsham, Me. Child :—

2712. i. ELIAS D., b. Jan. 4, 1815; m. Mary A. Blood.

792. Dr. DELANO[7] PIERCE, Jr. (*Delano[6], Benjamin[5], Timothy[4], Thomas[3], Thomas[2], Thomas[1]*), b. in Brooklyn, Conn., July 19, 1786; m. Nov. 22, 1813, Anna Nichols, b. 1791, d. Feb. 2, 1860. He d. Jan. 9, 1871, in Grafton, Mass.

He remained at home and worked on the farm in summer, attending school a part of the year, until seventeen years of age; then went to Plainfield Academy and spent two years in study, with intervals of teaching in winter. At nineteen years of age he commenced the study of medicine with the late Josias Fuller, M.D., of Plainfield, but was induced to take charge of a High School in Stonington for six months, intending to devote himself to the study of medicine at the expiration of that time, but consented to continue in the school the remainder of the year, having made an arrangement whereby he could read medicine with Dr. Hyde, a physician of the place, in his leisure hours. He then returned to Plainfield, and finished his medical studies with Dr. Fuller, at the age of twenty-three; was examined by, and received his diploma from the Connecticut State Medical Society, in August, and went in November into several towns in Connecticut and Rhode Island, introducing vaccination or cow-pock, which at that time was little known, and which met with much hostility owing to ignorance and prejudice on the subject, which, however, he was successful in overcoming to a great degree.

In the year 1811, he started on horseback from his father's house in pursuit of a place for the practice of his profession, and on arriving at Oxford, Mass., decided to locate there. On the 8th day of June, 1813, he was commissioned by His Excellency Caleb Strong, then Governor and Commander-in-Chief of the Commonwealth of Massachusetts, Surgeon of the Fifth Regiment of Infantry in the First Brigade and Seventh Division of the Militia of this Commonwealth, which office he held until he tendered his resignation and from which he was honorably discharged on the 6th day of November, 1818. He was energetic and persevering in whatever he engaged, and carried through every undertaking with remarkable vigor and unfaltering trust in his own ability. The first start in life financially he obtained in the manufacture of cotton cloth. Some time during the early introduction of machinery in the manufacture of cotton cloth, he had a conference with Mr. Slater of Webster, who was then making it by hand looms, he made a proposition to him to furnish material and pay a fixed sum per yard for making cloth by machinery. An arrangement was made, he hired a grist-mill, placed in it a few looms and employed hands to weave. This in connection with his practice, he carried on one or two years with satisfaction to Mr. Slater, who at first had doubts that cloth could be made by machinery equal in quality to that made by hand.

After an extensive and successful practice in Oxford, of about twenty-three years, and having disposed of his practice to Dr. Knight, he removed to East Douglas in 1834, and formed a co-partnership with the late Dr. Ezekiel Wood, which lasted two years with much cordiality and unusual harmony. While there a select school was established through his influence, it being the first in the village where classical studies were pursued. In the spring of 1836, he came to Grafton, and purchased of Mr. Ephraim Wilson the estate now owned by Mr. Charles A. Pierce, where he lived until 1841, when he removed to the estate formerly occupied by the Rev. John Miles.

The old house was removed to the rear, remodeled and rebuilt, and was his residence until his death, which occurred Jan. 9, 1871. This house is now the residence of Dr. T. T. Griggs, who married his daughter and only child.

Dr. Pierce was a faithful and skillful physician, and loved his profession—merciful in his charges—and very considerate to the poor. He was a man of good natural abilities, sound judgment, social and gentle in disposition; of vigorous muscular powers, and never seemed to tire or become weary in responding to the various duties attendant upon his profession. He was industrious and economical in his habits, and was ever ready to aid those who made any exertions to help themselves to an honest living. He was charitable in all those little things which contribute so much to make life happy, and which, perhaps, accomplish more than greater charities but seldom performed. He practised medicine nearly fifty-nine years, and by strictly temperate habits was enabled to endure this vast labor with scarcely any interruption until within about two years of his decease. Watching the symptoms of approaching dissolution and conscious that his end was near, he resigned peacefully to his fate with hopes of a more glorious and brighter day in realms of light and life.—[*History of Grafton, Mass., by F. C. Peirce, Esq.*

Children :—

2713. i. JULIA, b. July 25, 1823; m. Feb. 16, 1842, Dr. Thomas T. Griggs, b. Jan. 31, 1818. Ch. : Anna, b. June 7, 1845, d. Aug. 13, 1845; Frances Helen (adopted in infancy), b. July 23, 1859.

Dr. Thomas T. Griggs, in early life, was employed in a store, attending school in Sutton. He attended a commercial school in Boston to qualify himself for book-keeping and mercantile pursuits. He subsequently attended school at Northfield Academy, and also at Wrentham Academy. In March, 1839, he came to Grafton, and was associated with his brother, Salem Griggs, for a short time in the sale of drugs and medicines, and general merchandise, occupying the brick store erected by the late Lovel Stow. After which he studied medicine with Dr. Delano Pierce, whose daughter he married, Feb. 16, 1842. He also pursued the study of medicine in Brunswick, and in Boston, and received the degree of M. D. from the medical department of Harvard University, July 18, 1849, and immediately commenced the practice of his profession in Grafton, in connection with his father-in-law, continuing it to the present time. He is a member of the Massachusetts Medical Society; has held a Justice's commission; served on the board of selectmen; and in 1875, represented his district in the General Court, where he was assigned a place on the committee on towns.—[*History of Grafton, Mass., by F. C. Peirce, Esq.*

795. PAYSON G.[7] PIERCE (*Timeus*[6], *Benjamin*[5], *Timothy*[4], *Thomas*[3], *Thomas*[2], *Thomas*[1]), b. Sept. 10, 1781 ; m. Nov., 1808, Mary Shepard, d. Oct. 9, 1869. He d. Dec. 12, 1845. Res. Brooklyn, Conn., and Butternuts, N. Y. Children :—

2714. i. LUCIAN, b. Sept. 2, 1809; d. Feb., 1812.
2715. ii. S. PUTNAM, b. Aug. 25, 1811; m. Cornelia Andrews and Sarah E. Brown.
2716. iii. MARTHA S., b. Nov. 11, 1813; m. B. Gates.
2717. iv. MARY E., b. Oct. 22, 1815; d. Sept. 22, 1844.
2718. v. LUCIAN G., b. Sept. 4, 1818; d. Nov., 1853.
2719. vi. GEORGE W., b. Nov. 8, 1825; m. Melissa Sexton.

826. JONAS[7] PIERCE (*Jonas*[6], *Oliver*[5], *Stephen*[4], *Stephen*[3], *Thom*-

21

as², *Thomas¹*), b. Jan. 20, 1780 ; m. ———— ———— ; d. May 30, 1810. Res. E. Chelmsford.

Jonas Peirce

Children :—

2720. 1.　JONAS, b. 1807; m. Elizabeth Patch.
2721. ii.　HEZEKIAH.

831.　RICHARD W.[7] PIERCE (*Jonathan⁶*, *Oliver⁵*, *Stephen⁴*, *Stephen³*, *Thomas²*, *Thomas¹*), b. Oct. 15, 1782 ; m. Nov. 4, 1804, Sarah Farrar, b. May 4, 1780, d. Jan. 31, 1835 ; m. 2nd, Apr. 28, 1835, Susan Keep, by whom he had no issue. He d. Apr. 9, 1845. They res. in Townsend, Mass.

Richard W Pierce

Children :—

2722. i.　RICHARD, b. Nov. 2, 1805; m. Mary A. Hartwell.
2723. ii.　SALLY D., b. July 23, 1807; d. 1823.
2724. iii.　THIRZA, b. June 24, 1809; m. May 13, 1830, Calvin Boutell, b. May 4, 1806. Ch.: Newton C., b. June 10, 1832, m. Ann C. Winchester and Abby G. Adams; Thirza A., b. May 25, 1835, d. May 16, 1837; Angela, b. Feb. 11, 1837, m. Anson D. Fessenden; Abigail, b. Oct. 29, 1839, d. Aug. 10, 1840; Mortimer, b. June 26, 1842, d. Oct. 12, 1846; Thirza A., b. Oct. 17, 1844; John W., b. Jan. 16, 1848, m. Julia A. E. Ball. Res. Townsend.
2725. iv.　ESTHER, b. July 16, 1811; m. May 22, 1834, John Spalding, b. May 10, 1794, d. May 15, 1866. Ch.: Ellen M., b. Nov. 21, 1838; Isabella A., b. Nov. 13, 1842, m. Leander Rowell; Theodore L., b. April 21, 1845; Lyman B., b. Feb. 25, 1847; Theodore L., b. May 3, 1849; Ellen R., b. Feb. 23, 1854. Res. Townsend.
2726. ·· LUCY, b. Oct. 15, 1813; m. Nov. 28, 1833, John Proctor, b. July 6, 1808. Ch.: Myra A., b. Oct. 12, 1834; Lucy A., b. Dec. 31, 1837; John M., b. Sept. 12, 1839, d. Feb. 15, 1866. Res. Townsend.
2727. vi.　JONATHAN, b. Oct. 17, 1815; m. Dec. 28, 1837, Abigail Turner; m. 2nd, Apr. 22, 1859, Sophia Hills.
2728. vii.　LAURA, b. Oct. 11, 1817; d. 1822.
2729. viii.　REBECCA, b. Feb. 1, 1820; m. Sept. 5, 1876, Andrew Rockwood, b. Jan. 22, 1812. No issue. Res. Brookline, N. H.
2730. ix.　ABEL, b. Feb. 20, 1822; m. Nov. 4, 1844, Catherine E. Kemp, d. Dec. 8, 1853. He d. Nov. 2, 1852, in Groton.

836.　STEPHEN[7] PIERCE (*Stephen⁶*, *Oliver⁵*, *Stephen⁴*, *Stephen³*, *Thomas²*, *Thomas¹*), b. April 5, 1786 ; m. April 12, 1814, Abigail Bateman, b. Dec. 1, 1790, d. Sept. 10, 1826 ; m. 2nd, Jan., 1831, Mary Cory, b. March 4, 1800, d. Nov. 6, 1853. He d. Feb. 19, 1854. Res. Chelmsford, Mass.　Children :—

2731. 1.　GEORGE, b. Jan. 28, 1815; m. Reuhamah Stearns.

2732. ii. NANCY B., b. Oct. 9, 1816; m. Jan. 16, 1840, Eli B. Parker.
2733. iii. MILO, b. May 28, 1818; m. three times.
2734. iv. LUCINDA, b. Oct. 30, 1820; d. Oct. 2, 1826.
2735. v. ANN E., b. Nov. 20, 1832; m. S. A. Marshall.
2736. vi. NEWELL, b. Aug. 9. 1834; d. June 12, 1835.
2737. vii. JOEL E., b. March 27, 1836; m. Harriet A. Upham.
2738. viii. JULIA, b. May 31, 1838; m. M. Hutchins.
2739. ix. CHARLES H., b. April 13, 1840; m. Maria T. French.
2740. x. JOHN, b. July 15, 1845; m. Asa E. Ripley.

838. JESSE[7] PIERCE (*Stephen[6], Oliver[5], Stephen[4], Stephen[3], Thomas[2], Thomas[1]*), b. Feb. 2, 1790 ; m. Dec. 27, 1814, Hannah Harrington, dau. of Eben Harrington, of Lexington, Mass. He d. June, 1820. She m. 2nd, Jonathan Pierce [841]. Res. Chelmsford, Mass.

Jesse Pierce

Children :—

2741. i. WILLIAM S., b. Sept. 14, 1815: m. three times.
2742. ii. EDWIN, b. Jan. 19, 1818; m. Eliza S. Milliken.
2743. iii. SARAH J., b. Aug. 19, 1820; m. S. T. French.

839. MOSES[7] PIERCE (*Stephen[6], Oliver[5], Stephen[4], Stephen[4], Thomas[2], Thomas[1]*), b. Jan. 22, 1792 ; m. 1814, Mary Barron, b. 1797. He d. in Boston in 1829. Res. Tyngsboro', and Boston, Mass.
Children :—

2744. i. PRESCOTT, b. Oct., 1816; d. April, 1818.
2745. ii. WINSLOW S., b. May 3, 1819; m. three times.
2746. iii. OLIVE; d. infancy.
2747. iv. FRANKLIN B., b. Jan. 7, 1823; m. Melissa Hinman.
2748. v. GEORGE B., b. Feb. 28, 1824; m. Mary C. Brittan.

840. MARSHALL[7] PIERCE (*Stephen[6], Oliver[5], Stephen[4], Stephen[3], Thomas[2], Thomas[1]*), b. Nov. 14, 1793 ; m. Mary Stearns. Res. Chelmsford, Mass. Children :—

2749. i. SANBORN, b. Dec. 6, 1818; d. Feb. 1, 1874.
2750. ii. MARY ANN.
2751. iii. SUSAN, b. Aug. 22, 1822; m. George Woods.
2752. iv. LUCINDA.
2753. v. ELIZA.

841. JONATHAN[7] PIERCE (*Stephen[6], Oliver[5], Stephen[4], Stephen[3], Thomas[2], Thomas[1]*), b. Oct. 16, 1796 ; m. May 8, 1827, Hannah H. Pierce [838], d. Nov. 27, 1867. He d. Oct. 8, 1878. Res. Chelmsford, Mass. Children :—

2754. i. MARIA, b. Jan. 21, 1828; m. Ira Atwood.
2755. ii. HERMON, b. Sept. 26, 1829.
2756. iii. ORRIN, b. Aug. 7, 1831; m. Elmira S. Bolton.
2757. iv. HENRY C., b. Sept. 8, 1833; d. Feb. 5, 1834.

843. WILLIAM[7] PIERCE (*John[6], William[5], Stephen[4], Stephen[3], Thomas[2], Thomas[1]*), b. Oct. 8, 1776 ; m. June 4, 1809, Ruth Hub-

bard, b. 1783, d. June 23, 1832. He d. June 4, 1854. Res. Lyndon, Vt.

Children :—

2758. i.   EMILY, b. Feb. 18, 1812; d. Aug. 14, 1862.
2759. ii. WILLIAM E., b. June 12, 1813; m. Helen A. Houghton.
2760. iii. GEORGE W., b. Feb. 5, 1815; m. Ruth Bey.

845. JOHN[7] PIERCE, Jr. (*John[6]*, *William[5]*, *Stephen[4]*, *Stephen[3]*, *Thomas[2]*, *Thomas[1]*), b. June 1, 1780 ; m. 1799, Judith Thompson, d. Nov. 14, 1860. He d. Apr. 27, 1857. Res. Londonderry, Vt.

Children :—

2761. i.   ABIGAIL, b. Dec. 12, 1800; m. Alanson Chamberlin.
2762. ii.   ALFRED, b. Dec. 23, 1802; m. 1829, Abigail Rockwood.
2763. iii. IRENA, b. Jan. 15, 1805; d. Sept., 1806.
2764. iv.   LAURA, b. Sept. 19, 1807 ; m. Sept., 1831, Sam'l H. Walker, d.
            Oct. 4, 1864. She d. Jan. 28, 1861, leaving Laura C., b. June,
            1832, m. Almon White.
2765. v.   AMANDA, b. Mar. 14, 1809; m. Apr., 1835, Lyman Brittan, d.
            June, 1866. She d. Dec. 21, 1836, leaving no issue.
2766. vi.   LUCINDA, b. Oct. 12, 1811; d. Mar. 2, 1814.
2767. vii. MARY, b. Oct. 27, 1813; d. Aug. 20, 1839.
2768. viii. LUCY, b. Feb. 17, 1817; m. Capt. Charles W. Clarke; no issue.
2769. ix.   JOHN L., b. Nov. 16, 1819; m. Dec., 1846, Ellen E. Marsh.
2770. x.   ELIZABETH F., b. July 27, 1822; m. Marshall H. Day.

847. EZEKIEL P.[7] PIERCE (*John[6]*, *William[5]*, *Stephen[4]*, *Stephen[3]*, *Thomas[2]*, *Thomas[1]*), b. Apr. 20, 1785 ; m. Mar. 1, 1808, Susanna Porter, b. May 4, 1785, d. Jan. 11, 1866. He d. May 23, 1865, in Chesterfield, N. H., where he resided. He was a very large manufacturer of bits. He was one of the most prominent men of the place. He was for a long term of years Trial Justice and Justice of the Peace.

Ezekiel P. Pierce

Inscription on Ezekiel P. Pierce's monument in the Joslin Cemetery, Chesterfield :—

"Ezekiel P. Pierce, Esq., died May 23d, 1865, Æ. 80 yrs. Susanna, his wife, died Jan. 11th, 1866, Æ. 80 yrs. 6 mos.

No more on earth dear Father,
Shall we see thy smiling face.
No more on earth dear mother,
Shall we feel thy fond embrace.
No more on earth dear brother,
Shall we greet thy coming home,
And little smiling Andrew,
We shall never cease to mourn."

Children :—

2771. i. Susanna P., b. Dec. 2, 1809; m. Nov. 12, 1840, Bethuel. Farley. They res. in Marlow, N. H. Ch.: Lucius P., b. May, 1843, m. Jane Knight; Dallas J., b. 1845.
2772. ii. Theresa J., b. Feb. 23, 1812; unm.
2773. iii. Ezekiel P., Jr., b. Aug. 18, 1814; m. 1844, Sarah Webster.
2774. iv. Julia A., b. Oct. 28, 1817; unm.
2775. v. Lucius D., b. Aug. 9, 1820; m. Jan., 1854, Lucy C. Fuller.
2776. vi. Horace T. H., b. Feb. 22, 1822; m. June 12, 1850, Sophia Dickinson.
2777. vii. Lafayette W., b. May 19, 1826; m. Sept. 15, 1859, Cleopatra S. Bang; m. 2nd, Oct. 5, 1865, Lydia M. Piper; m. 3rd, Mar. 29, 1875, Hannah E. Derby.
2778. viii. Andrew J., b. May 19, 1828; d. Nov. 20, 1828.
2779. ix. Augusta E., b. Jan. 29, 1830; unm.
2780. x. Benj. Franklin, b. Aug. 1, 1833; unm.

848. Ebenezer[7] Pierce (*John*[6], *William*[5], *Stephen*[4], *Stephen*[3], *Thomas*[2], *Thomas*[1]), b. June 22, 1788; m. June, 1808, Alpha Randall, b. Feb. 27, 1791, d. July 6, 1869. He d. March 11, 1874. Res. Chesterfield, N. H.

Children :—

2781. i. Britton, b. Nov. 23, 1812.
2782. ii. Charles, b. March 8, 1813; m. Caroline Scribner.
2783. iii. Lloyd, b. Dec. 20, 1815.
2784. iv. Alson, b. June 8, 1817; m. Lorany P. Wheeler.
2785. v. Dexter, b. Oct. 11, 1819; m. R. C. Wing.
2786. vi. Ebenezer, b. Nov. 23, 1826; d. April 21, 1864.

857. Col. Benjamin K.[7] Pierce (*Benjamin*[6], *Benjamin*[5], *Stephen*[4], *Stephen*[3], *Thomas*[2], *Thomas*[1]), b. Aug. 29, 1790; m. —— La-Flambou, d. Jan. 17, 1854 ; m. 2nd, Amanda —— ; m. 3rd, —— Reed. He d. Apr. 1, 1850. Res. New York City.

He entered Dartmouth College, and began reading law, but when the war of 1812 opened, his enthusiasm was so great that he forsook his situation for the army, where he soon rose to a high rank. He was

appointed 1st Lieut. of 3rd U. S. Artillery in 1812 ; Capt. in 1817 ;
Major in 1823.   In 1836 Brevet Lieut.-Col. for distinguished service
at Fort Drame, Florida, in which he commanded ; Col. of a Regiment
of Creek Mounted volunteers in Florida War in 1836 ; Lieut.-Col. of 1st
Artillery in 1842.   He was a brave and accomplished officer and gentleman, and was in many respects like his brother, Franklin Pierce.   He
was exceedingly amiable and kind, was graceful in his manners, and
everywhere he was known was loved and respected.   Children :—

2787. i.   HARRIET J. ; m. Gen. James B. Ricketts.
2788. ii.   ——— ; d. young.
2789. iii. ELIZABETH ; never m.
2791. iv. AMANDA ; m.
2792. v.   CHARLOTTE ; m. Gen. Wm. M. Graham, of Fort Warren, Boston,
            Mass.

859.   JOHN SULLIVAN[7] PIERCE (*Benjamin*[6], *Benjamin*[5], *Stephen*[4],
Stephen[3], *Thomas*[2], *Thomas*[1]), b. Nov. 5, 1796 ; m. Feb. 10, 1828,
Marietta O. Putthoff, b. April 12, 1802, d. March 25, 1829.   He d.
Sept. 28, 1824.   Res. Detroit, Mich.   Children :—

2793. i.   MARY O., b. Dec. 5, 1820 ; m. A. B. Warburgh.
2794. ii.   ANNE K., b. Dec. 19, 1824 ; m. Dr. C. E. Parker, of Springfield, Ill.

862.   President FRANKLIN[7] PIERCE (*Benjamin*[6], *Benjamin*[5], *Stephen*[4], *Stephen*[3], *Thomas*[2], *Thomas*[1]), b. Nov. 23, 1804 ; m. Nov. 10,
1834, Jane M. Appleton, b. 1806, d. Dec. 2, 1863.   He d. Oct. 8, 1869,
in Concord, N. H.

FRANKLIN PIERCE was the fourth son of the late Gov. Benj. Pierce of
Hillsborough, N. H., and was born Nov. 23, 1804.   His father sent him
to an out-of town school at an early age ; an elder brother, then in the
army, had the sagacity to perceive the powers of his mind, and was
exceedingly anxious that he should receive a thorough education.   For
several years he attended school in the neighboring towns of Hancock
and Francestown ; while a resident of the latter town he lived with
the mother of the lamented Judge Woodbury, who was a lady of superior mind and attractions.   Over Frank she had a most beneficial influence, as he very often acknowledged.   He left Francestown for
Exeter Academy where he completed his preparatory studies, and entered Bowdoin College at the precocious age of sixteen, in the year
1820.   During his first two years in college Frank Pierce was not distinguished for his devotion to his studies.   He was not dissipated,
but having naturally a full flow of spirits, he was a little wild ; but
among all his classmates he was extremely popular.   Possessing frank
manners and a generous disposition, it could not well be otherwise.
While in college his young friends formed a military company and
elected him its Captain.   Mr. Pierce took his degree in the year 1824
with high honors, and left Bowdoin College and his numerous circle of
friends there with regret, for among them he had spent some of the
happiest portions of his life.   The three following years were spent successively in the offices of the Hon. Edmund Parker at Amherst, N. H.,
Hon. Levi Woodbury at Portsmouth, N. H., and in the law school of
Judge Howe at Northampton, Mass.   In 1827 Mr. Pierce was admitted

to the bar and opened an office opposite to his father's residence in Hillsborough. At this time Gov. Benj. Pierce enjoyed a commanding influence in New Hampshire. His popularity was such as is not often witnessed in the world of politics. As a matter of course, the success of Franklin was almost instantaneous. Under common circumstances a young lawyer is obliged to make his abilities known to the world before he can hope for success; but in this case the high position and popularity of Gov. Pierce gained for his son immediate practice. But had he lacked eminent abilities, it would soon have been discovered, and he would have lost that patronage which he had secured from the reputation of his father. He needed not only great abilities but severe and constant labor to maintain the position which it was on all hands conceded he must take. We need not say that he not only met the highest expectations of his friends, but far exceeded them. He rose daily in their esteem and admiration. Mr. Pierce at once espoused the cause of the Democrats with unbounded zeal, and such was the confidence reposed in him by his fellow-townsmen that in the second year of his practice, at the age of 25, he was elected to represent the town of Hillsborough in the State Legislature at Concord. The three successive years he was elected to that body, and such was their opinion of his abilities that in 1832 and 1833 he was made Speaker of the House of Representatives. At this time there was great agitation throughout N. H. in reference to Gen. Jackson. The State in the year 1829 came out boldly and grandly in favor of the hero of New Orleans, Benj. Pierce being elected Governor by more than 2,000 majority, and an entire Congressional delegation in favor of Jackson's administration and a legislature returned thoroughly Democratic. Through all these exciting scenes Mr. Pierce, though a young man, took an important part. Thus in a few years Frank Pierce had raised himself to a commanding position in his native State. In his own party, among his own adherents, his position was most amicable, and indeed he was beloved and admired by his political enemies. Although young yet, he continued to conduct himself in so modest yet able a manner as to raise the admiration of the older leaders among the Granite Democracy of N. H. A political critic, noticing his career at this portion of his life, remarks : "Thus, in five years, he attained an enviable position among his associates ; and won it, not by undermining his rivals, or by adroitness in political intrigue, but by a firm adherence to political principle, eloquence in debate, unquestioned capacity for public business, unvarying courtesy and exhibition of frankness and manliness of character. So honorable was his ambition, that while he was ranking his associates, he retained their love and commanded their respect.

In the summer of 1833, Mr. Pierce was elected from his native district to the lower house of Congress for the term of two years, and took his seat in that body in December of the same year. In 1837, Mr. Pierce was elected by a large majority of the New Hampshire Legislature to the U. S. Senate. He took his seat in that body the 4th of March, 1837, the day on which Martin Van Buren was inaugurated as President. While in the Senate Mr. Pierce served on some of the most important of the committees,—on the Judiciary, on Military affairs, on Pensions, etc., etc. He was emphatically a working member. In June, 1838, one year after his election to the U. S. Senate, Mr. Pierce changed his residence from his native town of Hillsborough to Concord, the capital. His large circle of friends in Hillsborough could not allow the occasion to pass without a testimonial of their affection for Mr. Pierce, and consequently invited him to a public dinner.

In Feb., 1842, Mr. Pierce resigned his seat in the Senate, to the great sorrow not only of his constituents but of his friends in Washington. The causes for this step were mainly of a personal nature. His wife was always of a retiring disposition, and was ill-suited with the excitement of Washington life, and when to this was added the misfortune of poor health, she was compelled to leave Washington and Mr. Pierce felt it to be his duty to accompany her to Concord, and therefore resigned his seat in the Senate. For three successive years Mr. Pierce had little visible connection with politics, though he was the most influential man in the Democratic party of N. H. In 1845, Mr. Pierce was appointed by the Governor to fill the vacancy in the U. S. Senate, occasioned by the resignation of Judge Woodbury, he having been appointed by President Polk to the Superior bench. Such was Mr. Pierce's popularity, that at once all the presses in the State pointed him out as the most suitable man to fill the vacancy. He was urged with vehemence by the most influential men in the State to accept the position, but he positively declined the honor. About this time the President offered him the office of District Attorney of N. H., which he accepted, as the duties which belonged properly to it came in the line of his profession. He continued to hold this office until 1847.

In 1845 a convention of the Democracy of the State nominated Mr. Pierce to the office of Governor, but in a most eloquent speech, he declined this honor. In 1846, his old friend, President Polk, with whom he had served in Congress before, offered him a seat in his Cabinet. He was well aware of the great abilities and thorough devotion to principle which characterized Mr. Pierce, and was anxious to secure his services at Washington. This honor also was declined.

Gen. Pierce was during his whole political life a modest and retiring man. We see him resigning his seat in the most august legislative body in the Union at the call of affection. We see him refusing the highest office within the gift of his native State, refusing to accept an appointment to the U. S. Senate, and finally refusing a seat in the Cabinet of the President when invited in the most flattering and pressing manner. Truly, this is not an ordinary political character; and in looking at his life and acts, one is carried back to the earlier days of our republic, when offices sought men, not men sought offices. When the Mexican war broke out Mr. Pierce enlisted as a *private soldier* and went through the drill exercise as such. He however was appointed Col. of the old Ninth N. H. by Pres. Polk, and subsequently raised to Brigadier-General. Gen. Pierce sailed from Newport in the bark *Keple*, and arrived after a tedious voyage at Vera Cruz, June 28, 1847. After landing, his line of march was a most harassing one, beset on all sides by Mexicans and Guerrilla bands whose object was to intercept all recruits. Fifteen miles from Vera Cruz, the courage and decision of Gen. Pierce were put to trial. He was there attacked by a fierce guerrilla party, and gave an order to charge upon the chaparal. His Colonel "The brave Ransom!" disputed the propriety of the movement, but Pierce replied firmly and boldly : "I have given the order." The enemy was completely routed after some severe fighting. At the National Bridge he was attacked by the guerrillas, who barricaded the bridge with chaparal. He ordered Capt. Dupreau to dash over the barricade and charge the enemy. The order was promptly executed, and with success. In this skirmish, Gen. Pierce received two bullets through his hat. The men under his care were principally Northern recruits ; they had suffered much by disease ; had been attacked five times by guerrilla parties, and yet Gen. Pierce had lost scarcely a man though in the heart of an enemy's country. After the surrender of the Mexicans, Gen. Pierce resigned his commission in the army, and returned to his residence in Concord.

In 1852, the Democrats of N. H. presented Gen. Pierce as their candidate for the Presidency. This he also declined. It is not necessary to give a detailed account of the doings of the Democratic National Convention held in Baltimore. After four days spent in earnest attempts to come to a decision, on the 36th ballot the Virginia delegation cast their vote for Franklin Pierce of N. H. State after State wheeled in to the support of the General, until the vote stood : Gen. Pierce 282 ; all others 11. He was triumphantly elected and his record stands unblemished.

The following letter, in Nathaniel Hawthorne's handwriting, seems very curious in its accurate foreshadowings. It was written forty-five years ago to Franklin Pierce, when both young men could not have been long out of college. Its prophetic intimations, in the light of what has since occurred in Pierce's career, sound weird and startling, and the epistle is worth perusal. It is addressed to " Colonel Franklin Pierce, Hillsborough, New Hampshire " :—

" SALEM, June 28, 1832..

Dear Mr. Speaker.—I sincerely congratulate you on all your public honors, in possession or in prospect. If they continue to accumulate so rapidly you will be at the summit of political eminence by that time of life when men are usually just beginning to make a figure. I suppose there is hardly a limit to your expectations at this moment; and I really cannot see why there should be any. If I were in your place I should like to proceed by the following steps,—after a few years in Congress, to be chosen governor, say at thirty years old; next a senator in Congress; then minister to England; then to be put at the head of one of the departments (that of War would suit you I should think), and lastly,—but it will be time enough to think of the next step some years hence. You cannot imagine how proud I feel when I recollect that I myself was once in office with you on the standing committee of the Athenian society. That was my first and last appearance in public life.

I read the paper which you sent me from beginning to end, not forgetting Colonel Pierce's neat and appropriate address. I also perused ———'s speech in favor of grog-shops ; he seems to have taken quite a characteristic and consistent course in this respect, and I presume he gives the retail dealers as much of his personal patronage as ever. I was rather surprised at not find-

22

ing more of my acquaintance in your legislature. Your own name and ———'s were all that I recognized.

I was making preparations for a Northern tour when this accursed cholera broke out in Canada. It was my intention to go by way of New York and Albany to Niagara; from thence to Montreal and Quebec, and home through Vermont and New Hampshire. I am very desirous of making this journey on account of a book by which I intend to acquire an (undoubtedly) immense literary reputation, but which I cannot commence writing till I have visited Canada. I still hope that the pestilence will disappear, so that it may be safe to go in a month or two. If my route brings me into the vicinity of Hillsborough I shall certainly visit you. As to the cholera, if it comes, I believe I shall face it here. By the by, I have been afflicted for two days past with one of the symptoms of it, which makes me write rather a tremulous hand. I keep it secret, however, for fear of being sent to the hospital.

I suppose your election to Congress is absolutely certain. Of course, however, there will be an opposition, and I wish you would send me some of the newspapers containing articles laudatory or abusive of you. I shall read them with great interest, be they what they may. It is a pity that I am not in a situation to use my pen in your behalf, though you seem not to need the assistance of newspaper scribblers.

I do not feel very well, and will close my letter here, especially as your many associations would not permit you to read a longer one. I shall be happy to hear from you as often as you can find leisure or inclination to write.

I observe that the paper styles you the ' Hon. Franklin Pierce.' Have you already an official claim to that title?

Your friend,
NATH. HAWTHORNE,
alias ' HATH.' "

Children :—

2795. i.   FRANKLIN, b. Feb. 2, 1836; d. Feb. 5, 1836.
2796. ii. FRANK R., b. Aug. 27, 1839; d. Nov. 14, 1843.
2797. iii. BENJAMIN, b. Apr. 13, 1841; killed by the cars while riding by the side of his father and mother on his way to Andover, Mass., Jan. 6, 1853.

864. HENRY D.[7] PIERCE (*Benjamin[6], Benjamin[5], Stephen[4], Stephen[3], Thomas[2], Thomas[1]*), b. Sept. 19, 1812 ; m. Nov., 1841, Susan Tuttle, b. 1815, d. Oct., 1874. Res. Hillsborough, N. H.

Children :—

2798. i. KIRK D., b. Aug., 1846; m. Mary A. Collins.
2799. ii. FRANK H., b. Jan. 10, 1848.

870. MERRILL[7] PIERCE (*Merrill*[6], *Benjamin*[5], *Stephen*[4], *Stephen*[3], *Thomas*[2], *Thomas*[1]); m. Mary Dickinson. Res. Utica, N. Y. Children :—

2800. i. JESSE, b. 1830; d. 1832.
2801. ii. ——; d. young.

873. JONATHAN[7] PIERCE (*Jonathan*[6], *Stephen*[5], *Jacob*[4], *Stephen*[3], *Thomas*[2], *Thomas*[1]), b. Dec. 3, 1751 ; m. June 9, 1778, Abigail Prescott, b. Jan. 22, 1755, d. Jan. 9, 1840. He d. May 12, 1806. Res. Groton, Mass. Children :—

2802. i. MARY, b. Oct. 8, 1778; m. Joseph Tuttle; d. Sept., 1822.
2803. ii. ABIGAIL, b. May 27, 1780; m. —— Tibbetts ; d. 1839.
2804. iii. EUNICE, b. May 20, 1782; m. John Nutting; d. 1862.
2805. iv. ANN, b. Feb. 19, 1785; d. Feb. 22, 1785.
2806. v. SARAH, b. May 23, 1786; m. Aaron Brown.
2807. vi. JONATHAN, b. Jan. 29, 1789; m. Olive Hale.
2808. vii. MOSES, b. Feb. 2, 1792.
    He studied medicine with Dr. Hitchcock of Boston and removed to Beaufort, S. C., where he engaged in an extensive and lucrative practice for a number of years. He died unm., of yellow fever, Sept., 1818.
2809. viii. ASENATH, b. June 8, 1794; m. Aaron Place.
2810. ix. STEPHEN, b. Sept. 20, 1797; d. young.

874. Sergt. BENJAMIN[7] PIERCE (*Jonathan*[6], *Stephen*[5], *Jacob*[4], *Stephen*[3], *Thomas*[2], *Thomas*[1]), b. June 5, 1754 ; m. June 13, 1782, Rebecca Wright, b. Feb. 28, 1764, d. June 13, 1844. He d. Nov. 27, 1829. Res. Cavendish, Vt.

He enlisted as a soldier in the Revolutionary War, was at the battle of Bunker Hill, taken prisoner at Quebec and subsequently escaping was recaptured on Arnold's march through Vermont. Benjamin Pierce held the rank of Orderly Sergeant and was the first to scale the walls of Quebec. Children :—

2811. i. REBECCA, b. April 9, 1783 ; d. July 24, 1805.
2812. ii. BRIDGET, b. May 7, 1785; d. Aug. 28, 1873.
2813. iii. BENJAMIN, b. Dec. 21, 1786; m. Tamar Gannett.
2814. iv. LYDIA, b. Mar. 17, 1789; d. Dec. 2, 1848.
2815. v. POLLY, b. Jan. 31, 1791; d. Apr. 10, 1793.
2816. vi. JOSEPH, b. Feb. 11, 1792; m. Bridget Davis.
2817. vii. CYRUS, b. Jan. 5, 1794; d. war of 1812.
2818. viii. JOHN, b. Sept. 24, 1795; m. Lydia Putnam.
2819. ix. SOLOMON, b. June 10, 1797; d. June 10, 1801.
2820. x. ASENATH, b. Feb. 20, 1799; m. Feb. 22, 1823, Alvah Thompson, b. Apr. 7, 1792. Res. Ludlow, Vt. Ch.: William H., b. Jan. 31, 1824, m. Abby P. Bates; Benjamin G., b. Mar. 20, 1826, m. Mary A. Newton; Ann N., b. June 2, 1827, m. Austin Constantine; Eliza R., b. Aug. 21, 1834, m. Wesley Grover.
2821. xi. RHODA, b. Apr. 5, 1801; d. Apr. 8, 1861.
2822. xii. SARAH, b. Feb. 7, 1803; m. John Sawtell, and d. Apr. 25, 1875, s. p.
2823. xiii. STEPHEN, b. May 2, 1804; m. Almira Tarbell.
2824. xiv. ROXANNA, b. July 29, 1806; d. 1856.
2825. xv. DAVID, b. Feb. 27, 1808; m. Susan Kendall.

881. SAMUEL[7] PIERCE (*Samuel*[6], *Samuel*[5], *Samuel*[4], *Samuel*[3],

Thomas², *Thomas¹*), b. June 11, 1779; m. ———— Butler. Res. Rome, N. Y. Child:—

2826. i.   OLIVER B.; m. ————; d. about 15 years ago.

887.   SETH⁷ PIERCE (*Josiah⁶*, *Samuel⁵*, *Samuel⁴*, *Samuel³*, *Thomas²*, *Thomas¹*), b. June 16, 1785; m. Dec. 12, 1811, Cynthia Hawkes, b. 1785, d. Mar. 29, 1834. He d. Jan. 21, 1822. Res. Charlemont, Mass.   Children :—

2827. i.   CASIDARA, b. Oct. 12, 1812; m. Charles B. Wells.
2828. ii.   AUSTIN, b. Oct. 14, 1814; d. Aug., 1842.
2829. iii. CYNTHIA H., b. Jan., 1816; d. May 24, 1824.
2830. iv.   HENRY A., b. Dec. 8, 1818; m. Cornelia Seward.

888.   JOSIAH⁷ PIERCE (*Josiah⁶*, *Samuel⁵*, *Samuel⁴*, *Samuel³*, *Thomas²*, *Thomas¹*), b. June 18, 1787; m. Oct. 13, 1814, Jemima Thornton, b. June 12, 1788. Res. North Adams, Mass. and Geneva, Ill.

Children :—

2831. i.   JUDITH R., b. July 11, 1815; m. Ambrose Bliss.
2832. ii.   ELIZABETH, b. Feb. 2, 1817; m. Lawson McCloud.
2833. iii. HARRIET J., b. June 30, 1819; d. 1849.
2834. iv.   JOSIAH S., b. July 20, 1821; m. Chloe Hammond.
2835. v.   JOHN H., b. Nov. 19, 1823; unm.; res. Chagrin Falls, Ohio.
2836. vi.   POLLY T., b. Feb. 14, 1825; m. Jerome B. Kingsley.
2837. vii. MARYETTA P., b. Nov. 2, 1829; m. C. B. Wells.
2838. viii. HENRY B., b. June 24, 1834; m. Eliza Wilson and Addie L. Potter.

889.   DAVID⁷ PIERCE (*Josiah⁶*, *Samuel⁵*, *Samuel⁴*, *Samuel³*, *Thomas²*, *Thomas¹*), b. Oct. 14, 1789; m. Providence ————. Res. Dresden, Ohio.   No children.

891.   RICHARD⁷ PIERCE (*Josiah⁶*, *Samuel⁵*, *Samuel⁴*, *Samuel³*, *Thomas²*, *Thomas¹*), b. June 9, 1794; m. Oct. 23, 1817, Sally Rudd, b. June 1, 1794, d. Nov. 10, 1877. He d. Nov. 18, 1848. Res. Buckland and Charlemont, Mass.   Children :—

2839. i.   HORACE R., b. July 5, 1818; d. May, 1849.
2840. ii.   DORCAS E., b. Oct. 28, 1819; m. Allen Logan.
2841. iii. ROBERT W., b. Feb. 14, 1821; m. Elizabeth M. Burditt.
2842. iv.   SETH, b. Dec. 14, 1822; d. Dec. 20, 1822.
2843. v.   SARAH F., b. Oct. 28, 1823; d. July 29, 1829.
2844. vi.   ALBERT L., b. Jan. 27, 1825; m. Sarah McFarland.
2845. vii. ————, b. May 9, 1826; d. May 9, 1826.
2846. viii. CORNELIA M., b. May 6, 1827; m. Thomas Mayhew.
2847. ix.   RICHARD M., b. Oct. 6, 1828; d. Jan. 15, 1829.
2848. x.   SARAH F., b. Apr. 17, 1830; d. May 9, 1835.
2849. xi.   RICHARD M., b. May 26, 1832; d. July 21, 1832.

2850. xii. MINERVA M., b. Oct. 30, 1833; d. Sept. 4, 1838.
2851. xiii. HARRIET E., b. Dec. 26, 1835; m. J. K. Sherman.
2852. xiv. SYLVIA H., b. Mar. 22, 1838; m. O. S. Bartlett.
2853. xv. OSCAR H., b. July 6, 1840; m. Martha Horning.
2854. xvi. JANE E., b. Sept. 6, 1842; d. Dec., 1848.

897. DAVID[7] PIERCE (*Josiah*[6], *Josiah*[5], *Samuel*[4], *Samuel*[3], *Thomas*[2], *Thomas*[1]), b. Mar. 31, 1780; m. July 9, 1825, Miriam Cook, b. May 16, 1801, d. Apr. 12, 1873. He d. Mar. 6, 1850. Res. Hadley, Mass. Children:—

2855. i. ELIZA, b. Feb. 13, 1826. Res. Hadley.
2856. ii. WILLIAM M., b. Dec. 30, 1827; m. Fanny M. Shyrock.
2857. iii. SARAH, b. Mar. 23, 1829; m. Alfred Hawkes.
2858. iv. JOHN N., b. Dec. 8, 1833; m. Lucy M. Brackett and Mrs. Calista M. Root.
2859. v. ALMIRA, } twins, b, Oct. 1, 1835; { d. April 3, 1836.
2860. vi. ALMINA, } { res. Hadley.
2861. vii. CHARLES, b. Aug. 19, 1839; d. May 26, 1841.

898. ELIHU[7] PIERCE (*Josiah*[6], *Josiah*[5], *Samuel*[4], *Samuel*[3], *Thomas*[2], *Thomas*[1]), b. Jan. 27, 1782; m. Dec. 31, 1804, Nancy Dunnakin, b. Oct. 20, 1784, d. Mar., 1839. He d. Nov. 15, 1825. Res. Hadley, Mass. Children:—

2862. i. ROSWELL, b. May 3, 1806; d. May 21, 1806.
2863. ii. LUCY, b. May 27, 1807; m. David Boynton.
2864. iii. CYNTHIA, b. Aug. 3, 1809; m. Feb. 1, 1827, Quartus Clapp, b. Sept. 25, 1796.
2865. iv. MARY, b. Sept. 23, 1811; m. Henry Drury.
2866. v. BELINDA, b. July 1, 1814; m. Nathan Pierce. Res. N. Amherst.
2867. vi. PHEBE, b. May 23, 1817; m. Ebenezer Jones and Isaac Smith.
2868. vii. NANCY, b. Mar. 15, 1820; d. Oct., 1838.
2869. viii. SAMUEL, b. May 9, 1822; d. May 30, 1822.
2870. ix. JOSIAH, b. Feb. 4, 1824; m. Hannah M. Muzzey.
2871. x. MARTHA, b. July 1, 1826; m. Wm. Crossman. Res. Shutesbury.

899. JOB[7] PIERCE (*Josiah*[6], *Josiah*[5], *Samuel*[4], *Samuel*[3], *Thomas*[2], *Thomas*[1]), b. July 8, 1785; m. Dec. 10, 1810, Thankful Fairfield, b. Jan. 19, 1784, d. Dec. 21, 1857. He d. May 10, 1879. Res. Hadley, Mass., and Lyme, N. H. Children :—

2872. i. JOHN F., b. July 14, 1811; m. Nancy Bardwell.
2873. ii. DAVID, b. 1813; d. 1813.
2874. iii. FRANCIS N., b. 1817; res. Hadley.
2875. iv. DAVID, b. July 24, 1822; res. Australia.
2876. v. RUFUS S., b. 1824; res. California.
2877. vi. LEWIS, b. Jan. 20, 1826; m. Frances Emerson and Louise M. Ives.

903. GORDON[7] PIERCE (*Seth*[6], *Seth*[5], *Samuel*[4], *Samuel*[3], *Thomas*[2], *Thomas*[1]), b. Aug. 31, 1773; m. 1796, Thirsa Smalley, d. 1861. He d. Feb. 7, 1875. They res. in Thetford and Norwich, Vt., and Pitcher, N. Y. Children:—

2878. i. ALMINA, b. 1798; m. Jan. 7, 1818, John Coy, b. Sept. 6, 1799. Ch.: William W., b. Jan. 14, 1820, m. Nancy Smith and Mary J. Paddock; Orlando P., b. Aug. 11, 1821, m. Helen Hyslop; John A., b. Nov. 11, 1822, m. Ada Hulbert; Bela A., b. July 8, 1824, m. Delett R. Craudal; Thirsa L., b. Apr. 5, 1826, m. Josiah Flint; Daniel T., b. May 21, 1828, d. Mar. 21, 1852; Gurdon P., b. June 15, 1830, m. Maria Flanders; Irus, b. July

25, 1832, m. Augusta Manchester; Lucien, b. Aug. 31, 1834, d.
Oct. 9, 1834; Winfield S., b. July 8, 1838; Milton A., b. Feb.
21, 1841; Julia M., b. Nov. 22, 1843, m. J. D. Fox.
2879. ii. AUSTIN, b. Sept. 2, 1799; m. Mar. 17, 1826, Mary A. Sterling.
2880. iii. MINERVA P., b. Jan. 25, 1803; m. Feb. 10, 1829, Jethro Hatch, b.
1791, d. Feb. 7, 1875.   Ch.: Misulla P., b. Jan. 4, 1830, m. Dr.
Lawson A. Winslow; Fayette S., b. Oct. 9, 1832, m. Teresa M.
Pierce (———); Jethro A., b. June 18, 1836; Mattie, b. Jan.
13, 1840, m. D. C. Winslow; Austin P., b. June 24, 1843, m.
Melissa J. Snow.
2881. iv. FRANCIS S., b. Feb. 6, 1806; m. Oct. 25, 1831, Rebecca Page.
2882. v. ROYAL S., b. Jan. 8, 1812; m. Sept. 30, 1835, Juliet Morton.

906. SAMUEL[7] PIERCE (*Seth*[6], *Seth*[5], *Samuel*[4], *Samuel*[3], *Thomas*[2],
Thomas[1]), b. May 20, 1779; m. 1800, Persis Barrows, b. Oct., 1783,
d. Feb. 5, 1858. He d. Aug. 17, 1849. They res. in Brimfield and
Hardwick, Mass.
The house of Samuel Pierce stood on the boundary line between
Hardwick and Ware. It is related that he slept in a bed which was
in two towns and two counties at the same time; his head in Ware in
Hampshire county and his feet in Hardwick in Worcester county, and
vice versa.   Children :—

2883. i. SETH, b. May 15, 1802; m. Sept. 22, 1831, Fidelia Barrett.
2884. ii. CHESTER, b. June 20, 1803; m. Mar. 15, 1831, Abigail Marsh.
2885. iii. ELIZA, b. Feb. 7, 1805; m. Feb. 10, 1825, William Pepper, b.
Mar. 17, 1804. Ch.: Abbie F., b. June 24, 1832, m. Daniel A.
Sampson; Caroline W., b. Mar. 4, 1828, m. Geo. F. Tyler;
Samuel J., b. Nov. 2, 1829, m. Sarah Torrey; Wm. A., b. June
25, 1834; Ashbell, b. Apr. 7, 1838, m. Martha Sibley; Elijah, b.
Apr. 27, 1840; Austin, b. Jan. 23, 1845, m. Eva Burnett.
2886. iv. GRANGER, b. 1806; m. Mercy Stockwell.
2887. v. S. AUSTIN, b. Oct. 6, 1808; m. Jan. 28, 1831, Roxanne Harwood.
2888. vi. WILLIAM, b. Mar. 4, 1810; m. Sarah Witherell.
2889. vii. BRIGHAM, b. 1812; m. Mrs. Cook.
2890. viii. MANDLEY, b. Oct. 31, 1817; m. May 3, 1842, Emily Thomas.
2891. ix. OCTAVIA, b. Dec. 18, 1819; m. Dec. 15, 1844, Byram H. Hervey.
They res. in New Braintree. Ch.: Elizabeth F., b. Nov. 8,
1846, m. J. Edward Barr; George Fred'k, b. Nov. 24, 1850, m.
Catherine Twombley.

907. ELIJAH[7] PIERCE (*Seth*[6], *Seth*[5], *Samuel*[4], *Samuel*[3], *Thomas*[2],
Thomas[1]), b. Apr. 27, 1781; m. Feb. 8, 1801, Patty Moulton, b. Feb.
5, 1782, d. Apr. 17, 1838. He d. Apr. 7, 1832. They res. in Brimfield, Mass., and Homer, N. Y.   Children :—

2892. i. ALMA, b. Feb. 10, 1802; m. Sept. 2, 1827, Lucas Welch. Ch.:
Martha J., b. Dec. 5, 1828, m. Walter Jones; Maria S., b. May
31, 1833, m. Sam'l Harris, M. D.; Adeline L., b. Apr. 13, 1837,
m. E. H. Coon; Clarissa A., b. Jan. 24, 1840, d. Jan. 21, 1843;
Calvin S., b. Aug. 14, 1846, d. Oct. 9, 1846.
2893. ii. JUSTIN M., b. Nov. 9, 1804; m. Aug. 21, 1833, Mary Trowbridge.
2894. iii. DANIEL, b. Feb. 12, 1807; m. Jan. 8, 1835, Sarah S. Sharp.
2895. iv. HORACE, b. Dec. 28, 1809; m. Jan. 21, 1835, Sarah A. Smith.
2895½. v. ADELINE, b. Jan. 23, 1815; m. Aug. 17, 1847, Seth Ferguson, b.
Jan. 6, 1810. Ch.: Mary A., b. Oct. 25, 1848; John H., b. Nov.
22, 1851. They res. in Homer, N. Y.

913. ALGERNON[7] PIERCE (*Enoch*[6], *Enoch*[5], *Samuel*[4], *Samuel*[3],
Thomas[2], *Thomas*[1]), b. Jan. 17, 1786; m. March, 22, 1818, Phebe,

Evans, d. May 26, 1861. He d. April 20, 1826. Res. North Pitcher, N. Y. Children :—

2896. i. LUCIUS E., b. Jan. 19, 1819; m. Chloe Chevalier and Clarinda Porter.
2897. ii. JULIUS S., b. Nov. 5, 1820; d. June 24, 1849.
2898. iii. HENRY E., b. June 10, 1823; m. Lydia E. Hyde and Maria L. Ishanger.
2899. iv. S. ALGERNON, b. Aug. 7, 1826; d. June, 1833.

916. ENOCH[7] PIERCE (*Enoch*[6], *Enoch*[5], *Samuel*[4], *Samuel*[3], *Thomas*[2], *Thomas*[1]), b. July 17, 1795 ; m. April 25, 1821, Laura Dean, b. 1797, d. Jan. 24, 1857. He d. Sept. 30, 1854. Res. Eastford. Children :—

2900. i. ELIZABETH T.; d. young.

917. EARL[7] PIERCE (*Enoch*[6], *Enoch*[5], *Samuel*[4], *Samuel*[3], *Thomas*[2], *Thomas*[1]), b. April 3, 1798 ; m. Sept. 17, 1823, Olive Stearns, b. Jan. 3, 1799, d. Feb. 24, 1870. Res. Mansfield, Conn.

Composed by EARL PIERCE, *on his eightieth birthday, April 3, 1878, at Mansfield.*

My eightieth birthday now has come,
North Mansfield is my native home;
It seems the most like home to me
Of any place where I can be.

I think I live among my friends
On whom my happiness depends ;
I like this eastern country best,
Instead of going further west.

If I should live another year,
Perhaps my friends will find me here ;
The time is short for me to stay—
I may not live another day.

I 'm growing older every breath,
I ought to be prepared for death,
And strive to act the better part,
And serve the Lord with all my heart.

Composed by the same on his eighty-first birthday, April 3, 1879, at Mansfield.

Another birthday now is mine,
The third of April, 'seventy-nine ;
Another year is now begun—
My present age is eighty-one.

I thank the Lord for blessings past,
For special favors first and last ;
And hope to meet Him as a friend,
When birthdays here shall have an end,
And find an everlasting Home,
To praise Him in the world to come.

Earl Pierce.

Children :—

2901. i. LATHROP S., b. Sept. 24, 1824; m. Julia M. Gurley.
2902. ii. WILLIAM P., b. Aug. 14, 1827; d. June 23, 1849.

2903. iii. SHEPPARD H., b. Nov. 14, 1830; m. Frances Haven and Olive Fox.
2904. iv. CORNELIA M., b. Oct. 19, 1833; d. Feb. 16, 1840.
2905. v. DELIA J., b. Jan. 1, 1842; d. Sept. 20, 1852.

926. Major JOSEPH H.[7] PIERCE (*Joseph*[6], *Isaac*[5], *Isaac*[4], *Samuel*[3], *Thomas*[2], *Thomas*[1]), b. March 8, 1773 ; m. Dec., 1791, Frances Temple Cordis, dau. of Joseph Cordis, Esq., of Charlestown, Mass., b. Dec. 3, 1776, d. Apr. 8, 1815; m. 2nd, Aug. 16, 1819, Abby Robinson, of Newport, R. I., b. Feb. 16, 1790, d. Dec. 3, 1832. He d. Dec. 3, 1832.

Major Pierce was a man of most elegant presence. He passed several years abroad. In 1802-5 was Lieutenant, with rank of Major of the Independent Corps of Cadets ; was also some years aide-de-camp to several Governors ; was Secretary of the Board of War ; Clerk of the Municipal Court and from his dignified presence was often mistaken for the Judge. In 1824 he was appointed agent of Massachusetts for claims against the General Government growing out of the war of 1812, and passed the season in Washington. His daughters were celebrated beauties; Frances, the eldest, a blonde, was said by Joseph Bonaparte, who met her at a ball in Boston, to be the handsomest lady he had ever seen in America. Major Pierce was lost at sea with his wife while on a passage from New York to Mobile and New Orleans.

Joseph H. Peirce

Children :—

2906. i. JOSEPH, b. May 9, 1792; d. Sept. 3, 1823.
2907. ii. FRANCES, b. Jan. 17, 1794; m. Oct. 24, 1810, Henry Gray, a son of Lieut.-Governor William Gray, the famous merchant, d. Dec. 10, 1854. She d. Mar. 22, 1830. Ch. : Frances E., b. July 2, 1811; William H., b. Oct. 22, 1812; John, b. Nov. 18, 1813; Henry, Jr., b. Apr. 25, 1815, d. 1851; Francis, b. Nov. 22, 1816, d. Sept. 4, 1817; Caroline, b. Jan. 18, 1818, m. John Haskins; Charles R., b. Feb. 11, 1819; Lydia F., b. Jan. 11, 1820, m. Elias Cornelius ; Mary C., b. Apr. 16, 1821, m. Charles A. Winthrop; a son, b. June 29, 1822, d. July 1, 1822; Frederick W., b. Oct. 7, 1823; Arthur, b. Dec. 14, 1824; Frances, b. Feb. 5, 1826; Francis, b. Mar. 7, 1827; Horatio, b. Dec. 13, 1828; Anna E. C., b. Mar. 19, 1830, m. Rev. William H. Brooks.
2908. iii. DELIA, b. Feb. 16, 1796; m. May 10, 1852, Gen. Jos. L. C. Amee, b. 1800, d. Feb. 4, 1867. They had no issue. He was at one time Chief of the Boston Police force and during the late Rebellion was Quartermaster-General in Gen. Sheridan's command.
2909. iv. MARCIA, b. Apr. 29, 1797; m. Nov. 7, 1835, Thomas Blanchard, d. Feb. 4, 1864. She d. Nov. 15, 1861. Ch. : Henrietta P., b. Nov. 11, 1836, d. Mar. 8, 1837; Thomas H. P., b. Aug. 7, 1838, d. Oct. 29, 1845; Delia P., b. Sept. 25, 1840, d. Apr. 25, 1867.

A brief biography of Thomas Blanchard, the inventor of the mechanical combination for turning irregular forms, who died at Boston in 1865, has just been issued. The writer, Asa

H. Waters, says that although the name of Thomas Blanchard is not so popularly known as many others who have achieved fame from single inventions, the writer boldly asserts that •—It may be questioned whether another inventor can be named in this country or in Europe, during the last century, who has produced so many different labor-saving machines, applicable to such a great variety of uses, and which have contributed so largely to the common necessities, comforts and economies of life. This language may seem extravagant, but it must be remembered that not an armory exists in this country or in England where guns are made—hardly a human being that wears boots or shoes—scarcely a vessel that sails upon the ocean—not a school where slates are used—not a carpet laid down, but that owes tribute to the genius of Thomas Blanchard for producing articles cheaper and better. The same may be said of carriage wheels, ploughs, shovels and various articles of furniture. Latterly, his machines have been applied to carving, to architectural designs and even to statuary—much to the surprise of artists. Indeed, there seems to be no limit to the uses made of Blanchard's inventions, and it is impossible at present to enumerate them. One can hardly go into a tool shop, a machine shop, or a workshop of any kind, wood or iron, where motive power is used, in which he will not find more or less of Blanchard's mechanical motions.

Blanchard was a native of Sutton, Mass., and was born June 24, 1788. His father, Samuel, was a farmer, and lived on a poor, remote strip of land, where there was absolutely nothing to suggest a mechanical motion. While on the farm Thomas gave little if any promise of the latent powers within him. There was nothing in his surroundings to excite them. He was misplaced; schools were remote, and he seldom attended, for he was afflicted with a perverse impediment of speech, so that the boys called him "Stammering Tom." At the age of 18 he was engaged by his elder brother, Stephen, to assist him in his tack-mill, which he had just started in West Millbury. Young Thomas's duty it was to head the tacks in a vise, with a hand hammer, one by one. Once in a mechanic shop his dormant genius began to wake up. Ere he had spent many months heading tacks, one by one, he had designed, constructed and put in operation a machine which would cut and head them at one motion twice as fast as the ticking of a watch, and better finished than those made by hand. So perfect was it in design and construction it was continued in use more than twenty years. It is said to be still in existence, and experts who have seen it say no essential improvement has ever been made upon it. The reputation of the boy's success in his brother's tack factory led Mr. Asa Waters, who had in the same town of Millbury an armory, where he manufactured arms for the government, to send for the budding inventor, and there young Blanchard, at almost a glance at the old processes for shaping gun barrels, suggested an improvement by which the irregular butt of the barrel could be turned by machinery, and afterward produced a machine for turning out the gun stock. The germ of the stocking machine lay in that cam motion, and it was then and there, as he afterwards said, that the idea of his world-renowned machine for turning irregular forms first flashed through his mind, although it required some months to elaborate and bring it out. Blanchard was afterwards called to the Springfield armory, where his machines were introduced and adopted by the government. His machine for producing irregular forms was applied to a vast number of special purposes. Unlike many other in-

23

ventions, this was really the discovery of a new principle in mechanics, whereby the machine is made the obedient, faithful servant of man, to work out his designs after any given model, be it round or square, crooked or straight, however irregular and made to reproduce the original shape exactly, every time. This perfect uniformity of Blanchard's work suggested the idea of having all the parts of the guns made at the armories perfectly uniform, so as to be interchangeable. Hitherto they had been fitted separately, like Swiss watches, and carefully lettered or numbered. This is the method in all our workshops, even to the bolts of a carriage or a common bedstead, and woe to him who misplaced one. It was Blanchard who first rendered possible the accomplishment of the desired result with respect to arms, and to him the writer gives the credit of the origin of the "uniformity system" which has revolutionized mechanic processes in all our workshops; perfected and greatly cheapened mechanic products, and driven from use the old system of numbering.

Blanchard realized but little pecuniarily on his patents, for they were so pirated upon that he had to spend many thousands of dollars in defending his rights in the courts. He succeeded in getting an extension of his patent for producing irregular forms, but at the end of the extension he had made practically nothing on it, and began to think of trying for a second extension; but such a thing was unprecedented, and Blanchard, knowing that great opposition would be made to another renewal, thought he would resort to a little stratagem. He fitted up a machine for turning busts from marble blocks, took it to Washington, obtained plaster casts of the heads of Webster, Clay, Calhoun, and others, and exhibited the busts in the rotunda of the capitol. The members were quite astonished when they found that these busts were wrought out by a machine and that they were more exactly like the originals than any human hand could make them. It produced a great sensation. They all supposed it a new invention. Blanchard said, "No, not a new invention, but a new application of an old one of mine from which I never realized much, and I want the patent renewed." A resolution was introduced in the Senate by Webster to renew it for a term of years, and it was rushed through without delay.

When the news was first proclaimed from Springfield of a machine which turned gun-stocks, mechanics came floating from near and far to see it. Among those attracted were two members of the British parliament, then traveling in this country. When they returned to England they reported the wonderful invention of Blanchard, by whom the Americans were getting greatly in advance of them in gun manufacture, and moved a resolution for the purchase of similar machines. A true John Bull member then arose and ridiculed them unmercifully for being so badly sold and played upon by the cunning Yankees. "The very idea of turning a gun-stock is absurd on the face of it, as all must know who ever saw one." Finding the resolution would fail the two members withdrew it and moved for a committee to go to the United States armory and report upon the facts. The committee came over, examined the workings of the machine, returned and reported the facts to be as at first stated. The doubting Thomas rose and said the Americans might have got up something to work their soft woods, pine and poplar, but it would never stand the test of "our tough English oak and hickory." Upon this, doubting Thomas himself was chosen a committee to go over and examine. He was not to be imposed upon; he would expose this humbug. Selecting three rough stocks of the hardest, toughest timber he could find, he went to the Springfield armory incognito, brought his stocks to the stocking room, and inquired of the overseer if he would grant him the favor of turning them. "Certainly, sir; take a seat." Without making the least alteration of the machine the overseer run the stocks through in a few minutes, and then went on with his work as though nothing unusual had happened. The Englishman examined the stocks, found they were turned all the better for being of hard wood, and he was completely dumbfounded. After musing awhile, he frankly confessed who he was, why he came, and his thorough conviction of the utility of the machine. Before he left the city he gave an order in behalf of the British government for this and the accompanying machines, some six or eight, which amounted to some $40,000. The machines were built at Chicopee, shipped to England, and have been in use there from that day to this.

2910. v. MARCUS T., b. May 17, 1799; m. Apr. 28, 1830, Sarah C. E. Wood, dau. of Judge Wood, of Savannah, Georgia.
2911. vi. CONSTANTIUS, b. May 9, 1801; m. Nov. 25, 1823, Mary Steer.
2912. vii. ISAAC, b. Jan. 21, 1803; d. prob. 1848; unm.
2913. viii. LAURA, b. Apr. 28, 1804; m. Sept. 6, 1825, Captain S. M. Holland, b. Dec. 14, 1798, d. Jan. 18, 1833. Ch.: Frances T., b. Sept. 17, 1826, m. Franklin Blanchard; John, b. Nov. 23, 1827, m. Eliza P. Cosgrove; Laura P., b. Aug. 12, 1830; Sarah M., b. Aug. 21, 1833, m. Harrison Ellery. She res. in Chelsea.
2914. ix. ANN, b. Apr. 30, 1805; m. Sept. 22, 1835, Ed. A. West, b. 1805, d. Mar. 11, 1871. Ch.: Walter, b. Aug. 10, 1836; Frances A., b. Dec. 29, 1837, d. Aug. 24, 1840; Mary L., b. Dec. 20, 1840, d. Nov. 20, 1841; Frances C., b. 1843; Frederick, b. Dec. 28, 1844, d. May 31, 1846; Clifford H., b. Nov. 10, 1846.
2914½. x. MARY ELIZABETH, b. Mar. 31, 1807; m. Jan. 29, 1826, Col. Edward Fitch Hall, b. Mar. 15, 1798, of Medford, Mass., where they reside. He is a Commission Merchant, of Boston. Children: Delia Cordis, b. Dec. 5, 1826, d. 1829; Delia Frances, b. May 19, 1830, d. 1830; George Brown, b. Oct. 21, 1831, d. 1834; Georgianna, b. Dec. 27, 1833, d. 1842; Mary Ellen, b. July 20, 1835, m. Oct., 1855, Edward Richmond. He d. 1871. She d. Oct. 26, 1859. Henrietta, b. Jan. 23, 1837, m. Jan. 23, 1859, Wm. S., son of Rev. John Turner Sargent; Edward Fitch, b. Nov. 15, 1838, m. Lottie Brown; Marcus, b. 1844, m. Delia Page.
2915. xi. HENRY A., b. Dec. 15, 1808; m. July 3, 1838, Susan R. Thompson.
2916. xii. JOHN D., b. Aug. 6, 1812; m. Mrs. Smith.
2917. xiii. HARDY, b. Mar. 21, 1814; d. May 1, 1838.
2918. xiv. SARAH R., b. 1820; d. 1820.
2919. xv. EMMA, b. 1821; d. 1826.

The five daughters of Major Joseph Hardy Pierce while in Washington attended a grand ball given by Mrs. John Quincy Adams, on the 8th of January, 1824, the anniversary of the battle of New Orleans. It was estimated that one thousand persons were present, many very distinguished. The *Washington Republican* at that time published the famous poem by "Orlando," which is still remembered by many of our older people. In it the Pierces were gallantly noticed as follows:—

    "Wend you with the world to-night?
      Sixty gray—and giddy twenty,
    Flirts that court and prudes that slight,
      State coquettes and spinsters plenty.

Mrs. Sullivan is there,
  With all the charms that Nature lent her;
Gay McKim, with city air;
  And winning Gates and Vanderventer;
Forsyth, with her group of graces;
  Both the Crowninshields in blue;
The *Pierces*, with their heavenly faces,
  And eyes like suns that dazzle through.
Belles and matrons—maids and maidens,
All are gone to Mrs. Adams'."

Lines written by Thomas Bulfinch, author of "The Age of Fable," etc., on board the schooner *Zephyr*, at Alexandria, May 13, 1824, on the departure of the five daughters of Major Joseph Hardy Pierce, for Boston:—

Brave vessel! know'st thou what a freight
  Thy gallant timbers soon shall bear?
The famed Venetian bark of State
  Ne'er bore a freight so rich and rare.

Fair Delia with the dimpled cheek,
  And Marcia with the pensive brow,
And Laura with the eyes that speak,
  Ere from her lips the accents flow.

And Ann, the conqueror of hearts,
  With charms at will—a very fairy;
And there arrayed in Beauty's darts,
  Hebe—(the mortals call her Mary).

Brave vessel—may thy oaken sides
  Cleave old Potomac's billowy breast,
And homeward speed as swift as glides
  The parent swallow to her nest.

939. Asa[7] Pierce (*William*[6], *William*[5], *Sommers*[4], *William*[3], *Thomas*[2], *Thomas*[1]), b. Dec. 6, 1788; m. Mar. 13, 1817, Hannah Higgins, b. Mar. 30, 1798, d. Dec. 30, 1872. He d. Feb. 3, 1874. Res. Clarendon, Mount Holly and Weston, Vt.

Children :—

2920.	i.	CALVIN H., b. Jan. 20, 1818; d. Dec. 26, 1827.
2921.	ii.	WILLIAM J., b. Oct. 4, 1820; m. Serepta Hossiter.
2922.	iii.	SARAH A., b. Apr. 8, 1825; m. July 4, 1844, Henry Burton.
2923.	iv.	MARY, b. Oct. 28, 1827; m. Aug., 1852, Nelson Miller.
2924.	v.	WARREN A., b. July 14, 1831; m. Frances J. Davis.
2925.	vi.	WESLEY, b. Nov. 18, 1833; d. Aug. 29, 1864.
2926.	vii.	ALBERT H., b. Mar. 10, 1836; m. Eugenia Hossiter.

942. William[7] Pierce (*William*[6], *William*[5], *Sommers*[4], *William*[3], *Thomas*[2], *Thomas*[1]), b. Sept. 20, 1785; m. Mary Moncrief, b. Oct. 4, 1786, d. Jan. 5, 1847. He d. May 26, 1867. Res. Salem, N. Y.

Children :—

2927. i. HUGH, b. Nov. 12, 1818; m. Mary Rogers.
2928. ii. WILLIAM, b. June 7, 1820; m. Adelaide Bristol.
2929. iii. JOHN, b. Mar. 31, 1824; m. Ann E. Tucker.
2930. iv. SARAH J., b. Mar. 3, 1822; m. Almon Botsford.

951. Capt. ABIEL[7] PIERCE (*Benjamin[6]*, *William[5]*, *Sommers[4]*, *William[3]*, *Thomas[2]*, *Thomas[1]*), b. Mar. 21, 1791; m. July 20, 1717, Nancy Holt, b. Nov. 24, 1793, d. Jan. 13, 1828; m. 2nd, Apr. 13, 1830, Hannah K. Manning, b. Sept. 4, 1792, d. Jan. 1, 1878. He d. Nov. 30, 1871. Res. Andover, Vt., and Dodge's Corner, Wis. Abiel Pierce was born in Wilton, N. H. When he was four years old his parents moved to Andover, Windsor Co., Vt. When old enough to leave home and care for himself he bought a farm in Andover, and remained there until 1838, when he moved to Vernon, Wis., where he lived the remainder of his life. He was Captain of the State Militia for a number of years and was familiarly known as "Captain Pierce." He was one of the first settlers in Waukesha Co. Children :—

2931. i. DORCAS L., b. Jan. 30, 1818; m. July 18, 1837, Orrin B. Haseltine, b. Feb. 22, 1816. She d. Mar. 7, 1874. They res. in Dodge's Corner, Wis. Children: Calista D., b. July 1, 1838, m. Wesley R. Park; Jane N., b. Aug. 16, 1840, m. Warren W. Carlton; Ellen L., b. May 11, 1842, m. Warren Walker; Oren P., b. May 4, 1846, m. Mary Downs; Rollin B., b. April 20, 1848; Ewin M., b. June 22, 1850, m. Susan Davis; Nora E., b. Sept. 11, 1860.
2932. ii. DOROTHY G., b. July 26, 1819; m. July 18, 1837, John Dodge, b. Sept. 10, 1813; d. July 29, 1858, s. p.
2933. iii. ABIEL H., b. May 23, 1822; m. Cordelia B. Finton.
2934. iv. LUCINDA W., b. Oct. 26, 1824; m. Feb. 24, 1849, Curtis Carlton, b. Aug. 6, 1823; d. Aug. 11, 1854. Res. Dodge's Corner, Wis. Ch.: Fred. M., b. Nov. 27, 1852.

952. ASA[7] PIERCE (*Benjamin[6]*, *William[5]*, *Sommers[4]*, *William[3]*, *Thomas[2]*, *Thomas[1]*), b. Mar. 17, 1793; m. Sept. 29, 1818, Betsey Dodge, b. Dec. 29, 1789. He d. Dec. 7, 1858. Res. Adrian, Mich., and Fort Wayne, Ind. Children :—

2935. i. ASA W., b. Sept. 22, 1821; m. Annie Poinsett and Hester Corey.
2936. ii. BETSEY L., b. Oct. 18, 1822; m. Jan. 16, 1842, Samuel Cartwright. Res. Fort Wayne, Ind. Ch.: Lewis A., b. April 9, 1844; Betsey, b. May 17, 1854, d. May 20, 1854; Jas. W., b. July 9, 1856.
2937. iii. PARYNTHIA D., b. Nov. 22, 1824; m. Aug. 16, 1850, Solomon P. Haswell. She d. Jan. 24, 1873. Res. Fort Wayne, Ind. Ch.: Altha L., b. Aug. 13, 1851; Amelia W., b. Feb. 16, 1856.
2938. iv. JAMES S., b. Mar. 6, 1827; m. Mary Rockwill and Phebe Strout.
2939. v. MARY J., b. Nov. 29, 1837; d. July 30, 1866.

953. ALVAH[7] PIERCE (*Benjamin[6]*, *William[5]*, *Sommers[4]*, *William[3]*, *Thomas[2]*, *Thomas[1]*), b. Oct. 6, 1796; m. Sept. 21, 1817, Dolly Baker, b. May 9, 1795, d. Aug. 17, 1879. He d. Sept. 22, 1818. She m. 2nd, Oliver Atwood. Res. Andover, Vt. Child :—

2940. i. ALVAH W., b. June 26, 1818; m. Lydia W. Atwood and Lucy C. Allen.

955. ALANSON[7] PIERCE (*Benjamin*[6], *William*[5], *Sommers*[4], *William*[3], *Thomas*[2], *Thomas*[1]), b. Aug. 27, 1801 ; m. May 1, 1825, Hannah Burton, d. April 20, 1851. Res. Weathersfield, Vt. Children :—

2941. i.   FERNANDO A., b. Apr. 25, 1826; m. Betsey A. Hoyt.
2942. ii   AUGUSTA H., b. July 11, 1829.
2943. iii. HARRIET J., b. Sept. 4, 1835 ; d. July 11, 1838 ;
2944. iv.   SAMUEL B., b. Sept. 5, 1839 ; m. Mary E. Bond.

956. ABEL[7] PIERCE (*Benjamin*[6], *William*[5], *Sommers*[4], *William*[3], *Thomas*[2], *Thomas*[1]), b. Apr. 1, 1804 ; m. May 8, 1825, Harriet Dodge, b. Aug. 1, 1809, d. June 26, 1838. He d. June 25, 1832. Children :—

2945. i.   LORENZO A., b. Jan. 27, 1826; m. Charlotte L. Davis.
2946. ii.   ROYAL A., b. Feb. 23, 1828; m. Eliza A. Ashdown.
2947. iii. MARTHA H., b. Oct. 13, 1830 ; m. Hascal Hazeltine.

965. JAMES[7] PIERCE (*Nathan*[6], *James*[5], *James*[4], *James*[3], *Thomas*[2], *Thomas*[1]), b. June 7, 1790 ; m. Apr. 19, 1813, Polly Wood, b. Jan. 12, 1792. He res. in Hubbardston and d. there, Oct. 16, 1838. She was an inmate of the Old Ladies' Home in Charlestown for a number of years, where she d. Oct. 9, 1877. Children :—

2947½. i. MARY, b. Jan. 9, 1815; m. Apr. 20, 1829, George W. Foster, d. 1862. Ch.: George W., Jr., b. June 7, 1835, m. Abbie B. Woodward; Josephine, b. Jan. 17, 1836, d. Dec., 1837 ; Lydia A., b. Jan. 17, 1840, d. May 19, 1840; Mary J., b. Dec. 8, 1844, m. Samuel W. Bradley.
2948. ii.   DEBORAH, b. Aug. 30, 1816; d. Nov. 30, 1816.
2949. iii. JAMES, b. Dec. 17, 1818; d. Dec. 8, 1821.
2950. iv.   ELLEN M., b. Sept. 8, 1819 ; d. Dec. 29, 1820.
2951. v.   SYLVANUS W., b. Jan. 27, 1821 ; d. Dec. 8, 1822.
2952. vi.   JAMES, b. Dec. 24, 1822 ; d. Sept. 7, 1823.
2953. vii. JAMES, Jr., b. July 4, 1824 ; m. Jane Hunt.
2954. viii. ELLEN, b. Oct. 14, 1825 ; d. Nov. 25, 1826.
2955. ix.   LUCY, b. Feb. 20, 1827 ; d. Aug 30, 1827.
2956. x.   GEORGE, b. March 1, 1828 ; m. Mary E Trask.
2957. xi.   LYDIA, b. Jan. 3, 1831 ; d. Dec. 1, 1838.
2958. xii. SARAH, b. June 21, 1833 ; m. Uriah Gatchell. They res. in So. Wolfboro', N. H.
2959. xiii. NATHAN. b. Feb. 11, 1836 ; d. Dec. 27, 1836.

966. SAMUEL[7] PIERCE (*Nathan*[6], *James*[5], *James*[4], *James*[3], *Thomas*[2], *Thomas*[1]), b. 1800 ; m. —— Merriam ; m. 2nd, Priscilla E. Moore. He d. Sept. 12, 1873. Res. Hubbardston, Mass. Children :—

2960. i.   LEANDER, b. July 4, 1837 ; killed at battle of Newbern, N. C., March 14, 1862.
2961. ii.   ASA, b. Jan. 2, 1841 ; d. young.
2962. iii. ELIZA, b. March 16, 1832 ; m. William Pierce. [2963].

968. JOSIAH[7] PIERCE (*Nathan*[6], *James*[5], *James*[4], *James*[3], *Thomas*[2], *Thomas*[1]), b. 1804 ; m. Nov. 9, 1826, Ellen Davis, b. 1788, d. July 13, 1850 ; m. 2nd, 1857, Polly Baker. He d. Oct. 12, 1860. Children :—

2963. i.   WILLIAM, b. July 20, 1828 ; m. Eliza Pierce [2962].
2964. ii.   HARVEY L., b. Oct. 22, 1838 ; m. Louise J. Bruce.
2965. iii. IRA A., b. July 29, 1845 ; m. Jane Ekis.
2966. iv.   ANNA E. ; m. —— Mowry.

971. ABEL.[7] PIERCE, Jr. (*Abel*[6], *James*[5], *James*[4], *James*[3], *Thomas*[2], *Thomas*[1]), b. Jan. 25, 1797 ; m. Apr. 4, 1822, Almira Russell, b. 1804, d. Oct. 15, 1836 ; m. 2nd, Jan. 17, 1840, Mary C. Dickson, b. 1809, d. Feb. 1, 1848 ; m. 3rd, Jan. 17, 1849, Eliza Dickson, b. July 18, 1811. They res. in Arlington. He is noted for his eccentric habits.

Abel Pierce

Children :—

2967. i. ABEL, Jr., b. Aug. 15, 1831 ; d. May 22, 1833.
2968. ii. OLIVER H., b. Oct. 1, 1825 ; m. May 16, 1850, Mary P. Warren.
2969. iii. SARAH H., b. Jan. 2, 1834 ; m. Nov. 16, 1852, Varnam Frost. Ch. : Alma L., b. Oct. 1, 1856 ; Howard, b. Apr. 19, 1861 ; Louis P., b. Jan. 1, 1866. Res. Arlington.
2970. iv. ALMIRA R., b. Sept. 7, 1829 ; m. Dec. 21, 1848, Samuel Wells, b. Aug. 2, 1820. Ch. : Sarah R., b. Oct. 16, 1849, m. Wm. W. Benjamin ; Henry W., b. Nov. 12, 1851, m. Flora A. Richardson ; Frank W., b. Jan. 4, 1854 ; Abel P. and Ella J., b. Mar. 7, 1853. She d. Nov 3, 1863 ; Maria H., b. Sept. 20, 1866 ; Carrie G., b. Jan. 13, 1868. Res. Winchester.
2971. v. MARY E., b. Aug. 27, 1850.

975. WILLIAM[7] PIERCE (*Abel*[6], *James*[5], *James*[4], *James*[3], *Thomas*[2], *Thomas*[1]), b. Apr. 30, 1807 ; m. June 19, 1828, Lydia Sleeper, d. Nov. 24, 1853 ; m. 2nd, May 12, 1856, Jane Clark. He d. Jan. 31, 1880. He res. in Woburn.

William Pierce

Children :—

2972. i. SULLIVAN, b. June 18, 1828 ; m. 1854, Ruth Bosworth.
2973. ii. LYDIA J., b. Sept. 26, 1829 ; d. May 10, 1831.
2974. iii. ANNA M., b. June 10, 1831 ; m. —— Chamberlin.
2975. iv. WILLIAM H., b. Dec. 10, 1832 ; d. infant.
2976. v. ELIZA A., b. Mar. 4, 1835 ; m. May 29, 1871, Lowell W. Chamberlin ; no issue. Res. Charlestown.
2977. vi. FIDELIA, b. May 1, 1836 ; m. George Means.
2978. vii. ELLA W., b. Nov. 18, 1843 ; m. Aug. 25, 1863, Captain J. Harvey Symonds. Ch. : William P., b. Feb. 15, 1865. She is quite a noted writer and res. in Woburn.
2979. viii. WILLIAM E., b. Dec. 17, 1847 ; d. infant.

976. GEORGE W.[7] PIERCE (*Abel*[6], *James*[5], *James*[4], *James*[3], *Thomas*[2], *Thomas*[1]), b. July 14, 1819 ; m. Sept. 26, 1840, Eliza B. Hutchinson, b. Feb. 25, 1824, d. Nov. 4, 1848 ; m. 2nd, Hannah C. Merrill, b. July 14, 1825. Res. Lynn, Mass.

George Pierce

Children :—

2980. i. WILLIAM H., b. July 18, 1841 ; m. Sarah E. Ellis.
2981. ii. LEWIS H., b. Aug. 29, 1843 ; m. Sarah J. Ingalls.

2982. iii. GEORGIANNA E., b. Nov. 7, 1845; d.
2983. iv. BENJAMIN F., b. Sept., 1848; d.
2984. v.   GEORGIANNA, b. Feb. 24, 1853; d. Dec. 14, 1864.

977. SEWALL W.[7] PIERCE (*Abel*[6], *James*[5], *James*[4], *James*[3],
Thomas[2], *Thomas*[1]), b. Dec. 11, 1813 ; m. Feb. 7, 1838, Margaret R.
Adams, b. Dec. 11, 1816, d. July 31, 1878. He d. May 13, 1871.
Res. Winchester, Mass.

Sewell Pierce

Children :—

2985. i.   MARY E., b. June 19, 1839; m. L. L. Thaxter.
2986. ii.   FRANKLIN S., b. March 7, 1841; m. Mary L. Bragg.
2987. iii. EMMA A., b. Nov. 12, 1842; d. Oct. 28, 1844.
2988. iv.   EDWARD A., b. May 16, 1846; m. Julia E. Hatch.
2989. v.   WINSLOW, b. May 12, 1848; m. Mary A. Townsend.
2990. vi.   EMMA J., b. April, 19, 1850; m. Frank W. Danforth.
2991. vii. MARGARET, b. Dec. 19, 1852; m. L. W. Erskine. Res. Pond-St.,
             Winchester.

981. JOSHUA[7] PIERCE, Jr. (*Joshua*[6], *Joshua*[5], *James*[4], *James*[3],
Thomas[2], *Thomas*[1]), b. July 9, 1787 ; m. Mar. 10, 1810, Dolly
Hutchins, b. May 18, 1790, d. Sept. 24, 1828. He d. Sept. 16, 1828.
They res. in Hudson and Nashua N. H.   Children :—

2992. i.   SARAH L., b. Mar. 26, 1811; m. Mar. 21, 1829, Hervey Bugbee, b.
             July 17, 1809, d. Feb. 9, 1865. Ch.: Edwin F., b. Dec. 6, 1830,
             m. J. H. Hills; Edward H., b. Aug. 11, 1832, d. Mar. 11, 1837;
             James H., b. July 29, 1834, d. July 1, 1863; Edward H., b. Jan.
             29, 1837, d. July 30, 1838; Albert P., b. Apr. 29, 1840; m.
             Mattie Rice; Clara I., b. Nov. 21, 1842; Clinton P., b. Jan. 3.
             1851; m. Hannah J. Weston; Frederick P., b. Mar. 7, 1853,
             They res. in Hancock, Me.
2993. ii.   JOSHUA D., b. Mar. 22, 1813; m. Jan. 8, 1835, Louisa L. Corbin.
2994. iii. HANNAH L., b. Jan. 29, 1815; m. Jan. 22, 1837, William E. Graves,
             b. Aug. 15, 1814. Ch.: Edward P., b. Dec. 31, 1840, m. Sarah
             A. Ulman; Sarah R., b. July 31, 1845, m. Eugene H. Clapp.
             Res. 48 East Springfield-St., Boston.
2995. iv.   NANCY H., b. June 3, 1817; m. C. P. Danforth.
2996. v.   ANDREW J., b. Jan. 30, 1821; m. Caroline Holmes.
2997. vi.   DOLLY J., b. Mar. 6, 1823; m. J. A. Woodward.

982. JAMES[7] PIERCE (*Joshua*[6], *Joshua*[5], *James*[4], *James*[3], *Thomas*[2], *Thomas*[1]), b. Mar. 31, 1792 ; m. Apr. 11, 1821, Belinda Cross, b.
July 24, 1794, d. Mar. 15, 1861. He d. May 10, 1871, in Nashua, N. H.

James Pierce

Children :—

2998. i.   BELINDA A., b. Mar. 25, 1822; m. Dec. 4, 1845, Edward A. Galli-
             son. She d. Jan. 14, 1850. Ch.: James E., b. Aug. 3, 1846, d.
             Nov. 11, 1847; James P., b. Dec. 26, 1847.

2999. ii. CAROLINE P., b. June 9, 1823; m. May 15, 1847, Benjamin H. Kidder. She d. Apr. 23, 1848.
3000. iii. JAMES L., b. Aug. 6, 1824; m. Oct. 5, 1851, Martha J. Cross.
3001. iv. JOHN P., b. July 25, 1828; m. Oct. 29, 1854, Martha E. Case.
3002. v. NANCY T., b. Jan. 12, 1830; d. Aug. 8, 1847.
3003. vi. JOSHUA C., b. Dec. 8, 1831; m. Oct. 29, 1861, Kate H. Chase.
3004. vii. COSMO L., b. Aug. 11, 1833; d. Sept. 1, 1834.

987. NATHAN[7] PIERCE, Jr. (*Nathan*[6], *Joshua*[5], *James*[4], *James*[3], *Thomas*[2], *Thomas*[1]), b. Jan. 15, 1789; m. June 1, 1831, Abigail Graves, b. May 4, 1798. He d. June 1, 1839. Res. Bradford, N. H. Children :—

3005. BENJAMIN F., b. May 2, 1832; m. Harriet J. Goodwin.
3006. CYNTHIA C., b. Nov. 23, 1835; m. L. P. Jameson.

992. DANIEL[7] PIERCE (*Nathan*[6], *Joshua*[5], *James*[4], *James*[3], *Thomas*[2], *Thomas*[1]), b. July 17, 1801; m. Nov., 1829, Lucy Wheelock, b. May 23, 1809, d. Mar., 1877. He d. Aug. 28, 1848. Res. Eden, Vt.

Daniel Pierce

Child :—

3007. i. LAURA, b. Oct., 1831; m. Edwin Wheelock.

993. CUMMINGS[7] PIERCE (*Nathan*[6], *Joshua*[5], *James*[4], *James*[3], *Thomas*[2], *Thomas*[1]), b. May 22, 1803; m. Feb. 22, 1833, Caroline Dowlin, d. Apr. 14, 1874. Res. Bradford, N. H. Children :—

3008. i. LUCRETIA, b. May 12, 1838; m. John H. Ewins.
3009. ii. ANNIE M., b. Aug. 18, 1849; m. Freeman Gillingham.

994. STEPHEN C.[7] PIERCE (*Nathan*[6], *Joshua*[5], *James*[4], *James*[3], *Thomas*[2], *Thomas*[1]), b. Nov. 4, 1807; m. Dec. 29, 1834, Martha Collins, d. Apr. 21, 1873. Res. Bradford, N. H. Child :—

3010. i. DANIEL, b. Sept. 12, 1852; m. Nancy H. Morgan.

995. ALVAH[7] PIERCE (*James*[6], *Joshua*[5], *James*[4], *James*[3], *Thomas*[2], *Thomas*[1]), b. July 30, 1795; m. 1832, Leafee Miller, b. 1805, d. Aug. 29, 1866. He d. Jan. 20, 1869. Res. Bellows Falls, Vt. No children.

998. DANIEL[7] PIERCE (*James*[6], *Joshua*[5], *James*[4], *James*[3], *Thomas*[2], *Thomas*[1]), b. Oct. 24, 1801; m. Sept. 25, 1826, Ursula Caldwell, b. Aug. 24, 1808. He d. Aug. 18, 1874. Res. W. Swanzey, N. H., and Bolton, Mass. Children :—

3011. i. DANIEL, b. Dec. 14, 1827; m. Sarah Jones.
3012. ii. ENOCH C., b. Jan. 1, 1830.
3013. iii. JAMES S., b. Feb. 6, 1832; m. Mary A. Casey.
3014. iv. JOHN C., b. May 5, 1834; d. May 25, 1834.
3015. v. MARSHALL W., b. Apr. 4, 1836; m. Liza Booth.
3016. vi. MARY E., b. Aug. 24, 1841; d. July 20, 1861.
3017. vii. LEANDER F., b. Dec. 6, 1843; d. Jan. 13, 1844.
3018. viii. LODENA W., b. Jan. 27, 1847; d. Apr. 27, 1866.

24

1002. Gen. James[7] Pierce, Jr. (*James*[6], *Joshua*[5], *James*[4], *James*[3], *Thomas*[2], *Thomas*[1]), b. Sept. 24, 1810; m. Jan. 1, 1839, Chloe Holbrook, b. Mar. 20, 1816. He d. Dec. 2, 1874, in Sharpsville, Pa.

General James Pierce was born in Swanzey, Cheshire county, New Hampshire, on the twenty-fourth day of September, 1810, and remained with his father, working on the farm, until he was twenty-one years of age, receiving in the meantime such limited education as country schools of that period furnished.

The history of those who, under adverse circumstances have, by their own unaided efforts and native force of character, achieved success in any department of human enterprise, is always interesting, and should be especially so to young men about to engage in the active duties of life, as examples for their imitation.

In the hurried preparation of a newspaper article, we can only expect to give a brief outline of the General's life, but even this will serve to show what can be accomplished by a man possessing an indomitable will, enterprise and perseverance,—the three leading characteristics so peculiar to Mr. Pierce.

At the age of twenty-one he left his father's house and hired himself by the month to work at the lumber business, at which employment he continued about two years, and then commenced the same business on his own account, which was the manufacture of shooks for sugar hogsheads, conveying them to market down the Connecticut river.

He and a cousin, named Jervis Bates, came to Erie county in 1844, bringing with them cotton and woolen cloths, which they disposed of and turned the proceeds into horses, which they took back with them, when they returned home. They made the journey out in wagons and sleighs. Mr. P. came here again in December of the same year, and staid all winter. This time he was engaged in selling clocks through Erie and Crawford counties. There being very little money in this section at that time, his accumulations, about $1,000, consisted wholly of Pennsylvania and Erie canal bonds. Being unable to obtain the interest on the bonds at Erie, he disposed of them for a lot of stoves.

Possessing an enterprising spirit, and desiring a wider field for the display of his energies, he sold his property in New Hampshire, and in the year 1845 emigrated with his young family into Pennsylvania, settling at Cranesville, in Erie county, where he remained until the spring of 1847, when he removed to Clarksville, Mercer county. The first business enterprise in which he engaged here was mining and shipping coal in the vicinity of Clarksville, in the year 1847. Coal then found its market at Erie, and was transported to that point via the Pennsylvania and Erie Canal, the business being then in its infancy in the Shenango Valley. This first adventure was only moderately successful,—the mine, being limited in extent, soon became exhausted. He then opened new mines near to his late residence at Mount Hickory. These proved very valuable, and here was laid the foundation of his subsequently eminently successful business career. To convey the coal from these mines he constructed a *tram road*, operated

Gilary Pub. Co. Philadelphia

James Pierce.

by horse-power, which was regarded at that time as a wonderful achievement of individual enterprise, and which answered a most valuable purpose until it was superseded by the completion of the Erie and Pittsburgh and the Sharpsville and Oakland Railroads.

In the construction of both these roads he took a most active interest. In the former he was a large stockholder and a director; in the latter the principal stockholder and its President and General Manager from the beginning to his death.

These roads have performed an indispensable part in the development of the iron, coal and other industries of the country through which they pass, and to the energy and public spirit of Mr. Pierce is the community indebted for the existence and beneficial results of these improvements.

Among the first to engage in the coal business in Mercer county, so had he continued until the day of his death to be among the more prominent and successful operators, being connected with extensive mines both in Mercer and Lawrence counties.

His connection with the furnace business commenced in the year 1859. Becoming the proprietor of the Sharpsville Furnace, he put the same in blast that year, and with the exception of occasional stoppages for repairs, it has been in successful operation until the late depression in the iron business made it expedient to lessen the production of Pig iron throughout the country. He was President and principal owner of the Iron Banking Company, of this place, and a stockholder in the Sharon Banking Company.

His farming operations were conducted on a very extensive scale, and with more science and system than is generally employed. Mt. Hickory is a model farm. The mansion and outbuildings are superior to any in the county, and perhaps not surpassed by any of their kind in Western Pennsylvania. The land is in the highest state of cultivation, abounding in all the fruits suitable to this latitude; and, in short, with everything to make it a most pleasant and desirable residence. His extensive herd of thorough-bred cattle was greatly admired by farmers and stockbreeders. That he had very superior stock is evidenced by the many premiums awarded him this year at the North Western Pennsylvania Fair and elsewhere.

He had just completed, and had nearly ready for occupancy, at a cost of over $100,000, a palatial residence in this place, which for architectural design, beauty of finish, and convenience of arrangement, will compare most favorably with the best city or suburban residences to be found anywhere.

He always manifested a deep interest in the cause of education, devoting much personal attention—as a director for a number of years—to our common schools and in liberal contributions in lands and money for the erection of school-houses, aside from the large amount of taxes paid by him annually for their support. A noted instance of his liberality is seen in the contribution of $10,000, made in the name of his wife, towards endowing a female professorship in Buchtel College, Akron, Ohio, to be called the "Chloe Pierce" professorship. This is a new

institution of learning, of which he was one of the trustees, and is in a
very prosperous condition.

Several of the churches in Sharpsville also received generous donations from his hand, while public and private enterprises have been
greatly aided and fostered through his liberality.

THE OBSEQUIES.

Friday afternoon, at one o'clock, was fixed as the time for the
obsequies. All the business houses in Sharpsville were closed and
work generally suspended during the day. An hour or more before the
time announced for the ceremonies to begin numbers of carriages could
be seen on their way to the residence of the deceased. By one o'clock
a very large gathering of people had assembled, many of them, however, being unable to gain admission to the house on account of the
crowd present. The casket was placed in the library, and the religious
services were conducted in the hall, at the door of the parlor. The
Universalist choir opened the services by singing "We shall know
each other there," after which Rev. S. H. McCollester, President of
Buchtel College, Akron, Ohio, read a portion of Scripture and offered
up a fervent prayer to the Throne of Grace. Rev. Charles Shipman,
of Girard, then delivered a very sympathetic, eloquent and appreciative
sermon, at the close of which the choir sang "He has gone to the silent
land."

The pall-bearers were Hon. Wm. L. Scott, of Erie; Major J. W.
Ormsby, of Sharon; Dr. Wm. Gibson, of Jamestown; Dr. J. M.
Irvine, of Sharon; Samuel Sherman, of Albion, Erie county; Alex.
Nimick, of Pittsburg; Judge Maxwell, of Greenville; John Phillips,
of Neshannock; John McCleary, of New Castle; A. McIntyre, of
Neshannock; Hugh Young, of Hermitage; Robert Oaks, of Oakland;
Seth Hoftus and A. J. Nickel, of Sharpsville.

Mr. Sherman, one of the pall-bearers, was the first person with whom
Mr. Pierce became acquainted when he settled in Erie county.

The procession, as it slowly wended its way to Riverside cemetery,
which is about three miles from the residence of the deceased, presented a sight seldom seen in this section. Its entire length was fully a
mile, 250 carriages being in the procession. Every follower seemed
impressed with the idea that he had lost in the deceased a personal
friend. On arriving at the burial-ground, the school children, numbering about three hundred, were formed in line and sang "Bright
Jewels" as the procession passed in, after which they marched by the
casket and took a view of the corpse.

Editorial from the *Sharpsville Advertiser.*—It is with no ordinary
feelings of sadness that we chronicle his sudden death. The news
came to all who knew Mr. Pierce with a feeling of personal bereavement, for he was a noble man, whose kind heart was ever prompting
him to good deeds and a conscientious fulfillment of his highest con-
ceptions of duty. His kindnesses passed from his hand not as credits
to be returned with use, but as souvenirs sacred to his memory, and as
such will be cherished in perpetual remembrance. His memory will

long be retained in the hearts of those whom he has befriended and assisted by counsel, advice, and pecuniary aid—and among them can be numbered many poor men who have been brought to a prosperous condition, if not to affluence and wealth. The strict rule of rectitude was the magnet by which he moved, and the guide-star of his business career. Honesty, and not cupidity, governed him. Purity of purpose and of principle crowned him as a chief of excellence, and by these he merited no common exaltation. He was, indeed, a shining mark ; and as death courts a glittering prize, we must bow submissively to the mandate that called him hence, leaving us to grieve with no common grief, and sigh with no common sorrow, that we are bereft of one of our most useful and upright citizens. The members of this community are not the only ones that grieve over his loss. There are others whose hearts are stricken with sadness. His home has been mantled in the drear habiliments of mourning. There they weep that will not be comforted, because he is not. Let them have our sympathy and condolence.

The loss of such a man to any community cannot be estimated. It is irreparable. His enterprise knew no bounds, and but for the intervention of the business depression, many projects of a valuable character, that he had in contemplation, would now be under way.

Children :—

3019. i. JONAS J., b. Sept. 23, 1839; m. Apr. 6, 1865, Kate Pritzel.
3020. ii. WALTER, } b. Oct. 19, 1842; { m. June 28, 1871, Alice M. Mower.
3021.   WALLACE,
3022. iii. FRANK, b. Nov. 10, 1852.
3023. vi. JAMES B., b. Sept. 2. 1856. He was graduated from Stevens Institute of Technology, Hoboken, N. J., with Degree of Mechanical Engineer, in June, 1877.

1003.   WILLIAM[7] PIERCE (*James[6]*, *Joshua[5]*, *James[4]*, *James[3]*. *Thomas[2]*, *Thomas[1]*), b. Jan. 6, 1813 ; m. Mar. 13, 1844, Martha M. Whitcomb, b. Mar. 7, 1823. They res. at Empire Prairie, Missouri. Children :—

3024. i. JOB W., b. Nov. 25, 1845 ; m. Dec. 19, 1866, Hortense E. Thompson.
3025. ii. FRANK D., b. Feb. 7, 1863.

1004.   SAMUEL[7] PIERCE (*Daniel[6]*, *Joshua[5]*, *James[4]*, *James[3]*, *Thomas[2]*, *Thomas[1]*), b. March 25, 1784 ; m. 1805, Abigail Davis, d. 1856. He d. 1876. Res. Brownington, and Albany, Vt.

Children :—

3026. i. HEROD, b. 1806; m. Eliza Thurston and Mrs. Chubb.
3027. ii. CHARLES F., b. Nov. 7, 1808; m. Nancy Church.
3028. iii. MARY, b. 1810; m. Luke Whitney.
3029. iv. SARAH A., b 1812; m. Luke Whitney.
3030. v. ELBRIDGE G., b. Jan. 12, 1814; m. Betsey Cochran.
3031. vi. WILLIAM, b. 1816; d. 1818.

3032. vii. WILLIAM, P., b. April 16, 1818; m. Fidelia A. Booth.
3033. viii. CAROLINE, b. May 7, 1820; m. Wm. Whitney.
3034. ix. SUSAN E., b. 1822; d. June 1, 1846.
3035. x. SAMUEL M., b. April, 1824; d. April 27, 1851.
3036. xi. HUDSON, b. Feb., 1826.
3037. xii. ABIGAIL, b. April 16, 1828; m. Harvey Coolidge.
3038. xiii. EDMOND B., b. Aug., 1830; m. Jane Bancroft.
3039. xiv. MARTHA J., b. June 7, 1832; m. Mar. 24, 1853, Addison P. Wheelock, b. July 27, 1826. Ch.: Emma J., b. Dec. 9, 1857, m. Samuel S. Crosby; Nellie S., b. June 9, 1859, d. June 1, 1879; Frank A., b. July 9, 1862.

1006.   I .NIEL⁷ PIERCE (*Daniel⁶, Joshua⁵, James⁴, James³, Thomas², Thomas¹*), b. May 31, 1789 ; m. Clarissa Hardy, b. March 26, 1791, d. Feb. 15, 1866. He d. Sept. 28, 1861. Res. Hopkinton, N. H.

Daniel Pierce

Children :—

3040. i. ALMIRA, b. March 9, 1810; m. Moses Hale.
3041. ii. GEORGE W., b. Sept. 26, 1812; d. Feb. 2, 1832.
3042. iii. KATHERINE, b. May 2, 1814; d. Jan. 17, 1829.
3043. iv. HANNAH M., b. Nov. 2, 1816; d. April 25, 1829.
3044. v. HORACE, b. Oct. 14, 1819; m. Mary A. Startup.
3045. vi. ROXANNA, b. May 16, 1822; d. April 10, 1829.
3046. vii. HENRY. b. Dec. 24, 1825; d. Oct. 1, 1844.
3047. viii. KATHERINE, b. March 20, 1829; m. Langdon Brown.
3048. ix. GEORGE W., b. July 1, 1832; m. Myra F. Copp.
3049. x. ROXANNA, b. Feb. 17, 1836; m. Anson White.

1007. ROBERT F.⁷ PIERCE (*Daniel⁶, Joshua⁵, James⁴, James³, Thomas², Thomas¹*), b. Oct. 5, 1790 ; m. 1812, Sarah Harvey, b. May 1, 1790, d. April 30, 1856. He d. May 8, 1860. Res. New London and Bradford, N. H. Children :—

3050. i. MATHEW H., b. Oct. 24, 1813; m. Hannah J. Jones.
3051. ii. WALTER H., b. April 19, 1817; m. Lydia Bean and Rebecca Phillips.
3052. iii. DRUSILLE H., b. Dec. 7, 1823; m. J. Fred. Buswell.

1008. ISAAC⁷ PIERCE (*Daniel⁶, Joshua⁵, James⁴, James³, Thomas², Thomas¹*), b. July 13, 1793 ; m. April, 1818, Mary Floyd, b. Jan. 16, 1797, d. Feb. 1, 1868. He d. Oct. 28, 1865. Res. Norwich, Vt. He was in the war of 1812.

Isaac Pierce

Children :—

3053. i. NATHANIEL F., b. Feb. 16, 1820; m. three times.
3054. ii. NANCY F., b. Jan. 4, 1823; m. W. W. Baker.
3055. iii. MARY J., b. March 11, 1825; m. Nelson E. Smith.
3056. iv. HAROD, b. April 27, 1827; d. Sept. 10, 1829.

3057. v. ABBY C., b. March 27, 1830; m. Richard Waterman.
3058. vi. ADELAIDE, b. Jan. 11, 1832; d. Oct. 6, 1839.

1009. JOSHUA[7] PIERCE (*Daniel*[6], *Joshua*[5], *James*[4], *James*[3], *Thomas*[2], *Thomas*[1]) ; m. Apr. 3, 1817, Sarah Barnard, b. Apr. 12, 1798; m. 2nd, Polly Kenson. Res. Warner, N. H. Children :—

3059. i. JOSEPH B., b. 1818; m. Elizabeth Elliott. Res. Manchester, N. H.
3060. ii. NANCY, b. 1820; d. 1837.
3061. iii. MARK W., b. Aug. 2, 1825; m. Harriet D. Burbank and Lucy A. E. Sinclair.
3062. iv. BETSEY H., b. Sept. 15, 1827; m. July 31, 1844, Jo⸢ ⸣H. Morrill, b. July 31, 1820. Ch.: Frank H., b. Feb. 23, 1846, d. Dec. 1, 1848; Fred. S., b. May 29, 1848, m. Helen, Burrows, res. Waterloo, Iowa; Minnie H., b. Oct. 35, 1857, m. Walter B. Dean, res. Vermillion, Da.; Nellie M., b. May 8, 1865, res. Rockford, Ill.
3063. v. OLIVE, b. 1829; m. Edward P. Dean. Res. Newark, Ill. Ch.: Fenton; and three other children, all dead. She d. 1856.
3063¼. vi. GEORGE J., b. Sept. 3, 1833; m. Carrie A. Kent.
3063½. vii. CHARLES A., b. Jan. 13, 1838; m. Mary O. Harvey.

1010. WILLIAM M.[7] PIERCE (*Daniel*[6], *Joshua*[5], *James*[4], *James*[3], *Thomas*[2], *Thomas*[1]), b. June 15, 1806; m. June 4, 1825, Lois C. Kenniston, b. May 3, 1804. Res. Salisbury, N. H. Children :—

3064. i. MELISSA B., b. Dec. 2, 1826; m. H. C. W. Moore.
3065. ii. NANCY W., b. July 15, 1828; m. S. C. Forsaith.
3066. iii. WILLIAM R., b. July 3, 1831; d. Sept. 15, 1854.
3067. iv. BETSEY J., b. Oct. 19, 1836; m. J. A. Fellows.

1014. JACOB[7] PIERCE, Jr. (*Jacob*[6], *Jacob*[5], *James*[4], *James*[3], *Thomas*[2], *Thomas*[1]), b. June 20, 1789 ; m. Sept. 26, 1816, Melicent Lawrence, b. May 17, 1798, d. Oct. 25, 1842. He d. Oct. 10, 1872. They res. in Woburn.

J. Pierce

Children :—

3068. i. ROSANNA, b. Aug. 2, 1817; m. Oct. 8, 1836, Wilder S. Thurston. She d. Dec. 14, 1846 in Lynn. Ch.: Clara W., m. —— Frye; Louisa; Ella, m. —— Leonard.
3069. ii. EBENEZER L., b. June 16, 1819; m. Mary Gardner. [See 1012.]
3070. iii. CAROLINE J., b. Sept. 4, 1830; m. William Bateman. They res. at 48 Waltham-St., Boston.
3071. iv. JACOB F., b. July 15, 1833; d. 1865.

1016. EPHRAIM[7] PIERCE, Jr. (*Ephraim*[6], *Jacob*[5], *James*[4], *James*[3], *Thomas*[2], *Thomas*[1]), b. Oct. 2, 1783 ; m. May 3, 1806, Sarah Leathe, b. Oct. 11, 1784, d. Sept. 18, 1854. He d. Feb. 12, 1845. They res. in Woburn and Stoneham.

Ephraim Pierce

Children :—

3072. i. EPHRAIM, b. Feb. 15, 1807; d. Apr. 30, 1831.
3073. ii. SARAH L., b. Apr. 1, 1808; d. Feb. 5, 1828.
3074. iii. JAMES, b. Oct. 10, 1809; m. Nov. 10, 1835, Eliza Porter.

3075. iv. SARAH, b. Apr. 3, 1811; m. Sept. 28, 1830, Benjamin M. Perry. She d. Apr., 1844. Ch.: Sarah J., m. Thos. Greene; Ira; Augustus E.

3076. v. ELIZABETH A., b. July 29, 1813; m. July 2, 1839, Luther Richardson. She d. Aug. 3, 1853, without issue.

3077. vi. ABIGAIL B., b. Jan. 13, 1817; d. Aug. 24, 1863.

3078. vii. JOHN, MARY J., } b. Feb. 20, 1820; { m. Nov. 5, 1846, Agnes Goodhue.

3079. viii. RUFUS L., b. May 16, 1822; m. Apr. 5, 1849, Eliza J. McIntire; no issue.

3080. ix. LAVINA, b. July 20, 1824; d. Sept. 6, 1854.

3081. x. WILLIAM H., b. Aug. 4, 1827; m. July 15, 1849, Sarah A. Mooney.

3082. xi. ELLEN R., b. June 17, 1831; m. Sept. 22, 1852, Noah Worcester, d. Mar. 20, 1865. Ch.: Joseph F., b. July 10, 1853, d. Dec. 15, 1875; Sarah E., b. Oct. 16, 1857; Charles, b. June 10, 1859, d. Sept. 15, 1876.

1024. HENRY[7] PIERCE (*Heman[6], Jacob[5], James[4], James[3], Thomas[2], Thomas[1]*), b. Nov. 25, 1798; m. May 10, 1819, Mary Newton, b. Nov. 23, 1802. He d. Nov. 10, 1843. She m. 2nd, ——— Parker. He d. ———. She res. in Hammondsville, Reading, Vt.

Children :—

3083. i. AUGUSTUS H., b. Aug. 3, 1821; d. Dec. 26, 1822.

3084. ii. JOSIAH S., b. Sept. 24, 1823; rev. to Big Rapids, Mich.

3085. iii. CHRISTHANA M., b. Mar. 21, 1825; d. Aug. 10, 1827.

3086. iv. LAURA J., b. Mar. 22, 1827; m. Mar. 27, 1861, Forest G. Persons. Ch.: Gertrude, b. July 4, 1863, res. Felchville, Vt.

3087. v. CHARLES L., b. May 16, 1829; d. Sept. 25, 1848.

3088. vi. RUFUS F., b. Jan. 20, 1832; d. in Army Hospital Apr. 2, 1865.

3089. vii. SAMUEL B., b. Nov. 2, 1834; rev. to Cal., never heard from.

3090. viii. LOUISA C., b. Dec. 26, 1836; m. Nov. 25, 1856, Oliver Sherwin, b. Nov. 23, 1832. Ch.: Jennie L., b. Mar. 18, 1858; Dean, b. Nov. 28, 1867. Res. Woodstock, Vt.

1025. JAMES[7] PIERCE (*Heman[6], Jacob[5], James[4], James[3], Thomas[2], Thomas[1],*) b. Mar. 7, 1803; m. Oct. 15, 1828, Mary Slayton, b. Sept. 8, 1808. He d. Mar. 5, 1868. They res. in Reading and Woodstock, Vt. The widow now res. in Stoneham.

Children :—

3090½. i. MARY E., b. Aug. 1, 1833; d. Apr. 5, 1843.

3091. ii. SUSAN A., b. Apr. 10, 1835; m. Mar. 20, 1876, Oliver S. Quimby, b. Mar. 9, 1830. No issue. Res. Stoneham.

3091½. iii. W. H. HARRISON, b. Sept. 5, 1837; m. Oct. 26, 1859, Emma H. Cooley.

3092. iv. GEORGE E., b. Aug. 6, 1845; d. Oct. 6, 1845.

3093. v. ADALINE E., b. July 31, 1848; m. ———.

3093½. vi. FRANK, b. Apr. 14, 1853; d. Oct. 30, 1869.

1026. SAMUEL B.[7] PIERCE (*Heman*[6], *Jacob*[5], *James*[4], *James*[3], *Thomas*[2], *Thomas*[1]), b. Aug. 11, 1806; m. Dec. 17, 1829, Hannah R. Homer, dau. of Joseph Warren Homer, of Boston, b. Dec. 25, 1806. He res. in Dorchester District, Boston.

Samuel B. Pierce was born on a farm in Reading, Vt., to which place his father, who was born in Woburn, Mass., moved Aug. 11, 1806. He lived on the farm until he was fourteen years old, attending the public schools of the town whenever practicable, going over long steep hills to do so. His father having died when he was young he started for Boston, riding all the way on top of an ox load of produce, driven by his elder brother, who on his return carried back goods to the merchants of the town—arriving at the Hub of the Universe he found employment at the crockery store of Moses Pierce, then located near Hanover street and Marshall lane, where he remained for three years, going then to work for Robert Briggs for four years, at the end of which time he went into business for himself putting out his own sign on his 21st birthday. He continued in the crockery business until 1869, when he retired from active business, being one of the oldest living merchants in that line in the county, many of the older merchants in this business in Boston, have been boys in his store. In 1844 he moved to what was then Dorchester, building a large house for himself at Upham's corner, which was then considered some distance out of town. He continued to reside there until a few years ago, when he moved into a handsome residence which he had then just finished, three of his children living within a stone's throw of him. He has built quite a number of houses in that part of the city and is at present building more.

Children :—

3094. i.   MARY L., b. Oct. 4, 1830; m. May 18, 1853, Samuel Quincy, b. Sept. 5, 1825. Ch.: Samuel, Jr., b. Feb. 13, 1857; Annie L., b. Oct. 8, 1859. They res. in Brooklyn, N. Y.
3095. ii.   SAMUEL B., Jr., b. Oct. 19, 1832; d. June 19, 1864.
3096. iii. FRANK, b. Nov. 24, 1834; d. June 11, 1859.
3097. iv.   MARTHA C., b. Dec. 14, 1837; m. Oct. 11, 1866, Charles H. Clark, b. Oct. 22, 1836. Ch.: Homer P., b. July 6, 1868; Mary B., b. Aug. 20, 1871. Res. St. Paul, Minn.
3098. v.   J. HOMER, b. Oct. 27, 1840; m. June 16, 1869, Eliza C. Bradford.
3099. vi.   ANNA E., b. June 3, 1843; d. Oct. 24, 1844.
3100. vii. FREDERIC B., b. May 1, 1845; m. Oct. 16, 1873, Mary R. Davis.
3101. viii. GERTRUDE, b. June 7, 1847; m. Apr. 2, 1873, Nathaniel H. Henchman, Jr., b. June 12, 1845. She d. without issue June 22, 1873.
3102. ix.   HELEN H., b. July 3, 1852; m. June 19, 1873, William H. Canterbury, b. Feb. 10, 1852. Ch.: Gertrude P., b. June 19, 1874; Alice T., b. Aug. 14, 1876; d. June 10, 1881; George W., b. Feb. 25, 1878; Harold S., b. Sept. 14, 1880; d. June 17, 1881. Res. Dorchester.

25

1031. LUTHER[8] PIERCE (*Benjamin[7], Benjamin[6], Thomas[5], Thomas[4], Thomas[3], Thomas[2], Thomas[1]*), b. Aug. 21, 1791 ; m. Jan. 6, 1818, Betsey Brackett, b. Aug. 30, 1789. He was a shoemaker by trade and lived in Needham, Sudbury, Framingham and South Boston. He fell overboard while out mackerel fishing and was drowned, about the year 1828.

Children :—

3103. i.   LUTHER, b. Nov. 25, 1819; m. Feb. 27, 1873, Hannah Bacon.
3104. ii.   JOSEPH W., b. Mar. 4, 1821.
3105. iii. DAVID B., b. Nov. 5, 1822; d. Aug. 21, 1880.
3106. iv.   EMMA S., b. Mar., 1824 ; m. William Holliday, and d. Apr., 1845.
3107. v.   SAMUEL H., b. 1828; d. 1828.

1032. BENJAMIN[8] PIERCE, Jr. (*Benjamin[7], Benjamin[6], Thomas[5], Thomas[4], Thomas[3], Thomas[2], Thomas[1]*), b. Jan. 3, 1794 ; m. Mar. 10, 1818, Almira Harrington, b. Feb. 22, 1799, d. June 23, 1880. He d. Oct. 5, 1863.

He began business as a baker in Mendon, lived there about five years, moved back to Weston, where he carried on the business about twelve years, then retired to the farm formerly owned by Capt. Boyd, where he died. He filled many town offices ; was a whig in politics ; was three times candidate for Representative, but his party being in a minority, he failed of an election. He was a Justice of the Peace for a number of years.

Children :—

3108. i.   BENJAMIN, Jr., b. June 25, 1819; m. Oct. 3, 1843, Maria A. Warren.
3109. ii.   ALMIRA L., b. May 10, 1821; d. Jan. 17, 1877.
3110. iii. HARRIET M., b. Apr. 5, 1823 ; m. June 12, 1845, Samuel A. Minor, d. July 3, 1852, on board the steamer *S. S. Lewis*, bound for California.
3111. iv.   EMILY M., b. Apr. 23, 1825 ; m. Apr. 26, 1848, John Coburn. Ch. : Elizabeth S., b. Sept. 26, 1849 ; Emily F., b. Sept. 21, 1851 ; Agnes P., b. Sept. 15, 1857 ; Mary E., b. July 5, 1861.
3112. v.   EDWARD, b. Mar 31, 1827. Res. Weston.
3113. vi.   CAROLINE, b. May 6, 1829 ; m. May 23, 1854, Albert L. Cooley. Ch. : Charles A., b. May 17, 1855 ; Edward, b. Aug. 12, 1859 ; George P., b. Jan. 30, 1856. Res. Cambridgeport.
3114. vii. MARY F., b. June 9, 1831. She is First Assistant Teacher in the Cambridge High School, where she has taught for the last twenty-five years.
3115. viii. MARGARET, b. May 1, 1833.
3116. ix.   JOSEPH, b. Aug. 9, 1837.
3117. x.   GEORGE, b. Aug. 21, 1843 ; m. Sept. 15, 1875, Anna G. Bartlett.

1035. JOHN[7] PIERCE (*John*[6], *Benjamin*[5], *Thomas*[4], *Benjamin*[3], *Thomas*[2], *Thomas*[1]), b. Jan. 16, 1789 ; m. 1815, Ann Cragin, b. Dec. 28, 1793, d. May 16, 1819 ; m. 2nd, Oct. 22, 1822, Sarah Spalding, b. Jan. 16, 1799. He d. Oct. 26, 1858. Res. Embden, Me.
Children :—

3118. i. SARAH, b. Oct. 29, 1815; d. Sept. 28, 1870.
3119. ii. JOHN, b. Aug. 31, 1823; m. June 1, 1851, Sophronia Goodrich.
3120. iii. MERIAR S., b. Mar. 13, 1826; m. Feb. 22, 1865, Sarah Selley.
3121. iv. ANNA E., b. Aug. 10, 1828; d. May 10, 1850.
3122. v. WALTER S., b. Aug. 14, 1833; m. Feb. 5, 1866, Flavilla Nichols.

1036. DAVID W.[7] PIERCE (*John*[6], *Benjamin*[5], *Thomas*[4], *Benjamin*[3], *Thomas*[2], *Thomas*[1]), b. Feb. 7, 1791 ; m. May 12, 1819, Ruth Andrews, b. Aug. 21, 1801. He d. 1835. Res. Des Moines, Iowa.
Children :—

3123. i. JOSIAH A., b. June 20, 1820; d. Oct. 18, 1824.
3124. ii. ALEXANDER P., b. Mar. 15, 1822; d. Oct. 18, 1824.
3125. iii. DAVID, b. Jan. 2, 1824; d. Jan. 15, 1824.
3126. iv. MARK A., b. July 18, 1825; m. Mary E. Palmer and Annie Hughes.
3127. v. SAMUEL B. P., b. Sept. 27, 1827; m. Mrs. Anna R. Young.
3128. vi. HARRIET, b. June 15, 1830; m. Jan. 20, 1853, Wm. F. Conrad, b. Nov. 7, 1826. Ch. : William F., Jr., b. Aug. 2, 1856; Hattie L., b. Sept. 30, 1866. Res. Des Moines, Iowa.

1037. BENJAMIN[7] PIERCE (*John*[6], *Benjamin*[5], *Thomas*[4], *Benjamin*[3], *Thomas*[2], *Thomas*[1]), b. March 6, 1795 ; m. Dec. 18, 1817, Hannah Cragin, b. 1799, d. June 20, 1838 ; m. 2nd, May 30, 1841, Lois H. Bartlett. He d. Oct. 10, 1845. Res. Norridgewock, Me.

Children :—

3129. i. EDITH, b. Sept. 20, 1818; m. Ozias McFadden. Had one child.
3130. ii. DAVID W., b. July 5, 1820; m. Olive Albee.
3131. iii. SIMEON C., b. Feb. 25, 1822. Res. Selma, Ala.
3132. iv. ELEANOR C., b. Jan. 22, 1824; m. Llewellyn Crommett.
3133. v. MARY, } twins, b. July 31, 1827; { d. Nov. 24, 1857.
3134. vi. SARAH, }   { d. Sept. 15, 1844.
3135. vii. BENJAMIN F., b. July 30, 1829; d. Dec. 14, 1856.

3136. viii. HENRY C., b. Dec. 26, 1834; m. Sarah H. Lancaster.
3137. ix. GEORGE W., b. Jan. 3, 1837; unm. Res. Baraboo, Wis.
3138. x. JOHN, b. June 2, 1844.

1043. JAMES[7] PIERCE (*Amos*[6], *Benjamin*[5], *Thomas*[4], *Benjamin*[3], *Thomas*[2], *Thomas*[1]), b. Aug. 20, 1801 ; m. Apr. 7, 1835, Martha W.

Warren, b. Mar. 24, 1809. He d. Dec. 30, 1872. Res. Ashburnham and Bolton, Mass.

Children :—

3139. i. JAMES W., b. Sept. 18, 1839; m. Annie L. Clark.
3140. ii. MARTHA, b. June 18, 1846.

1045. LEVI[7] PIERCE (*Joseph[6], Thomas[5], Thomas[4], Benjamin[3], Thomas[2], Thomas[1]*), b. June 27, 1785 ; m. Betsey Eaton, b. July, 1785, d. 1809 ; m. 2nd, Jan. 2, 1811, Eunice Green, b. Mar. 17, 1790, d. 1854. He d. Sept. 6, 1825. Res. Leicester, Mass., and Chester, Vt.

Children :—

3141. i. ELIZA E., b. Aug. 30, 1807; m. —— Williams.
3142. ii. JOSEPH G., b. Sept. 21, 1809 ; m. Hannah Hemmenway.
3143. iii. CLARISSA B., b. Sept. 27, 1812 ; m. —— Curtis.
3144. iv. LEVI L., b. May 28, 1816 ; m. Fidelia A. Eastman.
3145. v. —— ——; d. young.
3146. v. EUNICE, b. June 26, 1821 ; d.

1047. ABEL G.[7] PIERCE (*Joseph[6], Thomas[5], Thomas[4], Benjamin[3], Thomas[2], Thomas[1]*), b. Feb. 10, 1792 ; m. 1811, Susan H. Rice, b. Nov. 4, 1794. He d. Feb. 15, 1865. Res. Chester, Vt., and Renssalear Falls, N. Y.

A G Pierce —

Children :—

3147. i. ELVIRA, b. Feb. 26, 1812; m. Feb. 28, 1832, George W. Cooper. Ch. : Frances E., b. Oct. 6, 1844. Res. De Kalb, N. Y.
3148. ii. MARY R., b. Dec. 3, 1813; m. Oct. 12, 1843, Dr. Josiah C. Chandler. Ch : Carrie A., b. Sept. 18, 1844; Mary C., b. Mar. 11, 1847, d. Sept. 4, 1848; Nellie M., b. Sept. 8, 1849, d. July 31, 1864. Res. Rensselear Falls, N. Y.
3149. iii. SUSAN E., b. Dec. 14, 1815; m. Feb., 1837, Harrison Ames. Ch. : Ennias M., b. Mar., 1839, d. at Yorktown, Va., July 29, 1863, a member of Co. G, 142nd Regt., N. Y. S. Vols.; Julia S., b. May 21, 1844, m. John Thornhill; Emma, b. Jan. 30, 1849, d. Oct. 10, 1866. She d. July 18, 1849.
3150. iv. ALFRED A., b. Dec. 25, 1817; d. Jan. 5, 1847.
3151. v. FERDINAND, b. Dec. 24, 1820; drowned July 23, 1831.
3152. vi. HANNAH, b. Mar. 3, 1823; m. June 5, 1841, Levi O. Chappel. Ch. : Addie L., b. Dec. 19, 1843, d. Aug. 24, 1848; Addie A., b. Aug. 21, 1848, d. Dec. 24, 1849. She d. Dec. 11, 1849.
3153. vii. ARVILLA D., b. Apr. 29, 1830; m. Nov. 1, 1849, Edward Sayer. Ch. : Fred. E., b. Jan. 11, 1852 ; m. Larissa Ruberley.
3154. viii. JASON R., b. Nov. 11, 1833; m. Celina Vanderhender.
3155. ix. EMOGENE, b. July 30, 1838.

1051. IRA[7] PIERCE (*Eliab[6], Thomas[5], Thomas[4], Benjamin[3], Thomas[2], Thomas[1]*), b. March 28, 1794 ; m. Dec., 1830, Mary J.

Brown, b. April 26, 1811, d. March 14, 1867. He d. Aug. 26, 1862. Res. Rochester Depot, Ohio. Children :—

3156. i. EZRA B., b. Dec. 22, 1831; m. Adeline Sparks.
3157. ii. HENRY D., b. April 30, 1833; m. Melvina J. Bennett and Mrs. Anna Drake Marble.
3158. iii. SUSAN M., b. Oct. 3, 1834.
3159. iv. MARY A., b. June 8, 1837; m. Nathan Goodwill.
3160. v. GEORGE G., b. Jan. 13, 1840; m. Bettie G. Durand.
3161. vi. WILBUR E., b. Jan. 11, 1844; m. Addie M. Clifford.
3162. vii. HARLOW W., b. Nov. 10, 1852; m. Maria C. Sutton.

1055. CHAUNCEY[7] PIERCE (*Thomas*[6], *Thomas*[5], *Thomas*[4], *Benjamin*[3], *Thomas*[2], *Thomas*[1]), b. Sept. 17, 1796 ; m. June 29, 1821, Lydia Wells. He d. Feb. 27, 1842. She m. 2nd, —— Keeney. Res. Muir, Mich.

Chauncey Pierce (signature)

Children :—

3163. i. CASSANDRA E., b. July 25, 1822; m. Milton House.
3164. ii. JOSEPH, b. July 2, 1824; d. March 7, 1838.
3165. iii. BETSEY, b. March 18, 1827.
3166. iv. EDWIN M., b. March 5, 1830; m. Nancy Armstrong.
3167. v. SARAH, b. Dec. 3, 1840; d. Feb. 1, 1862.

1057. THOMAS[7] PIERCE (*Thomas*[6], *Thomas*[5], *Thomas*[4], *Benjamin*[3], *Thomas*[2], *Thomas*[1]), b. Dec. 8, 1800 ; m. Nov. 2, 1829, Catherine Weber, d. Apr. 17, 1865 ; m. 2nd, Oct. 15, 1866, Mary Etta Scobey. Res. Springville, N. Y.

Thomas Pierce has been, and still is, a deacon in the Baptist church at Springville, N. Y., for about fifty years, and while a resident of the town of Ashford, N. Y., he held the offices of Supervisor, Justice of the Peace, Town Superintendent of Schools, etc., for several terms. He is a man who is honored wherever he is known for high moral and christian integrity of character. Children :—

3168. i. HARRIET A., b. Nov. 19, 1830; m. B. A. Lowe.
3169. ii. ANN H., b. May 29, 1834; unm. Res. Springville, N. Y.
3170. iii. THOMAS W., b. Sept. 3, 1836; m. Esther A. Cook.

1059. GIFFORD[7] PIERCE (*Thomas*[6], *Thomas*[5], *Thomas*[4], *Benjamin*[3], *Thomas*[2], *Thomas*[1]), b. Feb. 2, 1805 ; m. March, 1835, Henrietta Wells, b. Feb. 8, 1810, d. Apr. 8, 1837 ; m. 2nd, Jan. 19, 1841, Nancy Mayo, b. July 25, 1814, d. April 21, 1846 ; m. 3rd, Jan. 14, 1847, Mayette P. Brown, d. March 5, 1864 ; m. 4th, June 13, 1865, Mrs. Sarah W. Dow, b. June 27, 1808. He d. April 12, 1878.

Giffard Peirce (signature)

Children :—

3171. i. HELEN A.; m. George P. Kellogg.
3172. ii. ALICE H., b. Jan. 29, 1837; d. April 16, 1837.
3173. iii. JULIA, b. May 2, 1842; d. Oct. 8, 1842.
3174. iv. D. GIFFORD, b. April 22, 1844; d. Jan. 21, 1846.
3175. v. ———, b. April 18, 1846; d. April 20, 1846.

1063. HAVEN[7] PIERCE (*Moses H.*[6], *Thomas*[5], *Thomas*[4], *Benjamin*[3], *Thomas*[2], *Thomas*[1]), b. Nov. 12, 1797 ; m. March 11, 1819, Hannah Rice, b. July 21, 1797, d. Jan. 22, 1869. He d. Feb. 1, 1875. Children : —

3176. i. MARY, b. Nov. 7, 1819; m. William J. Eveleth.
3177. ii. MARSHALL, b. March 3, 1821; m. Elizabeth L. Jones.
3178. iii. LEVI, b. April 15, 1823; m. Almira Wilson.
3179. iv. HARDING, b. March 13, 1825; m. Mary Johnson.
3180. v. SOPHIA, b. Feb. 27, 1827; m. Charles Goodspeed.

1064. LEVI[7] PIERCE (*Moses H.*[6], *Thomas*[5], *Thomas*[4], *Benjamin*[3], *Thomas*[2], *Thomas*[1]), b. Jan. 7, 1799 ; m. April 1, 1830, Mary M. Clark. He d. April 25, 1875. Res. Worcester, Mass. Children :—

3181. i. HENRIETTA, b. March 10, 1831; d. Aug. 29, 1831.
3182. ii. THEODORE H., b. Aug. 10, 1832.
3183. iii. HENRIETTA M., b. Nov. 4, 1833.
3184. iv. FRED'K L., b. 1837; d. May 7, 1858.
3185. v. ALFRED W., b. Jan. 1, 1841; .d. March 11, 1871.

1065. ASA[7] PIERCE (*Moses H.*[6], *Thomas*[5], *Thomas*[4], *Benjamin*[3], *Thomas*[2], *Thomas*[1]), b. Sept. 13, 1800; m. Harriet Wheeler, b. Sept., 1803, d. Oct. 20, 1852. He d. Jan. 7, 1875. Res. Hubbardston. Children :—

3186. i. ORRIN, b. Sept. 29, 1826; m. Fidelia Holden.
3187. ii. CHARLOTTE, b. March 21, 1828; d. Oct. 20, 1847.
3188. iii. WATSON I., b. May 31, 1830; m. Adelphia C. Clark.
3189. iv. HARRIET W., b. April 21, 1833; m. May 23, 1854, Sewell Grimes.
3190. v. HANNAH A., b. July 2, 1835; m. Dec. 1, 1854, Charles Hunting.
3191. vi. MOSES D., b. Jan. 30, 1839; res. unm. in Holden, Mass.
3192. vii. ELSIE, b. Dec. 24, 1841; m. Julius Fitts.

1067. J. HERVEY[7] PIERCE (*Moses H.*[6], *Thomas*[5], *Thomas*[4], *Benjamin*[3], *Thomas*[2], *Thomas*[1]), b. Nov. 23, 1804 ; m. Eunice Davis, d. Nov. 4, 1842. He d. Jan. 25, 1846. Res. Hubbardston and Princeton. Children :—

3193. i. ELLEN M., b. Dec. 29, 1829; m. James Goodrich.
3194. ii. SYLVANUS O., b. Feb. 1, 1832; d. unm. in California, July 7, 1866.
3195. iii. HERSCHEL O., b. Mar. 31, 1834.
3196. iv. SELVIA A., b. May 10, 1836; d.
3197. v. WESLEY H., b. April 2, 1841; d. Dec. 12, 1857.

1073. JAMES[8] PIERCE (*Joseph*[7], *Silas*[6], *Joseph*[5], *Joseph*[4], *Jonathan*[3], *Samuel*[2], *Thomas*[1]), b. June 19, 1819 ; m. June 4, 1844, Ellen L. Weatherbee, b. May 3, 1820, d. Jan. 21, 1862 ; m. 2nd, Aug. 13, 1864, Elvira Sibley, b. Mar. 19, 1822, d. Feb. 5, 1874. He res. in Fitchburg.

James Peirce

Children :—

3198. i. MARCIA E., b. June 12, 1846; d. Feb. 7, 1861.
3199. ii. HARRIET A., b. Sept. 3, 1848; m. Dec. 31, 1871, Frank Scott, b. Mar. 14, 1844. Res. Fitchburg; no issue.
3200. iii. JOSEPH M., b. Oct. 21, 1850; m. Nov. 26, 1878, Helen F. Moore.
3201. iv. ELIZA E., b. Dec. 25, 1853; m. Dec. 22, 1875, Alfred A. Marshall; no issue. Res. Fitchburg.
3202. v. ANN M., b. Jan. 5, 1855; m. Nov. 17, 1874, William A. Cook, b. Aug. 5, 1853; no issue. Res. Leominster.
3203. vi. JAMES E., b. July 30, 1857.
3204. vii. NELLIE L., b. Oct. 19, 1859.

1078. LEVI A.[8] PIERCE (*Levi*[7], *Levi*[6], *Silas*[5], *Joseph*[4], *Jonathan*[3], *Samuel*[2], *Thomas*[1]), b. Sept. 2, 1818 ; m. Nov. 27, 1847, Rachel A. Lovejoy. He res. in Wilton, N. H.

Levi A. Pierce

Children :—

3205. i. EMILY F., b. Jan. 14, 1849; m. July 4, 1869, Henry A. Holt. Ch.: Harry P., b. June 7, 1870; Myrtie F., b. July 12, 1873. Res. Wilton, N. H.
3206. ii. CHARLES A., b. Mar. 11, 1851; d. Sept. 27, 1867.
3207. iii. FRANK W., b. Aug. 3, 1857; d. Dec. 10, 1878.

1083. JOSEPH B.[8] PIERCE (*Joseph*[7], *Levi*[6], *Joseph*[5], *Joseph*[4], *Jonathan*[3], *Samuel*[2], *Thomas*[1]), b. Mar. 10, 1819 ; m. Mary B. Cummings. Res. White River Junction, Vt.

J. B. Pierce

Children :—

3208. i. WASHINGTON B., b. May 28, 1841; m. Effie M. ——
3209. ii. WALLACE W., b. Nov. 9, 1843.
3210. iii. CHARLES H., b. Jan. 7, 1846.
3211. iv. FRANK W., b. Dec. 11, 1849.
3212. v. MARY E., b. Nov. 30, 1854.
3213. vi. EMMA C., b. Aug. 2, 1858.
3214. vii. WALTER E., b. Mar. 24, 1863.

1089. REV. EPAMINONDAS J.[8] PIERCE (*Erasmus J.*[7], *Erasmus*[6], *Isaac*[5], *Isaac*[4], *Jonathan*[3], *Samuel*[2], *Thomas*[1]), b. Oct. 24, 1823 ; m. Nov. 20, 1853, Susan Savery, b. 1826, d. Feb. 8, 1855. He grad. at Dart. Coll. in 1845. Was a missionary at Gaboon River, Equatorial Africa, where his wife died, for five years. Res. Farmingdale, New Jersey. Children :—

3214½. i. ——, b. Feb. 8, 1855; d. Feb. 8, 1855.

1093. ROBERT M.[8] PIERCE (*Peter*[7], *Erasmus*[6], *Isaac*[5], *Isaac*[4],

Jonathan³, Samuel², Thomas¹), b. Aug. 19, 1828 ; m. Nov. 12, 1857, Elizabeth G. Hodgson, b. July 12, 1832. Res. Lewisville, Pa.

Children :—
3215. i.   GEORGE H., b. July 30, 1859.
3216. ii. NORRIS A., b. Dec. 28, 1861; d. Aug. 17, 1877.
3217. iii. JAMES H., b. May 2, 1864.
3218. iv. SARAH E., b. Aug. 24, 1867.
3219. v.   ELIZABETH G., b. July 21, 1872.

2004. Dr. HARVEY L.⁸ PIERCE (*Daniel⁷, Erasmus⁶, Isaac⁵, Isaac⁴, Jonathan³, Samuel², Thomas¹*), b. Aug. 24, 1839 ; m. —— Perrington. He was a surgeon in the army. Was taken prisoner at Winchester, Va., and died in Libby Prison. She m. 2nd, —— Bunting. Res. Washington, D. C.   Child :—
3219½. i.   ——.

2005. JOSEPH⁸ PIERCE (*Joseph⁷, Joseph⁶, Isaac⁵, Isaac⁴, Jonathan³, Samuel², Thomas¹*), b. May 23, 1809 ; m. July 2, 1831, Mary Thrives, b. Sept. 4, 1810, d. July 12, 1850. He d. July 16, 1851. Res. Cincinnati, Ohio.   Children :—
3220. i.   MARY A., b. July 2, 1832; d. July 17, 1833.
3221. ii. WILLIAM, b. Dec. 13, 1833; m. Alice R. Campbell.
3222. iii. THOMAS S., b. March 27, 1839. Thomas S. Pierce was killed at the Battle of Shiloh while fighting the rebel cause, Sept. 10, 1863.
3223. iv. CHARLES H., b. Nov. 24, 1841; d. Nov. 10, 1866.
3224. v.   SALLY A., b. Dec. 31, 1844; d. Dec. 15, 1867.
3225. vi. LEWIS W., b. Feb. 6, 1848; m.

2007. WILLIAM H.⁸ PIERCE (*Joseph⁷, Joseph⁶, Isaac⁵, Isaac⁴, Jonathan³, Samuel², Thomas¹*), b. Feb. 23, 1813 ; m. Eveline Jackson ; m. 2nd, Elizabeth Garrison ; m. 3rd, Elizabeth Jacques. Res. Cincinnati, Ohio.   No children.

2008. JAMES W.⁸ PIERCE (*Joseph⁷, Joseph⁶, Isaac⁵, Isaac⁴, Jonathan³, Samuel², Thomas¹*), b. March 25, 1814 ; m. Mary Woods. Res. Cincinnati, Ohio.   No children.

2012. BENJAMIN F.⁸ PIERCE (*Joseph⁷, Joseph⁶, Isaac⁵, Isaac⁴, Jonathan³, Samuel², Thomas¹*), b. June 2, 1827 ; m. July 14, 1859, Frances A. Rockinfeld. Res. Cincinnati, Ohio.   Children :—
3226. i.   SALLY H., b. Oct. 14, 1860.
3227. ii. CHARLES J., b. May 14, 1862.

2015. CHARLES[8] PIERCE (*Isaac[7], Joseph[6], Isaac[5], Isaac[4], Jonathan[3], Samuel[2], Thomas[1]*), b. Oct. 1, 1815 ; m. Sept. 13, 1839, Hannah Eaton, b. July 16, 1822. He d. April 5, 1851. Res. Charlestown, Mass. Children :—

3228. i. CHARLES P., b. ——— ; d.
3229. ii. CHARLES P., b. ——— ; d.
3230. iii. ALICE B., b. Dec. 15, 1847 ; d.

2017. JOSEPH[8] PIERCE (*Isaac[7], Joseph[6], Isaac[5], Isaac[4], Jonathan[3], Samuel[2], Thomas[1]*), b. Nov. 21, 1819 ; m. Elizabeth Huff. Res. Boston, Mass. Children :—

3231. i. JEANETTE.
3232. ii. JOSEPHINE.
3233. iii. HELEN L.

2018. GEORGE J.[8] PIERCE (*Isaac[7], Joseph[6], Isaac[5], Isaac[4], Jonathan[3], Samuel[2], Thomas[1]*), b. Sept. 30, 1821 ; m. Nov. 24, 1839, Emeline C. Canterbury, b. 1818, d. Sept. 27, 1872. Res. Boston, Mass. Children :—

3234. i. EMMA C., b. June 21, 1841; m. W. C. Anderson.
3235. ii. GEORGE W. W., b. Aug. 1, 1844; m. Lydia M. Dana.
3236. iii. FRANCES L., b. Feb. 10, 1846.
3237. iv. CORA; d.
3238. v. NELLIE; d.
3239. vi. THEODORE; d.
3240. vii. CHARLES F., b. May 11, 1856; m. Nellie J. Bowen.

2021. EDWARD F.[8] PIERCE (*Isaac[7], Joseph[6], Isaac[5], Isaac[4], Jonathan[3], Samuel[2], Thomas[1]*), b. Feb. 22, 1828 ; m. Harriet E. Deguio. Children :—

3241. i.
3242. ii. HARRIET E.
3243. iii. CHARLES.
3244. iv. GEORGE.
3245. v. FRANK.

2027. JAMES W.[8] PIERCE (*James[7], Joseph[6], Isaac[5], Isaac[4], Jonathan[3], Samuel[2], Thomas[1]*), b. July 8, 1820 ; m. Sept. 14, 1840, Sarah E. D. B. Wilson, b. May 23, 1822, d. He d. June 15, 1854. Res. Boston, Mass. Children :—

3246. i. SARAH A., b. Jan. 12, 1842; m. George A. Leonard.
3247. ii. JAMES W., b. Jan. 26, 1844; m. Anna M. Billings.
3248. iii. CHARLES E., b. Oct. 31, 1847; m. Harriet E. Thurston.
3249. iv. ANNA E., b. Oct. 7, 1853.

2030. THOMAS P.[8] PIERCE (*James[7], Joseph[6], Isaac[5], Isaac[4], Jonathan[3], Samuel[2], Thomas[1]*), b. Nov. 30, 1825 ; m. Sept. 20, 1848, Anna Clapp, b. Sept. 17, 1827, d. July 10, 1874 ; m. 2nd, Nov. 3, 1874, Annie Sutherland. He d. June 15, 1880. Res. Halifax, N. S., and Boston, Mass. Children :—

3250. i. ANNA E., b. Oct. 14, 1849; d. Nov. 5, 1850.
3251. ii. JOSEPHINE W., b. Dec. 17, 1851; d. Aug. 5, 1853.
3252. iii. THEODORE H., b. July 11, 1854; m. Oct. 28, 1880, Lucy E. Ware.
3253. iv. BEATRICE J., b. Oct. 10, 1857; m. Henry C. Wilson.
3254. v. WILLIETTA W., b. Feb. 10, 1861; d. 1863.

2032. WILLIAM J.[8] PIERCE (*James*[7], *Joseph*[6], *Isaac*[5], *Isaac*[4], *Jonathan*[3], *Samuel*[2], *Thomas*[1]), b. April 19, 1829 ; m. May 29, 1856, Sarah L. Bunten. He d. Jan. 14, 1879. Res. Boston, Mass. Children :—

3255. i.   FORESTER H., b. July 9, 1858.
3256. ii.   RALPH F., b. Aug. 6, 1860.
3257. iii.   HUBERT W., b. May 19, 1864.
3258. iv.   BESSIE L., b. March 13, 1869.
3259. v.   HAROLD B., b. July 2, 1871.
3260. vi.   WILBER J., b. Nov. 20, 1878.

2033. ISAAC[8] PIERCE (*James*[7], *Joseph*[6], *Isaac*[5], *Isaac*[4], *Jonathan*[3], *Samuel*[2], *Thomas*[1]), b. Dec. 27, 1830 ; m. Sept. 2nd, 1862, Jennie Hayes, d. He d. March 6, 1868. Res. Boston, Mass. No children.

2036. JOSEPH[8] PIERCE (*James*[7], *Joseph*[6], *Isaac*[5], *Isaac*[4], *Jonathan*[3], *Samuel*[2], *Thomas*[1]), b. Aug. 26, 1835 ; m. March 9, 1865, Emily A. Norwood. Res. 32 Anderson-St., Boston, Mass. No children.

2041. S. WINSLOW[8] PIERCE (*Samuel*[7], *Samuel*[6], *Samuel*[5], *Stephen*[4], *Jonathan*[3], *Samuel*[2], *Thomas*[1]), b. July 19, 1835 ; m. Sept. 30, 1858, Fannie Whitney, b. Sept. 12, 1838. Res. Davenport, Iowa.

Children :—

3261. i.   CHARLES A., b. April 24, 1864.
3262. ii.   FANNIE M., b. Dec. 30, 1865.
3263. iii.   CARRIE L., b. Dec. 25, 1868.
3264. iv.   NELLIE A., b. Nov. 12, 1871.
3265. v.   EMMA J., b. Sept. 14, 1874.

2048. E. HENRY[8] PIERCE (*Edward K.*[7], *Samuel*[6], *Samuel*[5], *Stephen*[4], *Jonathan*[3], *Samuel*[2], *Thomas*[1]), b. July 2, 1847 ; m. June 13, 1872, Luella Lake, b. April 22, 1855. Res. Davenport, Iowa. Children :—

3266. i.   EDNA L., b. July 30, 1876.
3267. ii.   ALBERT L., b. Sept. 5, 1878 ; d. Sept. 20, 1878.

2051. WILLIAM[8] PIERCE (*Barzillai*[7], *Jonathan*[6], *Joseph*[5], *Daniel*[4], *John*[3], *Thomas*[2], *Thomas*[1]), b. Jan. 13, 1803 ; m. Nov. 20, 1827, Jane Spratt. Res. So. Thomaston, Me. Children :—

3268. i.   JOHN S., b. Aug. 26, 1828 ; m. July 20, 1857, Sarah L. Dean.
3269. ii.   SAMUEL D., b. April 27, 1832 ; d. at sea, 1852.
3270. iii.   ALMIRA, b. April 14, 1839 ; m. Oct. 27, 1859, Elbridge F. Haskell.

2052. ISRAEL S.[8] PIERCE (*Barzillai*[7], *Jonathan*[6], *Joseph*[5], *Daniel*[4], *John*[3], *Thomas*[2], *Thomas*[1]), b. Jan. 1, 1805 ; m. Oct. 23, 1828, Mary Snow. He d. March 18, 1851. Res. Rockland, Me. Children :—

3271. i.   NATHANIEL J., b. Aug. 3, 1830 ; d. at sea about 1845.
3272. ii.   ISRAEL T., b. Jan. 8, 1834 ; d. at N. Y.
3273. iii.   MARY H., b. Sept. 30, 1835 ; d.
3274. iv.   CAROLINE E., b. Sept. 24, 1837 ; m. Charles Vertoux.

3275. v. GEORGE W., b. April 12, 1834; d. at N. Y.
3276. vi. SUSAN A., b. June 22, 1841.

2055. JOSEPH S.[8] PIERCE (*Barzillai*[7], *Jonathan*[6], *Joseph*[5], *Daniel*[4], *John*[3], *Thomas*[2], *Thomas*[1]), b. Feb. 5, 1811 ; m. Jan. 16, 1836, Margaret Snow. Res. Rockland, Me. Children :—

3277. i. JOSEPH H., b. March 7, 1839. Res. Rockland, Me. Was in the U. S. Navy during the war.
3278. ii. ROSE C., b. Aug. 15, 1840. Res. Rockland, Me.
3279. iii. MARGARET, b. June 28, 1841; d. Oct., 1854.
3280. iv. DELIA, b. May 7, 1844; m. ―― Smith.

2057. GEORGE W.[8] PIERCE (*Barzillai*[7], *Jonathan*[6], *Joseph*[5], *Daniel*[4], *John*[3], *Thomas*[2], *Thomas*[1]), b. May 13, 1816 ; m. Oct. 27, 1847, Nancy F. Martin, b. Sept. 24, 1824, d. Sept. 23, 1860 ; m. 2nd, Dec. 8, 1861, Mrs. Harriet N. McLane, b. Nov. 10, 1823. Res. South Thomaston, Me.

George W. Pierce

Children :—

3281. i. SIDNEY H., b. Sept. 27, 1849; m. Abbie L. Dean.
3282. ii. SARAH T., b. March 1, 1852; m. B. Hinckley Clay.
3283. iii. ANNIE M., b. Nov. 3, 1854; m. B. Hinckley Clay.
3284. iv. EMMA E., b. Sept. 23, 1856; d. Sept. 24, 1873.
3285. v. NANNIE M., b. Nov. 10, 1862; d. May 18, 1877.

2063. CYRUS[8] PIERCE (*Simon*[7], *David*[6], *Daniel*[5], *Daniel*[4], *John*[3], *Thomas*[2], *Thomas*[1]), b. Aug. 18, 1793 ; m. Julia Sewall, d. April 5, 1857. He d. April 28, 1851. Res. Chesterville, Me. No children.

2069. ABNER[8] PIERCE (*Simon*[7], *David*[6], *Daniel*[5], *Daniel*[4], *John*[3], *Thomas*[2], *Thomas*[1]), b. Jan. 17, 1809 ; m. Abigail Walton. He d. June 30, 1862. She m. 2nd, Rev. M. Wright. Res. Waupon, Wis. Children :—

3286. i. HOWARD.
3287. ii. HELEN.
3288. iii. ――.
3289. iv. CHARLES.

2071. MOSES C.[8] PIERCE (*Calvin*[7], *David*[6], *Daniel*[5], *Daniel*[4], *John*[3], *Thomas*[2], *Thomas*[1]), b. May 4, 1791 ; m. March 14, 1815, Temperance Savage, b. Jan. 6, 1799, d. Sept. 28, 1865. He d. April 7, 1831. Children :—

3290. i. HANNAH, b. April 6, 1816; m. John Graves.
3291. ii. CALVIN, b. July 21, 1817; d. Sept. 28, 1852.
3292. iii. MARTHA, b. Feb. 24, 1819; m. Hiram Cousins.
3293. iv. LUTHER, b. Aug. 25, 1820; m. Nancy T. Greenwood.

3294. v. MARY, b. June 6, 1822; m. William Howes.
3295. vi. JOTHAM S., b. Feb. 26, 1824; m. Mary Chapman.
3296. vii. CYRUS, b. Sept. 29, 1826; d. Feb. 13, 1845.
3297. viii. EZRA, b. May 22, 1827; m. Hannah Holway.
3298. ix. JOEL M., b. May 2, 1830; m. Cordelia Clark.
3299. x. BETSEY P., b. May 18, 1831; m. Ira Dole.

2072. NATHANIEL[8] PIERCE (*Calvin[7], David[6], Daniel[5], Daniel[4], John[3], Thomas[2], Thomas[1]*), b. March 25, 1793 ; m. Nov. 13, 1814, Ardear Baker, b. March 28, 1798, d. Aug. 6, 1875. Res. Carritunk Plantation, Me. Children :—

3300. i. HARRIET, b. July 28, 1817; m. Thomas Brown and William Knapp.
3301. ii. JAMES, b. Aug. 29, 1819; m. Lucinda Holway.
3302. iii. IRENA, b. July, 1821; m. Aaron Sanborn and William Arno.
3303. iv. OSBORN, b. Feb. 7, 1823; m. Sybil Paine.
3304. v. FIDELIA, b. May 25, 1825; m. John Holway.
3305. vi. HANNAH B., b. Nov. 7, 1828; m. Jeremiah S. Spalding.
3306. vii. SETH B., b. Oct. 20, 1830; m. Vesta Kimball.
3307. viii. ESTHER, b. Aug. 1, 1835; m. Henry Durgin.
3308. ix. HENRIETTA, b. June 1, 1840; m. Orland Young.

2074. JAMES S.[8] PIERCE (*Calvin[7], David[6], Daniel[5], Daniel[4], John[3], Thomas[2], Thomas[1]*), b. Feb. 3, 1797 ; m. Mercy B. Hale, b. March 25, 1804, d. May 11, 1855 ; m. 2nd, ———— ————, d. March 20, 1876. He d. March 20, 1876. Res. Solon, Me. Children :—

3309. i. FRANCES C., b. Sept. 7, 1823; m. Chas. K. White.
3309½. ii. M. LOUISA, b. July 23, 1825; m. John P. Cobb.
3310. iii. LEWELLYN, b. Nov. 30, 1826; m. Catherine Spillane.
3311. iv. JOSIAH H., b. May 3, 1828; d. May 7, 1833.
3312. v. CHARLOTTE W., b. June 20, 1830; d. Aug. 19, 1833.
3313. vi. JOPHANES H., b. June 10, 1832; d. Aug. 23, 1833.
3314. vii. ROMANDEL, b. Sept. 20, 1834; m. Mrs. ———— Lyford.
3315. viii. ARDELIA, b. Oct. 10, 1836; d. Dec. 25, 1840.
3316. ix. CASKALINE, b. Sept. 17, 1838; m. Chas. Ingalls.
3317. x. HELVENA, b. Nov. 3, 1840; d. July 11, 1861.

2075. JOSHUA B.[8] PIERCE (*Calvin[7], David[6], Daniel[5], Daniel[4], John[3], Thomas[2], Thomas[1]*), b. Feb. 19, 1799 ; m. Oct. 2, 1821, Hannah Bean, b. Nov. 27, 1797. He d. Aug. 27, 1836. She m. 2nd, Edward Howes. Res. Bingham, Me. Children :—

3318. i. MOSES, b. Oct. 29, 1827; m., left home in '54 and went to Cal.
3319. ii. CLARISSA C., b. Sept. 14, 1829; d. March 3, 1845.
3320. iii. SETH B., b. May 6, 1831; d. Jan. 20, 1867, unm.
3321. iv. DOLLY A., b. Jan. 25, 1836; m. John Steward.

2079. EZEKIEL[8] PIERCE (*Calvin[7], David[6], Daniel[5], Daniel[4], John[3], Thomas[2], Thomas[1]*), b. Jan. 17, 1807 ; m. Jan. 1, 1833, Content B. Pierce [2116], b. Aug. 12, 1810, d. June 8, 1856. Res. Clinton, Me.

Children :—

3322. i. LOIS, b. Jan. 20, 1834; m. John Mears.
3323. ii. EMILY, b. Apr. 2, 1835; m. Stephen Runnells and Hollis Spencer.

3324. iii. JULIA A., b. Dec. 16, 1836; d. Oct. 26, 1857.
3325. iv. JOHN G., b. July 22, 1838; d. June, 1876.
3326. v. JOEL C., b. May 2, 1840; res. N. Berwick, Me.
3327. vi. HELENA B., b. May 7, 1844; d. Sept. 17, 1846.
3328. vii. PETER, b. Feb. 18, 1846; d. Sept. 4, 1846.
3329. viii. CHARLES E., b. June 15, 1848.
3330. ix. JOSEPH, b. Jan. 31, 1850; d. June 8, 1850.

2082. JOHN[8] PIERCE (*Luther*[7], *David*[6], *Daniel*[5], *Daniel*[4], *John*[3], *Thomas*[2], *Thomas*[1]), b. March 2, 1795 ; m. Oct. 4, 1846, Rachel L. Nudd, b. Oct. 27, 1820. Res. Solon, Me. Children :—

3330¼. i. HARRIET F., b. Aug. 22, 1848; m. Joseph Maynard.
3330½. ii. RACHEL O., b. Jan. 19, 1853; m. Joseph Maynard.

2083. LUTHER[8] PIERCE (*Luther*[7], *David*[6], *Daniel*[5], *Daniel*[4], *John*[3], *Thomas*[2], *Thomas*[1]), b. Feb. 8, 1797 ; m. April 12, 1819, Lucinda Pierce [2064], b. Sept. 20, 1797, d. Jan. 14, 1845 ; m. 2nd, June 4, 1846, Mary S. Burns, b. Aug. 17, 1808. He d. Oct. 2, 1871. Res. Solon, Me. Children :—

3331. i. NAOMI, b. Nov. 8, 1820; m. George G. Burns; res. Brandon, Wis.
3332. ii. ELIZABETH, b. Jan. 13, 1823; m. Howard B. Wilson.
3333. iii. LUTHER, b. March 19, 1826; d March 22, 1826.
3334. iv. CYRUS B., b. Nov. 26, 1829; m. Harriet Moore.
3335. v. JOHN L., b. Sept. 29, 1832; m. Achsa Andrews and Sarah B. Merrill.
3336. vi. JULIA O., b. Jan. 2, 1837; m. Wickliff Goodrich; Res. Ripon, Wis.
3337. vii. MARY E., b. March 25, 1850 ; m. Samuel Albee.

2084. JESSE[8] PIERCE (*Luther*[7], *David*[6], *Daniel*[5], *Daniel*[4], *John*[3], *Thomas*[2], *Thomas*[1]), b. Jan. 17, 1799 ; m. Dec. 25, 1826, Catherine Reed, b. April 10, 1801, d. Sept. 27, 1877. He d. May 6, 1854. Res. Madison, Me. Children :—

3338. i. CATHERINE, b. Feb. 18, 1828; d. June 24, 1832.
3339. ii. ADELINE S., b. March 16, 1829; m. Dudley L. Fogg.
3340. iii. JESSE, b. April 27, 1831; d. Oct. 16, 1831.

2086. ISAAC R.[8] PIERCE (*David*[7], *David*[6], *Daniel*[5], *Daniel*[4], *John*[3], *Thomas*[2], *Thomas*[1]), b. Oct. 15, 1795 ; m. 1820, Eliza Chute, b. Aug. 27, 1803. He d. Oct., 1872. Res. Smithfield, Me. Children :—

3341. i. ELIZA A., b. Aug. 27, 1822; m. Silas V. Tuck; res. Brockton, Mass.
3342. ii. OLIVE R., b. May 8, 1824; m. Nathaniel Page.
3343. iii. DAVID, b. July 26, 1826; d. July 10, 1843.
3344. iv. ISAIAH, b. Nov. 19, 1828; m. —— Thompson.
3345. v. MARTHA D., b. Feb. 1, 1835; m. John M. Clark.
3346. vi. CELESTIA, b. 1843; m. Leonard W. Hunnewell.

2087. SAMUEL D.[8] PIERCE (*David*[7], *David*[6], *Daniel*[5], *Daniel*[4], *John*[3], *Thomas*[2], *Thomas*[1]), b. Jan. 18, 1797 ; m. Dec. 2, 1819, Lucy Barstow, b. May 18, 1794, d. Sept. 1, 1856. He d. May 3, 1867. Res. Norridgewock, Me. Children :—

3347. i. OBED W., b. Sept. 23, 1820; m. Sarah R. Haines.
3348. ii. WELLINGTON, b. March 29, 1822; m. Silvinia Albee.
3349. iii. ALFRED, b. March 9, 1824; m. Hannah C. Clark.
3350. iv. SETH, b. July 30, 1826; d. Oct. 8, 1852.
3351. v. SUMNER, b. Oct. 7, 1829; m. Emily Clark.

3352. vi. CAROLINE, b. Feb. 22, 1831; m. Feb. 23, 1861.
3353. vii. SABINIA, b. March 2, 1833; m. Tobias C. Walton.
3354. viii. LUCY B., b. July 5, 1835; m. William Toothaker.

2089. RUFUS W.[8] PIERCE (*David*[7], *David*[6], *Daniel*[5], *Daniel*[4], *John*[3], *Thomas*[2], *Thomas*[1]), b. Dec. 31, 1805; m. June 20, 1833, Sally Hosmer, b. 1803, d. Feb. 12, 1845; m. 2nd, Sept. 29, 1847, Martha Nutting, b. July 5, 1818. Res. Smithfield, Me. Children :—

3355. i. MARY H., b. Apr. 1, 1834; m. Harper Allen.
3356. ii. SARAH R., b. June 3, 1836; m. Samuel A. Marston.
3357. iii. JOHN C., b. Sept. 9, 1838; m. Louise V. Morton.
3358. iv. JOSEPH H., b. June 15, 1841; m. Helen M. Hale.
3359. v. EMMA M., b. Sept. 16, 1848.
3360. vi. ELLEN, b. Feb. 18, 1852; d. May 10, 1872.
3361. vii. CALVIN R., b. May 22, 1853.
3362. viii. SARIA, b. June 22, 1855; d. July 13, 1873.

2092. CALEB S.[8] PIERCE (*David*[7], *David*[6], *Daniel*[5], *Daniel*[4], *John*[3], *Thomas*[2], *Thomas*[1]), b. Jan. 13, 1812; m. Dec. 22, 1830, Eliza Young, b. 1810. He d. Oct. 4, 1876. Res. Ionia, Mich. Children :—

3363. i. HENRY. 3364. ii. SEWALL. 3365. iii. MARTHA; m. ——— Gibbs.

2093. SIMON D.[8] PIERCE (*David*[7], *David*[6], *Daniel*[5], *Daniel*[4], *John*[3], *Thomas*[2], *Thomas*[1]), b. June 10, 1813; m. Oct., 1835, Sarah A. Parsons, b. Aug. 14, 1819. Res. Smithfield, Me.

Simon D. Pierce was born in Norridgewock, Me., June 10, 1813, and resided for some years in No. 2 Plantation, in the County of Somerset, and during that residence was considerably engaged in lumbering on the upper Kennebec and its tributaries. In 1855 he removed to Smithfield, Me., where he has since resided, being engaged in agriculture.

S D Pierce

Children :—

3366. i. ANNIE, b. Dec. 16, 1837; d. May 6, 1863.
3367. ii. HENRY W., b. Jan. 30, 1840; m. Sarah E. Allen.
3368. iii. FRANCES W., b. May 3, 1843; m. 1859, Luther A. Rowe, b. Sept. 16, 1839. Ch.: Laura E., b. Feb. 9, 1860; Mary F., b. Jan. 20, 1862; Arthur S., b. Feb. 6, 1864; Alma A., b. May 29, 1865; res. So. Norridgewock, and Smithfield, Me.
3369. iv. LAURA A., b. Mar. 3, 1845; d. July 6, 1857.
3370. v. DAVID R., b. Feb. 4, 1848; m. Lucie A. Burnham.
3371. vi. WILLIAM S.; Res. Berwick, Me.

2095. CALVIN[8] PIERCE (*David*[7], *David*[6], *Daniel*[5], *Daniel*[4], *John*[3], *Thomas*[2], *Thomas*[1]), b. July 13, 1818; m. Nov. 29, 1841, Julia A. Swan. He d. July 18, 1849. Res. Auburn, Me. Children :—

3372. i. JOHN F.
3373. ii. LAURA, b. 1844; m. July 3, 1864, Francis A. Thurston, b. Oct. 19, 1837. Ch.: Marion F., b. Nov. 12, 1865; Herbert R., b. Mar. 24, 1869. They res. in Auburn, Me. He is master mechanic in the Little Androscoggin Water Power Company at Auburn, and belongs to the Universalist denomination while his wife is a Congregationalist.
3374. iii. ORLANDO.

2100. HARRY[8] PIERCE (*Charles[7], David[6], Daniel[5], Daniel[4], John[3], Thomas[2], Thomas[1]*), b. July 23, 1803; m. Fidelia Quint. Res. Parkersburg, Iowa. Children :—

3375. i. MOSES.
3376. ii. WILLIAM.
3377. iii. ORILLA.
3378. iv. DAVID.

2101. PETER[8] PIERCE (*Charles[7], David[6], Daniel[5], Daniel[4], John[3], Thomas[2], Thomas[1]*), b. Nov. 20, 1804; m. Dec. 30, 1830, Lydia Watters, b. 1802, d. Dec., 1869; m. 2nd, Nov. 27, 1872, Delia McMaster, b. Apr., 1829. Res. Brooklyn, N. Y. Children :—

3379. i. WILLIAM A., b. July 6, 1835; d. Oct. 27, 1836.
3380. ii. DELIA, b. July 7, 1843; d. Feb. 20, 1868.
3381. iii. ———.

2102. WILLIAM[8] PIERCE (*Charles[7], David[6], Daniel[5], Daniel[4], John[3], Thomas[2], Thomas[1]*), b. Apr. 22, 1806; m. Anula Quint. Res. Moston, Wis. No children.

2108. CHARLES T.[8] PIERCE (*Charles[7], David[6], Daniel[5], Daniel[4], John[3], Thomas[2], Thomas[1]*), b. Feb. 14, 1821; m. Apr. 6, 1841, Polly Strickland, b. Oct. 28, 1822. Res. Ferdinand, Ill. Children :—

3382. i. HANNAH A., b. Feb. 28, 1842; m. Cornelius L. Jackson.
3383. ii. PETER O., b. Aug. 8, 1843; killed at battle of Resaca, Ga., May 15, 1864.
3384. iii. ELIAS, b. Nov. 22, 1845; wounded at battle of Resaca, Ga., and d. Feb. 1, 1869.
3385. iv. WILLIAM A., b. Mar. 31, 1848; m. March 7, 1872, Mary A. Livingston.
3386. v. FANNY O., b. Jan. 26, 1850; d. Aug. 3, 1853.
3387. vi. ABIGAIL A., b. Dec. 14, 1851; m. Charles S. Bigelow.
3388. vii. MANLY W., b. Dec. 10, 1853; m. March 19, 1876, Sarah J. Taylor.
3389. viii. MARY A., b. Aug. 31, 1855; d. Apr. 19, 1858.
3390. ix. TRUMAN, b. Sept. 17, 1857.
3391. x. ELLEN, b. Aug. 8, 1859.
3392. xi. IDA A., b. Apr. 9, 1861.
3393. xii. OBED A., b. Feb. 18, 1865; d. Mar. 2, 1865.

2110. ELIAS M.[8] PIERCE (*Charles[7], David[6], Daniel[5], Daniel[4], John[3], Thomas[2], Thomas[1]*); m. Feb. 18, 1854, Mary E. Allen. Res. Warren, Pa. Children :—

3394. i. FRED. C., b. July 18, 1855.
3395. ii. FRANK A., b. Feb. 6, 1857.
3396. iii. EDWARD W., b. June 13, 1865.

2111. ALVIN B.[8] PIERCE (*Peter[7], David[6], Daniel[5], Daniel[4], John[3], Thomas[2], Thomas[1]*), b. Aug. 13, 1800; m. Sally Baker; d. Nov. 23, 1870. Res. Bingham, Me. Children :—

3397. i. REUBEN B., b. Oct. 4, 1829; m. Lydia M. Chase and Elizabeth (Baker) Pierce.
3398. ii. OBED, b. May 2, 1832; m. Elizabeth Baker.
3399. iii. PETER; m. Apprinda Blake.
3400. iv. ALVIN; m. ———.
3401. v. SEWELL, b. 1839; d. ———.

3402.   vi.   ELIZABETH; m. Luther Moore and Samuel Paine.
3403.   vii. SARAH; m. Justus Washburn.

2113. CHARLES[8] PIERCE (*Peter[7], David[6], Daniel[5], Daniel[4], John[3], Thomas[2], Thomas[1]*), b. Nov. 25, 1804; m. Feb. 15, 1828, Hannah R. Jones, b. Nov. 1, 1806, d. ———. He d. ———. Res. Waupun, Wis. Children :—

3404.   i.   ASA G., b. Jan. 13, 1829; m. Rhoda Collins; res. Waupun, Wis.
3405.   ii.   CLARISSA F., b. Sept. 22, 1830; m. B. H. Harkness; res. Humboldt, Iowa.
3406.   iii. EDWIN R., b. Mar. 13, 1832; m. Algenir Morse; res. Riverside, Cal.
3407.   iv.   CHARLES B., b. Feb. 9, 1834; res. Custer City, Dak.
3408.   v.   RUFUS K., b. Dec. 10, 1835; m. Elizabeth Minton; res. Waupun, Wis.
3409.   vi.   FLORA S., b. Dec. 27, 1840; m. Rollin Amadon; res. Waupun, Wis.
3410.   vii. JOHN G.
3411.   viii. SIMON.
3412.   ix.   DANIEL.

2115. HEMAN[8] PIERCE (*Peter[7], David[6], Daniel[5], Daniel[4], John[3], Thomas[2], Thomas[1]*), b. Dec. 15, 1808; m. Achsah Holman. Res. Bangor, Me. Children :—

3412¼. i.   BOWEN; m. ———.
3412½. ii.   HELEN; m. George Pierce.

2117. SIMON[8] PIERCE (*Peter[7], David[6], Daniel[5], Daniel[4], John[3], Thomas[2], Thomas[1]*), b. Feb. 10, 1813; m. Betsey Graves. Res. Somerset Mills, Me. Children :—

3413.   i.   MARY; m. ——— Sheppard.
3414.   ii.   FANNY; m. Fred. Morse.
3415.   iii. LIVONIA; m. ———.

2119. REUBEN[8] PIERCE (*Jedediah[7], Reuben[6], Daniel[5], Daniel[4], John[3], Thomas[2], Thomas[1]*), b. Dec. 9, 1809; m. Dec. 15, 1837, Cornelia Jewell, b. Aug. 20, 1809. Res. Jaffrey, N. H. Children :—

3416.   i.   ELOISE N., b. Feb. 2, 1839.
3417.   ii.   DELIA J., b. Feb. 20, 1850.

2123. ABIJAH A.[8] PIERCE (*Abijah[7], Reuben[6], Daniel[5], Daniel[4], John[3], Thomas[2], Thomas[1]*), b. Mar. 9, 1818; m. Apr. 16, 1838, Caroline Maivel, b. July 25, 1814. Res. St. Albans, Vt. Children :—

3418.   i.   MARION B., b. Aug. 16, 1841; m. L. O. Stone.
3419.   ii.   EDWARD A., b. Apr. 13, 1844.
3420.   iii. CASSIUS W., b. Oct. 3, 1849; m. M. Emma Pierce.

2124. LEWIS L.[8] PIERCE (*Abijah[7], Reuben[6], Daniel[5], Daniel[4], John[3], Thomas[2], Thomas[1]*), b. Mar. 28, 1820; m. May 2, 1841, Christina M. Billings, b. Aug. 10, 1819. Res. E. Jaffrey, N. H. Children :—

3421.   i.   SARAH E., b. Sept. 4, 1843; d. May 18, 1874.
3422.   ii.   ZENOPHON J., b. Apr. 9, 1846; m. Dora Bowman.
3423.   iii. ELLELY C., b. Aug. 12, 1848; d. Nov. 14, 1864.

2128. R. PARKER[8] PIERCE (*Abijah[7], Reuben[6], Daniel[5], Daniel[4], John[3], Thomas[2], Thomas[1]*), b. June 4, 1831; m. Charlotte Morris; m. 2nd, Mar. 27, 1860, Susan P. Davis, b. Nov. 22, 1834, d. Aug. 28, 1879. Res. New York.

Children :—

3424. i.   CHARLOTTE.   3425. ii.   HENRY N., b. Feb. 25, 1861.
3426. iii. WALTER M., b. Sept. 6, 1863; d. Aug. 7, 1864.

2130. SAMUEL[8] PIERCE (*Asaph[7], Samuel[6], Daniel[5], Daniel[4], John[3], Thomas[2], Thomas[1]*), b. Dec. 23, 1799; m. 1824, Matilda Bailey, d. July 10, 1873. Res. Moretown, Vt. Children :—

3427. i.   SCHUYLER, b. Jan. 17, 1826; m. Almira Marble.
3428. ii. ALVIN M., b. Feb. 16, 1828; m. L. S. Bagley.

2136. LUKE C.[8] PIERCE (*Samuel[7], Samuel[6], Daniel[5], Daniel[4], John[3], Thomas[2], Thomas[1]*), b. Jan. 11, 1807; m. May 5, 1836, Margaret Smith, b. Sept. 5, 1814, d. Mar. 9, 1851; m. 2nd, Dec, 16, 1851, Hester E. Lammons, b. Apr. 25, 1830. He d. Jan. 4, 1855, in Franklin, Mich. Children :—

3429. i.   SARAH T., b. Nov. 25, 1839; m. July 5, 1865, Frank Meeker, b. Dec. 15, 1837. Ch. : Sarah L., b. May 20, 1867; Frank L., b. July 23, 1869; Guy A., b. Apr. 19, 1876; res. Marshalltown, Iowa.
3430. ii. CAROLINE P., b. May 12, 1841; d. Sept. 27, 1841.
3431. iii. LUKE, b. Dec. 12, 1843; d. Dec. 15, 1843.
3432. iv. SAMUEL W., b. Apr. 29, 1853; unm.

2137. LUTHER B.[8] PIERCE (*Samuel[7], Samuel[6], Daniel[5], Daniel[4], John[3], Thomas[2], Thomas[1]*), b. Jan. 11, 1807; m. Sept. 29, 1831, Mary A. Wilson, b. July 4, 1804. They res. in Boston, 15 Groton street. Children :—

3433-4. i. MARTHA S., b. Jan. 27, 1834; m. June 1, 1853, John Hughes; res. 337 N. Charles street, Boston.
3435. ii. ROSINA S., b. Mar. 5, 1836; m. May 3, 1857, Charles W. Huntress, b. Oct. 18, 1830, d, Oct. 14, 1874. Ch. : Eddie B., b. Aug. 27, 1860, d. May 18, 1864.
3436. iii. SAMUEL W., b. Feb. 3, 1837; m. Mrs. Anna Hewer, Feb. 5, 1880.
3437. iv. MARY E., b. Feb. 22, 1841; m. Apr. 1, 1858, George V. Leicester, b. 1830; d. Mar. 31, 1871, leaving Walter P., b. July 31, 1865.
3438. v.   LUCINDA M., b. Aug. 2, 1844; m. Aug. 16, 1863, Wm. K. Gerrish, b. 1835. Ch. : Abbie R., b. Mar. 17, 1866; Mabel F., b. Mar. 18, 1868; Nellie G., b. Jan. 16. 1870; Willie R., b. 1875; Flora E., b. Aug. 5, 1876. Res. 182 Tudor street, So. Boston.
3439. vi. ELIZA T., b. May 13, 1846.

2138. SAMUEL W.[8] PIERCE (*Samuel[7], Samuel[6], Daniel[5], Daniel[4], John[3], Thomas[2], Thomas[1]*), b. Aug. 31, 1808; m. Apr. 27, 1837, Mary Dutton, b. Apr. 4, 1813, d. Jan. 1, 1847; m. 2nd, Sept. 28, 1847, Martha Plummer, b. Nov. 3, 1817. They res. E. Jaffrey, N. H.

Children :—

3440. i. MARY E., b. Apr. 30, 1838; m. Feb. 24, 1861, Joseph F. Carr, b.
            Apr. 28, 1835. Ch.: Mary A., b. Sept. 5, 1862; Emma F., b.
            Feb. 2, 1867, d. Sept. 8, 1869; Frank F., b. Aug. 18, 1869;
            Walter A., b. Jan. 1, 1875; res. Carlisle, Mass.
3441. ii. HENRY W., b. Mar. 21, 1842; m. June 4, 1867, Helen V. Buttrick.
            Res. Winchendon, Mass.
3442. iii. ALBERT S., b. Mar. 15, 1845; m. Dec. 11, 1872, Mary A. Chamber-
            lin, b. May 25, 1849. No issue. Res. Fitchburg, Mass.
3443. iv. J. PLUMMER, b. Feb. 25, 1851; m. June 10, 1874, Lizzie P Morse,
            b. Jan. 21, 1856. Res. Jaffrey, N. H.

2140. Col. CHARLES W.[8] PIERCE (*Samuel[7], Samuel[6], Daniel[5],
Daniel[4], John[3], Thomas[2], Thomas[1]*), b. May 27, 1812 ; m. May 27,
1835, Abigail G. Going, b. May 15, 1811. He d. Aug. 25, 1865, in
Dublin, N. H.

Charles W. Pierce was a miller by occupation and had repeatedly
held the office of selectman and was for a number of years Colonel of
the 12th Regiment of N. H. State Militia. Children:—

3444. i.   PHEBE, b. Feb. 18, 1836; d. Jan. 1, 1857.
3445. ii.   CHARLES H., b. June 6, 1837; d. Apr. 5, 1860.
3446. iii. JAMES E., b. July 1, 1839; d. Mar. 21, 1866.
3447. iv.   ASAPH W., b. Sept. 28, 1840.

            Asaph W. Pierce died in Poolesville, Md., Jan. 21, 1862. He
            was corporal of Company A, 14th Regt. N. H. Vols.

3448. v.   HARRIET A., b. Oct. 6, 1842; m. May 13, 1864, John E. Baldwin,
            b. July 28, 1842. Ch. : Charles E., b. Apr. 28, 1865; M. Abbie,
            b. Mar. 9, 1868, d. Mar. 11, 1868; Edwin P., b. Jan 4, 1869;
            Almon A., b. Oct. 15, 1870; Carl F., b. July 30, 1872; Mark E.,
            b. Mar. 22, 1874; Claribell, b. Nov. 19, 1875. Res. Jaffrey, N. H.
3449. vi.   ALMON G., b. Oct. 29, 1843.

            Almon G. Pierce died in New Orleans, La., June 8, 1864. He
            was Orderly Sergeant of Company C, 14th Regt. N. H. Vols.

3450. vii. RUFUS P., b. May 11, 1846; m. July 1, 1874, Sarah M. Gleason.
3451. viii. EUDORA F., b. Oct. 31, 1847; d. Mar. 19, 1869.
3452. ix.   WILLARD H., b. Feb. 5, 1849; m. Mar. 30, 1872, Ellen Simmons.
3453. x.   CLARA G., b. Mar. 23, 1851; d. Apr. 15, 1871.
3454. xi.   FRANK E., b. Feb. 3, 1853.
3455. xii. FRED. A., b. Oct 12, 1854; m. Urania Parker.
3456. xiii. ABBIE G., b. May 22, 1856; d. Apr. 20, 1857.

2148. CALEB W.[8] PIERCE (*Caleb[7], Samuel[6], Daniel[5], Daniel[4],
John[3], Thomas[2], Thomas[1]*), b. Feb. 28, 1810 ; m. Nov. 2, 1835, Mary
M. Miles, b. Oct. 25, 1816; He d. Sept. 5, 1872. Res. Flint, Mich.

Child :—

3457. i. LUCINDA A., b. Oct. 28, 1836; m. July 6, 1862, George A. Patrick.

2150. SILAS R.[8] PIERCE (*Caleb[7], Samuel[6], Daniel[5], Daniel[4],
John[3], Thomas[2], Thomas[1]*), b. June 27, 1817 ; m. Apr. 24, 1844,
Mary A. Wolverton, b. June 2, 1817, d. Sept. 2, 1848; m. 2nd, Jan.

3, 1851, Caroline Crocker, d. Feb. 28, 1856; m. 3rd, Dec. 7, 1865, Jennie McEwen, b. Feb. 14, 1831. Res. Flint, Mich.

Silas P. Pierce

Children :—

3458. i. LUCY, b. Feb. 16, 1845; m. Gilbert Hobbs. No issue.
3459. ii. MARY, b. Aug. 23, 1847; m. Ira D. Stannard, and d. Oct. 7, 1877.
        Ch. : Burt, b. July 12, 1872; Jennie, b. Apr. 16, 1875.
3460. iii. GEORGE C., b. Dec. 15, 1852.
3461. iv. SILAS R., Jr., b. Mar. 14, 1854.
3462. v. CARRIE C., b. Feb. 14, 1856.
3463. vi. FANNIE, b. Dec. 6, 1867.
3464. vii. ADDIE, b. May 10, 1869.

2153. FREDERICK S.[8] PIERCE (*Joseph*[7], *Samuel*[6], *Daniel*[5], *Daniel*[4], *John*[3], *Thomas*[2], *Thomas*[1]), b. Sept. 10, 1822; m. Dec. 10, 1848, Martha Tolman, b. Jan. 3, 1823, d. May 3, 1850; m. 2nd, Jan. 29, 1853, Mary A. Grant, b. Jan. 11, 1820. He is Dept. Sheriff of Hillsboro and Cheshire counties, and res. in E. Jaffrey, N. H.

Frederick Sumner Pierce

No issue.

2156. SAMUEL S.[8] PIERCE (*Joseph*[7], *Samuel*[6], *Daniel*[5], *Daniel*[4], *John*[3], *Thomas*[2], *Thomas*[1]), b. July 14, 1828; m. Apr. 9, 1851, Stella L. Clark. b. Sept. 13, 1830. Res. Worcester. Children :—

3465. i. EMMA A., b. Feb. 25, 1852; m. Nov. 27, 1873, Charles F. Wood, b. Feb. 26, 1851.
3466. ii. EDWIN S., b. June 14, 1855.
3467. iii. CARRIE E., b. Aug. 27, 1857.
3468. iv. JENNIE V., b. Oct. 3, 1861; d. Sept. 9, 1865.
3469. v. FRANK S., b. Mar. 1, 1871.

2165. ORVILLE W.[8] PIERCE (*Jacob*[7], *Jacob*[6], *Daniel*[5], *Daniel*[4], *John*[3], *Thomas*[2], *Thomas*[1]), b. Dec. 6, 1806; m. Amanda Templeton, b. 1816, d. July 21, 1857; m. 2nd, Feb. 15, 1858, Mrs. Lydia Flanders Griffing, b. Jan. 14, 1818. He d. May 3, 1880. Res. Langdon, N. H. Children :—

3470. i. MELICIA A.; m. Henry Nevers.
3471. ii. JACOB S.; m. Mary O. Ray.
3472. iii. FRANKLIN O.; m. ———.
3473. iv. MARY A.; m. Charles Gates.
3474. v. ORILLA M., b. Mar., 1841; d. Nov. 2, 1861.
3475. vi. GEORGE H., b. Jan. 9, 1844; m. Clara ———.
3476. vii. SARAH E., b. Aug 9, 1847; m. Charles Gates.
3477. viii. HARRIET A., b. Oct. 18, 1849; m. Willard F. Inman.
3478. ix. CLEMENTINE, b. Mar. 21, 1859; d. Mar. 14, 1873.
3479. x. CHARLES F., b. Feb. 2, 1860.

2166. DANIEL[8] PIERCE (*Jacob[7], Jacob[6], Daniel[5], Daniel[4], John[3], Thomas[2], Thomas[1]*), b. Aug. 24, 1808; m. Oct. 18, 1836, Almira Black, b. Nov. 26, 1807. Res. Chesterfield Factory, N. H.
Children :—

3480. i. HENRY D., b. Apr. 8, 1839; m. Feb. 24, 1862, Mary A. Starkey.
3481. ii. DAVID H., b. May 25, 1841; m. Jan. 19, 1870, Angie M. Bennett.
3482. iii. WILLIAM H., b. Dec. 9, 1842; m. Ella L. Hunt.

2172. SAMUEL G.[8] PIERCE (*Jacob[7], Jacob[6], Daniel[5], Daniel[4], John[3], Thomas[2], Thomas[1]*), b. Jan. 13, 1825; m. Nov. 29, 1853, Almira E. Kimball, b. Nov. 6, 1832. He d. Jan. 12, 1862, and she then m. Warren Bingham.

Child :—

3483. i. FRED. O., b. Oct. 1, 1857.

2173. BENJAMIN[8] PIERCE, Jr. (*Benjamin[7], Jacob[6], Daniel[5], Daniel[4], John[3], Thomas[2], Thomas[1]*), b. Dec. 8, 1814; m. Feb. 13, 1838, Louisa A. R. Scott, b. June 19, 1819. Res. Pulaski, N. Y.

Children :—

3484. i. WINSLOW N., b. July 21, 1842; m. Oct., 1870, Hattie M. Walworth.
3485. ii. EVA A., b. July 23, 1850.
3486. iii. WARD E., b. Dec. 14, 1855.

2174. HILLMAN[8] PIERCE (*Benjamin[7], Jacob[6], Daniel[5], Daniel[4], John[3], Thomas[2], Thomas[1]*), b. June 9, 1815; m. Nov. 26, 1839, Sarah A. Wood, b. June 5, 1820, d. Aug. 26, 1872. Res. Pulaski, N. Y., and Collegeville, Cal. Children :—

3487. i. LEWIS O., b. Mar. 5, 1845; m. Oct. 6, 1869, Martha W. Allen.
3488. ii. WILLARD J., b. Jan. 12, 1848; m. Nov. 9, 1869, Orpha T. Wright.
3489. iii. HATTIE M., b. June 24, 1855; m. Dec. 10, 1875, William S. Lane, b. Mar. 5, 1850. Res. Pulaski, N. Y.

2175. MARSHALL[8] PIERCE (*Benjamin[7], Jacob[6], Daniel[5], Daniel[4], John[3], Thomas[2], Thomas[1]*), b. Nov. 30, 1819; m. May 15, 1849, Sarah A. Stowe, b. Mar. 31, 1823. Res. Pulaski, N. Y. Children :—

3490. i. JULIUS M., b. Aug. 28, 1852; m. Jan. 23, 1875, Isa H. Reed, b. Feb. 27, 1849. Res. Pulaski, N. Y.
3491. ii. SARAH J., b. Dec. 19, 1856.

2177. BENJAMIN W.[8] PIERCE (*Reuben*[7], *Jacob*[6], *Daniel*[5], *Daniel*[4], *John*[3], *Thomas*[2], *Thomas*[1]), b. May 31, 1825; m. Oct. 21, 1847, Salina Wiggins, b. Mar. 1, 1826. She d. Apr. 30, 1865. Res. Feltonville, Mich.

Benjamin W Pierce

Children :—
3492. i. WILLIAM O., b. Sept. 3, 1848; m. July 5, 1871, —— ——.
3493. ii. ELLA J., b. June 24, 1852; d. Feb. 19, 1876.
3494. iii. MARY A., b. Sept. 21, 1857; m. Sept. 21, 1876, Alpheus P. Beaver, b. Jan. 6, 1852. Ch.: Alpheus P. Jr., b. Aug. 27, 1877. Res. Vernon, Mich.
3495. iv. FREDERICK H., b. Dec. 20, 1863; d. May 18, 1870.

2185. FRANKLIN K.[8] PIERCE (*Reuben*[7], *Jacob*[6], *Daniel*[5], *Daniel*[4], *John*[3], *Thomas*[2], *Thomas*[1]), b. Nov. 11, 1841; m. Mar. 16, 1871, Mrs. Sarah Peck Raines, b. Feb. 7, 1838. Res. North Bloomfield, N. Y. Children :—
3496. i. FRED. S., b. July 21, 1872; d. Sept. 10, 1872.
3497. ii. ADDISON E., b. Mar. 1, 1874.
3498. iii. BERTHA I., b. July 14, 1876.

2188. CHARLES R.[8] PIERCE (*Reuben*[7], *Jacob*[6], *Daniel*[5], *Daniel*[4], *John*[3], *Thomas*[2], *Thomas*[1]), b. May 17, 1849; m. Apr. 24, 1869, Mary A. Woodward, b. May 30, 1848. She d. Feb. 21, 1876. Res. North Bloomfield, N. Y. Children :—
3499. i. CORA M., b. June 2, 1870.
3500. ii. WILLIAM R., b. Dec. 14, 1872.
3501. iii. LEWIS W., b. Aug. 7, 1874.

2193. AUGUSTUS J.[8] PIERCE (*Josiah*[7], *Jacob*[6], *Daniel*[5], *Daniel*[4], *John*[3], *Thomas*[2], *Thomas*[1]), b. Nov. 29, 1828; m. Dec. 25, 1850, Louisa A. Evarts, b. Feb. 13, 1830. He d. Mar. 2, 1875. Res. Mexico, N. Y. Child :—
3502. i. JOSEPHINE, b. June 2, 1858.

2207. JOHN E.[8] PIERCE (*John*[7], *Calvin*[6], *John*[5], *Daniel*[4], *John*[3], *Thomas*[2], *Thomas*[1]), b. Aug. 22, 1819; m. Mar. 4, 1849, Elizabeth Lovejoy, b. Nov. 15, 1813, d. Apr. 6, 1858; m. 2nd, May 12, 1859, Emeline A. Trufant, b. July 18, 1829, d. Mar. 8, 1868; m. 3rd, Sept. 1, 1869, Elizabeth C. Woodbury, b. June 28, 1828. Res. Charlestown.

John E Pierce

No children.

2208. ALBERT[8] PIERCE (*John*[7], *Calvin*[6], *John*[5], *Daniel*[4], *John*[3], *Thomas*[2], *Thomas*[1]), b. May 17, 1821; m. Dec. 25, 1844, Abigail Moody. Res. Boston, Pinckney street. Children :—
3503. i. JOHN A., b. Oct. 21, 1845.
3504. ii. JUDSON J., b. Apr. 15, 1848; m. Carrie Gile.

2209. ADDISON B.[8] PIERCE (*John[7], Calvin[6], John[5], Daniel[4], John[3], Thomas[2], Thomas[1]*), b. May 16, 1826; m. Dec. 30, 1852, .Mary W. Sanderson. Children :—

3505. i.   SUSAN M., b. Apr. 17, 1853; m. Jan. 24, 1870, John L. Hart.
            Ch. : Albert L., b. June 19, 1871. Res. Newtonville, Mass.
3506. ii. HARRIET E., b. Dec. 31, 1854.
3507. iii. GRACE C., b. Feb. 6, 1857.

2210. JOHN[8] PIERCE (*John[7], Ebenezer[6], Ebenezer[5], Ebenezer[4], John[3], Thomas[2], Thomas[1]*), b. June 12, 1797; m. Dec. 23, 1818, Laura Barrett, b. Mar. 20, 1798, d. Sept. 12, 1858. He d. May 28, 1872. Res. Hinsdale, Mass.

Children :—

3508. i.   CHRISTOPHER C., b. Nov. 8, 1819; m. Eliza M. Cloughan.
3509. ii. DEXTER P., b. Aug., 1821; m. Miriam Roberts.
3510. iii. HENRY A., b. Sept. 23, 1826; m. Mary Ely.
3511. iv. EDWARD C., b. Nov. 25, 1832; m. Martha Bartlett.
3512. v.   ELIZABETH A., b. Mar. 4, 1845.

2214. ERASTUS[8] PIERCE (*John[7], Ebenezer[6], Ebenezer[5], Ebenezer[4], John[3], Thomas[2], Thomas[1]*), b. Jan. 8, 1805; m. Apr. 3, 1833, Sophia Morgan, b. Aug. 28, 1809. Res. Hinsdale, Mass.

Child :—

3513. i.   CHARLES M., b. Oct. 13, 1834; m. Eliza Peabody.

2215. MARSHAL[8] PIERCE (*John[7], Ebenezer[6], Ebenezer[5], Ebenezer[4], John[3], Thomas[2], Thomas[1]*), b. Sep. 26, 1808; m. Nov. 8, 1832, Mary P. Francis, b. Aug. 31, 1811. Res. Hinsdale, Mass.

Children :—

3514. i.   ADELINE M., b. Nov. 16, 1833; m. Mar. 6, 1860, Edwin Tremaine.
            Ch. : Frank, b. June 11, 1862; George, b. May 20, 1868. Res.
            Hinsdale, Mass.
3515. ii. CLARISSA B., b. July 3, 1836; m. Samuel H. Rossiter. s. p.
3516. iii. HARLAN A., b. Aug. 21, 1840; m. Mary J. Rowley.
3517. iv. LORENZA A., b. July 25, 1842; m. Osman P. Clark.
3518. v.   FRANCIS M., b. Oct. 21, 1847; m. Nov. 26, 1874, Mrs. Tilly Smith.
            Res. Brooklyn, N. Y.

2216. ASHLEY S.[8] PIERCE (*John[7], Ebenezer[6], Ebenezer[5], Ebenezer[4], John[3], Thomas[2], Thomas[1]*), b. Jan. 6, 1810; m. Mary McGee, d. Mar. 23, 1869. Res. Kansas City, Kansas.

Child :—

3519. i. MAUD, b. ——— ; d. ———.

2219. LEWIS[8] PIERCE (*John[7], Ebenezer[6], Ebenezer[5], Ebenezer[4], John[3], Thomas[2], Thomas[1]*), b. July 14, 1817 ; m. Mary Aiken, b. 1816, d. Apr. 13, 1852. Res. Lyndon, Ills. Children :—

3520. i. SARAH, b. Nov. 29, 1845.
3521. ii. MARY, b. Dec. 8, 1848.
3522. iii. MARTHA, b. Mar. 2, 1850 ; m. ——— Gould.

2220. LUCIUS[8] PIERCE (*John[7], Ebenezer[6], Ebenezer[5], Ebenezer[4], John[3], Thomas[2], Thomas[1]*), b. July 14, 1817 ; m. Apr. 25, 1847, Matilda Spencer, b. Sept. 3, 1827. Res. Emporia, Kansas.

Lucius Peirce

Children :—

3523. i. CLARA, b. Jan. 31, 1849 ; m. Dr. John Schultz.
3524. ii. SALLY S., b. June 15, 1858.
3525. iii. HARRY M., b. Mar. 11, 1862.
3526. iv. JESSE E., b. Apr. 20, 1868.

2223. WARREN[8] PIERCE (*Asa[7], Ebenezer[6], Ebenezer[5], Ebenezer[4], John[3], Thomas[2], Thomas[1]*), b. Nov. 25, 1811 ; m. May 14, 1837, Clemence Morgan, b. Oct. 21, 1813, d. Feb. 6, 1838 ; m. 2nd, June 20, 1838, Abigail Wright, b. Mar. 1, 1815. Res. Vergennes, Vt. Child :—

3527. i. WYATT W., b. Apr. 11, 1840 ; m. Addie L. Ross.

2226. Dr. ELBRIDGE G.[8] PIERCE (*Asa[7], Ebenezer[6], Ebenezer[5], Ebenezer[4], John[3], Thomas[2], Thomas[1]*), b. Aug. 26, 1816 ; m. Jan. 1, 1841, Electa Rockwell, b. July 7, 1823, d. Dec. 29, 1848. He d. Aug. 7, 1862, at Fortress Monroe. He was Surgeon to the 8th New York Battery in the late Rebellion. Res. New York. Children :—

3528. i. FRANCES F., b. Oct. 8, 1843 ; d. June 19, 1856.
3529. ii. ALICE R., b. Mar. 18, 1845.
3530. iii. ELECTRA, b. Dec. 29, 1848 ; d. Aug. 7, 1849.

2227. Rev. ASA C.[8] PIERCE (*Asa[7], Ebenezer[6], Ebenezer[5], Ebenezer[4], John[3], Thomas[2], Thomas[1]*), b. July 17, 1819 ; m. Oct. 24, 1855, Mary Wilson, b. Feb. 25, 1834. Res. Brookfield Centre, Conn.

He was the son of Asa and Caroline (Worthington) Pierce, and was born in Hinsdale, Berkshire county, Mass., July 17, 1819. By the death of his father he became an orphan when but six weeks old. In consequence of the largeness of his mother's family (the four youngest born were two pairs of twins, with but fourteen months difference in age), he was taken when yet an infant into the family of Mr. and Mrs. Lemuel Frissell of Peru, Mass., with whom he spent most of his time until he was sixteen years of age, though his mother did not resign her claim to him, and he remained with them by mutual consent. These earlier years were devoted to ordinary farmer-boy pursuits, varied only by the privilege of going to the district school three months each winter and three in the summer until he had reached the age of ten years, after which his schooling was confined to the winter months.

In the year 1831 his mind became subject to religious influences, and cherishing a hope that he had entered upon a Christian life, with many others, subjects of a general revival which visited the place that year, he made public profession of religion, his mother and his foster-parents giving their approval. In connection with this change of feeling he received his first impression that he ought to devote his life to preaching the Gospel, but as he saw no way in which a suitable education could be acquired as preparative to the work, the notion was dismissed and other life-plans began to take shape and importance before his mind for the present.

He studied at "Green Mountain Seminary" and at Monson Academy, and closed at Amherst College. He was entered in that institution in the autumn of 1839 and graduated in the class of 1843—each winter term being spent in teaching. After graduation about two years were spent in the effort to liquidate some obligations incurred in the College course and also in securing funds with which to prosecute the theological course, the first year in charge of a "Select School" at Granby, Mass., and the second as principal of the Academy at Madison, Morris county, New Jersey.

In the spring of 1845 he connected himself with the "Theological Institute of Connecticut," then located at East Windsor, Conn., and since removed to Hartford—his Theological Professor being Rev. Dr. Tyler. During the course here he was obliged to resort to teaching, in which occupation he engaged two terms at Ware Village, Mass.

The theological course was completed in the summer of 1847, and he had already received "licensure" from the "Berkshire County Ministerial Association." Before leaving the Seminary, and for a few months after, he engaged in pulpit labors as a temporary supply at Westminster, Conn., where a blessing attended the "Word," and the feeble church was strengthened by an addition of about twenty to its membership.

In January, 1848, he commenced religious services at Holyoke, Mass., then in the infancy of its days, where a church was at length gathered and was duly recognized in the May of 1849. He received a "call" to the pastorate of this church and was ordained by Council which was convened September 20, 1849. The sermon was preached by Rev. Walter Clark, D.D., then of Hartford, Conn., but since deceased. In consequence of the financial reverses which came upon the place and the removal of a large part of his people, in June, of 1851, he sought and obtained a dismission from this society.

In January, 1853, he began pulpit labors in Hartford, Conn. He remained here until July 1, 1866, when on account of financial troubles he obtained a dismission. He entered immediately into an engagement with the church of Durham, Conn., where he was engaged from year to year, until Sept. 1st, 1870, when preferring a regular settlement in the pastoral office, he accepted a call to his present parish, Brookfield, Conn., where his installation took place October 19, Rev. Nahum Gale, D.D., of Lee, Mass., preaching the sermon.

Children :—

3531. i. WILSON H., b. Oct. 11, 1857.
3532. ii. ELBRIDGE W., b. June 18, 1862.

2231. AARON[8] PIERCE (*Ebenezer*[7], *Ebenezer*[6], *Ebenezer*[5], *Ebenezer*[4], *John*[3], *Thomas*[2], *Thomas*[1]), b. June 6, 1819 ; m. Martha Thompson, b. 1820. He d. Nov. 7, 1851. Res. Peru and Worthington, Mass. Child :—

3533. i. CARLTON A., b. March 7, 1851.

2234. MARTIN[8] PIERCE (*Ebenezer*[7], *Ebenezer*[6], *Ebenezer*[5], *Ebenezer*[4], *John*[3], *Thomas*[2], *Thomas*[1]), b. March 21, 1833 ; m. March 4, 1853, Malvina M. Thompson, b. Dec. 4, 1833. Res. Peru and Holyoke, Mass.

Children :—

3534. i. MYRLETTA M., b. Aug. 14, 1858.
3535. ii. WILBUR M., b. Jan. 4, 1864.
3536. iii. WALLACE A., b. Oct. 24, 1868.

2235. ARTHUR G.[8] PIERCE (*Enoch*[7], *Ebenezer*[6], *Ebenezer*[5], *Ebenezer*[4], *John*[3], *Thomas*[2], *Thomas*[1]), b. Feb. 19, 1822 ; m. March 17, 1853, Dolly Thompson. He d. March 3, 1879. Res. Greenwich, N. Y. Children :—

3537. i. ARTHUR K., b. Oct. 21, 1857. Res. Greenwich, N. Y.
3538. ii. JENNIE E., b. Dec. 26, 1859.

2236. DAVID S.[8] PIERCE (*Enoch*[7], *Ebenezer*[6], *Ebenezer*[5], *Ebenezer*[4], *John*[3], *Thomas*[2], *Thomas*[1]), b. Aug. 22, 1825 ; m. August 9, 1853, Charlotte Todd, b. June 6, 1824. Res. Saratoga Springs, N. Y. Child :—

3539. i. EMMA M., b. Nov. 29, 1858.

2239. LUTHER[8] PIERCE (*Luther*[7], *John*[6], *Ebenezer*[5], *Ebenezer*[4], *John*[3], *Thomas*[2], *Thomas*[1]), b. June 23, 1804 ; m. Aug. 11, 1826, Mary A. Ashley, b. Nov. 27, 1802, d. Oct. 10, 1873. Res. South Hadley Falls, Mass.

Children :—

3540. i. LUTHER A., b. July 8, 1827; d. Aug. 16, 1848.
3541. ii. MARY ANN, b. Nov. 5, 1828; d. Jan. 10, 1866.
3542. iii. JOHN H., b. Jan. 21, 1831; m. Ellen E. Cheney.

28

3543. iv. CLARISSA E., b. Feb. 10, 1833; m. Amos Wood.
3544. v. ALMON D., b. Sept. 17, 1835; d. Nov. 15, 1848.
3545. vi. JOSEPH A., b. July 23, 1837; m. Mary E. Moore.
3546. vii. MARTHA M., b. Feb. 26, 1840; m. Henry Converse.
3547. viii. EDWIN G., b. April 20, 1842; m. Susan Nelson.
3548. ix. LEWIS P., b. Nov. 22, 1845; m. Eva Bowers.

2246. Rev. NEHEMIAH P.[8] PIERCE, D.D. (*Luther*[7], *John*[6], *Ebenezer*[5], *Ebenezer*[4], *John*[3], *Thomas*[2], *Thomas*[1]), b. Aug. 28, 1817 ; m. Apr. 8, 1846, Frances Ann Ely, b. Oct. 22, 1817. He d. Apr. 11, 1880. Res. Warren, Mass.

The Doctor entered Amherst College in his twenty-first year and was graduated in the class of 1842. After teaching a year he became a member of Union Theological Seminary, New York. Receiving his license to preach 1846, he became pastor of a small church in Whippany, near Morristown, New Jersey. So successful were his ministrations and so strong a hold did he gain upon the affections of his people that they refused to hear of his leaving them. At the expiration of his fifth year, however, his health, never strong, made a temporary rest necessary. He determined to allow a year for recuperation, but chancing to supply the pulpit of the 12th St. Reformed Church of Brooklyn, N. Y., they extended to him a hearty call and he became their pastor, preaching his first sermon as their settled minister the first Sabbath of April, 1851. Here was his field for the greater part of his life work. For nearly twenty-five years he went in and out among this people breaking unto them the bread of life. No greater testimony of his success is needed than this long pastorate. He that can hold a city congregation for nearly a quarter of a century, in spite of "itching ears" and desire for a change, must be one of rare ability and able to gain the love of his people. One by one the senior ministers of his denomination in Long Island dropped away till Dr. Pierce became the patriarch of the classis. The church increased from a membership of forty to nearly four hundred, and the Sabbath school numbering less than one hundred at first grew to more than one thousand two hundred, becoming the largest school in that city of churches. In 1871 the degree of Doctor of Divinity was conferred upon him by Rutgers College and for several years he was a member of the examining committee of the Theological Seminary in New Brunswick. At last the intense activity of his mind wore out the body. Despite the protestations of his people he resigned his charge, hoping that a sea voyage and rest in Europe would improve his health. In May, 1875, his farewell sermon was preached and in June he went abroad for four months. Though somewhat benefited in health it was too late for perfect recovery, and to his intense disappointment he was obliged to give up all hopes of another pastorate. It was a heavy trial. He would have preferred to die with the harness on, but God willed it otherwise. Coming to Warren, he took up his abode in our midst. What his life has been we all know. Earnest and active in every good work he could not remain idle and often his zeal outran his bodily strength. His sermons preached at the Congregational Church and especially his address at the Dedication of the Town Hall, will linger long in our memories. A year ago he was elected a member of the School Committee and was appointed its chairman. Accepting the trust he carried it with him night and day, endeavoring to benefit the schools. As a member of the library committee he assisted them by advice and counsel. His interest led him to contribute many valuable books from his private library. At several different times it was supposed his end was near but his determination to live triumphed over his body till last Sabbath evening when murmuring "Come quickly, Lord Jesus, come quickly, " he fell asleep.

Funeral services were held in the Congregational Church, Tuesday afternoon, with a sermon by Rev. Jesse F. Forbes, who paid an eloquent and glowing tribute to the memory of the deceased. The schools in town were all closed during the afternoon. Yesterday forenoon the remains were interred in the cemetery at West Springfield.

Children :—

3549. i.   HOMER E., b. May 5, 1847; m. Catherine S. Chamberlain.
3550. ii.   GEORGE A., b. March 11, 1849; m. Anna C. Morford.
3551. iii. ANNA K., b. Nov. 24, 1851; m. George McKenzie.
3552. iv.   WILLIAM H., b. Jan. 4, 1854; d. Sept. 5, 1854.

2247. FRANCIS R.[8] PIERCE (*Luther*[7], *John*[6], *Ebenezer*[5], *Ebenezer*[4], *John*[3], *Thomas*[2], *Thomas*[1]), b. Oct. 22, 1821; m. April 22, 1846, Cynthia E. Hitchcock, b. May 17, 1821, d. Sept. 8, 1848; m. 2nd, Nov. 27, 1849, Marietta E. Tuttle, b. July 20, 1817. Res. Thompsonville, Conn.

Children :—

3553. i.   ELVIRA H., b. Aug. 12, 1848; d. Sept. 9, 1849.
3554. ii.   IDA T., b. May 2, 1851.
3555. iii. EMMA L., b. Jan. 2, 1853; d. Jan. 30, 1866.
3556. iv.   EDWARD L., b. April 2, 1856; d. June 10, 1876.
3557. v.   FRANCIS A., b. Aug. 3, 1860.

2248. EBENEZER[8] PIERCE (*Luther*[7], *John*[6], *Ebenezer*[5], *Ebenezer*[4], *John*[3], *Thomas*[2], *Thomas*[1]), b. March 24, 1826; m. Dec. 25, 1841, Charlotte Kimball, b. March 13, 1818. He d. ———. Res. Thompsonville, Conn. No children. She m. 2nd, Rev. Rei Hills.

2250. CALVIN W.[8] PIERCE (*Calvin*[7], *John*[6], *Ebenezer*[5], *Ebenezer*[4], *John*[3], *Thomas*[2], *Thomas*[1]), b. May 5, 1811; m. April 6, 1833,

Catherine Lathrop, b. May 21, 1808. He d. April 8, 1876. Res. Worcester, Mass.

Children :—

3558. i.   SAMUEL, b. May 30, 1834; unm. Res. Worcester, clerk in the postoffice.
3559. ii. EDWIN, b. Feb. 13, 1836; m. Nov. 22, 1859, Ellen M. Morse.
3560. iii. CATHERINE, b. May 10, 1838; m. Oct. 19, 1864, Henry Bigelow.

2251. ANDREAS W.[8] PIERCE (*Hervey*[7], *John*[6], *Ebenezer*[5], *Ebenezer*[4], *John*[3], *Thomas*[2], *Thomas*[1]), b. Apr. 29, 1820; m. April 28, 1846, Mary Putnam, b. Nov. 17, 1821. Res. West Millbury, Mass.

Children :—

3561. i.   JOHN W., b. March 20, 1847; m. H. Catherine Hayden.
3562. ii. JULIA E., b. Sept. 6, 1853; m. John T. Brierly.

2260. JASON B.[8] PIERCE (*David*[7], *David*[6], *Ebenezer*[5], *Ebenezer*[4], *John*[3], *Thomas*[2], *Thomas*[1]), b. Dec. 13, 1821 ; m. Harriet Lemmix ; m. 2nd, ―――― ――――. Res. Anaheim, Cal.

2269. HENRY H.[8] PIERCE (*Aaron*[7], *David*[6], *Ebenezer*[5], *Ebenezer*[4], *John*[3], *Thomas*[2], *Thomas*[1]), b. Apr. 6, 1836 ; m. Sept. 5, 1865, Sarah E. Kirkland, b. Aug. 22, 1842. Res. Newark, N. J.

Children :—

3563. i.   LOUISA K., b. Sept. 5, 1866; d. April 26, 1874.
3564. ii. ABBY H., b. Aug 10, 1870.

2271. NELSON M.[8] PIERCE (*Dana*[7], *David*[6], *Ebenezer*[5], *Ebenezer*[4], *John*[3], *Thomas*[2], *Thomas*[1]), b. May 18, 1820; m. July, 27, 1848, Cynthia A. Brown, b. June 23, 1827, d. Feb. 7, 1879. Res. Ludlow, Vt.

Children :—

3565. i.   MARIA I., b. July 21, 1850.
3566. ii. GRACE M., b. Dec. 4, 1868.

2273. WILLIAM D.[8] PIERCE (*Dana*[7], *David*[6], *Ebenezer*[5], *Ebenezer*[4], *John*[3], *Thomas*[2], *Thomas*[1]), b. June 9, 1824 ; m. May 26, 1851,

Sophronia E. Sperry, b. Oct. 17, 1827. He d. Feb. 19, 1874. Res. Claremont, N. H. Children :—

3567. i.   ALBERT E., b. Sept. 28, 1852; d. Sept 2, 1859.
3568. ii. ARTHUR W., b. Aug. 31, 1859; d. June 11, 1865.
3569. iii. ANSON M., b. June 24, 1864.
3570. iv. BERTHA A., b. Feb. 18, 1870.

2274. Prof. EDWIN[8] PIERCE, A. M. (*Dana[7], David[6], Ebenezer[5], Ebenezer[4], John[3], Thomas[2], Thomas[1]*), b. June 25, 1826 ; m. April 10, 1855, Sarah L. De Forrest, d. March 23, 1865 ; m. 2nd, Dec, 29, 1868, Harriet M. Goddard, d. Oct. 30, 1871 ; m. 3rd, Dec. 23, 1873, Phebe T. Marsh. Res. Ashburnham, Mass.

EDWIN PIERCE, A. M., grad. at Dartmouth College in the class of 1852. Taught the classics at Seneca Collegiate Institute at Ovid, N. Y., from Sept., 1852, to Apr., 1856. Was then Professor of Languages at Yellow Springs College, Des Moines, Iowa. Removed to Jersey City, N. J., in May, 1863, as Principal of Pavonia Grammar School. Was in 1879, Principal of the Academy at Ashburnham, Mass.

Children :—

3571. i.   ALICE G., b. Oct. 12, 1869.
3572. ii. EDWIN D., b. April 11, 1871.

2275. RODNEY C.[8] PIERCE (*Dana[7], David[6], Ebenezer[5], Ebenezer[4], John[3], Thomas[2], Thomas[1]*), b. May 24, 1828; m. Sept. 16, 1849, Mary R. Severance, b. Oct, 24, 1826. Res. Nos. 19 and 21 Leonard Street, New York, N. Y.

Children :—

3573. i.   ADA A., b. April 6, 1851; m. April 23, 1870, Hugh H. Weber. Res. New York City.
3574. ii. ANNA B., b. June 16, 1855; m. Oct. 3, 1876, Frank E. Doling. Res. New York City.
3575. iii. EDWIN DE F., b. Dec. 29, 1859; d. Oct. 26, 1873.
3576. iv. CLARENCE P., b. June 26, 1869.

2278. Dr. SAMUEL N.[8] PIERCE (*Dana[7], David[6], Ebenezer[5], Ebenezer[4], John[3], Thomas[2], Thomas[1]*), b. May 6, 1832 ; m. Dec. 28, 1856, Margaret N. Peirce, b. June 27, 1833. [See Peirce Gen., p. 202.] Res. Cedar Falls, Iowa.

Dr. SAMUEL N. PIERCE was born in Windsor County, Vt., May 6th, 1832. He received an academic education at Meriden, N. H., and at West Randolph, Vt., completing the Sophomore course of studies at West Randolph under the tutorage of Austin Adams, now of Iowa, and at present one of the Supreme Judges of the State. He began the study of medicine at Woodstock in 1853 as a pupil of Prof. Benjamin Palmer. After Prof. Palmer removed to Louisville, Ky., he studied with Dr. W. C. Pierce, then of Woodstock, but now of Alton, Ill. Attended medical lectures at Dartmouth and at Woodstock. Graduated in medicine at Vt. Med. Coll. at Woodstock in June, 1856. He went west in Sept., 1856, located in Cedar Falls, Iowa, in Oct., 1856, and that has been his residence ever since. Served as Surgeon of the 14th Iowa Vols. from Oct., 1861, to June, 1863, at which time he was obliged to resign his commission, owing to ill health. Excepting the time he was in the Army, has been in the practice of medicine in Cedar Falls since 1856. He has been Pension Examining Surgeon since 1864 ; was Clerk of that city four years, and connected with the School Board as clerk for five years. Held the position of attending Physician and Surgeon to the Soldier's Orphan Home for five years. Was Coroner for Black Hawk County two years. Is a member of the Iowa State Medical Society and of the American Medical Association.

Children :—

3577. i. CHARLES D., b. Oct. 5, 1862; d. Feb. 5, 1867.
3578. ii. NELLIE B., b. Aug. 5, 1865.
3579. iii. FRANK, b. Nov. 2, 1867.
3580. iv. HARRY, b. Feb. 10, 1872.

2279. LUCIAN F.[8] PIERCE (*Dana*[7], *David*[6], *Ebenezer*[5], *Ebenezer*[4], *John*[3], *Thomas*[2], *Thomas*[1]), b. April 7, 1834 ; m. July 28, 1860, Susan Heizer, b. July 13, 1839. Res. Kossuth, Iowa. Children :—

3581. i. ALBERT W., b. Aug. 1, 1861.
3582. ii. GEORGE W., b. Oct. 20, 1863; d. Oct. 30, 1868.
3583. iii. MARY L., b. May 26, 1869.
3584. iv. ELLEN R., b. March 14, 1872; d. Nov. 2, 1876.
3585. v. EDWIN P., b. July 28, 1875.
3586. vi. ELIZABETH B., b. Oct. 29, 1878.

2281. PAYSON A.[8] PIERCE (*Dana*[7], *David*[6], *Ebenezer*[5], *Ebenezer*[4], *John*[3], *Thomas*[2], *Thomas*[1]), b. Feb. 26, 1836 ; m. Sept. 17, 1861, Frances M. Swain, b. Oct. 26, 1840. Res. Woodstock, Vt. Children :—

3587. i. HATTIE J., b. Nov. 9, 1862.
3588. ii. GARDNER S., b. March 16, 1868.

2284. WORTHINGTON W.[8] PIERCE (*Dana*[7], *David*[6], *Ebenezer*[5], *Ebenezer*[4], *John*[3], *Thomas*[2], *Thomas*[1]), b. June 1, 1843 ; m. July 21,

1870, Mary J. Bennett, b. Dec. 25, 1845. Res. Des Moines, Iowa. Children :—

3589. i. ELIZA D., b. May 20, 1871.
3590. ii. CHARLES N., b. Dec. 25, 1872.
3591. iii. EMMA J., b. Oct. 28, 1874.

2287. HENRY B.[8] PIERCE (Edmund[7], David[6], Ebenezer[5], Ebenezer[4], John[3], Thomas[2], Thomas[1]), b. April 14, 1827 ; m. May 1, 1854, Laura A. Hoyt. Res. San Francisco, Cal.

2288. CLAUDIUS B.[8] PIERCE (Edmund[7], David[6], Ebenezer[5], Ebenezer[4], John[3], Thomas[2], Thomas[1]), b. April 10, 1829 ; m. Dec. 1, 1864, Mary E. Fairchild, b. Oct. 19, 1839. Res. Leavenworth, Kansas.
CLAUDIUS B. PIERCE graduated at Dartmouth College in the class of 1854. Taught in Texas one year. Read law at Albany, N. Y., Law School and is now in practice at Leavenworth, Kansas.

Children :—
3592. i. CATHERINE L., b. Jan. 14, 1867.
3593. ii. WILLIAM E., b. June 2, 1869.
3594. iii. EDWARD B., } b. July 3, 1873.
3595. iv. EDWIN DE F., }

2291. LYMAN B.[8] PIERCE (Edmund[7], David[6], Ebenezer[5], Ebenezer[4], John[3], Thomas[2], Thomas[1]), b. Jan. 14, 1835 ; m. June 25, 1865, Lea A. Bandy, b. Jan. 7, 1838. Res. Kossuth, Iowa. Children :—

3596. i. CLAUDE H., b. June 23, 1866.
3597. ii. GRACE M., b. Feb. 7, 1868.
3598. iii. JOHN E., b. July 31, 1870.
3599. iv. MARY L., b. Feb. 6, 1872.
3600. v. KATIE H., b. Oct. 1, 1873.
3601. vi. NELLIE, b. June 27, 1876; d. March 27, 1877.

2299. AUGUSTUS[8] PIERCE (Thomas S.[7], Joshua[6], Joshua[5], Ebenezer[4], John[3], Thomas[2], Thomas[1]), b. Dec. 29, 1795 ; m. Mar. 28, 1824, Eliza Whitney, b. June 19, 1805, d. Jan. 20, 1857, He d. April 27, 1830. Res. Leominster, Mass. Children :—

3602. i. THEODORE W., b. Nov. 6, 1824; m. Laura A. Peasley.
3603. ii. FIDELIA, b. Aug. 19, 1826; m. John H. Hawes.

2303. HOUGHTON[8] PIERCE (Thomas S.[7] Joshua[6], Joshua[5], Ebenezer[4], John[3], Thomas[2], Thomas[1]), b. Apr. 20, 1802 ; m. Apr. 10, 1825, Mira Snow. He d. Apr. 23, 1842. Res. Leominster, Mass. Children :—

3604. i. THOMAS E., b. Jan. 29, 1826; m. Sarah Brown.
3605. ii. GEORGE A., b. Apr. 21, 1830; m. Mary E. Brown.
3606. iii. CAROLINE A., b. May 21, 1832; m. Wm. H. Johnson.
3607. iv. ELLEN A., b. March 19, 1834; m. Charles B. Benedict.

3608.   v.   CHARLES P., b. Sept. 8, 1836; m. Adelaide Carter.
3609.   vi.   AUSTIN S., b. Nov. 1, 1838; d. Sept., 1849.
3610.   vii.   MIRA E., b. April 1, 1841; d. March 30, 1842.

2309.   SYLVESTER[8] PIERCE (*Asa[7], Joshua[6], Joshua[5], Ebenezer[4], John[3], Thomas[2], Thomas[1]*), b. Jan. 24, 1802 ; m. Abigail Taylor, b. June 20, 1815. He d. April 17, 1849. Res. Leominster, Mass. Children :—

3611.   i.   GEORGE F., b. March 6, 1836; d. April 16, 1836.
3612.   ii.   ALBERT F., b. June 3, 1838; m. Annie E. Wilder.
3613.   iii.   GEORGE S., b. Sept. 15, 1840; m. Ellen A. Balch.
3614.   iv.   MARY J., b. May 31, 1843; m. Charles Wilder.
3615.   v.   MARTHA, b. July 18, 1845; m. Adin Rice.

2311.   JOSEPH[8] PIERCE (*Asa[7], Joshua[6], Joshua[5], Ebenezer[4], John[3], Thomas[2], Thomas[1]*), b. Dec. 10, 1804 ; m. 1829, Roxanna B. March, d. July 2, 1836; m. 2nd, 1839, Susan A. W. Goodrich, b. Aug. 14, 1818. Res. North Leominster, Mass. Children :—

3616.   i.   JOSEPH B., b. Feb. 22, 1830; m. Estelle M. Holden.
3617.   ii.   ADELIA F., b. June 11, 1833; d. Feb., 1851.
3618.   iii.   HENRY E., b. Apr. 4, 1834; d. in army, 1863.
3619.   iv.   CATHERINE W., b. July 11, 1842; m. Wm. W. Adams.
3620.   v.   CHARLES D., b. Sept. 11, 1844; m. Hattie A. Phelps.
3621.   vi.   CHARLOTTE L., b. Jan. 29, 1847.
3622.   vii.   CAROLINE F., b. Mar. 16, 1849; d. May, 1863.
3623.   viii.   CLARA, b. Oct. 20, 1850.
3624.   ix.   ELLEN B., b. May 2, 1854; d. May 2, 1863.
3625.   x.   FRANK, b. Apr. 3, 1856.

2318.   WILLIAM D.[8] PIERCE (*Asa[7], Joshua[6], Joshua[5], Ebenezer[4], John[3], Thomas[2], Thomas[1]*), b. Jan. 31, 1825 ; m. Nov. 29, 1849, Maria Whitney, b. April 13, 1824. Res. Shrewsbury, Mass. No children.

2326.   JONATHAN[8] PIERCE (*Jonathan[7], Jonathan[6], Joshua[5], Ebenezer[4], John[3], Thomas[2], Thomas[1]*), b. Aug. 26, 1836 ; m. Oct. 23, 1858, Hannah Warren. Res. Boston, Mass. Child :—

3626.   i.   LUCY E., b. June 15, 1859.

2328.   WILLIAM H.[8] PIERCE (*Jonathan[7], Jonathan[6], Joshua[5], Ebenezer[4], John[3], Thomas[2], Thomas[1]*), b. April 28, 1841 ; m. July 11, 1866, Sarah A. Moore. He d. Dec. 28, 1870. She m. 2nd, Hiram W. Wheeler. Res. Chelsea, Mass. Children :—

3627.   i.   HENRY A., b. Sept. 5, 1868.
3628.   ii.   CHARLES W., b. Dec. 12, 1870; d. July 16, 1872.

2331.   JOSIAH[8] PIERCE (*Josiah[7], Josiah[6], Josiah[5], Josiah[4], John[3], Thomas[2], Thomas[1]*), b. June 14, 1827 ; m. April 23, 1858, Martha D. Lander, d. Dec. 13, 1873 ; m. 2nd, Oct. 29, 1877, Isabel Millett, b. June 10, 1842. Res. No. 12 Beaufort Gardens, London, E. C., England.

JOSIAH PIERCE, son of Hon. Josiah and Evelina Pierce, was born at Gorham, Maine, June 14th, 1827.

Was prepared for College at the Academies in Gorham and Limerick, Me. Was matriculated as Freshman at Bowdoin College, July, 1842. Graduated with the degree of B. A. at Bowdoin College, July,

1846. Member of the Phi Beta Kappa Society, and received the degree of A. M. in 1849. Read law with his father at Gorham, and with Augustine Haines, U. S. Att'y, at Portland ; was admitted to the Bar in Cumberland County, Maine, in 1849. Passed nine months traveling in Europe, in the British Islands, Holland, Germany, Switzerland, Italy and France. Commenced practice as Counsellor and Attorney at Law in Portland, Maine, in 1850, and continued this till 1855, when in September, being appointed U. S. Secretary of Legation to Russia, he went to St. Petersburg, and remained in that office till the spring of 1858, when he resigned the office, came to America, was married to Martha Lander (youngest child of Edward and Eliza [West] Lander, born June 24th, 1833), and returned to St. Petersburg, and was engaged professionally by the firm of Winans, Harrison & Winans, railway contractors, in their business in Russia, till its termination in 1863. Returned to Portland in May, 1863, and resided there till August, 1865, when he went again to Russia, employed professionally by Wm. L. Winans in the business of a new contract. Received in October, 1865, from the Emperor of Russia, Knighthood of the 3rd Class of the Order of St. Anne. Went to London in 1870, at the termination of the Winans contract and has since been engaged there in business of Wm. L. Winans. Is a Fellow of the Royal Geographical Society, and of the Zoölogical Society, and member of the Royal Institution, in London ; a member of the Cincinnati Society of Massachusetts (as representing his grandfather Archelaus Lewis, an officer in the Revolutionary War) and member of the Maine Historical Society ; and of the American Episcopal Church. His first wife died at Portland, Dec., 1873. By her he has one surviving child, Josiah, born Jan. 30, 1861 ; and he was married to his second wife, Isabella Lucia Millett, (b. June 10, 1842), at Petersham, Eng., Oct. 29, 1877.

Josiah Pierce

Children :—

3629. i. ELIZA, b. April 13, 1859 ; d. May 20, 1877.
3630. ii. JOSIAH, b. Jan. 30, 1861.
3631. iii. ALEXANDER, b. July 16, 1867 ; d. June 7, 1874.

2334. LEWIS[8] PIERCE (*Josiah[7], Josiah[6], Josiah[5], Josiah[4], John[3], Thomas[2], Thomas[1]*), b. April 15, 1832 ; m. June 13, 1860, Emily Hall Willis, b. June 13, 1837, d. Oct. 16, 1864 ; m. 2nd, Dec. 10, 1874, Mary Bellows Hill, b. Sept. 19, 1846. Res. Portland, Me.

Lewis Pierce, L.L.B., the son of Hon. Josiah and Evaline (Lewis) Pierce, was born in Gorham, was graduated at Bowdoin College in the class of 1852. After graduation he taught schools for a year or two in Hollis and Dennysville. He then read law in Portland, took a course at the Dane Law School, Harvard University, graduating L.L.B. 1855,

29

and settled in the profession in Portland, where he now resides. He has represented the city in the Legislature, has been Public Administrator for the County of Cumberland, and has served on the School Committee of Portland. He is a member of the Historical Society of Maine.

Lewis Pierce

Children :—

3632. i. EMILY W., b. Dec. 11, 1861.
3633. ii. LEWIS, b. July 12, 1863; d. Dec. 2, 1868.
3634. iii. CHARLOTTE H., b. July 20, 1864.
3635. iv. HENRY H., b. Nov. 7, 1875.
3636. v. THOMAS L., b. July 6, 1877.
3637. vi. JOHN A., b. Sept. 14, 1878.

2342. DANIEL T.[8] PIERCE (*Daniel T.[7], Josiah[6], Josiah[5], Josiah[4], John[3], Thomas[2], Thomas[1]*), b. May 15, 1835 ; m. May 31, 1871, Annie M. Pitcher, b. June 24, 1849. Res. Washington, D. C. Children :—

3638. i. ANNIE L., b. Aug. 27, 1872.
3639. ii. DANIEL M., b. March 22, 1875.
3640. iii. ISABELLA K., b. Oct. 27, 1877.
3641. iv. LEWIS W., b. March 2, 1880.

2352. JOHN[8] PIERCE (*John[7], John[6], Josiah[5], Josiah[4], John[3], Thomas[2], Thomas[1]*), b. July 30, 1827 ; m. Jan. 27, 1852, Harriet M. Craig, b. Jan., 1830, d. March 27, 1877. Res. Hiram, Me. Children:—

3642. i. FRANCELLIS, b. Sept. 9, 1857; m. Geo. W. Copp.
3643. ii. RUTH L., b. 1862.

2361. WILLIAM B.[8] PIERCE (*William[7], John[6], Josiah[5], Josiah[4], John[3], Thomas[2], Thomas[1]*), b. July 17, 1826 ; m. Dec. 15, 1850, Augusta Berry, b. 1831. He d. Oct. 6, 1864. Res. Biddeford, Me. Children :—

3644. i. CLARENCE M., b. June 26, 1852; d. Jan. 1, 1866.
3645. ii. GEORGE E., b. June 17, 1855; m. Clara G. Whiton.
3646. iii. ORVILLE C., b. Feb., 1857.
3647. iv. LILLIAN A., b. Mar., 1860.
3648. v. FRANCES E., b. April, 1863.

2363. CHARLES W.[8] PIERCE (*William[7], John[6], Josiah[5], Josiah[4], John[3], Thomas[2], Thomas[1]*), b. July 21, 1831 ; m. Oct. 6, 1858, Ann E. Scammon, b. Oct. 29, 1833. Res. Biddeford, Me. Child :—

3649. i. INGILLA, b. Feb. 10, 1860; m. Henry Hawkins.

2365. ARTHUR[8] PIERCE (*William[7], John[6], Josiah[5], Josiah[4], John[3], Thomas[2], Thomas[1]*), b. April 15, 1835 ; m. Nov. 30, 1856, Lizzie Gile. He d. Jan. 27, 1864. Res. Lynn, Mass. Children :—

3650. i. EFFIE, b. Feb. 10, 1861.
3651. ii. ANGIE, b. Feb., 1863.

2372. DANIEL W.[8] PIERCE (*Daniel[7]*, *John[6]*, *Josiah[5]*, *Josiah[4]*, *John[3]*, *Thomas[2]*, *Thomas[1]*), b. June 26, 1834; m. Sept. 28, 1856, Lois G. Lane. Member of the firm of Libbey, McNeil & Libbey, the great pork packers. Res. Chicago, Ill. Children :—

3652. i. LORIN E., b. Aug. 13, 1857; d. Aug. 17, 1859.
3653. ii. ALLEN M., b. Jan. 18, 1869.

2373. JOHN H.[8] PIERCE (*Daniel[7]*, *John[6]*, *Josiah[5]*, *Josiah[4]*, *John[3]*, *Thomas[2]*, *Thomas[1]*), b. Dec. 31, 1837 ; m. 1855, Fidelia Temple ; m. 2nd, May 1, 1864, Sarah Spikins. Res. Chicago, Ill. Children :—

3654. i. FRANK.
3655. ii. CHARLES.
3656. iii. JOHN L.
3657. iv. PERLEY.

2376. HUBBARD L.[8] PIERCE (*Joseph[7]*, *Joseph[6]*, *John[5]*, *Josiah[4]*, *John[3]*, *Thomas[2]*, *Thomas[1]*), b. March 1, 1795; m. June 6, 1822, Amy Spalding, d. Dec. 15, 1841 ; m. 2nd, Feb. 23, 1842, Matilda H. Brockway. He d. April, 1867. She m. 2nd, Hon. Titus Hutchinson. Res. Cavendish and St. Johnsbury, Vt.

Children :—

3658. i. CHARLES O., b. Apr. 21, 1824; m. Lovina Sargent.
3659. ii. MARY A., b. Jan. 22, 1826; d. May 14, 1828.
3660. iii. FRANKLIN O., b. Apr. 8, 1829; m. Eliza Webster.
3661. iv. ELMORE A., b. Aug. 11, 1843; m. Mary ———.
3662. v. MARION A., b. Oct. 11, 1845; m. Charles West.
3663. vi. EUGENE F., b. Feb. 5, 1849 ; m. Nellie Walters.
3664. vii. MATILDA J., b. April 1, 1853; m. George Griswold.

2377. LEWIS[8] PIERCE (*Joseph[7]*, *Joseph[6]*, *John[5]*, *Josiah[4]*, *John[3]*, *Thomas[2]*, *Thomas[1]*), b. Dec. 21, 1796 ; m. Nov. 27, 1826, Abigail Stowell, b. 1787, d. March, 1871. He d. Dec. 25, 1876. Res. St. Johnsbury, Vt. Child :—

3665. i. FREEMAN, b. July 12, 1827; d. Aug. 19, 1846.

2383. WILLARD M[8]. PIERCE (*Joseph[7]*, *Joseph[6]*, *John[5]*, *Josiah[4]*, *John[3]*, *Thomas[2]*, *Thomas[1]*), b. Aug. 12, 1813 ; m. April 9, 1840, Lucinda C. Witherell, b. Dec. 24, 1815. Res. Sandusky, Ohio. Children :—

3666. i. MARION C., b. Dec. 27, 1844.
3667. ii. JOHN W., b. Sept. 13, 1846.
3668. iii. FRANK W., b. May 9, 1849.

2393. CHARLES K.[8] PIERCE (*Jotham[7]*, *Joseph[6]*, *John[5]*, *Josiah[4]*, *John[3]*, *Thomas[2]*, *Thomas[1]*), b. June 11, 1818 ; m. Sept. 28, 1840, Sarah Barker, b. Dec. 23, 1820, d. June 23, 1853 ; m. 2nd, Mary A. Barker, b. Dec. 18, 1826. Res. Chicago, Ill. Children :—

3669. i. JOTHAM B., b. Jan. 7, 1842; d. Dec. 22, 1868. Jotham Pierce died at San Francisco, Cal., in 1868. During the rebellion of

1861, he was telegraph operator in the Secretary of War's office at Washington and at the Headquarters of the Army of the Potomac throughout the campaign in Virginia. At the close of the war, he with others, went to Kamschatka and Siberia in the interest of the American and Russian Governments to survey and complete a Telegraph Line to St. Petersburg and London. While the party were in Siberia, the Atlantic Cable was laid between England and America, in consequence of which the project was abandoned and they were recalled to San Francisco, where he died.

3670. ii.   SARAH M., b. Dec. 26, 1844; m. Geo. R. Underwood.
3671. iii. ELLEN M., b. Oct. 21, 1846; m. C. E. Plimpton.
3672. iv.   RANSOM T., b. Sept. 17, 1848; m. Hattie Rice.
3673. v.   FRANK H., b. May 8, 1851.
3674. vi.   LESLIE E., b. May 1, 1853; d. Aug. 15, 1874.
3675. vii. JOSIE A., b. Dec. 7, 1854.
3676. viii. GEORGE B., b. May 19, 1858.

2400.   FREDERICK[8] PIERCE (*Martin[7]*, *Joseph[6]*, *John[5]*, *Josiah[4]*, *John[3]*, *Thomas[2]*, *Thomas[1]*), b. May 1, 1804; m. March 26, 1832, Mary Briggs, b. Jan. 22, 1812. Res. Stanbridge, P. Q. Children :—

3677. i.   LUCINA B., b. March 29, 1835; m. Rev. Samuel Jackson.
3678. ii.   NELSON; d. infancy.
3679. iii. INFANT; d. infancy.
3680. iv.   INFANT; d. infancy.

2401.   VARNUM[8] PIERCE (*Martin[7]*, *Joseph[6]*, *John[5]*, *Josiah[4]*, *John[3]*, *Thomas[2]*, *Thomas[1]*,) b. Nov. 26, 1805; m. Philome Claflin, d. Dec. 23, 1839; m. 2nd, Feb. 23, 1840, Evaline Goss. He d. Apr. 4, 1873. Res. St. Albans, Vt. Children :—

3681. i.   LUCINDA, b. Feb. 2, 1832; m. Joshua Gray.
3682. ii.   WILLARD, b. Sept. 3, 1834; m. Sarah Gray.
3683. iii. EMILY, b. July 22, 1836; d. Aug. 11, 1863.
3684. iv.   HUBBARD, b. Apr. 20, 1838; d. May 22, 1839.
3685. v.   MARY, b. Dec. 6, 1840.
3686. vi.   MARTIN, b. Nov. 12, 1844; m. Della Streeter.

2404.   CURTIS[8] PIERCE (*Martin[7]*, *Joseph[6]*, *John[5]*, *Josiah[4]*, *John[3]*, *Thomas[2]*, *Thomas[1]*), b. Mar. 16, 1811; m. Feb., 1837, Mary Dunham, b. July, 1816, d. Oct. 17, 1844; m. 2nd, Feb. 3, 1845, Sarah Dunham, b. July 16, 1820. Res. St. Albans, Vt. Children :—

3687. i.   ALONZO, b. June, 1838; d. Oct., 1857.
3688. ii.   CAROLINE, b. Feb. 23, 1841; m. Hiram Perkins.
3689. iii. LUTHER, b. 1843; d. 1844.
3690. iv.   EDNA, b. Oct. 12, 1844; m. Henry Green.

2405.   HENRY[8] PIERCE (*Martin[7]*, *Joseph[6]*, *John[5]*, *Josiah[4]*, *John[3]*, *Thomas[2]*, *Thomas[1]*), b. Nov. 16, 1812; m. Aug. 16, 1848, Lucinda Stockwell, b. Oct. 4, 1824. Res. Otsego, Mich. Children :—

3691. i.   WILLARD, b. Nov. 7, 1849; d. Apr. 9, 1850.
3692. ii.   ALONZO, b. June 8, 1850; m. Sarah Minkler.
3693. iii. LUTHER, b. Apr. 2, 1852.
3694. iv.   MARSHALL, b. Feb. 16, 1857.
3695. v.   AMANDA, b. Dec. 25, 1859.

2407.   HIRAM[8] PIERCE (*Martin[7]*, *Joseph[6]*, *John[5]*, *Josiah[4]*, *John[3]*, *Thomas[2]*, *Thomas[1]*), b. June 7, 1818; m. Aug. 9, 1843, Anna

Beattie, b. Jan. 19, 1822. He d. Sept. 3, 1875. Res. St. Albans, Vt.
Children :—

3696. i. A. JENNIE, b. June 7, 1844; m. James Holway.
3697. ii. GEORGE M., b. Sept. 29, 1845; m. Maritt Fields.
3698. iii. M. ABBIE, b. Feb. 8, 1847; d. Feb. 9, 1869.
3699. iv. HIRAM M., b. July 31, 1849; m. Carrie L. Baldwin.
3700. v. M. EMMA, b. Oct. 21, 1851; m. Cassius W. Pierce.
3701. vi. JAMES W., b. Sept. 18, 1857.

2408. MILO[8] PIERCE (*Martin*[7], *Joseph*[6], *John*[5], *Josiah*[4], *John*[3],
Thomas[2], *Thomas*[1]), b. Mar. 23, 1820; m. Amanda Baker, d. Dec.
29, 1866. Res. Otsego, Mich. Children :—

3702. i. CLARA.
3703. ii. MARY.

2418. ANDREW M.[8] PIERCE (*Leonard*[7], *Joseph*[6], *John*[5], *Josiah*[4],
John[3], *Thomas*[2], *Thomas*[1]), b. Aug. 8, 1829; m. Mar. 3, 1852,
Rodaska Paddleford, b. Nov. 7, 1832. Res. Brownington, Vt.
Children :—

3704. i. CARLOS W., b. Dec. 25, 1853.
3705. ii. MARY A., b. Sept. 16, 1855; d. Oct. 20, 1868.
3706. iii. HATTIE L., b. Mar. 1, 1860.
3707. iv. EMMA N., b. Dec. 29, 1862.
3708. v. KATIE W., b. Mar. 13, 1866.
3709. vi. MYRA A., b. Aug. 5, 1870.
3710. vii. GEORGE T., b. Jan. 10, 1873.

2419. CHARLES W.[8] PIERCE (*Wilder*[7], *Joseph*[6], *John*[5], *Josiah*[4],
John[3], *Thomas*[2], *Thomas*[1]), b. Apr. 23, 1818; m. Jan. 22, 1845,
Mary F. Horton. Res. Boston.

Children :—

3711. i. CHARLES F., b. Jan. 10, 1846; m. Jennie Morse.
3712. ii. MARY W., b. June 1, 1847; m. Rev. A. Lee Holmes.
3713. iii. EMILY F., b. June 29, 1851.
3714. iv. ELIZABETH F., b. Nov. 17, 1853.
3715. v. GEORGE A., b. Dec. 2, 1855; m. Jennie E. Thornton.
3716. vi. WILLIAM A., b. June 1, 1857.

2422. GEORGE[8] PIERCE (*Wilder*[7], *Joseph*[6], *John*[5], *Josiah*[4], *John*[3],
Thomas[2], *Thomas*[1]), b. May 31, 1825; m. Sept. 15, 1864, Mary
Motley Clapp, b. Mar. 12, 1834. He d. Dec. 12, 1864. Res. Boston.
No children.

2423. HENRY G.[8] PIERCE (*Wilder*[7], *Joseph*[6], *John*[5], *Josiah*[4],
John[3], *Thomas*[2], *Thomas*[1]), b. June 9, 1827; m. June 9, 1857, Mary
C. Benton, b. Jan. 27, 1836. He d. Oct. 9, 1870. Res. Stanstead,
P. Q. Children :—

3717. i. NANCY A., b. Apr. 23, 1858; m. O. W. Ellis.
3718. ii. HENRY F., b. Jan. 27, 1862.
3719. iii. ROSE M., b. Apr. 23, 1865.

2425. Carlos[8] Pierce (*Wilder[7]*, *Joseph[6]*, *John[5]*, *Josiah[4]*, *John[3]*, *Thomas[2]*, *Thomas[1]*), b. May 20, 1831 ; m. June 24, 1858, Mary A. Mills. He d. Aug. 20, 1870. She m. again and res. Bangor. Res. Boston, Mass., and Stanstead, P. Q.

Carlos Pierce was a man of remarkable energy and perseverance in mercantile pursuits. He retired from it at an early age on account of ill health, and thereafter devoted most of his time to agricultural pursuits. He will be remembered as having raised and presented for exhibition the famous white ox " Gen. Grant," which was on exhibition for some years. His liberality to the church and to the village of Stanstead, where he was born and died, will not soon be forgotten by its citizens. No children.

2437. James M.[8] Pierce (*Thomas[7]*, *Joseph[6]*, *John[5]*, *Josiah[4]*, *John[3]*, *Thomas[2]*, *Thomas[1]*), b. Nov. 1, 1826 ; m. Feb. 5, 1862, Emily Barras, b. Nov. 7, 1836. Res. Martinsville, P. Q.   Child :—

3720. i.   Ida F., b. Dec. 25, 1866 ; d. Oct. 6, 1875.

2439. William A.[8] Pierce (*Thomas[7]*, *Joseph[6]*, *John[5]*, *Josiah[4]*, *John[3]*, *Thomas[2]*, *Thomas[1]*), b. Aug. 31, 1834 ; m. Jan. 11, 1861, Maria Merrill, b. Jan. 2, 1845. Res. Martinsville, P. Q.
Children :—

3721. i.   Wilder A., b. Aug. 21, 1863.
3722. ii. Wilber, b. Feb. 17, 1873.

2442. Albert C.[8] Pierce (*Thomas[7]*, *Joseph[6]*, *John[5]*, *Josiah[4]*, *John[3]*, *Thomas[2]*, *Thomas[1]*), b. Oct. 29, 1842 ; m. Oct. 17, 1871, Minnie A. Ayer, b. Nov. 4, 1851. Res. Boston. Children :—

3723. i.   George H., b. Jan. 28, 1873.
3724. ii. Mary O., b. Oct. 17, 1876.

2443. Henry T.[8] Pierce (*Thomas[7]*, *Joseph[6]*, *John[5]*, *Josiah[4]*, *John[3]*, *Thomas[2]*, *Thomas[1]*), b. Aug. 17, 1846 ; m. May 20, 1874, Annie P. L. Manning, b. Mar. 26, 1856, d. May 14, 1877 ; m. 2nd, Oct. 8, 1879, Sarah M. Hogan, b. Sept. 29, 1858. Res. Martinsville, P. Q. Child :—

3725. i.   Jennie O., b. June 2, 1876.

2445.   Warren[8] Pierce (*Daniel[7]*, *Daniel[6]*, *John[5]*, *Josiah[4]*, *John[3]*, *Thomas[2]*, *Thomas[1]*), b. 1789 ; m. July 1, 1810, Sally McManus, b. June 28, 1788, d. Jan. 6, 1839. She was a dau. of Patrick and Grace McManus. He was an Irish soldier and was a member of the army that was surrendered by Gen. Burgoyne. He d. Sept. 12, 1847. Res. St. Johnsbury, Vt.

Children :—
3726. i.   Daniel W., b. Apr. 3, 1811 ; m. Lucy Edson.

3727. ii. WILLARD A., b. Oct. 15, 1812; m. —— Powers and Mary Jane Northrop.
3728. iii. SABRINA A., b. Oct. 13, 1814; m. Samuel Averill and ——Cooper.
3729. iv. LUCINDA, b. Jan. 8, 1817; d. June 17, 1846.
3730. v. GEORGE W., b. May 4, 1819; m. Harriet Severns.
3731. vi. WARREN, b. June 20, 1821; m. Lucy M. Streeter.
3732. vii. ABEL, b. Apr. 18, 1823; m. three times.
3733. viii. TRUMAN L., b. Feb. 14, 1826; d. Apr. 18, 1828.
3734. ix. HENRY R., b. Jan. 2, 1828; m, A. Frances Tillinghast.

2446. ARETAS[8] PIERCE (*Aretas*[7], *Daniel*[6], *John*[5], *Josiah*[4], *John*[3], *Thomas*[2], *Thomas*[1]), b. Mar. 27, 1799; m. May 8, 1823, Matilda Stedman, b. Jan. 29, 1801. He d. Apr. 19, 1872. Res. Rome, N. Y.

Children :—

2735. i. SOPHRONIA, b. Feb. 25, 1824; m. David Webster.
3736. ii. GEORGE W., b. May 1, 1826; m. Ellen A. Southworth.
3737. iii. JOHN Q., b. Jan. 4, 1828; m. Julia M. Bennett and Sarah L. Keyes.
3738. iv. MARY, b. Apr. 27, 1832; m. Alonzo F. Stedman.
3739. v. JOSEPH B., b. May 23, 1836; m. Emma A. Brown.
3740. vi. AMANDA C., b. Sept. 1, 1843; m. Sterns Albert.

2465. ABEL A.[8] PIERCE (*Abel*[7], *Daniel*[6], *John*[5], *Josiah*[4], *John*[3], *Thomas*[2], *Thomas*[1]), b. Apr. 28, 1825; m. Mar. 9, 1848, Rosetta Ayer, b. Nov. 24, 1829, d. June 29, 1876; m. 2nd, Oct. 11, 1878, Sarah McGrath, b. Oct. 11, 1841. Res. St. Johnsbury Centre, Vt.

Children :—

3741. i. FREEMAN A., b. May 6, 1849; m. Olive Raney.
3742. ii. TRUMAN L., b. June 24, 1851; d. June 24, 1851.
3743. iii. JOSIAH W., b. Nov. 20, 1852.
3744. iv. EDWARD C., b. Aug. 9, 1857; m. Mary Williams.
3745. v. CHARLES S., b. Nov 6, 1859.
3746. vi. ETTA B., b. Oct. 14, 1867.
3747. vii. HIRAM L., b. Oct. 9, 1873.
3748. viii. LETTIE V., b. May 29, 1879.

2466. JOHN S.[8] PIERCE (*Reuben*[7], *Daniel*[6], *John*[5], *Josiah*[4], *John*[3], *Thomas*[2], *Thomas*[1]), b. Jan. 8, 1809; m. Sarah Gould. He d. Sept. 10, 1862. Res. St. Johnsbury, Vt. Children :—

3749. i. SOLON; d. ——.
3750. ii. HORACE; d. ——.

2468. HORATIO A.[8] PIERCE (*Reuben*[7], *Daniel*[6], *John*[5], *Josiah*[4], *John*[3], *Thomas*[2], *Thomas*[1]), b. Mar. 7, 1812; m. Feb. 21, 1837,

Clarissa Stearns. He d. Sept. 16, 1840. She m. 2nd, John Proctor.
Res. St. Johnsbury, Vt. Children :—

3751. i.   CANDACE C., b. June 8, 1839; m. Irving Frost.
3752. ii.   STELLA, b. 1841; d. 1857.

2470. PRENTICE L.[8] PIERCE (*Reuben*[7], *Daniel*[6], *John*[5], *Josiah*[4], *John*[3], *Thomas*[2], *Thomas*[1]), b. May 5, 1829 ; m. June 20, 1854, Martha J. Powers, b. Mar. 28, 1834. Res. St. Johnsbury Centre, Vt.

No children.

2472. HIRAM[8] PIERCE (*Thomas*[7], *Thomas*[6], *John*[5], *Josiah*[4], *John*[3], *Thomas*[2], *Thomas*[1]), b. June 3, 1803 ; m. Oct. 16, 1825, Lois Stiles, b. May 29, 1807, d. Sept. 15, 1832; m. 2nd, Jan. 19, 1833, Diantha Fuller, b. May 18, 1803, d. Jan. 19, 1877. He d. Feb. 28, 1875. Res. St. Johnsbury, Vt. Children :—

3753. i.   LUCIA M., b. June 1, 1827; m. Archibald Stark and William Aldrich.
3754. ii.   HOLLIS S., b. Mar. 19, 1829; m. Aurora Hill.
3755. iii. EMELINE L., b. Oct. 8, 1834; m. Stephen W. Hunter.
3756. iv.   ANN S., b. Apr. 21, 1835; d. Aug. 15, 1850.
3757. v.   HIRAM D., b. Mar. 1, 1838; m. Marian Hopkins.

2475. MILO[8] PIERCE (*Thomas*[7], *Thomas*[6], *John*[5], *Josiah*[4], *John*[3], *Thomas*[2], *Thomas*[1]), b. June 6, 1808; m. Dec. 9, 1840, Eliza Bennett. Res. E. Albany, Vt. Children :—

3758. i.   ANGONIA, b. Dec. 8. 1841; m. David Hunter.
3759. ii.   ADELAIDE ; m. Francis Hunter.
3760. iii. MATILDA; m. Wm. Brockway.

2482. JABEZ[8] PIERCE (*Thomas*[7], *John*[6], *Thomas*[5], *Thomas*[4], *Thomas*[3], *Thomas*[2], *Thomas*[1]), b. May 9, 1794; m. June 22, 1828, Ann Mary King, b. Apr. 17, 1799. Res. Chatham Village, N. Y. Children :—

3761. i.   REBECCA, b. July 22, 1830.
3762. ii.   JOHN R., b. Aug. 10, 1834.

2488. WILLIAM L.[8] PIERCE (*Spalding*[7], *John*[6], *Thomas*[5], *Thomas*[4], *Thomas*[3], *Thomas*[2], *Thomas*[1]), b. Feb. 16, 1810 ; m. Nov. 16, 1853, Susan Barringer, b. Feb. 16, 1822. Res. Suequoit, N. Y. No children.

2490. SYLVESTER P.[8] PIERCE (*Spalding*[7], *John*[6], *Thomas*[5], *Thomas*[4], *Thomas*[3], *Thomas*[2], *Thomas*[1]), b. Sept. 19, 1814 ; m. Nov. 18, 1841, Cornelia Marsh, b. Mar. 25, 1819. Res. Syracuse, N. Y.

Children :—

3763. i. MARSH C., b. Feb. 19, 1847; m. Jennie Cook.
3764. ii. CHARLES H., b. Aug. 8, 1849.
3765. iii. WILLIAM K., b. May 11, 1851.
3766. iv. EUNICE C., b. Dec. 11, 1852; m. W. A. Butler.

2492. JOHN S.[8] PIERCE (*Spalding*[7], *John*[6], *Thomas*[5], *Thomas*[4], *Thomas*[3], *Thomas*[2], *Thomas*[1]), b. May 8, 1819; m. May 28, 1843, Fidelia Griffith, b. Aug. 15, 1825. Res. Phoenix, N. Y. Children :—

3767. i. GRANVILLE G., b. Jan. 14, 1845.
3768. ii. J. EMMETT, b. Feb. 18, 1847.

2500. CHARLES[8] PIERCE (*Phineas*[7], *Lemuel*[6], *Ebenezer*[5], *Thomas*[4], *Thomas*[3], *Thomas*[2], *Thomas*[1]), b. 1798; m. 1818, Emily Edson, d. 1833; m. 2nd, 1834, Maria White. He d. 1847. Res. Killingly and Pomfret, Conn. Children :—

3769. i. MARY, b. 1819; m. Henry Bradford and —— ——.
3770. ii. WILLIAM, b. 1821; m. Mary Barstow.
3771. iii. NATHANIEL, b. 1825; m. Amy Adams.
3772. iv. GEORGE A., b. Dec. 25, 1835; m. Ellen Rich.
3773. v. JANE, b. 1837; d. 1854.
3774. vi. ALMYRA, b. 1839.
3775. vii. CHARLES, b. 1846; d. in army hospital.

2501. MARTIN[8] PIERCE (*Phineas*[7], *Lemuel*[6], *Ebenezer*[5], *Thomas*[4], *Thomas*[3], *Thomas*[2], *Thomas*[1]), b. Sept., 1803; m. Sept. 19, 1826, Julia Hall, b. June 16, 1806. Res. Wauregan, Conn. Children :—

3776. i. ALBERT W., b. Mar. 3, 1827.
3777. ii. JULIA A., b. Aug. 31, 1828.
3778. iii. EDWIN M., b. Dec. 8, 1831; m. Martha Kenyon.
3779. iv. MARY L., b. Oct. 18, 1833; d. Oct. 18, 1833.
3780. v. JEREMIAH H., } twins, b. Apr. 21, 1836; { m. Almira Place.
3781. vi. JOHN W.,
3782. vii. CALEB H. A., } twins, b. Oct. 18, 1838; { d. July 2, 1839.
3783. viii. EMELINE J.,
3784. ix. ALONZO S., b. May 31, 1841, d. Dec. 13, 1861.

2504. DARIUS[8] PIERCE (*Phineas*[7], *Lemuel*[6], *Ebenezer*[5], *Thomas*[4], *Thomas*[3], *Thomas*[2], *Thomas*[1]), b. 1809; m. 1840, Cornelia Crandall, b. 1817. He d. 1844. Children :—

3785. i. NORMAN S., b. Nov. 14, 1842; m. Mary L. J. McMaine.
3786. ii. ANNA E., b. Mar. 20, 1844; m. Edwin Pinney.

2512. ALVARES[8] PIERCE (*Samuel*[7], *Thomas*[6], *Amos*[5], *Thomas*[4], *Thomas*[3], *Thomas*[2], *Thomas*[1]), b. Dec. 3, 1791; m. June 21, 1818, Polly Booth, b. 1802, d. July 11, 1835; m. 2nd, July 22, 1838, Sarah M. Ryan, b. Nov. 17, 1806. He d. Sept. 19, 1871. Res. Groton, Mass., Penn., and Eldora, Iowa. Alvares Pierce with three motherless children moved into the wilds of Northern Penn. some time about the year 1837–8. He was then about 46 years old, and for several years with his children experienced the hardships incident to a new country. He penetrated farther than any who had preceded him, and for some time his home was at the "end of the road." A large territory around was then an almost unbroken forest, and the few scattered settlers had little

30

food for themselves and none for those that followed them : so the only alternative was to go to Egypt, and that Egypt was some 70 miles off, part of the way over barren mountains with scarce any inhabitants save wild animals and rattlesnakes. Great hardships were endured by those who went to buy food, and equally great perhaps were the trials of those who tarried at home. On one occasion while Mr. P. was gone for supplies the meal barrel was exhausted and he did not return,—and their poor neighbors had none to spare. The children had a step-mother then, and she contrived to drive the wolf of hunger from the door. Taking a little girl, the youngest, she went to the field near the house and dug up the newly-planted potatoes, although somewhat sprouted, washed and boiled them, and with the addition of cooked leeks, milk and a few trout, subsisted until he came home. The town in which he lived had two settlements, one on the north and the other on the south side of a large forest. To go from one to the other a foot path was used. One day Mr. P. went from home to the other settle-ment three or four miles to procure a pig, which having got he swung in a bag over his shoulder and started for home. After going some distance he lost the path, and towards night found it quite certain he could not get home before dark. A thunder storm came on and dark-ness set in and he could proceed no further, and laying his bundle at the foot of a tree he passed the rainy night, standing up most of the time to prevent being wet through. In the morning he found himself on the banks of the same brook that ran past his log house, but some distance off. He took up his bundle and went to the hut of a neighbor, got some breakfast and then started home, which he reached all right with his burden.

Alvares Pierce

Children :—

3787.   i.   GEORGE, b. Feb. 20, 1820; d. April 29, 1825.
3788.   ii.   JULIA, b. Oct. 22, 1821; m. Trumann Kebbel.
3789.   iii.   JAMES, b. Aug. 5, 1823; m. Sarah R. Preston.
3790.   iv.   THEODOTIA, b. Aug. 3, 1831; m. Albert A. Presho.
3791.   v.   MARY S., b. Aug. 27, 1842; m. Stephen Small.
3792.   vi.   ANN H., b. Nov. 16, 1844; m. J. B. Wilson.

2514.   RODNEY[8] PIERCE (*Samuel[7], Thomas[6], Amos[5], Thomas[4], Thomas[3], Thomas[2], Thomas[1]*), b. April 1, 1796 ; m. Oct. 7, 1830, Eliza Severance, b. Aug. 24, 1805, d. July 5, 1877. He d. Aug. 16, 1871. Res. Brandon, Vt. Children :—

3793.   i.   FREDERICK F., b. Sept. 2, 1832; m. Margaretta E. Coe.
3794.   ii.   HENRY M., b. March 29, 1834; m. Mary Spaulding.
3795.   iii.   HARRIET E., b. May 10, 1836; m. Wm. P. Corvel.
3796.   iv.   MARETTA M., b. Dec. 1, 1837.
3797.   v.   EMMA A., b. July 10, 1839; m. G. H. Plumly.

2516. S. WILLIAM[8] PIERCE (*Samuel[7]*, *Thomas[6]*, *Amos[5]*, *Thomas[4]*, *Thomas[3]*, *Thomas[2]*, *Thomas[1]*), b. Dec, 26, 1801 ; m. June 2, 1827, Eliza Bigelow, d. Aug. 27, 1853. He d. Dec. 10, 1878. Res. Salisbury, Vt. Children :—

3798. i. ALFRED I., b. May 7, 1828; m.
3789. ii. ———, b. Oct. 7, 1829; d. Oct. 10, 1829.
3800. iii. SAMUEL A., b. July, 1, 1831; m. Harriet E. Wilson.
3801. iv. WILLIAM B., b. Jan. 21, 1833.
3802. v. LOUISE A., b. Feb. 2, 1836; m. Willard Allen.
3803. vi. ANN E., b. Oct. 24, 1839; m. Henry Perry.
3804. vii. ARRABELLA I., b. March 6, 1841; d. Sept., 1867.
3805. viii. HARRIET L., b. May 21, 1845.

2519. RODNEY[8] PIERCE (*John[7]*, *Thomas[6]*, *Amos[5]*, *Thomas[4]*, *Thomas[3]*, *Thomas[2]*, *Thomas[1]*), b. July 12, 1807 ; m. Jan. 1, 1831, Harriet Kelsey, b. Apr. 20, 1813, d. June 12, 1841 ; m. 2nd, Aug. 30, 1841, Jane Dalton, b. Sept. 13, 1812, d. Jan. 21, 1864 ; m. 3rd, July 30, 1865, Emeline Mulholland, b. Oct. 15, 1826. Res. Garrettsville, Ohio. Children :—

3806. i. LOUISE M., b. June 10, 1832; m. July 30, 1853, Omar C. Stocking, b. Oct. 14, 1828.
3807. ii. ELIZA, b. Oct. 30, 1834; d. Jan. 23, 1856.
3808. iii. CHARLES K., b. Apr. 18, 1837; m. Ellen S. Goodall.
3809. iv. GEORGE, b. June 2, 1839; m. Caroline Westlake.
3810. v. HENRY W., b. June 12, 1841; d. Sept. 7, 1842.
3811. vi. HENRY D., b. July 12, 1842; m. Charlotte Stocking.
3812. vii. JOHN, b. July 14, 1844; d. Feb. 1, 1857.
3813. viii. HARRIET, b. Oct. 27, 1846; d. March 3, 1857.
3814. ix. JANE, b. Feb. 1, 1849; m. Nov. 25, 1868, Frank A. Clark. Res. Courtland, Ohio.
3815. x. RODNEY, b. June 15, 1851; m. Mary E. Askin.

2520. ANDREW[8] PIERCE (*John[7]*, *Thomas[6]*, *Amos[5]*, *Thomas[4]*, *Thomas[3]*, *Thomas[2]*, *Thomas[1]*), b. July 21, 1814 ; m. March 10, 1836, Mary A. Cleveland. He d. Oct. 2, 1851. Res. Conn. Children :—

3816. i. JOHN I., b. Dec. 19, 1837; m. Harriet Cobb.
3817. ii. HENRY S., b. Nov. 23, 1840.
3818. iii. SARAH J., b. July 25, 1850; d. Sept. 29, 1866.

2521. JOHN D.[8] PIERCE (*John[7]*, *Thomas[6]*, *Amos[5]*, *Thomas[4]*, *Thomas[3]*, *Thomas[2]*, *Thomas[1]*), b. May 5, 1817 ; m. Jan. 1, 1838, Mary West, b. Aug. 2, 1817. Res. Garrettsville, Ohio.

John D. Pierce

Child :—
3819. i. EDWARD R., b. Nov. 18, 1840; m. Mary E. McGahan.

2523. HENRY M.[8] PIERCE (*Samuel[7]*, *Amos[6]*, *Amos[5]*, *Thomas[4]*, *Thomas[3]*, *Thomas[2]*, *Thomas[1]*), b. Aug. 11, 1810 ; m. Oct. 28, 1844, Cornelia C. Campbell. Res. Elbridge, N. Y.

2527. WILLIAM[8] PIERCE (*Samuel[7]*, *Amos[6]*, *Amos[5]*, *Thomas[4]*, *Thomas[3]*, *Thomas[2]*, *Thomas[1]*), b. Dec. 19, 1818 ; m. July 28, 1842, Aurelia Bowker. He. d. June 30, 1858.

2529. Amos[8] Pierce (*William[7], Amos[6], Amos[5], Thomas[4], Thomas[3], Thomas[2], Thomas[1]*), b. Nov. 12, 1814 ; m. May 13, 1841, Marianna Butler, d. Dec. 9, 1861 ; m. 2nd, Oct. 5, 1864, Mrs. Saloma E. Lewis, b. March 5, 1820, d. April 29, 1876. Res. Elmwood, Ill. Children :—

   3820. i.   William N., b. April 18, 1843 ; m. Eliza Richards.
   3821. ii. Amos A., b. June 28, 1856 ; m. Fredonia T. Jarmain.

2530. Rev. William G.[8] Pierce (*William[7], Amos[6], Amos[5], Thomas[4], Thomas[3], Thomas[2], Thomas[1]*), b. Nov. 27, 1816 ; m. May 1, 1843, Jane E. Adams, b. Nov. 16, 1815. Res. Champaign, Ill. He lived with his father and worked upon his farm until he was 21 years of age. Then went to the Weslyan University, Middletown, Conn., where he was graduated in the class of 1842. Read law in Poughkeepsie, N. Y., in 1843–1844 and 1845, in the last named year admitted to the bar. In 1843 was married to Jane Elizabeth Adams of Canaan, Conn. While in Poughkeepsie was Deputy Clerk of the Court of Chancery of the 2nd Circuit. In 1846 moved to Canaan, Ct., and was there engaged in the iron and mercantile business for several years. Held the office of Judge of Probate for Canaan District, of Litchfield Co. Sold out his interest in the iron business in 1858, and commenced preparing for the ministry. Opened an Academy in Canaan, and taught during a portion of the time from 1859 to 1861. Licensed to preach by the North Litchfield Association of Congregational ministers in March, 1861. In April, 1861, by previous invitation went to Elmwood, Peoria Co., Illinois ; received a call to preach, and settled there. Remained as pastor of the Congregational Church at Elmwood ten or eleven years. In August, 1862, enlisted as private in Co. E. 77th Regt. Ill. vols. He was elected Chaplain of the same regiment soon after. Connected with the army for about a year and a half, was with his regiment during the siege of Vicksburg, and in many of the battles during that campaign. His health failing entirely, he was obliged to leave the service, and sent in his resignation, which was accepted in the winter of '63—'64. He then returned to his pastorate. He resigned his charge at Elmwood in the fall of 1871. Took several months rest, and afterwards for a short time preached in Springfield, Mo. Declined a call there to the pastorate of the Congregational Church. Accepted a call to Champaign, Ill., in the fall of 1872, where he is now the settled pastor of the Congregational Church. Children :—

   3822. i.   Lucy, A., b. Sept, 16, 1844 ; d. Dec. 20, 1847.
   3823. ii. Jeannie, b. July 4, 1846 ; m. Mar. 10, 1868, Theo. H. Tracy, b. May 16, 1846. Children : Fanny M., b. Dec. 16, 1868 ; Wm. A., b. Dec. 3, 1871 ; Jeanie R., b. Jan. 14, 1875 ; Theo. P., b. Nov. 19, 1876. Res. Elmwood, Ill.
   3824. iii. Frank, b. June 25, 1848 ; d. July 19, 1856.
   3825. iv. Fanny, b. June 5, 1851.
   3826. v.   John L., b. Aug. 24, 1853 ; m. Margaret H. Harris.

2533. Daniel L.[8] Pierce (*William[7], Amos[6], Amos[5], Thomas[4], Thomas[3], Thomas[2], Thomas[1]*), b. Jan. 1, 1824 ; m. June 5, 1850, Ann E. Rood. Res. Canaan, Conn. Children :—

   3827. i.   Mary E., b. March 15, 1853 ; d. Aug. 29, 1854.

3828. ii. ELSIE D., b. Sept. 19, 1855.
3829. iii. MINNIE E., b. Aug. 23, 1858.
3830. iv. MARY E., b. Ang. 21, 1860.
3831. v. ALICE L., b. Dec. 16, 1863.
3832. vi. BURTON A., b. April 21, 1867.
3833. vii. ROBERT D., b. Oct. 9, 1868.

2535. SAMUEL R.[8] PIERCE (*Phineas*[7], *Phineas*[6], *Amos*[5], *Thomas*[4], *Thomas*[3], *Thomas*[2], *Thomas*[1]), b. Jan. 23, 1813 ; m. April 24, 1834, Sylvia J. Comstock, b. Sept. 15, 1815, d. Aug., 1871 ; m. 2nd, Oct. 6, 1872, Fanny Holman, b. May 10, 1851. Res. Bedford, Ind.

S. R. Pierce

Children :—

3834. i. WILLIAM O., b. Oct. 28, 1835 ; m. Zerelda Fall.
3835. ii. CHLOE A., b. Feb. 3, 1841 ; m. Francis M. Miles.
3836. iii. JAMES W., b. Jan. 5, 1845 ; d. Aug. 10, 1870.
3837. iv. DORSEY C., b. July 24, 1848 ; m. Mary J. Martin.
3838. v. MARY E., b. Dec. 19, 1851 ; d. Feb. 2, 1853.
3839. vi. EDA B., b. Jan. 14, 1859 ; m. —— Houser.
3840. vii. C. WALTER, b. March 3, 1874.
3841. viii. STANLEY R., b. Dec. 4, 1878.

2536. CLEMENT PIERCE (*Amos*[7], *Phineas*[6], *Amos*[5], *Thomas*[4], *Thomas*[3], *Thomas*[2], *Thomas*[1]), b. Sept. 24, 1813 ; m. Mar. 6, 1834, Nancy Farr, b. Jan. 13, 1814. Res. Roseville, Ill. Children :—

3842. i. MARIETTA, b. Aug. 2, 1835.
3843. ii. LAURA A., b. Jan. 26, 1837 ; m. Alex. H. Bramhall.
3844. iii. AMOS, b. Dec. 10, 1843 ; m. Mary J. Barr.
3845. iv. PHEBE J., b. Oct. 10, 1845 ; m. Thomas J. Newburn.
3846. v. ZACHARAH T., b. Apr. 23, 1848 ; d. Sept. 23, 1860.

2537. WILLIAM H.[8] PIERCE (*Amos*[7], *Phineas*[6], *Amos*[5], *Thomas*[4], *Thomas*[3], *Thomas*[2], *Thomas*[1]), b. Jan. 23, 1816 ; m. Sept. 10, 1837, Angeline Waldron, b. Apr. 17, 1819, d. July 9, 1842 ; m. 2nd, March 22, 1846, Harriet Woods, b. Feb. 27, 1826. He d. Feb. 25, 1880. Res. Galesburg, Ill.

William H. Pierce

Children :—

3847. i. ALMIRAN G., b. July 4, 1838 ; m. Caroline C. Sanford.
3848. ii. CHARLES H., b. Feb. 1, 1840 ; m. Elizabeth Long.
3849. iii. MARIETTA L., b. March 28, 1847 ; m. Benj. A. Griffiths.
3850. iv. JULIA P., b. May 10, 1849 ; m. Wm. E. Day.
3851. v. EMMA J., b. May 11, 1851.
3852. vi. FRANK A., b. Aug. 3, 1853 ; d. Aug. 1, 1854.
3853. vii. HARRIET L., b. June 22, 1856 ; m. John F. Perry.
3853½. viii. FLORA A., b. Apr. 9, 1858 ; d. Oct. 13, 1862.
3854. ix. EFFIE, b. Oct. 7, 1860 ; d. Sept. 11, 1862.
3855. x. PERLIE, b. Sept, 21, 1863 ; d. Aug. 16, 1864.

238   PIERCE PEDIGREE.

2539. STEPHEN[8] PIERCE (*Amos*[7], *Phineas*[6], *Amos*[5], *Thomas*[4], *Thomas*[3], *Thomas*[2], *Thomas*[1]), b. Sept. 24, 1820 ; m. Dec. 23, 1847, Elizabeth Hanan, b. Sept. 19, 1829, d. Apr. 30, 1855 ; m. 2nd, Dec. 24, 1857, Lottie Johnson, b. June 28, 1834. Res. Roseville, Ill. Children :—

3856. i.   SARAH E., b. Dec. 25, 1851; m. J. H. Sayler.
3857. ii.   IDA A., b. Oct. 26, 1858; d. June 4, 1863.
3858. iii. CASSIUS E., b. Apr. 1, 1860; d. March 21, 1865.
3859. iv.   BROWNLOW, b. Feb. 10, 1862; d. Feb. 4, 1863.
3860. v.   HERBERT O., b. June 6, 1864.
3861. vi.   JANE I., b. Dec. 11, 1865.
3862. vii. STEPHEN B., b. July 11, 1867; d. Jan. 1, 1872.
3863. viii. CLARA R., } twins, b. Sept. 2, 1870; { d. July 7, 1871.
3864. ix.   MARY A.,
3865. x.   JESSE K., b. March 29, 1875.
3866. xi.   DAISY L., b. April 12, 1877.

2542. CHRISTOPHER E.[8] PIERCE (*Abiram*[7], *Phineas*[6], *Amos*[5], *Thomas*[4], *Thomas*[3], *Thomas*[2], *Thomas*[1]), b. Sept. 24, 1809 ; m. May 7, 1838, Emeline Pierce, b. Aug. 11, 1814. Res. Smithfield, Pa.

Children :—

3867. i.   ELIZABETH, b. Feb. 10, 1845; m. Dec. 18, 1873, F. C. Proctor. Res. Smithfield.
3868. ii. FRANK L., b. Apr. 10, 1853; m. Mattie Cooley.

2543. WILLIAM S.[8] PIERCE (*Abiram*[7], *Phineas*[6], *Amos*[5], *Thomas*[4], *Thomas*[3], *Thomas*[2], *Thomas*[1]), b. July 9, 1811 ; m. Jan. 12, 1847, Sarah Hermon, b. Aug. 19, 1820. He d. Apr. 22, 1878. Res. E. Smithfield, Pa.

Children :—

3869. i.   GEORGIANNA, b. Mar. 26, 1848; d. Apr. 20, 1857.
3870. ii. BELLE K., b. Dec. 17, 1856.
3871. iii. WILLIAM, b. Mar. 31, 1858.

2544. STEPHEN[8] PIERCE (*Abiram*[7], *Phineas*[6], *Amos*[5], *Thomas*[4], *Thomas*[3], *Thomas*[2], *Thomas*[1]), b. Aug. 29, 1813 ; m. Aug. 23, 1838, Mary Ransom, b. Oct. 2, 1813. He d. Feb. 12, 1868. Res. Troy, Pa.

Children :—

3872. i. EMMA J., b. July 3, 1839 ; m. Oct. 30, 1865, G. F. Reddington.
3873. ii. ROLLIN A., b. May 27, 1842.
3874. iii. CLARENCE W., b. Dec. 19, 1848 ; d. May 19, 1870.
3875. iv. JOHN R., b. Oct. 7, 1851 ; d. June 20, 1873.

2546. AMOS[8] PIERCE (*Abiram*[7], *Phineas*[6], *Amos*[5], *Thomas*[4], *Thomas*[3], *Thomas*[2], *Thomas*[1]), b. Oct. 12, 1820 ; m. June 1, 1843, Laura Pomeroy, b. 1824, d. Nov. 22, 1861. He d. July 12, 1871. Res. Troy, Pa. Children :—

3876. i. MARY J., b. June 2, 1844 ; m. Oct. 21, 1873, R. F. Reddington. She d. Sept. 24, 1876. Ch. : Laura M., b. Aug. 14, 1864 ; infant d. Sept. 15, 1866 ; Fanny, b. Jan. 16, 1870, d. Jan. 14, 1873 ; Jenny L., b. Oct. 11, 1873 ; Frank S., b. Feb. 14, 1875.
3877. iii. EDWARD S., b. Sept. 5, 1845 ; d. Aug. 5, 1866.

2551. STEPHEN[8] PIERCE (*Stephen*[7], *Phineas*[6], *Amos*[5], *Thomas*[4], *Thomas*[3], *Thomas*[2], *Thomas*[1]), b. Nov. 8, 1828 ; m. 1855, Elizabeth Miller, d ———. He d. ———. Res. Henrietta, Clay Co., Texas.

2554. WALTER[8] PIERCE (*Horace*[7], *Phineas*[6], *Amos*[5], *Thomas*[4], *Thomas*[3], *Thomas*[2], *Thomas*[1]), b. Oct. 3, 1834 ; m. Apr. 17, 1859, Lorancy Carpenter, d. Dec. 18, 1878. Res. E. Smithfield, Pa. Children :—

3878. i. GEORGE W., b. Jan. 8, 1860.
3879. ii. STANLEY E., b. Feb. 7, 1867.
3880. iii. JESSE, b. Jan. 28, 1870.
3881. iv. IDA M., b. Feb. 26, 1876.

2555. HARRY[8] PIERCE (*Horace*[7], *Phineas*[6], *Amos*[5], *Thomas*[4], *Thomas*[3], *Thomas*[2], *Thomas*[1]), b. Dec. 22, 1842 ; m. Dec. 30, 1866, Harriet Campbell. Res. E. Smithfield, Pa. Children :—

3882. i. MARY E., b. Jan. 16, 1870.
3883. ii. ANNIE M., b. Dec. 9, 1872.
3884. iii. EDIE S., b. Feb. 25, 1876.

2557. CLARENCE H.[8] PIERCE (*Harry*[7], *Phineas*[6], *Amos*[5], *Thomas*[4], *Thomas*[3], *Thomas*[2], *Thomas*[1]), b. July 29, 1838 ; m. Aug. 15, 1861, Marion Morley, b. July 24, 1837. Res. Burlington, Pa. Children :—

3885. i. J. MARIA, b. Jan. 3, 1863.
3886. ii. HARRIET A., b. Aug. 16, 1866 ; d. Apr. 2, 1871.
3887. iii. PERLEY C., b. July 14, 1870.
3888. iv. CLARENCE L., b. Apr. 29, 1872.
3889. v. THOMAS M., b. Apr. 19, 1874.
3890. vi. HUGH E., b. Feb. 11, 1876.
3891. vii. HAROLET W., b. Mar. 11, 1878.

2562. CHARLES[8] PIERCE (*Harry*[7], *Phineas*[6], *Amos*[5], *Thomas*[4], *Thomas*[3], *Thomas*[2], *Thomas*[1]), b. Nov. 7, 1855 ; m. Nov. 24, 1877, Nellie K. Wood, b. Apr. 13, 1857. Res. E. Smithfield, Pa.

2573. EARL[8] PIERCE (*Palmer*[7], *Timothy*[6], *Timothy*[5], *Timothy*[4], *Thomas*[3], *Thomas*[2], *Thomas*[1]), b. Aug. 5, 1785 ; m. Oct. 22, 1806, Orry Woodward, d. Nov. 24, 1860. He d. Oct. 30, 1836. Res. Jackson, Chesterfield and Peru, N. Y. Earl Pierce, after his marriage, in 1806, resided in Washington County for fifteen years, dividing the time about equal between the two towns. During all of this time he was engaged in farming and lumbering. In 1820, he formed a business connection with Thomas McLean and Isaac Huestis and purchased a tract of pine timber land, embracing a valuable water-power and privilege, in Peru, Clinton County, N. Y. It was then an almost unbroken wilderness. As Mr. Pierce was to be the pioneer in the erection of dams, mills, &c., in this wilderness section, he moved his family from Greenwich, Washington County, to Peru, Clinton County, in May, 1821. The distance, 120 miles, was made in a covered wagon in just six days time. There were eight persons in the family besides two servants. Having got his family comfortably settled he went immediately at the work in hand, which consisted in clearing the lands, erecting dams, flumes, saw-mills, forge, blacksmith shops, store, dwelling houses, barns, fences, &c., &c., which consumed about three years time to put things in good working order. A school-house of suitable size to answer also for a place of worship was early provided for. So in truth it might be said that the desert was made to blossom like the rose. Mr. Pierce being well settled in a comfortable home, after the great strain upon him during the first few years of his pioneer life, finds himself at the head of a large manufacturing business, of both lumber and iron, and also has a large farming interest, and other industries to look after, has but a sparse time to devote to objects outside of his business. His office was in his store for the convenience of his business.

But amid all his hurry and press of business he always took time to attend to his religious duties. He was an active and devoted christian, an ardent temperance man, and strict observer of the Sabbath. His standing in the community was high, and he was regarded as a shrewd, energetic, industrious and persevering business man. In the midst of his active busy life the Lord called for him. A ladder on which he was descending, slipped on the barn prostrating him to the floor, a distance of 20 feet, and fatally injuring him so that after four days of suffering he died. When his family physician told him that he could live but a short time he looked around wishfully and said, "if it is the Lord's time it is my time," and continued to talk while his strength lasted. He was perfectly conscious to the last, and bade his wife and each of his children an affectionate farewell—dying in the triumphs of faith, at the age of 51 years and over.

Earl Pierce

Children :—

3892. i.   JANE, b. May 30, 1807; d. July 6, 1816.
3893. ii. ELIZA ANN, b. Mar. 22, 1809; m. Jan. 1, 1828, Joshua C. Finch. Ch. : Earl P., b. 1830; Eliza A., b. 1832, d. Aug. 27, 1848; Mary J., b. 1834; Frances, b. 1836, d. 1836. They res. in Jay, N. Y.

3894. iii. LEWIS W., b. Nov. 20, 1810; m. Perley H. Sanford.
3895. iv. BENJAMIN C., b. Sept. 12, 1812; m. Catherine R. Finch.
3896. v. MARY K., b. June 26, 1815; m. Sept. 12, 1834, Daniel W. Dewel, d. Oct. 5, 1863. She d. May 24, 1858. They res. in Ausable, N. Y. Ch.: Carter, b. June 25, 1835, d. June 25, 1835; Mary E., b. June 5, 1836; Rollin, b. Jan. 8, 1839; Orry I., b. Aug. 16, 1841; William C., b. Sept. 24, 1843, d. July 20, 1844; Maria L., b. Nov. 4, 1845; Emma I., b. Sept. 17, 1848.
3897. vi. HENRY P., b. Dec. 13, 1817; m. Maria O. Wright.
3898. vii. EUNICE O., b. Jan. 17, 1820; m. Dec. 20, 1842, Daniel W. Wright, d. Aug. 27, 1848. They res. in Argyle, N. Y. Ch.: Josephine B., b. May, 1844; James, b. May, 1846, d. 1848; Daniel, b. May 8, 1848.
3899. viii. WILLIAM C., b. Sept. 19, 1822; m. Catherine Boynton and Margaret M. Myers.
3900. ix. LYMAN P., b. Mar. 22, 1825; d. Oct. 26, 1825.
3901. x. JAMES H., b. Aug. 26, 1826; m. Carrie O. Lennon.
3902. xi. DANIEL W., b. Oct. 20, 1828; m. Adelaide R. Finch.
3903. xii. EDWIN R., b. Nov. 27, 1831; m. Maria Bentley.

2574. PALMER[8] PIERCE (*Palmer[7], Timothy[6], Timothy[5], Timothy[4], Thomas[3], Thomas[2], Thomas[1]*), b. July 27, 1787 ; m. Sept. 20, 1810, Anna A. Brewster, b. July 15, 1781, d. July 15, 1868. He d. Oct. 25, 1859. Res. Lebanon, Conn., and North East, Pa. Children :—

3904. i. ELIZA P., b. July 29, 1811; d. 1813.
3905. ii. JOHN L., b. Feb. 7, 1813; m. Cynthia Whitcomb.
3906. iii. ARNOLD Y., b. Feb. 25, 1815; m. Wealthy Austin.
3907. iv. JANE, b. Dec. 9, 1818; m. A. Jones.
3908. v. EARL, b. Dec. 19, 1820; m. Louisa L. Hested.
3909. vi. CAROLINE, b. Mar. 17, 1823; m. F. C. Keeler.

2577. JOHN[8] PIERCE (*Palmer[7], Timothy[6], Timothy[5], Timothy[4], Thomas[3], Thomas[2], Thomas[1]*), b. Oct. 29, 1793 ; m. Oct. 20, 1822, Clarissa Pratt, b. Sept. 19, 1802, d. Aug. 11, 1876. He d. Nov. 16, 1865. Res. ———. Children :—

3910. i. MORDAUNT M., b. Mar. 21, 1827; m. Tarrissa C. Willers.
3911. ii. BRENDA F., b. Oct. 27, 1828; m. Marshall Stewart.
3912. iii. JOHN E., b. Oct. 22, 1830; d. Sept., 1832.
3913. iv. MARY J., b. Mar. 14, 1834; d. Aug. 26, 1847.
3914. v. EUNICE A., b. Feb. 22, 1836.
3915. vi. LYDIA C., b. Apr. 5, 1839; d. Apr. 15, 1842.
3916. vii. MARTHA M., b. Mar. 22, 1842; d. Aug. 20, 1849.
3917. viii. LUCY M., b. Dec. 15, 1844.

2586. Dr. JOHN G.[8] PIERCE (*John L.[7], Timothy[6], Timothy[5], Timothy[4], Thomas[3], Thomas[2], Thomas[1]*), b. Nov. 14, 1802 ; m. June 1, 1840, Sarah A. Babcock. He d. Feb. 11, 1861. Res. Westerly, R. I.

Sarah A. Pierce

Children :—

3918. i. SARAH A., b. Mar. 24, 1841; d. Jan. 28, 1861.
3919. ii. LEVERETT, b. Mar. 2, 1845.
3920. iii. WILLIAM B., b. Dec. 11, 1847; d. June 6, 1849.

2588. SHEPARD[8] PIERCE (*Job[7]*, *Josiah[6]*, *Timothy[5]*, *Timothy[4]*, *Thomas[3]*, *Thomas[2]*, *Thomas[1]*); m. Apr. 27, 1826, Mary E. Pitkin. Res. New York. Children :—

3921. i.   CHARLES; banker on Wall street, N. Y. city.
3922. ii. FRANCES; m. Dr. —— Durrell and Prof. —— Burton.

2590. JOSEPH S.[8] PIERCE (*Job[7]*, *Josiah[6]*, *Timothy[5]*, *Timothy[4]*, *Thomas[3]*, *Thomas[2]*, *Thomas[1]*), b. Apr. 22, 1802 ; m. Apr. 29, 1828, Celina Strong, b. May 6, 1806, d. Apr. 25, 1834 ; m. 2nd, Jan. 1, 1840, Elizabeth Branch, b. Mar. 23, 1814. He d. May 9, 1877. Res. Bellevue, Ohio. Children :—

3923. i.   SARAH C., b. Oct. 24, 1829 ; m. Welcome S. Browning.
3924. ii.   SOPHRONIA, b. Nov. 25, 1840 ; m. Jacob Johnson.
3925. iii. JOHN S., b. Nov. 28, 1842 ; m. Jane A. Auckland.
3926. iv.   SAMUEL B., b. Oct. 18, 1845. Res. Bellevue.
3927. v.   WILLIAM, b. Jan. 25, 1849 ; m. Lucy A. Banta.
3928. vi.   CHARLES S., b. Sept. 8, 1855. Res. Bellevue.

2598. ALFRED B.[8] PIERCE (*Azel[7]*, *Josiah[6]*, *Timothy[5]*, *Timothy[4]*, *Thomas[3]*, *Thomas[2]*, *Thomas[1]*), b. Jan. 22, 1803 ; m. May 25, 1831, Harriet Worthington, b. Dec. 9, 1807. Res. Colchester, Conn. Child :—

3929. i.   INFANT, b. Apr., 1834 ; d. Apr., 1834.

2605. CHESTER[8] PIERCE (*Shepard[7]*, *Josiah[6]*, *Timothy[5]*, *Timothy[4]*, *Thomas[3]*, *Thomas[2]*, *Thomas[1]*), b. Mar. 22, 1815 ; m. Sept. 27, 1843, Harriet S. Lilley, b. June 23, 1821, d. Oct. 9, 1854 ; m. 2nd, Oct. 29, 1855, Charlotte I. Brown, b. Sept. 14, 1824. Res. North Aurora, Ills. Children :—

3930. i.   MAHLON H., b. Sept. 9, 1844 ; m. Mira Kennedy.
3931. ii.   EUGENIA A., b. Dec. 2, 1845 ; m. Oct. 10, 1866, W. H. Carpenter.
           Res. Centerpoint, Ind.
3932. iii. M. ESTELLE, b. June 28, 1847.
3933. iv.   ALFRED L., b. Sept. 28, 1849 ; m. Mary Bowman.
3934. v.   CHESTER L., b. Aug. 11, 1853 ; m. Alice Eisor.

2609. WILLIAM A.[8] PIERCE (*Shepard[7]*, *Josiah[6]*, *Timothy[5]*, *Timothy[4]*, *Thomas[3]*, *Thomas[2]*, *Thomas[1]*), b. May 9, 1822 ; m. Apr. 10, 1844, Anna M. Nagle, b. Aug. 8, 1824, d. Nov. 26, 1861 ; m. 2nd, May 25, 1863, Anna A. Newell, b. Aug. 20, 1840. Res. Myersburg, Pa.

Children :—

3935. i.   SAMUEL N., b. June 28, 1846 ; m. Hattie Wood.
3936. ii.   HENRY N., b. Feb. 18, 1848 ; m. Fannie Hunter.
3937. iii.   WILLIAM A., b. Oct. 8, 1850 ; m. Ruth A. Inscko.
3938. iv.   MARY A., b. July 21, 1864.
3939. v.   GEORGE C., b. Feb. 3, 1866.
3940. vi.   REUBEN B., b. Nov. 23, 1869.
3941. vii.   SARAH E., b. Feb. 28, 1872.
3942. viii. WILLIAM A., b. Aug. 28, 1875.
3943. ix.   WARREN L.

2612. SHEPPARD S.[8] PIERCE (*Shepard*[7], *Josiah*[6], *Timothy*[5], *Tim-othy*[4], *Thomas*[3], *Thomas*[2], *Thomas*[1]), b. Mar. 2, 1828; m. June 16, 1852, Sarah A. Lilley, b. Mar. 3, 1827. Res. Towanda, Penn.

Children:—

3944. i. EARNEST B., b. Jan. 22, 1854; m. Clara Wright.
3945. ii. HATTIE E., b. Jan. 13, 1856; m. Sept. 13, 1872, Earnest Frost; res. Ithaca, New York.
3946. iii. JOHN S., b. Oct. 6, 1862; d. Sept. 22, 1864.

2617. PHINEAS[8] PIERCE (*Willard*[7], *Nathaniel*[6], *Nathaniel*[5], *Tim-othy*[4], *Thomas*[3], *Thomas*[2], *Thomas*[1]), b. July 13, 1787; m. Sept. 30, 1813, Charlotte S. Parkhurst, b. May 2, 1792, d. May 29, 1869. He d. Nov. 15, 1875. They res. in So. Royalton, Vt.

Children:—

3947. i. CHARLOTTE S., b. Oct. 7, 1814; m. Jan. 11, 1848, George W. Bradstreet, d. Feb. 16, 1873, in Royalton. Ch.: George P., b. Dec. 23, 1848; Frank W., b. July 26, 1852.
3948. ii. SUSAN W., b. Oct. 9, 1816; m. June 7, 1842, Horace P. Allen, Ch.: Parkhurst P., b. Apr. 22, 1843, m. E. Maria Geldert.
3949. iii. PHINEAS D., b. Aug. 3, 1818; m. Nov. 29, 1842, Eleanor D. Kibbee.
3950. iv. MARTHA P., b. Jan. 22, 1820; m. Apr. 12, 1842, D. Bryan Cox, d. Sept. 23, 1872. She d. Oct. 1, 1847, and left Fred. B., b. June 3, 1846.
3951. v. PRISCILLA W., b. Apr. 19, 1826; m. Oct. 31, 1855, Silas H. Clark. Ch.: Henry P., b. July 18, 1859, d. Aug. 13, 1875; res. Royalton.
3952. vi. JOHN H., b. Aug. 8, 1829; d. Aug. 20, 1842.
3953. vii. FRANCES C., b. Nov. 10, 1831.
3954. viii. ELLEN A., b. Dec. 8, 1833.

2618. Dr. ALBIGENCE[8] PIERCE (*Willard*[7], *Nathaniel*[6], *Nathan-iel*[5], *Timothy*[4], *Thomas*[3], *Thomas*[2], *Thomas*[1]), b. May 23, 1789; m. June 12, 1813, Lucy Bryant, d. Feb. 26, 1846; m. 2nd, Nov. 15, 1848, Mrs. Louise Bryant, b. 1810, d. Sept. 14, 1850; m. 3rd, Jan. 11, 1855, Mrs. Ruth Hochstrasser, b. 1810, d. Feb. 28, 1857. He d. Nov. 10, 1873, in So. Royalton, Vt. .

Children:—

3955. i. NATHAN W., b. Aug. 30, 1813; m. 1846, Sophia Spaulding.
3956. ii. GEORGE B., b. Aug. 26, 1815; m. May 1, 1850, Adaline E. Duncklee.
3957. iii. ELIZABETH M., b. Oct. 19, 1819; m. Francis Johnson and a Bennett. Ch.: Lucy, m. Henry Van Hooser; Gertrude and Charles; res. So. Norwalk, Ct.

3958.   iv.   ALBIGENCE M., b. Apr. 27, 1823.
3959.   v.   JOHN S., b. Feb. 2, 1828.
3960.   vi.   LUCY E., b. June 27, 1831; m. Jan., 1855, James Moore; res. Scituate.
3961.   viii.   MARIA L., b. July 31, 1850.

2619.   JOHN D.[8] PIERCE (*Willard*[7], *Nathaniel*[6], *Nathaniel*[5], *Timothy*[4], *Thomas*[3], *Thomas*[2], *Thomas*[1]), b. July 14, 1791; m. Nancy Fogg, d. June 22, 1875. He d. Sept. 8, 1872, in Stafford, Vt.
Children :—

3962.   i.   GEORGE, b. May 4, 1827; m. 1856, Sarah Phillips.
3963.   ii.   LUCY A., b. Jan. 1, 1829; m. Ira Morrill, d. 1877.   Ch.: David; Nathan; Fred.; res. Stafford.
3964.   iii.   SUSAN, b. Feb. 6, 1831; d. Mar. 22, 1832.
3965.   iv.   ARTHUR W., b. Jan. 6, 1833; unm.
3966.   v.   SUSAN W., b. Mar. 26, 1836; unm.
3967.   vi.   ARABELLA B., b. Aug. 20, 1838; unm.
3968.   vii.   MARTHA M., b. June 15, 1841; unm.

2623.   DANIEL W.[8] PIERCE (*Willard*[7], *Nathaniel*[6], *Nathaniel*[5], *Timothy*[4], *Thomas*[3], *Thomas*[2], *Thomas*[1]), b. Jan. 20, 1803; m. Dec. 25, 1826. Olive Hutchinson, b. Dec. 25, 1806, d. Feb. 8, 1876. He d. Feb. 28, 1876, in Sharon, Vt.

Daniel W. Pierce

Children :—

3969.   i.   JEANNETTE, b. Nov. 18, 1827; m. George Ames of Warren, Pa.
3970.   ii.   EDGAR, b. Apr. 22, 1830; m. Emma Chapman.
3971.   iii.   HELEN, b. Nov. 22, 1833; d. Feb. 13, 1855.
3972.   iv.   CHARLES, b. Apr. 12, 1845; d. May 28, 1861.

2625.   Dr. CALEB[8] PIERCE (*Bester*[7], *Nathaniel*[6], *Nathaniel*[5], *Timothy*[4], *Thomas*[3], *Thomas*[2], *Thomas*[1]), b. Aug. 6, 1799; m. Feb. 13, 1827, Sarah E. Farnsworth, b. Apr. 23, 1807, d. Jan. 1, 1865. Res. Madrid, N. Y.
He was born in the State of Vermont in the year 1799. Is a physician practicing his profession at Madrid, New York. Was graduated at Dartmouth College, New Hampshire.
Children :—

3973.   i.   WILLIAM C., b. Feb. 22, 1828; m. Harriet C. Reddington.
3974.   ii.   JAMES F., b. Apr. 8, 1830; m. Anna Reddington.
3975.   iii.   HENRY C., b. Mar. 6, 1833; d. Sept. 16, 1854.
3976.   iv.   JOHN H., b. Aug. 6, 1835; d. Sept. 6, 1850.
3977.   v.   HARRIET, b. Sept. 6, 1838; d. Jan. 4, 1841.
3978.   vi.   GEORGE T., b. Apr. 3, 1843; d. May 18, 1843.

2626.   COLLINS[8] PIERCE (*Bester*[7], *Nathaniel*[6], *Nathaniel*[5], *Timothy*[4], *Thomas*[3], *Thomas*[2], *Thomas*[1]), b. 1801; m. Mrs. Sabrina

[2625. The following sketch of the life of Dr. Caleb Pierce of Madrid, New York, was received too late for publication in its proper place, and is therefore inserted here].

In the front rank of the honorable profession of medicine in St. Lawrence County, New York, he of whom we write has for many years occupied a prominent and honorable position, and deservedly and justly so. Winning this place by skill and erudition, he has maintained it well in the general estimation of his fellow-citizens.

Dr. Caleb Pierce is the first son of Bester Pierce and grandson of Nathaniel Pierce, of Plainfield, Conn., the family being of English descent, and claiming ancestry among the Percys of Northumberland. The first wife of Bester Pierce was a daughter of Eden Burroughs and was the mother of Caleb, Collins R., Minerva, and Laura Pierce. She died April 4th, 1813. About the year 1816 Bester Pierce married Margaret McChesney, a native of the State of New York, who bore to him two sons, John and Robert. The only surviving children of both unions are Caleb, John, and Robert. Dr. Caleb Pierce was born in Royalton, Vt., August 6th, 1800, and at the age of six years came with his father and family to St. Lawrence County, and settled in Potsdam. He was reared as a farmer, and attended the common district schools until the opening of St. Lawrence Academy, when he entered that institution, and pursued its course of studies for three years.

At the age of nineteen he evinced a strong desire to prepare himself for the practice of the medical profession, but owing to the limited circumstances in which his father was placed, no assistance beyond a mere pittance could be awarded from that source. The young man, however, was undaunted, and had the courage and will sufficient to face even poverty in the struggle to accomplish his cherished desire. He therefore went to Lebanon, N. H., and began the study of medicine with Dr. Phineas Parkhurst and Prof. R. D. Muzzy, members of the Faculty of Dartmouth College. During his stay with these gentlemen he attended three full courses of medical lectures, and received a diploma as a doctor of medicine in the fall of 1822, and also a diploma from the Vermont State Medical Society. In the year 1823 Dr. Pierce settled in Madrid for the practice of his profession. Here for a few years the shades, as well as a few of the lights, of the practice of medicine in a new country fell on his pathway. Though he was struggling with poverty, and money was hard to get to replenish the soon depleted stock of medicines, yet he never refused to attend the calls of his chosen profession, though they came from those unable to pay even for the necessaries that made them whole. Rich and poor were alike served well, and his ministrations to those engaged in the sister profession of the Gospel have ever been gratuitously supplied, whatever their doctrines or creeds. Soon after his arrival in Madrid he connected himself with the St. Lawrence Medical Society, of which he is still a member, receiving from that society in 1821 its certificate of authority to practice his profession. He has been the President and Vice-President, and repeatedly one of the censors of the society; and has also a diploma of honorary membership from the Castleton Medical College of Vermont, granted in 1848. He received also in 1871 the honorary degree of M. D. from Dartmouth College. He has represented the County society many times in the State medical society as a delegate to its annual meetings. Thus was he thrown into the circle of cultivated and enlarged minds at a period in his life when his enthusiasm was enlisted in an honorable pursuit; and the influences then surrounding him so moulded and directed the student that the practitioner of later years felt and acknowledged their power and benefit.

At the age of twenty-five years he married an estimable lady, Miss Sarah, daughter of General James Farnsworth of Fairfax, Franklin County, Vt. She was a woman of no ordinary ability; and possessed of a finely cultivated mind, and ever-willing heart to lend a helping hand to those in distress. As a wife and mother she performed her duties and obligations with a scrupulous regard for right, but always full of sympathy for the poor and afflicted, a well-chosen mate for her husband, who reciprocated her generosity and charities. Her religious belief was in consonance with her early training, coupled with her own logical deductions. She was an active member of the Congregational Church of Madrid for many years. To Dr. and Mrs. Pierce six children have been given: William Cornelius, James Farnsworth, Henry Clark, John Horton, Harriet Melinda, and Granville S., of whom James F. alone survives.

In politics Dr. Pierce has been a life-long Democrat of the Jacksonian school; always active in public affairs, but never soliciting office nor neglecting professional business for political preferment.

As a physician of over half a century's practice in the County of St. Lawrence, he has met with great success, and from bare-handed circumstances has by prudence and economy, gathered to himself a sufficiency of this world's goods to give him comfort and ease to his declining days.

Tiffany, b. 1803, d. June 28, 1857. He d. ———. Res. Madrid, N. Y.
Children :—

3979. i. DARWIN C., b. June 16, 1838; m. Anna M. Robinson.
3980. ii. LIZZIE E., b. Sept. 18, 1843; d. Sept. 18, 1860.

2629. JOHN[8] PIERCE (*Bester*[7], *Nathaniel*[6], *Nathaniel*[5], *Timothy*[4], *Thomas*[3], *Thomas*[2], *Thomas*[1]), b. Sept. 30, 1820 ; m. July 8, 1852, Marcia C. Hoyt, b. Mar. 17, 1827. Res. Potsdam, N. Y.
Children :—

3981. i. JOHN, b. Dec. 20, 1853; d. Aug. 15, 1854.
3982. ii. HERBERT I., b. Dec. 27, 1855.
3983. iii. HENRY C., b. July 9, 1859.
3984. iv. HELEN J., b. June 8, 1864.

2630. ROBERT[8] PIERCE (*Bester*[7], *Nathaniel*[6], *Nathaniel*[5], *Timothy*[4], *Thomas*[3], *Thomas*[2], *Thomas*[1]), b. June 18, 1821 ; m. June 4, 1843, Mary Rugg, b. June 10, 1822. Res. Potsdam, N. Y.

Children :—

3985. i. MINERVA, b. Mar. 8, 1844; m. John Gage.
3986. ii. LUCY A., b. Dec. 15, 1845; d. May 18, 1875.
3987. iii. LAURA, b. Feb. 1, 1848; m. John Robinson.
3988. iv. FRANKLIN B., b. May 8, 1852; d. Apr. 1, 1868.
3989. v. HENRY R., b. Apr. 24, 1859; d. July 29, 1879.

2634. HORACE[8] PIERCE (*Isaac*[7], *Nathaniel*[6], *Nathaniel*[5], *Timothy*[4], *Thomas*[3], *Thomas*[2], *Thomas*[1]), b. June 8, 1805 ; m. Feb. 17, 1836, Maria Cooley, b. Nov. 30, 1805. He d. May 20, 1877. She res. in Barton, Vt.

Children :—

3990. i. CHARLES H., b. Apr. 27, 1838; d. June 13, 1841.
3991. ii. JULIA, b. June 15, 1840; m. Dec. 9, 1862, Rinaldo A. Barker.
    Ch. : Julia M., b. May 15, 1865; Ellen M., b. Sept. 30, 1867; res. Chicago, Ill.
3992. iii. MARY A., b. June 6, 1842; d. Mar. 18, 1844.
3993. iv. FRANCES M., b. July 21, 1844; d. July 24, 1846.
3994. v. SUSAN H., b. Nov. 21, 1846; m. Oct. 27, 1867, Solon C. Currier.
    Ch. : Marion M., b. Apr. 7, 1869; Florence L., b. Aug. 21, 1875; res. Barton, Vt.
3995. vi. HORACE C., b. Oct. 14, 1850; m. Sept. 9, 1874, Althea L. Dalton; no issue; res. Barton.

2635. John S.[8] Pierce (*Isaac*[7], *Nathaniel*[6], *Nathaniel*[5], *Timothy*[4], *Thomas*[3], *Thomas*[2], *Thomas*[1]), b. Mar. 6, 1807; m. Feb. 10, 1836, Julia Huntington, b. Oct. 4, 1809. He d. Apr., 1879. They resided at 28 Somerset street, Boston. Children :—

3996. i. Henry H., b. Nov. 17, 1836; d. May 5, 1864.
3997. ii. Sidney C., b. Sept. 21, 1843; m. Nov. 6, 1866, Sarah V. White.

2644. Seth[8] Pierce (*Joseph*[7], *Jedediah*[6], *Nathaniel*[5], *Timothy*[4], *Thomas*[3], *Thomas*[2], *Thomas*[1]), b. Oct. 19, 1796; m. Dec. 25, 1826, Sarah Shepard, b. Jan. 23, 1806, d. May 26, 1852; m. 2nd, Apr. 19, 1853, Ellen M. Eaton ; m. 3rd, Nov. 11, 1858, Mrs. Catherine Doyle. Res. Lockport, N. Y. Children :—

3998. i. Sarah C., b. July 15, 1828; m. Sept. 29, 1847, Marvin H. Webber. Ch: Martha C., b. June 28, 1848, d. July 7, 1848; Frederick W., b. Sept. 5, 1849; Emma Kate, b. Nov. 9, 1851, d. March 12, 1852; Carrie Emiline, b. Feb. 12, 1854; Sarah Elizabeth, b. Feb. 18, 1856, d. March 12, 1860; Hortense Valean, b. Feb. 20, 1862; Charles Wadsworth, b. Aug. 11, 1864.
3999. ii. Harriet S., b. Jan. 4, 1831; m. Oct. 6, 1852, Alfred M. Leonard, b. Nov. 11, 1821. Ch.: Frank P., b. July 10, 1853; Willie C., b. March 12, 1855; Ada F., b. June 9, 1858; Fred., b. Jan. 22, 1862, d. Apr. 9, 1866; Mark, b. Nov. 27, 1866.
4000. iii. Joseph S., b. July 10, 1838; m. Matilda Weaver.
4001. iv. Frederic C., b. Oct. 15, 1842. Went to the war and never returned.
4002. v. Frank, b. Sept. 5, 1859.
4003. vi. Albert, b. Nov. 7, 1861.

2649. John[8] Pierce (*Joseph*[7], *Jedediah*[6], *Nathaniel*[5], *Timothy*[4], *Thomas*[3], *Thomas*[2], *Thomas*[1]), b. Apr. 10, 1806; m. May 18, 1841, Margaret Watson, b. July 3, 1825. He d. Jan. 10, 1874. Res. Lockport, N. Y. Children :—

4004. i. Jane F., b. July 20, 1843; m. Sept. 6, 1866, James Cobb.
4005. ii. Susan, b. Dec. 25, 1846; d. June 29, 1848.
4006. iii. Harriet R., b. Jan. 25, 1849; d. June 11, 1851.
4007. iv. Eliza A., b. Aug. 29, 1851; m. Dec. 24, 1867, Albert V. Gould.
4008. v. Margaret, b. May 22, 1854; d. July 18, 1854.
4009. vi. John E., b. Dec. 14, 1855; d. Nov. 10, 1861.
4010. vii. Sally A., b. July 7, 1858; m. Sept. 27, 1873, George Allen.
4011. viii. George W., b. Apr. 28, 1861; d. May 14, 1863.
4012. ix. Charles E., b. Feb. 8, 1863.

2653. William[8] Pierce, Jr. (*William*[7], *Jedediah*[6], *Nathaniel*[5], *Timothy*[4], *Thomas*[3], *Thomas*[2], *Thomas*[1]), b. Apr. 15, 1801; m. Nov. 7, 1833, Orpha B. Pierce [2668], d. May 8, 1839 ; m. 2nd, May 22, 1840, Hannah Brockway, b. Nov. 7, 1819. They res. in Royalton, Vt.

William Pierce

Children :—

4013-4. i. Louis A., b. Aug. 1, 1834; m. May 18, 1861, Mary A. Bronson.
4015. ii. Charles, b. June 14, 1837; m. Nancy A. Winslow.
4016. iii. Perry F., b. Apr. 17, 1841; d. May 1, 1863.
4017. iv. Harriet B., b. Aug. 22, 1842; m. Aug. 6, 1863, Nelson M. Grant, b. May 7, 1840. Ch.: Minnie J., b. Oct. 25, 1865; Fred. P., b. Nov. 8, 1872. Res. Stockbridge, Vt.

4018. v. WILLIAM L., b. June 14, 1846; m. Ella L. Winslow.
4019. vi. ORPHA B., b. Jan. 14, 1849; m. Dec. 31, 1873, Edwin Bent, b. Sept. 13, 1846; no issue. Res. Stockbridge, Vt.
4020. vii. ESTHER E., b. Dec. 5, 1852; m. Ezra S. Burnham.
4021. viii. JENNIE L., b. May 18, 1854.
4022. ix. ELNORA, b. Feb. 14, 1856; m. May 15, 1876, Alva Learned, b. Sept. 14, 1850; no. issue. Res. Stockbridge, Vt.

2654. BESTER[8] PIERCE (*William[7], Jedediah[6], Nathaniel[5], Timothy[4], Thomas[3], Thomas[2], Thomas[1]*), b. Jan. 20, 1803 ; m. June 13, 1839, Sarah A. Shepard, b. Mar. 5, 1811, d. Mar. 21, 1879. They res. De Kalb, Ill.

BESTER PIERCE was born in Royalton, Vt., where he spent the first fifty-two years of his life and never was away from home for the length of a year. In 1855 he sold his property and removed with his family, consisting of his wife and four children, to what was then the small village of De Kalb, De Kalb Co., Ill. The country was then very sparsely settled, not a building to be seen, but a few in the village, for miles.

Children :—

4023. i. JOSEPHINE I., b. Aug. 12, 1840; m. Mar. 30, 1858, Fred'k C. Skeales, b. Feb. 3, 1836. She d. Jan. 12, 1874. Ch.: Kendrick, b. July 29, 1866, d. Apr. 14, 1867; Charles, b. Mar. 10, 1868, d. Aug. 10, 1868.
4024. ii. WASHINGTON F., b. Feb. 23, 1843; m. Dec. 23, 1866, Louisa A. Shumway.
4025. iii. ANDREW J., b. Mar. 23, 1845; d. Feb. 4, 1863.
4026. iv. MARY E., b. Feb. 13, 1848; m. Jan. 7, 1874, Zachary T. Wheeler, b. Oct. 6, 1848. She d. childless, Sept. 25, 1877.

2655. IRA[8] PIERCE (*William[7], Jedediah[6], Nathaniel[5], Timothy[4], Thomas[3], Thomas[2], Thomas[1]*), b. Jan. 20, 1805 ; m. Oct. 25, 1832, Emily Sheppard, b. Feb. 19, 1809, d. March, 1874 ; m. 2nd, April 27, 1874, Hannah J. Ashley, b. Feb. 25, 1820. He d. June 22, 1879. Res. So. Royalton, Vt.

Children :—

4027. i. HENRY, b. Jan. 16, 1834; m. Mary Remick.
4028. ii. DESIRE E., b. May 1, 1838; m. Charles A. Slack. Res. Norwich, Vt.

2657. LEVI W.[8] PIERCE (*William[7], Jedediah[6], Nathaniel[5], Timothy[4], Thomas[3], Thomas[2], Thomas[1]*), b. June 14, 1808 ; m. Mar. 10,

1835, Maria Berndock, b. 1813, d. March, 1845 ; m. 2nd, Mar. 1, 1854, Celia Munson, b. Aug. 12, 1820. Res. New York. Children :—

4029. i.   HARRIET B., b. Jan. 18, 1837; m. Joseph Patterson.
4030. ii.   SARAH; d. young.
4031. iii. GEORGE W.; d. young.
4032. iv.   ——; d. young.
4033. v.   ——; d. young.
4034. vi.   CHARLES M., b. Nov. 2, 1854.

2660. CHARLES[8] PIERCE (*William[7], Jedediah[6], Nathaniel[5], Timothy[4], Thomas[3], Thomas[2], Thomas[1]*), b. April 20, 1814 ; m. July, 1873, Mary A. Griffith. He. d. Feb. 28, 1874. No children. She m. 2nd, —— Grimley.

2661. HENRY B.[8] PIERCE (*William[7], Jedediah[6], Nathaniel[5], Timothy[4], Thomas[3], Thomas[2], Thomas[1]*), b. Oct. 6, 1816 ; m. March 22, 1838, Abigail M. Parish, b. Sept. 6, 1817. They res. in So. Barre, Vt. Children :—

4035. i.   HARRY B., b. Oct. 8, 1839; d. Nov. 1, 1839.
4036. ii.   PARISH, b. May 29, 1841; d. Aug. 12, 1847.
4037. iii. ARTHUR L., b. Oct. 2, 1843; m. Dec. 6, 1871, Sarah J. Peyton.
4038. iv.   HARRY, b. Sept. 16, 1845; d. Aug. 10, 1847.
4039. v.   HARRY P., b, Jan. 29, 1848; m. May 19, 1872, Abbie M. Hitchcock.
4040. vi.   WALTER W., b. Jan. 21, 1850.
4041. vii. ABBIE P., b. Feb. 12, 1852; m. Feb. 22, 1876, Herbert O. Camp, b. June 16, 1851 ; no issue. Res. Barre, Vt.
4042. viii. AGNES A., b. Apr. 4, 1855; m. Apr. 24, 1876, Edwin A. Waldron, b. Apr. 9, 1851 ; no issue. Res. 642 Union-St., Manchester, N. H.
4043. ix.   GEORGE F., b. Apr. 20, 1858.

2663. CHESTER[8] PIERCE (*William[7], Jedediah[6], Nathaniel[5], Timothy[4], Thomas[3], Thomas[2], Thomas[1]*), b. Jan. 2, 1819 ; m. Oct. 26, 1842, Caroline R. Briggs, b. June 24, 1822, d. Mar. 1, 1869. They res. in Rochester, Vt.

Child :—

4044. i.   EDWARD L., b. July 26, 1843 ; m. Oct. 24, 1871, Julia A. Ashley.

2664. EDWIN[8] PIERCE (*Elisha[7], Jedediah[6], Nathaniel[5], Timothy[4], Thomas[3], Thomas[2], Thomas[1]*), b. Oct. 27, 1800 ; m. Jan. 25, 1827, Susan H. Kimball, b. Aug. 1, 1805. He d. Mar. 28, 1873, in Royalton, Vt. Children :—

4045. i.   STEPHEN H., b. Oct. 26, 1827; m. Jan. 1, 1854, Nancy M. Holmes.
4046. ii.   MARY M., b. Aug. 14, 1830; m. Oct. 16, 1853, Joseph W. Bailey, b. July 19, 1829. Ch.: Lulu E., b. May 24, 1866. Res. Royalton, Vt.
4047. iii. GEORGE W., b. Aug. 21, 1836; d. Sept. 27, 1866.

2669. ARCHIBALD T.[8] PIERCE (*Elisha*[7], *Jedediah*[6], *Nathaniel*[5], *Timothy*[4], *Thomas*[3], *Thomas*[2], *Thomas*[1]), b. Jan. 6, 1811 ; m. Feb. 9, 1837, Harriet M. Baker, d. April 26, 1859 ; m. 2nd, June 2, 1862, Sarah D. White. Res. White River Junction, Vt. Children :—

4048. i. SIDNEY E., b. May 9, 1838; m. Mary B. Kimball.
4049. ii. ELLA A., b. June 7, 1840; m. Geo. W. Holmes.
4050. iii. ADA M., b. June 16, 1842.
4051. iv. WRIGHT G., b. July 22, 1844.
4052. v. ALMA H., b. May 26, 1847.
4053. vi. ARTHUR L., b. Sept. 7, 1850.
4054. vii. HATTIE A., b. Aug. 27, 1857.

2671. EBENEZER F.[8] PIERCE (*Ebenezer*[7], *Jedediah*[6], *Nathaniel*[5], *Timothy*[4], *Thomas*[3], *Thomas*[2], *Thomas*[1]), b. Oct. 16, 1805 ; m. Nov. 1, 1841, Betsey J. Luce, b. 1823, d. July 4, 1859. Res. Royalton, Vt.

Children :—

4055. i. MARY J., b. Sept. 24, 1844; m. June 25, 1877, Lyman A. Peck. Res. Royalton, Vt.
4056. ii. LEVI L., b. March 7, 1847; m. Sarah Doyle.
4057. iii. FRANKLIN E., b. June 20, 1852; m. Addie J. Woodward.
4058. iv. ELBRIDGE I., b. May 9, 1854; m. Josephine Waldo.
4059. v. LUCY ANN, b. April 13, 1855.

2672. HOSEA[8] PIERCE (*Ebenezer*[7], *Jedediah*[6], *Nathaniel*[5], *Timothy*[4], *Thomas*[3], *Thomas*[2], *Thomas*[1]), b. April 26, 1808 ; m. Mar. 18, 1834, Charity Russell. Went West—nothing heard of him for some years.

2673. HIRAM[8] PIERCE (*Ebenezer*[7], *Jedediah*[6], *Nathaniel*[5], *Timothy*[4], *Thomas*[3], *Thomas*[2], *Thomas*[1]), b. April 12, 1816 ; m. May 4, 1848, Martha A. Mason, b. April 22, 1826. Res. Greenville, Ala. Children :—

4060. i. FRANCES M., b. July 14, 1849.
4061. ii. THOMAS A., b. March 21, 1852; d. Jan. 29, 1853.
4062. iii. WILLIAM, b. March 28, 1854.
4063. iv. MARY L., b. Feb. 1, 1856; m. —— Windham. Res. Hope Hull, Ala.
4064. v. ELLEN A., b. Jan. 25, 1859.
4065. vi. HENRY C., b. May 13, 1862. Res. Hope Hull, Ala.

32

2679. DAVID[8] PIERCE (*Benjamin*[7], *Nehemiah*[6], *Benjamin*[5], *Timothy*[4], *Thomas*[3], *Thomas*[2], *Thomas*[1]), b. Nov. 5, 1787 ; m. May 15, 1832, Elizabeth Allin, daughter of Capt. Daniel Allin, of Pomfret, Conn., formerly of Providence, R. I., b. March 6, 1802. He d. June 6, 1874. Res. Castile, N. Y. Children :—

4066. i. GEORGE G., b. Nov. 2, 1834; d. June 30, 1864. Hon. George G. Pierce at 21 years of age emigrated to Kansas to practice surveying. It was at the time of the Border Ruffian War there, and he being a strong anti-slavery man was obliged to leave Leavenworth and go to Nebraska for a time until the excitement was allayed a little; he then returned and helped to make Kansas a free State, and was twice chosen to the Territorial Legislature. He enlisted in the union army against the rebellion, and died June 30, 1864, of wounds received before Petersburg. He is buried at Arlington, D. C. In an article written by Senator Lane at the time, he says :

"I learn that the Hon. George G. Pierce who represented this district in the Territorial Legislature for two years is dead. He died in a hospital at Washington, D. C., of wounds received before Petersburg. George G. Pierce was a good man: his friends loved him, his enemies respected him. Of an indomitable and persevering spirit, sanguine temperament, and a fervent enthusiast in the cause of liberty, no obstacle was too great for him to overcome, no path too rugged for him to climb, no night too cold, too dark or too stormy for him to labor; and recognizing these qualities while he was among us, the friends of freedom in North-Western Kansas proudly acknowledge him their first successful champion. Sacred is his memory. He sleeps the sleep of the brave; he rests like an American upon the bosom of his country for which he gave his life that she might live."

4067. ii. ABBY A., b. May 1, 1839 ; d. Oct. 7, 1839.
4068. iii. EDWARD A., b. Jan. 12, 1841 ; m. Jane Lynch.

2681. HENRY[8] PIERCE (*Benjamin*[7], *Nehemiah*[6], *Benjamin*[5], *Timothy*[4], *Thomas*[3], *Thomas*[2], *Thomas*[1]), b. Apr. 14, 1791 ; m. Sept. 2, 1817, Lucia Cleveland, b. Mar. 8, 1797, d. Jan. 9, 1832 ; m. 2nd, May 2, 1833, Mrs. J. Stowe, b. Jan. 29, 1801, d. Jan. 3, 1874. He d. Sept. 3, 1847. Res. Livonia, N. Y.

H. Pierce

Children :—

4069. i. LUCIA A., b. Mar. 24, 1834.
4070. ii. HENRY S., b. Apr. 25, 1836.
4071. iii. EDWARD L., b. June 17, 1838.
4072. iv. FANNY W., b. July 31, 1840.

2684. GEORGE F.[8] PIERCE (*Benjamin*[7], *Nehemiah*[6], *Benjamin*[5], *Timothy*[4], *Thomas*[3], *Thomas*[2], *Thomas*[1]), b. Apr. 14, 1802 ; m. Oct. 10, 1844, Mary A. Ashley, b. Aug. 25, 1812. He d. Sept. 5, 1872. Res. Castile, N. Y. Children :—

4073. i. MARIETTA E., b. Dec. 22, 1845.
4074. ii. HENRY A., b. Oct. 1, 1847.

2685. CHARLES P.[8] PIERCE (*Benjamin[7], Nehemiah[6], Benjamin[5], Timothy[4], Thomas[3], Thomas[2], Thomas[1]*), b. Apr. 14, 1802 ; m. Feb. 29, 1832, Elizabeth Fowler, b. 1813, d. Apr. 24, 1837. He d. Sept. 2, 1851. Res. Castile, N. Y. Children :—

4075. i. CHARLES F., b. Jan., 1833; d. Sept. 14, 1844.
4076. ii. MARIETTA, b. 1837; d. Jan. 9, 1840.

2687. JACOB G.[8] PIERCE (*Benjamin[7], Nehemiah[6], Benjamin[5], Timothy[4], Thomas[3], Thomas[2], Thomas[1]*), b. Dec. 8, 1806 ; m. Sept. 20, 1836, Fanny W. Bliss, b. Aug., 1817, d. July 5, 1842 ; m. 2nd, May 6, 1845, Emily S. Hall. Res. Grinnell, Iowa. Children :—

4077. i. JACOB, b. Apr. 6, 1837 ; d. Apr. 7, 1838.
4078. ii. ELIZABETH E., b. Sept. 20, 1840 ; d. Aug. 19, 1841.
4079. iii. CHARLES F., b. July 12, 1850.
4080. iv. ALICE L., b. Sept. 17, 1855.

2694. NEHEMIAH N.[8] PIERCE (*Frederick[7], Nehemiah[6], Benjamin[5], Timothy[4], Thomas[3], Thomas[2], Thomas[1]*), b. Oct. 25, 1818 ; m. Jan. 8, 1861, Emily W. Pullman, b. Sept. 8, 1834. Res. Bridgewater, N. Y.

Nehemiah Nathaniel Pierce

Child :—

4081. i. FREDERICK P., b. Sept. 11, 1864.

2695. OLIVER W.[8] PIERCE (*Nehemiah[7], Nehemiah[6], Benjamin[5], Timothy[4], Thomas[3], Thomas[2], Thomas[1]*), b. Apr. 2, 1795 ; m. Jan. 20, 1826, Rebecca Carlton, b. Sept. 26, 1801, d. Mar. 27, 1854 ; m. 2nd, Nov. 10, 1855, Mrs. Delia Morris, b. Mar. 25, 1805. He d. Jan. 19, 1871. Res. Monmouth, Me.

Oliver W. Pierce

Children :—

4081¼. i. LUCY A. H., b. Aug. 25, 1827 ; d. June 2, 1851.
4082. ii. HENRY O., b. Feb. 7, 1830 ; m. Martha C. Storr.
4083. iii. REBECCA C., b. July 7, 1831 ; d. Feb. 17, 1833.
4084. iv. HARRIET M., b. Sept. 30, 1832 ; d. Feb. 11, 1853.
4085. v. REBECCA C., b. May 11, 1834 ; d. June 17, 1860.
4086. vi. JOSEPH A., b. Sept. 1, 1837 ; d. July 14, 1840.
4087. vii. JOSEPH A., b. Sept. 11, 1840 ; d. Apr. 26, 1865.

2696. BELA[8] PIERCE (*Nehemiah[7], Nehemiah[6], Benjamin[5], Timothy[4], Thomas[3], Thomas[2], Thomas[1]*), b. Jan. 2, 1797; m. Mar. 27, 1822, Elizabeth Wilcox, b. May 8, 1799. They res. in Wales, Me.

Bela Pierce

Children :—

4088. i. CLARISSA W., b. Feb. 7, 1823; m. June 8, 1847, William L. Small, b. Oct. 29, 1819. Ch.: Charles W., b. Apr. 15, 1848; Chester W., b. Dec. 17, 1851; Fred. W., b. Apr. 27, 1854; Edward P., b. Dec. 6, 1870; res. Fayette, Me.
4089. ii. CHARLES H., b. July 8, 1824; m. Nov. 12, 1863, Sarah M. Sprague.
4090. iii. ELIZABETH M., b. Feb. 18, 1827; d. Sept. 15, 1831.
4091. iv. WILLIAM, b. Apr. 1, 1830; m. Aug. 1, 1865, Jane Barron and Lena C. Allen.
4092. v. ELIZABETH, b. Aug. 20, 1832; d. May 21, 1864.
4093. vi. EDWARD P., b. Oct. 7, 1834; m. June 5, 1873, Nellie F. Kenney.
4094. vii. ANN M., b. Mar. 17, 1836; m. Nov. 30, 1871, Thos. H. Sprague, b. Jan. 29, 1838. Ch.: Edward B., b. Dec. 20, 1872; Alice P., b. Jan. 11, 1874; res. Topsham, Me.
4095. viii. MERIBAH T., b. Feb. 8, 1840.

2697. JESSE[8] PIERCE (*Nehemiah[7], Nehemiah[6], Benjamin[5], Timothy[4], Thomas[3], Thomas[2], Thomas[1]*), b. Dec. 4, 1798; m. Oct. 22, 1822, Catherine Johnson, b. Oct. 31, 1803. He d. Apr. 13, 1842. Res. No. Andover. Children :—

4096. i. JESSE A., b. Aug. 31, 1824; d. at Andover, 1844.
4097. ii. CATHERINE J., b. Sept. 23, 1825; d. Mar. 19, 1849.
4098. iii. JOHN M., b. Apr. 10, 1826; res. Albany, N. Y.
4099. iv. SAMUEL, b. June 12, 1832; d. Mar. 13, 1833.
4100. v. MARTHA A., b. Mar. 2, 1830; m. L. P. Merriam; res. London, Eng.
4101. vi. HARRIET F., b. Dec. 29, 1833; m. C. A. Brown; res. Portland, Me.
4102. vii. MASSY E., b. July 21, 1836; m. G. H. Clarke; res. Brooklyn, N. Y.
4103. viii. GEORGE W., b. Jan. 14, 1840; m. June 7, 1866, Isabell Scovel.

2700. Dr. JOHN[8] PIERCE (*Nehemiah[7], Nehemiah[6], Benjamin[5], Timothy[4], Thomas[3], Thomas[2], Thomas[1]*), b. Nov. 25, 1805; m. Nov. 2, 1840, Chloe McLellan, b. Aug. 31, 1816. Res. Edgartown, Mass.

J. Pierce

Children :—

4104. i. CLARISSA, b. 1844; d.———.
4105. ii. JOHN N., b. Apr. 7, 1851.
        John Nehemiah Pierce is a graduate of Wesleyan University, Middletown, Conn., degree A. M., and studying law.
4106. iii. FRANKLIN W., b. Sept. 11, 1852.
        Franklin W. Pierce, B. A., is a graduate of Yale, New Haven, Conn.

2701. DANIEL[8] PIERCE (*Nehemiah[7]*, *Nehemiah[6]*, *Benjamin[5]*, *Timothy[4]*, *Thomas[3]*, *Thomas[2]*, *Thomas[1]*), b. Apr. 5, 1808 ; m. Apr. 18, 1833, Caroline Shorey, b. Apr. 3, 1811. They res. in Monmouth, Me. Children :—

4107. i. GEORGE B., b. Feb. 27, 1834; m. Apr. 26, 1860, Mary A. Kingsbury.
4108. ii. FRANCES C., b. June 6, 1836; m. Aug. 19, 1863, H. M. Blake, A. M., M. D., b. Nov. 29, 1836. Ch.: Fredk., b. Oct. 17, 1868; res. Monmouth, Me.
4109. iii. JOHN E., b. Sept. 22, 1838; m. July 8, 1868, Lizzie A. Grey.
4110. iv. MARIA A., b. June 19, 1841.
4111. v. MARY J., b. July 18, 1843; m. Feb. 20, 1870, Moses B. Sylvester, b. Sept. 16, 1842; res. Wayne, Me.
4112. vi. DANIEL O., b. Sept. 28, 1845; m. Ida N. Williams.
4113. vii. ELLEN A., b. Nov. 7, 1857; d. Sept. 9, 1880.

2712. ELIAS D.[8] PIERCE (*Elias[7]*, *Delano[6]*, *Benjamin[5]*, *Timothy[4]*, *Thomas[3]*, *Thomas[2]*, *Thomas[1]*), b. Jan. 4, 1815 ; m. Sept. 19, 1836, Mary A. Blood, b. Sept. 23, 1817. He d. Feb. 14, 1872, in Lowell. Child :—

4114. ABBIE A., b. Apr. 27, 1839 ; m. May 23, 1857, Otis A. Coburn, b. Aug. 4, 1837. Ch.: Charles A., b. Mar. 6, 1858, d. Sept. 14, 1858; Mary A., b. July 10, 1859; Lizzie A., b. Aug. 4, 1861, d. Aug. 19, 1863; Nellie A., b. June 21, 1864; Carrie, b. Jan. 10, 1873, d. Mar. 12, 1873 ; Henry S., b. Aug. 17, 1875; res. Lowell.

2715. S. PUTNAM[8] PIERCE (*Payson G.[7]*, *Timeus[6]*, *Benjamin[5]*, *Timothy[4]*, *Thomas[3]*, *Thomas[2]*, *Thomas[1]*), b. Aug. 25, 1811 ; m. May 17, 1832, Cornelia Andrews, b. Jan. 31, 1813, d. July 7, 1842 ; m. 2nd, Nov. 23, 1842, Sarah E. Brown, b. July 18, 1810. Res. Norwich, N. Y. Children :—

4115. i. FRANCES M. ; d. in infancy.
4116. ii. SARAH C., b. June 11, 1835 ; d. Feb. 27, 1854.
4117. iii. WILLIAM W.; d. in infancy.
4118. iv. MARY E., b. Aug. 12, 1839 ; m. S. F. Schell.
4119. v. HENRY A., b. July 2, 1842 ; d. Feb. 8, 1865.

2719. GEORGE W.[8] PIERCE (*Payson G.[7]*, *Timeus[6]*, *Benjamin[5]*, *Timothy[4]*, *Thomas[3]*, *Thomas[2]*, *Thomas[1]*), b. Nov. 8, 1825 ; m. Mar. 7, 1856, Melissa A. Sexton, b. Dec. 22, 1831. Res. Rome, Pa. Children :—

4120. i. EDWARD P., b. Nov. 7, 1858.
4121. ii. WILLIS H., b. Sept. 16, 1862.
4122. iii. MARY J., b. Nov. 16, 1871 ; d. Aug. 23, 1875.

2720. JONAS[8] PIERCE (*Jonas[7]*, *Jonas[6]*, *Oliver[5]*, *Stephen[4]*, *Stephen[3]*, *Thomas[2]*, *Thomas[1]*), b. 1807 ; m. Elizabeth Patch. He d. May 16, 1839. Res. E. Chelmsford. Child :—

4123. i. JONAS V., b. 1839; d. June 21, 1863.

2722. RICHARD[8] PIERCE (*Richard W.[7]*, *Jonathan[6]*, *Oliver[5]*, *Stephen[4]*, *Stephen[3]*, *Thomas[2]*, *Thomas[1]*), b. Nov. 2, 1805 ; m. June 16, 1831, Mary A. Hartwell, b. Oct. 1, 1811. Res. Pepperell, Mass.

Richard Pierce

Children :—

4124. i.   HARRIET A., b. Oct. 1, 1833; m. Nov. 30, 1854, George C. Lewis, of Pepperell. Ch.: Charles A., b. Apr. 16, 1859.
4125. ii.   SARAH A., b. Sept. 26, 1840; m. Dec. 13, 1860, George T. Fletcher, of Hollis, N. H. He d. Oct. 29, 1879. Ch.: Anna A., b. Apr. 8, 1865, d. Apr. 13, 1874; William, b. Jan. 12, 1877, d. Oct. 17, 1877.

2727.   JONATHAN[8] PIERCE (*Richard W.*[7], *Jonathan*[6], *Oliver*[5], *Stephen*[4], *Stephen*[3], *Thomas*[2], *Thomas*[1]), b. Oct. 17, 1815; m. Dec. 28, 1837, Abigail Turner, b. Jan. 5, 1817, d. Dec. 19, 1858; m. 2nd, Apr. 22, 1859, Sophia Hills, b. March 6, 1819. Res. Townsend Harbor, Mass.

He was born in Townsend, Middlesex Co., Mass., Oct. 17, 1815. His father was a farmer, as was his grandfather before him, and he himself has followed that calling all his life. He received his education at the common school. At the age of 22 he married Abigail Turner, who died of consumption, December, 1858. He afterwards married Sophia G. Hills (widow of Dr. E. P. Hills of Shirley, Mass.), his present wife. By his first wife he had three children, who still live—Susan, Richard and Granville. Richard is now at work on the old farm. He is married and lives near his father's home. Susan is now a widow, and is living at her father's. She has one child.

Mr. Pierce has been in town office several times—has twice served as Selectman, Overseer of the Poor, and Assessor. In 1868 he was representative in the State Legislature. In the various offices he has filled he has been distinguished for his good judgment in practical matters quite as much as for anything else. He is not wealthy, but well-to-do. The estate of his father was left him—under certain conditions relating to the other children and the widow to be fulfilled— and he has improved the estate very much—both the land and the buildings, beside adding thereto both land and outbuildings. He has been a hard-working man nearly all of his life. He is a member of the Unitarian Church, as is also his present wife.

Jona Pierce

Children :—

4126. i.   SUSAN, b. Nov. 26, 1838; m. Oct. 17, 1867, Israel Wetherbee, b. June 21, 1815. Ch.: Arthur, b. Dec. 16, 1873; res. Westminster.
4127. ii.   RICHARD, b. May 17, 1842; m. Mary E. Kinser.
4128. iii.   GRANVILLE, b. Dec. 17, 1847; m. Jennie C. Emerson and Georgia H. Damon.

2730.   ABEL[8] PIERCE (*Richard W.*[7], *Jonathan*[6], *Oliver*[5], *Stephen*[4], *Stephen*[3], *Thomas*[2], *Thomas*[1]), b. Feb. 20, 1822; m. Nov. 4, 1844, Catherine E. Kemp, d. Dec. 8, 1853. He. d. Nov. 2, 1852. Res. Groton, Mass. No children.

2731.   GEORGE[8] PIERCE (*Stephen*[7], *Stephen*[6], *Oliver*[5], *Stephen*[4],

*Stephen*³, *Thomas*², *Thomas*¹), b. Jan. 28, 1815; m. Reuhamah Stearns. Res. Philadelphia, Pa. Children :—

4129.	i.	——.	4130. ii.	——.
4131.	iii.	——.	4132. iv.	——.
4133.	v.	——.	4134. vi.	——.

2733. MILO⁸ PIERCE (*Stephen*⁷, *Stephen*⁶, *Oliver*⁵, *Stephen*⁴, *Stephen*³, *Thomas*², *Thomas*¹), b. May 28, 1818; m. Nov. 3, 1842, Mary A. Spaulding, b. Sept. 1, 1823, d. Jan. 28, 1849; m. 2nd, Nov. 18, 1849, Maria D. Farrington, b. June 9, 1825, d. Dec. 13, 1864; m. 3rd, Apr. 22, 1865, Sarah B. Cooper, b. Feb. 17, 1828. Res. Vineland, N. J.

Children :—

4135. i. MARY F., b. June 19, 1843; m. Jarvis C. Cooper.
4136. ii. MILO S., b. Dec. 8, 1844.
4137. iii. EDWARD A., b. July 18, 1847.
4138. iv. ARTHUR, b. Nov. 18, 1850; d. Feb. 16, 1851.
4139. v. STEPHEN, b. Jan. 5, 1854.
4140. vi. ——, b. Mar. 2, 1855; d. Nov. 5, 1855.
4141. vii. LILLA M., b. Sept. 28, 1858; d. Oct. 23, 1870.
4142. viii. DANA, b. Aug. 24, 1862.
4143. ix. MINNIE I., b. Nov. 12, 1864; d. May 13, 1865.

2737. JOEL A.⁸ PIERCE (*Stephen*⁷, *Stephen*⁶, *Oliver*⁵, *Stephen*⁴, *Stephen*³, *Thomas*², *Thomas*¹), b. Mar. 27, 1836; m. Dec. 15, 1856, Harriet A. Upham, b. Dec. 2, 1838. He d. May 12, 1878. Res. St. Paul, Minn. Children :—

4144. i. FRED. A., b. Feb. 23, 1859.
4145. ii. FRANK A., b. Mar. 22, 1860.
4146. iii. WILLIAM E., b. Apr. 16, 1866; d. July 26, 1866.

2739. CHARLES H.⁸ PIERCE (*Stephen*⁷, *Stephen*⁶, *Oliver*⁵, *Stephen*⁴, *Stephen*³, *Thomas*², *Thomas*¹), b. Apr. 13, 1840; m. Apr. 13, 1864, Maria T. French, b. Nov. 10, 1841. Res. Springfield, Ohio. Children :—

4147. i. BERTHA F., b. Oct. 7, 1865.
4148. ii. WALTER C., b. Nov. 9, 1867.
4149. iii. ROSCOE, b. Aug. 24, 1869.

2740. JOHN⁸ PIERCE (*Stephen*⁷, *Stephen*⁶, *Oliver*⁵, *Stephen*⁴, *Stephen*³, *Thomas*², *Thomas*¹), b. July 15, 1845; m. Ada E. Ripley, b. Sept. 21, 1849, d. Nov. 7, 1878. Res. So. Paris, Me. No children.

2741. WILLIAM S.⁸ PIERCE (*Jesse*⁷, *Stephen*⁶, *Oliver*⁵, *Stephen*⁴, *Stephen*³, *Thomas*², *Thomas*¹), b. Sept. 14, 1815; m. Apr. 2, 1840, Sarah Butler, b. Jan. 18, 1817, d. Sept. 1, 1853; m. 2nd, Dec. 26, 1853, Mary A. Merrow, d. Mar. 28, 1874; m. 3rd, Nov. 15, 1878, Priscilla Smith. Res. Lowell, Mass. Children :—

4150. i. IRA, b. Apr. 30, 1842; d. Jan. 27, 1864.
4151. ii. LEVI O., b. Feb. 14, 1844; d. Dec. 22, 1848.

4152. iii. IDA M., b. Jan. 25, 1846; m. John Coolidge.
4153. iv. MARY E., b. Mar. 7, 1848; m. Riley Davis.
4154. v. HENRY M., b. Feb. 17, 1850; d. May 24, 1853.
4155. vi. CHARLES L., b. Oct. 13, 1854; m. Lowella Murphy.
4156. vii. SARAH A., b. April 30, 1859.

2742. EDWIN[8] PIERCE (*Jesse*[7], *Stephen*[6], *Oliver*[5], *Stephen*[4], *Stephen*[3], *Thomas*[2], *Thomas*[1]), b. Jan. 19, 1818; m. Sept. 30, 1845, Eliza S. Milliken, b. Jan. 31, 1820. Res. Lynn, Mass.

Edwin Pierce

Children :—
4157. ELIZA, b. June 29, 1846.
4158. EDWIN W., b. Dec. 16, 1849; m. Mary J. Southworth.

2745. WINSLOW S.[8] PIERCE (*Moses*[7], *Stephen*[6], *Oliver*[5], *Stephen*[4], *Stephen*[3], *Thomas*[2], *Thomas*[1]), b. May 3, 1819; m. July 22, 1847, Georgianna C. Moore; m. 2nd, April 17, 1855, Jane Webb, d. Apr. 27, 1865; m. 3rd, Ann Hendricks. Res. Indianapolis, Ind.

He was born in Chelmsford, and by the death of his father and mother was left an orphan at the age of nine years. Since he was eleven years of age he has been the architect of his own fortunes. He graduated as M. D. from Dartmouth College. Practiced medicine several years in Illinois, where he had previously settled. He emigrated to California in 1849, and in 1851 was elected Comptroller of the State, in which office he served one term.

Winslow S. Pierce

Children :—
4159. i. HENRY D., b. Apr. 9, 1848; m. Elizabeth S. Vinton.
4160. ii. JOHN H., b. Feb. 16, 1856.
4161. iii. WINSLOW S., b. Oct. 23, 1857.
4162. iv. HELEN M., b. Jan. 8, 1860.
4163. v. MARY H., b. Oct. 19, 1862.
4164. vi. VIRGINIA, b. 1863; d. Feb. 10, 1863.

2747. FRANKLIN B.[8] PIERCE (*Moses*[7], *Stephen*[6], *Oliver*[5], *Stephen*[4], *Stephen*[3], *Thomas*[2], *Thomas*[1]), b. Jan. 7, 1823; m. Sept. 17, 1843, Melissa Hinman, b. Aug. 30, 1827. Res. Ludington, Mich.

Franklin B. Pierce

Children :—

4165. i. MARY M., b. May 5, 1844; m. D. L. Filer.
4166. ii. FRANKLIN B., b. July 11, 1850.
4167. iii. NEWTON B., b. Sept. 26, 1856.

2748. GEORGE B.[8] PIERCE (*Moses*[7], *Stephen*[6], *Oliver*[5], *Stephen*[4], *Stephen*[3], *Thomas*[2], *Thomas*[1]), b. Feb. 28, 1824; m. Apr. 3, 1853, Mary C. Brittan, b. Oct. 4, 1834. Res. Pleasanton, Mich.
Children :—

4168. i. WINSLOW B., b. Aug. 6, 1855.
4169. ii. MARY B., b. Apr. 29, 1859.
4170. iii. KENT B., b. June 7, 1861.
4171. iv. NOTT F., b. Nov. 29, 1863; d. July 26, 1865.
4172. v. PAUL, b. Nov. 19, 1866.
4173. vi. JESSE E., b. Feb. 11, 1867.

2756. ORRIN[8] PIERCE (*Jonathan*[7], *Stephen*[6], *Oliver*[5], *Stephen*[4], *Stephen*[3], *Thomas*[2], *Thomas*[1]), b. Aug. 7, 1831; m. Aug. 25, 1855, Elmira S. Bolton, b. 1833. Res. Chelmsford, Mass. Children :—

4174. i. CARRIE A., b. Sept. 8, 1857; m. William H. Smith.
4175. ii. ADELLA F., b. Oct. 27, 1859.

2759. WILLIAM E.[8] PIERCE (*William*[7], *John*[6], *William*[5], *Stephen*[4], *Stephen*[3], *Thomas*[2], *Thomas*[1]), b. June 12, 1813; m. Oct. 10, 1865, Helen A. Houghton, b. Nov. 20, 1834, d. Jan. 9, 1878. Res. Lyndon, Vt.

Wm. E. Pierce

Children :—

4176. i. EMILY A., b. Mar. 14, 1869.
4177. ii. GEORGE W., b. Jan. 8, 1875.

2760. GEORGE W.[8] PIERCE (*William*[7], *John*[6], *William*[5], *Stephen*[4], *Stephen*[3], *Thomas*[2], *Thomas*[1]), b. Feb. 5, 1815; m. July 26, 1840, Ruth Bey, b. Sept. 4, 1818. Res. Charleston, Vt.
Children :—

4178. i. ALFRED I., b. Aug. 18, 1841.
4179. ii. RUTH E., b. Apr. 23, 1848.

2762. ALFRED[8] PIERCE (*John*[7], *John*[6], *William*[5], *Stephen*[4], *Stephen*[3], *Thomas*[2], *Thomas*[1]), b. Dec. 23, 1802; m. Oct. 11, 1829, Abigail M. Rockwood, b. Jan. 15, 1811. He d. Apr. 22, 1880. Res. Hartland, Vt.

Alfred Pierce

Children :—

4180. i. MARY H., b. June 30, 1831; d. Feb. 24, 1833.
4181. ii. FRANCIS M., b. Jan. 7, 1834; m. Helen Bishop.

4182. iii. MARY H., b. Oct. 24, 1836; m. Gen. Lewis A. Grant.
4183. iv. ABBIE L., b. Feb. 19, 1842; m. Charles H. Smith.

2769. JOHN L.[8] PIERCE (*John*[7], *John*[6], *William*[5], *Stephen*[4], *Stephen*[3], *Thomas*[2], *Thomas*[1]), b. Nov. 16, 1819; m. Dec. 20, 1846, Ellen E. Marsh, b. Dec. 24, 1826. Res. Chester, Vt.

John L. Pierce

Children :—
4184. i. FRED. M., b. Oct. 18, 1851; m. Ella N. Albee.
4185. ii. CORA E., b. Apr. 16, 1862.

2773. Gen. EZEKIEL P.[8] PIERCE (*Ezekiel P.*[7], *John*[6], *William*[5], *Stephen*[4], *Stephen*[3], *Thomas*[2], *Thomas*[1]), b. Aug. 18, 1814 ; m. 1844, Sarah Webster. Res. Cambridgeport, Mass.

Ezekiel, Gen.

Children :—
4186. i. GEORGIANNA, b. Mar. 21, 1847.
4187. ii. EDWARD E., b. May 17, 1848; m. Fanny Chandler.

2775. LUCIUS D.[8] PIERCE (*Ezekiel P.*[7], *John*[6], *William*[5], *Stephen*[4], *Stephen*[3], *Thomas*[2], *Thomas*[1]), b. Aug. 9, 1820; m. Jan., 1854, Lucy C. Fuller, d. May 8, 1858. Res. Chesterfield, N. H.

LUCIUS DARWIN PIERCE, son of Ezekiel Porter Pierce, Esq. and Susannah Porter, was born August 9th, 1820, at Chesterfield, N. H., nurtured in a tavern and upon his father's farm. In boyhood and youth he enjoyed such limited advantages for acquiring an education as the common schools and Academy in Chesterfield afforded. About the year 1841 he entered Norwich University, Vt., gained a commendable proficiency in the Ancient languages, and while yet an under-graduate was appointed to and accepted the position of Professor of Languages in a seminary in Portsmouth, Va., and served in that capacity in Virginia till he found the climate did not suit his constitution, when he resigned and returned, and graduated A. B. in full Collegiate Course at Norwich University in the class of 1846. He studied law in the office of Hon. William P. Wheeler, at Keene, N. H., and was admitted to the Bar in New Hampshire in 1849, successfully practiced Law in Marlow, N. H., till November, 1853, when he moved to Winchendon, Mass., and formed a Law copartnership with Benj. O. Tyler, Esq., a lawyer in extensive practice ; continued with Tyler for a year, when Tyler, who was also engaged in manufacturing, becoming financially embarrassed, he withdrew from Tyler and opened an office by himself, and from the first did an extensive, increasing and lucrative business in his profession to the time of his death, which occurred May 8, 1858.

He was a gentleman of culture and refinement; had a genial, affable disposition, courteous, obliging address, and studious, industrious habits. While in practice in New Hampshire, he, held a commission as Justice of the Peace and at the time of his death held commissions as Justice of the Peace and Notary Public for Massachusetts, and Commissioner for New Hampshire and Vermont. Jan. 2d, 1854, he married Miss Lucy C. Fuller, daughter of John H. Fuller, Esq., of Keene, N. H., but died without issue.

Lucius J. Pierce

2776. Capt. HORACE T. H.[8] PIERCE (*Ezekiel P.*[7], *John*[6], *William*[5], *Stephen*[4], *Stephen*[3], *Thomas*[2], *Thomas*[1]), b. Feb. 22, 1822; m. June 12, 1850, Sophia E. Dickinson. He d. Jan. 7, 1877. Res. Keene, N. H.

Captain HORACE TRUMAN HAWKS PIERCE, son of Ezekiel Porter Pierce, Esq., and Susannah Porter, was born at Chesterfield, N. H., Feb. 22, 1822; was brought up on the farm and in the tavern of his father and enjoyed such advantages as the common schools and Academy in Chesterfield afforded, and pursued a partial course of studies at Norwich University, Vt., which, in addition to the usual Collegiate and Scientific course of studies, required its members to be instructed in military tactics, to which, while he remained in the University, he gave considerable attention, being naturally of a military turn of mind, and in after years turned his acquirements to good advantage. On leaving the University, he became a mechanic, for a while manufactured, and later became a brick mason, and followed that trade, residing with his family in Keene, N. H., till the War of the Rebellion broke out, when, upon the first call of President Lincoln for 75,000 three months' volunteers, he was among the first to offer his services in defence of the Union; and having raised a company of men, as Lieutenant, he joined the 2nd Infantry Regiment New Hampshire Volunteers and served out his term of enlistment with credit. On being discharged from the three months' service, he at once set himself about raising three years' men, and succeeded in raising a company at Keene, which joined the 5th Regiment New Hampshire Volunteers as Co. "F," and he was commissioned by the Governor of New Hampshire its captain; served under Colonel Cross and General McClellan all through the Peninsula Campaign against Richmond in the spring and summer of 1862, was in command of his company in the memorable battle of Antietam, September 17, 1862, and in pursuit of the enemy on their retreat to Fredericksburg, soon after which he was honorably discharged for physical disability. He was an intrepid, resolute officer, cared for and beloved by his men; he fearlessly discharged his duty, with dignity and honor. Upon his return from the war he resumed his occupation as a brick-mason, at Keene, which he followed with his characteristic resolution and enterprise till his health and strength gave out. He married Miss Sophia E. Dickinson, daughter of Mr. William Dickinson of Hinsdale, N. H., June 12, 1850, by whom he had three children—Julia L., William E. and Frank, and died at Keene, N. H., Jan. 7, 1877. Children :—

4188. i. JULIA L., b. Mar. 17, 1851; m. Jan., 1874, Frank A. Hardy. She d. Apr. 30, 1875, s.p.
4189. ii. WILLIAM E., b. 1853.
4190. iii. FRANK D., b. Nov. 15, 1855.

2777. LAFAYETTE W.[8] PIERCE (*Ezekiel P.*[7], *John*[6], *William*[5], *Stephen*[4], *Stephen*[3], *Thomas*[2], *Thomas*[1]), b. May 20, 1825; m. Sept. 15, 1859, Cleopatra S. Bang, b. Apr. 24, 1832, d. Nov. 12, 1864; m. 2nd, Oct. 5, 1865, Lydia M. Piper, b. July 22, 1840, d. May 15, 1872; m. 3rd, Mar. 29, 1875, Hannah E. Derby, b. July 31, 1846. Res. Winchendon, Mass.

LAFAYETTE WASHINGTON PIERCE, Esq., son of Ezekiel Porter Pierce and Susannah Porter, was born at Chesterfield, New Hampshire, May 20th, 1825, and was reared in the tavern and upon the farm of his father. In boyhood and youth, obliged to labor when not attending school, his opportunities for acquiring an education were meagre indeed, and confined to the very limited advantages of the public schools in Chesterfield; notwithstanding, in the autumn of 1844, at the age of nineteen years, he entered Norwich University at Norwich, Vt., though he was obliged to earn for himself means for defraying his expenses at the University and other institutions of learning which he attended in pursuing his collegiate and law courses of studies; this, in the practice of the most rigid economy and untiring industry by manual labor and teaching schools, he was able to accomplish, and graduated in full Collegiate course at Norwich University, August 22d, 1850. After graduating he followed teaching for a while, in connection with studying law, becoming successively principal of the Cæsar Seminary at Swanzey, N. H., at Wilmington, Vt., and Alstead, N H., High Schools, meeting with a good degree of success teaching. He was one of the constituent members of the "Cheshire County, N. H., Musical Convention and Institute," at its original organization in August, 1853, and was elected and served as its first President through its several sessions that year. He studied law with Hon. F. F. Lane, of Keene, N. H., and Messrs. Tyler & Pierce, counsellors at law, at Winchendon, Mass., and upon examination by Judge Thomas of the Supreme Judicial Court, was admitted to practice law in all the courts of Massachusetts, at the Worcester County Bar, at the April Term of the Supreme Judicial Court, April 28, 1854. He practiced law one year in Oxford, Mass., then between three and four years in Westborough, in the same County, finally removing to and opening a law office in Winchendon, Mass., and there continuing the practice of his profession in the courts of Massachusetts and New Hampshire to the present time. He has made a specialty of the prosecution of pension and other government claims in which he has been quite successful, making glad many a worthy soldier and dependent relatives, in the successful

Lafayette W. Pierce.

prosecution of their claims. He is and for thirteen years has been a
confidential contributor of a leading journal in Worcester County. He
was commissioned a Justice of the Peace by Gov. Emory Washburn
in 1854, and holds that office at the present time. Was commissioned
in 1858, by Gov. Wm. Hale, a Commissioner of New Hampshire for
Massachusetts. He is a member of the Right Worthy Grand Lodge
of the Independent Order of Odd Fellows of Massachusetts. And has
several times been elected by his lodge its special representative to
and attended upon the sessions of the Grand Lodge of I. O. O. F., and
been promoted to many positions of honor and trust in the Order.

Children :—
4191. i.   CHARLES L., b. Mar. 6, 1864.

4192. ii.   JOHN A., b. July 23, 1866.

2779. AUGUSTA E.[8] PIERCE (*Ezekiel P.*[7], *John*[6], *William*[5],
Stephen[4], *Stephen*[3], *Thomas*[2], *Thomas*[1]), b. Jan. 29, 1830. She is
unm. and resides in Chesterfield, N. H.

Miss AUGUSTA ELIZABETH PIERCE, youngest daughter of Ezekiel
Porter Pierce, Esq., and Susannah Porter, was born near Spofford's
Lake in what is called the Lake House on the "Old Pierce Homestead,"
Chesterfield, New Hampshire, January 29, 1830. Her parents, in point
of character, were among the most respectable inhabitants of the community. Her father, a manufacturer, merchant and farmer, was a
representative man of great energy and enterprise, and of sterling
integrity. Her mother was a remarkable woman of excellent character,
possessing a high degree of refinement and more than ordinary intellec-
tual qualifications, having been educated at Farmington Academy, Me.
Augusta is a woman of refinement and culture, having inherited
many of the sterling qualities of her parents, she is industrious, enterprising and energetic. Like her brothers, her early education was
acquired in the public schools and at Chesterfield Academy, which for
many years stood prominent in the State as a literary and scientific
institution.

When but six years of age, she resolved to qualify herself for
teaching, and in after years followed up that resolution. At the age of
eighteen she commenced teaching public schools in her native town.
Success crowned her efforts and she zealously devoted her time to
teaching and attending school at different seminaries of learning. Entering Mount Holyoke Seminary in 1856, she pursued a partial course of

studies there, fitted for and chose teaching as a profession, and followed it with marked success for many years, insomuch that her services were eagerly sought far and near, being for several years Principal of Wilmington, Vt., High School, and Preceptress in Wilmington Academy, Vt. Taught several terms of school in the City of Keene, N. H., and the High Schools in Marlow and Hinsdale, N. H., and was principal of the Grammar School at Shelburne Falls, Mass., and Chesterfield Academy, N. H.—having taught seventy-seven different terms of school with usual success. She has always taken great interest in all moral and religious reforms, being a staunch advocate and supporter of the Union cause during the "Great Rebellion." At times she has been elected to fill public offices in her own district and as a member upon the board of education in her own town, being elected to the office of superintending school committee of Chesterfield, and has always resided at what is now called the "Old Pierce Homestead" or "Lake House," Chesterfield, N. H.

2782. CHARLES[8] PIERCE (*Ebenezer*[7], *John*[6], *William*[5], *Stephen*[4], *Stephen*[3], *Thomas*[2], *Thomas*[1]), b. Mar. 8, 1813; m. Jan., 1850, Caroline Scribner. Res. Boston, and rem. to Cal. Child:—

4193. i. Edith J., b. Jan. 31, 1853.

2784. ALSON[8] PIERCE (*Ebenezer*[7], *John*[6], *William*[5], *Stephen*[4], *Stephen*[3], *Thomas*[2], *Thomas*[1]), b. June 8, 1817; m. June 27, 1852, Lorany P. Wheeler, b. July 11, 1827, d. Dec. 25, 1872. Res. Chesterfield, N. H. Children :—

4194. i. FRANK A., b. Apr. 24, 1854; m. Persis Prentice.
4195. ii. LORANY, b. Oct. 27, 1856; d. Oct. 29, 1856.
4196. iii. WILLIAM B., b. Aug. 11, 1858; d. Aug. 28, 1858.
4197. iv. ELLA E., b. Mar. 20, 1860; m. Ferdinand Springer.
4198. v. FRED. M., b. Feb. 12, 1864; d. Aug. 24, 1864.

2785. DEXTER[8] PIERCE (*Ebenezer*[7], *John*[6], *William*[5], *Stephen*[4], *Stephen*[3], *Thomas*[2], *Thomas*[1]), b. Oct. 11, 1819; m. July 14, 1856, R. C. Wing. Res. E. Westmoreland, N. H. Children :—

4199. i. HASKINS, b. Oct. 21, 1864.
4200. ii. CORA M., b. Oct. 10, 1866.

2798. KIRK D.[8] PIERCE (*Henry D.*[7], *Benjamin*[6], *Benjamin*[5], *Stephen*[4], *Stephen*[3], *Thomas*[2], *Thomas*[1]), b. Aug. 11, 1846; m. Feb. 17, 1879, Mary A. Collins, b. May 6, 1845. Res. Hillsboro, N. H. No children.

2807. JONATHAN[8] PIERCE (*Jonathan*[7], *Jonathan*[6], *Stephen*[5], *Jacob*[4], *Stephen*[3], *Thomas*[2], *Thomas*[1]), b. Jan. 29, 1789; m. Oct., 1811, Olive Hale, b. Jan. 12, 1788, d. Feb. 24, 1868. He d. Mar. 26, 1866. Res. Groton, Mass. Children :—

4201. i. CHARLES H., b. Sept. 17, 1812; m. Lovey J. Brown.
4202. ii. ELIZA, b. June 3, 1814; m. Francis Flagg.
4203. iii. CHARLOTTE, b. Apr. 13, 1816; d. Aug. 29, 1837.
4204. iv. GEORGE, b. Feb. 13, 1819; m. Ann Hartwell.
4205. v. MARY A., b. Sept. 9, 1821; d. July 10, 1845.
4206. vi. JOHN, b. Oct. 29, 1823; m. Elizabeth J. Flagg.

2813. BENJAMIN[8] PIERCE (*Benjamin*[7], *Jonathan*[6], *Stephen*[5], *Jacob*[4], *Stephen*[3], *Thomas*[2], *Thomas*[1]), b. Dec. 21, 1786; m. Tamar Gannett, b. Apr. 19, 1786, d. June 12, 1862. He d. Oct. 9, 1865. Res. Ludlow, Vt. No children.

2816. JOSEPH[8] PIERCE (*Benjamin*[7], *Jonathan*[6], *Stephen*[5], *Jacob*[4], *Stephen*[3], *Thomas*[2], *Thomas*[1]), b. Feb. 11, 1792; m. Bridget Davis. Children :—

4207. i. MARY, b. ———; d. ———.
4208. ii. WILLARD.
4209. iii. ELIZA, b. ———, 1820; m.———

2818. JOHN[8] PIERCE (*Benjamin*[7], *Jonathan*[6], *Stephen*[5], *Jacob*[4], *Stephen*[3], *Thomas*[2], *Thomas*[1]), b. Sept. 24, 1795; m. Feb. 3, 1823, Lydia Putnam, b. Feb. 11, 1796, d. Aug. 15, 1856. He d. June 1, 1858. Res. Andover, Vt.

John Piesee.

Children :—

4210. i. RODNEY M., b. July 22, 1825; m. Malinda Butterfield.
4211. ii. CALISTA A., b. Aug. 13, 1834; d. Sept. 19, 1856.

2823. STEPHEN[8] PIERCE (*Benjamin*[7], *Jonathan*[6], *Stephen*[5], *Jacob*[4], *Stephen*[3], *Thomas*[2], *Thomas*[1]), b. May 2, 1804; m. Dec. 10, 1836, Almira Tarbell, b. Nov. 22, 1806, d. Sept. 26, 1875. Res. Mount Pleasant, Iowa.

Stephen Pierce

Children :—

4212. i.   BENJAMIN T., b. Aug. 25, 1843; d. Mar. 13, 1862.
4213. ii. OLIVER W., b. May 20, 1845; d. Apr. 24, 1877.
4214. iii. ESTELLA A., b. July 27, 1850; m. ——— Harris.

2825. DAVID[8] PIERCE (*Benjamin*[7], *Jonathan*[6], *Stephen*[5], *Jacob*[4], *Stephen*[3], *Thomas*[2], *Thomas*[1]), b. Feb. 27, 1808; m. Dec. 4, 1836, Susan Kendall, b. Sept. 6, 1816. He d. Sept. 20, 1845. Res. Montpelier, Ind. Children :—

4215. i.   ELIZABETH, b. June 18, 1837; d. 1845.
4216. ii. DAVID J., b. July 18, 1841; m. Marietta A. Hall.
4217. iii. STEPHEN B., b. Mar. 5, 1843; m. Annie B. Holt.
4218. iv. JOHN K., b. Apr. 8, 1845; m. Helen M. French.

2830. HENRY A.[8] PIERCE (*Seth*[7], *Josiah*[6], *Samuel*[5], *Samuel*[4], *Samuel*[3], *Thomas*[2], *Thomas*[1]), b. Dec. 8, 1818; m. Oct. 28, 1850, Cornelia Seward, b. Sept. 27, 1818, d. May 22, 1866. Res. Zoar, Mass. No children.

2834. JOSIAH F.[8] PIERCE (*Josiah*[7], *Josiah*[6], *Samuel*[5], *Samuel*[4], *Samuel*[3], *Thomas*[2], *Thomas*[1]), b. July 20, 1821; m. May 19, 1850, Chloe Hammond, b. Oct. 3, 1827. He d. Mar. 27, 1875. Res. Barrington, Ill. Children :—

4219.　i.　CHARLES A., b. May 7, 1851; m. Annie E. Dean.
4220.　ii.　LYDIA M., b. Oct. 5, 1854; d. Oct. 5, 1879.
4221.　iii.　H. JUDSON, b. Mar. 23, 1862; d. Sept. 27, 1879.

2838. HENRY B.[8] PIERCE (*Josiah*[7], *Josiah*[6], *Samuel*[5], *Samuel*[4], *Samuel*[3], *Thomas*[2], *Thomas*[1]), b. June 24, 1834; m. Aug. 26, 1856, Eliza Wilson, b. Nov. 14, 1836, d. May 27, 1867; m. 2nd, July 21, 1869, Addie L. Potter, b. Oct. 2, 1842. He d. Aug. 26, 1878. Res. Geneva, Ill. Children :—

4222.　i.　MARIETTA, b. Oct. 20, 1857.
4223.　ii.　E. MAUDE, b. Aug. 26, 1860; m. Fred. G. Underwood.
4224.　iii.　HARRY B., b. Apr. 28, 1864; d. Dec., 1864.
4225.　iv.　ELSIE I., b. Mar. 8, 1866.
4226.　v.　MILLICENT L., b. Nov. 28, 1870.
4227.　vi.　LOUIS W., b. Apr. 9, 1874; d. Feb. 17, 1876.
4228.　vii.　HENRY B., b. Sept. 13, 1877.

2841. ROBERT W.[8] PIERCE (*Richard*[7], *Josiah*[6], *Samuel*[5], *Samuel*[4], *Samuel*[3], *Thomas*[2], *Thomas*[1]), b. Feb. 14, 1821; m. June 24, 1846, Elizabeth M. Burditt, b. July 5, 1827. Res. Milwaukee, Wis.

Robert W. Pierce

Children :—

4229.　i.　RICHARD W., b. June 24, 1848; d. Aug 21, 1849.
4230.　ii.　——, b. Mar. 14, 1851; d. Apr. 15, 1851.
4231.　iii.　EDGAR F., b. Mar. 16, 1852.
4232.　iv.　FLORA I., b. Aug. 31, 1856; d. July 1, 1857.
4233.　v.　LOUIS W., b. Sept. 24, 1858.
4234.　vi.　MARION, b. June 21, 1861; d. Aug. 16, 1866.
4235.　vii.　ROBERT W., b. Nov. 20, 1865.
4236.　viii.　CHESTER B., b. Sept. 25, 1870.

2844. ALBERT L.[8] PIERCE (*Richard*[7], *Josiah*[6], *Samuel*[5], *Samuel*[4], *Samuel*[3], *Thomas*[2], *Thomas*[1]), b. Jan. 27, 1825; m. Oct. 22, 1863, Sarah McFarland; d. Nov. 14, 1865. Child :—

4237.　i.　NELLIE McF., b. Sept. 19, 1864.

2853. OSCAR H.[8] PIERCE (*Richard*[7], *Josiah*[6], *Samuel*[5], *Samuel*[4], *Samuel*[3], *Thomas*[2], *Thomas*[1]), b. July 6, 1840; m. Jan. 24, 1867, Martha Horning, b. May 15, 1841. Res. Milwaukee, Wis. Children :—

4238.　i.　MARION, b. July 7, 1869.
4239.　ii.　ELLA, b. Dec. 25, 1870.

2856. Prof. WILLIAM M.[8] PIERCE (*David*[7], *Josiah*[6], *Josiah*[5], *Samuel*[4], *Samuel*[3], *Thomas*[2], *Thomas*[1]), b. Dec. 30, 1827; m. Dec. 28, 1860, Fanny M. Shyrock, d. Jan. 7, 1871. Res. Hadley, Mass.

He graduated at Amherst College, in Class of 1853. He was Professor of Mathematics and Principal of Senior Male Department two years in the Virginia Male and Female Collegiate Institute, Portsmouth, Va. Studied law one year in Portsmouth, Va., two years with Judge Wells in Geneva Co., Ill., and was there admitted to the bar, but never practiced. After this for several years was Professor of Languages in Wyman's City University, St. Louis, Mo. When the war broke out he was teaching in Ironton, Mo.; troops were stationed in that place. His school building was taken for a hospital and his school broken up. In 1869 he received an appointment from the Government as Notary Public, Surveyor and Land Agent. He followed this to the time of his death, Jan. 7, 1871.

Child :—

4240. i. HELEN CARSON, b. Nov. 30, 1861. Res. Butte City, Montana.

2858. JOHN N.[8] PIERCE (*David*[7], *Josiah*[6], *Josiah*[5], *Samuel*[4], *Samuel*[3], *Thomas*[2], *Thomas*[1]), b. Dec. 8, 1833 ; m. Apr. 17, 1861, Lucy M. Brackett, b. Dec., 1833, d. May 26, 1864 ; m. 2nd, Nov. 14, 1867, Mrs. Calista M. Root, b. Jan. 31, 1838. Res. Hadley, Mass.

Child :—

4241. i. MARTIN S., b. Nov. 10, 1868.

2870. JOSIAH[8] PIERCE (*Elihu*[7], *Josiah*[6], *Josiah*[5], *Samuel*[4], *Samuel*[3], *Thomas*[2], *Thomas*[1]), b. Feb. 4, 1824 ; m. May 3, 1848, Hannah M. Muzzy, b. Apr. 21, 1828, d. Oct. 5, 1875. Res. New Haven, Conn.

JOSIAH PIERCE, the youngest and only son of Elihu Pierce that survived infancy, was born in Hadley, Mass., February 4th, 1824. The death of his father in his fifth year compelled the restriction of his school days to the few short winter months preceding his fourteenth year.

The death of his mother during the following year, left him entirely dependent upon himself for support, which he earned by farm labor until sixteen years of age; serving the remainder of his minority as cabinet-maker's apprentice in Northampton. At the expiration of this time he went to Bristol, Conn., where he obtained employment in the clock manufactory, a business which he followed during the greater portion of his life. In this village upon the third of May, 1848, he married Hannah M. Muzzy, who became in good time the proud and happy mother of four boys.

While his eldest son was yet an infant he removed to Ansonia, Conn., where he remained until the spring of 1866, when he removed to the city of New Haven, his present home. In this quiet old " City of Elms " he buried his wife upon the 7th of October, 1875, and four years later, upon the 9th of the same month, he laid his oldest boy by her side. Children :—

4242. i. CHARLES F., b. July 3, 1849 ; d. Oct. 9, 1879.
4243. ii. DWIGHT E., b. May 13, 1854 ; m. Fannie E. Lloyd.

34

4244. iii. WILLIAM J., b. Mar. 1, 1856; m. Edna Scofield.
4245. iv. HARRY S., b. June 23, 1859.

2872. JOHN F.[8] PIERCE (*Job*[7], *Josiah*[6], *Josiah*[5], *Samuel*[4], *Sam uel*[3] *Thomas*[2], *Thomas*[1]), b. July 14, 1811; m. July 27, 1841, Nancy Bardwell, b. Sept. 9, 1806, d. Dec. 24, 1865. Res. Hadley, Mass.
Child :—

4246. i. LORAIN B., b. Apr. 6, 1845; m. Henry Belden.

2877. LEWIS[8] PIERCE (*Job*[7], *Josiah*[6], *Josiah*[5], *Samuel*[4], *Samuel*[3], *Thomas*[2], *Thomas*[1]), b. Jan. 20, 1826; m. Nov. 21, 1857, Frances Emerson, b. June, 1831, d. Dec. 20, 1861; m. 2nd, Sept. 19, 1872, Louise M. Ives, b. Feb. 26, 1839. Res. Salem, Mass.

Children :—

4247. i. FRANK H., b. Nov. 20, 1857.
4248. ii. ELLA F., b. Nov., 1859.
4249. iii. GEORGE L., b. Nov., 1861.
4250. iv. CHARLES S., b. Mar. 21, 1874.

2879. AUSTIN[8] PIERCE (*Gordon*[7], *Seth*[6], *Seth*[5], *Samuel*[4], *Samuel*[3], *Thomas*[2], *Thomas*[1]), b. Sept. 2, 1799; m. Mar. 17, 1826, Mary Ann Sterling. He d. June 17, 1861. Res. Villenova, N. Y.

AUSTIN PIERCE was born in Thetford, Vt., in 1799; he moved to Villenova, New York, in 1829, while the country was quite new and just being settled. He practiced medicine till 1850, when he was attacked with a spinal disease and was confined to his bed for nearly twelve years. He died June 17, 1861, a firm believer in Christianity, a consistent Christian, and a member of the Presbyterian church. He was Supervisor of his town for a number of years, and represented his district in the State Assembly in the winter of 1841 and 1842.
Children :—

4251. i. JULIA M., b. Oct. 9, 1829; m. Sept. 3, 1846, Charles L. Mark, b. Aug. 12, 1822. Ch.: Ed. L., b. May 30, 1847; res. Fredonia, N. Y.
4252. ii. WILLIAM P., b. Mar. 25, 1830; m. Dec. 18, 1856, Mary F. Rood.
4253. iii. ELLEN E., b. Dec. 18, 1831; m. July 10, 1858, George White, b. Sept. 11, 1829. Ch.: Squire, b. June 11, 1859; Austin P., b. May 16, 1864, d. Mar. 22, 1865; res. Fredonia, N. Y.
4254. iv. LUCIUS G. C., b. Feb. 5, 1836; m. Sept. 27, 1860, Esther Snow.
4255. v. THERESA M., b. Sept. 2, 1838; m. Mar. 3, 1858, Fayette S. Hatch. Ch.: Mary S., b. Nov. 30, 1858; Lawson W., b. Feb. 21, 1861; Austin S., b. Dec. 7, 1870. Res. Kankakee, Ill.
4256. vi. GORDON L., b. Jan. 25, 1841; d. June 1, 1864.
4257. vii. HENRY A., b. Oct. 11, 1843; m. Sarah E. Sessions.
4258. viii. AUSTIN L., b. June 9, 1848; d. Nov. 30, 1870.

2881. FRANCIS S.[8] PIERCE (*Gordon[7]*, *Seth[6]*, *Seth[5]*, *Samuel[4]*, *Samuel[3]*, *Thomas[2]*, *Thomas[1]*), b. Feb. 6, 1806; m. Oct. 25, 1831, Rebecca Page, b. Aug. 18, 1806. Res. Frankton, Ind.
Children :—

4259. i. HENRY E., b. Oct. 10, 1833; m. Feb. 14, 1855, Scineathy Sinsor.
4260. ii. FRANCIS N., b. July 25, 1835; m. Aug. 22, 1861, Susan Moore.
4261. iii. EDMUND G., b. Apr. 30, 1837; m. Oct. 17, 1858, Lydia P. Duell; m. 2nd, May 15, 1864, Catherine Groandyke.
4262. iv. ALBERT O., b. June 2, 1839; m. Dec. 10, 1863, Elizabeth Pike.
4263. v. MARGARET P., b. Oct. 18, 1840; m. Sept. 3, 1868, William H. H. Sommers; res. Ossian, Ind.
4264. vi. AMANDA P., b. Dec. 20, 1842; d. Feb. 22, 1845.
4265. vii. MINERVA, b. Dec. 6, 1846; m. Dec. 31, 1868, Daniel Sigler. Res. Elwood, Ind.
4266. viii. ALMIRA P., b. Mar. 8, 1849; m. Sept. 3, 1868, Andrew J. Sigler, b. Mar. 8, 1846. Ch.: John H., b. Feb. 8, 1869; Jerry A., b. July 20, 1872; Charles, b. Dec. 14, 1874; res. Frankton, Ind.
4267. ix. EMMA P., b. Feb. 20, 1851; d. Aug. 15, 1853.

2882. Dr. ROYAL S.[8] PIERCE (*Gordon[7]*, *Seth[6]*, *Seth[5]*, *Samuel[4]*, *Samuel[3]*, *Thomas[2]*, *Thomas[1]*), b. Jan. 8, 1812; m. Sept. 30, 1835, Juliet Morton, b. Sept. 11, 1809. He d. Mar. 16, 1845, in Mina, N. Y.
ROYAL S. PIERCE, born in Germantown, N. Y., Jan. 8, 1812. Grad uated at the Medical College at Fairfield, Herkimer Co., N. Y., 1835. Practiced his profession at Mina, N. Y., until his death in 1845. His widow m. 2nd, —— Leavitt. Res. in Sparta, Wis., with her daugh· ter. Children :—

4268. i. AMELIA J., b. Dec. 13, 1836; d. Feb. 17, 1848.
4269. ii. LUTHER M., b. June 4, 1838; d. Oct. 18, 1840.
4270. iii. WM. H. H., b. Apr. 4, 1841; m. Jan. 22, 1876, Elizabeth H. Harwell.

2883. SETH[8] PIERCE (*Samuel[7]*, *Seth[6]*, *Seth[5]*, *Samuel[4]*, *Samuel[3]*, *Thomas[2]*, *Thomas[1]*), b. May 15, 1802; m. Sept. 22, 1831, Fidelia Barrett, d. Oct. 30, 1876. He. d. Nov. 20, 1876. Res. Ware, Mass. Children :—

4271. i. DELIA A., b. Sept. 10, 1835; m. Dec. 27, 1857, John H. Storrs. She d. Oct. 12, 1859.
4272. ii. EMILY E., b. Feb. 12, 1839; d. May 11, 1861.

2884. CHESTER[8] PIERCE (*Samuel[7]*, *Seth[6]*, *Seth[5]*, *Samuel[4]*, *Samuel[3]*, *Thomas[2]*, *Thomas[1]*), b. June 20, 1803; m. March 15, 1831, Abigail Marsh, b. Aug. 15, 1807, d. Nov. 30, 1851; m. 2nd, April, 1853, Angeline Titus, b. Feb. 23, 1812. Res. Ware, Mass.

Children :—

4273. i. CORDELIA, b. Dec. 29, 1838; m. George Armitage. Ch. : Lettie, Angeline, Cora and Waldo.
4274. ii. WALDO, b. Nov. 17, 1844; m. Annie Belcher.

2886. GRANGER[8] PIERCE (*Samuel[7], Seth[6], Seth[5], Samuel[4], Samuel[3], Thomas[2]. Thomas[1]*), b. 1806 ; m. Mercy Stockwell. Res. Worcester, Mass. Children :—

4275. i. RUFUS J., b. Jan. 12, 1839 ; m. Sarah Nye.
4276. ii. THEODORE S., b. June 20, 1841 ; d.

2887. S. AUSTIN[8] PIERCE (*Samuel[7], Seth[6], Seth[5], Samuel[4], Samuel[3], Thomas[2], Thomas[1]*), b. Oct. 6, 1808 ; m. Jan. 28, 1831, Roxanna Harwood. Res. Ware, Mass. Children :—

4277. i. JAMES S., b. June 8, 1831 ; m. May 1, 1856, Mary Ellis, b. May 29, 1832 ; no issue. Res. Ware.
4278. ii. THIRIZA, b. Nov. 11, 1833 ; m. Dec. 27, 1849, Stephen E. Newton, b. Feb. 12, 1826. Ch.: Amy L., b. June 6, 1851 ; Rollin D., b. Apr. 20, 1857 ; Willie A., b. July 14, 1859 ; Lewis E., b. Aug. 23, 1867 ; Stephen E. Jr., b. Mar. 12, 1875.
4279. iii. LEVERETT, b. Jan. 28, 1835 ; m. Mar. 31, 1858, Mary L. Benway.
4280. iv. WALDO, b. Feb. 28, 1838 ; m. Sept. 15, 1860, Abigail Bassett.
4281. v. ELLEN, b. Dec. 5, 1841 ; m. Geo. P. Campbell and has two children. Res. Ware, Mass.
4282. vi. MARY, b. July 26, 1848 ; m. Feb. 14, 1871, Augustus Cummings, b. May 26, 1841. Ch.: Roy E., b. Aug. 4, 1873 ; Guy A., b. July 19, 1875 ; Grenville, b. June 10, 1877. Res. Ware, Mass.

2888. WILLIAM[8] PIERCE (*Samuel[7], Seth[6], Seth[5], Samuel[4], Samuel[3], Thomas[2], Thomas[1]*), b. March 4, 1810 ; m. April 11, 1837, Sarah Witherell, b. 1811. Res. Ware, Mass. Children :—

4283. i. WILLIAM W., b. July 2, 1838.
4284. ii. GEORGE, b. Oct. 29, 1841 ; d. 1841.
4285. iii. JOHN W., b. Oct., 1851 ; m. Mary Sumner.

2889. BRIGHAM[8] PIERCE (*Samuel[7], Seth[6], Seth[5], Samuel[4], Samuel[3], Thomas[2], Thomas[1]*), b. Aug. 15, 1812 ; m. Jan. 19, 1866, Mrs. Mary E. K. Cook, b. Dec. 12, 1823. Res. Rutland, Mass. Child :—

4286. i. EUGENE, b. July 10, 1867.

2890. MANDLEY[8] PIERCE (*Samuel[7], Seth[6], Seth[5], Samuel[4], Samuel[3], Thomas[2], Thomas[1]*), b. Oct. 31, 1817 ; m. May 3, 1842, Emily Thomas, b. Feb. 23, 1816. Res. West Brookfield. Children :—

4287. i. R. JENNIE, b. Apr. 23, 1843 ; m. May 1, 1867, Wm. A. Sturdy. Ch.: Willie M., Emily V., Alice W., Willie M., Arthur T. Res. Lane Station, Norton, Mass.
4288. ii ELLA F., b. Apr. 27, 1845.
4289. iii. EMMA F., b. Dec. 10, 1847 ; m. June 20, 1875, Dr. Watson E. Rice. Watson E. Rice, M. D., was born in Shrewsbury, Mass., December 15th, 1846, the son of Rev. Gardner Rice. He was fitted for College by his father, and then followed the profession of teaching for four years. Subsequently, beginning the study of medicine under Dr. W. F. Breakey of Ann Arbor, Mich., he entered the University of Michigan in September, 1869, and was graduated from that institution March 27th, 1872, and settled at New England Village June 14th, 1872. [*See History of Grafton, Mass., by F. C. Pierce, Esq.*
4290. v. LUTHERIA R., b. Dec. 2, 1850 ; m. July 1, 1874, Jas. E. Hills, b. Oct. 3, 1841. Ch.: J. Mandley, b. Apr. 28, 1875. Res. Brooklyn, N. Y., 82 South Elliott Place.

4291. v. LOUISE T., b. Feb. 18, 1852.

2893. JUSTIN M.[8] PIERCE (*Elijah*[7], *Seth*[6], *Seth*[5], *Samuel*[4], *Samuel*[3], *Thomas*[2], *Thomas*[1]), b. Nov. 9, 1804 ; m. Aug. 21, 1833, Mary Trowbridge, b. Dec. 5, 1807. Res. Homer, N. Y.

Children :—

4292. i.   MARY A., b. May 21, 1834; d. April 23, 1847.
4293. ii.   GEORGE R., b. Jan. 16, 1836; m. Elizabeth Cummings.
4294. iii. HELEN L., b. April 10, 1838; d. Jan. 10, 1862.
4295. iv.   CAROLINE S., b. June 29, 1840; m. Willet Fisher.
4296. v.   FRANCIS L., b. May 4, 1849; d. Dec. 24, 1860.
4297. vi.   WILLIAM E., b. Feb. 22, 1853; m. Harriet Shorley.
4298. vii. EDGAR L., b. May 12, 1856.

2894. DANIEL[8] PIERCE (*Elijah*[7], *Seth*[6], *Seth*[5], *Samuel*[4], *Samuel*[3], *Thomas*[2], *Thomas*[1]), b. Feb. 12, 1807 ; m. Jan. 8, 1835, Sarah S. Sharp, b. March 29, 1805. Res. Homer, N. Y. Child :—

4299. i.   SARAH E., b. Jan. 12, 1839; m. Nov. 1, 1860, A. S. Merrill. b. Mar. 15, 1830. Ch.: Frances C., b. Sept. 29, 1861; Chas. R., b. Mar. 1, 1863; Katie F., b. July 11, 1865; Lewis P., b. June 25, 1870; John S., b. July 11, 1872.

2895. HORACE[8] PIERCE (*Elijah*[7], *Seth*[6], *Seth*[5], *Samuel*[4], *Samuel*[3], *Thomas*[2], *Thomas*[1]), b. Dec. 28, 1809 ; m. Jan. 21, 1835, Sarah A. Smith, b. Sept. 8, 1815. Res. Middleport, N. Y. Children :—

4300. i.   LIBBIE W., b. Oct. 11, 1835; m. Nov. 21. 1855, Ezra B. DeLane, b. Mar. 20, 1829. Res. Middleport, N. Y.
4301. ii.   MOULTON N., b. July 21, 1837; m. Mary Swain.

2896. LUCIUS E.[8] PIERCE (*Algernon*[7], *Enoch*[6], *Enoch*[5], *Samuel*[4], *Samuel*[3], *Thomas*[2], *Thomas*[1]), b. Jan. 19, 1819 ; m. Jan. 1, 1844, Chloe A. Chevalier, b. July, 1824, d. July 27, 1846 ; m. 2nd, Aug. 25, 1846, Clarinda Porter, b. March 16, 1820. Res. North Pitcher, N. Y.

Children :—

4302. i.   CHLOE A., b. Oct. 28, 1847; d. Mar. 11, 1857.
4303. ii.   HENRY E., b. Oct. 1, 1853; d. Mar. 8, 1856.
4304. iii. MILFORD H., b. Mar. 23, 1858.

2898. HENRY E.[8] PIERCE (*Algernon*[7], *Enoch*[6], *Enoch*[5], *Samuel*[4], *Samuel*[3], *Thomas*[2], *Thomas*[1]), b. June 10, 1823 ; m. June 21, 1849, Lydia E. Hyde, d. April 10, 1852 ; m. 2nd, Jan. 24, 1854, Maria L. Ishauger, b. Dec. 12, 1829. He d. Nov. 8, 1858. Res. North Pitcher, N. Y.

Children :—

4305. i. NELLIE L., b. June 2, 1854; d. March 10, 1861.
4306. ii. LYDIA M., b. Jan. 24, 1856.

2901. LATHROP S.[8] PIERCE (*Earl[7]*, *Enoch[6]*, *Enoch[5]*, *Samuel[4]*, *Samuel[3]*, *Thomas[2]*, *Thomas[1]*), b. Sept. 24, 1824 ; m. May 6, 1852, Julia M. Gurley. He d. Nov. 27, 1862. Res. Bolton, Conn. Child :—

4307. i. HATTIE, b. Sept. 27, 1859; m. A. A. Bosworth.

2903. SHEPPARD H.[8] PIERCE (*Earl[7]*, *Enoch[6]*, *Enoch[5]*, *Samuel[4]*, *Samuel[3]*, *Thomas[2]*, *Thomas[1]*), b. Nov. 14, 1830 ; m. July 6, 1851, Frances Haven, b. Oct. 13, 1832, d. March 26, 1856 ; m. 2nd, Apr. 10, 1861, Olive Fox, b. Oct 26, 1830. Res. Leslie, Mich. Children :—

4308. i. ADELBERT, b. July 31, 1852.
4309. ii. LORETTA, b. July 20, 1855; m. A. C. Johnson.

2910. Capt. MARCUS T.[8] PIERCE (*Joseph H.[7]*, *Joseph[6]*, *Isaac[5]*, *Isaac[4]*, *Samuel[3]*, *Thomas[2]*, *Thomas[1]*), b. May 17, 1799 ; m. April 28, 1830, Sarah C. E. Wood, daughter of Judge Jacob Wood of Savannah, Georgia. He d. April 19, 1833. He was a sea captain. Child :—

4310. i. SARAH F. T., b. Apr. 14, 1831.

2911. Col. CONSTANTIUS[8] PIERCE (*Joseph H.[7]*, *Joseph[6]*, *Isaac[5]*, *Isaac[4]*, *Samuel[3]*, *Thomas[2]*, *Thomas[1]*), b. May 9, 1801 ; m. Nov. 25, 1823, Mary Steer. He d. 1839.

Colonel CONSTANTIUS PIERCE of Baton Rouge, La., of the U. S. A., died at San Jacinto while acting as colonel in the Texan war. He was proprietor of the plantations, "Gartness" and "Arlington." His son, Hamilton McKee Pierce, was a colonel of volunteers in the Mexican war.

Children :—

4311. i. HAMILTON McKEE, b. Sept. 23, 1824; d. May 1, 1866.
4312. ii. FRANCES T., b. Feb. 9, 1826; m. Bertrand Harolson.
4313. iii. GRENVILLE M., b. Dec. 5, 1827; m. Mary C. Baker.
4314. iv. MARY S., b. Feb. 28, 1830; m. Joseph Mather.
4315. v. LAURA; m. Fergus Harolson.
4316. vi. SARAH.

2915. Hon. HENRY A.[8] PIERCE (*Joseph H.[7]*, *Joseph[6]*, *Isaac[5]*, *Isaac[4]*, *Samuel[3]*, *Thomas[2]*, *Thomas[1]*), b. Dec. 15, 1808 ; m. July 3, 1838, Susan R. Thompson, b. Mar. 15, 1818.

HENRY A. PIERCE, educated at the public schools of Boston, excepting for a period of a year or so, while he was a member of Gideon F. Thayer's school. In 1824 at the age of sixteen he embarked in the *Griffin*, accompanied by his brother Marcus Tullis for a voyage to the N. W. Coast country, known as the territory of Alaska, where he was engaged in the fur trade until 1829, when he sailed for Honolulu,

Sandwich Islands, where he resided as a merchant until his return to Boston with a moderate fortune in 1842, where he became an extensive merchant and ship owner engaged in commerce with the Hawaiian Islands, Russian Settlements in Asia, California, Manilla and China; during the Civil war he encountered severe losses; in 1867, having withdrawn in a great measure from business he settled in Yazoo County, Miss., as a cotton planter; owing to unprosperous seasons and also to unfortunate speculations in the cotton market he lost nearly all the remainder of a once large fortune accumulated by so much toil and enterprise. Through the interest of the Hon. Hamilton Fish, Secretary of State of the U. S., he was in Mar. 1869 appointed U. S. minister resident at Honolulu, Sandwich Islands; now res. San Francisco, Cal.

Henry A. Peirce,

Children :—
4317. i. ELLA A., b. Oct. 3, 1839; m. Apr. 15, 1862, Fred. Clapp. Ch.:
Anna, b. Oct. 6, 1864, m. Silas A. Gurney.
4318. ii. HENRY M., b. Nov. 23, 1846.

2916. JOHN D.[8] PIERCE (*Joseph H.*[7], *Joseph*[6], *Isaac*[5], *Isaac*[4], *Samuel*[3], *Thomas*[2], *Thomas*[1]), b. Aug. 6, 1812 ; m. 1837, Ruth Stockton Smith, b. ——, d. Nov. 7, 1865. He d. Oct 19, 1870. Res. Cincinnati, Ohio. Children :—
4319. i. FRANCES T., b. June 18, 1838; d. May 11, 1839.
4320. ii. ANNA T., b. Apr. 4, 1840; m. —— Borham.
4321. iii. WILLIAM, b. Oct. 8, 1844; m. ——.
4322. iv. HARDY, b. June 25, 1847.
4323. v. CATHARINE, b. Feb. 19, 1849; m. —— Meader.
4324. vi. FRANCES L., b. May 23, 1853.

2921. WILLIAM J.[8] PIERCE (*Asa*[7], *William*[6], *William*[5], *Sommers*[4], *William*[3], *Thomas*[2], *Thomas*[1]), b. Oct. 4, 1820 ; m. 1846, Serepta Hossiter. Res. Springville, N. Y.

2924. WARREN A.[8] PIERCE (*Asa*[7], *William*[6], *William*[5], *Sommers*[4], *William*[3], *Thomas*[2], *Thomas*[1]), b. July 14, 1831 ; m. Feb. 18, 1856, Frances J. Davis, b. July 18, 1838. Res. Rolla, Miss. Children :—
4325. i. CARRIE A., b. June 16, 1858.
4326. ii. FRANK W., b. March 21, 1862.
4327. iii. FRED. H., b. May 21, 1864.
4328. iv. ADA J., b. Nov. 9, 1871.
4329. v. WARREN D., b. April 10, 1873.

2926. ALBERT H.[8] PIERCE (*Asa*[7], *William*[6], *William*[5], *Sommers*[4], *William*[3], *Thomas*[2], *Thomas*[1]), b. March 10, 1836 ; m. Eugenia Hossiter. Res. Springville, N. Y.

2927. HUGH[8] PIERCE (*William*[7], *William*[6], *William*[5], *Sommers*[4], *William*[3], *Thomas*[2], *Thomas*[1]), b. Nov. 12, 1818 ; m. Feb. 22, 1848, Mary Rogers, b. March 22, 1824. Res. West Hebron, N. Y. Child :—
4330. i. DAVID T., b. Feb. 10, 1850; m. Etta Burt.

2928. WILLIAM[8] PIERCE (*William[7]*, *William[6]*, *William[5]*, *Sommers[4]*, *William[3]*, *Thomas[2]*, *Thomas[1]*), b. June 7, 1820 ; m. Jan. 24, 1848, Adelaide Bristol, b. May 21, 1821. Res. Sandgate, Vt. No children.

2929. JOHN[8] PIERCE (*William[7]*, *William[6]*, *William[5]*, *Sommers[4]*, *William[3]*, *Thomas[2]*, *Thomas[1]*), b. March 31, 1824 ; m. March 21, 1848, Ann Eliza Tucker. He d. May 11, 1848. Res. Sandgate, Vt. No children. She m. 2nd, Cheney Bowker. Res. Belleville, Wis.

2933. ABIEL H.[8] PIERCE (*Abiel[7]*, *Benjamin[6]*, *William[5]*, *Sommers[4]*, *William[3]*, *Thomas[2]*, *Thomas[1]*), b. May 23, 1822 ; m. Dec. 23, 1847, Cordelia B. Finton, b. Oct. 24, 1821. Res. Dodge's Corner, Wis. Children :—

4331. i.   JOHN B., b. April 2, 1856 ; m. Priscilla Kyburg.
4332. ii. FRANK A., b. Sept. 30, 1858 ; m. Laura L. Jackson.
4333. iii. WILLIAM A., b. April 25, 1864.
4334. iv. CLEMENT H., b. Sept. 27, 1868.

2935. ASA W.[8] PIERCE (*Asa[7]*, *Benjamin[6]*, *William[5]*, *Sommers[4]*, *William[3]*, *Thomas[2]*, *Thomas[1]*), b. Sept. 22, 1821 ; m. Mar. 20, 1845, Ann Poinsett, d. July 29, 1868 ; m. 2nd, Oct. 31, 1869, Hester Corey. Res. Fort Wayne, Ind.   Children :—

4335. i.   JAMES E., b. Jan. 24, 1846 ; d. Oct. 10, 1865.
4336. ii.   MARY E., b. Apr. 23, 1849 ; d. Apr. 20, 1860.
4337. iii. PARYNTHIA O., b. Sept. 13, 1858.
4338. iv.   JOSEPH M., b. Aug. 17, 1862.
4339. v.   W. DELLA, b. Aug. 26, 1870.
4340. vi.   MILOW S., b. Aug. 26, 1872.
4341. vii. ARTHUR, b. Sept. 4, 1874.
4342. viii. CECIL R., b. Oct. 1, 1876.

2938. JAMES S.[8] PIERCE (*Asa[7]*, *Benjamin[6]*, *William[5]*, *Sommers[4]*, *William[3]*, *Thomas[2]*, *Thomas[1]*), b. March 6, 1827 ; m. Apr. 28, 1851, Mary Rockhill, d. Sept. 19, 1855 ; m. 2nd, Feb. 19, 1856, Phebe Strout. Res. Fort Wayne, Ind.

Children :—

4343. i.   FLORENCE M., b. Nov. 30, 1854.
4344. ii. INDIANA L., b. July 31, 1859 ; d. April 22, 1860.
4345. iii. J. FRANK, b. Feb. 13, 1862.

2940. ALVAH W.[8] PIERCE (*Alvah[7]*, *Benjamin[6]*, *William[5]*, *Sommers[4]*, *William[3]*, *Thomas[2]*, *Thomas[1]*), b. June 26, 1818 ; m. May 9, 1841, Lydia W. Atwood, d. May 7, 1854 ; m. 2nd, Apr. 5, 1855, Lucy C. Allen. Res. Londonderry. Vt.

Children :—

4346. 1.   LEROY M., b. Jan. 10, 1842 ; m. Catherine Billings.

4347. ii. LILLIE A., b. Dec. 6, 1844; m. Apr. 25. 1865, Rev. Robert B. Snowden.
Robert B. Snowden was born in New York City, Nov. 21, 1833, graduated at Williams College, Mass., 1854, at present (1881), Presbyter in the Protestant Episcopal Church, Rector of St. Albans Hall, Brooklyn, N. Y., Editor of the *Church Magazine*, and Rector of St. John's Church, Fort Hamilton, N. Y. Harbor. Ch.: Mary M., b. Feb. 17, 1866; Willard, b. Apr. 7, 1868; Laura H., b. Dec. 19, 1870; Lillian P., b. Sept. 11, 1872; Edith A., b. Aug. 26, 1873, d. May 5, 1875; Evelyn S., b. Jan. 25, 1876.

4348. iii. MARY, b. Sept. 7, 1848; m. Moses M. Martin. Mary Pierce, daughter of Alvah Pierce, has devoted herself to the profession of teaching, in which she has been successful. She graduated at Monticello Seminary, Godfrey, Ill., in 1869. She taught one year in the public schools of Belleville, Ill., one year in Alton, Ill., and three years as Preceptress of Black River Academy of Ludlow, Vt. She was in 1878 a teacher in the institution where she graduated. She has scholarly and literary tastes and is quite skillful in painting.

4349. iv. FRANK, b. Aug. 26, 1853; d. March 10, 1854.

4350. v. CLARA, b. March 16, 1856. Clara Pierce, daughter of Alvah, has also devoted herself to the profession of teaching. She was educated at Black River Academy, where she took high rank as a scholar. She was in 1878 a teacher in the public schools of Ludlow, Vt. In 1880, she was engaged as a missionary teacher among the Scandinavian Mormons at Mount Pleasant, San Pete County, Utah. She is one of the sixteen young ladies employed in this work by the Presbyterian Board of Home Missions in Utah.

4351. vi. FRANK, b. April 3, 1857. Frank Pierce, son of Alvah, graduated at Barr & Barton's Seminary, Manchester, N. H., in June, 1877, the valedictorian of his class. In the autumn of the same year he entered Williams College, from which institution he graduated with honors in the summer of 1881. President Chadbourne says of him " he was one of the very best scholars in his class."

4352. vii. EDWARD, b. Feb. 10, 1859.
4353. viii. JESSIE, b. July 29, 1861.
4354. ix. NATHAN, b. Sept. 24, 1865.
4355. x. CARSON, b. April 1, 1868.
4356. xi. FLORENCE, b. Jan. 29, 1870; d. Feb. 15, 1875.
4357. xii. FANNIE, b. Feb. 18, 1877.

2941. FERNANDO A.[8] PIERCE (*Alanson*[7], *Benjamin*[6], *William*[5], *Sommers*[4], *William*[3], *Thomas*[2], *Thomas*[1]), b. April 25, 1826; m. Nov. 25, 1847, Betsey A. Hoyt. He d. Oct. 5, 1856. Res. Manchester, N. H. Children :—

4358. i. HATTIE A., b. Sept. 26, 1848; m. June 29, 1872, Edwin P. Taylor. Res. Cavendish, Vt.
4359. ii. MARY F., b. May 9, 1851.
4360. iii. NELLIE J., b. March 3, 1854; m. Mar. 10, 1876, Everett Bingham. Res. Springfield, Vt.
4361. iv. BESSIE A., b. July 31, 1855; m. Nov. 10, 1876, L. C. Atherton. Res. Leominster, Mass.

2944. SAMUEL B.[8] PIERCE (*Alanson*[7], *Benjamin*[6], *William*[5], *Sommers*[4], *William*[3], *Thomas*[2], *Thomas*[1]), b. Sept. 5, 1839; m. Jan. 3, 1865, Mary E. Bond. She d. Feb., 1880. Res. Weathersfield, Vt.

35

Children :—
4362. i.   MARY E., b. July 18, 1868.
4363. ii. BERTIE B., b. Mar. 24, 1869.
4364. iii. DAISY, b. April 29, 1871.
4365. iv. EDNA, b. Oct. 11, 1874.
4366. v.   SUSIE L., b. Nov. 7, 1875.

2945. LORENZO A.[8] PIERCE (Abel[7], Benjamin[6], William[5], Sommers[4], William[3], Thomas[2], Thomas[1]), b. Jan. 27, 1826 ; m. Aug. 16, 1845, Charlotte L. Davis, b. April 13, 1829. Res. Minneapolis, Kansas. He received his education at the common schools, and at the age of nineteen began the study of law in the office of A. M. Able, Esq., in Londonderry, Vt. After pursuing his studies here for two years, he removed to the State of Wisconsin and was admitted to practice as an attorney in 1852. He remained here until 1864 when he crossed the Rocky Mountains. In 1869 he returned and settled in Kansas, where he now resides. He conducts farming with his law practice.

Lorenzo A. Pierce

Children :—
4367. i.   HARRIET M., b. Dec. 20, 1846 ; m. Feb. 27, 1870, Joseph Decker. Res. Young Co., Texas.
4368. ii.   ROYAL L., b. April 23, 1851.
4369. iii. CURTIS D., b. Aug. 27, 1854 ; d. June 17, 1863.
4370. iv.   JOHN D., b. Aug. 12, 1858.
4371. v.   MARY E., b. Oct. 6, 1862.
4372. vi.   FRANK S., b. Aug. 23, 1870.
4373. vii. WILLIAM A., b. Oct. 5, 1872.

2946. ROYAL A.[8] PIERCE (Abel[7], Benjamin[6], William[5], Sommers[4], William[3], Thomas[2], Thomas[1]), b. Feb. 23, 1828 ; m. Dec. 18, 1853, Eliza A. Ashdown, b. Feb. 8, 1832. Res. Baker City, Oregon. He was born at North Derry, in Londonderry, Vt., and lived with a relative, Sumner Wait, after his father's death in 1832. The following year he resided with his uncle Abel. In 1843 he resided in Wisconsin with an uncle. In 1845 attended a select school at Caldwell's Prairie, Racine County, and the following year taught school. He studied law and practiced quite successfully. His name is closely linked with the founding of the towns of Black Earth, Dane County, Wisconsin, and Baker City, Baker County, Oregon. Children :—
4374. i.   LILY E., b. Apr. 20, 1854 ; d. July 14, 1854.
4375. ii.   ROYAL A., b. Jan. 27, 1856 ; d. Aug, 26, 1856.
4376. iii. JAMES A., b. June 26, 1857.
4377. iv.   ABEL G., b. Aug. 2, 1858.
4378. v.   NELLY A. A., b. Nov. 21, 1860.
4379. vi.   MARTHA H. D., b. Nov. 16, 1863.
4380. vii. WILLIAM A. D., b. Feb. 23, 1866.
4381. viii. MARY E. V., b. March 22, 1868.
4382. ix.   ROYAL A., b. Jan. 4, 1871.

2953. JAMES[8] PIERCE (*James[7], Nathan[6], James[5], James[4], James[3], Thomas[2], Thomas[1]*), b. July 4, 1824 ; m. Sept. 28, 1855, Jane Hunt, b. Nov. 25, 1834. Res. Leroy, Minn.

James Pierce,

Children :—

4383. i. FANNIE W., b. Oct. 2, 1856.
4384. ii. GEORGE G., b. Sept. 14, 1858.
4385. iii. THOMAS L., b. Mar. 24, 1860.
4386. iv. ALFRED W., b. May 1, 1862.
4387. v. WILLIAM A., b. Mar. 8, 1865.
4388. vi. HENRY O., b. Nov. 7, 1871.
4389. vii. ELIZABETH J., b. June 6, 1874.
4390. viii. JESSIE, b. Apr. 5, 1876.

2956. GEORGE[8] PIERCE (*James[7], Nathan[6], James[5], James[4], James[3], Thomas[2], Thomas[1]*), b. March 1, 1828 ; m. Dec. 5, 1847, Mary E. Trask, b. Nov. 25, 1830. Res. Leroy, Minn., and Charlestown, Mass. Children :—

4391. i. JAMES O., b. Sept. 2, 1848; m. Rosabel Mason.
4392. ii. GEORGE B., b. May 25, 1855; d. Sept. 28, 1855.
4393. iii. GEORGE W., b. Jan. 10, 1857.
4394. iv. WILLIAM H., b. Jan. 10, 1864.
4395. v. HATTIE B., b. Jan. 26, 1867.
4396. vi. MAMIE W., b. July 15, 1869.
4397. vii. FRANK H., b. May 28, 1872.

2963. WILLIAM[8] PIERCE (*Josiah[7], Nathan[6], James[5], James[4], James[3], Thomas[2], Thomas[1]*), b. July 20, 1828 ; m. Eliza Pierce [2962], b. March 16, 1832. Res. Woburn. No children.

2964. HARVEY L.[8] PIERCE (*Josiah[7], Nathan[6], James[5], James[4], James[3], Thomas[2], Thomas[1]*), b. Oct. 22, 1838 ; m. April 22, 1863, Louise J. Bruce, b. April 27, 1841. Res. Westminster, Mass. Children :—

4398. i. STELLA L., b. Feb. 9, 1864.
4399. ii. J. MABEL, b. Oct. 4, 1871.

2965. IRA A.[8] PIERCE (*Josiah[7], Nathan[6], James[5], James[4], James[3], Thomas[2], Thomas[1]*), b. July 29, 1845 ; m. Aug. 13, 1868, Jane Ekis, b. Nov. 14, 1839. Res. Braddock's Field, Pa. No children.

2968. OLIVER H.[8] PIERCE (*Abel[7], Abel[6], James[5], James[4], James[3], Thomas[2], Thomas[1]*), b. Oct. 1, 1825 ; m. May 16, 1850, Mary P. Warren, b. Aug. 15, 1824. He. d. Aug. 17, 1872. Res. Arlington, Mass. Child :—

4400. i. FRANCES A., b. Sept. 9, 1851.

2972. SULLIVAN[8] PIERCE (*William[7], Abel[6], James[5], James[4], James[3], Thomas[2], Thomas[1]*), b. June 18, 1828 ; m. 1854, Ruth Bosworth. He d. Jan. 9, 1860. Child :—

4401. i. GEORGIANA, b. Feb. 5, 1856.

2980. WILLIAM H.[8] PIERCE (*George W.[7], Abel[6], James[5], James[4], James[3], Thomas[2], Thomas[1]*), b. July 18, 1841 ; m. Dec. 25, 1871, Sarah E. Ellis, b. Feb. 18, 1857. Res. Lynn, Mass. Child :—

4402. i.   ALBERT A., b. Aug. 17, 1873.

2981. LEWIS H.[8] PIERCE (*George W.[7], Abel[6], James[5], James[4], James[3], Thomas[2], Thomas[1]*), b. Aug. 29, 1843 ; m. May 26, 1869, Sarah J. Ingalls, b. Jan. 27, 1849. Res. Lynn, Mass, Child :—

4403. i.   GEORGIANA, b. May 20, 1875.

2986. FRANKLIN S.[8] PIERCE (*Sewall W.[7], Abel[6], James[5], James[4], James[3], Thomas[2], Thomas[1]*), b. Mar. 7, 1841 ; m. Apr. 4, 1867, Mary L. Bragg, b. Nov. 1, 1851. Res. Raleigh, N. C. Children:—

4404. i.   MARY F., b. Jan. 10, 1868.
4405. ii.   BERTHA, b. June 9, 1870.
4406. iii. GERTRUDE, b. Apr. 10, 1872.

2988. EDWARD A.[8] PIERCE (*Sewall W.[7], Abel[6], James[5], James[4], James[3], Thomas[2], Thomas[1]*), b. May 16, 1846; m. Nov. 20, 1866, Julia E. Hatch. Res. Lynn, Mass. Children :—

4407. i.   LILLIAN, b. Oct. 21, 1869.
4408. ii.   GEORGE E., b. Feb. 22, 1872.
4409. iii. WILLARD F., b. Apr. 3, 1875.

2989. WINSLOW[8] PIERCE (*Sewall W.[7], Abel[6], James[5], James[4], James[3], Thomas[2], Thomas[1]*), b. May 12, 1848; m. Apr., 1871, Mary A. Townsend. Res. Winchester, Mass. Children :—

4410. i.   ———; d. infancy.
4411. ii.   ———; d. infancy.

2993. JOSHUA D.[8] PIERCE (*Joshua[7], Joshua[6], Joshua[5], James[4], James[3], Thomas[2], Thomas[1]*), b. Mar. 22, 1813 ; m. Jan. 8, 1835, Louisa L. Corbin, b. Feb. 21, 1813. Res. Augusta, Me.

Children :—
4412. i.   EDWARD C., b. Jan. 30, 1836; m. Mary C. Sayward.
4413. ii.   CHARLES A., b. Apr. 11, 1839; d. Aug. 20, 1868.
4414. iii. ANDREW J., b. Nov. 11, 1841.
4415. iv.   JOSHUA F., b. May 28, 1844; m. Emma A. Hutchinson.
4416. v.   HARRIET S., b. June 24, 1848.
4417. vi.   GEORGE M., b. June 30, 1851.
4418. vii. ROBERT W., b. May 16, 1854.

2996. ANDREW J.[8] PIERCE (*Joshua[7], Joshua[6], Joshua[5], James[4], James[3], Thomas[2], Thomas[1]*), b. Jan. 30, 1821 ; m. Sept. 19, 1859, Caroline Holmes, b. June 3, 1815. Res. Watertown, Mass.
No children.

3000. JAMES L.[8] PIERCE (*James[7], Joshua[6], Joshua[5], James[4], James[3], Thomas[2], Thomas[1]*), b. Aug. 6, 1824; m. Oct. 5, 1851, Martha J. Cross, b. Oct. 12, 1830. Res. Nashua, N. H.

Children :—

4419. i. FRANK J., b. July 16, 1852.
4420. ii. GEORGE R., b. Feb. 22, 1857.

3001. JOHN P.[8] PIERCE (*James[7], Joshua[6], Joshua[5], James[4], James[3], Thomas[2], Thomas[1]*), b. July 25, 1828; m. Oct. 29, 1854, Martha E. Case, b. June 28, 1835, d. Apr. 3, 1863. He d. Nov. 8, 1864. Child :—

4421. i. ARTHUR P., b. Nov. 10, 1855.

3003. JOSHUA C.[8] PIERCE (*James[7], Joshua[6], Joshua[5], James[4], James[3], Thomas[2], Thomas[1]*), b. Dec. 8, 1831; m. Oct. 29, 1861, Kate H. Chase, b. Mar. 14, 1839. Res. Red Wing, Mich. No children.

3005. BENJAMIN F.[8] PIERCE (*Nathan[7], Nathan[6], Joshua[5], James[4], James[3], Thomas[2], Thomas[1]*), b. May 2, 1832; m. Sept. 3, 1855, Harriet J. Goodwin, b. Jan. 17, 1836. Res. Stoughton, Mass.

Children :—

4422. i. ABBIE E., b. Aug. 9, 1856; d. Oct. 20, 1863.
4423. ii. ANNIE M., b. Feb. 26, 1858.
4424. iii. BERTHA F., b. May 26, 1861.
4425. iv. MARTHA A., b. Oct. 11, 1866.
4426. v. ABBIE L., b. Apr. 17, 1872.
4427. vi. THOMAS W., b. Dec. 23, 1875.

3010. DANIEL[8] PIERCE (*Stephen C.[7], Nathan[6], Joshua[5], James[4], James[3], Thomas[2], Thomas[1]*), b. Sept. 12, 1852; m. Sept. 3, 1872, Nancy H. Morgan.
Children :—

4428. i. MARTHA E., b. Nov. 14, 1874.
4429. ii. ALICE M., b. Aug. 4, 1876.
4430. iii. ANNA M., b. Sept. 19, 1878.

3011. DANIEL[8] PIERCE (*Daniel[7], James[6], Joshua[5], James[4], James[3], Thomas[2], Thomas[1]*), b. Dec. 14, 1827; m. 1860, Sarah Jones. Res. Fort Wayne, Ind.

3013. JAMES S.[8] PIERCE (*Daniel*[7], *James*[6], *Joshua*[5], *James*[4], *James*[3], *Thomas*[2], *Thomas*[1]), b. Feb. 6, 1832 ; m. July 10, 1858. Mary A. Casey. Res. New Haven, Conn. Children :—

4431. i.   JAMES D., b. Oct. 1, 1862.
4432. ii. HATTIE W., b. Aug. 10, 1865.

3015. MARSHALL W.[8] PIERCE (*Daniel*[7], *James*[6], *Joshua*[5], *James*[4], *James*[3], *Thomas*[2], *Thomas*[1]), b. Apr. 4, 1836 ; m. Oct. 15, 1861, Liza Booth, d. Mar. 4, 1874 ; m. 2nd, Apr. 14, 1876, Sarah Wilson, Res. New York city. Children :—

4433. i.   WILLIE, b. Aug. 1, 1862.
4434. ii.   LIZA R., b. Jan. 24, 1866.
4435. iii. WALTER, b. Nov. 23, 1867.

3019. JONAS J.[8] PIERCE (*James*[7], *James*[6], *Joshua*[5], *James*[4], *James*[3], *Thomas*[2], *Thomas*[1]), b. September 23, 1839 ; m. April 6, 1865, Kate Pritzl, b. December 19, 1841. He was born in Swanzey, New Hampshire, and came to Pennsylvania with his father's family in 1845. Until twenty-one he was employed at his father's coal and iron works, and received an academical education. At the breaking out of the Rebellion in 1861 he enlisted in the United States service in Company K, 63d Regiment, P. V. Army of the Potomac. Received a commission as first lieutenant, 111th Regiment, P. V. After recruiting and organization in January 1862 was appointed Captain in Company K. Served with the regiment in the Army of Virginia, and resigned in the fall of 1862. Engaged in business with his father until 1870. At that time organized the firm of Pierce, Kelley & Co., for the erection of the Douglass Furnaces at Sharpsville, for the manufacture of Pig Iron. Is interested with his brothers in the mining of Lake Superior iron ores in Michigan, Iron Banking Company, Sharpsville, also Railroad and Coal Companies. Is now and has been a member of the school board since the organization of the borough. Has served twice as Burgess. Present residence and address Sharpsville, Pa.

Children :—

4436. i.   SCOTT, b. Jan. 18, 1866.
4437. ii.   JAMES A., b. Oct. 27, 1867.
4438. iii. CHLOE H., b. June 25, 1869.
4439. iv.   JONAS, b. Aug. 5, 1874.
4439½. v.   FREDERICK P., b. Mar. 11, 1880.

3020. WALTER[8] PIERCE (*James*[7], *James*[6], *Joshua*[5], *James*[4], *James*[3], *Thomas*[2], *Thomas*[1]), b. Oct. 19, 1842 ; m. June 28, 1871, Alice M. Mower, b. Feb. 17, 1850. Res. Sharpsville, Pa. Children :—

4440. i.   ALICE M., b. Nov. 6, 1872.
4441. ii.   MARY J., b. Mar. 17, 1874.
4441½. iii. KATE, b. May 30, 1879.

3022. FRANK[8] PIERCE (*James*[7], *James*[6], *Joshua*[5], *James*[4], *James*[3], *Thomas*[2], *Thomas*[1]), b. Nov. 10, 1852 ; m. Oct. 21, 1880, Minnie Andrews, b. Nov. 15, 1859. Res. Sharpsville, Pa.

Walter Pierce

Wallace Pierce

Jonas G. Pierce

Samuel Pierce

James B. Pierce

3023. JAMES B.⁸ PIERCE (*James⁷, James⁶, Joshua⁵, James⁴, James³, Thomas², Thomas¹*), b. Sept. 2, 1856; m. June 17, 1880, Albertina Pomplitz, b. Mar. 7, 1856. Res. Sharpsville, Pa.

3024. JOB W.⁸ PIERCE (*William⁷, James⁶, Joshua⁵, James⁴, James³, Thomas², Thomas¹*), b. Nov. 25, 1845; m. Dec. 19, 1866, Hortense E. Thompson, b. Sept. 28, 1844. Res. Empire Prairie, Missouri. No children.

3026. HEROD⁸ PIERCE (*Samuel⁷, Daniel⁶, Joshua⁵, James⁴, James³, Thomas², Thomas¹*), b. 1806; m. 1836, Eliza Thurston, b. 1809, d. June 20, 1865; m. 2nd, Mrs. Chubb. Res. Albany, Vt.

Herod Pierce

Child :—
4442. i. IRA T., b. June, 1838; m. Mary Kelley.

3027. CHARLES F.⁸ PIERCE (*Samuel⁷, Daniel⁶, Joshua⁵, James⁴, James³, Thomas², Thomas¹*), b. Nov. 7, 1808; m. Mar. 24, 1836, Nancy Church, b. Mar. 24, 1812, d. Aug. 10, 1877. Res. Barton, Vt. Children ;—
4443. i. SIDNEY, b. Apr. 4, 1838; d. Sept. 17, 1862.
4444. ii. ELLEN, b. May 16, 1840; m. Henry Dudley.
4445. iii. EDWIN, b. Aug. 31, 1850; m. Abby Woodward.
4446. iv. ARTHUR, b. May 1, 1855; d. May 1, 1858.

3030. ELBRIDGE G.⁸ PIERCE (*Samuel⁷, Daniel⁶, Joshua⁵, James⁴, James³, Thomas², Thomas¹*), b. Jan. 12, 1814; m. Betsey Cochran, b. Aug. 6, 1817. Res. Northfield, Vt.

E. G. Pierce

Children :—
4447. i. CHARLES H., b. June 20, 1846.

C. H. Pierce

4448. ii. KATIE, b Oct. 16, 1851.

3032. WILLIAM P.⁸ PIERCE (*Samuel⁷, Daniel⁶, Joshua⁵, James⁴, James³, Thomas², Thomas¹*), b. April 16, 1818 ; m. March 15, 1849, Fidelia A. Booth, b. Jan. 5, 1825. Res. Boston, Mass. Children :—
4449. i. CAROLINE E., b. Jan. 20, 1852; d. Aug. 11, 1853.
4450. ii. CAROLINE E., b. July 27, 1855.

3038. EDMOND B.⁸ PIERCE (*Samuel⁷, Daniel⁶, Joshua⁵, James⁴,*

James³, Thomas², Thomas¹), b. Aug., 1830 ; m. 1853, Jane Bancroft.
He d. Feb. 27, 1854.   Res. Albany, Vt.   No children.

3044. HORACE⁸ PIERCE (*Daniel⁷, Daniel⁶, Joshua⁵, James⁴,
James³, Thomas², Thomas¹*), b. Oct. 14, 1819 ; m. 1847, Mary A.
Startup, b. March 31, 1828.   Children :—

4451. i.   KATE, b. Dec. 1, 1847 ; m. Wm. C. Osman.
4452. ii. DANIEL I., b. Aug. 17, 1849 ; m. Carrie J. Lawrence.

3048. GEORGE W.⁸ PIERCE (*Daniel⁷, Daniel⁶, Joshua⁵, James⁴,
James³, Thomas², Thomas¹*), b. July 1, 1832 ; m. April 26, 1855,
Myra F. Copp, b. Feb. 4, 1832.   Children :—

4453. i.   GEORGE H., b. Jan. 24, 1859.
4454. ii. ELLEN M., b. Aug. 5, 1864.

3050. MATTHEW H.⁸ PIERCE (*Robert F.⁷, Daniel⁶, Joshua⁵, James⁴,
James³, Thomas², Thomas¹*), b. Oct. 24, 1813 ; m. Sept. 3, 1836,
Hannah J. Jones, b. March 25, 1816.   He d. May 1, 1859.   Res. West
Andover, N. H.

Children :—

4455. i.   AURILLA L., b. Jan. 12, 1838 ; m. A. J. Seavey,
4456. ii.   PHILONA C., b. Oct. 1, 1843 ; d. Feb. 15, 1863.
4457. iii. BURTT H., b. Sept. 1, 1846 ; d. April 12, 1874.
4458. iv.   FRANK J., b. Feb. 24, 1852 ; d. Dec. 24, 1877.

3051. WALTER H.⁸ PIERCE (*Robert F.⁷, Daniel⁶, Joshua⁵, James⁴,
James³, Thomas², Thomas¹*), b. April 19, 1817 ; m. Lydia Bean ; m.
2nd, 1844, Rebecca Phillips, d. May, 1848.   He d. Nov., 1847.   Res.
New London, N. H.   Children :—

4459. i.   ARABELLA, b. June 2, 1845 ; d. 1864.
4460. ii. ———, b. July, 1846 ; d. young.

3053. NATHANIEL F.⁸ PIERCE (*Isaac⁷, Daniel⁶, Joshua⁵, James⁴,
James³, Thomas², Thomas¹*), b. Feb. 16, 1820 ; m. Sept., 1842, Sarah
M. Smith, b. Jan. 13, 1825, d. March 8, 1865 ; m. 2nd, Nov., 1865, Mrs.
Eliza Little Burnham, d. Aug., 1870 ; m. 3rd, Lovina Breck.   He d.
Dec. 22, 1875.   Res. Norwich, Vt.   Children :—

4461. i.   HELEN I., b. May 26, 1845 ; m. J. B. Smith.
4462. ii.   ELBRIDGE S., b. July 30, 1849 ; m. Henrietta Benton.
4463. iii. HORACE A., b. Aug. 24, 1860.

3061. MARK W.⁸ PIERCE (*Joshua⁷, Daniel⁶, Joshua⁵, James⁴,
James³, Thomas², Thomas¹*), b. Aug. 2, 1825 ; m. July 4, 1848,
Harriet D. Burbank, b. March 26, 1830, d. Sept. 28, 1851 ; m. 2nd,

Jan. 2, 1862, Lucy A. E. Sinclair, b. April 9, 1842, d. Nov. 19, 1878. Res. Centre Bartlett, N. H.

Mark W⁰ Pierce

Children :—

4464. i.   ——, b. May 6, 1849; d. infancy.
4465. ii. SARAH E., b. March 18, 1850.
4466. iii. ——, b. July 28, 1851; d. infancy.

3063¼. GEORGE J.[8] PIERCE (*Joshua[7], Daniel[6], Joshua[5], James[4], James[3], Thomas[2], Thomas[1]*), b. Sept. 3, 1833 ; m. April. 16, 1857, Carrie A. Kent, b. March 8, 1834. Res. West Newbury, Mass. Children :—

4467. i.   GEORGE G., b. Sept. 1, 1859.
4468. ii. J. HENRY, b. Nov. 3, 1860.
4469. iii. EVERETT S., b. June 20, 1864; d. Dec. 9, 1878.
4470. iv. CARRIE F., b. July 14, 1866.

3063½. CHARLES A.[8] PIERCE (*Joshua[7], Daniel[6], Joshua[5], James[4], James[3], Thomas[2], Thomas[1]*), b. Jan. 13, 1838; m. Oct. 29, 1861, Mary O. Harvey, b. Oct. 9, 1839. Res. Manchester, N. H. Child :—

4471. i.   FRED. C., b. May 14, 1863.

3069. EBENEZER L.[8] PIERCE (*Jacob[7], Jacob[6], Jacob[5], James[4], James[3], Thomas[2], Thomas[1]*), b. June 16, 1819 ; m. May 17, 1848, Mary Gardner [1012], b. Oct. 1, 1820. Res. Woburn, Mass.

E L Pierce,

Children :—

4472. i.   GARDNER M., } b. Aug. 13, 1849; { d. Feb. 13, 1850.
4473. ii. THEODORE L., }

Theodore L Pierce.

4474. iii. EDWARD G., b. Aug. 16, 1852.
4475. iv. ROSCOE P., b. May 4, 1856; m. Mabel N. Boutwell
4476. v.   E. WINSLOW, b. June 2, 1859.

E Winslow Pierce

4477. vi. MARY C., b. July 22, 1861; d. Sept. 5, 1861.

36

3074. JAMES[8] PIERCE (*Ephraim*[7], *Ephraim*[6], *Jacob*[5], *James*[4], *James*[3], *Thomas*[2], *Thomas*[1]), b. Oct. 10, 1809 ; m. Nov. 10, 1835, Eliza Porter, b. Oct. 30, 1807. He d. Jan. 25, 1871. Res. Stoneham, Mass.

Children :—

4478. i. JAMES, b. Feb. 15, 1837; d. Feb. 15, 1837.
4479. ii. ELIZA A., b. Sept. 10, 1838; d. Sept. 2, 1864.
4480. iii. ABBY J., b. Jan. 20, 1840; d. May 25, 1862.
4481. iv. JAMES H., b. Sept. 30, 1841; m. April 18, 1865, Alice J. Weston.
4482. v. WILLIAM B., b. Dec. 30, 1843; d. Jan. 25, 1845.
4483. vi. SARAH E., b. Oct. 16, 1845; m. Oct. 16, 1865, John H. Cook. She d. Nov. 8, 1871, leaving Earnest F., b. July 21, 1866.
4484. vii. MARY F., b. May 13, 1850; m. Sept. 5, 1877, Henry E. Grenville, b. 1850. Children: Walter E., b. June 25, 1878; Elmer K., b. Mar. 9, 1880.

3078. JOHN[8] PIERCE (*Ephraim*[7], *Ephraim*[6], *Jacob*[5], *James*[4], *James*[3], *Thomas*[2], *Thomas*[1]), b. Feb. 20, 1820 ; m. Nov. 5, 1846, Agnes Goodhue, b. April 4, 1818. Res. Reading, Mass. Children :—

4485. i. AUGUSTA A., b. July 3, 1850; m. James F. Cook.
4486. ii. JOHN M., b. Dec. 16, 1853.
4487. iii. FLORA E., b. May 10, 1857.

3079. RUFUS L.[8] PIERCE (*Ephraim*[7], *Ephraim*[6], *Jacob*[5], *James*[4], *James*[3], *Thomas*[2], *Thomas*[1]), b. May 16, 1822 ; m. Apr. 5, 1849, Eliza J. McIntire, b. March 4, 1832, d. Nov. 5, 1878. He m. 2d Rebecca E. Ripley, Nov. 25, 1879, b. ——— ———. Res. Lynn, Mass.

Child :—

4487¼. i. Mary Elma, b. June 22, 1881.

3081. WILLIAM H.[8] PIERCE (*Ephraim*[7], *Ephraim*[6], *Jacob*[5], *James*[4], *James*[3], *Thomas*[2], *Thomas*[1]), b. Aug. 4, 1827; m. July 15, 1849, Sarah A. Mooney, b. Feb. 23, 1828. Res. Breed-Street, Lynn, Mass.

Children :—

4487½. i. SARAH L., b. Oct. 29, 1851.

4488. ii. IDA M., b. July 18, 1855.
4489. iii. WILLIAM H., b. July 27, 1857; d. Oct. 8, 1859.

3091½. WILLIAM H. H.[8] PIERCE (*James*[7], *Heman*[6], *Jacob*[5], *James*[4], *James*[3], *Thomas*[2], *Thomas*[1]), b. Sept. 5, 1837 ; m. Oct. 26, 1859, Emma H. Cooley, b. Nov. 27, 1839. Res. Wakefield, Mass.

Children :—

4490. i. HOMER I., b. Oct. 27, 1860.
4491. ii. LOUISA S., b. Oct. 4, 1863.
4492. iii. HENRY L., b. June 6, 1865.
4493. iv. EMMA F., b. July 29, 1868.
4494. v. GRACE B., b. Feb. 8, 1873.
4495. vi. CHARLES S., b. July 30, 1874.
4496. vii. MARY L., b. Sept. 27, 1875.

3098. JAMES HOMER[8] PIERCE (*Samuel B.*[7], *Heman*[6], *Jacob*[5], *James*[4], *James*[3], *Thomas*[2], *Thomas*[1]), b. Oct. 27, 1840 ; m. June 16, 1869, Eliza C. Bradford, b. Sept. 23, 1846. They res. in Dorchester. He is in the wholesale crockery business on Pearl-St., in Boston, and on Barclay-St., in New York. The firm style is J. H. Pierce & Robertson. He has been a member of the Common Council of the City of Boston from his ward in Dorchester.

Children :—

4497. i. MARY B., b. March 11, 1870.
4498. ii. LOUISA Q., b. Sept. 17, 1871.
4499. iii. KATHERINE K., b. Mar. 9, 1878.
4500. iv. NANETTE R., b. July 15, 1879.

3100. FREDERIC B.[8] PIERCE (*Samuel B.*[7], *Heman*[6], *Jacob*[5], *James*[4], *James*[3], *Thomas*[2], *Thomas*[1]), b. May 1, 1845 ; m. Oct. 16, 1873, Mary R. Davis, b. Sept. 1, 1853. They res. in Dorchester. He is engaged in business at No. 47, Broad-St., in Boston, in the oil business; his refinery, The Union Oil Works, is at East Boston. His brother-in-law, Wm. H. Canterbury, is in company with him. They are the largest oil refiners and one of the largest dealers in the State.

Children :—
4501. i.   SAMUEL B., b. Nov. 27, 1874.

SAMUEL B. PIERCE

4502. ii.   ANDREW D., b. Mar. 5, 1876.
4503. iii. MILDRED R., b. May 19, 1877.
4504. vi.   MARGERY M., b. Oct. 22, 1880.

3108. BENJAMIN[8] PIERCE (*Benjamin[7], Benjamin[6], Benjamin[5], Thomas[4], Benjamin[3], Thomas[2], Thomas[1]*), b. June 25, 1819 ; m. Oct. 3, 1843, Maria A. Warren, b. Feb. 5, 1824. He was born in Mendon and moved to Weston with his parents. He succeeded his father in the baking business, which he carried on until 1859. The next year he was appointed Assistant Marshal to take the United States Census, in the towns of Weston, Wayland, Sudbury, Marlborough and Framingham. He was Constable and Tax Collector for ten years, and also held the offices of Selectman, Assessor and Overseer of the Poor. In 1862 he removed to a farm, where he still lives in Weston, Mass.

Benjamin Peirce

Children :—
4505. i.   AMANDA W., b. Mar. 26, 1846.
4506. ii.   ELLEN M., b. Dec. 31, 1848; m. Oct. 27, 1869, Wm. G. Childs; b. Apr. 12, 1853. Ch.: Arthur G., b. Apr. 4, 1871; Alice P., b. May 4, 1874; Wm. B., b. Feb. 4, 1876.
4507. iii. IDA M., b. Dec. 9, 1856.

3117. GEORGE[8] PIERCE (*Benjamin[7], Benjamin[6], Benjamin[5], Thomas[4], Benjamin[3], Thomas[2], Thomas[1]*), b. Aug. 21, 1843 ; m. Sept. 15, 1875, Anna G. Bartlett. Res. Boston, Mass. Child :—
4508. i.   J. GILBERT, b. Oct. 11, 1879.

3119. JOHN[8] PIERCE (*John[7], John[6], Benjamin[5], Thomas[4], Benjamin[3], Thomas[2], Thomas[1]*), b. Aug. 31, 1823 ; m. June 1, 1851, Sophronia Goodrich, b. Aug. 5, 1822, d. Feb. 2, 1875. Res. Skowhegan, Me.

John Pierce Jr.

Children :—
4509. i.   HATTIE E., b. April 6, 1852; m. Nov. 30, 1873, Frank B. Ward, b. June 25, 1842. Ch.: Pierce, b. Jan. 18, 1875.
4510. ii.   STEPHANIA G., b. Feb., 1855.

3120. MERARI S.[8] PIERCE (*John[7], John[6], Benjamin[5], Thomas[4],*

Benjamin³, Thomas², Thomas¹), b. March 13, 1826 ; m. Feb. 22, 1865, Sarah Seley, b. Oct. 1, 1845. He d. Feb. 2, 1869.

Children :—

4511. i. ISAAC S., b. Sept. 10, 1866.
4512. ii. MERARI S., b. Sept. 13, 1868; d. Feb. 21, 1869.

3122. WALTER⁸ S. PIERCE (*John⁷, John⁶, Benjamin⁵, Thomas⁴, Benjamin³, Thomas², Thomas¹*), b. Aug. 14, 1833 ; m. Feb. 5, 1866, Flavilla Nichols, b. March 28, 1843. Res. Eureka, Cal.

Child :—

4513. i. GEORGIE, b. Feb. 11, 1868.

3126. MARK A.⁸ PIERCE (*David W.⁷, John⁶, Benjamin⁵, Thomas⁴, Benjamin³, Thomas², Thomas¹*), b. July 18, 1825 ; m. May 11, 1853, Mary E. Palmer, b. Oct. 22, 1829, d. Dec. 2, 1861 ; m. 2nd, March 11, 1869, Annie Hughes, b. July 17, 1844. Res. Arcade, N. Y. Children :—

4514. i. FRANK B., b. Oct. 28, 1855.
4515. ii. RUTH A., b. Oct. 8, 1858.
4516. iii. HARRIET M., b. Mar. 23, 1861.
4517. iv. T. ALTON, b. June 8, 1871.

3127. SAMUEL B. P.⁸ PIERCE (*David W.⁷, John⁶, Benjamin⁵, Thomas⁴, Benjamin³, Thomas², Thomas¹*), b. Sept. 27, 1827 ; m. May 26, 1875, Mrs. Anna R. Young, b. Nov. 16, 1844. Residence, Paradise, Nev.

Children :—

4518. i. JAMES B., b. May 24, 1876; d. Jan. 24, 1879.
4519. ii. HATTIE C., } b. Dec. 4, 1879; } d. infancy.
4520. iii. HETTIE C., }

3130. DAVID W.⁸ PIERCE (*Benjamin⁷, John⁶, Benjamin⁵, Thomas⁴, Benjamin³, Thomas², Thomas¹*), b. July 5, 1820 ; m. Jan. 30, 1847, Olive Albee. He d. Oct. 3, 1870. Children :—

4521. i. GEORGE A., b. Aug. 25, 1848.
4522. ii. FRED. B., b. July 18, 1850.
4523. iii. MARY F., b. Feb. 18, 1852.
4524. iv. FRANK A., b. Jan. 15, 1855.

4525.   v.   FLORA E., b. Jan. 6, 1859.
4526.   vi.   EDITH M., b. Oct. 9, 1861.
4527.   vii. EMMA F., b. Dec. 21, 1863.

3136.   HENRY C.[8] PIERCE (*Benjamin*[7], *John*[6], *Benjamin*[5], *Thomas*[4], *Benjamin*[3], *Thomas*[2], *Thomas*[1]), b. Dec. 26, 1834 ; m. Feb. 5, 1865, Sarah H. Lancaster, b. July 11, 1844. Res. Embden, Me.

Child :—

4528.   i.   ROSA M., b. Feb. 10, 1866.

3139.   JAMES W.[8] PIERCE (*James*[7], *Amos*[6], *Benjamin*[5], *Thomas*[4], *Benjamin*[3], *Thomas*[2], *Thomas*[1]), b. Sept. 18, 1839 ; m. Jan. 5, 1862, Annie L. Clark, b. Aug. 19, 1839. Res. Bolton, Mass. Children :—

4529.   i.   MARTHA L., b. July 17, 1865.
4530.   ii.   FRANCIS W., b. Jan. 30, 1867.
4531.   iii. ALBERT J. P., b. Aug. 30, 1874; d. Oct. 4, 1875.
4532.   iv.   WARREN C., b. Sept. 5, 1876.

3142.   JOSEPH G.[8] PIERCE (*Levi*[7], *Joseph*[6], *Thomas*[5], *Thomas*[4], *Benjamin*[3], *Thomas*[2], *Thomas*[1]), b. Sept. 21, 1809 ; m. Feb. 2, 1837, Hannah Hemmenway, b. May 17, 1807. Res. Chester, Vt. Children :—

4533.   i.   LEVI O., b. Dec. 27, 1837 ; d. Aug. 20, 1862.
4534.   ii.   ELIZABETH H., b. Apr. 17. 1839; m. D. B. Dennison.
4535.   iii. GEORGE A., b. Jan. 20, 1843 ; m. Jessie Carney.
4536.   iv.   FRANKLIN J., b. Aug. 5, 1847 ; m. M. E. Wheeler.
4537.   v.   LYDIA M., b. Sept. 4, 1850 ; d. Aug. 23, 1852.
4538.   vi.   ALVA J., b. Jan. 20, 1852 ; d. Aug. 2, 1853.

3144.   LEVI L.[8] PIERCE (*Levi*[7], *Joseph*[6], *Thomas*[5], *Thomas*[4], *Benjamin*[3], *Thomas*[2], *Thomas*[1]), b. May 28, 1816 ; m. Aug. 2, 1840, Fidelia A. Eastman, b. May 2, 1818. Res. Winchendon, Mass. Children :—

4539.   i.   JANE, b. Feb. 17, 1842 ; m. George A. Smith.
4540.   ii.   FRANK, b. Aug. 1, 1844.
4541.   iii. EUNICE, b. June 25, 1846 ; m. Andrew J. Flagg. Res. Fitchburg, Mass.
4542.   iv.   ELLA, b. Aug. 21, 1848.
4543.   v.   ULAH, b. May 1, 1851 ; m. Charles G. Ball.
4544.   vi.   AMY, b. June 28, 1854 ; m. Russell J. Flagg and Milton Lane.

3154.   JASON R.[8] PIERCE (*Abel G.*[7], *Joseph*[6], *Thomas*[5], *Thomas*[4], *Benjamin*[3], *Thomas*[2], *Thomas*[1]), b. Nov. 11, 1833 ; m. Dec. 24, 1852, Celina Vanderhender. Res. Bay City, Mich. Children :—

4545.   i.   CHARLES G., b. Nov. 10, 1853.
4546.   ii.   MINNIE M., b. Oct. 11, 1855 ; m. June 10, 1873, David Twombly. Ch. : Charles E., b. Oct. 23, 1875 ; Iva M., b. Aug. 30, 1877.
4547.   iii. EVA H., b. Jan. 26, 1858 ; m. June 24, 1875, Alfred W. Beers. Ch. : Alfred W. Jr., b. Aug. 16, 1876.
4548.   iv.   ELLIE, b. Apr. 13, 1862.
4549.   v.   WILLIAM L., b. Apr. 12, 1864.
4550.   vi.   FRED. E., b. Mar. 4, 1866.

3156. Rev: EZRA B.⁸ PIERCE (*Ira⁷*, *Eliab⁶*, *Thomas⁵*, *Thomas⁴*, *Benjamin³*, *Thomas²*, *Thomas¹*), b. Dec. 22, 1831 ; m. Aug. 15, 1860, Adeline Sparks, b. Feb. 19, 1831. Res. Spencertown, N. Y.

E. B. Peirce

Children :—
4551. i. CLARENCE W., b. June 13, 1862.
4552. ii. WALTER M., b. July 24, 1864.

3157. HENRY D.⁸ PIERCE (*Ira⁷*, *Eliab⁶*, *Thomas⁵*, *Thomas⁴*, *Benjamin³*, *Thomas²*, *Thomas¹*), b. Apr. 30, 1833 ; m. June 29, 1859, Melvina J. Bennett, b. May 5, 1857, d. Feb. 10, 1871 ; m. 2nd, Mar. 25, 1874, Mrs. Anna Drake Marble, b. May 21, 1827. Res. Hastings, Mich.

3160. GEORGE G.⁸ PIERCE (*Ira⁷*, *Eliab⁶*, *Thomas⁵*, *Thomas⁴*, *Benjamin³*, *Thomas²*, *Thomas¹*), b. Jan. 13, 1840 ; m. Jan. 15, 1862, Bettie G. Durand, b. Sept. 16, 1837. Res. Elyria, Ohio.

Geo. G. Peirce

3161. WILBUR E.⁸ PIERCE (*Ira⁷*, *Eliab⁶*, *Thomas⁵*, *Thomas⁴*, *Benjamin³*, *Thomas²*, *Thomas¹*), b. Jan. 11, 1844 ; m. Mar. 29, 1866, Addie M. Clifford, b. Nov. 28, 1842. Res. Wellington, Ohio.
Children :—
4553. i. ALBERT H., b. Jan. 28, 1867.
4554. ii. C. DELL., b. Oct. 26, 1868.
4555. iii. EDITH M., b. May 10, 1876.

3162. HARLOW M.⁸ PIERCE (*Ira⁷*, *Eliab⁶*, *Thomas⁵*, *Thomas⁴*, *Benjamin³*, *Thomas²*, *Thomas¹*), b. Nov. 10, 1852 ; m. Jan. 1, 1874, Maria C. Sutton, b. May 6, 1850. Res. Wellington, Ohio.

3166. EDWIN M.⁸ PIERCE (*Chauncey⁷*, *Thomas⁶*, *Thomas⁵*, *Thomas⁴*, *Benjamin³*, *Thomas²*, *Thomas¹*), b. Mar. 5, 1830 ; m. Nancy Armstrong. He d. Dec., 1872. Res. Muir, Mich.
Children :—
4556. i. CHAUNCEY M.
4557. ii. JOSEPHINE.

3170. THOMAS W.⁸ PIERCE (*Thomas⁷*, *Thomas⁶*, *Thomas⁵*, *Thomas⁴*, *Benjamin³*, *Thomas²*, *Thomas¹*), b. Sept. 3, 1836 ; m. 1862, Esther A. Cook of Yorkshire, N. Y. Res. Sioux Falls, Dakota. He received a common school education and for some time was in business in Yorkshire. He is engaged in teaching school in Dakota. No children living.

3177. MARSHALL⁸ PIERCE (*Haven⁷*, *Moses H.⁶*, *Thomas⁵*, *Thomas⁴*, *Benjamin³*, *Thomas²*, *Thomas¹*), b. Mar. 3, 1821 ; m. Apr. 20, 1847, Elizabeth L. Jones, b. Jan. 15, 1821. He d. Dec. 15, 1856. Res. Worcester, Mass. Child :—
4558. i. LIZZIE L., b. Apr. 12, 1848 ; m. James E. Jenkins.

3178. Levi[8] Pierce (*Haven*[7], *Moses H.*[6], *Thomas*[5], *Thomas*[4], *Benjamin*[3], *Thomas*[2], *Thomas*[1]), b. Apr. 15, 1823 ; m. Oct. 11, 1855, Almira Wilson, b. Jan. 16, 1830. Res. Worcester, Mass. No children.

3179. Harding[8] Pierce (*Haven*[7], *Moses H.*[6], *Thomas*[5], *Thomas*[4], *Benjamin*[3], *Thomas*[2], *Thomas*[1]), b. Mar. 13, 1825 ; m. Oct. 2, 1845, Mary W. Johnson, b. Aug. 16, 1829. Res. Worcester, Mass.

Harding Peirce.

Children :—

4559. i. Mary E., b. Dec. 18, 1846.
4560. ii. William H., b. Mar. 24, 1849.
4561. iii. Frederick M., b. Oct. 21, 1850; m. March 4, 1879, Sarah E. Whitney.
4562. iv. Caroline H., b. June 17, 1852.

3186. Orrin[8] Pierce (*Asa*[7], *Moses H.*[6], *Thomas*[5], *Thomas*[4], *Benjamin*[3], *Thomas*[2], *Thomas*[1]), b. Sept. 29, 1826; m. Apr. 20, 1853, Fidelia Holden, b. Oct. 9, 1829. Res. North Rutland, Mass.

Orrin Peirce

Children :—

4563. i. Emma F., b. Jan. 27, 1857 ; m. Lyman Wilson.
4564. ii. Florence A., b. May 24, 1868.
4565. iii. George G., b. Jan. 17, 1870.

3188. Watson J.[8] Pierce (*Asa*[7], *Moses H.*[6], *Thomas*[5], *Thomas*[4], *Benjamin*[3], *Thomas*[2], *Thomas*[1]), b. May 31, 1830 ; m. Apr. 27, 1861, Adelphia C. Clark. Res. Athol, Mass. No children.

3200. Joseph M.[9] Pierce (*James*[8], *Joseph*[7], *Silas*[6], *Joseph*[5], *Joseph*[4], *Jonathan*[3], *Samuel*[2], *Thomas*[1]), b. Oct. 21, 1850 ; m. Nov. 26, 1878, Helen F. Moore. Res. Fitchburg, Mass.

3221. William[9] Pierce (*Joseph*[8], *Joseph*[7], *Joseph*[6], *Isaac*[5], *Isaac*[4], *Jonathan*[3], *Samuel*[2], *Thomas*[1]), b. Dec. 13, 1833 ; m. Aug. 16, 1858, Alice R. Campbell, b. Dec. 27, 1834. Res. New Orleans, La.

Wm Peirce

No children.

3235. GEORGE W. W.[9] PIERCE (*George J.*[8], *Isaac*[7], *Joseph*[6] *Isaac*[5], *Isaac*[4], *Jonathan*[3], *Samuel*[2], *Thomas*[1]), b. Aug. 1, 1844 ; m. June 1, 1875, Lydia M. Dana, b. Apr. 10, 1852. Res. Boston, Mass.
Child :—
4566. i. LAWRENCE W., b. Sept. 17, 1877.

3240. CHARLES F.[9] PIERCE (*George J.*[8], *Isaac*[7], *Joseph*[6], *Isaac*[5], *Isaac*[4], *Jonathan*[3], *Samuel*[2], *Thomas*[1]), b. May 11, 1856 ; m. Dec. 29, 1880, Nellie J. Bowen, b. Sept. 23, 1860. Res. Boston.

3247. JAMES W.[9] PIERCE (*James W.*[8], *James*[7], *Joseph*[6], *Isaac*[5], *Isaac*[4], *Jonathan*[3], *Samuel*[2], *Thomas*[1]), b. Jan. 26, 1844 ; m.?Mar. 13, 1867, Anna M. Billings, b. Apr. 25, 1847. Res. Cambridge, Mass.

Children :—
4567. i. CHARLES F., b. Jan. 28, 1869.
4568. ii. WILLIAM F., b. July 20, 1870.
4569. iii. MARTHA E., b. Nov. 4, 1873.

3248. CHARLES E.[9] PIERCE (*James W.*[8], *James*[7], *Joseph*[6], *Isaac*[5], *Isaac*[4], *Jonathan*[3], *Samuel*[2], *Thomas*[1]), b. Oct. 31, 1847 ; m. Dec. 7, 1869, Harriet E. Thurston, b. Apr. 22, 1849. Res. Cambridge, Mass.
Children :—
4570. i. JAMES W., b. Aug. 28, 1870.
4571. ii. FLORENCE T., b. Sept. 29, 1879.

3268. JOHN S.[9] PIERCE (*William*[8], *Barzillai*[7], *Jonathan*[6], *Joseph*[5], *David*[4], *John*[3], *Thomas*[2], *Thomas*[1]), b. Aug. 26, 1828 ; m. July 20, 1851, Sarah L. Deane. Res. South Thomaston, Me.
Children :—
4572. i. SAMUEL D., b. 1853.
4573. ii. EDWIN, b. 1855.

3281. SYDNEY H.[9] PIERCE (*George W.*[8], *Barzillai*[7], *Jonathan*[6], *Joseph*[5], *David*[4], *John*[3], *Thomas*[2], *Thomas*[1]), b. Sept. 27, 1849 ; m. Nov. 20, 1873, Abbie L. Dean, b. Oct. 24, 1850. He d. Apr. 23, 1876. Res. South Thomaston, Me. Child :—
4574. i. FLORENCE, b. Mar. 31, 1875.
37

290   PIERCE PEDIGREE.

3293. LUTHER[9] PIERCE (*Moses C.*[8], *Calvin*[7], *David*[6], *Daniel*[5], *Daniel*[4], *John*[3], *Thomas*[2], *Thomas*[1]), b. Aug. 25, 1820; m. June 15, 1848, Nancy T. Greenwood, b. Aug. 2, 1824. Res. Brewer, Me. Children :—

4575. i.   CYRUS A., b. Apr. 16, 1849.
4576. ii. AMOS G., b. May 26, 1850; d. Aug. 17, 1851.
4577. iii. LIVONIA E., b. Nov. 21, 1851; m. —— Copeland.
4578. iv. DORA E., b. Feb. 24, 1853; m. —— Dole.
4579. v.   LUCINDA B., b. Feb. 8, 1855; d. Sept. 23, 1857.
4580. vi. CLARA J., b. Jan. 27, 1857.
4581. vii. ROSA L., b. Oct. 8, 1858.
4582. viii. MELVIN L., b. Jan. 20, 1861.
4583. ix. CORA M., b. Apr. 19, 1863.
4584. x.   RANDALL S., b. Apr. 23, 1866.
4585. xi. LYMAN G., b. Dec. 26, 1869.

3295. JOTHAM S.[9] PIERCE (*Moses C.*[8], *Calvin*[7], *David*[6], *Daniel*[5], *Daniel*[4], *John*[3], *Thomas*[2], *Thomas*[1]), b. Feb. 26, 1824; m. Apr. 29, 1851, Mary Chapman. Res. Brewer, Me. Children :—

4586. i.   FRANK E., b. Apr. 15, 1852; m. Maria Western.
4587. ii. WILBUR E., b. Nov. 4, 1858.
4588. iii. FLORY A., b. Jan. 1, 1861; d. May 8, 1865.
4589. iv. PHEBE B., b. Oct. 11, 1862; d. Jan. 11, 1865.

3297. EZRA[9] PIERCE (*Moses C.*[8], *Calvin*[7], *David*[6], *Daniel*[5], *Daniel*[4], *John*[3], *Thomas*[2], *Thomas*[1]), b. May 22, 1827; m. July 23, 1854, Hannah Holway, b. Feb. 25, 1828. Res. Carritunk Plantation, Me. Children :—

4590. i.   MOSES C., b. July 4, 1857; d. Oct. 24, 1873.
4591. ii. LUCY, b. Jan. 4, 1864; d. Feb. 6, 1870.
4592. iii. MARY H., b. Dec. 31, 1866.
4593. iv. BERTIE, b. Nov. 8, 1870; d. Nov. 6, 1874.

3298. JOEL M.[9] PIERCE (*Moses C.*[8], *Calvin*[7], *David*[6], *Daniel*[5], *Daniel*[4], *John*[3], *Thomas*[2], *Thomas*[1]), b. May 2, 1830; m. May 30, 1855, Cordelia Clark, b. Aug. 14, 1828. Res. Solon, Me. Children :—

4594. i.   INGRAM C., b. July 23, 1860.
4595. ii. WILLIE H., b. Feb. 15, 1862.
4596. iii. GEORGE B., b. Nov. 18, 1863.
4597. iv. JOSEPH C., b. Aug. 27, 1870.

3301. JAMES[9] PIERCE (*Nathaniel*[8], *Calvin*[7], *David*[6], *Daniel*[5], *Daniel*[4], *John*[3], *Thomas*[2], *Thomas*[1]), b. Aug. 29, 1819; m. May 28, 1839, Lucinda Holway, b. Oct. 15, 1819, d. Nov. 28, 1858. He d. Nov. 27, 1865. Res. The Forks Plantation, Me. Children :—

4598. i.   JOHN H., b. Apr. 1, 1840; d. Dec. 24, 1861.
4599. ii. HARRIET B., b. Mar. 4, 1842; m. Young Stafford.
4600. iii. HIRAM, b. Jan. 27, 1844; m. Lucinda Durgin.
4601. iv. CHARLES H., b. Sept. 10, 1846; d. Mar. 27, 1864.
4602. v.   ELIZA A., b. July 16, 1852; m. Joseph Pratt. Res. E. Weymouth, Mass.
4603. vi. ESTHER W., b. Jan. 9, 1855; m. Luther W. Howes.

3303. OSBORN[9] PIERCE (*Nathaniel*[8], *Calvin*[7], *David*[6], *Daniel*[5], *Daniel*[4], *John*[3], *Thomas*[2], *Thomas*[1]), b. Feb. 7, 1823; m. Mar. 3, 1860, Sybil Paine, b. Oct. 26, 1831. Res. Carritunk Plantation, Me.

Children :—

4604. i. EFFIE F., b. Nov. 27, 1860.
4605. ii. ETTA N., b. Nov. 11, 1861.
4606. iii. ELMORE L., b. Sept 23, 1871.

3306. SETH B.[9] PIERCE (*Nathaniel*[8], *Calvin*[7], *David*[6], *Daniel*[5], *Daniel*[4], *John*[3], *Thomas*[2], *Thomas*[1]), b. Oct. 20, 1830 ; m. July 23, 1856, Vesta Kimball, b. Dec. 12, 1834. Res. Moose River, Me.

Seth B. Pierce

Children :—

4607. i. FRED., b. Oct. 28, 1858.
4608. ii. MILFORD.

3310. LLEWELLYN[9] PIERCE (*James S.*[8], *Calvin*[7], *David*[6], *Daniel*[5], *Daniel*[4], *John*[3], *Thomas*[2], *Thomas*[1]), b. Nov. 30, 1826 ; m. Oct. 27, 1855, Catherine Spillane, b. Dec. 27, 1836. Res. Shaw's Flat, Cal.

Llewellyn Pierce

4609. i. LLEWELLA, b. Apr. 1, 1857; m. Edwin H. Clough.
4610. ii. LLEWELLYN, b. June 18, 1859.
4611. iii. JAMES S., b. Jan. 26, 1861.
4612. iv. EVA M., b. Mar. 7, 1863.
4613. v. IDA F., b. Apr. 20, 1867; d. Dec. 8, 1868.
4614. vi. FRANKLIN, b. Oct.. 4, 1868; d. Oct. 25, 1868.

3314. ROMANDELL[9] PIERCE (*James S.*[8], *Calvin*[7], *David*[6], *Daniel*[5], *Daniel*[4], *John*[3], *Thomas*[2], *Thomas*[1]), b. Sept. 20, 1834 ; m. Mrs. Lyford, b. Sept. 20, 1830, d. Oct. 8, 1876. Res. Quincy, Cal.
No children.

3334. CYRUS B.[9] PIERCE (*Luther*[8], *Luther*[7], *David*[6], *Daniel*[5], *Daniel*[4], *John*[3], *Thomas*[2], *Thomas*[1]), b. Nov. 26, 1829 ; m. June 5, 1855, Harriet Moore. He d. Jan. 28, 1875. Res. Brandon, Wis.
No children.

3335. JOHN L.[9] PIERCE (*Luther*[8], *Luther*[7], *David*[6], *Daniel*[5], *Daniel*[4], *John*[3], *Thomas*[2], *Thomas*[1]), b. Sept. 29, 1832 ; m. Oct. 7, 1861, Achsa Andrews, b. Nov. 25, 1834, d. July 3, 1863 ; m. 2nd, May 24, 1871, Sarah B. Merrill, b. Dec. 19, 1853. Res. Solon, Me.

John L. Pierce

Child :—

4615. i.   ZELMA A., b. July 22, 1862; d. May 16, 1864.

3344. ISAIAH⁹ PIERCE (*Isaac R.*⁸, *David*⁷, *David*⁶, *Daniel*⁵, *Daniel*⁴, *John*³, *Thomas*², *Thomas*¹), b. Nov. 19, 1828; m. ——— Thompson. He d. Sept. 6, 1854.

3347. OBED W.⁹ PIERCE (*Samuel D.*⁸, *David*⁷, *David*⁶, *Daniel*⁵, *Daniel*⁴, *John*³, *Thomas*², *Thomas*¹), b. Sept. 23, 1820; m. July 11, 1845, Sarah R. Haines, b. Oct. 2, 1820. He d. Feb. 23, 1870. Res. Lexington, Me.   Children :—

4616. i.   ALFREDA, b. Feb. 20, 1847; m. John B. Briggs.
4617. ii. D. DECATUR, b. Feb. 5, 1853; d. 1856.
4618. iii. FREMONT, b. Aug. 1, 1857.

3348. WELLINGTON⁹ PIERCE (*Samuel D.*⁸, *David*⁷, *David*⁶, *Daniel*⁵, *Daniel*⁴, *John*³, *Thomas*², *Thomas*¹), b. Mar. 29, 1822; m. May 4, 1843, Silvinia Albee, b. June 25, 1822. Res. New Richmond, Wis.

Wellington Pierce

Children :—

4619. i.   SAMUEL H., b. May 21, 1844; m. Asa Samson.
4620. ii. WILLIAM SCOTT, b. 1848; m. Emma Pease.

3349. ALFRED⁹ PIERCE (*Samuel D.*⁸, *David*⁷, *David*⁶, *Daniel*⁵, *Daniel*⁴, *John*³, *Thomas*², *Thomas*¹), b. Mar. 9, 1824; m. Nov. 7, 1852, Hannah C. Clark.   Res. New Richmond, Wis.   Child :—

4621. i.   LOVINIA I., b. Sept. 18, 1853; m. M. S. Wells.

3351. SUMNER⁹ PIERCE (*Samuel D.*⁸, *David*⁷, *David*⁶, *Daniel*⁵, *Daniel*⁴, *John*³, *Thomas*², *Thomas*¹), b. Oct. 7, 1829; m. Oct. 25, 1857, Emily Clark, b. July 4, 1841.   Res. Lexington, Me.   No children.

3357. JOHN C.⁹ PIERCE (*Rufus W.*⁸, *David*⁷, *David*⁶, *Daniel*⁵, *Daniel*⁴, *John*³, *Thomas*², *Thomas*¹), b. Sept. 9, 1838; m. Apr. 12, 1868, Louisa V. Morton.   Child :—

4622. i.   ONA L., b. 1871.

3358. JOSEPH H.⁹ PIERCE (*Rufus W.*⁸, *David*⁷, *David*⁶, *Daniel*⁵, *Daniel*⁴, *John*³, *Thomas*², *Thomas*¹), b. June 15, 1841; m. Jan. 17, 1871, Helen M. Hale.   Children :—

4623. i.   JAY M., b. 1873.
4624. ii. WALTER B., b. 1875.

3367. HENRY W.⁹ PIERCE (*Simon D.*⁸, *David*⁷, *David*⁶, *Daniel*⁵, *Daniel*⁴, *John*³, *Thomas*², *Thomas*¹), b. Jan. 30, 1840; m. Dec. 24, 1859, Sarah E. Allen, b. Mar. 13, 1842.   Res. Cumberland Mills, Me.

Henry W. Pierce

Children :—

4625. i.   A. A., b. Nov. 22, 1860; d. Dec. 9, 1862.
4626. ii. GEORGE H., b. Oct. 21, 1862.

3370. DAVID R.[9] PIERCE (*Simon D.*[8], *David*[7], *David*[6], *Daniel*[5], *Daniel*[4], *John*[3], *Thomas*[2], *Thomas*[1]), b. Feb. 4, 1848; m. Nov. 19, 1872, Lucie A. Burnham, b. June 16, 1857. David R. Pierce was born Feb. 4, 1848, in No. Two Plantation. When he was seven years of age his father removed to Smithfield, Me. At the age of 14 he began attending school at Bloomfield Academy, Skowhegan, Me., and continued there until 16 years of age, when he began teaching in Waterville, Me. In Sept., 1864, he enlisted in the 7th Maine Battery and served as a private until the close of the war, in 1865, when he returned to his studies. In 1867, he went to California and was clerk for the Pacific Mail Steamship Co. between San Francisco and China and Japan ; he returned to Maine in 1871. After his marriage he taught in Kennebunkport and is now (1878) Grammar Master in the Schools of Great Falls, N. H. ; he is also A. A. G. of the N. H. Dept. of the G. A. R. Res. Great Falls, N. H.

No children.

3397. REUBEN B.[9] PIERCE (*Alvin B.*[8], *Peter*[7], *David*[6], *Daniel*[5], *Daniel*[4], *John*[3], *Thomas*[2], *Thomas*[1]), b. Oct. 4, 1829 ; m. Sept. 22, 1851, Lydia M. Chase, b. March 21, 1835, d. Feb. 14, 1871 ; m. 2nd, April 3, 1874, Elizabeth Baker Pierce [3398], b. Aug. 8, 1826. Res. Bingham, Me. Children :—

4627. i.   SARAH E., b. Apr. 2, 1855 ; m. James Merrill.
4628. ii. DAVIS C., b. Jan. 2, 1856.
4629. iii. ESTHER C., b. Jan. 13, 1858.
4630. iv. CHARLES E., b. Dec. 25, 1860.
4631. v.   HATTIE E., b. Sept. 1, 1863.
4632. vi. OBED P., b. Jan. 30, 1865.

3398. OBED[9] PIERCE (*Alvin B.*[8], *Peter*[7], *David*[6], *Daniel*[5], *Daniel*[4], *John*[3], *Thomas*[2], *Thomas*[1]), b. May 2, 1832 ; m. July 1, 1854, Elizabeth Baker [3397], b. Aug. 8, 1826. He d. Aug. 15, 1864. Res. Moscow, Me. Children :—

4633. i.   DANVILLE, b. March 22, 1855.
4634. ii. EMMA, b. June 13, 1856 ; m. Thomas Whitney.
4635. iii. FANNY, b. Sept. 9, 1859.

3399. PETER[9] PIERCE (*Alvin B.*[8], *Peter*[7], *David*[6], *Daniel*[5], *Daniel*[4], *John*[3], *Thomas*[2], *Thomas*[1]), b. May 31, 1824 ; m. June 27, 1848, Apprinda Blake, b. Jan. 9, 1824. Res. Waterville, Me.

Children :—

4636. i.   ELLA S., b. Apr. 27, 1853.
4637. ii. HIRAM O., b. May 8, 1857.
4638. iii. HENRY K., b. Oct. 10, 1859.
4639. iv. FRED., b. Nov. 15, 1861; d. Nov. 14, 1862.

3420.   CASSIUS W.[9] PIERCE (*Abijah A.*[8], *Abijah*[7], *Reuben*[6], *Daniel*[5], *Daniel*[4], *John*[3], *Thomas*[2], *Thomas*[1]), b. Oct. 3, 1849 ; m. Oct. 12, 1870, M. Emma Pierce [3700], b. Oct. 21, 1851. Res. St. Albans, Vt. Children :—

4640. i.   GUY C., b. Dec. 11, 1873.
4641. ii. SEVLA V., b. July 18, 1878.

3422.   ZENOPHON J.[9] PIERCE (*Lewis L.*[8], *A'bijah*[7], *Reuben*[6], *Daniel*[5], *Daniel*[4], *John*[3], *Thomas*[2], *Thomas*[1]), b. Apr. 9, 1846 ; m. July 18, 1876, Dora Bowman. Res. Clinton, Mass.

3427.   SCHUYLER[9] PIERCE (*Samuel*[8], *Asaph*[7], *Samuel*[6], *Daniel*[5], *Daniel*[4], *John*[3], *Thomas*[2], *Thomas*[1]), b. Jan. 17, 1826 ; m. March 22, 1855, Almira Marble. He d. Oct. 17, 1869. Children :—

4642. JENNIE M., b. Dec. 26, 1855.
4643. ALICE O., b. Sept., 1863.

3428.   ALVIN M.[9] PIERCE (*Samuel*[8], *Asaph*[7], *Samuel*[6], *Daniel*[5], *Daniel*[4], *John*[3], *Thomas*[2], *Thomas*[1]), b. Feb. 16, 1828 ; m. Nov. 28, 1855, L. S. Bagley. Res. Moretown, Vt. Children :—

4644. i.   EMMA C., b. March 16, 1857; d. Dec. 16, 1859.
4645. ii. LEWIS S., b. Aug. 31, 1860.
4646. iii. EDWARD A., b. June 25, 1862.
4647. iv. HATTIE M., b. Aug. 26, 1868.

3436.   SAMUEL W.[9] PIERCE (*Luther B.*[8], *Samuel*[7], *Samuel*[6], *Daniel*[5], *Daniel*[4], *John*[3], *Thomas*[2], *Thomas*[1]), b. Feb. 3, 1837 ; m. Feb. 5, 1880, Mrs. Anna Hewer. Res. Boston, Mass.

3441.   HENRY W.[9] PIERCE (*Samuel W.*[8], *Samuel*[7], *Samuel*[6], *Daniel*[5], *Daniel*[4], *John*[3], *Thomas*[2], *Thomas*[1]), b. Mar. 21, 1842 ; m. June 4, 1867, Helen V. Buttrick, b. June 8, 1849. Res. Winchendon, Mass. No children.

3442.   ALBERT S.[9] PIERCE (*Samuel W.*[8], *Samuel*[7], *Samuel*[6], *Daniel*[5], *Daniel*[4], *John*[3], *Thomas*[2], *Thomas*[1]), b. Mar. 15, 1845 ; m. Dec. 11, 1872, Mary A. Chamberlain, b. May 25, 1849. Res. Fitchburg, Mass. No. children :—

3443.   J. PLUMMER[9] PIERCE (*Samuel W.*[8], *Samuel*[7], *Samuel*[6], *Daniel*[5], *Daniel*[4], *John*[3], *Thomas*[2], *Thomas*[1]), b. Feb. 25, 1851 ; m. June 10, 1874, Lizzie P. Morse, b. Jan. 21, 1856. Res. Jaffrey, N. H. No children.

3450.   RUFUS P.[9] PIERCE (*Charles W.*[8], *Samuel*[7], *Samuel*[6], *Daniel*[5], *Daniel*[4], *John*[3], *Thomas*[2], *Thomas*[1]), b. May 11, 1846 ; m. July 1, 1874, Sarah M. Gleason. Res. Dublin, N. H. Children :—

4648. i.   E. GERTRUDE, b. Nov. 17, 1877.
4649. ii. ELSIE G., b. July 26, 1880; d. March 7, 1881.

3452. WILLARD H.[9] PIERCE (*Charles W.*[8], *Samuel*[7], *Samuel*[6], *Daniel*[5], *Daniel*[4], *John*[3], *Thomas*[2], *Thomas*[1]), b. Feb. 5, 1849 ; m. March 30, 1872, Ellen Simmons, b. May 9, 1852. Res. Dublin, N. H.

Child :—
4650. i. HENRY H., b. Nov. 7, 1876; d. June 25, 1879.

3455. FRED. A.[9] PIERCE (*Charles W.*[8], *Samuel*[7], *Samuel*[6], *Daniel*[5], *Daniel*[4], *John*[3], *Thomas*[2], *Thomas*[1]), b. Oct. 12, 1854 ; m. May 11, 1879, Urania Parker. Res. Peterborough, N. H.

3471. JACOB S.[9] PIERCE (*Orville W.*[8], *Jacob*[7], *Jacob*[6], *Daniel*[5], *Daniel*[4], *John*[3], *Thomas*[2], *Thomas*[1]) ; m. Mary O. Ray. He d. Dec., 1863. Child :—
4651. i. HATTIE E., b. June, 1864.

3475. GEORGE H.[9] PIERCE (*Orville W.*[8], *Jacob*[7], *Jacob*[6], *Daniel*[5], *Daniel*[4], *John*[3], *Thomas*[2], *Thomas*[1]), b. Jan. 9, 1844 ; m. Clara ———. He d. Jan. 13, 1877. Child :—
4652. i. ARTHUR; d. infancy.

3480. HENRY D.[9] PIERCE (*Daniel*[8], *Jacob*[7], *Jacob*[6], *Daniel*[5], *Daniel*[4], *John*[3], *Thomas*[2], *Thomas*[1]), b. Apr. 8, 1839 ; m. Feb. 24, 1862, Mary A. Starkey, b. Aug. 6, 1840. Res. Graniteville, Mass. Children :—
4653. i. MARY J., b. June 21, 1865.
4654. ii. NELLIE M., b. Nov. 5, 1875.

3481. DAVID H.[9] PIERCE (*Daniel*[8], *Jacob*[7], *Jacob*[6], *Daniel*[5], *Daniel*[4], *John*[3], *Thomas*[2], *Thomas*[1]), b. May 25, 1841 ; m. Jan. 19, 1870, Angie M. Bennett, b. March 11, 1847. Res. Fitchburg, Mass. Children :—
4655. i. CARRIE E., b. Oct. 22, 1871.
4656. ii. ELLA A., b. Nov. 28, 1875; d. Sept. 19, 1876.

3482. WILLIAM H.[9] PIERCE (*Daniel*[8], *Jacob*[7], *Jacob*[6], *Daniel*[5], *Daniel*[4], *John*[3], *Thomas*[2], *Thomas*[1]), b. Dec. 9, 1842 ; m. Jan. 30, 1878, Ella L. Hunt. Res. Chesterfield, N. H.

3484. WINSLOW N.[9] PIERCE (*Benjamin*[8], *Benjamin*[7], *Jacob*[6], *Daniel*[5], *Daniel*[4], *John*[3], *Thomas*[2], *Thomas*[1]), b. July 21, 1842 ; m. Oct., 1870, Hattie M. Walworth, b. Nov. 29, 1844. Res. Pulaski, N. Y. Child :—
4657. i. MATTIE L., b. Feb. 15, 1872.

3487. LEWIS O.[9] PIERCE (*Hillman*[8], *Benjamin*[7], *Jacob*[6], *Daniel*[5], *Daniel*[4], *John*[3], *Thomas*[2], *Thomas*[1]), b. Mar. 5, 1845 ; m. Oct. 6, 1869, Martha W. Allen, b. Aug. 19, 1849. Res. Oswego, N. Y.

Children :—

4658. i.   NELLIE A., b. Nov. 27, 1875.
4659. ii. FANNIE I., b. Feb. 3, 1877.

3488. WILLARD J.[9] PIERCE (*Hillman*[8], *Benjamin*[7], *Jacob*[6], *Daniel*[5], *Daniel*[4], *John*[3], *Thomas*[2], *Thomas*[1]), b. Jan. 12, 1848 ; m. Nov. 9, 1869, Orpha T. Wright, b. Aug. 16, 1842. Res. Pulaski, N. Y.

3490. JULIUS M.[9] PIERCE (*Marshall*[8], *Benjamin*[7], *Jacob*[6], *Daniel*[5], *Daniel*[4], *John*[3], *Thomas*[2], *Thomas*[1]), b. Aug. 28, 1852 ; m. Jan. 23, 1875, Isa H. Reed, b. Feb. 27, 1849. Res. Pulaski, N. Y. No children.

3504. JUDSON J.[9] PIERCE (*Albert*[8], *John*[7], *Calvin*[6], *John*[5], *Daniel*[4], *John*[3], *Thomas*[2], *Thomas*[1]), b. Apr. 15, 1848 ; m. July 15, 1875, Carrie Gile. Res. Boston, Mass. Child :—

4660. i. ———.

3508. CHRISTOPHER C.[9] PIERCE (*John*[8], *John*[7], *Ebenezer*[6], *Ebenezer*[5], *Ebenezer*[4], *John*[3], *Thomas*[2], *Thomas*[1]), b. Nov. 8, 1819 ; m. June 17, 1850, Eliza M. Cloughan, b. Aug. 26, 1820. Res. Hinsdale, Mass. Children :—

4661. i.   ELMA M., b. Aug. 2, 1851.
4662. ii.   ALDEN•H., b. Mar. 24, 1853.
4663. iii. ALSTON, b. Aug. 1, 1858; d. Sept. 3, 1858.
4664. iv.   SARAH A., b. Jan. 19, 1860.
4665. v.   GEORGE D., b. Nov. 2, 1862; d. Feb. 18, 1873.

3509. DEXTER P.[9] PIERCE (*John*[8], *John*[7], *Ebenezer*[6], *Ebenezer*[5], *Ebenezer*[4], *John*[3], *Thomas*[2], *Thomas*[1]), b. Aug., 1821 ; m. Dec. 21, 1854, Miriam Roberts, b. June 12, 1827. He d. Oct. 18, 1861. Res. Bristol, Kane Co., Ill. Child :—

4666. i. ELLEN, b. July 23, 1856.

3510. HENRY A.[9] PIERCE (*John*[8], *John*[7], *Ebenezer*[6], *Ebenezer*[5], *Ebenezer*[4], *John*[3], *Thomas*[2], *Thomas*[1]), b. Sept. 23, 1826 ; m. Sept., 1852, Mary Ely. Res. Lansingburg, N. Y. No children.

3511. EDWARD C.[9] PIERCE (*John*[8], *John*[7], *Ebenezer*[6], *Ebenezer*[5], *Ebenezer*[4], *John*[3], *Thomas*[2], *Thomas*[1]), b. Nov. 25, 1832 ; m. Martha Bartlett. Res. Marshall, Lyon Co., Minn. Children :—

4667. i.   WILLIAM H., b. Jan. 24, 1860.
4668. ii.   LAURA, b. 1867.
4669. iii. MARTHA, b. 1871.
4670. iv.   ADDIE, b. 1872.

3513. Rev. CHARLES M.[9] PIERCE (*Erastus*[8], *John*[7], *Ebenezer*[6], *Ebenezer*[5], *Ebenezer*[4], *John*[3], *Thomas*[2], *Thomas*[1]), b. Oct. 13, 1834 ; m. Aug. 12, 1863, Elizabeth M. Peabody. Res. Middlefield, Mass.
    Rev. CHARLES M. PIERCE was born in Hindsdale, Mass., Oct. 13,

1834. His early life was spent on the farm, with such opportunities for education as his native town offered in its public schools and academy. He entered Williams College in 1853, and graduated in 1857. After graduation he taught for one year in an Academy in Topsfield, Mass. In 1859 he entered Andover Theological Seminary and completed a two years' course of study, when he was called to a tutorship of Mathematics and Latin in Williams College. Here he remained two years, and during this time was licensed as a preacher. Resigning his tutorship he returned to Andover Seminary to complete his course. At the same time he took the supply of the Congregational Church in West Boxford, Mass., over which he was installed Sept. 2nd, 1863, Rev. S. M. Worcester preaching the ordination sermon. August 12th, 1863, he was married to Elizabeth M. Peabody, of Salem, Mass. He was dismissed from the church in Boxford, July 17th, 1867, and spent the year following as instructor in Mathematics in Williams College. In April, 1868, he assumed the supply of the Congregational Church in Middlefield, Mass., over which he was installed July 1st, 1868.

Child :—

4671. i. CHARLES P., b. Oct. 19, 1869.

3516. HARLAN A.[9] PIERCE (*Marshal*[8], *John*[7], *Ebenezer*[6], *Ebenezer*[5], *Ebenezer*[4], *John*[3], *Thomas*[2], *Thomas*[1]), b. Aug. 21, 1840 ; m. Mar. 19, 1867, Mary A. Rowley. Res. New York, N. Y.

Children :—

4672. i. ADDIE, b. Jan. 31, 1868.
4673. ii. FANNIE, b. May, 1871.
4674. iii. WINONA, b. Apr., 1872.

3518. FRANCIS M.[9] PIERCE (*Marshal*[8], *John*[7], *Ebenezer*[6], *Ebenezer*[5], *Ebenezer*[4], *John*[3], *Thomas*[2], *Thomas*[1]), b. Oct. 21, 1847 ; m. Nov. 26, 1874, Mrs. Matilda M. Smith, b. Dec. 15, 1847. Res. New York, N. Y.

No children.

3527. WYATT W.[9] PIERCE (*Warren*[8], *Asa*[7], *Ebenezer*[6], *Ebenezer*[5], *Ebenezer*[4], *John*[3], *Thomas*[2], *Thomas*[1]), b. Apr. 11, 1840; m. Sept. 20, 1865, Addie L. Ross, b. Dec. 19, 1843. Res. Franklin Furnace, N. Y.

Children :—

4675. i.   HELEN, b. May 29, 1866.
4576. ii. WILLIAM, b. June 23, 1867.
4677. iii. CHESTER, b. Dec. 25, 1871; d. Apr. 21, 1877.

3542. JOHN H.[9] PIERCE (*Luther*[8], *Luther*[7], *John*[6], *Ebenezer*[3], *Ebenezer*[4], *John*[3], *Thomas*[2], *Thomas*[1]), b. Jan. 21, 1831 ; m. Aug. 30, 1852, Ellen E. Cheney, b. Aug. 3, 1832. He d. Apr. 24, 1878. Res. So. Hadley Falls, Mass. Children :—

4678. i.   GEORGE E., b. Oct. 16, 1857.
4679. ii. JOHN E., b. Dec. 8, 1863; d. July 11, 1864.
4680. iii. NELLIE E., b. May 10, 1866.
4681. iv. M. GERTRUDE, b. May 9, 1868.

3545. JOSEPH A.[9] PIERCE (*Luther*[8], *Luther*[7], *John*[6], *Ebenezer*[5], *Ebenezer*[4], *John*[3], *Thomas*[2], *Thomas*[1]), b. July 23, 1837 ; m. Sept. 13, 1861, Mary E. Moore. He d. Aug. 28, 1875. Res. So. Hadley Falls, Mass. Children :—

4682. i.   IDA, b. Oct., 1862.
4683. ii. JOSEPH, b. June 30, 1868.

3547. EDWIN G.[9] PIERCE (*Luther*[8], *Luther*[7], *John*[6], *Ebenezer*[5], *Ebenezer*[4], *John*[3], *Thomas*[2], *Thomas*[1]), b. Apr. 20, 1842 ; m. Oct. 12, 1861, Susan Nelson, b. Jan. 27, 1842. Res. So. Hadley Falls, Mass. Children :—

4684. i.   CLARA B., b. June 18, 1863; d. Feb. 20, 1867.
4685. ii. EDWIN N., b. Aug. 1, 1864; d. Feb. 18, 1867.
4686. iii. JENNIE G., b. Sept. 7, 1868.
4687. iv. LEWIS N., b. Jan. 13, 1872; d. May 15, 1873.
4688. v.   FRANK A., b. Oct. 21, 1876.
4689. vi. JOSEPH H., b. Sept. 21, 1878.

3548. LEWIS P.[9] PIERCE (*Luther*[8], *Luther*[7], *John*[6], *Ebenezer*[5], *Ebenezer*[4], *John*[3], *Thomas*[2], *Thomas*[1]), b. Nov. 22, 1845 ; m. Nov. 24, 1870, Eva J. Bowers, b. Aug. 19, 1853. Res. Collinsville, Conn. Children :—

4690. i.   MABEL M., b. Apr. 20, 1875.
4691. ii. GRACE E., b. Apr. 16, 1878.

3549. HOMER E.[9] PIERCE (*Nehemiah P.*[8], *Luther*[7], *John*[6], *Ebenezer*[5], *Ebenezer*[4], *John*[3], *Thomas*[2], *Thomas*[1]), b. May 5, 1847 ; m. Mar. 4, 1869, Catherine S. Chamberlain. Res. Brooklyn, Conn. Children :—

4692. i.   HENRY O., b. Dec. 19, 1869.
4693. ii. ALBERT P., b. July 3, 1874.

3550. GEORGE A.[9] PIERCE (*Nehemiah P.*[8], *Luther*[7], *John*[6], *Ebenezer*[5], *Ebenezer*[4], *John*[3], *Thomas*[2], *Thomas*[1]), b. Mar. 11, 1849 ; m. Jan. 30, 1871, Anna C. Morford, b. May 23, 1854. Res. Concord, N. H.

Geo A Pierce

Child :—

4694. i. F. BLANCHE, b. Sept. 1, 1878.

3559. EDWIN[9] PIERCE (*Calvin W.*[8], *Calvin*[7], *Ebenezer*[6], *Ebenezer*[5], *Ebenezer*[4], *John*[3], *Thomas*[2], *Thomas*[1]), b. Feb. 13, 1836; m. Nov. 22, 1859, Ellen M. Morse, b. Mar. 8, 1837. Res. Worcester, Mass. Children :—

4695. i. EDGAR B., b. Aug. 19, 1863.
4696. ii. MABEL, b. May 5, 1865.

3561. JOHN W.[9] PIERCE (*Andreas W.*[8], *Harvey*[7], *Ebenezer*[6], *Ebenezer*[5], *Ebenezer*[4], *John*[3], *Thomas*[2], *Thomas*[1]), b. Mar. 20, 1847; m. Jan. 17, 1872, H. Catherine Hayden, b. Feb. 14, 1845. Res. W. Millbury, Mass.

Children :—

4697. i. MABEL E., b. Mar. 10, 1874.
4698. ii. ALICE M., b. Sept. 23, 1876.
4698½. iii. HERVEY C., b. July 13, 1881.

3602. THEODORE W.[9] PIERCE (*Augustus*[8], *Thomas S.*[7], *Joshua*[6], *Joshua*[5], *Ebenezer*[4], *John*[3], *Thomas*[2], *Thomas*[1]), b. Nov. 6, 1824; m. Oct. 26, 1847, Laura A. Peasley, b. Mar. 27, 1828. Res. Nashua, N. H.

Children :—

4699. i. EDWARD T., b. Nov. 6, 1848; m. Louisa M. Peebles and Emma J. Shoens.
4700. ii. GEORGE W., b. Sept. 24, 1850.
4701. iii. FRANCES A., b. Jan. 18, 1853; d. Sept. 12, 1857.
4702. iv. ELLA E., b. Oct. 23, 1854; d. Feb. 17, 1857.
4703. v. CHARLES J., b. Sept. 21, 1859.
4704. vi. FRED. A., b. Sept. 7, 1861.
4705. vii. FLORA E., b. Aug. 11, 1867.

3604. THOMAS E.[9] PIERCE (*Houghton*[8], *Thomas S.*[7], *Joshua*[6], *Joshua*[5], *Ebenezer*[4], *John*[3], *Thomas*[2], *Thomas*[1]), b. Jan. 29, 1826; m. Sept. 9, 1849, Sarah Brown, b. Dec., 1829. Res. New York, N. Y.

No children.

3605. GEORGE A.[9] PIERCE (*Houghton*[8], *Thomas S.*[7], *Joshua*[6], *Joshua*[5], *Ebenezer*[4], *John*[3], *Thomas*[2], *Thomas*[1]), b. Apr. 21, 1830; m. 1860, Mary E. Brown. Res. Kansas. Child:—

4706. i. CORA, b. May, 1871.

3608. CHARLES P.[9] PIERCE (*Houghton*[8], *Thomas S.*[7], *Joshua*[6], *Joshua*[5], *Ebenezer*[4], *John*[3], *Thomas*[2], *Thomas*[1]), b. Sept. 8, 1836; m. 1857, Adelaide Carter. Res. Leominster, Mass. Child:—

4707. i. HERBERT F., b. Jan. 13, 1860.

3612.. ALBERT F.[9] PIERCE (*Sylvester*[8], *Asa*[7], *Joshua*[6], *Joshua*[5], *Ebenezer*[4], *John*[3], *Thomas*[2], *Thomas*[1]), b. June 3, 1838; m. May 28, 1862, Annie E. Wilder, b. Feb. 9, 1843, d. Aug., 1876. Res. Troy, N. H. Children:—

4708. i. ANNIE F., b. June 9, 1865; d. Apr., 1866.
4709. ii. EDWIN L., b. Sept. 24, 1867.
4710. iii. NELLIE A., b. July 22, 1869.
4711. iv. HARRY N., b. Jan. 22, 1873.

3613. GEORGE S.[9] PIERCE (*Sylvester*[8], *Asa*[7], *Joshua*[6], *Joshua*[5], *Ebenezer*[4], *John*[3], *Thomas*[2], *Thomas*[1]), b. Sept. 15, 1840; m. Sept. 1, 1870, Ellen A. Balch, b. July 8, 1844. Res. No. Leominster, Mass. Children:—

3616. JOSEPH B.[9] PIERCE (*Joseph*[8], *Asa*[7], *Joshua*[6], *Joshua*[5], *Ebenezer*[4], *John*[3], *Thomas*[2], *Thomas*[1]), b. Feb. 22, 1830; m. Sept. 25, 1862, Estelle M. Holden, b. June 26, 1844. Res. Northfield, Mass. Children:—

4712. i. JEROME S., b. Nov. 11, 1865.
4713. ii. W. MYRTLE, b. Mar. 20, 1879.

3620. CHARLES D.[9] PIERCE (*Joseph*[8], *Asa*[7], *Joshua*[6], *Joshua*[5], *Ebenezer*[4], *John*[3], *Thomas*[2], *Thomas*[1]), b. Sept. 11, 1844; m. Dec. 29, 1869, Hattie A. Phelps, b. June 2, 1849. Res. No. Leominster, Mass. Children:—

4714. i. GRACE R., b. Nov. 26, 1872.
4715. ii. GILMAN H., b. Oct. 18, 1875.

3645. GEORGE E.[9] PIERCE (*William B.*[8], *William*[7], *John*[6], *Josiah*[5], *Josiah*[4], *John*[3], *Thomas*[2], *Thomas*[1]), b. June 17, 1855; m. June 10, 1877, Clara G. Whiton, b. June 25, 1852. Res. Biddeford, Me. Child:—

4716. i. GRACE E., b. Mar. 14, 1878.

3658. CHARLES O.[9] PIERCE (*Hubbard L.*[8], *Joseph*[7], *Joseph*[6], *John*[5], *Josiah*[4], *John*[3], *Thomas*[2], *Thomas*[1]), b. Apr. 21, 1824; m. Oct. 28, 1849, Lovina Sargent, b. Aug. 25, 1829. Res. St. Johnsbury Centre, Vt. Children:—

4717. i. ELLA F., b. Dec. 18, 1855.
4718. ii. SADIE S., b. Feb. 16, 1860.

3660. FRANKLIN O.[9] PIERCE (*Hubbard L.*[8], *Joseph*[7], *Joseph*[6], *John*[5], *Josiah*[4], *John*[3], *Thomas*[2], *Thomas*[1]), b. Apr. 8, 1829; m. Jan.

24, 1854, Mary E. Webster, b. May 12, 1833. He d. Dec. 14, 1872. Res. Norwich, Conn. Children :—

4719. i. CHARLES F., b. Feb. 12, 1856; d. Sept. 23, 1858.
4720. ii. CHARLES W., b. Apr. 5, 1859.

3663. EUGENE F.[9] PIERCE (*Hubbard L.*[8], *Joseph*[7], *Joseph*[6], *John*[5], *Josiah*[4], *John*[3], *Thomas*[2], *Thomas*[1]), b. Feb. 5, 1849; m. Nov. 17, 1868, Nellie Walters, b. 1845. Children :—

4721. i. NORA.
4722. ii. ELENOR.
4723. iii. ELWIN.
4724. iv. NELLIE.

3672. RANSOM T.[9] PIERCE (*Charles K.*[8], *Jotham*[7], *Joseph*[6], *John*[5], *Josiah*[4], *John*[3], *Thomas*[2], *Thomas*[1]), b. Sept. 17, 1848 ; m. Sept. 28, 1876, Hattie Rice. Res. Benton Harbor, Mich. Child :—

4725. i. L. EDWIN, b. July, 1877.

3682. WILLARD[9] PIERCE (*Varnum*[8], *Martin*[7], *Joseph*[6], *John*[5], *Josiah*[4], *John*[3], *Thomas*[2], *Thomas*[1]), b. Sept. 3, 1834 ; m. Apr. 23, 1864, Sarah A. Gray, b. Jan. 29, 1845. Res. St. Albans, Vt.

Children :—

4726. i. CHARLES A., b. July 26, 1865.
4727. ii. FRANK V., b. Oct. 5, 1866.
4728. iii. NELLIE, b. Jan. 16, 1869.
4729. iv. WILLARD M., b. Oct. 2, 1870.
4730. v. JOSEPHINE E., b. Oct. 19, 1878.

3686. MARTIN[9] PIERCE (*Varnum*[8], *Martin*[7], *Joseph*[6], *John*[5], *Josiah*[4], *John*[3], *Thomas*[2], *Thomas*[1]), b. Nov. 12, 1844 ; m. Della Streeter. Res. Allegan, Mich. Children :—

4731. i. ———.
4732. ii. ———.
4733. iii. ———.
4734. iv. ———.
4735. v. ———.

3692. ALONZO[9] PIERCE (*Henry*[8], *Martin*[7], *Joseph*[6], *John*[5], *Josiah*[4], *John*[3], *Thomas*[2], *Thomas*[1]), b. June 8, 1850 ; m. Jan. 2, 1870, Sarah Minkler, b. Feb. 27, 1853. Res. Kendall, Mich. Children :—

4736. i. ARTHUR, b. July 22, 1872.
4737. ii. FRED., b. Sept. 22, 1874.
4738. iii. CHARLES, b. May 28, 1877.

3697. GEORGE M.[9] PIERCE (*Hiram*[8], *Martin*[7], *Joseph*[6], *John*[5], *Josiah*[4], *John*[3], *Thomas*[2], *Thomas*[1]), b. Sept. 29, 1845 ; m. July 10, 1873, Maritt Fields. Res. St. Albans, Vt. Child :—

4739. i. WEST M., b. Aug. 25, 1875.

3699. HIRAM M.[9] PIERCE (*Hiram*[8], *Martin*[7], *Joseph*[6], *John*[5], *Josiah*[4], *John*[3], *Thomas*[2], *Thomas*[1]), b. July 31, 1849 ; m. Apr. 7, 1880, Carrie L. Baldwin, b. Aug. 31, 1867. Res. Baldwin, Wis.

Hiram M. Pierce

3711. CHARLES F.[9] PIERCE (*Charles W.*[8], *Wilder*[7], *Joseph*[6], *John*[5], *Josiah*[4], *John*[3], *Thomas*[2], *Thomas*[1]), b. Jan. 10, 1846 ; m. Dec. 31, 1868, Jennie Morse, b. Aug. 13, 1843. Res. Chicago, Ill.

Children :—

4740. i. CARL H., b. Jan. 24, 1870.
4741. ii. ADA, b. Jan. 8, 1879.

3715. GEORGE A.[9] PIERCE (*Charles W.*[8], *Wilder*[7], *Joseph*[6], *John*[5], *Josiah*[4], *John*[3], *Thomas*[2], *Thomas*[1]), b. Dec. 2, 1855 ; m. Sept. 27, 1877, Jennie E. Thornton, b. July 19, 1877. Res. Stanstead, P. Q.

No children.

3726. DANIEL W.[9] PIERCE (*Warren*[8], *Daniel*[6], *Daniel*[6], *John*[5], *Josiah*[4], *John*[3], *Thomas*[2], *Thomas*[1]), b. April 3, 1811 ; m. Lucy Edson, b. Jan. 3, 1816. Res. Salem, Nebraska.

Children :—

4742. i. DANIEL W., b. Aug. 31, 1835 ; m. Belinda B. Laythe.
4743. ii. EDGAR E., b. Jan. 9, 1837.
4744. iii. GEORGE W., b. Nov. 13, 1838.
4745. iv. HENRY H., b. June 2, 1840.
4746. v. LUCY A., b. Feb. 26, 1844 ; m. Harrison H. Cornell.
4747. vi. LUCINDA O., b. Nov. 19, 1847 ; m. Shedrick Chafin.
4748. vii. CHARLES L., b. Dec. 12, 1851.

3727. WILLARD A.[9] PIERCE (*Warren*[8], *Daniel*[7], *Daniel*[6], *John*[5], *Josiah*[4], *John*[3], *Thomas*[2], *Thomas*[1]), b. Oct. 15, 1812 ; m. March 17, 1836, Emily Powers ; m. 2nd, Mary J. Northrop. Children :—

4749. i. DANIEL E., b. July 1, 1840 ; d. Oct., 1840.
4750. ii. ELVIRA L., b. May 3, 1842 ; d. Jan. 30, 1843.
4751. iii. CHARLES P., b. Oct. 26, 1844.
4752. iv. DANIEL, b. Jan. 21, 1847.

3730. GEORGE W.[9] PIERCE (*Warren*[8], *Daniel*[7], *Daniel*[6], *John*[5],

Josiah[4], *John*[3], *Thomas*[2], *Thomas*[1]), b. May 4, 1819 ; m. Sept. 22, 1846, Harriet Severns, b. July 3, 1822. Res. Vineland, N. J.

Geo. W. Pierce

Child :—

4753. i. IRWIN S., b. March 14, 1860.

3731. WARREN[9] PIERCE (*Warren*[8], *Daniel*[7], *Daniel*[6], *John*[5], *Josiah*[4], *John*[3], *Thomas*[2], *Thomas*[1]), b. June 20, 1821 ; m. 1844, Lucy M. Streeter, b. Feb. 8, 1827. Res. Westmore, Vt. Child :—

4754. i. J. HENRY, b. Oct., 1845; m.

3732. ABEL[9] PIERCE (*Warren*[8], *Daniel*[7], *Daniel*[6], *John*[5], *Josiah*[4], *John*[3], *Thomas*[2], *Thomas*[1]), b. April 18, 1823 ; m. April 18, 1847, Mary H. Vanderpoole ; m. 2nd, 1855, Mary Webster, d. 1857 ; m. 3rd, 1859, Laurana Powers, b. 1831. Res. Vineland, N. J. Children :—

4755. i. CLARENCE A.
4756. ii. EUGENE W.
4757. iii. EARNEST A., b. Nov. 30, 1864.

3736. GEORGE W.[9] PIERCE (*Aretas*[8], *Aretas*[7], *Daniel*[6], *John*[5], *Josiah*[4], *John*[3], *Thomas*[2], *Thomas*[1]), b. May 1, 1826 ; m. Feb. 16, 1854, Ellen A. Southworth, b. Sept. 7, 1834. Res. Wellsville, N. Y. Children :—

4758. i. ELLA S., b. Jan. 7, 1855.
4759. ii. EMMA R., b. Nov. 6, 1859 ; d. Feb. 17, 1869.
4760. iii. GRACE M., b. Aug. 1, 1866.

3737. JOHN Q.[9] PIERCE (*Aretas*[8], *Aretas*[7], *Daniel*[6], *John*[5], *Josiah*[4], *John*[3], *Thomas*[2], *Thomas*[1]), b. Jan. 4, 1828 ; m. Oct. 4, 1855, Julia M. Bennett, b. Oct. 3, 1831, d. Sept. 12, 1868 ; m. 2nd, June 1, 1874, Sarah L. Keyes, b. Sept. 23, 1849. Res. St. Johns, Mich.

J. Q. Pierce

Children :—

4761. i. ADA J., b. Oct. 17, 1859 ; d. July 30, 1870.
4762. ii. FLORA M., b. May 29, 1867 ; d. Dec. 4, 1868.
4763. iii. BENJAMIN, b. July 23, 1875 ; d. Dec. 30, 1875.
4764. iv. BURT K., b. Jan. 9, 1878.

3739. JOSEPH B.[9] PIERCE (*Aretas*[8], *Aretas*[7], *Daniel*[6], *John*[5], *Josiah*[4], *John*[3], *Thomas*[2], *Thomas*[1]), b. May 23, 1836 ; m. May 10, 1860, Emma A. Brown, b. 1840. Res. Holly, N. Y. Children :—

4765. i. EDITH, b. 1863.
4766. ii. FANNY E., b. 1864.
4767. iii. FLORENCE E., b. 1869.
4768. iv. NELLIE M., b. 1872.

3741. FREEMAN A.⁹ PIERCE (*Abel A.*⁸, *Abel*⁷, *Daniel*⁶, *John*⁵, *Josiah*⁴, *John*³, *Thomas*², *Thomas*¹), b. May 6, 1849 ; m. Oct. 30, 1874, Olive Raney, b. Sept. 20, 1852. Res. St. Johnsbury Centre, Vt. Children :—

4769. i. ETHEL R., b. Aug. 18, 1877.
4770. ii. GEORGE A., b. Feb. 2, 1880.

3744. EDWARD C.⁹ PIERCE (*Abel A.*⁸, *Abel*⁷, *Daniel*⁶, *John*⁵, *Josiah*⁴, *John*³, *Thomas*², *Thomas*¹), b. Aug. 9, 1857 ; m. Sept. 6, 1879, Mary Williams, b. Sept. 6, 1856. Res. St. Johnsbury Centre, Vt.

3754. HOLLIS S.⁹ PIERCE (*Hiram*⁸, *Thomas*⁷, *Thomas*⁶, *John*⁵, *Josiah*⁴, *John*³, *Thomas*², *Thomas*¹), b. March 19, 1829 ; m. Oct. 3, 1850, Aurora Hill, b. July 30, 1832. Res. St. Johnsbury Centre, Vt. Children :—

4771. i. EVA, b. May 19, 1853; m. Alexander Allbee.
4772. ii. GEORGE H., b. Oct. 15, 1861.

3757. HIRAM D.⁹ PIERCE (*Hiram*⁸, *Thomas*⁷, *Thomas*⁶, *John*⁵, *Josiah*⁴, *John*³, *Thomas*², *Thomas*¹), b. March 1, 1838 ; m. Oct. 8, 1862, Marian Hopkins, b. June 11, 1837. Res. St. Johnsbury Centre, Vt. Children :—

4773. i. ABBIE M., b. Feb. 5, 1864.
4774. ii. FLORENCE J., b. Oct. 10, 1866; d. Oct. 25, 1876.
4775. iii. MABLE, b. May 16, 1873; d. May 1, 1878.
4776. iv. MARY B., b. Sept. 1, 1878.

3763. MARSH C.⁹ PIERCE (*Sylvester P.*⁸, *Spalding*⁷, *John*⁶, *Thomas*⁵, *Thomas*⁴, *Thomas*³, *Thomas*², *Thomas*¹), b. Feb. 19, 1847 ; m. Nov. 7, 1872, Jennie Cook, b. Aug. 14, 1848, d. Oct. 17, 1873. Res. Syracuse, N. Y. Child :—

4777. HARRY C., b. Oct. 8, 1873.

3770. WILLIAM⁹ PIERCE (*Charles*⁸, *Phineas*⁷, *Lemuel*⁶, *Ebenezer*⁵, *Thomas*⁴, *Thomas*³, *Thomas*², *Thomas*¹), b. 1821 ; m. 1848, Mary Barstow. He d. 1851.

3771. NATHANIEL⁹ PIERCE (*Charles*⁸, *Phineas*⁷, *Lemuel*⁶, *Ebenezer*⁵, *Thomas*⁴, *Thomas*³, *Thomas*², *Thomas*¹), b. 1825 ; m. 1845, Amy Adams. Children :—

4778. i. ———.
4779. ii. ———.
4780. iii. ———.

3772. GEORGE A.⁹ PIERCE (*Charles*⁸, *Phineas*⁷, *Lemuel*⁶, *Ebenezer*⁵, *Thomas*⁴, *Thomas*³, *Thomas*², *Thomas*¹), b. Dec. 25, 1835 ; m. Aug. 22, 1859, Ellen Rich. Res. Rockville, Conn.

George A. Pierce

Children :—

4781. i.   JANE, b. Nov. 26, 1860; d. Jan. 18, 1862.
4782. ii. GEORGE, b. March 26, 1862; d. Oct., 1863.
4783. iii. CHARLES, b. 1868.

3778. EDWIN M.[9] PIERCE (*Martin*[8], *Phineas*[7], *Lemuel*[6], *Ebenezer*[5], *Thomas*[4], *Thomas*[3], *Thomas*[2], *Thomas*[1]), b. Dec. 8, 1831 ; m. Martha Kenyon. Res. Grosvenordale, Conn.

3781. JOHN W.[9] PIERCE (*Martin*[8], *Phineas*[7], *Lemuel*[6], *Ebenezer*[5], *Thomas*[4], *Thomas*[3], *Thomas*[2], *Thomas*[1]), b. April 21, 1836 ; m. Almira Place. Children:—

4784. i.   ELIPHALET H., b. Nov. 3, 1857.
4785. ii. JOHN W., b. Dec. 3, 1859.
4786. iii. ALONZO S., b. Jan. 31, 1862.
4787. iv. JULIAN H., b. Dec. 13, 1863.

3785. NORMAN S.[9] PIERCE (*Darius*[8], *Phineas*[7], *Lemuel*[6], *Ebenezer*[5], *Thomas*[4], *Thomas*[3], *Thomas*[2], *Thomas*[1]), b. Nov. 14, 1842 ; m. July 28, 1862, Mary L. J. McMaine. Res. Portland, Oregon.

Children :—

4788. i.   KATIE E., b. Apr. 28, 1867.
4789. ii. ANNIE, b. May 10, 1869.
4790. iii. ALICE C., b. Mar. 17, 1871.
4791. iv. NORMAN S., b. June 3, 1874.

3789. JAMES[9] PIERCE (*Alvares*[8], *Samuel*[7], *Thomas*[6], *Amos*[5], *Thomas*[4], *Thomas*[3], *Thomas*[2], *Thomas*[1]), b. Aug. 5, 1823 ; m. Nov. 11, 1845, Sarah R. Preston, b. Dec. 22, 1824. Res. Moline, Mich. Children :—

4792. i.   WILLIAM W., b. Oct. 15, 1848; m. Annie E. Jones and Huldah H. Millifor.
4793. ii. ORPHA J., b. Dec. 18, 1852; m. Fred. Waderman.

3793. FREDERICK F.[9] PIERCE (*Rodney*[8], *Samuel*[7], *Thomas*[6], *Amos*[5], *Thomas*[4], *Thomas*[3], *Thomas*[2], *Thomas*[1]), b. Sept. 2, 1832; m. Sept. 14, 1864, Margaretta E. Coe, b. Sept. 14, 1839. Res. Brandon, Vt.

39

Children :—

4794. i. FREDERICK W., b. Dec. 1, 1865; d. Mar. 30, 1866.
4795. ii. MABEL C., b. Mar. 12, 1870.
4796. iii. HERBERT F., b. Sept. 26, 1872.

3794. HENRY M.[9] PIERCE (*Rodney*[8], *Samuel*[7], *Thomas*[6], *Amos*[5], *Thomas*[4], *Thomas*[3], *Thomas*[2], *Thomas*[1]), b. Mar. 29, 1834; m. Nov. 7, 1865, Mary Spaulding, b. May 27, 1845. Res. Lowell, Mass. Child :—

4797. i. CORA E., b. May 10, 1867.

3800. SAMUEL A.[9] PIERCE (*S. William*[8], *Samuel*[7], *Thomas*[6], *Amos*[5], *Thomas*[4], *Thomas*[3], *Thomas*[2], *Thomas*[1]), b. July 1, 1831 ; m. Nov. 26, 1859, Harriet E. Wilson, b. Feb. 4, 1836. Res. W. Salisbury, Vt. Child :—

4798. i. EDNA W., b. Apr. 12, 1872.

3808. CHARLES K.[9] PIERCE (*Rodney*[8], *John*[7], *Thomas*[6], *Amos*[5], *Thomas*[4], *Thomas*[3], *Thomas*[2], *Thomas*[1]), b. Apr. 18, 1837 ; m. Aug. 27, 1861, Ellen L. Goodall, b. May 25, 1841. Res. Hiram, Ohio. Children :—

4799. i. LOUISA N., b. Nov. 10, 1863.
4800. ii. HATTIE L., b. Mar. 28, 1868; d. Feb. 15, 1869.
4801. iii. CARRIE E., b. Aug. 13, 1870.

3809. GEORGE[9] PIERCE (*Rodney*[8], *John*[7], *Thomas*[6], *Amos*[5], *Thomas*[4], *Thomas*[3], *Thomas*[2], *Thomas*[1]), b. June 2, 1839 ; m. Mar. 19, 1860, Caroline Westlake. He was killed by the Rebels at Cold Harbor, June 1, 1864. Res. ———. Child :—

4802. i. ALBERT W., b. Aug. 13, 1862.

3811. HENRY D. PIERCE (*Rodney*[8], *John*[7], *Thomas*[6], *Amos*[5], *Thomas*[4], *Thomas*[3], *Thomas*[2], *Thomas*[1]), b. July 12, 1842 ; m. May 9, 1866, Charlotte Stocking, b. Nov. 27, 1839. Res. Alliance, Ohio. Children :—

4803. i. NELLIE C., b. Oct. 31, 1867; d. July 11, 1869.
4804. ii. FRANK H., b. Feb. 1, 1871.
4805. iii. MABEL C., b. Aug. 28, 1875; d. Dec. 14, 1875.

3815. RODNEY[9] PIERCE (*Rodney*[8], *John*[7], *Thomas*[6], *Amos*[5], *Thomas*[4], *Thomas*[3], *Thomas*[2], *Thomas*[1]), b. June 15, 1851 ; m. Sept. 1, 1875, Mary E. Askin, b. Mar. 30, 1855. Res. Danville, Pa. Child :—

4806. i. GYE, b. Nov. 29, 1877.

3816. JOHN I.[9] PIERCE (*Andrew*[8], *John*[7], *Thomas*[6], *Amos*[5], *Thomas*[4], *Thomas*[3], *Thomas*[2], *Thomas*[1]), b. Dec. 19, 1837 ; m. Nov., 1859, Harriet Cobb. Children :—

4807. i. MARY A., b. Feb. 15, 1862.
4808. ii. GEORGE A., b. June 7, 1869.

3819. EDWARD R.[9] PIERCE (*John D.*[8], *John*[7], *Thomas*[6], *Amos*[5], *Thomas*[4], *Thomas*[3], *Thomas*[2], *Thomas*[1]), b. Nov. 18, 1840 ; m.

Dec. 24, 1861, Mary E. McGahan, b. Sept. 7, 1839. Res. Hiram Centre, Ohio. Children :—

4809. i. ELLA R., b. May 20, 1863.
4810. ii. JOHN F., b. May 6, 1865; d.$Mar. 31, 1867.

3820. WILLIAM N.^{9} PIERCE ($Amos^8$, $William^7$, $Amos^6$, $Amos^5$, $Thomas^4$, $Thomas^3$, $Thomas^2$, $Thomas^1$), b. Apr. 18, 1843; m. Sept. 1, 1870, Eliza Richards, b. Feb. 21, 1847. Res. Elmwood, Ill.

William N. Peirce [signature]

Children :—

4811. i. RICHARD A., b. Aug. 31, 1871.
4812. ii. MIRIAM J., b. May 30, 1876.
4813. iii. LOIS E., b. Dec. 29, 1877.

3821. AMOS A^9. PIERCE ($Amos^8$, $William^7$, $Amos^6$, $Amos^5$, $Thomas^4$, $Thomas^3$, $Thomas^2$, $Thomas^1$), b. June 28, 1856; m. May 12, 1878, Fredonia T. Jarmain. Res. Elmwood, Ill.

3826. JOHN L.^{9} PIERCE ($William$ $G.^8$, $William^7$, $Amos^6$, $Amos^5$, $Thomas^4$, $Thomas^3$, $Thomas^2$, $Thomas^1$), b. August 24, 1853, m. Margaret H. Harris. Res. Champaign, Ill. John L. Pierce was born in Canaan, Conn., Aug. 24, 1853. Educated at Knox College, Galesburg, Ill., and the Illinois Industrial University, Champaign, Ill., where he graduated in 1874. Read law in the office of Black & Gere.

John L. Pierce [signature]

3834. WILLIAM O.^{9} PIERCE ($Samuel$ $R.^8$, $Phineas^7$, $Phineas^6$, $Amos^5$, $Thomas^4$, $Thomas^3$, $Thomas^2$, $Thomas^1$), b. Oct. 28, 1835; m. Oct. 31, 1859, Zerelda Fall, b. Jan. 29, 1835. Res. Winchester, Ind.
Children :—

4814. i. FRANCES L., b. July 31, 1860; d. Feb. 21, 1865.
4815. ii. JENNY L., b. Mar. 12, 1865; d. Aug. 26, 1868.

3837. DORSEY C.^{9} PIERCE ($Samuel$ $R.^8$, $Phineas^7$, $Phineas^6$, $Amos^5$, $Thomas^4$, $Thomas^3$, $Thomas^2$, $Thomas^1$), b. July 24, 1848; m. Dec. 17, 1867, Mary J. Martin, b. Apr. 11, 1848. Res. Nashville, Tenn.

Dorsey C. Pierce [signature]

Children :—

4816. i.   EDA R., b. July 26, 1873.
4817. ii. MARY E., b. Nov. 25, 1875.

3844. AMOS[9] PIERCE (*Clement*[8], *Amos*[7], *Phineas*[6], *Amos*[5], *Thomas*[4], *Thomas*[3], *Thomas*[2], *Thomas*[1]), b. Dec. 10, 1843 ; m. Apr. 24, 1867, Mary J. Barr, b. May 28, 1839. Res. Bellville, Kansas.
Children :—

4818. i.   JOHN O., b. Jan. 24, 1868; d. Dec. 16, 1868.
4819. ii.   HARLEY L., b. Dec. 10, 1870.
4820. iii. GEORGE C., b. July 27, 1874.
4821. iv.   MABEL M., b. Sept. 16, 1877; d. May 28, 1879.

3847. ALMIRON G.[9] PIERCE (*William H.*[8], *Amos*[7], *Phineas*[6], *Amos*[5], *Thomas*[4], *Thomas*[3], *Thomas*[2], *Thomas*[1]), b. July 4, 1838 ; m. Nov. 1, 1860, Caroline C. Sanford, b. Mar. 19, 1839. Res. Galesburg, Ill.

Children :—

4822. i.   FRANCES R., b. Mar. 27, 1862.
4823. ii.   ELLEN M., b. Apr. 2, 1864.
4824. iii. MINERVA A., b. Nov. 20, 1871.
4825. iv.   KATE M., b. Mar. 26, 1873.
4826. v.   ARGUS B. C., b. June 23, 1874.

3848. CHARLES H.[9] PIERCE (*William H.*[8], *Amos*[7], *Phineas*[6], *Amos*[5], *Thomas*[4], *Thomas*[3], *Thomas*[2], *Thomas*[1]), b. Feb. 1, 1840 ; m. Feb. 1, 1862, Elizabeth Long, b. June 16, 1839. Res. Roseville, Ill. Children :—

4827. i.   Y. MAUDE, b. Dec. 31, 1862.
4828. ii.   WILLIAM H., b. Dec. 16, 1864
4829. iii. M. BLANCHE, b. Feb. 24, 1866.
4830. iv.   H. GRACE, b. June 26, 1871.
4831. v.   SEELY A., b. June 17, 1873.

3868. FRANK L.[9] PIERCE (*Christopher E.*[8], *Abiram*[7], *Phineas*[6], *Amos*[5], *Thomas*[4], *Thomas*[3], *Thomas*[2], *Thomas*[1]), b. Apr. 10, 1853 ; m. Nov. 15, 1876, Mattie Cooley, b. June 12, 1856. Res. Smithfield, Pa.
Child :—

4832. i.   JUD. S., b. Sept. 6, 1878.

3894. LEWIS W.[9] PIERCE (*Earl*[8], *Palmer*[7], *Timothy*[6], *Timothy*[5], *Timothy*[4], *Thomas*[3], *Thomas*[2], *Thomas*[1]), b. Nov. 10, 1810; m. July 9, 1834, Perley H. Sanford. Res. Plattsburgh, N. Y.
Mr. Pierce was born on the 10th of Nov., 1810. He is English, of Welsh descent. His father, Earl Pierce, died in 1836, in Au Sable,

Clinton County, where is mother is still living. He removed with his parents to that place in 1821. He was educated at Potsdam and Keeseville Academies, and in 1831 went to Jay, Essex County, N. Y., where he engaged in the sale of goods in connection with the manufacture of iron. On the death of his father he sold out his business and returned to Au Sable and was the acting administrator of his estate. In 1849 he disposed of all his business enterprises and in May, 1851, removed to Plattsburgh where he now resides. Mr. Pierce held almost continuously some town office from 1833 to 1851, when he was appointed Deputy Collector of Customs and clerk and cashier in the custom house at Plattsburgh, N. Y. This office he held till January, 1854, when he resigned to assume the duties of the office of County Clerk, to which office he was elected in November, 1853. This position he occupied for three years. He claims to have been formerly a Henry Clay whig and is now a republican, although elected to his present position by a combination of Americans and republicans. He is a man of fine business capacity and discharges his duties with an industry and promptness that commend him alike to his constituents and his legislative associates. Mr. Pierce was married in 1834 to Miss Perley H. Sanford, daughter of Hon. Reuben Sanford, and is an elder in the Presbyterian church. He is a staunch friend of temperance and education.

The foregoing was written in the winter of 1859.

On his return home from the legislature in the spring of that year, he was tendered the position of cashier and clerk of Clinton Prison, which he accepted and held for five years, when another position, much more to his taste and liking, was offered to him in the Plattsburgh custom house as deputy collector, clerk, cashier and special deputy, which he accepted, and entered upon the duties May 1, 1864, and this position he held and continued to fill for over twelve years, retiring June 1, 1876, since which time he has not engaged in any business enterprises. His two sons, Edgar, the oldest, is engaged in the manufacture and sale of furniture in all of its branches in Plattsburgh, and his other son, Fred, is a merchant at Morrisonville in this county, about five miles from this place. In looking after them it affords him very pleasant exercise and pastime in advising and assisting them in their business, and renders him less liable to rust out.

Lewis M Pierce

Children :—

4833. i. EDGAR W., b. Mar. 6, 1836; m. Frances A. Thorpe.
4834. ii. ANN M., b. July 6, 1840.
4835. iii. MARY H., b. Jan. 12, 1844.
4836. iv. FRED. E., b. Jan. 7, 1851.
4837. v. MARTHA E., b. Oct. 9, 1853.

3895. BENJAMIN C.[9] PIERCE (*Earl*[8], *Palmer*[7], *Timothy*[6], *Timo-*

thy⁵, Timothy⁴, Thomas³, Thomas², Thomas¹), b. Sept. 12, 1812; m. Sept. 12, 1832, Catherine R. Finch, b. Dec. 4, 1811. Res. Au Sable Forks, N. Y. He is the foreman in the out door-business of a large iron manufacturing establishment at Au Sable Forks, lying partly in Clinton and Essex counties.

Children :—

4838. i. HENRY I., b. May 9, 1833; m. Celia G. Clough.
4839. ii. ISABEL H., b. Aug. 16, 1836; m. N. A. Thorpe.
4840. iii. EARL, b. Apr. 23, 1841; m. Mary Adlam.
4841. iv. FRANK C., b. Oct. 26, 1851; m. Milla Kinealy.

3897. HENRY P.⁹ PIERCE (*Earl⁸, Palmer⁷, Timothy⁶, Timothy⁵, Timothy⁴, Thomas³, Thomas², Thomas¹*), b. Dec. 13, 1817; m. Dec. 12, 1842, Maria O. Wright. He has long been a lumber inspector. Res. West Troy, N. Y.

Children :—

4842. i. OSCAR W., b. Nov. 9, 1843; d. Nov. 30, 1843.
4843. ii. HELEN F., b. Jan. 8, 1845.
4844. iii. CHARLES H., b. Nov. 3, 1847.
4845. iv. SOPHRONIA I., b. Aug. 31, 1850.
4846. v. MARY E., b. Sept. 7, 1852.
4847. vi. FRED. W., b. April 9, 1860.

3899. WILLIAM C.⁹ PIERCE (*Earl⁸, Palmer⁷, Timothy⁶, Timothy⁵, Timothy⁴, Thomas³, Thomas², Thomas¹*), b. Sept. 19, 1822; m. June 5, 1851, Catherine Boynton, d. April 17, 1852; m. 2nd, Sept. 18, 1855, Margaret M. Myers. He resides on the old homestead and was formerly engaged in the manufacture of iron. Res. Au Sable Forks, N. Y.

Children :—

4848. i. WILLIAM W., b. Dec. 26, 1856.
4849. ii. MATHEW M., b. Dec. 22, 1859.

3901. JAMES H.⁹ PIERCE (*Earl⁸, Palmer⁷, Timothy⁶, Timothy⁵, Timothy⁴, Thomas³, Thomas², Thomas¹*), b. Aug. 26, 1826; m. Aug. 7, 1856, Carrie O. Lennon, b. June 7, 1835. He has been representative in the New York Assembly for four years in succession. He is now the proprietor of a large hotel in Blcomingdale.   Res. Bloomingdale, N. Y.

Children :—
4850. i.   JAMES H., b. Sept. 23, 1858.
4851. ii.   CAROLINE E., b. April 24, 1862.
4852. iii. ALMEDIA C., b. Feb. 13, 1867.

3902. DANIEL W.[9] PIERCE (*Earl*[8], *Palmer*[7], *Timothy*[6], *Timothy*[5], *Timothy*[4], *Thomas*[3], *Thomas*[2], *Thomas*[1]), b. Oct. 20, 1828 ; m. Adelaide R. Finch. He d. April 27, 1854, in Neenah, Wis. Child :—
4853. i.   CLIFTON W., b. 1853.

3903. EDWIN R.[9] PIERCE (*Earl*[8], *Palmer*[7], *Timothy*[6], *Timothy*[5], *Timothy*[4], *Thomas*[3], *Thomas*[2], *Thomas*[1]), b. Nov. 27, 1831 ; m. Dec. 27, 1866, Maria L. Bentley, b. Jan. 19, 1840. He is at the head of an insurance house doing a large business. Res. Minneapolis, Minn.

Children :
4854. i.   CHARLES E., b. April 6, 1870.
4855. ii.   GEORGE B., b. Nov. 11, 1872.

3905. JOHN L.[9] PIERCE (*Palmer*[8], *Palmer*[7], *Timothy*[6], *Timothy*[5], *Timothy*[4], *Thomas*[3], *Thomas*[2], *Thomas*[1]), b. Feb. 7, 1813 ; m. Oct. 25, 1836, Cynthia Whitcomb. He d. Nov. 9, 1836. Res. North East, Pa. No children.

3906. ARNOLD Y.[9] PIERCE (*Palmer*[8], *Palmer*[7], *Timothy*[6], *Timothy*[5], *Timothy*[4], *Thomas*[3], *Thomas*[2], *Thomas*[1]), b. Feb. 25, 1815 ; m. Sept. 26, 1838, Wealthy Austin, b. Jan. 28, 1819. Res. North East, Pa. Children :—
4856. i.   M. DELPHIUS, b. Dec. 15, 1839; m. John Higgins.
4857. ii.   EARL B., b. July 8, 1842; d. Dec. 13, 1862.
4858. iii. JOHN S., b. Sept. 7, 1844; m.
4859. iv.   WEALTHY L., b. Aug. 13, 1848; m. E. M. Putnam.
4860. v.   EPHRAIM A., b. Aug. 15, 1850; m. Maggie Williamson.

3908. EARL[9] PIERCE (*Palmer*[8], *Palmer*[7], *Timothy*[6], *Timothy*[5], *Timothy*[4], *Thomas*[3], *Thomas*[2], *Thomas*[1]), b. Dec, 19, 1820 ; m. May 15, 1844, Louisa L. Hested, b. July 6, 1822. Res. North East, Pa.

Children :—

4861. i. ROISE E., b. May 2, 1846; m. Josephine Brown.
4862. ii. WILLIAM, b. May 29, 1848; d. Jan. 8, 1860.
4863. iii. CHARLES, b. Aug. 16, 1854; d. Jan. 5, 1860.
4864. iv. GEORGE E., b. Dec. 25, 1860.

3910. MORDAUNT M.[9] PIERCE (*John*[8], *Palmer*[7], *Timothy*[6], *Timothy*[5], *Timothy*[4], *Thomas*[3], *Thomas*[2], *Thomas*[1]), b. March 21, 1827 ; m. April 11, 1852, Tarrissa C. Willers, b. June 9, 1825. Res. Milton, Vt. Child :—

4865. i. KATIE M., b. Oct. 6, 1858.

3925. JOHN S.[9] PIERCE (*Joseph S.*[8], *Job*[7], *Josiah*[6], *Timothy*[5], *Timothy*[4], *Thomas*[3], *Thomas*[2], *Thomas*[1]), b. Nov. 28, 1842 ; m. Mar. 2, 1870, Jane A. Auckland, b. June 23, 1848. Res. Monroeville, Ohio.

John, S., Peirce

No children.

3927. WILLIAM[9] PIERCE (*Joseph S.*[8], *Job*[7], *Josiah*[6], *Timothy*[5], *Timothy*[4], *Thomas*[3], *Thomas*[2], *Thomas*[1]), b. Jan. 25, 1849 ; m. Dec. 6, 1876, Lucy A. Banta, b. Jan. 18, 1858. Res. Lyme, Ohio. Child :—

4866. i. MARY C., b. Sept. 4, 1878.

3930. MAHLON H.[9] PIERCE (*Chester*[8], *Shepard*[7], *Josiah*[6], *Timothy*[5], *Timothy*[4], *Thomas*[3], *Thomas*[2], *Thomas*[1]), b. Sept. 9, 1844 ; m. April 10, 1867, Mira Kennedy, b. Jan. 1, 1848. Res. Turner, Ind.

Mahlon H Pierce

Children :—

4867. i. ELMER C., } b. Dec. 17, 1867.
4868. ii. ELMO M., }
4869. iii. HARRIET S., b. Nov. 8, 1869.
4870. iv. IDA L., b. April 3, 1872.
4871. v. LEMUEL, b. June 21, 1874.
4872. vi. GUY H., b. Sept. 3, 1876; d.

3933. ALFRED L.[9] PIERCE (*Chester*[8], *Shepard*[7], *Josiah*[6], *Timothy*[5], *Timothy*[4], *Thomas*[3], *Thomas*[2], *Thomas*[1]), b. Sept. 28, 1849 ; m. May 15, 1877, Mary Bowman, b. Dec. 14, 1856. Res. North Aurora, Ill. Child :—

4873. i. G. AUBREY, b. June 18, 1878.

3934. CHESTER L.[9] PIERCE (*Chester*[8], *Shepard*[7], *Josiah*[6], *Timothy*[5], *Timothy*[4], *Thomas*[3], *Thomas*[2], *Thomas*[1]), b. Aug. 11, 1853 ; m. Mar. 29, 1877, Alice Eisor. Res. Red Oak, Iowa.

3935. SAMUEL N.[9] PIERCE (*William A.*[8], *Shepard*[7], *Josiah*[6], *Timothy*[5], *Timothy*[4], *Thomas*[3], *Thomas*[2], *Thomas*[1]), b. June 28, 1846; m. Feb. 2, 1876, Hattie Wood, b. Jan. 14, 1843. Res. Chemung, N. Y. No children.

3936. HENRY N.[9] PIERCE (*William A.*[8], *Shepard*[7], *Josiah*[6], *Timothy*[5], *Timothy*[4], *Thomas*[3], *Thomas*[2], *Thomas*[1]), b. Feb. 18, 1848 ; m. May 9, 1874, Fannie Hunter. He d. March 25, 1877.   Res. Elmira, N. Y.   Child :—
4874.   i.   HENRY N., b. Feb. 6, 1876; d. July 2, 1877.

3937. WILLIAM A.[9] PIERCE (*William A.*[8], *Shepard*[7], *Josiah*[6], *Timothy*[5], *Timothy*[4], *Thomas*[3], *Thomas*[2], *Thomas*[1]), b. Oct. 8, 1850 ; m. Jan. 3, 1871, Ruth A. Inscko, b. June 27, 1850.   Res. Lawrenceville, Pa.   Children :—
4875.   i.   ELMA B., b. Dec. 23, 1872.
4876. ii.   ANNIE K., b. Jan. 5, 1875.

3944. EARNEST B.[9] PIERCE (*Shepard S.*[8], *Shepard*[7], *Josiah*[6], *Timothy*[5], *Timothy*[4], *Thomas*[3], *Thomas*[2], *Thomas*[1]), b. Jan. 22, 1854 ; m. Sept. 2, 1875, Clara A. Wright, b. July 1, 1856.   Res. Towanda, Pa.

Child :—
4877.   i.   JOHN S., b. March 19, 1877.

3949. PHINEAS D.[9] PIERCE (*Phineas*[8], *Willard*[7], *Nathaniel*[6], *Nathaniel*[5], *Timothy*[4], *Thomas*[3], *Thomas*[2], *Thomas*[1]), b. Aug. 3, 1818 ; m. Nov. 29, 1842, Eleanor D. Kibbee, b. Feb. 13, 1823.   Res. Royalton, Vt.   Children :—
4878.   i.   MARTHA L., b. April 8, 1848; m. Geo. H. Tracy.
4879. ii.   LUCY E., b. Oct. 22, 1852; m. Joseph Tracy.

3955. NATHAN W.[9] PIERCE (*Albigence*[8], *Willard*[7], *Nathaniel*[6], *Nathaniel*[5], *Timothy*[4], *Thomas*[3], *Thomas*[2], *Thomas*[1]), b. Aug. 30, 1813 ; m. 1846, Sophia Spaulding.   He d. Aug., 1853.   Res. Vernon, N. Y.   Child :—
4880.   i.   GEORGE W., b. June, 1851.

3956. GEORGE B.[9] PIERCE (*Albigence*[8], *Willard*[7], *Nathaniel*[6], *Nathaniel*[5], *Timothy*[4], *Thomas*[3], *Thomas*[2], *Thomas*[1]), b. Aug. 26, 1815 ; m. May 1, 1850, Adeline E. Duncklee, b. 1825.   Res. Lexington, Mass.

Children :—

4881.   i.   GEORGE A., b. Feb. 3, 1851; m. Lizzie A. Pitman.
4882. ii.   CHARLES B., b. Feb. 11, 1861.

3958.   ALBIGENCE M.^{9} PIERCE (*Albigence*^{8}, *Willard*^{7}, *Nathaniel*^{6}, *Nathaniel*^{5}, *Timothy*^{4}, *Thomas*^{3}, *Thomas*^{2}, *Thomas*^{1}), b. April 27, 1823 ; m. ———— ————. Res. Berlin, Wis.   Child :—

4883.   i.   GEORGE A.

3959.   JOHN S.^{9} PIERCE (*Albigence*^{8}, *Willard*^{7}, *Nathaniel*^{6}, *Nathaniel*^{5}, *Timothy*^{4}, *Thomas*^{3}, *Thomas*^{2}, *Thomas*^{1}), b. Feb. 2, 1828 ; m. ———— ————. Res. St. Louis, Mo.

3962.   GEORGE^9 PIERCE (*John D.*^{8}, *Willard*^{7}, *Nathaniel*^{6}, *Nathaniel*^{5}, *Timothy*^{4}, *Thomas*^{3}, *Thomas*^{2}, *Thomas*^{1}), b. May 4, 1827 ; m. 1856, Sarah Phillips, d. 1878.   He d. June 23, 1871.   Res. Stowe, Vt.   Children :—

4884.   i.   SIDNEY B., b. Nov. 16, 1856 ; d. May 23, 1874.
4885. ii.   JERRY, b. Dec. 14, 1862.

3970.   EDGAR D.^{9} PIERCE (*Daniel W.*^{8}, *Willard*^{7}, *Nathaniel*^{6}, *Nathaniel*^{5}, *Timothy*^{4}, *Thomas*^{3}, *Thomas*^{2}, *Thomas*^{1}), b. Apr. 22, 1830; m. Sept. 28, 1858, Emma Chapman ; m. 2nd, June 29, 1868, Lucy Pratt.   He d. June 22, 1872.   Res. Chicago, Ill.   Children :—

4886.   i.   NELLIE, b. Aug. 4, 1859.
4887. ii.   GEORGE W., b. May 13, 1869.
4888. iii.   FRANK S., b. Dec. 27, 1871.

3973.   WILLIAM C.^{9} PIERCE (*Caleb*^{8}, *Bester*^{7}, *Nathaniel*^{6}, *Nathaniel*^{5}, *Timothy*^{4}, *Thomas*^{3}, *Thomas*^{2}, *Thomas*^{1}), b. Feb. 22, 1828 ; m. Harriet C. Reddington, b. Mar., 1831.   He d. 1860.   Res. ————.   Child :—

4889.   i.   SARAH, b. 1858 ; m. Paul Brooks.

3974.   JAMES F.^{9} PIERCE (*Caleb*^{8}, *Bester*^{7}, *Nathaniel*^{6}, *Nathaniel*^{5}, *Timothy*^{4}, *Thomas*^{3}, *Thomas*^{2}, *Thomas*^{1}), b. Apr. 8, 1830 ; m. June 24, 1856, Anna Reddington, b. Dec. 14, 1835.   Res. No. 7 Montague Terrace, Brooklyn, N. Y.

James F. Pierce was born in Madrid, St. Lawrence County, New York, on the 8th of April, 1830.   His parents were both natives of New England.   His father, Dr. Caleb Pierce, is a physician, and a graduate of Dartmouth College, New Hampshire.   He was born in 1799 and removed in 1825 to Madrid, where for more than half a century he has been not only the physician, but the guide, counsellor and friend of several generations of patients.   He is still in active practice.

James F. Pierce was prepared to enter college, having been educated in the preliminary steps for the collegiate course in the St. Lawrence Academy at Potsdam ; but indications of pulmonary disease hereditary in his family, compelled him to abandon all ideas of further study.   By careful attention to his health he was enabled to enter upon the study of law in the office of Judge Henry L. Knowles.   He

Very truly yours
James F. Pierce

remained pursuing his studies for fifteen months, when he removed to the city of Troy and entered the law office of William A. Beach and Job Pierson, where he completed his studies. He was admitted to the Bar at Albany in the year 1851, just as he had attained his twenty-first year.

Shortly after his admission to the Bar, the disease which he had inherited made serious inroads upon his health, and under the advice of eminent physicians in New York, he sought the mild climate of St. Augustine, Florida, where he remained for nearly three years. The balmy air of that locality and a continuous residence there restored him to his usual health. While at St. Augustine, Mr. Pierce occupied an office with the Hon. Isaac H. Bronson, now deceased, then United States Judge for the Eastern District of Florida, whose friendship he retained up to the period of his death. He there formed the acquaintance of Gov. Marcy, which ripened into intimate personal relations. During the campaign which resulted in the election of Franklin Pierce, President, he took an active part on the stump and otherwise and was a frequent contributor to the Democratic paper then published at St. Augustine.

On his return to the North from Florida, he resumed the practice of his profession and in 1856 settled at Canton, the county seat of St. Lawrence County.

Mr. Pierce has at all times possessed an instinctive passion for politics. He seems to glory in the excitement incident to a political career and to be charmed by the vicissitudes of political life. In St. Lawrence County, as a Democrat, he was in a hopeless minority, the county having become at an early time in the history of the Republican party one of its firmest strongholds in the State of New York. For many years Mr. Pierce was a regular delegate to the Democratic State Convention from his district, and thus he became intimately acquainted with the representative men of the party of his State, whose confidence he always enjoyed.

At the breaking out of the Rebellion, Mr. Pierce became an ardent supporter of the cause of his country and took an active part in raising troops in St. Lawrence County to sustain the honor of the flag of the Union. He still, however, remained faithful in his adherence to the party and its principles, to which he has ever been warmly attached. In 1862 a union ticket was formed in St. Lawrence County and Mr. Pierce was nominated for one of the principal offices as a slight acknowledgment of his services in raising troops and the interest which he took in the cause of the Union. A strong and desperate effort was made to defeat him, but he came out of the contest successful, his majority being about one thousand. The idea of a Democrat at that time being elected to a county office in St. Lawrence County was looked upon as a remarkable event, and Mr. Pierce attending the Democratic State Convention while holding the important position he did in St. Lawrence County, was an object of interest and curiosity. In 1865, Mr. Pierce removed to the city of New York and entered into partnership with Mr. Robert Sewell, establishing the law firm of Sewell & Pierce. Very soon the firm became prominently known in legal circles in New York and were retained in many important cases, in a few years, working into a prominent position among the legal firms in the city. In the Fall of 1866, Mr. Pierce took up his residence in Brooklyn and in the following year was nominated by the Democrats of the Second Senatorial District for the Senate. The District had hitherto been represented by a Republican. Mr. Pierce was a comparative stranger in the District, yet he was elected by 4000 majority. At the expiration of his term, Mr. Pierce was again elected to the Senate and he served for two consecutive terms in that body. During the first session he acted on the committees of Commerce and Navigation, Insurance and Retrenchment, and during the second term on those of Railroads, Insurance, Commerce and Navigation, and Public Printing.

In 1877, Mr. Pierce was again put in nomination and was again triumphantly elected and took his seat in the Senate on the 1st of January, 1878, where he was placed upon the committees on Judiciary, Canals, Public Buildings, and Retrenchment.

In person Mr. Pierce is above the medium height, somewhat slightly built, straight and upright in his figure, with large hazel-gray eyes and dark brown hair, rapidly changing to gray, and now in his 51st year, Mr. Pierce bears upon his outward form but little trace of the physical sufferings which he has for many years endured. His hereditary disposition to pulmonary complaint, although conquered in his early years, frequently threatens to return, constantly suggesting to him the necessity of caring for his health. His physical sufferings, however, never affect his temper, and he preserves the same genial manners and kindly disposition in all conditions of his health.

It is, however, for the greatness of his heart that Mr. Pierce is most remarkable; it may safely be said of him that a larger one does not throb in any human breast. His sympathy for suffering knows no bounds of caste, religion or nationality, but extends, a broad and swiftly flowing stream, carrying with it gentle consolation and substantial relief to every suffering creature that comes within his ken. It need hardly be said that these qualities make him remarkably popular, whether in society, in his professional circles or in politics. The man who will toil all day to do another a kindness is sure to be loved of all men, and such in an especial way is the lot of Mr. Pierce. This accounts for his large majorities in popular elections in districts where his party do not usually prevail; and if his life is spared there is no doubt but that the people reserve for him still greater honors and higher positions in the State and Nation.

Children :—
4890. i.   MARY L., b. Nov. 1, 1858. She was graduated at the Packer Institute. Miss Mary L. Pierce, who is a daughter of Hon.

James F. Pierce, and who graduated at the recent Commencement, June 1877, at the Packer Institute, displayed in the poem, "The Three Knights," which she contributed as her part of the literary exercises of that beautiful occasion, a scope and depth of genuine poetical thought and expression noticeably greater than young ladies of her age often exhibit. The critical readers of the *Eagle* have already enjoyed the production which was published in the report of the Commencement proceedings, and it is due to say that in the reading of it to the audience the fair authoress demonstrated an elocutionary and dramatic ability of a very vigorous and refined order.—[*Brooklyn Eagle*.

4891. ii. WILLIAM R., b. Dec. 6, 1860; d. Apr. 23, 1871.
4892. iii. JENNIE R., b. Oct. 15, 1862.
4893. iv. ANNA, b. Feb. 22, 1871; d. Jan. 7, 1872.
4894. v. JESSIE F., b. Sept. 18, 1873.
4895. vi. JAMES F. Jr., b. Sept. 23, 1875.

3979. DARWIN C.[9] PIERCE (*Collins*[8], *Bester*[7], *Nathaniel*[6], *Nathaniel*[5], *Timothy*[4], *Thomas*[3], *Thomas*[2], *Thomas*[1]), b. June 16, 1838 ; m. Jan. 2, 1861, Anna M. Robinson, b. Oct. 31, 1841. Res. Rutland, Vt. Children :—

4896. i. LIZZIE A., b. Nov. 6, 1865.
4897. ii. HENRY C., b. Feb. 7, 1868.
4898. iii. DARWIN W., b. Sept. 2, 1873.
4899. iv. LYMAN R., b. Feb. 16, 1876; d. Apr. 17, 1877.

3995. HORACE C.[9] PIERCE (*Horace*[8], *Isaac*[7], *Nathaniel*[6], *Nathaniel*[5], *Timothy*[4], *Thomas*[3], *Thomas*[2], *Thomas*[1]), b. Oct. 14, 1850 ; m. Sept. 9, 1874, Althea L. Dalton, b. July 3, 1855. Res. Barton, Vt.

H C Pierce

No children.

3997. SIDNEY C.[9] PIERCE (*John S.*[8], *Isaac*[7], *Nathaniel*[6], *Nathaniel*[5], *Timothy*[4], *Thomas*[3], *Thomas*[2], *Thomas*[1]), b. Sept. 21, 1843 ; m. Nov. 6, 1866, Sarah V. White, b. Nov. 7, 1843. Res. Boston. Children :—

4900. i. HENRY C., b. Feb. 9, 1872; d. July 5, 1872.
4901. ii. FLORENCE G., b. May 17, 1873; d. Jan. 18, 1877.
4902. iii. MARTHA H., b. Sept. 21, 1876.

4000. JOSEPH S.[9] PIERCE (*Seth*[8], *Joseph*[7], *Jedediah*[6], *Nathaniel*[5], *Timothy*[4], *Thomas*[3], *Thomas*[2], *Thomas*[1]), b. July 10, 1838 ; m. Dec. 8, 1859, Matilda Weaver, b. Dec. 7, 1837. Res. Lockport, N. Y. Children :—

4903. i. SARAH E., b. July 21, 1861.
4904. ii. GEORGE A., b. Sept. 26, 1863.
4905. iii. HERBERT W., b. June 19, 1868.

4013-4. LOUIS A.[9] PIERCE (*William*[8], *William*[7], *Jedediah*[6], *Nathaniel*[5], *Timothy*[4], *Thomas*[3], *Thomas*[2], *Thomas*[1]), b. Aug. 1, 1834 ; m. May 18, 1861, Mary M. Bronson, b. July 21, 1840. Res. Chicago, Ill.

L A Pierce

Children :—
4906. i.   WILLIAM B., b. June 27, 1864.
4907. ii. EDITH M., b. Apr. 8. 1866.
4908. iii. ALICE E., b. Oct. 15, 1868.

4015. CHARLES⁹ PIERCE (*William*⁸, *William*⁷, *Jedediah*⁶, *Nathaniel*⁵, *Timothy*⁴, *Thomas*³, *Thomas*², *Thomas*¹), b. June 14, 1837 ; m. June 2, 1854, Nancy A. Winslow, b. Dec. 13, 1843. Res. Hartford, Vt. Child :—
4909. i.   ABBIE E., b. Sept. 22, 1866.

4018. WILLIAM L.⁹ PIERCE (*William*⁸, *William*⁷, *Jedediah*⁶, *Nathaniel*⁵, *Timothy*⁴, *Thomas*³, *Thomas*², *Thomas*¹), b. June 14, 1846 ; m. Nov. 8, 1869, Ella L. Winslow, b. Nov. 11, 1849. Res. Hartford, Vt. Children :—
4910. i.   EDWARD L., b. Sept. 2, 1871.
4911. ii. FRED. P., b. Oct. 2, 1873.

4024. WASHINGTON F.⁹ PIERCE (*William*⁸, *William*⁷, *Jedediah*⁶, *Nathaniel*⁵, *Timothy*⁴, *Thomas*³, *Thomas*², *Thomas*,¹), b. Feb. 23, 1843 ; m. Dec. 23, 1866, Louisa A. Shumway, b. July 14, 1843. Res. DeKalb, Ill. Children :—
4912. i.   GEORGE A., b. Aug. 12, 1870.
4913. ii. EDNA M., b. Aug. 28, 1876.

4027. HENRY⁹ PIERCE (*Ira*⁸, *William*⁷, *Jedediah*⁶, *Nathaniel*⁵, *Timothy*⁴, *Thomas*³, *Thomas*², *Thomas*¹), b. Jan. 16, 1834 ; m. Sept. 25, 1860, Mary N. Remick, b. Mar. 22, 1831. Res. Royalton, Vt. No children.

4037. ARTHUR L.⁹ PIERCE (*Henry B.*⁸, *William*⁷, *Jedediah*⁶, *Nathaniel*⁵, *Timothy*⁴, *Thomas*³, *Thomas*², *Thomas*¹), b. Oct. 2, 1843 ; m. Dec. 6, 1871, Sarah J. Peyton, b. Sept. 4, 1846. Res. St. Louis, Mo.

Children :—
4914. i.   JESSIE A., b. June 18, 1874.
4915. ii. HARRY B., b. Nov. 9, 1875 ; d. Mar. 16, 1876.

4039. HARRY P.⁹ PIERCE (*Henry B.*⁸, *William*⁷, *Jedediah*⁶, *Nathaniel*⁵, *Timothy*⁴, *Thomas*³, *Thomas*², *Thomas*¹), b. Jan. 29, 1848; m. May 19, 1872, Abbie M. Hitchcock, b. May 20, 1852. Res. So. Barre, Vt. Children :—
4916. i.   ARTHUR L., b. May 8, 1874.
4917. ii. SON, b. Sept. 6, 1880.

4044. EDWARD L.⁹ PIERCE (*Chester*⁸, *William*⁷, *Jedediah*⁶, *Nathaniel*⁵, *Timothy*⁴, *Thomas*³, *Thomas*², *Thomas*¹), b. July 26, 1843 ; m. Oct. 24, 1871, Julia A. Ashley, b. July 31, 1841. Res. Rochester, Vt.

Child :—

4918.   i.   LESLIE D., b. July 13, 1876.

4045.   STEPHEN H.[9] PIERCE (*Edwin*[8], *Elisha*[7], *Jedediah*[6], *Na-thaniel*[5], *Timothy*[4], *Thomas*[3], *Thomas*[2], *Thomas*[1]), b. Oct. 26, 1827 ; m. Jan. 1, 1854, Nancy M. Holmes. He d. Mar. 25, 1865. She m. 2nd, John B. Drake of Saratoga, N. Y. Children :—

4919.   i.   DEWITT E., b. May 23, 1857.
4920.   ii. IRVING K., b. Jan. 21, 1860; d. Mar. 23, 1863.

4048.   SIDNEY E.[9] PIERCE (*Archibald T.*[8], *Elisha*[7], *Jedediah*[6], *Na-thaniel*[5], *Timothy*[4], *Thomas*[3], *Thomas*[2], *Thomas*[1]), b. May 9, 1838 ; m. Apr. 24, 1868, Mary B. Kimball, b. June 17, 1850. Res. White River Junction, Vt. Children :—

4921.   i.   JAMES E., b. Dec. 11, 1868.
4922.   ii. BESSIE M., b. Mar. 27, 1872.

4056.   LEVI L.[9] PIERCE (*Ebenezer F.*[8], *Ebenezer*[7], *Jedediah*[6], *Na-thaniel*[5], *Timothy*[4], *Thomas*[3], *Thomas*[2], *Thomas*[1]), b. Mar. 7, 1847 ; m. May 13, 1871, Sarah Doyle. Res. St. Albans, Vt. Children :—

4923.   i.   ——.
4924.   ii. ——.
4925.   iii. ——.

4057.   FRANKLIN E.[9] PIERCE (*Ebenezer F.*[8], *Ebenezer*[7], *Jedediah*[6], *Nathaniel*[5], *Timothy*[4], *Thomas*[3], *Thomas*[2], *Thomas*[1]), b. June 20, 1852 ; m. Jan. 31, 1873, Addie J. Woodward. Res. So. Royalton, Vt. No children.

4058.   ELBRIDGE I.[9] PIERCE (*Ebenezer F.*[8], *Ebenezer*[7], *Jedediah*[6], *Nathaniel*[5], *Timothy*[4], *Thomas*[3], *Thomas*[2], *Thomas*[1]), b. May 9, 1854 ; m. Dec. 24, 1874, Josephine Waldo, b. Apr. 1, 1857. Res. Barnard, Vt.

4060.   FRANCIS M.[9] PIERCE (*Hiram*[8], *Ebenezer*[7], *Jedediah*[6], *Na-thaniel*[5], *Timothy*[4], *Thomas*[3], *Thomas*[2], *Thomas*[1]), b. July 14, 1849. Res. Greenville, Ala. Children :—

4926.   i.   ——.
4927.   ii. ——.
4928.   iii. ——.
4929.   iv. ——.

4068.   EDWARD A.[9] PIERCE (*David*[8], *Benjamin*[7], *Nehemiah*[6], *Benjamin*[5], *Timothy*[4], *Thomas*[3], *Thomas*[2], *Thomas*[1]), b. Jan. 12, 1841 ; m. Mar. 11, 1867, Jane Lynch. Res. Castile, N. Y. Children :—

4930.   i.   MARCIA C., b. Mar. 31, 1868.
4931.   ii. G. FREDERICK, b. Apr. 10, 1872.

4082.   Capt. HENRY O.[9] PIERCE (*Oliver W.*[8], *Nehemiah*[7], *Nehemi-ah*[6], *Benjamin*[5], *Timothy*[4], *Thomas*[3], *Thomas*[2], *Thomas*[1]), b. Feb. 7, 1830 ; m. Apr. 28, 1859, Marietta E. Storrs, b. May 10, 1841. Res. Monmouth, Me.

Captain Henry O. Pierce was born in Monmouth, Me., upon what is called the "Ridge," Feb. 7, 1830, where he resided until 1855. He received a common school and academic education and taught his first school at the age of 17. In the spring of 1858 he went to Wautoma, Wis., where he taught school until 1861, when he was elected County Superintendent of public schools, in which capacity he served for two years. He left Wautoma in 1864 for Fort Atkinson, Wis., where he remained teaching until 1865, when he enlisted in the army. He was mustered into the Volunteer service as Captain of Company H, 49th Regiment, Wisconsin Infantry Volunteers, March, 1865. His regiment was ordered to Missouri, where it remained doing guard and provost duty until the soldiers were mustered out, in November of the same year. He remained at Fort Atkinson until 1868, when he came to Monmouth, Me. His father dying in 1871, he succeeded to the estate. He has been a member of the board of Selectmen for several years, one of the School Committee for eight years, and has represented his district in the Legislature.

Children :—

4932. i.   HATTIE M., b. May 3, 1862.
4933. ii.   CARRIE C., b. Jan. 12, 1864.
4934. iii. MABEL S., b. Jan. 31, 1868.
4935. iv.   JOHN O., b. May 16, 1870.
4936. v.   HENRY R., b. June 15, 1876.
4937. vi.   FLORENCE, b. May 9, 1880.

4089. CHARLES H.⁹ PIERCE (*Bela⁸, Nehemiah⁷, Nehemiah⁶, Benjamin⁵, Timothy⁴, Thomas³, Thomas², Thomas¹*), b. July 8, 1824 ; m. Nov. 12, 1863, Sarah M. Sprague, b. March 9, 1839. Res. No. Berwick, Me.

Children :—

4938. i.   LIZZIE M., b. Sept. 24, 1865.
4939. ii.   CLARA S., b. Mar. 8, 1867.
4940. iii. CHARLES S., b. July 7, 1880.

4091. WILLIAM⁹ PIERCE (*Bela⁸, Nehemiah⁷, Nehemiah⁶, Benjamin⁵, Timothy⁴, Thomas³, Thomas², Thomas¹*), b. Apr. 1, 1830 ; m. Aug. 1, 1865, Jane Barron, b. May 8, 1836, d. Oct. 28, 1872; m. 2nd, Mar. 19, 1878, Lena C. Allen, b. July 8, 1850. He d. Sept. 12, 1879. Res. Berwick, Me. Children :—

4941. i.   WILLIAM B., b. Sept. 10, 1866.
4942. ii.   EDWARD E., b. Apr. 2, 1871.

4093. EDWARD P.⁹ PIERCE (*Bela⁸, Nehemiah⁷, Nehemiah⁶, Benjamin⁵, Timothy⁴, Thomas³, Thomas², Thomas¹*), b. Oct. 7,

1834; m. June 5, 1873, Nellie F. Kenney, b. Nov. 9, 1844. Res. Malden, Mass.

Edward Payson Pierce

Child :—

4943. i. EDWARD E., b. July 30, 1876.

4103. GEORGE W.[9] PIERCE (*Jesse*[8], *Nehemiah*[7], *Nehemiah*[6], *Benjamin*[5], *Timothy*[4], *Thomas*[3], *Thomas*[2], *Thomas*[1]), b. Jan. 14, 1840; m. June 7, 1866, Isabell Scovel, b. July 29, 1842. Res. Albany, N. Y.

Children :—

4944. i. HELEN V., b. Jan. 10, 1868.
4945. ii. LOUIS M., b. July 10, 1870.

4107. GEORGE B.[9] PIERCE (*Daniel*[8], *Nehemiah*[7], *Nehemiah*[6], *Benjamin*[5], *Timothy*[4], *Thomas*[3], *Thomas*[2], *Thomas*[1]), b. Feb. 27, 1834; m. Apr. 26, 1860, Mary A. Kingsbury, b. Sept. 5, 1836. Res. New Gloucester, Maine. Children :—

4846. i. GEORGE K., b. Jan. 21, 1861.
4947. ii. ALICE M., b. Oct. 15, 1864; d. Feb. 8, 1869.
4948. iii. JOHN C., b. Feb. 8, 1867.
4949. iv. MARY L., b. Dec. 18, 1869.
4950. v. EDWARD P., b. June 27, 1873.
4951. vi. MERTON W., b. Aug. 29, 1876.

4109. Rev. JOHN E.[9] PIERCE (*Daniel*[8], *Nehemiah*[7], *Nehemiah*[6], *Benjamin*[5], *Timothy*[4], *Thomas*[3], *Thomas*[2], *Thomas*[1]), b. Sept. 22, 1838; m. July 8, 1868, Lizzie A. Grey, b. Aug. 14, 1838. Res. Constantinople, Turkey.

Rev. J. E. Pierce was born in Monmouth, Me., entered Bowdoin College in 1858, and was graduated in 1862. He enlisted in the late war of the rebellion, was Orderly Sergeant of Company B, 39th Regiment Wisconsin Volunteers, in 1864; also private in the First Wisconsin Heavy Artillery, Company K; clerk at Headquarters, Fort Lyon, Va., 1865. He entered Bangor Theological Seminary in 1865, and graduated Aug., 1868. Ordained as a missionary of "A. B. C. F. M.," Aug. 3, 1868, and sailed for Eerzroom, Turkey, Aug. 15, 1868, arriving there Sept. 30th. He visited the United States in Nov., 1877, and returned to Turkey shortly after.

Children :—

4952. i. ARTHUE W., b. May 1, 1870.
4953. ii. BESSIE G., b. Nov. 15, 1872.
4954. iii. GEORGE E., b. June 15, 1875.

41

4112. Daniel O.[9] Pierce (*Daniel*[8], *Nehemiah*[7], *Nehemiah*[6], *Benjamin*[5], *Timothy*[4], *Thomas*[3], *Thomas*[2], *Thomas*[1]), b. Sept. 28, 1845; m. Ida N. Williams.

4127. Richard[9] Pierce (*Jonathan*[8], *Richard W.*[7], *Jonathan*[6], *Oliver*[5], *Stephen*[4], *Stephen*[3], *Thomas*[2], *Thomas*[1]), b. May 17, 1842; m. May 5, 1875, Mary E. Kinser, b. Apr. 9, 1844. Res. Townsend, Mass.

4128. Rev. Granville[9] Pierce (*Jonathan*[8], *Richard W.*[7], *Jonathan*[6], *Oliver*[5], *Stephen*[4], *Stephen*[3], *Thomas*[2], *Thomas*[1]), b. Dec. 17, 1847; m. Feb. 28, 1873, Jennie C. Emerson, b. Apr. 23, 1850, d. Oct. 19, 1873; m. 2nd, Sept. 12, 1876, Georgia H. Damon, b. Oct. 2, 1846. Res. Medfield, Mass.

Rev. Granville Pierce was born in Townsend, Mass., Dec. 17, 1847. After he was 21 years of age he pursued academic studies at Easthampton and Wilbraham, Mass., and during the winter months he taught school for pecuniary help. In Sept., 1871, he entered the Meadville Theological School and studied theology for nearly two years. He was ordained in Berlin, Mass., Nov. 19, 1873, the Rev. H. P. Cutting of Sterling preaching the sermon. He remained in Berlin until Oct., 1876, when he received a call from the First Unitarian church in Westboro for one year. In Oct., 1877, he was installed pastor of the church in Medfield. The societies at Berlin and Westboro were very anxious that Mr. Pierce should remain as their pastor, and on his departure they both passed resolutions highly complimentary to him as a spiritual adviser. He is now (1879) the pastor of the First Congregational Unitarian Society in Medfield, Mass.

4155. Charles L.[9] Pierce (*William S.*[8], *Jesse*[7], *Stephen*[6], *Oliver*[5], *Stephen*[4], *Stephen*[3], *Thomas*[2], *Thomas*[1]), b. Oct. 13, 1854; m. June 4, 1876, Lowella Murphy, b. Mar. 11, 1852. Res. Newfield, Me.

4158. Rev. Edwin W.[9] Pierce (*Edwin*[8], *Jesse*[7], *Stephen*[6], *Oliver*[5], *Stephen*[4], *Stephen*[3], *Thomas*[2], *Thomas*[1]), b. Dec. 16, 1849; m. Jan. 13, 1876, Mary J. Southworth, b. June 6, 1854. Res. Glover, Vt.

Rev Edwin W. Pierce

Children :—
4955. i. Fred. S., b. Mar. 7, 1877.
4956. ii. Edwin H., b. July 17, 1879.

4159. Henry D.[9] Pierce (*Winslow S.*[8], *Moses*[7], *Stephen*[6], *Oliver*[5], *Stephen*[4], *Stephen*[3], *Thomas*[2], *Thomas*[1]), b. Apr. 9, 1849; m. June 30, 1875, Elizabeth S. Vinton, b. Feb. 4, 1855. Res. Indianapolis, Ind.

The following is from "Citizens of Indianapolis."

Henry Douglas Pierce, or Harry Pierce as he is more generally known by his numerous friends, was born on the 9th of April, 1849, while his parents were en route to California. He was named in honor of the late Stephen A. Douglas, who was a personal as well as political friend of Henry's father, Doctor Winslow S. Pierce. In their younger days Doctor Pierce and Mr. Douglas agreed that whoever should first have a son he should name him for the other; hence the Douglas occupying a middle position in Harry's name. With his father he came to Indianapolis in 1854; he received regularly the rudiments of his education in the public schools preparatory to college. He was with the Rev. L. G. Hay and Luther H. Crull at their academy. He finished his education at Princeton College, New Jersey, attended two courses of medical lectures at the Ohio Medical College during Doctor Parvin's connection with it; the other at Berkshire Medical College when at the age of eighteen he passed the examination, standing fourth in a class of thirty, and received a certificate entitling him to a diploma of M. D. on becoming of age. At the age of twenty-one he received his diploma, but never intended to practice medicine, but wished a knowledge of it as a part of his education. He then studied law in the office of his uncle, Governor Thomas A. Hendricks, in this city (Indianapolis, Ind).

After he had finished the study of his profession, including a course at the Indianapolis Law School, he practiced one year alone. Since that time he has been connected as partner with ex-United States Senator David Turpie in the practice of law.

Child :—

4957. i.   THERESA VINTON, b. Mar. 4, 1877.

4181. FRANCIS M.^{9} PIERCE (*Alfred*^{8}, *John*^{7}, *John*^{6}, *William*^{5}, *Stephen*^{4}, *Stephen*^{3}, *Thomas*^{2}, *Thomas*^{1}), b. Jan. 7, 1834; m. Feb. 7, 1860, Helen Bishop, b. Apr. 16, 1834, d. Apr. 18, 1879. Res. Hartland, Vt.

Children :—

4958. i.   NINA E., b. Nov. 25, 1861.
4959. ii. INEZ L., b. Aug. 14, 1862.

4184. FRED. M.^{9} PIERCE (*John L.*^{8}, *John*^{7}, *John*^{6}, *William*^{5}, *Stephen*^{4}, *Stephen*^{3}, *Thomas*^{2}, *Thomas*^{1}), b. Oct. 18, 1851; m. Dec. 2, 1869, Ella N. Albee, b. Jan. 16, 1850. Res. Chester, Vt.
Child :—

4960. i.   JOHN F., b. July 10, 1871.

4187. EDWARD E.^{9} PIERCE (*Ezekiel P.*^{8}, *Ezekiel P.*^{7}, *John*^{6}, *William*^{5}, *Stephen*^{4}, *Stephen*^{3}, *Thomas*^{2}, *Thomas*^{1}), b. May 17, 1848; m. June 16, 1875, Fanny S. Chandler, b. Aug. 17, 1852. Res. Malden, Mass.

4194. FRANK A.⁹ PIERCE (*Alson*⁸, *Ebenezer*⁷, *John*⁶, *William*⁵, *Stephen*⁴, *Stephen*³, *Thomas*², *Thomas*¹), b. Apr. 24, 1854 ; m. Oct. 25, 1869, Persis M. Prentice, b. Nov. 19, 1849. Children :—

4961. i.   FRANK E., b. Jan. 8, 1871.
4962. ii. ANNA L., b. Oct. 26, 1874.
4963. iii. GUY L., b. June 14, 1878.

4201. CHARLES H.⁹ PIERCE (*Jonathan*⁸, *Jonathan*⁷, *Jonathan*⁶, *Stephen*⁵, *Jacob*⁴, *Stephen*³, *Thomas*², *Thomas*¹), b. Sept. 17, 1812 ; m. May 1, 1849, Lovey J. Brown, b. Feb. 3, 1817. He d. Aug. 7, 1875. Res. Hyde Park, Mass. Children :—

4964. i.   CHARLES H., b. Feb. 6, 1851; d. Sept. 13, 1851.
4965. ii. CHARLES H., b. Oct. 25, 1852; d. June 28, 1859.
4966. iii. NATHAN B., b. July 21, 1856; d. July 21, 1867.

4204. GEORGE⁹ PIERCE (*Jonathan*⁸, *Jonathan*⁷, *Jonathan*⁶, *Stephen*⁵, *Jacob*⁴, *Stephen*³, *Thomas*², *Thomas*¹), b. Feb. 13, 1819 ; m. Oct. 19, 1841, Ann Hartwell, b. Apr. 2, 1815. Res. Hyde Park, Mass. Children :—

4967. i.   ELLEN H., b. Apr. 2, 1847; m. C. H. Meiggs.
4968. ii. GEORGIA H., b. Sept. 10, 1852.

4206. JOHN⁹ PIERCE (*Jonathan*⁸, *Jonathan*⁷, *Jonathan*⁶, *Stephen*⁵, *Jacob*⁴, *Stephen*³, *Thomas*², *Thomas*¹), b. Oct. 29, 1823 ; m. Nov. 27, 1851, Elizabeth J. Flagg, b. Nov. 10, 1832. Res. Hyde Park, Mass. Children :—

4969. i.   FRANK H., b. June 15, 1853.
4970. ii.   ELMER L., b. Apr. 13, 1856; d. Nov. 7, 1857.
4971. iii. EMMA C., b. Oct. 25, 1858.
4972. iv.   JOHN E., b. June 10, 1860.
4973. v.   MYRON, b. Sept. 15, 1861.
4974. vi.   OTHO,   } twins, b. Apr. 3, 1864; { d. July 30, 1864.
4975. vii. OSWELL,
4976. viii. MARY E., b. Nov. 25, 1866.

4210. RODNEY M.⁹ PIERCE (*John*⁸, *Benjamin*⁷, *Jonathan*⁶, *Stephen*⁵, *Jacob*⁴, *Stephen*³, *Thomas*², *Thomas*¹), b. July 22, 1825 ; m. Nov. 12, 1850, Malinda Butterfield, b. Dec. 18, 1825. Res. Andover, Vt. Child :—

4977. i.   SADIE, b. Aug. 24, 1862.

4216. Rev. DAVID J.⁹ PIERCE (*David*⁸, *Benjamin*⁷, *Jonathan*⁶, *Stephen*⁵, *Jacob*⁴, *Stephen*³, *Thomas*², *Thomas*¹), b. July 18, 1841 ; m. July 7, 1870, Marietta A. Hall, b. Apr. 27, 1842. Res. Laramie City, Wyoming.

Rev. David Jonathan Pierce, oldest son of David, was born in Montpelier, Blackford County, Indiana, July 18, 1841, whither his parents had removed from Chester, Vt., two years before. At his father's death four years later the family returned to Vermont, where David was bound out to a cousin, Wm. H. Thomson, with whom he remained until 21 years of age, and left broken in health, to gain an education, against the protest of his physician. After five years' study in New Hampton Literary Theological Institute, Fairfax, Vt., he taught two years as Principal of Derby Academy, Vt., completed his studies in Newton Theological Institute, where he graduated in 1870, was married to Miss Marietta A. Hall at New London Literary Institute, N. H., July 7, 1870, the day after her graduation at the Institute, and the young couple started at once for Laramie, Wyoming, whither he was appointed as Pastor of the Baptist Church, then just formed by the American Baptist Home Mission Society. Being the second Protestant pastor in the place he labored at formation work for four years, building churches at Laramie, Evanston and Greeley, Col., acting as Principal of the Wyoming Institute at Laramie, and preaching for fifty miles along the U. P. R. R. After four years' pioneer labor he accepted a call to the Baptist Church, Portland, Oregon, where he labored for three years, baptizing over eighty members, twenty of whom were Chinese converted through a mission school. He left the church with 215 members, and returned to the mountains, broken down with bronchitis. The high, dry air of Wyoming has brought back his health, and he is now acting as pastor at Laramie and Cheyenne, Wyoming. Children :—

4978. i. Elizabeth A., b. Aug. 23, 1871; d. May 27, 1874.
4979. ii. Albert E., b. Mar. 23, 1875.
4980. iii. Winnifred l., b. Apr. 4, 1877.

4217. Stephen B.[9] Pierce (David[8], Benjamin[7], Jonathan[6], Stephen[5], Jacob[4], Stephen[3], Thomas[2], Thomas[1]), b. Mar. 5, 1843 ; m. Sept. 4, 1877, Annie B. Holt, b. May 23, 1856. Res. San Francisco, Cal.

4218. John K.[9] Pierce (David[8], Benjamin[7], Jonathan[6], Stephen[5], Jacob[4], Stephen[3], Thomas[2], Thomas[1]), b. Apr. 8, 1845 ; m. Feb. 26, 1867, Helen M. French, b. Nov. 29, 1847. Res. San Francisco, Cal. Children :—

4981. i. Archie B., b. Dec. 14, 1867.
4982. ii. William E., b. Sept. 19, 1872; d. Oct. 7, 1872.
4983. iii. Eugene I., b. Nov. 11, 1875.

4219. Charles A.[9] Pierce (Josiah T.[8], Josiah[7], Josiah[6], Samuel[5], Samuel[4], Samuel[3], Thomas[2], Thomas[1]), b. May 7, 1851 ; m. Nov. 20, 1879, Annie E. Dean, b. Oct. 29, 1855. Res. Dundee, Ill.

C. A. Pierce

4243. Prof. Dwight E.[9] Pierce (Josiah[8], Elihu[7], Josiah[6], Josiah[5], Samuel[4], Samuel[3], Thomas[2], Thomas[1]), b. May 13, 1854 ; m. June 26, 1877, Fannie E. Lloyd, b. Apr. 20, 1855. Res. Bethlehem, Pa.

Dwight Edward, the second son of Josiah Pierce, was born in Ansonia, Conn., May 13th, 1854. His early education in the three " R's " was tacked on or beaten in in accordance with the feruling custom then extant in the district schools. In the spring of 1866 his parents moved to the city of New Haven, where there were at his disposal many excellent educational advantages. At the age of eighteen he entered the scientific department of Yale College, where, notwithstanding the many petty interruptions belonging to a limited purse, he graduated with much honor in the summer of 1875. Immediately upon graduation he received an appointment as instructor in Mathematics in the Hopkins Grammar School or Preparatory Department for Yale, from which he had graduated but three years previous. Here he remained until called to fill the chair of Mechanical Engineering in the Lehigh University of Pennsylvania in the spring of 1877. On the 26th of June of the same year he married the only daughter of William R. Lloyd, who, after the manner of woman kind, presented him with a blushing daughter upon the 13th of February, 1879.

Child :—

4984. i. MARY L., b. Feb. 13, 1879.

4244. WILLIAM J.[9] PIERCE (*Josiah*[8], *Elihu*[7], *Josiah*[6], *Josiah*[5], *Samuel*[4], *Samuel*[3], *Thomas*[2], *Thomas*[1]), b. Mar. 1, 1856; m. Jan. 11, 1877, Edna Schofield. Res. New Haven, Conn. Child :—

4985. i. HARRY F., b. Oct. 25, 1878.

4252. Hon. WILLIAM P.[9] PIERCE (*Austin*[8], *Gordon*[7], *Seth*[6], *Seth*[5], *Samuel*[4], *Samuel*[3], *Thomas*[2], *Thomas*[1]), b. Mar. 25, 1830; m. Dec. 18, 1856, Mary F. Rood. Res. Lamont, Ill.

Hon. William P. Pierce was born in the village of Hamlet in the town of Villanova, Chautauqua County, New York, March 25, 1830. He graduated at the University of the City of New York in March, 1852. He practiced medicine in Marshall County, Mississippi, from the fall of 1852 until the spring of 1856, when he returned to Lisbon, Kendall County, Illinois. He was married to Miss Mary H. F. Rood, daughter of Levi H. Rood, Esq., of Sheridan, LaSalle County, Ill. On the breaking out of the war of the rebellion he raised a volunteer company, which was mustered into service as Company D, 36th Regiment Illinois Volunteers, and with which he served for about eighteen months as Captain. In the winter of 1862 and 1863 he applied for an examination for a transfer to the Medical Staff of the Army and received a commission in Feb., 1863, as Surgeon of the 88th Illinois Infantry Volunteers, in which capacity he served until the close of the war.

He was elected to the lower house of the Illinois Legislature from Kendall County, in 1867, and served one term. In 1868 he removed his residence to Minooka, Grundy County, and in 1869 was elected delegate from Grundy and Will Counties to the Illinois Constitutional Convention. He had the honor while in that convention to propose and carry out the provisions in our State Constitution limiting the capacity of Counties, Cities, and all municipal corporations to incur indebtedness, and also the provision forbidding all Municipalities from loaning money or making donations in aid of railroad or other corporations. In the winters of 1870, 1871 and 1872 he held a seat in the Illinois State Senate, representing the Counties of Grundy and Will

Then political duties so far interfered with his professional prospects that after the close of his Senatorial term he removed to the place he now resides in, Lamont, Ill., and renewed his practice and took himself out of the political field. In October of 1876 he stumped his old district for Hayes and was highly gratified with the result.

4254. LUCIUS G. C.[9] PIERCE (*Austin*[8], *Gordon*[7], *Seth*[6], *Seth*[5], *Samuel*[4], *Samuel*[3], *Thomas*[2], *Thomas*[1]), b. Feb. 5, 1836 ; m. Sept. 27, 1860, Esther Snow. Res. Grinnell, Iowa. Children :—

4986. i. PERLEY A., b. July 7, 1861.
4987. ii. BYRON B., b. Nov. 24, 1862.
4988. iii. EDNA L., b. July 18, 1864.
4989. iv. MARY G., b. Sept. 12, 1866.
4990. v. LUCIUS E., b. July 25, 1868.
4991. vi. GORDON D., b. June 14, 1870.
4992. vii. HELEN T., b. June 14, 1874.
4993. viii. WILLIAM S., b. Sept. 1, 1876.

4257. HENRY A.[9] PIERCE (*Austin*[8], *Gordon*[7], *Seth*[6], *Seth*[5], *Samuel*[4], *Samuel*[3], *Thomas*[2], *Thomas*[1]), b. Oct. 11, 1843 ; m. June 22, 1865, Sarah E. Sessions, b. Dec. 22, 1845. Res. Fredonia, N. Y.

Child :—

4994. i. JULIA L., b. July 28, 1876.

4259. HENRY E.[9] PIERCE (*Francis S.*[8], *Gordon*[7], *Seth*[6], *Seth*[5], *Samuel*[4], *Samuel*[3], *Thomas*[2], *Thomas*[1]), b. Oct. 10, 1833 ; m. Feb. 14, 1855, Scineathy Sinelsor. Res. Frankton, Ind. Children :—

4995. i. EMMA, b. May 18, 1857.
4996. ii. ROSSIE, b. July 24, 1859.
4997. iii. FRANK T., b. Aug. 21, 1861.
4998. iv. INDIE, b. Apr. 21, 1865.
4999. v. AMANDA, b. Jan. 9, 1871.
5000. vi. EVA, b. June 21, 1877.

4260. FRANCIS W.[9] PIERCE (*Francis S.*[8], *Gordon*[7], *Seth*[6], *Seth*[5], *Samuel*[4], *Samuel*[3], *Thomas*[2], *Thomas*[1]), b. July 25, 1835 ; m. Aug. 22, 1861, Susan Moore. Res. Arcola, Ill.

4261. EDMUND G.[9] PIERCE (*Francis S.*[8], *Gordon*[7], *Seth*[6], *Seth*[5], *Samuel*[4], *Samuel*[3], *Thomas*[2], *Thomas*[1]), b. Apr. 30, 1837 ; m. Oct. 17, 1858, Lydia P. Duell ; m. 2nd, May 15, 1864, Catherine Groandyke. Res. Anderson, Ind. Children :—

5001. i. WILLIAM F., b. July 10, 1865.
5002. ii. ELIAS A., b. Feb. 14, 1867.
5003. iii. MIRATHA, b. Nov. 6, 1868.
5004. iv. LYMAN, b. Mar. 8, 1871.
5005. v. MARGARET, b. Apr. 11, 1873.

4262. ALBERT O.[9] PIERCE (*Francis S.*[8], *Gordon*[7], *Seth*[6], *Seth*[5], *Samuel*[4], *Samuel*[3], *Thomas*[2], *Thomas*[1]), b. June 2, 1839 ; m. Dec. 10, 1863, Elizabeth Pike. Res. Anderson, Ind. Children :—

5006. i. STEPHEN F., } twins, b. Jan. 27, 1865.
5007. ii. JOHN H.,
5008. iii. EDWARD W., b. Mar. 21, 1867.
5009. iv. ROBERT P., b. May 27, 1868 ; d. Mar. 3, 1871.
5010. v. MARKIE, b. Aug. 31, 1877 ; d. Aug. 31, 1877.

4270. WILLIAM H. H.[9] PIERCE (*Royal S.*[8], *Gordon*[7], *Seth*[6], *Seth*[5],

Samuel[4], *Samuel*[3], *Thomas*[2], *Thomas*[1]), b. Apr. 4, 1841 ; m. Jan. 22, 1876, Elizabeth H. Harwell, b. Sept. 4, 1855. Res. Cedarville, Mo.

He was b. in Mina, N. Y. Soon after the first battle of Bull Run he volunteered in the 42d Ill's V. I. and accompanied Gen. Frémont's expedition to Springfield, Mo. Returning with the command to St. Louis in the winter, they descended the river and participated in the siege and capture of Island No. 10. After the siege of Corinth, they were organized in Gen. Rosecranz's Army of the Cumberland, and he was present during the campaign and battle of Murfreesboro, where he was captured by the enemy and subsequently taken to Richmond, Va., where he occupied quarters in Libby prison eighteen days—was paroled and delivered Feb. 3d, 1863 ; was exchanged during the following spring, returned to the command and participated in the battle of Chickamauga, where he received a ghastly flesh wound ; was then sent North. After his recovery he again joined the command and was present during the battle of Resaca, and Gen. Sherman's Atlanta campaign ; and in an unimportant engagement that occurred near Kenesaw Mountain, Ga., on June 18, 1864, he was again struck in the face by a ball which passed through his neck. After this last wound he obtained a discharge, and is now (1878) Preceptor of a school in Cedarville, Dade Co., Mo.

W. H. H. Peirce

Children :—

5011.	i.	ROYAL A., b. Mar. 14, 1879.
5012.	ii.	PAUL, b. Oct. 19, 1880.

4274. WALDO[9] PIERCE (*Chester*[8], *Samuel*[7], *Seth*[6], *Seth*[5], *Samuel*[4], *Samuel*[3], *Thomas*[2], *Thomas*[1]), b. Nov. 17, 1844; m. Annie Belcher. Res. Spencer, Mass.

4275. RUFUS J.[9] PIERCE (*Granger*[8], *Samuel*[7], *Seth*[6], *Seth*[5], *Samuel*[4], *Samuel*[3], *Thomas*[2], *Thomas*[1]), b. Jan. 12, 1839 ; m. Sarah Nye. Res. Worcester. Child :—

5013.	i.	SCOTT.

4277. JAMES S.[9] PIERCE (*S. Austin*[8], *Samuel*[7], *Seth*[6], *Seth*[5], *Samuel*[4], *Samuel*[3], *Thomas*[2], *Thomas*[1]), b. June 8, 1831 ; m. May 1, 1856, Mary Ellis, b. May 29, 1832. Res. Ware, Mass.
No children.

4279. LEVERETT[9] PIERCE (*S. Austin*[8], *Samuel*[7], *Seth*[6], *Seth*[5], *Samuel*[4], *Samuel*[3], *Thomas*[2], *Thomas*[1]), b. Jan. 28, 1835; m. Mar. 31, 1858, Mary L. Benway. Res. Natick, Mass. Children :—

5014.	i.	GEORGE F., b. June 17, 1859 ; d. Aug. 28, 1874.
5015.	ii.	NELSON H., b. Apr. 20, 1862.
5016.	iii.	ABBIE L., b. Mar. 8, 1866.
5017.	iv.	LILLIE J., b. June 7, 1868 ; d. Nov. 4, 1869.
5018.	v.	LILLIE A., b. Mar. 19, 1871.

5019. vi. LEVERETT, b. Feb. 18, 1873.
5020. vii. WALDO, b. May 24, 1875; d. Mar. 11, 1876.

4280. WALDO⁹ PIERCE (*S. Austin*⁸, *Samuel*⁷, *Seth*⁶, *Seth*⁵, *Samuel*⁴, *Samuel*³, *Thomas*², *Thomas*¹), b. Feb. 28, 1838; m. Sept. 15, 1860, Abigail Bassett. Res. Kensington, Conn. Children :—
5021. i. MINNIE, b. Mar. 18, 1862.
5022. ii. ERWIN L., b. May 22, 1866.
5023. iii. INEZ M., b. June 20, 1869.
5024. iv. EVA L., b. Aug. 15, 1872.

4285. JOHN W.⁹ PIERCE (*William*⁸, *Samuel*⁷, *Seth*⁶, *Seth*⁵, *Samuel*⁴, *Samuel*³, *Thomas*², *Thomas*¹), b. Oct. 28, 1851; m. Mary Sumner. Res. Ware, Mass. Child :—
5025. i. HARRY.

4293. GEORGE R.⁹ PIERCE (*Justin M.*⁸, *Elijah*⁷, *Seth*⁶, *Seth*⁵, *Samuel*⁴, *Samuel*³, *Thomas*², *Thomas*¹), b. Jan. 16, 1836; m. Oct. 29, 1868, Elizabeth Cummings, b. Aug. 12, 1848. Res. Oneida, N. Y. No children.

4297. WILLIAM E.⁹ PIERCE (*Justin M.*⁸, *Elijah*⁷, *Seth*⁶, *Seth*⁵, *Samuel*⁴, *Samuel*³, *Thomas*², *Thomas*¹), b. Feb. 22, 1853; m. Harriet Shorley. Res. Moravia, N. Y.

4301. MOULTON N.⁹ PIERCE (*Horace*⁸, *Elijah*⁷, *Seth*⁶, *Seth*⁵, *Samuel*⁴, *Samuel*³, *Thomas*², *Thomas*¹), b. July 21, 1837; m. Dec. 8, 1858, Mary Swain. Res. Middleport, N. Y. Child :—
5026. i. ALFRED H., b. Nov. 18, 1859.

4313. GRENVILLE M.⁹ PIERCE (*Constantius*⁸, *Joseph H.*⁷, *Joseph*⁶, *Isaac*⁵, *Isaac*⁴, *Samuel*³, *Thomas*², *Thomas*¹), b. Dec. 5, 1827; m. Mary C. Baker. Children :—
5027. i. GRENVILLE M., b. May, 1858; d. Dec. 2, 1862.
5028. ii. MARY S., b. ——; d. Oct. 19, 1865.
5029. iii. LEONTINE D., b. Dec. 19, 1861.
5030. iv. FRANCIS T., b. May 21, 1864.
5031. v. LULIE J., b. July 26, 1865.
5032. vi. HENRY A., b. Feb. 6, 1867.

4330. DAVID T.⁹ PIERCE (*Hugh L.*⁸, *William*⁷, *William*⁶, *William*⁵, *Sommers*⁴, *William*³, *Thomas*², *Thomas*¹), b. Feb. 10, 1850; m. June 23, 1875, Etta Burt. Res. Argyle, N. Y. Child :—
5033. i. MARY A., b. Dec. 15, 1877; d. Apr. 15, 1879.

4331. JOHN B.⁹ PIERCE (*Abiel H.*⁸, *Abiel*⁷, *Benjamin*⁶, *William*⁵, *Sommers*⁴, *William*³, *Thomas*², *Thomas*¹), b. Apr. 2, 1856; m. Oct. 3, 1877, Priscilla Kyburg. Res. Dodge's Corner, Wis.

4332. FRANK A.⁹ PIERCE (*Abiel H.*⁸, *Abiel*⁷, *Benjamin*⁶, *William*⁵, *Sommers*⁴, *William*³, *Thomas*², *Thomas*¹), b. Sept. 30, 1858; m. Sept. 28, 1874, Laura L. Jackson, b. Nov. 11, 1852. Res. Dodge's Corner, Wis. Child :—
5034. i. FRED. A., b. Nov. 27, 1876.

42

4346.   Rev. LEROY M.[9] PIERCE (*Alvah W.*[8], *Alvah*[7], *Benjamin*[6], *William*[5], *Sommers*[4], *William*[3], *Thomas*[2], *Thomas*[1]), b. Jan. 10, 1842; m. May 24, 1876, Catherine Billings, d. Dec. 6, 1837.   Res. Bernardston, Mass.

Rev. Leroy Matthew Pierce fitted for college at Springfield, Vt., where he united with the Congregational Church.   He entered Middlebury College in 1861.   In 1864 he served five months in the Christian Commission with the Union Army in front of Petersburg and Richmond, and in the hospitals in Washington and at City Point.   He graduated at Middlebury in 1866, and the same year entered Andover Theological Seminary, where he graduated in 1869.   After graduation he spent nearly two years at Glenwood, Mo., where he preached the gospel as a Home Missionary.   He returned East in 1871.   In October of that year he engaged to preach for the Congregational Church of Provincetown, Mass., for one year.   At the termination of his engagement he received a cordial invitation from both the Church and Society to become their settled pastor, but on account of the nervous prostration caused by typhoid fever, by the advice of physicians he declined their invitation.   After nearly a year of recreation, much improved in health he began to preach for the Orthodox Congregational Society in Bernardston, Mass., beginning Nov. 1, 1873.   He is still pastor of that church.   He married May 24, 1876, Catherine Billings, a daughter of Wm. Billings, Esq., of East Arlington, Vt., and a graduate of the Mount Holyoke Seminary.

Leroy M. Pierce

4391.   JAMES O.[9] PIERCE (*George*[8], *James*[7], *Nathan*[6], *James*[5], *James*[4], *James*[3], *Thomas*[2], *Thomas*[1]), b. Sept. 2, 1848; m. June 30, 1876, Rosabel Mason, b. Nov. 25, 1858.   Res. LeRoy, Mich.

Child :—

5035. i.   ROY, b. June 9, 1877.

4412.   EDWARD C.[9] PIERCE (*Joshua D.*[8], *Joshua*[7], *Joshua*[6], *Joshua*[5], *James*[4], *James*[3], *Thomas*[2], *Thomas*[1]), b. Jan, 30, 1836; m. Dec. 31, 1867, Mary C. Sayward, b. Oct. 31, 1842.   Res. Springfield, Mass.

E. C. Pierce

Children :—

5036.   i.   EDWARD S., b. Feb. 7, 1869.
5037.   ii.   CORA K., b. Oct. 31, 1870.
5038.   iii.   CHARLES C., b. Dec. 18, 1874.

4415. JOSHUA F.[9] PIERCE (*Joshua D.*[8], *Joshua*[7], *Joshua*[6], *Joshua*[5], *James*[4], *James*[3], *Thomas*[2], *Thomas*[1]), b. May 28, 1844; m. June 7, 1871, Emma A. Hutchinson, b. Oct. 30, 1848. Res, Augusta, Me. Children :—

5039. i. HENRY H., b. Dec. 17, 1874.
5040. ii. ANNIE L., b. Aug. 11, 1879.

4442. IRA[9] PIERCE (*Herod*[8], *Samuel*[7], *Daniel*[6], *Joshua*[5], *James*[4], *James*[3], *Thomas*[2], *Thomas*[1]), b. June, 1838 ; m. Oct. 25, 1866, Mary Kelley, b. Sept. 9, 1843. Res. Albany, Vt. Children :—

5041. i. LILLA B., b. Jan. 18, 1868.
5042. ii. FRED., b. Aug. 20, 1875.

4445. EDWIN[9] PIERCE (*Charles F.*[8], *Samuel*[7], *Daniel*[6], *Joshua*[5], *James*[4], *James*[3], *Thomas*[2], *Thomas*[1]), b. Aug. 31, 1850 ; m. July 6, 1875, Abby Woodward, b. July 6, 1854. Res. Barton, Vt.

Children :—

5043. i. BERTHA, b. July 1, 1876.
5044. ii. LILLIE, b. Aug. 14, 1878.

4452. DANIEL I.[9] PIERCE (*Horace*[8], *Daniel*[7], *Daniel*[6], *Joshua*[5], *James*[4], *James*[3], *Thomas*[2], *Thomas*[1]), b. Aug. 17, 1849 ; m. Feb. 18, 1874, Carrie J. Lawrence, b. Mar. 21, 1851. Res. Port Jervis, N. Y.

Children :—

5045. i. CHARLES L., b. Dec. 24, 1874.
5046. ii. DAU.; d. young.
5047. iii. EDITH, b. Sept. 26, 1878 ; d. Aug. 1, 1879.

4462. ELBRIDGE S.[9] PIERCE (*Nathaniel*[8], *Isaac*[7], *Daniel*[6], *Joshua*[5], *James*[4], *James*[3], *Thomas*[2], *Thomas*[1]), b. July 30, 1849 ; m. Nov. 22, 1873, Henrietta Benton, b. Jan. 21, 1849. Res. Manchester, N. H. Child :—

5048. i. JESSIE I., b. Jan. 7, 1877.

4474. EDWARD G.[9] PIERCE (*Ebenezer L.*[8], *Jacob*[7], *Jacob*[6], *Jacob*[5], *James*[4], *James*[3], *Thomas*[2], *Thomas*[1]), b. Aug. 16, 1852 ; m. June 1, 1881, Mary W. Gleason, b. Jan. 25, 1857. Res. Woburn, Mass.

4475. ROSCOE P.[9] PIERCE (*Ebenezer L.*[8], *Jacob*[7], *Jacob*[6], *Jacob*[5], *James*[4], *James*[3], *Thomas*[2], *Thomas*[1]), b. May 4, 1856; m. Jan. 13, 1881, Mabel N. Boutwell, b. Dec. 11, 1861. Res. Woburn, Mass.

4481. JAMES H.[9] PIERCE (*James*[8], *Ephraim*[7], *Ephraim*[6], *Jacob*[5], *James*[4], *James*[3], *Thomas*[2], *Thomas*[1]), b. Sept. 30, 1841; m. Apr. 18, 1865, Alice J. Weston, b. Aug. 4, 1843. Res. Stoneham.
Children :—
5049. i. HERBERT L., b. July 20, 1866.
5050. ii. FORRST C., b. July 7, 1869.
5051. iii. EUSTACE A., b. Apr. 25, 1873.
5052. iv. ARCHIE L., b. Oct. 24, 1877.

4535. GEORGE A.[9] PIERCE (*Joseph G.*[8], *Levi*[7], *Joseph*[6], *Thomas*[5], *Thomas*[4], *Benjamin*[3], *Thomas*[2], *Thomas*[1]), b. Jan. 20, 1843; m. Jessie Carney. Res. Claremont, N. H.

4536. FRANKLIN J.[9] PIERCE (*Joseph G.*[8], *Levi*[7], *Joseph*[6], *Thomas*[5], *Thomas*[4], *Benjamin*[3], *Thomas*[2], *Thomas*[1]), b. Aug. 5, 1847; m. M. E. Wheeler, b. May 30, 1854. Res. Newport, N. H.
Child :—
5053. i. ——.

4561. FREDERICK M.[9] PIERCE (*Harding*[8], *Haven*[7], *Moses H.*[6], *Thomas*[5], *Thomas*[4], *Benjamin*[3], *Thomas*[2], *Thomas*[1]), b. Oct. 21, 1850; m. Mar. 4, 1879, Sarah E. Whitney.

4586. FRANK E.[10] PIERCE (*Jotham S.*[9], *Moses C.*[8], *Calvin*[7], *David*[6], *Daniel*[5], *Daniel*[4], *John*[3], *Thomas*[2], *Thomas*[1]), b. Apr. 15, 1852; m. Dec. 1, 1871, Maria Western. Res. Brewer, Me.
Children :—
5054. i. ——, } twins, b. Oct. 14, 1878.
5055. ii. ——, }

4600. HIRAM[10] PIERCE (*James*[9], *Nathaniel B.*[8], *Calvin*[7], *David*[6], *Daniel*[5], *Daniel*[4], *John*[3], *Thomas*[2], *Thomas*[1]), b. Jan. 27, 1844; m. Lucinda Durgin. Res. The Forks Plantation, Me.

4699. EDWARD T.[10] PIERCE (*Theodore W.*[9], *Augustus*[8], *Thomas S.*[7], *Joshua*[6], *Joshua*[5], *Ebenezer*[4], *John*[3], *Thomas*[2], *Thomas*[1]), b. Nov. 6, 1848; m. Oct. 12, 1870, Louisa M. Peebles, b. May 12, 1849, d. Oct. 4, 1875; m. 2nd, Oct. 17, 1876, Emma J. Stevens, b. Nov. 27, 1853. Res. Nashua, N. H. Children :—
5056. i. WILLIE T., b. Sept. 12, 1871; d. July 17, 1872.
5057. ii. LOUISA M., b. Sept. 27, 1875.
5058. iii. EVA A., b. June 27, 1878; d. May 18, 1879.

4742. DANIEL W.[10] PIERCE (*Daniel W.*[9], *Warren*[8], *Daniel*[7], *Daniel*[6], *John*[5], *John*[4], *John*[3], *Thomas*[2], *Thomas*[1]), b. Aug. 31, 1835; m. Mar. 15, 1856, Belinda B. Laythe, b. Sept. 19, 1830. Res. Goldendale, Wash. Ter.

Children:—

5059. i. ELLA D., b. Dec. 17, 1856.
5060. ii. LONA B., b. Oct. 10, 1858; d. Oct. 30, 1858.
5061. iii. DANIEL W., b. May 11, 1861.
5062. iv. LIZZIE B., b. June 21, 1865.
5063. v. GEORGE E., b. Dec. 14, 1867.
5064. vi. ELI E., b. Feb. 12, 1870.
5065. vii. RUTH M., b. July 24, 1872.

4792. WILLIAM W.[10] PIERCE (*James*[9], *Alvares*[8], *Samuel*[7], *Thomas*[6], *Amos*[5], *Thomas*[4], *Thomas*[3], *Thomas*[2], *Thomas*[1]), b. Oct. 15, 1848; m. July 9, 1868, Annie E. Jones, divorced Nov. 7, 1878; m. 2nd, Aug. 12, 1879, Huldah H. Mullifor, b. Sept. 20, 1859. Res. Moline, Mich. Children :—

5066. i. CHARLES S., b. Sept. 25, 1870.
5067. ii. EDITH L., b. Feb. 13, 1874.

4833. EDGAR W.[10] PIERCE (*Lewis W.*[9], *Earl*[8], *Palmer*[7], *Timothy*[6], *Timothy*[5], *Timothy*[4], *Thomas*[3], *Thomas*[2], *Thomas*[1]), b. Mar. 6, 1836; m. Oct. 14, 1868, Frances A. Thorpe, b. June 17, 1837, d. Feb. 19, 1873. Res. Plattsburg, N. Y.
No children.

4838. HENRY I.[10] PIERCE (*Benjamin C.*[9], *Earl*[8], *Palmer*[7], *Timothy*[6], *Timothy*[5], *Tomothy*[4], *Thomas*[3], *Thomas*[2], *Thomas*[1]), b. May 9, 1833; m. Dec. 30, 1857, Celia G. Clough, b. July 10, 1835. Res. Milwaukee, Wis.

Children ;—

5068. i. HARRY S., b. May 21, 1860.
5069. ii. KATIE, b. Mar. 2, 1862.
5070. iii. ANNA B., b. Jan. 10, 1867.
5071. iv. JAMES C., b. May 11, 1869.
5072. v. WILLIAM H., b. Aug. 18, 1871.
5073. vi. DAISY M., b. Aug. 1, 1873.
5074. vii. CAROLINE S., b. May 23, 1875.

4840. EARL[10] PIERCE (*Benjamin C.*[9], *Earl*[8], *Palmer*[7], *Timothy*[6], *Timothy*[5], *Timothy*[4], *Thomas*[3], *Thomas*[2], *Thomas*[1]), b. Apr. 23, 1841; m. Mary Adlam. Res. Milwaukee, Wis.

4841. FRANK C.[10] PIERCE (*Benjamin C.*[9], *Earl*[8], *Palmer*[7], *Timothy*[6], *Timothy*[5], *Timothy*[4], *Thomas*[3], *Thomas*[2], *Thomas*[1]), b. Oct. 26, 1851; m. Feb. 18, 1873, Milla Kinealy, b. May 3, 1855. Res. Au Sable Forks, N. Y. Children :—

5075. i. JESSE C., b. Dec. 30, 1873.
5076. ii. HARRY A., b. June 26, 1879.

4858. JOHN S.[10] PIERCE (*Arnold Y.*[9], *Palmer*[8], *Palmer*[7], *Timothy*[6], *Timothy*[5], *Timothy*[4], *Thomas*[3], *Thomas*[2], *Thomas*[1]), b. Sept. 7, 1844; m. Jan. 16, 1878. Res. North East, Pa.

4860. EPHRAIM A.[10] PIERCE (*Arnold Y.*[9], *Palmer*[8], *Palmer*[7], *Timothy*[6], *Timothy*[5], *Timothy*[4], *Thomas*[3], *Thomas*[2], *Thomas*[1]), b. Aug. 15, 1850; m. Feb. 11, 1874, Maggie Williamson. Res. North East, Pa.

4861. ROISE S.[10] PIERCE (*Earl*[9], *Palmer*[8], *Palmer*[7], *Timothy*[6], *Timothy*[5], *Timothy*[4], *Thomas*[3], *Thomas*[2], *Thomas*[1]), b. May 2, 1846; m. Nov. 24, 1869, Josephine Brown. Res. Bradford, Pa.

Children :—

5077. i. BERTRAND, b. Jan. 25, 1873.
5078. ii. JULIA L., b. July 31, 1875.

4881. GEORGE A.[10] PIERCE (*George B.*[9], *Albigence*[8], *Willard*[7], *Nathaniel*[6], *Nathaniel*[5], *Timothy*[4], *Thomas*[3], *Thomas*[2], *Thomas,*[1]), b. Feb. 3, 1851; m. Lizzie A. Pitman. Res. Lexington, Mass.

Geo. A. Pierce

Children :—

5079. i. MAUD A., b. 1873.
5080. ii. CORA L., b. 1876.

APPENDIX.

APPENDIX.

WILL OF STEPHEN PEIRCE, OF CHELMSFORD.

In the nam of god amen the seventh Day of jun 1732 I stephen peirce of the town of chelmsford in the county of middelsex with in his maigests provnce of the masasuts Bay in nuengland be in parfit memory and in the rit exersis of my understanding and resen Blesed be god I Bele the mortalite of my body knowing it is apynti for all men once to Dy Do mack this my last will and testment that is to say first of all anprinceply I give and recommend my soul in to the hand of god that gave it and my Body to the earth to a decent christian Bural Be laveing at the genral reserection i shall reseve the sam again by the mity power of god

and as to shuch worly estet it hath plesed god to Bles me with in this life I give de spose of the same in In the folowing maner and form

Item my will is that all my dets shall be paid with all convent speed after my de seese if any be.

Item I give and bequeath to my deare and well Be loved wife Tabitha pierce all my movable estet with in my house and with out house wher any shall be found the sam to de spose of as she shall see met and convenent I all so give to my wife the free use of my house and Barn my will is that my wife shall have on third part of all the corn and half the apls that shall grow on my hom sted durin hur nateral life *Itm* my will is that my son Jacob shall have the whol use and improvmt of my hom sted above menshed and my rit in the neck field and of 2 wood lots Bounded north upon the hi way that gose by willam Fletchers he paing to my wife his mother the above said corn and aples and keepin a hors for his mother to rid to metin.

Itm my will is that after my wif shall dy my son Jacob Peirce shall have the free use and improvement of all the above named housen and land durin his nateral life and after my son Jacob shal dy my will is and I give all the above said house in and land to stephen Peirce my son Jacobs eldest son and to roBard Peirce and to Thomas Peirce my son Beimens son and to stephen Flecher my dafter Tabithas eldest son thay al being my gran sons thay may sel ther share on to another or to any of my children and to no other

43

Itm my will is and I give to my son stephen all my rit of land and
medo that is in his hom stedes that lieth a Both sides the hi way as
wel that: that he hath no deed of as that he hath   *Item* my wife
may sell my right in river medow and in concerd river neck Shee
decentle Buring me: *Item* I have to my son Benimen and to Sary
my dafter and to Tabitha my dafter given to ech of them there
poashon in full all redy my wil is that non of the airs of any of them
nor of any other parson from by or under them shall recouer any part
of my estet under any pretence whatsoever only my four gran sons
menshoned on the other sid.

Itm the reson why i have not settled non of my land on Jacob my
eldest son is bcause he went from me when he was young and lerned
a treade and so not profitabl to my estet   I also constitute mack and
ordain and apynt my wife and my son in law wilam Flecher the sol
excutors of this my last wil and testment and I du uterly dis a prov
of evry other testments or wils by me formerly med ratefiing this and
confarming this to be my last will and testment and no other

In witness heer of I have set to my hand and sel and sined seled
and and declered by me stephen peirce to be my last will and
testment

   In presents of us witnes
   Jonathan Barron
         his
   Joseph ✕ Warren
       mark
   Ephrim Warren

                              Stephen Peirce (Seal)

A Copy, Attest, J. H. Tyler, Register.

WILL OF TABITHA PIERCE, OF CHELMSFORD.

In the Name of God, Amen.

The Eighteenth Day of November Anno Domini One Thousand
Seven hundred & thirty five & in the Ninth Year of the Reign of
King George the second of great Britain &c Defender of the Faith
&c

I Tabitha Peirce relict Widow of Stephen Peirce late of Chelmsford deceas'd, being sich & weak of Body but of sound mind &
memory, knowing the Uncertainty of Life, do make this my last Will
& Testament, revoking & annulling by these Presents all & every
Will or Wills here to fore by me made whether in Word or Writing
& this to be taken only for my last Will & Testament and no other.

And first I commend my Soul to almighty God, hoping to receive
the Forgiveness of my Sins & be saved thro' the merit of Christ; and
my Body I comit to the Earth to be decently buried at the Discretion of my Executors hereafter named ; And as touching my worldly
Estate my Will & meaning is that it shall be disposed, employed &
bestowed in manner & form following that is to say.

Imprimis I give & bequeath to my Grandaughter Sarah Wheeler,
after my Decease, my best Bed & furniture, & warming Pan & Iron

Kettle & Pottage Pot & half a Dozen of Pewter Plates & two Pewter Platters & my Tramels & Box Iron

turn over *Item*

Item I give & bequeath to my Daughter Fletcher my other Bed & Furniture, as also my Brass Kettle & Box of Drawers, comonly called Case or Chest of Drawers.

Item Item I give all the Rest of my movable Estate to my afores'd Daughter Fletcher & Daughter Wheeler to be divided equally between them.

Lastly, I do constitute make & ordain my son Stephen Pierce & my Son in Law William Fletcher Executors of this my last Will & Testament & whereas my Grandson Oliver Pierce is indebted to me in the Sum of fifteen Pounds as appears by a Bond under his Hand, I order my Executor to take that money to defray my Funeral charges, & if that shall not suffice to sell for the same Purpose the Cow I have now in possession & employ the money as aforesd

In witness whereof I have hereto set my Hand & Seal the Day & Year first above written

Tabitha X Pierce (Seal)
her
Mark

Signed, sealed publish'd
pronounc'd & declar'd to
be her last Will & Testamt
In Presence of
Eleazer Tyng
Beniamin parker
Tabitha X Fletcher
her
mark

Middlesex Cambridge December 20th 1744

To Stephen Peirce Execu^r of the last Will and Testament of Tabatha Pierce late of Chelmsford deceased.—I find it necessary to acquaint you that the Law Subjects you to a very Severe penalty for your not Causing the probate of said Will to be made I do now again hereby Cite you to appear at my House in Cambridge on the Second monday of January next to take care that said Will be proved.

Jon^a Remington, J. Pro.

A Copy.

Attest J. H. Tyler, Register.

WILL OF JOHN PIERCE, OF STOW.

In the Name of God Amen the twenty sixth Day of April Annoy: Dom: 1753. I John Peirce of Stow in the County of Middlesex and Province or the Massachusetts Bay in New England Yeoman, being well in Body and of perfect mind and memory thanks be given to God: therefore calling to Mind the Mortality of my Body and knowing that it is appointed for all Men once to die. I do make and ordain this my last will & testament. That is to say, Principally and first of all, I give and recommend my Soul into the Hands of God that gave it, and my Body I recommend to the Earth to be buried in decent christian Burial at the discretion of my Executrix nothing doubting but at the general Resurrection I shall receive the same again by the mighty Power of God, and touching such worldly Estate wherewith it hath pleased God to bless me in this Life, I give demise and dispose thereof in the following manner and Form and to the following Persons hereby excluding all others that might claim any part of it from any Portion in it.

Imprimis. After my just Debts and Funeral charges are paid I give and bequeath to my beloved Wife Susanna the whole of my personal Estate for ever together with the Improvement of all my real Estate in Stow and Charlstown during her Life except that part of my Fathers Estate now in possession of and under the Improvement of my Brother James which came to Me by Heirship.

Item I give and Bequeath to my Brother James Peirce of Charlstown the Improvement of that part of my Fathers Estate in Charlstown which came to me by Heirship, as long as He lives and then my Will is that it go to his Children to be divided equally amongst them all except his Son John who is to have no Share therein.

Item I give and bequeath to my Brothers Son John Peirce of Charlstown the Son of my Brother James after my Wives decease one half part of my Farm in Stow both of Lands and Buildings as also that part of my Fathers Farm in Charlstown which I purchas'd. He paying to my neice Elisabeth Osborn £6. 13. 4 when she shall come of age: But in Case He should die without Heirs of his Body begotten then my will is that the sd Lands &c descend to Thomas Osborn next mentioned.

Item I give and bequeath to Thomas Osborn my Sisters Son after my Wives decease the other half part of my Farm in Stow Lands Buildings &c He paying to my neice Elizabeth Osborn his sister £6. 13. 4. when she shall come of age. But in Case the sd Thomas Osborn should die without Heirs of his Body begotten then my Will is that the sd Lands &c go to John Peirce above mentioned.

Item I give and bequeath to my Neice Elizabeth Osborn thirteen Pounds six shillings & eight pence to be paid to Her when she shall come of Age by my Nephews John Peirce and Thomas Osborn each an equal part as above mentioned.

turn over—

Item My Will and pleasure further is that if both my Nephews John Peirce and Thomas Osborn should die without Heirs of their Bodies begotten that then the Lands & Buildings &c which I have bequeathed unto them shoud go to my Brother James Children to be equally divided amongst them.

And I do herby constitute and appoint my beloved wife Susanna sole Executrix of this my last will and Testament. And I do hereby utterly disallow revoke & disannul all former wills or Bequests heretofore made by me hereby confirming this and no other to be my last will and Testament. In Witness whereof I have hereunto set my Hand and Seal the Day and Year above written.

Signed Sealed published   John Pierce (Seal)
pronounced & declared
in presence of.
Henry Barnes
Jonathan Loring
Samuel Brigham jun'.

A Copy, Attest, J. H. Tyler, Register.

No. 31.

A DEED GIVEN BY JOHN BURBEEN TO JAMES

PEIRCE, MARCH, 1693-4.

To all people before whome this Deed of sale shall come greeting, Now know ye that I, John Berbeene of Woodbourne in the County of Midd^x in their Maj^t province of the Massachusetts Bay in New England Tayler for and in consideration of the sume of four pounds and ten shillings in money to me well and truly pay^d in hand by James Pearce of the same Towne Husbandman, the receit whereof I do by these presents acknowlidge and therewith to be fully sattesfyed contented and pay^d and of every part and parsell thereof do fully freely and absolutely acquitt exonourate and discharge the said James Peirce his heirs exec^{rs} admi^{rs} and assignes for Ever by these presents, have given granted bargained and sold, and do by these presents further giue grant bargain sell Allien Enfeoffe and conferme vnto the said James Peirce, one peice of Woodland containeing six acres by measure little moore or less, and it is sittuate in the limmitts of Woobourne afors^d neer the said James Peirces hous, and it is bounded, North by the land of James Peirce, West by ye Woodland of Ebenezer and Jabez Brooks, South by the land of Matthew Johnson, North Easterly by ye Woodland of me ye I John Berbeene, and of this there is two acres and one halfe acre land and all lay^d out vpon ye account of Swamp Bottom, the premises as it is butted and bounded two acres and halfe land and all, and the other three acres and halfe only Woodland, with all the trees wood and timber standing lying and growing vpon the same with all that ever shall grow vpon it, with all the rights titles proffitts privelidges and advantages there vnto belonging to him the said James Peirce his heirs exec^{rs} admi^{rs} and assignes for ever, To haue and to hold, the aboue granted premises with all the proffitts and priveledges thereof, the two acres and halfe aboue mentioned land and timber wood, stones grass and hearbidge with all other the rights proffittss and privelidges thereof and the three acres and halfe of Woodland ye wood and timber only (the land to remaine the Towns for hearbidge) also the said James Peirce is to ·haue all the privelidges that belongs to ye same, as to take vp Swamp Bottom according to towns grant, and all other the proffitts privelidges and advantages therevnto belonging, to him the said James Peirce his heirs, exec^rs admi^rs and assignes for ever, to his and their own only propper vse bennifitt and behoofe, furthermoore I the said John Berbeen do for my selfe my heirs exec^rs admi^rs and assigne, promis Covenant and grant to and with the said James Peirce him his heirs exec^rs admi^rs and assignes, that I am at ye signing and sealing of this Instrument the true and rightfull owner of the premises, and therefore haue good right full power and lawfull authorety to make sale thereof, and that the said James Peirce his heirs or assignes shall or may att all times and from time to time for ever here after peacabley and quietly haue hold occuppie possess and enjoye the same in as full and ample manner as I myselfe did or might haue done, a good true absolute sure Indefeasable title of Inherrittance in ffee simple, without the lawfull just lett hinderance, molestation contradiction or expultion of me, or any other person or persons from by or vnd^er me warrantizing, the same from all former gifts grants sales leaces Joynters dowryes Mortgages Bonds or fforfittures, or any such like trouble or troubles by me had made or done at any time In wittness whereof I the said John Berbeen haue herevnto sett my hand and affixed my seale, this   day of March Annogs Domini sixteen hundred ninty three-four, and in the sixth yeare of their Maj^ts Reigne,

JOHN ‡ R. BORBEN his mark   [L. S.]

BENJAMIN PEIRCE.
JOHN EVANS.

This Indenture made the twelfth day of October Anno Domini one thousand seven hundred and thirty three between James Peirce of Woburn in the county of Middlesex in New England husbandman of the one part and Thomas Fitch of Boston in the County of Suffolk in New England aforesaid Esq &c^a in Trust for Elizabeth Peirce the wife of the said James Peirce of the other part. Witnesseth That the said James Peirce in consideration of the Love and affection which he hath for and beareth unto the said Elizabeth his present wife doth covenant promise grant & agree to and with the said Thomas Fitch qualified as aforesaid his heirs executors administrators and assigns that she the said Elizabeth Peirce and her heirs shall and will immediately after the Decease of the said James Peirce stand and be seized of and in a certain mansion house with one acre of Land about the same comprehending orcharding and lying partly on the east and partly on the west side of said house and so round the north end of the same butted and bounded as follows viz. Southerly on the Lane or Road leading to the meeting house Westerly on his land Easterly on land of Benjamin Peirce together with all and singular the Buildings on the said Land Profits Privileges and appurtenances thereto belonging and also all such Household goods or moveables as shall remain after his decease. To have and to hold the said House and Land and Personal Estate and all other the Premises before granted (immediately after the decease of the said James Peirce) unto the said Thomas Fitch Esqr qualified as aforesaid for the use of the said Elizabeth Peirce her heirs and assigns forever to her and their only sole and proper use benefit and behoof from henceforth and forever more and the said James Peirce doth covenant for himself and his heirs to and with the said Thomas Fitch qualified as aforesaid his executors administrators and assigns that he the said James Peirce is seized in fee of the said Real and Personal Estate and that he never will do anything whereby to alter change defeat or make void this present Deed which shall take effect and stand in full force to all Intents and Purposes in the Law whatsoever without any Revocation. In Witness Whereof the said Parties to these presents have interchangeably set their hands and seals the day and year first before written.

JAMES PEIRCE, & seal.

Signed sealed and delivered in presence of us,

> Samuel Tyler Junr,
> Malachy Salter Junr.

Suffolk, ss. Boston, October 12th, 1733. Mr. James Peirce acknowledged this Instrument to be his act and deed before me

Anthony Stoddard, Just. Peace.

Middlesex, Cambridge, Oct°. 12th, 1733. Rece'd and Entre^d by

Fra^s. Foxcroft, Reg^r.

A true Copy of Record Book 34 Page 340.

Attest Chas. B. Stevens, Reg.

No. 80.

DEED FROM JOHN PHERHAM, Sr. TO STEPHEN PEIRCE, Jr.

To All Christion People To whome thes presents shall come greeting know that I John Pherham Senr InThe Towne off Chelmsford In The covnty off Middx in Newingland Hosbandman sendeth Greeting Know Ye That I the Afore sd Pherham for and in consideration of A vallvaball som of Mony corrent off NewengLand To me in Hand Trevly And honestly Payd By Stephen Peirce Junr of the Towne And covnty Aforesd The Resaipt wheare of I do by Theas Presents Ackno^wledg And Thare with To be fully sattisfide contented And Payd And thare of and evry part & parcell thare of do Aqvit Exonerat and Clerely Descharg him The Afore sd Peirce him his Heirs Excvtors Administrators And Assignes ffor **euer** have granted bargened & sold Aliened enfeoffed conveyd and confirmed & by These presents doe fvlly and clerly freely And Absolvtly giue grant bargen sell Alyen enfeoffe convay pass over & conficat vnto him ye Afore sd Peirce his Hairs Excvtors Administrators And Assignes for ever one small lot of vpland citvate and lying within that parcell of Land knowne by the name of wamaset neck A Lying betwene m^r wentterops mado and chelmsford bovnds bovnded estrly by m^r wentrops mado westerly by y[e] Aboue sd Peirce et being The fefteth Loot marked with numbar fifty To Haue And To Hold All And singvlar y[e] Aboue graned & bargened primeses as before spesefide with all other the priveleges And Apvrtinancis thare vnto belonging Appartaining or in Any wise belonging vnto him y[e] Afore sd Peirce his Haires Excvtors Administrators And Asignes vnto his and thare & evrey of thare proper vse & benifit And behofe for ever And I The Aboue sd Pherham for my selfe my Haires Excvtors And Administrators And Asignes vnto His And thare & ev[e]ry of thare proper vse and benifit And Do covinant promass & grant to And with him the Afore sd Peirce his hairs And asignes that at Thes Present Time of signeing here of i Am The Trew And Lawf oner of y[e] primisis And thare for haue good right full powovr And Lawftll athority To seall & pase ovr the same & every part & parscell thare of vnto him The Afore sd Peirce Haires Excvtors And Asignes And that he The Afore sd Peirce him selfe His Hairs And asignes shall And May at All Times & from Time to time for evcer here Afgeor by force and vertue here of peacably & qviatly inioy haue & holde occvppy & porsese And inioy All The aboue granted & bargened premeses with all The preveleges and Apvrtinances thare vnto Appertaining or in Any wise belonging without the Lawfull Lott svte Molestatation erecttion expvltion contrediction or deniall of The sd Pherham my Heirs Execvtors or Administrators thame or any of Thame or any other parson or parsons by from or vndar Me or by any other Lawfull wayse what so euer hereby promasing to do Andperforme any further act or Acts thing or things Device or Devices that in the Law may be thovght nedfull for y[e] more perfeting thes Instrement That so y[e] premeses Aboue Granted may Abide And Remaine an Absolute And Indeferabl Inharitance in Fee simple vnto him The Afore sd Peirce his Hairs Excutors Administrators And Asignes for euer more In wetnes whare of I The Afore sd Pherham haue here vnto pvt my hand and seall This Aighte day of May In the yere of over Lord God seuenteen hvndred and seuen and In y[e] sixt yere of The Rayn off Queen Anne.

JOHN PHERHAM SENR.   [L. S.]

Signad sealed & delivered In the
    presence of vs

WILLIAM FLETCHER
JOSIAH FLETCHER
STEPHEN PEIRCE SENR.

Chelmsford May 14th 1707 John Pherham senr persnaly aperd and acknoleged the aboue riten instrument to be his free act and deed before me the subcriber   JONATHAN TYNG Jus[te]

No. 186–7.

DEED OF ROBERT PEIRCE TO OLIVER PEIRCE. 1751.

To ALL PEOPLE to whom these presents shall come, Greeting.
Know Ye, That I Robert Peirce of Chelmsford in the County of
Middlesex in his Majesty's Province of the Massachusetts Bay in New
England, Husbandman, For & in Consideration of the Sum of Seven-
teen Pounds Eleven Shillings Lawful Money of the Province aforesaid
to me in hand before the Ensealing hereof, well & truly paid by
Oliver Pierce of Chelmsford in the County & Province afors^d
Husbandman the Receipt whereof I do hereby acknowledge & myself
therewith fully Satisfyed & contented, and thereof, and of every Part
& Parcel thereof, do exonerate, acquit and discharge him the said
Oliver Peirce His Executors and Administrators forever by these
Presents : HAVE given, granted, bargained, sold, Aliened, conveyed
and confirmed ; and by these presents, do freely, fully and absolutely
give, grant, bargain, sell, aliene, convey and confirm unto him the said
Oliver Peirce his Heirs and Assigns forever the several certain pieces
of Upland Swamp Mowing Ground & Orchard Land following, all
situate in Chelmsford aforesaid, the first a Piece of Upland & Swamp
in Concord River Neck so called containing by Estimation Thirty
Acres, more or less, and is bounded as followeth, Southerly on Land of
Joseph Moors, Easterly on Land of Jerathmel Bowers, Northerly on
Land of Zebadiah Keyes and Westerly on a proprietors high-way.
Secondly a Piece of River Meadow containing by Estimation three
quarters of an acre, more or less, and is bounded as followeth, Northeasterly by Stakes and Meadows of Robert Peirce afores^d and on all
other Points and Parts on the River & on the upland of Joseph Moors.
Thirdly a Small Lott of upland in Concord River Neck aforesaid,
bounded on, and lying West of Joseph Moors Lott which he bought
of Samuel Perham, Southerly on a highway and on all other parts &
points as the s^d Lott hath been, or now is bounded.   Fourthly a Piece
of Orcharding & Mowing Land in the Home Stead of my Father
Stephen Peirce late of Chelmsford afores^d deceased containing by Estimation half an Acre, more or less, & is bounded at the Southeasterly
corner at a stake & heap of stones & from thence runs Northerly as
the Fence now stands about four Rods and an half to a stake and
heap of stones at the Northeasterly corner, from thence runs Westerly
on a straight line by the Land of Esther Peirce Twenty Rods to a
stake & heap of stones at the Northwest Corner, from thence runs
Southerly on a Straight Line by the Land of Stephen Peirce four Rods
and an half to a Stake & heap of Stones, at the Southwesterly Corner,
and from thence runs Easterly on a straight line by the Land of the s^d
Stephen Peirce to the bound first mentioned.   To HAVE AND TO HOLD
the s^d Granted & bargained Premises, with all the Appurtenances,
Priviledges & Commodities to the same belonging, or in any wise appertaining to him the s^d Oliver Peirce his Heirs & Assigns for ever.
To his and their only proper use, benefit & behoof forever.
44

And the s^d Robert Peirce for me my Heirs, Executors and Administrators do Covenant, Promise and Grant to & with him the said Oliver Peirce his Heirs and Assigns, that before the Ensealing hereof I am the true, sole, and Lawful owner of the above bargained Premises, and am Lawfully seized and possessed of the same in my own proper Right, as a good, perfect and absolute Estate of Inheritance in Fee Simple : And have in myself good Right, full Power and Lawful Authority to grant, bargain, sell, Convey and confirm, said bargained Premises in manner as aforesaid : and That he the s^d Oliver Peirce his Heirs & Assigns, shall & may, from Time to Time, and at all Times forever hereafter, by force and Virtue of these Presents, Lawfully peaceably and quietly Have, Hold, Use, Occupy, Possess and Enjoy the said demised and bargained Premises, with the Appurtenances, free and clear, and freely and clearly, acquitted, exonerated & discharged of, from all & all manner of former or other Gifts, Grants, Bargains, Sales, Leases, Mortgages, Wills, Entails, Joyntures, Dowries, Judgments, Executions or Incumbrances of what name or Nature soever, that might in any Measure or Degree obstruct or make void this present Deed.   Furthermore, I the s^d Robert Peirce for me my self my Heirs, Executors and Administrators, do Covenant & Engage the above demised Premises to him the s^d Oliver Peirce his Heirs and Assigns, against the Lawful Claims or Demands of any Person or Persons whatsoever forever hereafter to Warrant, Secure and Defend by these Presents.   In Witness whereof I the said Robert Peirce have hereunto set my hand & seal the Twenty Sixth Day of June, one Thousand seven hundred & fifty one, and in the Twenty fifth year of his Majesty's Reign King George the Second &c.

Signed Sealed & Delivered }
   in presence of us   }   ROBERT PEIRCE   [L. S.]
     OLIVER FLETCHER.

Middlesex ss Chelmsford July 12th 1753.

Then the above named Robert Peirce acknowledged the above Instrument to be his free Act & Deed.

before me OLIVER FLETCHER, Just^ce of the Peace.

To all people to whome this writeing shall come Know Ye, that I, Johanna Richardson, widow of Samuel Richardson of Oburne, in the County of Midlesex, decsd, for valluable consideration to mee well and truly payd by Thomas Peirce of the said Towne and Coun Husbandman, the receite whereof I do by these presents acknowledge, and therewith to be fully sattisfied, and of every part and parcell thereof do fully, clearly & absolutely acquitt and discharge the said Thomas Peirce his heyres, executo^rs, administrato^rs or assignes forever by these presents, have granted, bargained & sold, aliened, enfeoffed & confirmed, and by these presents do fully, clearly and absolutely grant, bargaine, sell, alien, enfeoffe, & confirme unto the said Thomas, his heyres, executo^rs, or assignes forever, Three parcells of land lyng & being in Oburne, in a feild comonly called New Bridge feilds, all of them conteyneing Twenty acres more or less, one parcell conteineing Ten acres, abutteth on Berry Meadow north, and upon dry poale Swamp, and George Pollyes Iland south, and it Joyneth to the land of the said George Polly west, and it adjoyneth to the land of the said Thomas Peirce whith hee purchased of Thomas Browne east. Another parcell conteyneing Seaven acres, more or less, lyeth ag^t the said Thomas Peirces owne land north, and abutteth on John Monsals meadow south, and adjoyneth to his owne land east & west, and the other parcell conteyneing Three acres more or less, joyneth to the land of George Polly south & east, & to the said Thomas Peirce his owne land north and west, all of them lyng in the said New Bridge feild part within & part without the fence of the said feild. To Have and to Hold occupy, possesse & injoy the said three parcells of land together with all the fences timber & timberlike trees, woodes underwoods growing on them, & all rights, priviledges and appurtenances there unto belonging to the said Thomas Peirce to him his heyres, executo^{rs}, admstrato^{rs}, or assignes forever, with warrantize from all former gifts, grants, bargaines, sales, mortgages, joynctures, dowers, titles, interests or any incomberance whatsoever. In Witness Whereof I have hereunto set my hand & seale the Tenth day of the Second month in the yeare of our Lord one thousand six hundred and sixty three.

† mark

JOHANNA RICHARDSON, & a seale.

JOHN RICHARDSON, & a seale.

Sealed, signed & delivded in the presence of John Farrow, Jonathan Thompson. February 15th, 1664. Johanna Richardson freely & fully acknowledged this instrumt to be her act and deed, before me, Thomas Danforth.

Entred & recorded 15, 12-64.

By Thomas Danforth Recorder.

A true Copy of Record—Book 3, Page 118

Attest Chas. B. Stevens Regr.

Know all Men by these Presents That I, Thomas Burges, of Charlestowne, in New England, have sold & made over unto Thomas Peirce of Woburne, in the Coun of Midlesex in New England, that peice of land lyng in the bounds of the said Towne of Woburne, which was formly given mee by Mr. George Bunkers, for my service with him, conteyneing about twenty acres (be it more or less) sittuate and bounded on the north by Bartholomew Persons land, and on the east & south by the widow Katherine Graves land, and on the west by the great pine hill of the said Mr. Bunkers land, which said twenty acres of land I do wholly resigne, with all my right, title & claime thereto unto the said Thomas Peirce, his heyres, executo^{rs}, admstrato^{rs} & assignes, for and in consideration of a Red Cow (of him bought in liew) haveing a long white strake on her back, being also big with calfe, whome the said Thomas Peirce is also sufficiently & carefully to feed & keep till shee be well delivd of her said calfe (except the said Thomas Burges demand her sooner) but then the said Thomas Peirce is to deliv[d] the said Cow & calfe (free of all charges for her said keeping in the interim) to the said Thomas Burges, his heyres, executo[rs], admstrato[rs] or assignes in consideration of the *pmify* with all his right, title & interest therein. In Witness Whereof both parties have each for themselves, their respective heyres, executo[rs], admstrato[rs] or assignes interchangeably put to their hands & seales this Twentieth day of January in the fourtenth yeare of the Reigne of our Soveraigne Lord King Charles ye Second, and yeare of our Lord God, one thousand six hundred sixty & two.

THOMAS BURGES, & a seale.
SARAH BURGES.

Signed, sealed & delivd in the presence of

JOHN GREENE.
ROBERT CUTLER.

This deed was legally acknowledged the 15th of the 11th, 1662. Before mee,

RICHARD RUSSELL.

Entred & Recorded Feb. 15th, 1664.

By THOMAS DANFORTH, Recorder.

A true Copy of Record—Book 3, Page 119.

Attest CHAS. B. STEVENS, Regr.

AGREEMENT REGARDING THE LOCATION OF A SCHOOL-HOUSE IN CHELMSFORD.

CHELMSFORD, *July the* 1, 1794.

Where as there is Disputes and uneasness aresun in this Squadon amung the peaple whare to set the schol hows altho we wich for peace we Dont find none and where to set it we can not agree and we the subscribers do agree to Leave it to the Selecmen of the town of Chelmsford for the present year and do promas to abide there judgment and to pay our eakel parts of the caust that shall arise if so be those gentlemen will come and give us there judgment where it aught to stand not regarding one more then another the rich and the pour being alike in matters of school.

OLIVER PEIRCE.
STEPHEN PEIRCE JUN.
SETH LIVINGSTON.
TIMOTHY MANNING.
JOSHUA MARSHALL.
JAMES MARSHALL.
ROBERDS X MEARS.
   his   mark
WILLIAM PARKER.
HENERY S. PARKER.
SAMUEL MARSHALL.

RECEIPT FOR BEQUESTS OF HANNAH PEIRCE.

CHELMSFORD, *Dec.* 20*th*, 1800.

This may Certify that we the Subscribers Children and Heirs to Hannah Pierce late of Chelmsford Deseas'd have receiv'd our full Potion and part of said Hannah Pierce's Estate which she gave us in her last will and Testament of Stephen Peirce Executor to said will.

We say received by us

> ELINOR PEIRCE.
> JONAS PEIRCE.
> JOHN DUNN.
> HANNAH DUNN.
> EPHR^M PARKHURST.
> ETHER PARKHURST.
> ABIJAH SPAULDING.
> OLIVER SPAULDING.
> ANDREW SPAULDING.
> RUTH SPAULDING.

INDEX I.

The Christian names of Pierces *only* are entered in this Index.   The figures refer to the pages of the book on which the names occur.

133, 163, 169, 170, 184, 211, 227, 245, 249, 252, 257, 286, 291, 315.

Fred., 207, 210, 212, 255, 258, 262, 271, 281, 285, 286, 291, 294, 299, 301, 309, 310, 318, 322, 329, 331.

Frederic, 193, 246.

Frederick, 22, 83, 121, 143, 158, 198, 213, 234, 251, 278, 288, 306, 319.

Freelove, 146.

Freeman, 227, 231.

Fremont, 292.

Forest, 332.

Forester, 202.

Gardner, 142, 222, 281.

Georganna, 138, 145.

George, 25, 26, 32, 77, 106, 115, 116, 124, 135, 142, 144, 145, 156, 158, 161, 162, 163, 164, 182, 190, 191, 192, 194, 195, 197, 200, 201, 203, 211, 219, 222, 224, 226, 228, 242, 243, 244, 246, 248, 252, 253, 257, 266, 268, 269, 275, 276, 277, 280, 281, 285, 286, 288, 290, 293, 296, 298, 299, 302, 304, 305, 306, 308, 311, 312, 313, 314, 317, 318, 321, 328, 333.

Georgia, 324.

Georgiana, 275, 276.

Georgianna, 184, 238, 258.

Georgie, 285.

Gershom, 58, 101.

Gertrude, 193, 276, 294, 298.

Gifford, 111, 198.

Gilbert, 284.

Gilman, 300.

Gordon, 102, 266, 327.

Grace, 214, 220, 223, 283, 298, 300, 303, 308.

Gratton, 58.

Granger, 174.

Granville, 233, 254.

Grenville, 240, 329.

Guy, 294, 312, 324.

Gye, 306.

Hamilton, 270.

Hammond, 159.

Hannah, 20, 21, 25, 28, 32, 36, 38, 43, 44, 46, 47, 48, 51, 52, 53, 54, 58, 68, 69, 71, 76, 77, 81, 83, 86, 87, 101, 104, 105, 111, 113, 120, 132, 142, 148, 153, 156, 189, 184, 190, 196, 198, 203, 204, 207.

Harding, 198.

Hardy, 60, 104, 147, 179, 271.

Harlan, 214,

Harley, 308.

Harlow, 197.

Harod, 190.

Harold, 202.

Harolet, 239.

Harriet, 77, 100, 106, 111, 115, 116, 119, 121, 124, 125, 131, 138, 142, 143, 144, 148, 156, 166, 172, 173, 182, 194, 195, 197, 198, 199, 201, 204, 205, 210, 211, 214, 234, 235, 237, 239, 244, 246, 248, 251, 252, 254, 274, 276, 285, 290, 312.

Harrison, 192.

Harry, 81, 119, 150, 215, 222,

248, 264, 266, 300, 304, 318, 326, 329, 333.

Harvey, 113, 182.

Haskins, 262.

Hattie, 212, 222, 239, 242, 249, 270, 273, 275, 278, 284, 285, 293, 294, 295, 303, 320.

Haven, 111.

Helen, 151, 193, 198, 201, 203, 208, 244, 245, 256, 265, 309, 321, 327.

Helena, 205.

Helvena, 204.

Heman, 63, 66, 67, 68, 119.

Henrietta, 111, 198, 204.

Henry, 100, 109, 116, 130, 132, 142, 144, 145, 149, 156, 158, 163, 172, 175, 179, 190, 195, 197, 206, 209, 210, 212, 214, 224, 226, 229, 231, 234, 235, 241, 242, 244, 245, 246, 247, 249, 250, 251, 253, 256, 264, 266, 267, 271, 275, 281, 283, 294, 295, 298, 302, 303, 310, 313, 317, 320, 329, 331.

Hepzibah, 43, 59, 68, 110, 119.

Herbert, 238, 245, 300, 306, 317, 332.

Hermon, 163.

Herod, 189.

Herschel, 198.

Hervey, 74, 111, 299.

Hettie, 285.

Hetty, 121.

Hezekiah, 83, 116, 162.

Hillman, 122.

Hiram, 143, 147, 153, 157, 229, 231, 232, 290, 294.

Hittie, 42.

Hollis, 232.

Homer, 193, 219, 283.

Horace, 81, 154, 165, 172, 174, 231, 245, 280.

Horatio, 146.

Hosea, 142, 157.

Houghton, 132.

Howard, 203.

Hubbard, 142, 228.

Hubert, 202.

Hudson, 190.

Hugh, 181, 239.

Huldah, 80.

Ichabod, 22, 23, 49, 51, 80.

Ida, 207, 219, 230, 238, 239, 256, 283, 284, 291, 298, 312.

Imogene, 122.

Indianna, 272.

Indie, 327.

Inez, 223, 329.

Ingilla, 226.

Ingram, 290.

Ira, 110, 156, 182, 255, 279.

Irena, 164, 204.

Irving, 319.

Irwin, 303.

Isaac, 24, 27, 28, 30, 31, 38, 39, 45, 57, 60, 71, 82, 104, 106, 107, 115, 118, 157, 179, 285.

Isabel, 310.

Isabella, 226.

Isaiah, 205.

Israel, 116, 202.

Jabez, 38, 53, 147.

Jacob, 24, 27, 38, 39, 40, 46, 47, 62, 63, 64, 65, 66, 67, 73, 108, 122, 158, 191, 211, 251.

James, 22, 23, 25, 26, 28, 29, 32, 39, 40, 42, 43, 46, 61, 62, 63, 64, 71, 83, 101, 105, 106, 107, 109, 110, 111, 114, 115, 117, 133, 145, 151, 152, 181, 182, 185, 189, 191, 196, 199, 200, 201, 204, 210, 229, 234, 237, 241, 244, 268, 272, 274, 275, 278, 282, 285, 289, 291, 311, 317, 319, 333.

Jane, 113, 116, 133, 150, 173, 233, 235, 238, 240, 241, 246, 286, 305.

Jason, 128, 196.

Jay, 292.

Jeannette, 201, 244.

Jeannie, 236.

Jeddediah, 37, 52, 83.

Jenetta, 145.

Jennie, 211, 217, 229, 230, 247, 268, 294, 298, 317.

Jenny, 307.

Jeremiah, 233.

Jerome, 300.

Jerry, 314.

Jerusha, 74, 83.

Jesse, 55, 88, 101, 118, 159, 171, 205, 215, 238, 239, 252, 257, 333.

Jessie, 273, 275, 317, 318, 331.

Joanna, 31, 44, 45, 66, 103.

Job, 82, 102, 152, 189.

Joel, 163, 204, 205.

John, 18, 20, 21, 22, 23, 24, 25, 26, 30, 31, 32, 33, 34, 35, 36, 37, 42, 43, 46, 47, 48, 49, 50, 51, 53, 54, 58, 59, 60, 68, 69, 70, 71, 73, 74, 78, 79, 80, 81, 87, 88, 100, 106, 111, 116, 118, 124, 126, 128, 141, 142, 144, 146, 147, 148, 151, 153, 154, 155, 156, 158, 163, 164, 171, 172, 173, 179, 181, 185, 192, 195, 202, 205, 206, 208, 213, 217, 220, 223, 226, 227, 231, 232, 233, 235, 236, 239, 241, 242, 243, 244, 245, 246, 252, 253, 256, 261, 262, 263, 268, 272, 274, 282, 290, 298, 305, 307, 308, 311, 313, 320, 321, 323, 324, 327.

Jonas, 54, 86, 132, 162, 189, 253, 278.

Jonathan, 20, 21, 23, 24, 25, 30, 31, 35, 42, 43, 47, 48, 54, 57, 71, 75, 76, 77, 87, 88, 101, 133, 162, 171.

Jophanes, 204.

Josenthia, 146.

Joseph, 20, 21, 22, 23, 24, 26, 28, 30, 35, 44, 46, 47, 48, 56, 57, 59, 69, 70, 71, 72, 82, 101, 106, 108, 111, 112, 114, 115, 116, 117, 122, 132, 133, 151, 152, 155, 171, 176, 191, 194, 196, 197, 199, 203, 205, 206, 218, 224, 231, 246, 272, 290, 298.

Josephine, 201, 213, 247, 287, 301.

Joshua, 31, 35, 39, 40, 46, 58, 62, 76, 77, 106, 107, 133, 184, 185, 276.

Josiah, 26, 30, 36, 38, 48, 51, 58, 73, 77, 78, 82, 101, 105, 115, 117, 135, 146, 172, 173, 192, 195, 204, 225, 231.

Josie, 228.

Jotham, 143, 204, 227.

INDEX TO NAMES OTHER THAN PIERCE.

This Index contains *other names* than that of Pierce of those who have intermarried, and of their descendants.

INDEX TO TOWNS AND CITIES.

ADDENDA.

285. JONATHAN[6] PIERCE (Ebenezer[5], Ebenezer[4], John[3], Thomas[2], Thomas[1]), b. Sept. 17, 1757; m. Apr. 15, 1781, Lydia Bowman, b. Jan. 8, 1763, d. June 28, 1841. He d. Aug. 20, 1808. They res. in Southboro, Mass. Children :—

(See page 75.)
597. i.   LYDIA, b. Feb. 4, 1782; m. ———.
598. ii. NANCY, b. June 30, 1783; m. Asa Holt.
599. iii. NATHAN, b. Jan. 6, 1785.
600. iv. JONATHAN, b. Apr. 21, 1788; went to China. N. f. k.
601. v.   LAVINA, b. Feb. 9, 1790; m. July 11, 1813, Wm. Robbins, b. Apr. 24, 1791. She d. Sept. 2, 1868. Ch.: Lavina, b. Aug. 25, 1814, d. Aug. 11, 1844; William, b. Apr. 14, 1816, d. June 21, 1819; Charles B., b. Nov. 28, 1817. He is a physician, and lives in Worcester.
602. vi. AARON, b. Feb. 15, 1793; m. Harriet Bellows.
603. vii. SINA, b. July 16, 1794; m. Nov. 11, 1816, Almond Ford, b Mar. 25, 1788. He d. Sept. 22, 1829. She d. Nov. 11, 1870. Ch.: Adaline, b. Jan. 3, 1819, d. Oct. 15, 1851; Joseph, b. Feb. 12, 1820; Hezekiah, b. Jan. 15, 1822; Henry P., b. Jan. 4, 1824. Lydia A., b. Feb. 19, 1826; Edwin P., b. Feb. 1, 1828.
604. viii. SILA, b. Nov. 20, 1799; d. Oct. 13, 1837.

ELIJAH BRIGHAM'S DEED TO JONATHAN PEIRCE.

Know all Men by these Presents That I Elijah Brigham of Southborough in the County of Worcester and Commonwealth of Massachusetts Gentleman. in Consideration of one hundred and thirty pounds lawful Money, paid by Jonathan Peirce of Southborough aforesaid Gentleman. the Receipt whereof I do hereby acknowledge, do hereby give, grant, sell and convey unto the said Jon[a] Peirce, a certain tract of Land in said Southborough situate on the easterly Side of cleanhill so cal'd, containing by estamation, Thirty one acres be the more or less, and is bounded as followeth viz Begining at the Southeasterly side of Said Land at a heap of Stones on the northerly Side of a town way, Thence easterly by said way 56. Rods to a corner. Thence northerly by an other town way 20 rods to a Large Rock, Thence S.°65. W. 10 Rods to a stake & stones. Thence N.° 59' W. 48 rods bounded partly by a ditch to a stake and stones, Thence West 12° S. 81½ rods to a stake & stones. Thence Southerly by Land of Jonas Ball Esq.[r] to a heap of Stones. Thence southerly by Land of David Woods and Land formerly belonging to Thomas Hudson Deca[d].

to the bound first mentioned, with all the priviledges there to belonging. ———

TO HAVE AND TO HOLD the afore-described Premises to the said Jon*ᵃ* Peirce—his Heirs and Assigns, to his and their Use and Behoof forever.

AND I do covenant with the said Jonathan Peirce and his Heirs and Assigns, That I am lawfully seized in Fee of the afore-described Premises; That they are free of all Incumbrances; That I have good Right to sell and convey the same to the said Jon*ᵃ*. Peirce———

AND that I will warrant and defend the same Premises to the said Jon*ᵃ*. Peirce and his Heirs and Assigns, forever, against the lawful Claims and Demands of all Persons.

In Witness whereof, I—the said Elijah Brigham—have hereunto set my Hand and Seal this first Day of May in the Year of our LORD *One thousand seven hundred and ninety four.*

ELIJAH BRIGHAM.   [Seal.]

Signed, sealed, and delivered
in Presence of us,

LUTHER STONE
JONAS BALL

Worcester ss. may Nineteenth 1794.   *THEN the above named Elijah Brigham personaly appeard and acknowledged the above Instrument to be his free Act and Deed— before me,*

JONAS BALL   { Justice of the Peace.

Worcester ss. April 20*ᵗʰ*. 1796 Rec*ᵈ* and Recorded in the Registry of Deeds Lib. 127. Pag. 506   pr DAN CLAP Reg*ʳ*.

Rec*ᵈ* April 20th 1796
                paid

602. AARON⁷ PIERCE (*Jonathan⁶, Ebenezer⁵, Ebenezer⁴, John³, Thomas², Thomas¹*), b. Feb. 15, 1793; m. ———, 1816, Harriet Bellows, b. Mar. 9, 1798, d. June 30, 1860. He d. July 16, 1856. Res. Chautauqua, N. Y. and Savanna, Ill. Children :—

2252. (*a*) i.   MARSHALL B., b. Nov. 27, 1816; m. twice.
2252. (*b*) ii.   HARRIET M., b. Sept. 5, 1819; m. V. L. Davidson, Etna, Cal.
2252. (*c*) iii. LORENZO D., b. Apr. 27, 1823; m. Fidelia E. Langford.
2252. (*d*) iv.   LILA C., b. Feb. 20, 1827; m. David L. Bowen.
2252. (*e*) v.   MARY J., b. Aug. 8, 1829; m. John B. Rodes.
2252. (*f*) vi.   LYDIA A., b. June 16, 1832; d. Aug. 2, 1838.
2252. (*g*) vii. HENRY C., b. Oct. 26, 1834; m. Laura Shepard.
2252. (*h*) viii. LEONORA, b. Feb. 2, 1841; m. Henry Carson, Compton, Cal.
2252. (*i*) ix.   ELIPHALET W., b. June 28, 1842; d. Mar. 24, 1843.

2252. (*a*) MARSHALL B.⁸ PIERCE (*Aaron⁷, Jonathan⁶, Ebenezer⁵, Ebenezer⁴, John³, Thomas², Thomas¹*), b. Nov. 27, 1816; m. Aug.

26, 1839, Julia A. Baker, d. July 10, 1854 ; m. 2nd, July 28, 1856, Mrs. Mary Jane Austin. Res. Savannah, Ill. Children :—

3562. (*a*) i.   LYDIA A., b. Aug. 6, 1840; d. Feb. 4, 1858.
3562. (*b*) ii.   WILLIAM H. H., b. May 5, 1844; m. 1870, Alice Etter. Res. Winona, Minn. s. p.
3562. (*c*) iii.   MARY, b. Dec. 15, 1845; d. July 6, 1846.
3562. (*d*) iv.   ORRIN S., b. Sept. 6, 1847 ; m. Belle Milligan.
3562. (*e*) v.   MARSHALL N., b. Nov. 17, 1849.
3562. (*f*) vi.   HARRIET, b. July 8, 1852; m. Dr. Fred. L. Pond, Aurora, Ill.
3562. (*g*) vii.   CHARLES C., b. Aug. 27, 1857.

2252. (*c*) LORENZO D.[8] PIERCE (*Aaron*[7], *Jonathan*[6], *Ebenezer*[5], *Ebenezer*[4], *John*[3], *Thomas*[2], *Thomas*[1]), b. Apr. 27, 1823 ; m. Dec. 25, 1845, Fidelia E. Langford. He d. Sept. 10, 1867. Res. ———.
Children :—

3562. (*h*) i.   GEORGE A., b. ———.
3562. (*i*) ii.   ANNA, b. ———; m. Charles E. Goodwin; res. Franktown, Virginia.

2252. (*f*) HENRY C.[8] PIERCE (*Aaron*[7], *Jonathan*[6], *Ebenezer*[5], *Ebenezer*[4], *John*[3], *Thomas*[2], *Thomas*[1]), b. Oct. 26, 1834 ; m. Oct. 23, 1855, Laura Shepard, b. Mar. 14, 1831. Res. Traer, Iowa.
Children :—

3562. (*j*) i.   HENRY S., b. Dec. 3, 1862.
3562. (*k*) ii.   PALMER E., b. Oct. 23, 1865.
3562. (*l*) iii.   RALPH H., b. Dec. 2, 1868.

3562. (*d*) ORRIN S.[9] PIERCE (*Marshall B.*[8], *Aaron*[7], *Jonathan*[6], *Ebenezer*[5], *Ebenezer*[4], *John*[3], *Thomas*[2], *Thomas*[1]), b. Sept. 6, 1847 ; m. March, 1872, Belle Milligan. Res. Winona, Mich. Children :—

4698. (*a*)   EVELINE B., b. Jan. 3, 1873.
4698. (*b*)   ALICE V., b. Aug. 13, 1874.
4698. (*c*)   ORRIN M., b. Oct. 20, 1875.
4698. (*d*)   CHARLES L., b., Apr. 20, 1877.
4698. (*e*)   EDWARD B., b. Nov. 23, 1880.

ERRATA.

Pages 18 and 19. Jeffs should read *Tufts*.
Page 20. May 17, 1716, should read *May 17, 1715*.
Page 31. May 20, 1724, " " *May 20, 1728*.
Page 74. Lina " " *Sina*.
Page 112. The account of Life of No. 492 should appear under head of *No. 495*.
Page 124. Chales should read *Charles*.
Page 124. Mar. 1, 1807, " " *Sept. 20, 1808*.
Page 126. Wood " " *Ward*.
Page 128. Maeia " " *Maria*.
Page 131. Stane " " *Stone*.
Page 166. Gen. Graham married a dau. of *No. 2787* instead of No. 2792.
Page 191. Bateman should read *Butman*.
Page 193. County " " *Country*.
Page 208. Ellely " " *Ellery*.
Page 234. Geoege " " *George*.
Page 242. No. 3942 " " *Son*.
Page 340. Mich. " " *Minn*.

On page 113 the numericals omitted by error from 1099 to 2000—which was not discovered until too late to be remedied.

ADDENDA.

Page 27. After No. 84, Jacob, m.—should be the word *Rachel*.
Page 31. After No. 130, Joshua, b. Aug. 28, 1740, should be the words *Sarah Saunders*.
Page 38. No. 84, after m. should be *Rachel*.
Page 68. *Mary (Lamson) Pierce d. Sept. 25, 1792*.
Page 124. No. 2209, m. *Mary W. Sanderson*.
Page 192. No. 3086, *Gertrude Persons, m. Oct. 26, 1881, Wm. L. Engrem*.
Page 219. No. 3554. *Ida T. Pierce m. Henry W. Davidson*.

www.ingramcontent.com/pod-product-compliance
Lightning Source LLC
Chambersburg PA
CBHW070541270326
41926CB00013B/2163